COURT AND CONSTITUTION IN THE TWENTIETH CENTURY

The Old Legality, 1889-1932

COURT
AND
CONSTITUTION
IN THE
TWENTIETH
CENTURY

The Old Legality
1889-1932

---

by William F. Swindler

THE BOBBS-MERRILL COMPANY, INC.
Indianapolis and New York

The Bobbs-Merrill Company, Inc.
A Subsidiary of Howard W. Sams & Co., Inc., Publishers
Indianapolis • Kansas City • New York

To My Wife

Benetta

for Devotion, Loyalty, Sacrifice

Foreword

What Henry Steele Commager has so aptly called "the water-shed of the nineties," dividing the older America from the new, also divided the constitutional experience of the American people, separating the earlier era of political theory from the newer one dominated primarily by economic and social issues. The year 1889, it may be noted, marked the end of the first century in the history of the Constitution of the United States, and the history of the modern Constitution may accordingly be dated roughly from the appointment of Melville W. Fuller to the Chief Justiceship in 1888. For although Fuller was not, personally or philosophically, in sympathy with the new propositions of economics and government which began to come before the Supreme Court of the United States during his tenure, it was his fate to have entered the scene at the point in time when the issues created by a changing society were reaching into every phase of American life. Thus the three-quarters of a century from the nineties to the mid-sixties has been the spawning period for a more sophisticated concept of federalism—a process which has been attended by a continuing ideological outcry.

This is so because the Constitution, and the Court which interprets it—and Congress which so often acts as a buffer between the judiciary and the lay public—could not escape the effect of all those events which fundamentally altered the domestic and international environment in this period. The passing of the frontier, the rise of an interstate industrialism, the shift from a rural to an urban distribution of population, the breakdown of nineteenth-century capitalism and the efforts to construct in its stead a twentieth-century capitalism, the breakthrough in science and technology, the change in the society of nations brought about by global wars and the militant dialectic of totalitarianism—the constitutional posture of the American people had to be readjusted in response to each of these.

Fuller's Court stood upon the watershed, with a powerful pull of ideological gravity toward the past. At least three of his colleagues when he came onto the bench dated from the constitutional golden age: Justices Bradley, Field and Miller all had begun their careers under men who in turn had known John Marshall and Joseph Story. From these venerated predecessors, who interpreted the Constitution with reference to a pioneer economy and an *ante-bellum* concept of the Federal function, Fuller and his intimate associates undertook to derive a jurisprudence to apply to issues never imagined by the early Federalist jurists. It is not surprising, therefore, that the first of the great constitutional crises of our modern age should have developed in this context.

This is a study of the turbulent progress of American constitutionalism through the first four (for there will be more) crises of twentieth-century change. From the Populist outburst of the nineties to the attempted reforms of the New Freedom, thence to the arduous decade of the Great Depression and finally to the fundamentally altered America emerging from World War II —this is the path over the peaks and pitfalls which has led from the watershed.

The constitutional history of the twentieth century has been decidedly cyclical, and so dramatic in its crises that the emotional involvement of its contemporaries has frequently made them lose sight of the fact that the issues of the moment have had their counterparts in the immediate past. Thus the uproar over the Court's doctrinaire opposition to the first New Deal reforms drowned out any recollection that fifteen years earlier the major legislative experiments of the first Wilson administration had been similarly nullified. And the vehement commentaries on the jurisprudence of the Warren Court which have been occasionally and widely broadcast sound all too familiar when one remembers what was said of the Fuller Court seventy-five years before.

It is, in fact, the cyclical nature of our constitutional dialogue which underlines the role of Congress in the whole history of this period. If the Constitution, in the oft-misunderstood aphorism of Chief Justice Hughes, is what the Supreme Court says it is, there is a great deal that Congress has also said, often in an emotional reaction to an unpopular judicial decision but even more often, and more significantly, with reference to contemplated legislative action and proposed amendments to the document itself. The present study, accordingly, has focused upon pertinent Congressional as well as judicial commentary in attempting to illustrate the emerging rationale of our constitutional development in the context of the present. Taken as a whole—as gleaned from the reported opinions, the arguments of counsel in critical cases, the perspectives afforded by professional literature and by commentators in the mass media, and in Congressional debate—the story reveals a fundamental shifting of ideological poles in this period. Particularly after the epochal decisions in the segregation, reapportionment and civil liberties cases of the past two decades, a new constitutionalism has been defined.

The present writer began his study of this subject three decades ago, in the heart of the depression thirties. Irving Brant's *Storm Over the Constitution* was one of the most dramatic reminders of that time that the stresses between the old and new orders, which had begun to build up under Fuller, had reached a final stage of fission under Charles Evans Hughes. Brant, with whom this writer worked at the time, was one of several discerning students of contemporary changes who recognized the ultimate significance of the dialogue of the thirties, and it is to his original observations that the present book must trace its inception. But the thirties, and the forties and fifties, represented only the more transitional chapters in the story; the actual writing has had to wait until some of the more significant consequences of the transition could be identified. The story, of course, is far from complete today, but now that a generation has passed since the catastrophic depression and the cataclysmic global war, we can at least discern the main outlines of the new constitutional environment.

To describe the fundamental changes in constitutional law which evolved from the nineties to the sixties is a complicated process, when the objective is to distinguish the forest from the trees. In the summary view the writer has tried to project through the narrative history which makes up the main part of the present work, both the leading constitutional decisions and the historical background of necessity have been highly condensed. To fill in some essential details which corroborate the main story, a comprehensive series of appendices has been added to the main text. As for the chief constitutional argument, it has been set out primarily in the words of the men who actually carried it on—Field and Harlan, Holmes and Brandeis, Taft and Sutherland, Hughes and Stone, Black and Douglas and Frankfurter, the second Harlan and Chief Justice Warren.

The history of constitutional change in the present—that is, since the second century of the Constitution itself began—has divided logically into two distinct eras, which in turn have seemed logically and accurately to be described by the titles given to each volume in the present study which deals respectively with them. The "old legality," to which the conservatives in law and government held with as deep and abiding a conviction as the conservative in religion would cling to the faith of his fathers, remained dominant from 1889 to 1932, when cataclysms theretofore unimagined began to come about. The "new legality" is the sum of the attempted responses to these cataclysms in the age since 1932. The "old legality" is, accordingly, the theme of the present volume.

The disputation is set against a background of human and public affairs which gave each historical era its peculiar temper—the nineties and the turn of the century, the first World War, the years of normalcy and depression, the second World War, and the chronic agitation of our own time. Of course, the story is incomplete in the telling and will be continued beyond the sixties. It is possible that before the next decade is much advanced, new developments in the argument will require an early restatement of the conclusions suggested here. The writer will welcome comments and suggestions from readers of the present work to compile against that possibility.

Some Americans look back in anger or frustration at the world we have left behind the watershed; others look about them with misgiving at the contemporary scene. This is perhaps the inevitable reaction of any group of wayfarers passing always from the familiar to the new and unfamiliar. The present writer, while he has his own conclusions which will be evident in the story, offers no palliative or panacea; his primary objective has been to tell the story itself, tracing the main milestones marking the movement of constitutional history in the direction we have come thus far. To demonstrate

the continuity of change under the circumstances of this century—as well
as the continuing viability of our constitutional process—is the hoped-for
product of this effort.

WILLIAM F. SWINDLER

Williamsburg, Virginia
March 1968

Contents

Appendices

COURT AND CONSTITUTION
IN THE TWENTIETH CENTURY

The Old Legality, 1889-1932

PART I

Transition to a New Century

The limitations upon legislative power, arising from the nature of the Constitution and its specific restraints in favor of private rights, cannot be disregarded without conceding that the legislature can change at will the form of our government from one of limited to one of unlimited powers.

Stephen J. Field, Address on the Centennial of the Federal Judiciary, 134 U.S. App. VI (1890)

Chart I   THE FULLER COURT

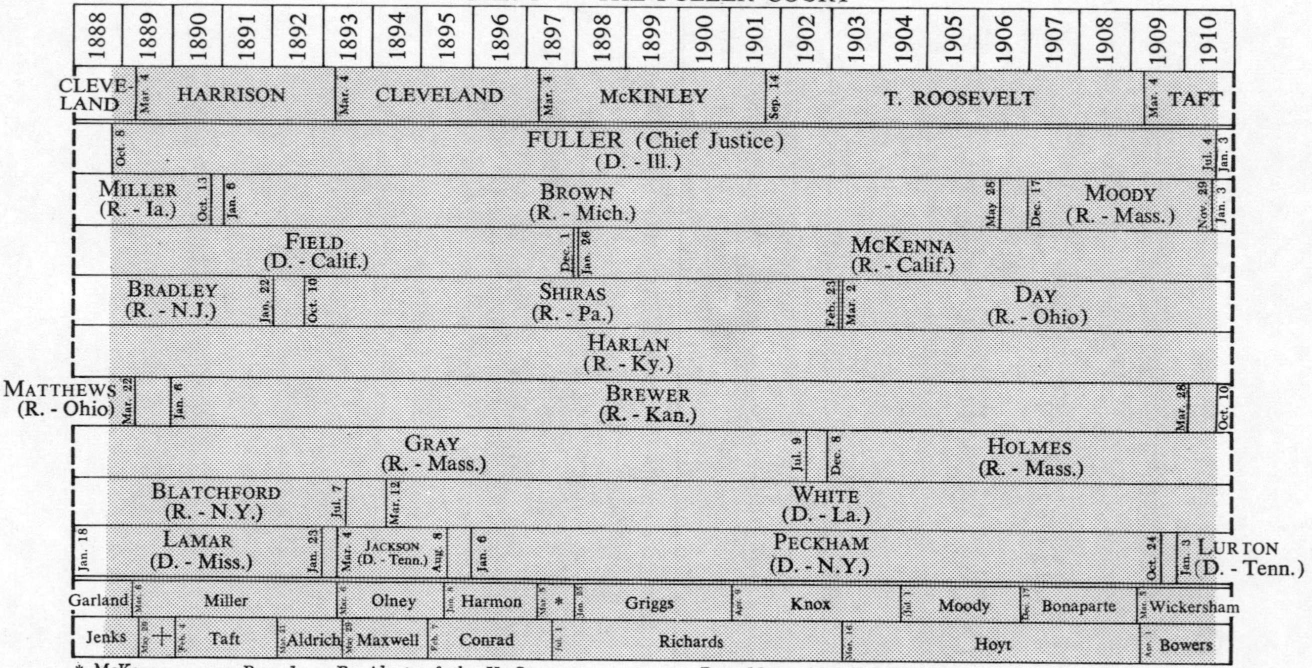

1888 1889 1890 1891 1892 1893 1894 1895 1896 1897 1898 1899 1900 1901 1902 1903 1904 1905 1906 1907 1908 1909 1910

CLEVE-LAND | HARRISON (Mar. 4) | CLEVELAND (Mar. 4) | McKINLEY (Mar. 4) | T. ROOSEVELT (Sep. 14) | TAFT (Mar. 4)

FULLER (Chief Justice) (D. - Ill.)

MILLER (R. - Ia.) Oct. 13

FIELD (D. - Calif.) Oct. 10

BROWN (R. - Mich.) Jan. 1 ... May 28

MOODY (R. - Mass.) Dec. 17

BRADLEY (R. - N.J.) Jan. 22

SHIRAS (R. - Pa.) Dec. 1 ... Feb. 23

McKENNA (R. - Calif.) Jan. 26

DAY (R. - Ohio)

HARLAN (R. - Ky.)

MATTHEWS (R. - Ohio) Mar. 22 ... Jan. 4

GRAY (R. - Mass.) Mar. 12 ... Jul. 9

BREWER (R. - Kan.) Jan. 1 ... Mar. 28

HOLMES (R. - Mass.) Dec. 8

JACKSON (D. - Tenn.) Mar. 4 ... Aug. 8

BLATCHFORD (R. - N.Y.) Jul. 7

WHITE (D. - La.)

LAMAR (D. - Miss.) Jan. 18 ... Jan. 23

PECKHAM (D. - N.Y.) Jan. 6 ... Oct. 24

LURTON (D. - Tenn.) Jan. 3

Garland | Miller | Olney | Harmon | Griggs | Knox | Moody | Bonaparte | Wickersham

Jenks | Taft | Aldrich | Maxwell | Conrad | Richards | Hoyt | Bowers

* McKenna
+ Chapman

Row 1 — Presidents of the U. S.
Rows 2-10 — Justices of the Supreme Court
Row 11 — Attorneys General
Row 12 — Solicitors General

The Fuller Court in terms of Presidential administrations, seniority and succession of Justices, and personnel of the Department of Justice are shown in the shaded area. Dates for Presidents, Attorneys General and Solicitors General represent the beginning of their terms. Dates for members of the Court represent (1) their swearing-in as Justice (see Tables in Appendix A), which is the effective beginning of their terms, and (2) the end of their service on the bench, whether occurring through resignation, retirement or death.

1/Apology for the Past

T HE SUPREME COURT of the United States, wrote an editor in Missouri, was guilty of "continually encroaching upon the legislative power of the States, on the one hand, and upon that of [Congress] on the other." A North Carolina jurist, alarmed at the current trend of decisions, suggested that Federal judges should henceforth be elected so that they would not be insulated by lifetime appointments from the needs and desires of the people. But the former governor of Oregon went furthest in his denunciation: "Our constitutional government has been supplanted by a judicial oligarchy," he declared. "The time has now arrived when the government should be restored to its constitutional basis. The duty is plain and the road is clear. If Congress, at its next session, would impeach the . . . judges for the usurpation of legislative power, remove them from office, and instruct the President to enforce the [law], the Supreme Court of the United States would never hereafter presume to trench upon the exclusive power of Congress."[1]

It was 1895, a memorable year in which the nation's highest tribunal had, in trip-hammer succession, cut much of the ground from under the anti-trust law, denied to the Federal government the power to levy an income tax, and confirmed the sentencing of the country's chief labor leader for his part in the vicious railroad dispute in Chicago the previous year. The mounting cadence of criticism had spread beyond the professional journals to the mass media. "The overthrow of the income tax," declared the *New York World,* "is the triumph of selfishness over patriotism. It is another victory of greed over need." In the Far West, the *Salt Lake Tribune* ominously spoke of the tax case: "It falls upon the fair-minded men of the country precisely as did the Dred Scott decision forty years ago." In the Midwest an Indianapolis editorial writer thundered: "Incorrect and strained as an alleged interpretation of the Constitution, it is something far worse. Clearly [the tax decision] has

3

been trumped up in the interest of the moneyed classes and carries with it a suspicion that it is corrupt in intent and procurement."[2]

Thus were the American people, in the closing decade of the century, invited to contemplate the prospect that the nation's ultimate tribunal had become the prisoner of the new plutocracy created in the thirty years since the Civil War. The growth of enormous new financial empires in this period, symbolized and implemented by the giant interstate corporations lacing the country in a network of tightly controlled railroads, had been both a dazzling and a dismaying spectacle unparalleled in human history. In every area of economic life the story had its individual chapters, most of which seemed to reach the same ending before courts uniformly sympathetic with the strong as they prevailed over the weak. It was this consistent judicial behavior which particularly concerned the influential *American Law Review* in its editorial criticism of the tax decision. The case, it warned, "has not strengthened the confidence of the American people in their Federal court of last resort. It has not escaped severe criticism that, on every essential point, the decision of the majority is in favor of the rich, and the talk is freely bandied about that the Court is and always has been a rich man's court and a corporation court. . . . It really seems that where the government, or the scattered and segregated people, stand on one side, and rich individuals or corporations stand on the other, the Federal judicial mind glides easily to a result favorable to the latter."[3] The rich had their spokesman also. A friend of the Eastern business interests wrote: "In a hundred years, the Supreme Court of the United States has not rendered a decision more important in its effect or reaching further in its consequences. . . . The wave of Socialist revolution has gone far, but it breaks at the foot of the ultimate bulwark set up for the protection of our liberties." The tax decision, added a Philadelphia paper, rejected "a vicious attempt at class and sectional legislation" which, as other metropolitan organs suggested, had been initiated by an unholy combination of Democrats and Populists.[4]

*   *   *

For the masses of Americans of the agricultural South and West, however, the decisions of the current term of the Court did indeed seem to bear out the complaint of the *St. Louis Post-Dispatch* that "the corporations and plutocrats are as securely entrenched in the Supreme Court as in the lower courts which they take such pains to control." The tax case and its companions in this closing decade of the century had brought to a boiling point the simmering discontents of the age. The brew had many ingredients, accumulated in the generation following a civil war which had destroyed a social system in the South and reoriented an economic system in the North; in both instances, the values and standards of the first century of national life had been called into question and a sense of lost innocence lay on the threshold of public consciousness.[5]

The dogmas of the Founding Fathers, the frontier tradition of independence, the Puritan ethic of virtue vindicated by hard work, still commanded the loyalty of the vast majority of men in public and private life; but it was becoming progressively more manifest that these alone did not dispose of the issues which were rising in the postwar economy. Since the beginning of the nation, the American yeoman had equated liberty of property with liberty of person; in recent years, the growth of corporate control over property, over the freedom to sell goods and services and even over the freedom to make or offer them for sale, had rendered the equation all but irrelevant. Although apologists for the credo of the past, like Thomas M. Cooley of Michigan, stoutly rejected the proposition that public authority should be invoked to preserve the system of competitive capitalism, the eighties had been witness to a succession of demands for legislative remedies to be applied to the changing character of the economy. Yet it seemed that every attempted accommodation of these demands was to be frustrated.

In January 1887, after more than a dozen years of unsuccessful attempts, Congress had passed the bill creating the Interstate Commerce Commission, hopefully regarded by the farmer and the consumer as an agency which would curtail the long catalog of rate abuses by the nation's railroads; but in less than three years thereafter a succession of judicial decisions had rendered the Commission almost totally impotent. In 1890, as this trend of court pronouncements reached its climax, Congress had enacted the Sherman Anti-Trust Law and hailed it as bringing under control the monopolistic march of the great postwar corporations; but the decision in the early part of the present year had stripped the law of most of its effectiveness and left the corporations as free as ever. Meantime, over the same period, the public had witnessed a steady and, indeed, accelerating movement of the Court away from the position it had taken in 1877 when it had affirmed the authority of the states, if not of the Federal government, to apply inherent police powers to the exercise of private economic power.[6]

The income tax decision in the spring of 1895 thus appeared to the average American as something more than a narrow construction of the tax law; it was taken to represent the judicial rebuttal of the whole case, built up over almost two decades, for the democratization of the capitalistic system of the postwar generation. The extent to which the Court, in this decision, had to overturn established law only served to underscore the ideology which the majority was impressing upon the whole fabric of constitutional law. Since the earliest days of the Republic, lawyers and laymen alike had assumed that the Court had recognized a broad taxing power in Congress, and during the Civil War a graduated income tax had first been introduced. While the Court, in 1871, had ruled that such a tax could not be laid upon the salaries of state officers,[7] it had, ten years later, unanimously rejected an argument that as a general constitutional principle such a revenue matter was illegal.[8] Now, however, as the *Harvard Law Review* bluntly put it, the current decision "not only overrules in effect three direct adjudications made by [the Court], but also refines away to the vanishing point two other of its decisions, and thereby cripples an important and necessary power and function of a coordinate branch of the government and delivers an opinion . . . contrary to what has been accepted as law for nearly one hundred years."[9]

*   *   *

The dispatch with which the attack upon the Income Tax Law had been brought before the high court further aggravated the sense of conspiracy. Under normal circumstances it would have been many months—or even years —before such a test of an act of Congress would have made its way from the original trial court to final judicial review. More than that, in the case of a tax the procedure prescribed for bringing about a test was well established: only after the tax was paid and protested would courts recognize the standing of a party to challenge the statute under which the tax had been collected. In this instance, however, the question had been raised, argued and conclusively adjudicated in less than five months.

On January 5, 1895, one Charles Pollock, a resident of Boston, had written the board of directors of the Farmers' Loan & Trust Company, a New York corporation, protesting as a stockholder against any attempt on the part of the corporation to comply with the tax law. Pollock's letter called upon the board to "take such steps as may be necessary to protect the rights of the Trust Company's shareholders and those for whom it acts in its numerous fiduciary capacities." Thirteen days later, on January 18, the board of directors had written Pollock declining to incur criminal liability for refusal to pay the tax. Thereupon, the following day a formal petition was filed by Pollock's attorneys in the United States Circuit Court for the Southern District of New York, demanding as a matter of equity that the corporation's board be directed to comply with his original request. On January 23 the company through its counsel demurred to the action, and on January 24 the demurrer was sustained. On that day—two weeks and five days after Pollock had sent his first letter— an appeal was being carried to the Supreme Court of the United States.*[10]

The fact that these proceedings were obviously collusive only added to the public sense of outrage; and when the Supreme Court, on January 28, expedited its own calendar and set the first Monday in March as the time for argument of the case, the laymen could readily be persuaded that the bench itself had entered into the collusion.[11] Finally, on April 8, or some ninety days after Pollock's original communication to the Trust Company, had come the first ruling of the Court, partially invalidating the tax. On the question of its constitutionality as a whole, the Court noted through its Chief Justice that there was a four-to-four division, the ninth Justice, Howell E. Jackson, not having participated because of a serious illness.[12]

As eager as the litigants to come to a final decision on the matter, the Court had then set the case for reargument upon the anticipated return of the ailing Justice. Even in accommodating the motion for a rehearing, the Court seemed to condone an irregularity in its own procedure in its zeal to meet the

---

*On the rules of appellate procedure applicable to constitutional questions for this period, see the annotation which follows Note 10.

constitutional issue; noting that "the Attorney General [had] presented a suggestion that if any rehearing were granted it should embrace the whole case," the Chief Justice had hastened to agree: "Treating this suggestion as amounting in itself to an application for a rehearing, and not desiring to restrict the scope of the argument," the Court on May 6 began reconsideration of the whole case.[13]

Even the lineup of the members of the Court on the ultimate constitutional question had developed an exaggerated air of mystery. How, indeed, had the eight Justices divided on the basic issues on April 8? Neither the minutes nor the journal of the Court identified the four who were reported on one side or the four on the other. In any event, it was assumed that when Justice Jackson returned to the bench he would become, as the *Washington Star* put it, "practically the judge of the entire question, as upon his vote upon the main point of the constitutionality of the law presumably rests the entire case."[14] But then, two days before the final decision was announced on May 20, the *Chicago Tribune* created a mild sensation by publishing a dispatch from its Washington correspondent stating that the outcome of the case had actually been settled by an about-face of one of the Justices in the original deadlock. Justice George Shiras of Pennsylvania, declared the *Tribune,* had gone over to the anti-tax side and thus insured a holding that the law was unconstitutional.[15]

Where the *Tribune*—or several other papers which published similar stories—got the information was never revealed, nor was the shift by Shiras ever definitely confirmed;[16] but it did indeed turn out that, by a five-to-four majority, Pollock's case against the Trust Company was upheld and the tax declared invalid. It was mildly surprising, though anticlimactic, that Jackson himself voted with the minority; this only made clearer the fact that some one of the other jurists had had a change of heart. There had been much soul-searching, and the sense of betrayal had reached onto the bench itself, as was evident in the intensity of emotion with which the several opinions of May 20 were handed down.

*   *   *

To capitalist and common man alike in the spring of 1895, the tax case had made the issue clear. As the business community saw it, "vested rights and invested wealth were surely in danger, and also the perpetuity of government," while to the man in the street the question was "whether consumption should pay all the taxes of the Federal government . . . or investment and speculation out of their increment of profit and gains, should bear their fair share of public burdens."[17] Rich and poor had come to grips, and the poor were not reassured by the observation of Justice Stephen J. Field in the split decision of April 8: "The present assault upon capital is but the beginning; it will be but the stepping stone to others larger and more sweeping, till our political contests will become a war of the poor against the rich, a war constantly growing in intensity and bitterness."[18] For thousands of men who had witnessed the crushing advance of corporate wealth in this generation, the war had already begun; and having read the uniform convictions of the Court in cases arising on other fronts in this war, they watched the outcome of the session of May 20 with a sullen pessimism.

Two hours before the customary noontime opening of the Court on this day, the people began to gather in the hallway of the Capitol, first outside the courtroom door and then in a lengthening file back through the corridors to the main rotunda. A steady murmur coursed along the line; the conversation had no gaiety, neither did it reflect belligerence—anxiety was the nearest to a common characteristic. The fact that such numbers of laymen had been moved to come to hear a relatively technical interpretation of constitutional law testified to the national concern which the Pollock litigation had aroused. Men and women, some shabby and others tailored, some obviously longtime familiars, but most of them equally obviously strangers to the Court, all were to be found in the continually growing crowd which waited, now with a slight surge of impatience as the hour for opening approached, then passed, without any sign of activity from the doorkeeper.

Finally, thirty minutes late, the door of the courtroom swung open and the line began to move forward, dividing to left and right and rapidly filling up the benches provided for the public in the little chamber. Extra chairs were brought, and were promptly occupied, until every vacant section of floor space had been taken. The fastidious little marshal, obviously upset at the unseemly vulgar interest in the coming decision and harrassed with the task of finding seating and standing room, looked at the packed audience and sighed. No one else, it was evident, could be squeezed in; and yet, there came one last *opéra-bouffe* episode before the marshal was allowed to return to his business.

In the doorway appeared a member of that self-assured and insistent species which the mid-nineties had come to recognize as the "new woman" —emancipated, imperious and doggedly involved in all important affairs of the forum. Such a one now stood, glancing about the room over the marshal's head, oblivious to his repeated whispers that there could be no more admittance. At length she located the vantage point she intended to occupy and, brushing aside him and his admonitions, pushed into the chamber, up through the packed aisles and planted herself in a spot at the end of the Justices' bench. The crowd watched the scene with titillated interest; would the diminutive marshal try to eject her? For a fleeting moment he apparently entertained the thought; then, recognizing the unfavorable odds, he shook his head and left the room, returning in a moment with an additional chair on which the spectator seated herself, aligned with and only slightly lower than the row of black leather chairs awaiting the members of the court.[19]

These were to be the eyewitnesses to history, seated or standing around the walls, filling the doorway and even yet stretching back down the corridor. The government counsel, and a number of Congressman-lawyers entitled to sit within the bar, had also made their way into the chamber; but conspicuously absent were the attorneys who had carried Pollock's case this far. Were they already aware of the outcome—and did they, in such event, seek to avoid the potential violence of the crowd's reaction? One could only speculate and in the meantime study the gilded eagle with outstretched wings placed above the bench and the row of portraits of past Chief Justices, from John Jay to Morrison R. Waite, looking down impassively upon the scene. Some of these men's opinions had helped shape the issue now in dispute; it was Oliver Ellsworth's Court, a century before, which had asserted a broad constitutional authority to levy taxes analogous to the income tax; Salmon P. Chase in the decade after the Civil War had strengthened the government's position on the question, and Waite himself, only fourteen years ago, had confirmed it still further.[20]

The low drone of voices was abruptly cut off. It was high noon, and the marshal, his self-confidence now restored, rose to announce in a loud voice the Chief Justice and Associate Justices of the United States, intoning thereafter the immemorial notice: "Hear ye, hear ye, hear ye: The honorable the Supreme Court of the United States is now in session. All persons having business with this Court draw near and give attention, and they shall be heard. God save the United States of America and this honorable Court." During this ritualistic pronouncement the nine Justices filed in behind the bench, acknowledged the grave bows of the members of the bar and now seated themselves in order of seniority and in varying attitudes of expectancy. In the now complete silence of the courtroom, the three men in the center of the bench at once became the focus of attention.

*   *   *

Melville W. Fuller of Illinois, as Chief Justice, occupied the center seat, while to his right sat the senior incumbent, Justice Field of California, and to his left the second in seniority, John Marshall Harlan of Kentucky. Thus Fuller himself seemed caught between the forces which, so vehemently championed and condemned by these respective associates, were coming headlong together this pleasant spring day. Under any circumstances the trio would have been an arresting combination—the presiding Justice with his long white hair parted in the middle and falling evenly over a clean-cut face, the patriarchal Westerner with his flowing beard, and the giant Kentuckian whose bald dome grew increasingly flushed as the tension of the occasion increased.

Without any preliminary comment to open the session, the Chief Justice leaned forward and began reading the majority opinion, rapidly but in a tone low enough to require the listener to strain to hear it.

"Whenever this Court is required to pass upon the validity of an act of Congress as tested by the fundamental law enacted by the people," he began, "the duty imposed requires in its discharge the utmost deliberation and care, and invokes the deepest sense of responsibility. And this is especially so when the question involves the exercise of a great governmental power." The Constitution, Fuller went on, had "divided Federal taxation into two great classes, the class of direct taxes, and the class of duties, imposts and excises; and prescribed two rules which qualified the grant of power as to each class." Direct taxes upon property were to be distributed among the states in proportion to their representation in the lower house of Congress, while indirect taxes were to be uniform throughout the Union. Accordingly, said the Chief Justice, "we are unable to conclude that the enforced subtraction from the yield of all of the owner's real or personal property, in the manner prescribed, is so different from a tax upon the property itself, that it is not a direct . . . tax, in the meaning of the Constitution."[21]

Imperceptibly, a tremor of relaxing tension ran through the crowded chamber; this, at least, settled any lingering doubt as to the majority opinion. The Federal income tax was unconstitutional. Yet the breathless silence remained unbroken as the quiet, almost melodious voice of the Chief Justice went on for a full forty-five minutes, his eyes fixed intently upon the manuscript before him and only once or twice in the course of his reading being raised to look at the courtroom. Most of his listeners, for their part, kept their eyes upon him; his calm dignity and personal warmth invited respect and even affection. As one pondered his career, it was not surprising that he should be with the majority on this decision. A lawyer of more than thirty years' experience and seasoned already by seven years as Chief Justice (his tenure would last for twenty-two), Fuller was the *beau idéal* of the new metropolitan practitioners of the last half of the nineteenth century. A native of Maine, he had moved west to the burgeoning community of Chicago in 1856 and there had grown as spectacularly as the town itself. His personal and professional philosophy was as firm as it was simple; transcendentalism had lighted his youth, and the Emersonian ideals of self-reliance and diligent labor were to him as literal standards of conduct as was the strict letter of the Constitution.

"It is vain," Justice Samuel F. Miller had observed early in Fuller's administration, "to contend with judges who have been, at the bar, the advocates of railroad companies, and all the forms of associated capital, when they are called upon to decide cases where such interests are in contest."[22] The statement did less than justice to Fuller's personal integrity and judicious moderation, but it served to underline the background of corporate practice which lay behind several prominent members of the bench. While Fuller as an attorney had handled cases in virtually every field of law, he had attained eminence in the profession for his expert knowledge of property and commercial law, and his retainers from various industrial clients, opportunely reinvested, had made him a wealthy man before he came onto the Court. It was a testimonial both to his frequent appearance as counsel before the Supreme Court and to his scrupulous avoidance of potential conflicts of interest, that he felt himself obliged not to participate in eight major decisions which came before the Court in the first four years of his Chief Justiceship, since he had been one of the lawyers in the cases when they had begun.[23] Banks, railroads and industrial corporations had been the clients in these cases, as in scores of others whose briefs he had handled over the years. He had witnessed at first hand, and often had actively aided in the creation of great new economic enterprises implemented by hard work and aggressive individual initiative; while he would, on frequent occasions, sustain the right of the injured and dispossessed to recover damages from employer or entrepreneur, he found the support for this in the rules of equity and utterly rejected any suggestion that such matters could ever be something of government concern.

*   *   *

The fact remained, however, that the Court's sympathies were generally assumed to lie with private capital and to be hostile to efforts at social restraint or regulation. Senator David B. Hill of New York, in the course of legislative debate on the Income Tax Law the previous year, had blurted out that he "hoped that with the Supreme Court as now constituted, this income tax will be declared unconstitutional." The indiscretion roused a Western Senator to decry the fact that the financial oligarchy "is not satisfied with reaching out its long bony fingers through the legislation of Congress, but that it is seeking to fasten itself upon the supreme tribunal of the land."[24] Still, the New Yorker knew his men on the bench; besides Fuller, there would be the ultra-conservative Field and his nephew, David Brewer of Kansas, and the traditionalist Horace Gray of Massachusetts. This would seem to assure four votes for the anti-tax argument and leave only one—for which Justice Shiras was the best prospect—to clinch a narrow but all-important majority.

Hill, himself a successful corporation lawyer and a vigorous exponent of sound currency—he would lead the Eastern Democratic opposition to William Jennings Bryan and "free silver" the following year—found substantial response from other members of the metropolitan bar. Half a dozen highly eminent attorneys, led by Joseph H. Choate of Boston, would appear as counsel for Pollock and for one Lewis H. Hyde in companion cases reviewing the legality of the tax in the March arguments, while a former Senator, George F. Edmunds of Vermont who had retired three years before to enter law practice in Philadelphia, argued with two other attorneys on behalf of John G. Moore, the appellant in a third case contesting the statute—in all, nine highly reputed lawyers concentrating their professional skills in the attack upon the tax.[25] Their briefs would run to massive volumes, and their oral arguments offered the Court every possible opportunity to distinguish the past cases upholding the tax, or, failing this, to override the precedents.

This legal phalanx had carried much of the field on April 8, and in the process had fatally breached the government's defenses in anticipation of the final decision on May 20. As to the rule handed down a century before, upholding the power of Congress to levy a tax on carriages without reference to apportionment and thus limiting direct taxes to land and fixed property, ex-Senator Edmunds bluntly urged the Court to "come back again to the true rule of the Constitution,"[26] which a co-counsel, Clarence A. Seward, insisted meant finding the original argument of Alexander Hamilton in the carriage tax case to be in error. That argument, said Seward, "was but a theory and advanced only as a presumption. The theory and presumption were not sustained by any

evidence." He then pleaded for justice for the rich by quoting Abraham
Lincoln: "In this country, nothing is ever finally decided until it is decided
right."[27] None of the decisions from 1796 to 1887, contended the foes of the
tax, had been "decided right," nor could the present law be held equitable when
(according to the complaining parties) it had the effect of laying 95 percent of the burden of the tax upon 2 percent of the population. Taxes
were a burden to be borne equally, contended the opponents—by which
they meant equally throughout the land by all individuals, and not equally in
terms of the benefits these individuals had received from the operation of the
economic system. Choate himself put it unequivocally in his closing statement:

> One of the fundamental objects of all civilized government [is] the preser-
> vation of the rights of private property. I have thought that it was the
> very keystone of the arch upon which all civilized government rests, and
> that this once abandoned, everything was at stake and in danger. . . .
> That was what Mr. Webster said, in 1820, at Plymouth, and I supposed
> that all educated, civilized men believed in that.[28]

This, actually, was the crux of the matter—the perpetuation of *laissez-
faire* capitalism and the proposal to bar Congress categorically from interference with the processes of that capitalism. This had placed upon the
present litigation an "immense pecuniary stake," in the words of the government's counsel, Attorney General Richard N. Olney. It was, he observed, a
stake "so large . . . that no legal or constitutional principle that stands in
the way, however venerable or however long and universally acquiesced in,
is suffered to pass unchallenged."[29] Olney, from the very tenor of his remarks,
seemed to accept the government's defeat; indeed, the opinion on April 8 had
left him little ground for optimism. By a six-to-two majority the Court had
held invalid one section of the law which had levied a Federal tax upon
income from land, and another on income from municipal bonds.[30] But on
the ultimate question of whether these findings amounted to a rule that a
tax upon income in general was beyond the power of Congress, the Court
had previously divided evenly.

So this day—May 20—had become the final fateful milestone in the
struggle, and early in his opinion Fuller had disposed of it. Now he continued
his reading, borrowing copiously from the arguments marshalled by the appellants' counsel to substantiate his contention that the present case was cor-
recting "a century of error." Meticulously he reviewed the reasoning of the
Constitutional Convention of 1787, the opinions of the several Justices in the
carriage tax case, and the opinions handed down in the cases of the past
thirty years, all having supported the proposition that such a tax was within
the constitutional powers of Congress. It was not so, he insisted; reiterating
his words in the opinion of April 8, he concluded: "If it be true that by
varying the form the substance may be changed, it is not easy to see that
anything would remain of the limitations of the Constitution, or of the rule of

taxation and representation, so carefully recognized and guarded in favor of the citizens of every state."[31]

*   *   *

At length the soft voice of the Chief Justice stopped. For a moment there was a total silence, then a scattering of handclapping which was promptly silenced by an indignant gesture from the marshal. Several reporters squeezed their way from the room to get the news to the telegraph wires, their emptied places instantly being filled by other bystanders. Everyone sensed that the drama was only half played, even though, like a Greek tragedy, the outcome was already known. The crowd's attention was shifting now from Fuller to Associate Justice Harlan, the first of four who were to read separate dissenting opinions. With Harlan, most knowledgeable observers linked Field, his only senior on the bench and his most consistent antagonist in constitutional ideology. Between them, as of this spring, a total of half a century of service on the Court was presented; Field had been appointed by President Lincoln in 1863 and Harlan by President Hayes in 1877. At the end of their careers, the Californian would have served longer than anyone else in the history of the bench—thirty-four years—and Harlan would claim a tenure only a few months shorter. Indeed, the length of service of several members of Fuller's Court—the Chief Justice included—accounted for a remarkably consistent constitutional dialogue from the beginning of the last decade of one century to the end of the first decade of the next.

Field's own career represented the demands of rugged individualism in the nation-building of the mid-nineteenth century; the brother of David Dudley Field, a leader of the New York City bar, Stephen had followed the Gold Rush to California in 1849. Within weeks of his landing at San Francisco, he had organized a government for the mining town of Marysville and been elected its mayor. There were claim-jumpers, however, in the practice of law as well as in the gold fields, and Field had almost immediately become embroiled in a violent quarrel with a local judge, William R. Turner, which found him twice disbarred and once jailed for contempt—before he won a seat in the state legislature, sponsored a bill reorganizing the judiciary and transferred his rival to an obscure district. Field's associations with California were tempestuous to the end; nearly four decades later, while riding the California circuit as Associate Justice of the Supreme Court of the United States, a tangled bit of litigation brought him to a confrontation with a former state chief justice, David S. Terry. An adverse ruling by Field's court against Terry and his wife led to threats and abuse which so alarmed the Justice's bodyguard, David Neagle, that he ultimately shot and killed Terry.[32]

To administer justice on the frontier was a bare-knuckled thing. For Stephen J. Field, having subdued one type of mob on more than one occasion in his lifetime, there was no question of yielding to another type of pressure of the masses in the form of legislation which would tend to limit the rewards which awaited the victor in the struggle for survival. This was his fundamental point of opposition to Harlan, who recognized that as the frontier passed, the methods demanded for life on the frontier had also to give way to a more civilized economic order. A Kentuckian who fought in the Union Army, Harlan saw in the settlement of the conflict the permanent disposition of the issue of the limits of national authority, as well as the permanent commitment of government to the guaranteeing of the rights of the individual within the impersonal structure of a new corporate society.

Fuller, Field and Brewer provided the nucleus of conservatism on the Court over most of these years, jointly concerned that "the task of the Court," as Field's biographer was later to write, should be "the prevention of dangerous changes in the good society." Or, as the Justice himself had put it in an address on the centennial of the judiciary in 1890: "As population and wealth increase . . . —as population in some quarters presses upon the means of subsistence, and angry menaces against order find vent in large denunciations—it becomes more and more the imperative duty of the Court to enforce with a firm hand all the guarantees of the Constitution."[33]

Harlan—usually supported by Edward D. White, the ex-Confederate from Louisiana who would succeed Fuller as Chief Justice—would be the author of more than three hundred dissents in the course of his long career. Where Congress had the power to act, it was no part of the judicial process to question the wisdom or efficacy of its actions, he told his colleagues in his first dissent in 1877; he would be repeating the theme in his final dissents in 1911. For Field, the rule of law was not to be compromised to accommodate the clamor for social change; for Harlan, the need for change was a need for change in the rule of law itself. Field, in his letter announcing his resignation in 1897, reiterated his concept of the judicial power as the "power of resistance," which was "the only safety of a popular government"; Harlan saw the effectuation of popular will as the only justification for government itself.[34]

So the ardent dialogue went. In dissenting in the present case, the Kentuckian was in essence making his reply to the propositions laid down by Field in his own opinion on the first Pollock case in April.

*   *   *

As he opened, it was noticeable that Harlan's voice trembled slightly; he controlled it by a deliberate slowing of his reading, and after a moment he regained full vigor of tone. His first point was sufficiently grave: "In my judgement," he said, "to say nothing of the disregard of the former adjudications of this Court and of the practice of the government for a century, this decision may well excite the gravest apprehensions. It strikes at the very foundations of national authority, in that it denies to the general government a power which is, or may, at some time in a great emergency, such as that of war, become vital to the existence and preservation of the Union." Now the voice began to rise in fervor. "The decision now made," said the Justice, "will inevitably provoke a contest in this country from which the American people had been spared, if the Court had not overturned its former adjudications and had adhered to those principles of taxation under which our government, following the repeated adjudications of this Court, had always been administered." If the majority opinion was henceforth to be the law of the land, he declared, then "the American people cannot too soon amend their Constitution."

But it was Field's dread of the "assault of the poor upon the rich" and Fuller's bland assumption of the corporation counsel's argument in favor of geographic uniformity of taxation that now goaded the dissenter to his climax. His voice was thundering, and the packed courtroom was transfixed; Harlan leaned forward over the bench to look beyond the Chief Justice at his chief antagonist. "Are those, in whose behalf the arguments are made that rest upon favoritism . . . to mere property and to particular sections of the country, aware that they are provoking a contest which in some countries has swept away in a tempest of frenzy and passion existing social organizations, and put in peril all that was dear to friends of law and order?" His finger stabbed at Field, and then his huge fist smote the bench before him. Could not the wealthy perceive, he demanded, that in entrenching themselves against the government's attempt at proportionate taxation, they merely armed the alien agitators who were increasingly articulate in the nation's political life and who "have neither respect for the rights of property nor any conception of what is liberty regulated by law?"[35]

Harlan's listeners knew the dangers to which he was referring. It was perhaps no coincidence that the Haymarket Riots of a decade before, generally alleged to have been fomented by anarchists, had occurred in the same period that Karl Marx's *Capital* was becoming the nation's best seller. Literate and thoughtful men were still discussing Edward Bellamy's *Looking Backward*, published in 1887 as a Socialistic forecast of the twenty-first century, while the Socialist Labor Party in the cities and the Populists in the rural West seemed on the verge of a coalition which might well sweep orthodox political faiths into oblivion. The mounting bitterness of the labor movement in the past five years, exacerbated by the Homestead strike in 1892 and the Pullman strike in 1894, had raised the grim prospect of a new Civil War fought on an economic front. Now, warned the Justice, the blind selfishness of the propertied and privileged was exposing their system to the concerted attack of all their foes.

"The practical, if not the direct effect of the decision today," Harlan concluded, "is to give to certain kinds of property a position of favoritism and advantage that is inconsistent with the fundamental principles of our social organization, and to invest them with power and influence that may be perilous to that portion of the American people upon whom rests the larger part of the burdens of government, and who ought not to be subjected to the domination of aggregated wealth any more than the property of the country should be at the mercy of the lawless."[36]

When Harlan stopped, the little chamber seemed still to reverberate with the indignant oratory which had filled the air for more than half an hour. There was no sound from the spectators except the rustle and collective sigh of relaxing emotions as the second scene in the drama came to its close. The weak voice of the next dissenter, Jackson of Tennessee, was all the more arresting because of its contrast and the racking cough which interrupted the reading at a number of points. This would be Jackson's last important case; when he finished his opinion he rose and left the chamber to return, as many believed, to the sick bed from which he had come. The deep bass of Justice Henry B. Brown of Michigan took up the thread of protest. To find Jackson and Brown on the side of the question was itself mildly surprising; Jackson's narrow and reactionary view of the Interstate Commerce Act a few years before on the Circuit Court had identified him generally with the conservatives. As for Brown, constitutional law was not his primary interest, and his specialty of commercial jurisprudence inclined him in most instances to sympathize with the business community. For men like this to protest the narrow construction of the tax power was to warn the country that the constitutional issue was not solely a doctrinaire opposition to liberalism.

Jackson's words were therefore all the more impressive: "The practical operation of the decision is not only to disregard the great principles of equality in taxation, but the further principle that in the imposition of taxes for the benefit of the government, the burdens thereof should be imposed upon those having the most ability to bear them. Considered in all its bearings, this decision is, in my judgment, the most disastrous blow ever struck at the constitutional power of Congress."[37] As for Brown, he agreed with Harlan that "the decision involves nothing less than the surrender of the taxing power to the moneyed class."[38]

For the spectators—now having been sitting or standing for more than three hours while the opinions were being read—the final scene in the drama was to be delivered by Justice White. Like Harlan, this was a military veteran who had personally experienced the cataclysm of a nation crumbling into chaos. Like the Kentucky Unionist, the Louisiana Confederate protested with an equal degree of fervor: "The grievous results sure to follow" from the prevailing opinion, he declared, "are so obvious that my mind cannot fail to see that if a tax on invested personal property were imposed by the rule of population, and there were no other means of preventing its enforcement, the red specter of revolution would shake our institutions to their very foundations."[39]

*   *   *

Caught by surprise, the courtroom suddenly became aware that the threnody of protest was at an end. White, who had delivered the peroration, dropped his voice and with scarcely a pause began to read the majority opinion on another case. After a moment or two, the spectators began to drift out into the Capitol corridors in silence that continued unbroken long after the individual was out of earshot of the chamber. It had been, as one observer later described it, "the most remarkable judicial performance of this generation"; but its ultimate consequences could not be grasped in the short space of time in which the performance had occurred. What indeed was the future of a Constitution, many were to ask, when a majority of five on a Court of nine wiped out the judicial declarations of a century? And as for the dissenters, equally divided between conservatives and liberals, to remember them as warning of—or perhaps even calling for—an uprising which would overturn the new interpretation of the fundamental law was a profoundly disquieting alternative. What, indeed, it all portended for the Court, the Constitution, or the country, no man this day was prepared to guess.[40]

2/The Jurisprudence of Industrialism

T HE CLOSING DECADE of the nineteenth century was variously described by its contemporaries. For those who had benefitted most from the events of the past generation, of course, the retrospect was pleasant indeed; Charles F. Clark, president of the Bradstreet Company, in the year of the Income Tax Case observed: "Not since the history of the world began has there been such a marvelous advancement of all factors creating wealth and developing trade and commerce." David A. Wells, former United States Commissioner of Revenue, saw the economic displacements of the seventies and eighties as insignificant in comparison to the gains. Poverty, he concluded, was proportionately no greater in the larger population of 1890 than it had been at the beginning of the Industrial Revolution; sweated labor in the garment trades at least had the beneficial effect of producing cheap clothing for the poor who would otherwise wear rags, and government, he hoped, had learned the lesson that any interference with private control of the economic system would only aggravate the vagaries of the business cycle.[1]

More objective commentators were not so tolerant; while confessedly dazzled by the remarkable technological advances of their time, they nonetheless cried shame at the human dislocations which accompanied the changes. Benjamin O. Flower called the whole nineteenth century a utilitarian age generally devoid of conscience, and the asthete Henry Adams had his own formula for coming to terms with this era:

> He had stood up for his eighteenth century, his Constitution of 1789, his George Washington, his Harvard College, his Quincy, and his Plymouth Pilgrims, as long as anyone would stand up with him. He had said it was hopeless twenty years before, but he had kept on, in the same old attitude, by habit and taste, until he found himself altogether alone. . . . The matter was settled at last by the people. For a hundred years, between 1793 and 1893, the American people had hesitated, vacillated, swayed forward and back, between two forces, one simply industrial, the other capitalistic, centralizing, and mechanical. In 1893, the issue came on the single gold

18

standard, and the majority at last declared itself, once and for all, in favor of the capitalistic system with all its necessary machinery. All one's friends, all one's best citizens, reformers, churches, colleges, educated classes, had joined the banks to force submission to capitalism; a submission long foreseen by the mere law of mass. Of all forms of society or government, this was the one he liked least, but his likes and dislikes were as antiquated as the rebel doctrine of state rights. A capitalistic system had been adopted, and if it were to be run at all, it must be run by capital and by capitalistic methods; for nothing could surpass the nonsensity of trying to run so complex and so concentrated a machine by Southern and Western farmers in grotesque alliance with city day-laborers, as had been tried in 1880 and 1828, and had failed even under simple conditions. [2]

Rank and file Americans, who seldom had occasion to read the confident pronouncements of men like Clark or the forebodings of men like Adams, nevertheless faced life with something of the same ambivalence. They still retained the optimism which was dedicated to the proposition that abundant opportunity for success lay within the reach of any normal, ambitious individual; they recalled that James J. Hill, the railroad king, had started out as a clerk in a country store, and that Andrew Carnegie, the steel lord, began as an immigrant messenger boy. Still, they did not deny—as they could not— that the mid-nineties marked the completion of twenty years of a chronic depression, which had begun with the catastrophic failure of the banking house of Jay Cooke and Company in 1873. In the decade following the Cooke collapse, prices had fallen almost 40 percent, and another 15 percent in the next decade. By 1896, almost one-third of the railroads in the country had gone into receivership, and as of this same date almost one-third of all farms had become tenant-operated. From an index figure of 112 in 1870, farm prices themselves had dropped to 56 in 1896.[3]

There were many second thoughts bred of the depression experience, as well. While the panic of 1893 had ruined many men, it had actually enriched others. Moreover, in spite of ailing markets for many small businesses, the closing decade of the century was characterized by what up to then had been the greatest gain in total wealth in the history of the United States—from $78,500,000,000 in 1890 to $126,700,000,000 in 1900. To an increasing number of men in private and public life, these statistics no longer vindicated the free enterprise system so much as they demonstrated the ultimate paradox inherent in it. Steadily improving technology and increasing productivity, as Henry George saw it, did not "act upon the social fabric from underneath, as was for a long time hoped and believed," but had instead the effect of a wedge driven into the midpoint of the economic system. "Those [who] are above the point of separation are elevated," he concluded, "but those who are below are crushed down."[4]

*   *   *

Another perspective of the nineties, two years after the decade's close, was to be found in the nineteen-volume *Report* of the United States Industrial

Commission, created by Congress in 1898 to assess the effects of the industrial outburst which had occurred in the closing quarter of the century. In a monumental compilation of testimony from captains of industry, spokesmen for the slowly coalescing labor organizations, government officials and academicians, the commissioners probed for an explanation of how late Victorian capitalism had come to its present position. More than any other documentary work, the *Report* of the Industrial Commission provided a text-book on the evolution of the post-Civil War corporation through the early system of voluntary associations into interlocking agreements and finally into the agency which represented the apex of nineteenth-century capitalistic achievement—the trust.

The history of the trust was virtually coincident with the last twenty-five years of the century; the progenitor, the Michigan Salt Association, was established in 1876. The problems of salt processing and marketing were the problems characteristic of most American industry—overproduction, conse-quent price wars, failure of the weaker competitors and unemployment re-sulting from continually advancing technologies. With the last problem, the capitalist of the seventies and eighties was unconcerned; as his favorite econ-omist, William Graham Sumner, had put it: "In a free state every man is held and expected to take care of himself and his family, to make no trouble for his neighbor, and to contribute his full share to public interests and com-mon necessities. If he fails in this he throws burdens on others. He does not thereby acquire rights against the others."[5]

The other problems, however, presented a direct threat to the profit system, and the capitalist cast about for their solution. One solution was the pool arrangement—in the case of the Michigan salt producers, a stock com-pany with shares equal to the barrels of salt each shareholder marketed. The arrangement proved so effective that within fifteen years it had brought the Michigan association into control of 85 percent of the industry throughout the country. The lesson was not lost on other manufacturers; in 1884 had come the Cottonseed Oil Trust, the next year the National Linseed Oil Trust, and 1887 marked the creation of both the National Lead Trust and the Sugar Refiners' Company. The sugar group would be destined to become the medium for testing the power of government to deal with this new dimension of capitalism. For the moment it was only one of a score of closely controlled industrial confederacies which had become the dominant feature of national business life.[6]

The pool was a secret, voluntary organization for controlling production and prices, and its effectiveness depended solely on the ability of all of its members to resist the temptation to take advantage of the others. Ambitious entrepreneurs and owners of idle capital eager for large profits looked for something better—a means of securing a firm grip on the production process itself, and a device for perpetuating the control thus gained. The search made separate careers for men like Samuel Calvin Tate Dodd, the attorney for the Standard Oil Company of Ohio, "Judge" William H. Moore, head of a Chicago firm of corporation lawyers. and Charles R. Flint, Jr., a banker who came to be acknowledged as the "father of trusts."[7]

For Flint, the trust was the symbol of capitalistic integrity, "an alliance of work, brains and money" which would in the nature of things make business better and thus benefit the public. A successful New York commission merchant who had also made a fortune as a munitions broker for foreign military powers, Flint regarded with disdain the domestic spectacle of planless, irrationally competitive business enterprise. Consolidation meant efficiency and economy, and he offered his services as "a disinterested intermediary" to industries willing to reorganize with these ends in view. Flint was responsible for the creation, in 1892, of the United States Rubber Company, and by the end of the decade he had brought about major consolidations in woolens, chicle, starch and a long list of other consumer products. He, and the numerous promoters who emulated him, brought into being the modern interstate corporation with its centralized management, diversified stockholder ownership and regional or national distribution of its products or services. What J. P. Morgan and E. H. Harriman had accomplished in the fields of banking and transportation, Flint and his contemporaries did for the manufacturing industries.[8]

More venturesome, and inclined to play fast and loose with other people's enterprises, was "Judge" Moore, whose initial consolidation of the Diamond Match Company was meteoric in both its rise and its fall. The company itself was successful in capturing most of the domestic market in a matter of a few years after its recapitalization—from an original $3,000,000 to an ultimate $11,000,000—in the late eighties. But Moore's zeal to inflate the value of the stock of the company on the Chicago Exchange, gambling on an expansion into foreign markets which never materialized, ultimately caused a collapse in the late summer of 1896 so shattering that the Chicago Exchange closed down for three months thereafter. Moore himself recouped his losses by organizing the National Biscuit Company in 1898 and, the following winter, the American Tin Plate Company, the National Steel Company and the National Steel Hoop Company—all precariously capitalized against anticipated profits. There followed the organization of the American Sheet Steel Company and the American Can Company at the turn of the century; thereupon the Moores turned to railroads, seizing control of the Chicago, Rock Island and Pacific and ultimately refinancing it with what *Harper's Weekly* was later to describe as "the most astounding piece of stock watering the world has ever seen." After nearly thirty years strewn with bankruptcies as well as solid triumphs, the Moores could boast that their organizational services had reshaped scores of American businesses "from the marshes of Maine to the Pacific Coast."[9]

*   *   *

Dodd of Standard Oil made the most spectacularly successful contribu-

tion of all—quite possibly because of the perceptiveness of John D. Rockefeller who found him so capable an opponent, in the early days of the oil
industry, that he made him his lifetime counsel. Rockefeller had already, in
1878, demonstrated his own business acumen by acquiring control of each
phase in the production and marketing of petroleum—from wells to refineries,
railroads and pipelines and finally the retail outlets—so that 90 percent of
the entire national output of the commodity was within his grasp. But this
centralized ownership of so many companies making up an entire industry
had brought indictments in Pennsylvania, Ohio and other states on common law conspiracy, and Rockefeller needed a new legal formula for accomplishing his purposes. Dodd was to provide this by adapting the
ancient concept of equitable ownership of property for the use of the legal
owner to the specific needs of the Standard Oil Trust Company, organized
in 1882.

The trust concept was an invention of necessity, the result of almost
universal state laws prohibiting a locally chartered corporation from holding
stock in another, out-of-state corporation. The statutes themselves were the
product of a decentralized frontier economy which had little relation to the
expanding areas of business in the eighties. The times presently required, as
Dodd was to write, "combinations of capital, persons and skill . . . sufficiently
great to meet the demands of our trade." Until the existing statutes could be
modernized, an alternative had to be found which would "use the corporations of different states as agencies in a joint business."[10]

Dodd and Rockefeller both understood the special need for such an
alternative in the oil industry. A native of Pennsylvania, Dodd had been admitted to the bar the same year that the first great oil discovery had been
made in Titusville. From the outset he had specialized in organizing new
petroleum companies, creating new contractual agreements between producers
and refiners and carriers, and witnessing at first hand the waste and ruin of
small operators coping with an industry which within a matter of a few years
had grown beyond their capacity to handle. Consolidation and systematic
managerial programming, he understood, had become imperative if the new
commodity was to be economically developed and delivered to farflung
markets. The central problem of the time, as Dodd described it, was that a
man engaged in a growing business "could have no assurance that he was
not transgressing the criminal laws."[11]

The solution, or rather the expedient, as Dodd devised it and described it
to Henry L. Flagler, secretary of the Rockefeller Ohio enterprises, had to
be a network of state corporations—Standard Oil of Ohio, New Jersey, New
York, and so on. "There is no way to perfectly consolidate the corporations
of different states," he wrote Flagler; but by placing the stock of each corporation in trust with a central trust company, in exchange for certificates of
ownership issued to the stockholders, "you could have a common name, a
common office, and a common management by means of a common executive

committee." This was a description of the Standard Oil Trust, and the plan became the model for a flood of reorganized industries within the decade, the word itself becoming a universally recognized synonym for big business.[12]

The state anti-monopoly statutes of the mid-nineteenth century, and the efforts of growing business to cope with them, exemplified the contradictions and frustrations of a transforming economy. Historically, the laws derived from early English efforts to control mercantile combinations which threatened to raise prices unconscionably; emotionally, they articulated the egalitarian ideals of the handicraft age and the early Industrial Revolution; economically, they presented an obstacle to commercial expansion which was manifestly demanded by the sheer size to which the United States was growing. Yet the small freeholder and the trust-builder of the type of Flint or Dodd could agree that consolidation in a major industry was but a step away from monopoly. The moral and legal issues were complicated and involved. In the closing years of the old century, the American was slowly to come to realize that henceforth he would find no simple answers to the demands of his society.

*   *   *

Certain facts about the new industrial America were already becoming clear: the Cooke collapse of the seventies demonstrated the interdependence of the economy as business firms for a generation thereafter felt, in varying degrees, the after-shocks of the disaster. In 1883 had come another demonstration of this interdependence when the operators for the Western Union Telegraph Company, which in that year transmitted forty million messages over four hundred thousand miles of wire, simultaneously struck in cities from coast to coast. The instant slowdown of business of every size throughout the country's commercial centers made clear that the modern industrial age was vitally dependent on fast and uninterrupted communications. It also demonstrated a dependence of another type: when Postmaster General John Wanamaker ten years later proposed government ownership of the telegraph, individual Congressmen mindful of the franking privilege provided them by Western Union declined to consider his recommendation.[13]

The importance of the telegraph—which in turn had facilitated the spectacular growth of the railroad system in the generation after the Civil War—was complemented in the fall of 1882 by the dramatic demonstration in New York City of the practical use of electric lighting by Thomas A. Edison and his associates. With lighting came electric power generally, so that by the early nineties the private and public utility had become another major element in the nation's economic life. The electric streetcar, successfully developed by an ex-naval officer, Frank J. Sprague, brought a practical transportation system to the cities and suburbs and still further accelerated their growth.[14]

But in the end it was the trust—a name applied popularly to any large-scale business, and with an increasing overtone of derogation—which remained the prototype of the industrialism of the eighties and nineties. And monopoly or near-monopoly appeared to be the natural history of the trust in transportation, utilities, communications, manufacturing and marketing. The trust was a readily identifiable symbol, as one Rockefeller associate ruefully observed, for "all that is evil, hard-hearted, oppressive, cruel." Each year seemed to bring more impressive examples of combination—in 1887, which witnessed the creation of the lead and sugar trusts, there also came a combination in whiskey and the most powerful of all, the National Cordage Trust. Cornering the entire world supply of manila hemp, it cast its shadow over most of the manufacturers in the United States which depended on this vital commodity.

By the end of the century, as Henry Demarest Lloyd was to observe, the trust as it had been developed by Dodd and his imitators controlled "an incredible number of the necessaries and luxuries of life, from meat to tombstones." Moreover, as first state legislatures and then Congress were importuned by constituents who were consumers at the mercy of the combinations, or competitors crushed by them, it seemed, as Lloyd put it, that "the forces of capital and industry have outgrown the forces of our government."[15]

*   *   *

Grover Cleveland, in his final message to Congress as his first Presidential term was ending, excoriated the trusts and monopolies for their "sordid disregard of all but personal interests" and their "refusal to abate for the benefit of others one iota of selfish advantage." But it was to be reserved for Benjamin Harrison's administration to witness the successful drive in Congress to enact a general statute dealing with the problem. Senator John Sherman of Ohio, younger brother of the Union military leader of the Civil War, saw the ruthless progress of the industrial combination as a devastation equal to the famed march through Georgia. As Secretary of the Treasury under Hayes, he had fought post-war inflation with a dogged integrity; as an expert on finance, he was persuaded that rampant and irresponsible manipulation of the business process was poisoning the springs of the whole capitalistic system. The anti-trust act which would bear his name evolved from a conviction that it was "the right of every man to work . . . and produce in any lawful vocation, and to transport his production on equal terms and conditions and under like circumstances. This is industrial liberty and lies at the foundation of the equality of all rights and privileges."[16]

Upon what constitutional basis was Federal anti-trust legislation to rely? The commerce clause of the First Article—"The Congress shall have power . . . to regulate commerce . . . among the several states"—was the most obvious starting point, but for the fact that many members shared the conviction expressed by Senator James Z. George of Mississippi: "The power of Congress commences with the initiation of interstate or foreign commerce and ceases with its termination"; manufacturing processes or commercial transactions occurring before or after this period were outside the scope of the Article.[17] Sherman replied that, assuming this to be true, the Federal law giving Federal courts jurisdiction over monopolistic activities in the area of interstate commerce would complement the jurisdiction of the state courts over activities before or after the interstate commerce.[18]

"The popular mind," Sherman observed, "is agitated with problems that may disturb social order, and among them all none is more threatening than the inequality of condition, of wealth, and opportunity that has grown within a single generation out of the concentration of capital into vast combinations to control production and trade and to break down competition . . . Congress alone can deal with them, and if we are unwilling or unable there will soon be a trust for every production and a master to fix the price for every necessity of life."[19]

It was one thing to concede the evils of monopoly—few voices in Congress or in industry were raised in its defense—but the sticking point came on the question of an effective and constitutional legislative enactment. "I am opposed to seeing any measure go out of this body . . . merely as a tentative proposition or one that is experimental upon a question of constitutional law," said John Tyler Morgan of Alabama, and he found many to agree with him. A sweeping prohibition of "unlawful restraints and monopolies," warned Henry M. Teller of Colorado, prophetically, would make it easier for labor organizations to be attacked than combinations of capital. Frank Hiscock of New York shrank from the prospect of extending the Federal authority into the states to reach goods or acts whose ultimate appearance in interstate commerce was purely hypothetical or conjectural. Orville H. Platt of Connecticut quibbled that the judicial jurisdiction proposed by the bill would deal with "agreements" between residents of different states when the Constitution spoke only of "controversies."[20]

The Congress of 1890 reflected the limitations of the country's own constitutional experience. Senator George Vest of Missouri frankly confessed that, in his view, the Founding Fathers had been incapable of foreseeing and therefore providing for problems of the sort now confronting the Fifty-first Congress. They could not, he observed, "ever have contemplated the immense country for which we are now legislating, and the enormous aggregation of wealth which startles and amazes the world. They undertook in the Constitution to meet contingencies, but here is one which beggars Aladdin's lamp in the reality that is before us and with us today." The doubts were not removed throughout the six months of debate; the bill was twice committed to the Senate judiciary committee, and after passing both houses was twice committed to conference committee to iron out remaining differences before it was finally enacted into law.[21]

The manifest fact was, as Justice Harlan would point out when the Sherman law came before the Supreme Court, that the American people, their legislatures and their judges, were unprepared to recognize that their national government had any power which was necessary to meet a national need. Most of them had never come to terms with John Marshall's concept of a

Constitution which, if "intended to endure for ages to come," of necessity had "to be adapted to the various crises of human affairs." Nor could they be expected to anticipate the doctrine of future Justices like Holmes and Cardozo, that "its principles are adaptable to changing events."

They could not rise to the challenge offered by Justice Harlan himself, speaking that same year in New York at the centennial of the Federal judiciary, when he offered four propositions for the America which was emerging:

> That while the preservation of the states, with authority to deal with matters not committed to national control, is fundamental in the American constitutional system, the Union cannot exist without a government for the whole;
> That the Constitution of the United States was made for the whole people of the Union, and is equally binding upon all the courts and all the citizens;
> That the general government, though limited as to its objects, is yet supreme with respect to those objects, is the government of all, its powers are delegated by all, and acts for all; and
> That America has chosen to be, in many respects and to many purposes, a nation, and for all these purposes her government is complete, to all these objects it is competent.[22]

For the majority of Americans, the Constitution of the United States was a charter of granted powers rather than a description of a national government possessed in latent form of all powers logically inherent in such government. The Fifty-first Congress searched for explicit permission to exercise its powers; the times were coming to demand a greater initiative. But the men of 1890 were no more clairvoyant than those of 1787; only the course of events would bring broader understanding and, as Justice Brandeis would put it, a willingness to let the mind be bold.*[23]

*   *   *

Self-doubt, which had produced a rather tentative document in the form of the Anti-Trust Act, also assailed the officers of the government who were charged with enforcing the statute. William H. H. Miller, Harrison's Attorney General, was not enthusiastic about this new responsibility—less, apparently, from sympathy for the trusts than from a lawyer's practical doubts as to the possibility of securing convictions. The kind of evidence to stand up at a trial —what constituted unfair acts in restraint of trade—was hard to come by, and Miller wrote ambivalently to a United States attorney:

> We do not want to undertake a prosecution and fail, especially a criminal indictment. It is always unfortunate to make a charge of crime against a person of otherwise good standing and subject him to the humiliation of making a defense, even though in the end he may be acquitted. At the same time, we cannot ignore our duty to enforce the penalties of this law, the same as any other, and parties must, of course, take their chances if

---

*For the basic provisions of the Sherman Act and other fundamental statutes, see Appendix D.

they get over the border line, even though it may be somewhat difficult to define that line.[24]

If Miller was reluctant, his Solicitor General, William Howard Taft, was substantially more so. Years later he was to cling to the conviction he expressed in the Harrison era, that the law was too vague and general to establish criminal intent in a business combination.[25]

With this lack of zeal for the task, it was not surprising that by the end of the Harrison administration only seven anti-trust cases had been begun by the government and only two of these concluded. Of the two, the one against the Whiskey Trust had been settled out of court, and the other, resulting in the enjoining of a combination of mining companies through the Nashville Coal Exchange, had been pushed through the United States District Court for the Middle District of Tennessee by the local Federal attorney, John Ruhm. No definitive judicial comment on the Sherman Act had emerged from this litigation, the court merely observing that "it should hesitate long and consider carefully before it should declare an act of Congress, passed after deliberation and debate, and approved by the President, unconstitutional."[26]

The returning President Cleveland did not seem to recognize in the statute the instrument for curbing the combinations which he had so vigorously criticized four years earlier. His selection for the office of Attorney General, Richard Olney, was a man who had actually been defense counsel in the Whiskey Trust prosecutions instituted a few months before. As attorney for the Chicago, Burlington & Olney Railroad, Olney had put himself into a position where there would be substantial conflicts of interest as well as loss of income in becoming the government's chief legal officer; the conflict, indeed, would become real enough in the bitter railroad strike in Chicago the next year. As for the Sherman Act, scarcely three months had passed since Olney had written to John G. Carlisle, now a colleague in Cleveland's Cabinet as Secretary of the Treasury, that a number of financiers in the Boston area were prepared to contribute funds and work for the repeal of the legislation, and he asked Carlisle for a list of Senators "who ought to be persuaded to see the thing in the right light."[27]

Humorless, austere in his integrity, and suffering chronically from what his biographer described as "lockjaw of the will," Olney could see no merit in the Anti-Trust Law, since "all ownership of property is of itself a monopoly," and every contract to a degree was a restraint of trade. It followed, in his mind, that "any literal application of the provisions of the statute [was] out of the question." The law was at best "an experimental piece of legislation" which did no more than make illegal by statute what was already recognized as illegal at common law. These statements in his first annual report echoed the arguments of the narrow constructionists in Congress as well as specifically citing a corroborating opinion by Circuit Judge Howell E. Jackson, who had subsequently been appointed to the Supreme Court.[28]

During his two years in office, Olney saw to it that no anti-trust cases were initiated—and, indeed, one begun by his subordinates against the Southern Pacific Railroad was dropped at his insistence. With so vague and novel a statute, he declared, it was necessary to seek a test of its constitutionality as soon as possible. He had selected his test case, the suit against the sugar trust, which had already been dismissed by the Federal trial court for the Eastern District of Pennsylvania and the dismissal upheld by the Circuit Court of Appeals. The lower courts had narrowed the justiciable issues; citing Circuit Judge Jackson's ruling that the statute was criminal and therefore to be strictly construed, the trial court had held that if any monopoly in sugar existed it was entirely intrastate and beyond the reach of the Federal government. The appellate court, on review, had ruled that even if the defendants had "acquired control of the business of refining and selling sugar in the United States," this did not tend to a monopoly in interstate commerce, since "manufacture and commerce are two distinct and very different things."[29]

*   *   *

The tenor of contemporary judicial opinion on the general subject of government's relationship to corporate enterprise corroborated Olney's confidence that the Sherman Act would be narrowly construed. Two cases the previous spring had revealed the trend: since 1877, when the Court by a seven-to-two majority had upheld an Illinois law regulating rate schedules for grain elevators, the margin in favor of a comparable New York law had dropped to six to three in 1892, and in 1894 had been barely five to four in support of a North Dakota grain elevator statute. The second 1894 case found a unanimous Court asserting a doctrine long to be reiterated thereafter, that the "reasonableness" of rate making by regulatory commissions was a reviewable question in the courts.[30]

The Illinois case (*Munn v. Illinois*) represented one pole of constitutional interpretation in the period of emergent capitalism, while the other pole was represented by arguments made by counsel and endorsed by the dissent in the Louisiana *Slaughterhouse Cases* of 1873. The assiduous strengthening of the *laissez-faire* position, inclining the preponderance of judicial disposition increasingly toward the former minority view of the Louisiana cases, was accomplished by brilliant attorneys whose arguments before the Court established the proposition of minimal government interference with free enterprise for half a century to come. In the process, the briefs of these counsel and the opinions of the bench which came more and more to echo them directed American constitutional law away from the long-accepted principle of the plenary power of government to regulate the activities of its citizens.

Many of the greatest names in the American bar were enlisted in this cause, which was nothing less than the emasculation of fundamental sovereignty in favor of the widest possible freedom for private capitalism. John A. Campbell of Georgia, a former member of the Supreme Court, appeared as counsel in the *Slaughterhouse Cases,* attacking the state-granted monopoly of meat packing as an improper exercise of the sovereign power. Within a decade would come Senator Roscoe Conkling of New York, appearing before the Court as counsel for railroad interests to assure the Justices that in extending the protection of due process to "persons" in the Fourteenth Amendment, the intent of Congress had been to include "legal persons" (i. e. corporations) and thus insulate them from the regulatory process. With arguments like these, zealously reiterated, constitutional jurisprudence of the last quarter of the nineteenth century was made to accommodate the desires of growing industrialism.[31]

With men like Campbell and Conkling to offer the argument, and men like Field and Bradley and later Brewer and Fuller to respond sympathetically, a case like the Sugar Trust prosecution was virtually pre-judged. In addition, confronting the unenthusiastic Olney as this case came on for argument, were corporation attorneys of a stature even more formidable than Campbell and Conkling. The counsel for the trust in the original trial had been John G. Johnson of Philadephia, who was the acknowledged leader of the American bar, and whose eminence in advocacy had earned him two offers of appointment to the Supreme Court and offers of the Attorney Generalship from three different Presidents. Johnson had refused them all; his total commitment, as a contemporary put it, was to the "defense of entrenched corporate interests." Between 1895, when he would argue the Sugar Trust Case before the Supreme Court, and 1917, he would be counsel for the business community in no less than eleven major constitutional cases. His methods, said another contemporary, "inspired among his adversaries anxiety and even terror."[32]

Joined with Johnson was John E. Parsons of New York, one of the founders of the Sugar Refining Company and himself an experienced counsel for major corporations. The two attorneys divided the strategy of defense between them; Parsons relied upon Justice Jackson's 1892 holding that the Act merely adopted the common law, and that common law tests of what constituted a monopoly were applicable. Under these tests, Parsons contended, only affirmative intention to restrain the rights of others could be acceptable proof of violation of the law. Johnson developed the argument he had successfully used in the courts below: interstate commerce, he repeated, was nothing more than the business of transporting goods, the goods themselves being distinguishable from their transportation and hence only "indirectly" affecting the commerce.[33]

Chief Justice Fuller and six of his colleagues eagerly accepted the Parsons-Johnson argument. Ironically enough, Justice Jackson, the intellectual godfather of the narrow construction of the Sherman Act, had already entered upon the long illness which would terminate his career the next summer, and took no part in the case. To the government's half-hearted argument that the control of sugar by the trust, then alleged to amount to 98 percent, was "a monopoly over a necessity of life," Fuller answered that the real question was not the nature of the commodity but whether the interstate power of Congress over commerce could reach an industry which manufactured or processed the commodity. Accepting the Johnson thesis, Fuller declared that while "the power to control the manufacture of a given thing involves in a certain sense the control of its disposition, . . . this is a secondary and not the primary sense." Although the disposition "may result in bringing the operation of commerce into play, it does not control it, and affects it only incidentally and indirectly. Commerce succeeds to manufacture, and is not a part of it."

In an apostrophe to narrow constructionism of constitutional law, the Chief Justice insisted that the Court must preserve the division between the commerce power of the Federal government and the police power of the states. He was not prepared to follow even the reluctant Congress in the direction of implementing a greater Federal police power. As for the monopoly problem, he concluded, "acknowledged evils, however grave and urgent they may appear to be, had better be borne, than the risk be run, in the effort to suppress them, of more serious consequences by resort to expedients of even doubtful constitutionality."[34]

*   *   *

No one would deny, said Justice Harlan in dissent, that "both the commercial power of the nation and the police powers of the states" had to be accommodated in the Constitution. The flaw in the majority reasoning, however, was in failing to recognize that "the preservation of the just authority of the general government is essential as well to the safety of the states as to the attainment of the important end" for which the Federal government was created by the people. "The Constitution which enumerates the powers committed to the nation for objects of interest to the people of all the states should not, therefore, be subjected to an interpretation so rigid, technical, and narrow that those objects cannot be accomplished."

Harlan then turned to the Johnson theory of a distinction between commerce and the goods transported in commerce, and the contention that the goods could only indirectly affect the commerce if they affected it at all. Why, he asked, had not the state courts, in their prosecution of monopolies to the extent of their jurisdiction, made such a distinction between manufacture and distribution? And if the states, in the limited extent of their police power, saw manufacture and distribution as integral parts of the same commerce, why were they not integral parts to the same degree when they came within the Federal jurisdiction? Finally, he asked, if the states themselves could not impose an unreasonable restraint upon goods leaving their borders, why should it be assumed that private combinations of individuals should be free to do so?[35]

Harlan concluded by quoting his great namesake: "Powerful and ingenious minds taking, as postulates, that the powers expressly granted to the government of the Union, are to be contracted by construction into the narrowest possible compass, and that the original powers of the states are retained if any possible construction will retain them, may . . . explain away the Constitution of our country and leave it, a magnificent structure, indeed, to look at, but totally unfit for use."[36]

The dissent, more perspicacious than the majority of either Court or Congress, voiced the constitutionalism of a distant future. For the present, the American people could only understand that the decision in the Sugar Trust Case had all but rendered the nation impotent in the face of the undiminishing threat of monopoly. As for the chief counsel of the nation, Olney was entirely satisfied with the outcome as well as disdainful of criticism. "You will observe that the government has been defeated in the Supreme Court on the trust question," he wrote his secretary. "I always supposed it would be and have taken the responsibility for not prosecuting under a law I believed to be no good—much to the rage of the *New York World*."[37]

         *   *   *

Constitutional law is a product of many ingredients—the temper of the times, which in turn is the sum of popular currents of conviction and dominant political control of the processes of government; the zeal and capability of the officers of government (when government happens to be a party to the legal action), and particularly the legal department's chief policy officer, the Attorney General, and its chief trial officer, the Solicitor General; the comparative zeal and capabilities of counsel for the private individuals and institutions whose cases happen to be the vehicles for the specific jurisprudential issues.

In an age like the twenty-five years concluding the nineteenth century, members of the Supreme Court, who presumably pronounced the law on the Constitution, inevitably bore the imprint of these various forces: they were nominated by Presidents who, uniformly from Grant through McKinley, were the choice of party organizations firmly in the control of conservative industrial interests of the Northeast and the most industrialized portions of the Midwest. Grant from Illinois, Harrison from Indiana, Garfield, Hayes and McKinley from Ohio, and Arthur and Cleveland from New York were unvarying in their economic and political orthodoxy. Their Cabinet members, including their Attorneys General, reflected the Presidents' own philosophies—and Presidential appointees to the Federal judiciary were of the same general type, and were confirmed by Senators who were of necessity the dominant figures in the majority parties of the state legislatures which then selected them.

Fuller was a prototype of this economically oriented process of selection. A "sound money" but low-tariff Democrat from the Midwest, he happily fitted President Cleveland's needs when Chief Justice Waite died suddenly in the spring of 1888. Confirmation had been bitterly contested, for the Republican Senate sensed victory coming in the November elections and demanded that such an important appointment ought not to be made by a prospectively retiring administration. Fuller's personal friendship with Cleveland, and the occasional reliance of the President on his advice, fed charges of "cronyism" in the course of the debates, while farm belt Senators protested against the candidate's corporation connections. Yet Fuller's professional credentials were totally acceptable to the dominant conservatives; Republican Senator Cullom of Illinois, after holding out briefly for a nominee less closely identified with the President's party, eventually assured Cleveland that he would support the nomination. Democratic Senator Edmunds of Vermont, who held out even longer for his own candidate—Edward J. Phelps, then Ambassador to Great Britain—subsequently became a firm friend.[38]

One other contemporary factor importantly affected the Court, and thus its jurisprudence: In the welter of economic and political rivalries in the post-Civil War generation—extending, indeed, into the nineties—the high tribunal had fallen to low estate among the separate and equal powers of government. The bench whose administration Fuller took over in the fall of 1888 had been an unhappy pawn (or perhaps shuttlecock) between factional interests ever since Chief Justice Taney, a gaunt ghost whose Dred Scott decision still haunted the land, had departed the scene in 1864. It was worth noting that seven of the nine Justices at the beginning of Fuller's Court had been confirmed only after varying degrees of dissension over their nominations; Matthews, for instance, had been nominated twice and had finally won confirmation by a single vote, while Fuller's own confirmation had been by a 41-20 vote. Bradley was the surviving member of a "packing" plan of President Grant, and one political stalwart—Roscoe Conkling—had been confirmed as a demonstration of party power, only to decline the appointment thereafter.*

Fuller's task would be to rebuild a respectable Court from the shambles which he had inherited—a task not made easier by a donnybrook between President Cleveland and Senator Hill in which two Cleveland nominees would be rejected by substantial Senate votes in 1894. It was Fuller's good fortune to remain in the Chief's chair long enough to outlast most of the political crudities of the decade in which his tenure began. He had a number of competent though hardly brilliant minds with which to develop the jurisprudence of his era. Field and Harlan were conspicuous intellectual giants on the Court in the nineties, followed at a rather wide interval by White and Fuller himself. The brilliant Miller—with Field, the surviving appointee of President Lincoln—served only two terms under Fuller; and Gray, whose seventeen years on the Massachusetts supreme judicial court had been loudly praised by the profession at the time of his nomination, left virtually no mark on the constitutional law of his time.[39]

This was the Court which addressed itself to the strange new issues created by the economic revolution of the last half of the century. The Justices responded in terms of the rules of law in which they had been trained and tempered by experience. The issues themselves were eloquently phrased by lawyers who had been trained and tempered in the same manner—and the government attorneys as well, called upon to assert the public interest, were almost to a man products of the same process. From the beginning of Harrison's administration to near the end of McKinley's, the five men who served as Attorneys General were as instinctively dedicated to *laissez-faire* capitalism as to the

---

*See tables and sketches in Appendix A.

traditions of constitutional precedent: William H. H. Miller, who studied law under Morrison R. Waite before Waite became Chief Justice, was a close political adviser to Benjamin Harrison and guided into the Federal judiciary many competent and orthodox attorneys of his own persuasion. Richard Olney was a railroad attorney; he was succeeded in Cleveland's Cabinet by Judson Harmon, an Ohioan who sought (with temporary success) to revive the original spirit of the Sherman Act.

Harmon had to work with the consequences of Olney's unenthusiastic test of the anti-trust statute in the Sugar Trust Case, and his earnest efforts to bring the statute back to some measure of vitality were, in the end, a study in frustration as well as an illustration of the consequences of indifferent or uninspired advocacy of the public interest on the part of the government's chief counsel. McKinley's appointments completed the process of frustration: his first Attorney General was Joseph McKenna, a California politician closely—many thought, too closely—identified with the western railroad's great friend, Senator Leland Stanford. McKenna's inactivity in the Department of Justice so far as the anti-trust law was concerned was only aggravated by his appointment to the Supreme Court. John W. Griggs of New Jersey, who succeeded him, inherited the same problems that Harmon had inherited from Olney; but his brief tenure, followed by his active participation in the organizing of the Steel Trust, added nothing to the record of anti-trust law enforcement.[40]

The Senate of the United States during the decade of the nineties was dominated by men of equally firm faith in the established order of things. In the Fiftieth Congress, when Fuller was confirmed as Chief Justice, California's two Senators were Leland Stanford and George Hearst; although neither was a leader of the entrenched conservative power, each represented the extent of business power control over the state legislatures which elected them. Stanford's chief prior political experience had been as governor of California during the Civil War, when he held the state in the Union and engineered the enactment of four statutes which placed the credit of both the state and its local government units solidly behind the project for the first transcontinental railroad. From the time he left the governor's office in 1863, having prepared the way for his own career in railroad building, until he was elected to the Senate in 1885—as many said, by the votes controlled by the Southern Pacific in Sacramento—Stanford's chief political activity had been the systematic blocking of regulatory legislation of all types. His philosophy was reiterated in the annual reports he made to the stockholders of the various carriers in which he owned controlling interests: The Granger cases he categorized as "pure communism," and the only form of civilized government, he declared, was the form which insured complete freedom of capitalism.[41]

Stanford, the Republican spokesman for Western railroad interests, had defeated Hearst, the Democratic representative of Western mining magnates, in the 1885 election; but two years later the California governor had named Hearst to fill an unexpired term in the Senate. Thus the spectrum of conservatism which dominated the California legislature was demonstrated to extend to both parties, although in practice Hearst was to prove more perceptive of the responsibilities of government to all classes in American life. His humanitarian instincts would be more flamboyantly demonstrated in the early newspaper career of his son, William Randolph, the youthful radical.[42]

The true prototype of the conservative establishment in the Senate of the turn of the century, however, was Nelson M. Aldrich of Rhode Island. The tenacity of industrialism's Republican representation in the national councils was exemplified by Aldrich's own thirty years in office, during much of which he dominated the Senate whenever his own party was in the majority. Men who demonstrated the capacity to survive the gyrations of national politics during this era—William B. Allison of Iowa, Eugene Hale of Maine, Orville Platt of Connecticut, Shelby M. Cullom of Illinois, George F. Hoar of Massachusetts, together with state bosses like Matthew S. Quay and later Boies Penrose of Pennsylvania and Marcus A. Hanna of Ohio—provided Aldrich with the close-knit group of party regulars necessary to keep an unbroken grip on party fortunes from the silver uprising of 1890 to the Congressional battles with the Square Deal through 1908.

A devout protectionist, Aldrich had a patrician's scorn for the "trooping of the beggars" who continually lobbied for higher tariffs in the bills of 1890, 1897 and 1909 with which he was identified. A self-made millionaire, he had a lifelong suspicion of social reforms and always pointed to Rhode Island's successful weathering of the Panic of 1893 as proof of the validity of an economy managed by an industrial elite. Over the years, the inner circle of Republicans constituted a select social club, presided over by the Rhode Islander and keeping a steady surveillance over the aberrations of the more changeable lower House as well as the occasional efforts at independence on the part of various occupants of the White House.[43]

In the final analysis, all of the branches of government—the Congress (and particularly the Senate), the Executive Department, and the judiciary—functioned throughout the nineties in the shining afternoon of conventional economic and political ideas. The hinterland might be seething with a variety of discontents, but the old orthodoxy still predominated in the nation's capital. Even Justice Harlan, the only consistent dissenter in this age, had his own world of absolutes; Justice Brewer was later to say of him that Harlan went confidently to sleep each night with one hand upon the Bible and the other upon the Constitution. For most Americans, the faith of the fathers, whether legal or theological, was not part of the order of affairs to be challenged. There were rumblings, but not yet war, in Eden.

*   *   *

With the decision in *United States v. E. C. Knight & Company* (the Sugar Trust Case), the makers of the new industrial order could breathe a sigh of relief; the Court had insured the validity of the trust, a device by which the interstate corporation had freed itself from the excessive inhibitions of state laws, by reducing virtually to a nullity the Federal power in the interstate area. Fuller and his colleagues had made a choice between the benefits to be derived from a modern form of corporate organization, threatened with an obsolete concept of localism on the one hand, and the dangers inherent in the trust structure where an adequate Federal police power was lacking, on the other hand. The choice was not universally applauded. Ardemus Stewart, associate editor of the *American Law Register*, complained that if the Sugar Trust Case meant, as it seemed to mean, "that the national government is powerless to protect the people" from the dangers of monopoly, "then this government is a failure."[44]

The *Knight* case was decided in the winter of 1895. The following spring came the *Pollock* case invalidating the income tax and by a one-vote majority, declared one jurist, saving the rich a tax liability of a billion dollars a year. The Court, within the first decade of Fuller's Chief Justiceship, did indeed seem to be committed to the interests of the new industrialism. At every turn, it appeared, important questions were decided in favor of corporations, railroads, or moneyed interests of every type. State taxes which burdened the services or trade of interstate shippers were held to infringe upon the commerce clause of the Constitution; laws which restricted private persons in the manner of paying taxes or other obligations to the government were held to be an impairment of contracts; state inspection of foodstuffs and livestock brought across state lines was struck down as an unreasonable or discriminatory burden on out-of-state business.[45]

The jurisprudence of the new industrialism centered around the doctrine that private commercial activity should be confronted with a minimum of public interference, and Fuller's Court in its first decade tended consistently to support the proposition. In his second year as Chief Justice, Fuller himself had written the opinion for the six-to-three majority which held unconstitutional an Iowa prohibition law as it had applied to interstate shipment of liquor in the original packages. The commerce clause of the Constitution gave Congress exclusive authority over the subject, he declared, and if Congress chose not to exercise its own authority it was *a fortiori* to be found that the states' laws could not affect the subject.[46]

The "unbroken package" doctrine was not wholly consistent with the arguments accepted by the majority in the *Knight* case, where it was necessary to distinguish the goods in interstate commerce from the commerce itself, in order to limit potential Federal authority over the subject. Indeed, the Court during the first decade under Fuller alternated between a broad and narrow interpretation of the commerce clause as it seemed necessary to preserve the principle of minimal governmental contact with the industrial process. It was, accordingly, consistent rather than inconsistent for the Chief Justice, who was almost single-minded in his belief in the principle, to support state taxes or regulation in certain instances where the alternative would be to tend to encourage the growth of a Federal power in interstate commerce.[47] It was, however, a testimonial to the degree to which legal precedent was committed to the preservation of property rights that on most constitutional cases the Court was unanimous in its opinions.*

The high-water mark in the judicial current against government intervention in the free enterprise system came in 1897, when the Court held invalid a Louisiana statute which penalized agents for insurance firms which did not comply with Louisiana insurance regulations. "In the privilege of pursuing an ordinary calling or trade and of acquiring, holding and selling property must be embraced the right to make all proper contracts in relation thereto," declared the unanimous opinion. Police power of the state could apply only to contracts in conflict with public policy when the contracts were within the state's jurisdiction; insurance policies issued in New York were without the jurisdiction.[48]

The year that witnessed *Allgeyer v. Louisiana* also marked the sweeping acceptance by the Court of a doctrine enunciated by Justice Field as early as 1882, including corporations within the definition of "persons" in the Fourteenth Amendment and hence entitled to the benefits of the Amendment's due process and equal protection clauses.[49] Although no opinion of the Court ever directly dealt with the proposition, it was confidently asserted before the end of Chief Justice Waite's term that all of the Justices subscribed to it, and by 1898 the Fuller Court unequivocally declared that "it is well settled that corporations are persons within the provisions of the Fourteenth Amendment."[50]

Within this congenial extension of the Fourteenth Amendment, due process as a description of procedure was now to become secondary to due process as a substantive right in itself—in the words of an anticipatory case in 1884, "the device . . . to protect the rights of individuals and minorities, as well against the power of numbers, as against the violence of public agents transcending the limits of lawful authority."[51] For the next half-century, this would be the refuge of the economic oligarchy against the cyclical movements of reform.

*   *   *

The sympathetic pronouncements of the judiciary were not the only bulwark for the jurisprudence of industrialism. The early treatises on American constitutional law had been replaced, in the generations following the Civil War, by a new authoritative literature even more ardent in its support of free enterprise. Joseph Story's *Commentaries* on the earlier Federalism had given place to Judge Thomas M. Cooley's *Constitutional Limitations,* a congeries of state constitutional law which treated this law as a restrictive covenant perpetually accommodating the interests of *laissez-faire* economics. Judge Peter Grosscup in 1902 was to state the philosophy aptly when he declared: "What is called tangible property has come to be, in most great enterprises, but the embodiment, physically, of an underlying life."

Cooley echoed the sentiment when he wrote: "The man or the class forbidden the acquisition or enjoyment of property in the manner permitted to

---

*Cf. statistical summaries in Appendix E.

the community at large would be deprived of *liberty* in particulars of primary importance to his or their happiness." Any general law which deprived parties of vested rights, Cooley continued, must be held obnoxious; any denial of freedom of action to the entrepreneur was by definition a denial of due process.[52]

Cooley's doctrines were powerfully supported by another impressive legal work by a young law professor at the University of Missouri. In his *Limitations of Police Power,* Christopher Tiedemann contended that "under *written* constitutions, Federal and state, democratic absolutism is impossible in this country." The *"unwritten* law of this country is in the main against the exercise of the police power," he continued; indeed, the most legitimate use of the power, in his view, would be in enforcement of freedom of contract.[53]

Cooley and Tiedemann were complemented by a third eloquent advocate of limited government in the context of contemporary industrialism. Judge John F. Dillon of Iowa was the author of a classic treatise on municipal corporations which took a similar narrow view of the powers of local authority. In the Storrs Lectures at Yale University in 1892, Dillon particularly addressed himself to the danger of government interference with corporate activity. This deprived the owner of property of its full enjoyment, he declared, and was a blatant example of "the despotism of the many—of the majority." Two years later, United States Circuit Judge William Howard Taft, speaking before the American Bar Association on "Recent Criticism of the Federal Judiciary," was heard to observe that the current hostility toward the courts stemmed from a willful refusal to recognize that the judges were charged with the responsibility for setting aside laws which involved "confiscation and the destruction of the principle of private property."[54]

This was the abrasive point of conflict between two eras—the mercantile and agrarian culture of the earlier America and the emerging corporate society of the new. For the majority of bench and bar, the constitutional doctrine seemed clear that government, whether state or Federal, was systematically to be restrained from infringing upon the rights of industry and corporate wealth. For the small farmer and businessman, conscious of a tightening economic encirclement, the process of government was becoming one of legislative thrust and judicial parry. The American yeoman had nowhere to turn; it was all very well for a Henry Adams to seek intellectual refuge elsewhere, but for the middle-class American the traditional route of escape—moving West to free land—was disappearing with the closing of the frontier.

Thus brought to bay, the average man of the nineties could only confirm the words of Henry Demarest Lloyd: "The world, enriched by thousands of generations of toilers and thinkers, has reached a fertility which can give every human being a plenty undreamed of even in the Utopias"—at least, it had seemed to have reached such a stage in the New World. But, Lloyd went on, "between this plenty ripening on the boughs of our civilization and the people hungering for it" were the manipulators of the productive process. "They assert the right, for their private profit, to regulate the consumption by the people of the necessaries of life, and to control production, not by the needs of humanity, but by the desires of a few for dividends." It was an age, Lloyd concluded, grown "gluttonous beyond its power of digestion," in which the concentration of control had become the basic reason for business existence. "What we call Monopoly," he said, "is Business at the end of its journey."[55]

Complaints like these were read by laymen, while lawyers and business executives read Cooley and Tiedemann. If the yeoman was concerned at what was happening to him in the new industrial system in which he found himself, the managers and beneficiaries of that system were not without their worries as well. The fateful constitutional issues of 1895 were not yet settled. With the trusts relieved of the threat of Federal attack after the *Knight* decision, and vested wealth relieved of the threat of an income tax after *Pollock,* there yet remained the growing threat of organized labor.

Seymour Thompson, senior editor of the *American Law Review,* saw the handwriting on the wall. By the Sugar Trust Case, he wrote, the Sherman Act had been "sponged out of existence, except for the purpose of enabling the Federal courts to enjoin railway strikes."[56] That final step in closing the ring of *laissez-faire* jurisprudence was now in the making.

3/The Conservative Crisis

T HE BOMB that exploded near Haymarket Square in Chicago on May 4, 1886 left the industrialists of the country in a state of shock for years following. For many, it was the opening gun in a war against capitalism; to others, recalling that violence and hatred had been festering among working classes for more than fifteen years, the "uprising" of the anarchists seemed the final battle. In any event, the reaction was swift and brutal. Only three days earlier, the first May Day parade of radical labor groups had brought tens of thousands of laborers from their jobs in Chicago, Detroit, New York and dozens of other cities in a massive show of solidarity in favor of the eight-hour day. It was, shuddered a conservative editor, an example of "Communism, lurid and rampant."[1]

Chicago was the main trouble center. European-born radicals, including the most rabid of anarchists, had congregated there over the years, recognizing its large foreign population, converging railroads and great new industries as offering some of the most fertile soil for their seed. Police hostility had made laboring men of the city regard the law enforcing agency as a natural enemy; Inspector John Bonfield's standard practice, reported an experienced observer, was to wade into any protest meeting where "he cracked all heads in sight until no man was left upright, and then announced that quiet was restored." The city's press, already launched upon its frenetic career, was committed to a prejudging of the issues; on May 1 it denounced the leaders of the parade as "dangerous ruffians" and urged that the authorities "hold them personally responsible for any trouble that occurs. Make an example of them if trouble occurs."[2]

Chicago was, by the latter eighties, a spectacular prototype of the new American urban economy. Soaring from its disastrous fire of 1871, it had doubled in population by the end of that decade and now, with the last half of the next decade setting in, it was rapidly approaching a million people. On the muck of its streets and the filth of its enormous slums it had constructed a wealthy business community; Marshall Field, who had fought back from destructive fires in both 1871 and 1877, now headed a department store giant to rival the pioneer Wanamaker's in Philadelphia, and was the acknowledged czar of the city's business men. Closely rivalling him in power was Cyrus Hall McCormick, whose great farm implement factory lay in the western part of the city. A self-taught, hard-bitten genius who had single-handedly fought off patent pirates and politically favored competitors, he regarded labor organizations as an intolerable intrusion into the state of industrial affairs. The right to hire and fire on his own terms and at his own pleasure, he had told a group of his employees a year before, "was something I would not surrender."[3]

The Haymarket "riot," as the conservatives called it, was primed by the McCormick "massacre," as the radicals called it. For many months the Harvester plant had been struck; in February McCormick had locked out the dissidents, and in the late spring he had begun importing strike-breakers under police escort. From a number of original grievances, the ex-workers had eventually settled upon a demand for an eight-hour day; by a singular irony, McCormick had now decided to introduce this work period, and had given his workers the afternoon of May 3 as a holiday to celebrate the event. The workers—"scabs"—leaving the plant had clashed with picketing strikers; these were reinforced by a group of striking lumbermen in an adjoining lot. In the fighting that immediately ensued, the police opened fire and six workmen were slain.[4]

So the meeting at Desplaines Street—a shabby thoroughfare a block from Haymarket and a half-mile from the main business district—had been called on the evening of May 4 to protest the shootings. The call for the meeting was hardly calculated to reassure the nervous city: "Revenge! Revenge! Workmen to arms!" had screamed the headline on five thousand handbills distributed through the slums within hours of the McCormick disorders. It was clear, too, that the chief anarchists of the area would be on hand to address the meeting: August Spies, editor of the radical German-language newspaper, *Arbeiter Zeitung;* Albert Parsons, of the anarchist publication *Alarm;* and Samuel Fielden, itinerant part-time preacher. Spies, indeed, had been addressing the striking lumbermen in the lot across from the McCormick works when the May 3 disorders had broken out; and his presses had run off the handbills for the May 4 meeting.

Yet to a man like tolerant, phlegmatic Mayor Carter H. Harrison, the speeches themselves seemed anything but inflammatory. He personally attended the Desplaines assembly to assure himself that there was no danger of an outbreak; at 10 o'clock, as rain began to fall and the crowd of fifteen hundred began to break up, he left for home, relieved at the turn of events. Most of the gathering, it was evident, consisted of typical immigrant laborers, many with their families accompanying them. While he would not be one to stand up vigorously against the hysteria which was about to burst its bounds, he was rational enough to realize, as Charles Edward Russell was to write in retrospect, that the real "physical force anarchists" in the city scarcely numbered a dozen.[5]

Harrison's departure was followed moments later by the appearance of "Black Jack" Bonfield, and one hundred and eighty armed policemen, in close military order. Only a third of the original crowd was still in the street, and the speaker, Fielden, was obviously ending his address. It was characteristic of Bonfield, however, that he should give orders for the assembly immediately to disperse. Fielden called back that the meeting was entirely peaceable; the crowd, apparently dazed at the sudden appearance of police in such numbers, seemed to hesitate. From somewhere in the darkness a black object with a small spark trailing from it sailed in an arc into the front ranks of policemen. An instant later, the street was shattered with a tremendous explosion.[6]

*   *   *

"Now it is Blood!" screamed the Chicago *Inter-Ocean* the next morning. The night had indeed been one of blood; gathered about their fallen brethren, Bonfield's police had fired wildly into the crowd in all directions. In the final accounting, seven policemen and four members of the assembly died, and several score were wounded, some being maimed for life. Swiftly, in cold fury, the police prepared a cleanout of known radical quarters, and with daylight the professional company detectives of the Pinkerton agency joined them. Search warrants were hardly considered; Julius S. Grinnell, the state's attorney, admonished the authorities: "Make the raids and look up the law afterwards."[7]

That some member of the extreme anarchists had thrown the bomb was reasonably certain; that he would ever be identified seemed unlikely even at the time. How, asked Grinnell, would it be possible to make arrests that would hold up and a case that would insure the conviction the whole country was now demanding? Melville S. Stone, publisher of the Chicago *Daily News,* suggested the strategy; the actual identity of the bomber was of little or no consequence, he urged, for "inasmuch as Spies and Parsons and Fielden had advocated over and over again the use of violence . . . their culpability was clear."[8]

The future founder of the Associated Press did not stop there. Having been called in on the case by Grinnell and City Attorney Fred S. Winston, he voluntarily "wrote out what I considered to be a proper verdict for the coroner's jury to render. In terms it was something like this: that [Police Officer] Mathias Degan had come to his death from a bomb thrown by a person or persons unknown, but acting in conspiracy with August Spies, Albert Parsons, Samuel J. Fielden, and others unknown." It was customary, Stone explained rather feebly, to dictate such verdicts to coroner's juries since it was "really a question of giving them the law on a case and not dictating as to their opinions."[9] What rule of law it was on which Stone was so confidently relying was unclear to a large segment of the professional bar after the hysteria had died.

It was obviously the same law understood by Judge Joseph E. Gary, to whom the case was assigned on the heels of a grand jury indictment which included Spies, Parsons, Fielden, and five others. To insure that the case would be heard by a petit jury who knew what was expected of them, Gary appointed a special bailiff, Henry L. Ryce, who selectively summoned new veniremen until the defense had exhausted its peremptory challenges. Thereafter, with Gary denying any challenge for cause if a prospective juryman conceded that he reasonably believed he could give a fair verdict, twelve were eventually picked—after three weeks and more than nine hundred talesmen. "Those fellows are going to be hanged as certain as death," Ryce had declared at the beginning of his project. The first step toward bearing out the prediction was accomplished: of the twelve good men and true, most were supervisory personnel from large factories, and not one was a laborer.[10]

The whole case was built around a conspiracy theory in which the radicals were accessories before the fact. Grinnell introduced evidence of a meeting on the night of May 3 at which a plot to blow up police stations was elaborated; the state hardly attempted to relate either the principal defendants to this meeting or the meeting to the bomb throwing. Gary overruled all defense objections. If the jury was satisfied that the evidence tended to show that the defendants favored overthrow of public institutions and that Policeman Degan had been killed "in pursuance of such conspiracy," said Gary in his instruction, it was enough to sustain a verdict of guilt. The jury accommodated, with recommendations of death for all but one.[11] (Two, condemned to the gallows, had their sentences commuted.)

The Supreme Court of Illinois, on review, found no irregularity or denial of justice in the trial. The Supreme Court of the United States declined to review; there was no Federal question involved, it declared, and no evidence that a right guaranteed by the Federal Constitution had been violated. In November 1887, eighteen months after the bombing, four were hanged while a fifth convicted defendant—Louis Lingg, a professional terrorist who apparently had made the Haymarket bomb—committed suicide in his death cell with another bomb smuggled to him by his sweetheart. It had, indeed, been a case of blood.[12]

*   *   *

The time of the Chicago anarchists' trial was a time of dread for middle class Americans; rumors flew widely and wildly that a general uprising was planned for the time of the executions. Charles Edward Russell reported that "newspaper offices, the banks, and the Board of Trade were guarded night and day," and that "nearly all citizens carried weapons." It was even more a time of decision for those entrepreneurs who hated the growing strength of organized labor; for them, it was no difficulty at all to ascribe to the raw new unions the intentions of violence that the anarchists openly proclaimed. For the more reactionary, the apochryphal remark of a Chicago businessman was accepted as a simple statement of the truth: Whether or not the anarchists were actually guilty of the bombing, "the labor movement must be crushed! The Knights of Labor will never dare to create discontent again if these men are hanged."[13]

There was fear in the statement and, indeed, conservative propertied persons in any of the industrial centers of the day had reason for misgiving. The generation after the Civil War had seen an enormous increase in immigration. In the decade of the eighties, nearly three million persons from Europe were to stream into the country, and increasing numbers of these were from strange southeastern lands rather than the dominant Anglo-Saxon, Celtic or Nordic stock of the past. Unskilled laborers, they crowded into the already teeming ghettos and tenements; hidden among them, it seemed, were untold numbers of revolutionists already bent on destroying the democracy where they had found refuge. Americans of older native stock recalled grimly that the anarchist Michael Bakunin and the father of Communism, Karl Marx, in 1876 had given their formal blessing to the creation of a Socialist-Labor party in the United States. The fact that it could attract any votes at all, in local elections in New York thereafter, seemed an affront to the ideals on which the nation had been founded.[14]

For half a dozen years after the Haymarket defendants were dispatched, the threat seemed to be turned away. Then John Peter Altgeld was elected governor of Illinois. German-born, self-educated, grindingly impoverished until he ultimately found the opportunities so many others found in the fabulous real estate developments in Chicago, Altgeld had risen in the Democratic ranks to become to the America of the eighties and early nineties what Lincoln had been to the America of the sixties—a compassionate spokesman for the downtrodden and forgotten. In 1884 Altgeld had published a pioneering book, *Our Penal Machinery and Its Victims,* which indicted the system of criminal justice on three counts: its tendency to make hardened malefactors out of convicts, its inability to take into account the immaturity of first offenders, and its inability to deter criminal acts through the severity of its threatened punishments.[15]

The boy who had left a ruined Ohio farm to seek a better life in the chaos of the post-Civil War period, who had known what it was to be broken in health and friendless on a strange frontier, who had taught himself law in Missouri and had finally found his true career in Chicago, had been elected on the eve of the Haymarket trials to the same Cook County court system where the trials were to take place. Altgeld would remember that carnival of vindictiveness when he became governor—the first Democratic governor of Illinois since the Civil War and the first foreign-born governor in the state's history. He would also remember the horrors of workingmen's tenements in the cities and the systematic reduction of the farmer toward a state of serfdom. His inaugural message sounded all of the changes of the future— abolition of child labor in industry, humane administration of state hospitals and prisons, minimum standards of industrial safety, and the like. Thereafter, the new governor sent for the records on the Haymarket trials.

What Altgeld found in the official transcripts shocked him; in the perspective of seven years, it was quite clear that the jury had been packed, the evidence of "constructive conspiracy" so confidently assumed by men like

Melville Stone was clearly insufficient to support the charges, and the behavior of the trial judge was outrageous. Gary, as Altgeld observed in his eighteen-thousand word message on the case, had "conducted the trial with malicious ferocity," and the record was filled with "insinuating remarks . . . made in the hearing of the jury, and with the evident intent of bringing the jury to his way of thinking."

The condemnation of Gary's behavior was, if anything, restrained; in the course of the trial, it had been noted with disapproval even by the public which insisted upon convictions that the judge daily invited three to five vivacious young ladies to sit beside him on the bench. When they lost interest in the technical details of the pleading, the judge amused one of the company by showing her a puzzle while argument was proceeding before him. As another jurist was to say, at a later date, Gary had been "ignoring every rule of law which was designed to assure a fair trial for a defendant on trial for his life."[16]

And yet, as Altgeld pondered the record, he had to recognize the consequence of what ought now to be done. The Haymarket convictions had been capitalism's answer to anarchistic protest; in the view of those who hated anarchy and radicalism in general, the sacrifice of the principle of a fair and impartial trial was a small price to pay for the death of an alien idea. Altgeld himself stood at the pinnacle of his personal fortunes, although he had substantially depleted them in the course of the election campaign; he also stood on the verge of a state administration which might carry Illinois a giant step forward into a new age of social and economic justice. Political, and probable economic, suicide awaited a man who, for the sake of a principle of equal justice for the unpopular and dispossessed in the good society, would expose the crime of which the good society was guilty. But for the German-born immigrant, this was not the question. "It is right," Altgeld declared, and signed the pardons.[17]

Thunderstruck, the nation's press recovered quickly enough to open floodgates of vituperation. The *Chicago Tribune* put it mildly; of the governor it declared that he "has apparently not a drop of true American blood in his veins. He does not reason like an American, not feel like one, and consequently does not behave like one." The *New York Times* felt that Altgeld was "too selfish to be a Socialist in fact," since he had made a fortune in real estate "too large to admit of his wishing to divide with those who work hard for a living." To this *non sequitur* the *Atlanta Journal* added: "Governor Altgeld has fired the hearts of the demons with fresh courage and fresh hatred of all that we consider sacred."[18]

The fury of the attack was unrelieved by any substantial counterforce, then or through the rest of the century, or at his death, at fifty-five, in 1902. It would be more than a generation after that when an Illinois poet would eulogize "The Eagle That Is Forgotten," and remind his countrymen of Altgeld's acceptance of his fate: "To live in mankind is far more than to live in a name."[19]

The Haymarket conflict was one of a succession of clashes in labor-industry relations that extended throughout the long depression from the early seventies to the mid-nineties. The nationalizing effects of the Civil War had provided the primary stimulus; between 1864 and 1873, craft unions had been established in printing, railroading, cigar manufacturing, cooperage and iron-mongering. The hard times brought on by the financial disasters of 1873 provided the next impetus toward a national organization of these and other laboring groups. The nucleus for such an organization was already at hand in the Noble and Holy Order of the Knights of Labor, which had been launched in December 1869 under the leadership of Uriah S. Stephens, a Baptist theological student turned tailor. Stephens envisioned in the movement a new brotherhood which would in time "cover the globe" and "include men and women of every craft, creed and color."[20]

For most of the seventies, militant employer opposition, widespread joblessness and chronic outbreaks of violence held back the efforts to establish a national labor organization. Anti-union industrialists systematically cultivated the popular disposition to link labor with lawlessness, and in the fetid economy of areas like the Pennsylvania coal mines the line of distinction was apt to be tenuous. For two decades—from the late 1850's to the mid-1870's—the railroad and mining interests there had been under attack by an outlaw secret society of Irish immigrants known as the Molly Maguires. The Ancient Order of Hibernians and the Workmen's Benevolent Association, the one a fraternal group and the other a labor group, periodically served as fronts for or were infiltrated by the "Mollies."

Franklin B. Gowen, general counsel and president of the Philadelphia & Reading Railroad, set out in the early seventies to run the membership to ground and break their power. His determination to tar the unions with the same brush was evident from the outset. "I do not charge this Workmen's Benevolent Association with it," he said in 1871, "but I say that there is an association which votes in secret, at night, that men's lives shall be taken, . . . and it happens that the only men who are shot are the men who dare to disobey the mandates of the . . . Association."[21] In engaging the Pinkerton's National Detective Agency to hunt for the evidence to convict the Mollies, Gowen was quoted as complaining that "men having their capital locked up in the coal beds are . . . fast losing sway over that which by right should be their own command"—a protest against creeping unionism as much as against the terrorists in the secret society.[22]

Allan Pinkerton's private detective agency began as a service to businessmen seeking to track down the robbers and embezzlers so prevalent in the mid-nineteenth century; during the Civil War he was active in ferreting out Southern saboteurs, and in the late sixties he found many clients among the burgeoning railroads. By the seventies, seeking new business to offset depression losses, Pinkerton found men like Gowen opening up lucrative fields of employment for him. The lawbreakers the Pinkertons were to hunt down, in the capitalist idiom of the time, were now increasingly to be troublemakers among the workers; the laws they broke were the various common-law precedents against impairment of contracts and interference with property rights.[23]

In agreement with Gowen, a young Pinkerton operative named James Mc-Parlan was assigned to ferret into the Mollies; he assumed the alias of James McKenna, went to Ireland to do preparatory research on various native secret societies, and then entered the Pennsylvania coal fields. An Irishman and Roman Catholic like the vast majority of the immigrant miners, he was soon accepted, initiated into the Hibernian order, and ultimately acquired the evidence Gowen was seeking. The Pinkerton Agency found the affair so successful that after it was over it commissioned a semi-fictional account under the title, *The Molly Maguires and the Detectives*. It would lead the Pinkertons into other lucrative engagements in the labor disturbances to follow.[24]

The men of the secret society who were brought to trial on the agents' evidence were provably guilty of criminal acts, including premeditated murder. But Gowen, who handled a major part of the prosecution as special counsel for the commonwealth, used the occasion to drive home an anti-union plea to the jury. "On behalf of the laboring people," he said in the climax to a three-hour speech, he was moved to protest "against the monstrous assumption that these villains are the representatives of the laboring people."[25]

The major prosecutions resulted in victories for the commonwealth; Mollies who were proved to have plotted and executed murders were convicted and several hanged. Gowen's own triumph was complete; not only had he destroyed the power of a lawless society which had terrorized both workers and employers for two decades, but by continuing innuendo he had all but destroyed the union idea in the mines. Other industrialists studied his methods for strategies which would become standard in fighting labor unions for the next half century; Pinkerton infiltrators, company police, and systematic surveillance of union plans and personalities were to be inseparable parts of the labor-capital struggle in that period.[26]

*   *   *

Four years of deepening depression brought the labor movement to a climax of violence in 1877; continual layoffs and wage cuts culminated that year in a spontaneous wave of strikes which spread over the land. A contemporary described it with only slight exaggeration: "Hundreds and thousands of men belonging to the laboring classes, alleging that they were wronged and oppressed, ceased to work, seized railroads, closed factories, foundries, shops and mills, laid a complete embargo on all internal commerce, interrupted travel, and bid defiance to the ordinary instruments of legal authority." Overnight, it seemed, the social and political system of the country had come to "the very brink of ruin."[27]

The railroads, bellwethers of industry then as steel would be three-quarters of a century later, precipitated the crisis in the early summer by announcing 10 percent cuts in wages—the second such cut in slightly more than three years. The Pennsylvania, New York Central and Baltimore & Ohio led the way; Gowen of the Reading, flushed with his recent triumph over the Molly Maguires, followed suit and at the same time warned his trainmen that they would be discharged if they did not withdraw from the railroad unions which were beginning to talk strike. Pinkertons, on the Reading and other lines, quickly broke some walkouts by recruiting and escorting new men onto the jobs.[28]

Around Pittsburgh, however, resistance began to stiffen, then to spread to key centers to the East. A brief outbreak occurred at Martinsburg, West Virginia on July 17, and another at Cumberland, Maryland three days later. Suddenly, a new pattern of employer militance manifested itself; as trains came to a halt in these and other centers, John W. Garrett, president of the B. & O., wired Governor Henry M. Mathews of West Virginia to request Washington for Federal troops. To lose a moment's time, he urged, would "imperil vast interests," but with the Army, "the rioters could be dispersed." At the moment there were no riots in progress or reasonably in prospect, but Garrett had little faith in a state militia force, comprised of men largely in sympathy with the strikers and in many instances related to them. With a sudden strike developing in Baltimore itself, Garrett also asked Governor John L. Carroll of Maryland to make a similar request.[29]

For Rutherford B. Hayes, settling uneasily into the White House after winning a hotly disputed election over Samuel J. Tilden, the requests for Army forces to deal with private labor disputes were most inopportune. The use of Federal forces against strikers was not unprecedented, as Hayes the lawyer was aware. But Hayes the lawyer also knew that the constitutionality of the action had never been satisfactorily documented. Yet if he took Mathews' request at face value, he would be justified in acting; the governor's wire declared that his military resources were inadequate to protect lives and property and that the legislature could not be convened in time to take any action to deal with the emergency. The President hesitated only briefly. Within hours after receiving the telegram, he directed Federal commanders at the Washington arsenal and at Fort McHenry in Baltimore to marshal all available men for Martinsburg.[30]

Still, the earlier precedents were hardly applicable to the present case; most of them had grown out of Civil War disturbances in sensitive border state areas, and in any event there had been a national emergency to override the local emergency. Although the strike of mid-July 1877 would quickly spread along major rail lines of the whole country, at the moment it was essentially a noisy crisis in a dispute between employers and workers. To introduce United States troops into the situation was to introduce an unfamiliar new concept into the economic process. With the political majority of the nation substantially opposed to government interference with the free play of the system of private enterprise, the use of Federal armed forces could benefit only the employers. If, on the other hand, the stoppage of transportation fundamentally affected the public interest, Federal intervention meant that the interest had become a national interest, a tacit concession that the labor question henceforth transcended the limits of individual states.

The appearance of the Army ended the demonstrations at Martinsburg and subsequently at Cumberland, but in the major centers of the B. & O.—in Baltimore and Pittsburgh—reaction to the carriers' tactics bred a greater violence. In the Maryland city, state militia were besieged in railroad company premises and had to fight their way out and run a gauntlet of bricks and rocks; ultimately, they leveled their rifles at the mobs and inflicted a number of casualties. But it was at Pittsburgh that the main battle of this summer of violence was to occur. At the root of the matter was the railroads' use of "double-headers"—single-crew trains hauling twice the normal number of cars—but the general causes were the same here as elsewhere: the hopelessness of the prospect of ever regaining a decent working wage, the hatred of the system which had bred the hopelessness, and, in the larger cities, the added provocative presence of mounting numbers of hoodlums, tramps and jobless youths spoiling for action.[31]

Pennsylvania considered that it had sufficient militia strength to cope with the situation, although it recognized that units from around Pittsburgh were likely to be too soft on the mobs. Accordingly, "strangers" from Philadelphia were called up and shipped across the state. On the same weekend that the Maryland forces were under siege in Baltimore, fighting began in the Smoky City; on a sweltering Saturday afternoon, the Philadelphia units fired into a shouting, brick-throwing mob at a main rail intersection inside the city limits. Twenty-six men were killed in the action, but the rioters only increased in numbers. The militiamen fell back to the roundhouse and machine shops and stood off a siege of almost twenty-four hours. Unable to bring the turbulence under control, state authorities then withdrew the forces to the outskirts of the city, and left Pittsburgh to the mob. For two more days the terror continued, and at the end $5,000,000 worth of property had been looted and put to the torch.[32]

By now the strike was truly interstate in nature and, like the Pittsburgh outbreak, beyond control. It spread to the Erie Railroad and thence in rapid paralysis to Toledo, Louisville, Chicago and St. Louis; at the far end of the rail network, San Francisco also was caught up in the stoppage of all transportation. Three million men, it was estimated by the last week of July, were now off their jobs. For Hayes, the problem had suddenly magnified a hundredfold; no man could answer the question which no one even dared to ask: Had the civil war between capital and labor, loudly predicted by the Marxists, actually begun?

*   *   *

Pennsylvania, with insurrection along many miles of its trackage, now added to the others its request to the White House for Army aid. The demands for men were beginning to tax the strength of the twenty-five thousand troops of the standing Army, many of them still tied down in Reconstruction areas and many others facing Indian threats in the West. General Winfield S. Hancock urged the President to follow Lincoln's example and issue a national call for volunteers; the situation, said Hancock and several Cabinet members, was fully as grave as in 1861. The Adjutant General of the Army reported to the President on the potentially disastrous condition of many of the Federal arsenals; the one at Rock Island, Illinois with its thousands of rifles and cartridges was guarded by forty men, the one in Pittsburgh by half that number, and another twenty held the depot at Indianapolis where rifles, field pieces and a million rounds of ammunition were stored.[33]

Abundant constitutional grounds for Federal action were now available. Aside from protecting government property and preserving order it was being insisted that the mails must go through unimpeded, and that Federal authority over interstate commerce extended to compelling the rail workers to resume work. Besides military property, there were other valuable items in danger; a vast amount of money was in the customhouse and subtreasury in New York, ultimately depending on the protection offered by thinly staffed garrisons in the adjacent forts. With Hayes' approval, Secretary of the Navy Richard W. Thompson ordered a gunboat to proceed to a point off the Battery and take up a station.[34]

Ironically, the hard times which had prepared the stage for the great strike also provided the government with another device for making a show of force. Many of the struck railroads were in receivership in the Federal courts, and the stoppage of these trains was a potential contempt of the judicial power. The Federal receiver in St. Louis, James H. Wilson, ardently urged the government to invoke the contempt power against any who obstructed the movement of the trains; the effort was actually made in several judicial districts in Illinois and Indiana, but the full implications of the use of contempt citations in labor disputes was to await a later development.[35]

The nation's radicals were in a frenzy of anticipation; they fully expected that the attempt to overthrow capitalism was imminent, and many capitalists agreed with them. But the real attitude of the discontented American workman was becoming apparent; wherever the Federal uniforms appeared, the assemblies tended to subside. The strike was a massive protest against the heartlessness of the existing economic system; it was not a calculated and concerted effort to destroy the system. The breakdown in state authority was essentially attributable to individual sympathy on the part of rank and file militiamen or of persons in authority, or both, for the dispossessed. It was also a tacit confession that the problem of dealing with the new industrialism was something beyond the capabilities of the several states. The great strike was a spontaneous, bitter cry for economic justice which, like a strangled scream, died away quickly; by the first days of August, the excitement was subsiding. But it left many lessons to be pondered for the future.

*   *   *

Thus battered by recurrent threats to his property, his values and perhaps his life, the conservative middle-class American was filled with misgivings as the century entered its final decade. The general railroad strike of 1877, the Haymarket anarchy of 1886, and the outbursts which were to come in 1892 and 1894 were crescendoes in a chorus of discontent and menace. Where, amid the accumulating dangers for the free enterprise system, was security to be sought? Private employers had their own methods of forestalling labor trouble; Pinkertons were now a characteristic feature of many factories, guarding company property or spying on incipient union movements, while dissidents were blacklisted and new employees required to take no-strike oaths. After 1877, most major cities had constructed armories for their militia in the form of fortresses frankly designed to defy attack. As for the legal process, the eighties had witnessed a revival of old common-law concepts of conspiratorial combination to be leveled against labor groups, and in many cases state legislatures had broadened these by statute.[36]

Yet the problem seemed to be hydra-headed; with every crisis and defeat, the workingmen moved a discernible step closer to solidarity and power. The first national convention of the Knights of Labor met in January following the great strike of 1877, and in the same year as the Haymarket affair, the American Federation of Labor was formally organized. The most militant and massive of the railroad unions up to that time was to be created between the strike years of 1892 and 1894. The three organizations, and the men who led them, epitomized the divergent philosophies of labor in particular and reformers in general.

Terence V. Powderly was the idealist, Samuel Gompers the pragmatist and Eugene V. Debs the radical activist, and their respective organizations reflected their own basic commitments. Powderly, and his Knights of Labor, served little more than to inform the American public of the seventies of the reality of the labor problem; indeed, "education and temperance" were his lifelong rules of conduct, a creed of meekness and rational dialogue in an age of brutal animosity between owners and workers. Committed to the goal of its founder, Uriah Stephens, of an all-inclusive brotherhood of labor, eschewing political action and defeatist in its attitude toward strikes, the Knights under Powderly inevitably disappointed the hopes of the membership for substantial material gains which could only be wrested from unwilling employers. Powderly's policy of restraint in the rail and packinghouse strikes of the eighties drove members by the thousands into the arms of the rising American Federation of Labor; the militance of the Knights was never more than a figment of capitalist imagination.[37]

Gompers, like Powderly, was essentially an organizer; unlike Powderly, he perceived that capital and labor, rather than having an identity of interests, were actually competitors for portions of the returns from the capitalist system. A product of the London slums, Gompers joined the Cigar Makers' Union at fourteen, the year after his family migrated to New York. Although his formal education had ended when he was ten, he studied the books and periodicals in the union's reading room, attended lectures at Cooper Union, read Marx and concluded that only Marx's pre-Communist arguments had pertinence in America. He quickly adopted the American habit of testing ideas and organizations by their workability and utility. He reorganized the Cigar Makers' Union in 1877 and the group which became the American Federation of Labor in 1886—both years of crisis—and established the model for both craft and inter-union structures thereafter.

Under Gompers' concept, cigar makers everywhere were to be members of a single international union—the "vertical" organization of trades and crafts which dominated the labor picture for half a century; a realistic dues schedule was to provide the union with adequate working funds; and a long-range program of member benefits to cover sickness, injuries, unemployment and retirement would unite the individuals in support of the organization. At the Federation level, Gompers proposed a membership by international unions only, and only one such union in each trade or craft, with each international free to follow its own policies on internal affairs without interference from the Federation.[38]

Gompers led the American labor movement away from the class-consciousness of the European radicals in the direction of the wage-consciousness characteristic of a capitalist economy. Powderly had had a vision of a partnership of employer and employee; Gompers saw them more realistically in terms of a continuing competition. For those who, in the aftermath of the radical influx of the seventies and eighties, held to the fixed idea that they were antagonists in a class war, a third concept of unionism was to be advocated by Eugene V. Debs.

*   *   *

The Chicago railroad strike of 1894 had elements of irrationality which vexed both industry and labor. The latter suffered from two fundamental commitments—to a course of violence, grossly exaggerated though this was by the metropolitan press, and to the support of a strike which only indirectly affected basic railroad union interests. Industry's leaders, increasingly obsessed with the spectre of a united front of workers prepared to paralyze the economic system in order to work their will, demanded (and at last got) a legal device which would prove consistently effective in turning back the danger.

The way had been prepared by twenty-four months of turbulence as the depression entered its third decade. Violent strikes in 1892 had been fought out at Homestead, Pennsylvania and Coeur d'Alene, Idaho in which desperate men had seized and held company properties while pitched battles had been fought with company police and Pinkerton agents. As in the past, the loss of these strikes only spurred labor to fresh organizational efforts, and in 1893 the two largest unions in American history to that date—the Western Federation of Miners and the American Railway Union—were founded. The year 1893 had been a period of successive political and economic crises; financial panic, a summer-long drought which all but destroyed the national corn and wheat crops, and the failure of more than fifteen thousand businesses. All were a prelude to the collapse of the second Cleveland administration that autumn, almost before it had fairly begun.

Convinced by "sound money" advocates among his Eastern advisers that the root of the current economic troubles was the Silver Purchase Act of 1890 —the second of the laws of that year to bear Senator Sherman's name—the President launched a campaign in August to repeal the statute. By marshalling all possible administration strength, his bill was finally rammed through House and Senate, but in the process the first Democratic Congress in forty years was split beyond repair. Moreover, the repeal did not bear out the hope that financial stability would return forthwith. On the contrary, the government's gold reserves continued to dwindle to disastrous levels during the following winter, and Cleveland felt compelled to turn to Wall Street bankers to borrow money, thereby outraging still more the Southern and Western wings of the party. A $60,000,000 loan in February 1895, it was widely averred, brought the lending syndicate of August Belmont and J. P. Morgan a profit of nearly $7,000,000.[39]

The year 1894 was bad enough; it was the year when the United States Commissioner of Labor reported an estimated 690,000 workers, or more than eight percent of the employed wage earners of the country, to be involved in labor disputes. It was in the spring of this year that an Ohio Populist named Jacob Coxey wrote a melodramatic footnote to history with his call for "armies" of jobless men to march on Washington to petition Congress for relief. The ominous knowledge that there were 2,000,000 persons unemployed in a total nonagricultural labor force of 15,000,000 suggested that Coxey's "armies" could reach formidable proportions. They were already on their way, according to rumor and news dispatch; trains were being seized in the West and taken over by hordes of men planning to keep a rendezvous with the Ohio leader.

Attorney General Olney had an answer for the train seizures, taken from the experiences of 1877. He sent Cleveland a memorandum pointing out that "most, if not all, of the railroads running between Oregon and the East were then in the hands of receivers of the United States courts." The seizures, in his view, were a challenge to the authority of the judicial arm of the government, and could be met by summary contempt process.[40] It did not prove necessary to employ the device on a large scale; most of the "armies" walked, and the distance cut down on their numbers so that only a few hundred ever reached the District of Columbia.[41]

*   *   *

George M. Pullman was one of the many post-Civil War millionaires who persuaded themselves that the evidence of their own success refuted any criticism of their methods. From the formation of his company in 1867, his "Palace Sleeping Car" had been one of the most popular advances since the practical development of the railroads; two decades after the formation of the company, its assets stood at $28,000,000, and they would have more than doubled by the year of the Pullman strike. It had been a rapid and spectacular advance for a poor farm boy of upstate New York, who hit upon a plan to adapt the luxurious accommodations of the proud river boat lines to the sleeping requirements of the transcontinental trains.[42]

The key to Pullman's success was his ingenious management operation; sleepers, parlor cars and diners not only were built by the company, but ownership was retained in the Pullman corporation and the cars themselves were leased to various railroads. Waiters, porters and conductors were all employees of Pullman and therefore technically not railroad men—a fact that contributed to the undoing of the strike in 1894. Rates for food and berths were fixed and inflexibly maintained by the company; many considered them extortionate. "I regard the Pullman Company and the Sugar Trust as the most outrageous monopolies of the day," declared Senator Sherman. "They make enormous profits and give their patrons little or nothing in return in proportion."[43] But the indirect relationship of the company to the carriers kept it out of the reach of the Interstate Commerce Commission. Moreover, unlike many trusts it was soundly financed; in 1892, on the eve of a financial panic, its stock was quoted at twice the par value, and with good reason since its cash reserves exceeded $25,000,000.[44]

Self-made man that he was, Pullman intended to brook no interference with his business from either government or labor. Brusque and domineering, thoroughly hostile to unionism, he nevertheless considered himself a peculiarly enlightened employer; the model town of Pullman, south of Chicago, was his case in point. Carefully laid out and developed some twenty years earlier, it was intended to be a comfortable suburban community for employees and their families. An efficient water system for every home, parks and tree-lined streets made it indeed the envy of many a laborer in other industries. Its plan and development also showed something more of Pullman's Midas touch; the four thousand acres which he had originally bought for $800,000 were now worth $5,000,000.[45]

As events turned out, however, the town had proved in 1893 to be something less than Utopia. Rents, for a number of years, had been consistently higher, by as much as 25 percent, than in neighboring communities. That winter this rent differential was sharply increased by a 25 percent cut in wages. Despite the deadly grip of financial collapse across the nation, Pullman had no more thought of reducing rents than he had of lowering the price of berths or diner meals. Moreover, the company's stockholders continued throughout the year of panic to receive their regular 8 percent dividends. To have lowered rents in proportion to wage cuts, or to have drawn upon the company's vast cash reserves to subsidize either, as Pullman later told the special Strike Commission appointed by the White House, "would have amounted to a gift of money to these men," unjustified in the face of declining orders.[46]

Eugene V. Debs, president of the new American Railway Union, was now led to a confrontation with Pullman and, inevitably and irrevocably, with the entire railroad industry. The Indiana native, then thirty-eight years old and a veteran of union action for fifteen, was a kindly, eloquent man; he had, declared Clarence Darrow, "the courage of a babe who had no conception of the world or its meaning." In a sense, he was even more of an idealist than Powderly, but an unflinching compulsion to fight for social justice spurred him continually into action. Like Powderly, too, he conceived of his new union as all-embracing, with membership open to all employees of railroads, skilled and unskilled. It was, however, a single big union confined to one industry, an idea which the Committee for Industrial Organization would adopt four decades later. Fatefully for the union and for Debs, the membership policy made it possible to include employees of the Pullman Company.[47]

Pullman, instinctively resentful of any questioning of his policies by lesser men, had fired three members of the American Railway Union when they waited upon him to protest the wage cuts and high rents. The union members of the Pullman Company appealed to Debs for support, and three thousand of them thereupon went on strike. Pullman retaliated by closing down all plant operations in the model town. Debs now found himself in a position of being compelled by circumstances to call for a general strike of the 160,000 members of the entire union to back up the complaints against a non-railroad company. Even more awkward was the fact that the only complaint of the majority of the membership, which would be directed against their own employers, the railroads, would have to be the existence of the carriers' contracts of lease with the Pullman Company—valid agreements which had no direct relation to the workmen.[48]

The situation illustrated the anomalies in law and economics which had been created by the labor contests of the time. "The steadily increasing concentration of workingmen in large numbers in mills and mines and at railroad terminals has changed all previous conditions," Chauncey F. Black had written a few months after the Homestead strike. "Capital massed on one side and men massed on the other side make a situation to which neither the common law nor the statute law of our foregoers is at all adequate."[49] For Debs, acutely aware that failure to support such a substantial part of his union's membership would send the whole union headlong after the Knights of Labor on the road to oblivion, there seemed to be no choice. For the business community, the irrationality of the situation emphasized that some new legal formula was imperatively needed to block massive work stoppages before they got out of hand.

*   *   *

The odds against the strike were substantial; the American Railway Union was new and untried, its treasury no match for the resources of the Pullman Company, particularly when complemented by the war chests of the railroads themselves. To bring in the railroads as parties to the controversy, indeed, was to prepare the way for a strike greater than any yet attempted in American labor history. Moreover, the employer front was formidable; since the mid-eighties, the twenty-four carriers with terminals in Chicago had maintained a common policy toward labor through its General Managers Association. The policy was twofold: to avoid competing for workers in certain classifications of jobs, the wage scales for these classifications were uniform; and in the event of work stoppage, the Association had a pool of jobless railroad men who could be recruited on short notice to break the strike.[50]

Once the issue was joined, events proceeded swiftly. Within a month, freight traffic in twenty-seven states of the American heartland had come to a standstill. Grain and cattle which normally filled the elevators and stockyards of a dozen Midwestern cities had to be unloaded from stranded cars; factories were shutting down from lack of coal to provide steam power; and passenger trains—denuded of Pullman cars—were hours late in arriving at their scheduled destinations, when they arrived at all. From Illinois to California, the Post Office Department reported it was unable to secure transportation of the mails —a fact upon which the Federal government could justify its intervention in due course.

But the threat, or the fact, of violence was the ultimate key to the issue, marshalling public opinion originally sympathetic to the Pullman strikers behind the employer forces as excitement mounted. Debs, realizing that the union would be the sole loser in such outbreaks, had given strict orders to avoid them. But the few established instances in which striking mobs got out of hand were enough to touch off wild exaggerations in the daily newspapers. On June 29, a thousand men had stopped the Chicago & Erie's New York Limited at Hammond, Indiana to detach two Pullman cars, while on July 2 at Blue Island, just outside Chicago, a gathering had blocked all traffic on the Rock Island main lines. These were enough to provide the sensationalist press with its standing headline: "Mob Rule in Chicago."[51]

*   *   *

In the confrontation between railroads and labor, it was generally noted that the leaders of the bar, and a substantial number of members of Congress and of the courts, were or had been railroad lawyers. President Cleveland himself had been one of this group, and his Attorney General had been counsel for several lines. In the Senate were railroad attorneys like William B. Allison of Iowa, Cushman K. Davis of Minnesota, Arthur P. Gorman of Maryland and John C. Spooner of Wisconsin. As for the Supreme Court, the Chief Justice had at one time been general counsel for the Chicago, Burlington & Quincy; in an 1884 case for his client, he had argued against an injured employee's claim by averring that an employer "is not bound to throw away his machinery because there may be others better calculated to insure safety."[52] Justices Brown, Jackson and Shiras had also represented various carriers in their former practice.[53]

It could hardly be questioned, therefore, that these attorneys in government would be intimately aware of the employer interests which were being challenged, however judicious they might be in these or other circumstances. (Olney, who was about to break the strike by government intervention, would later help draft the 1898 Erdmann Act outlawing anti-union "yellow-dog" contracts on interstate railroads, and would criticize the Supreme Court when it held the law unconstitutional.) In the present case, however, when the General Managers Association appealed to the Attorney General, his course of action was extraordinary.

At the Association's suggestion, Olney appointed Edwin Walker, counsel for the Milwaukee line, as special assistant to United States Attorney Thomas E. Milchrist in Chicago. Thereupon Olney sent—to Walker rather than to Milchrist—a set of instructions outlining his strategy: the "rights of the United States were [to be] vigorously asserted in Chicago, the origin and center of the demonstration," for when the strike was broken there it would be "a failure everywhere else and . . . prevent its spread over the entire country." To carry out this objective, Olney proposed two steps, one to be the obtaining of an injunction "which shall have the effect of preventing any attempts to commit the offense" of obstructing the mails or the movement of interstate commerce, and the second to be the dispatch of "a force which is overwhelming and prevents any attempt at resistance."[54]

The precedent of the second step—the use of the Army—had been definitively established in the Hayes administration in 1877. In Olney's view, which he was now to urge upon Cleveland and his Cabinet, the dimensions of the present strike were substantially greater than in that critical year; it was certainly a familiar story of mounting mob violence, burning properties, and the rapid evanescence of state authority. The Attorney General exhibited telegrams—which, as it was later shown, he had solicited—testifying to the growing threat of massive disorders in the Chicago area, whereupon Cleveland approved of the dispatch of troops.[55]

To Governor Altgeld's protests—he had not even been informed of the plans to put Federal forces on active duty in his state—the President replied that the Federal authority was paramount where the question was the halting of the mails and interfering with interstate commerce. That was hardly to be disputed, but to Altgeld's further protests against over-reacting to the one-sided advices of the General Managers Association, Cleveland observed that "in this hour of public danger and distress, discussion may well give way to active efforts on the part of all in authority to restore obedience to law and to protect life and property."[56]

Reasoned analysis of the justice of the claims on all sides, and the fixing of responsibility for all parties in various stages of the strike, had to await the report of Cleveland's Strike Commission which was appointed some weeks later. That report, indeed, tended to support Altgeld's position, unequivocably condemned the tactics of the managers' group, and placed responsibility for the whole matter upon "the people themselves, and . . . the government for not adequately controlling monopolies and corporations, and for failing to reasonably protect the rights of labor and redress its wrongs."[57]

By that time, the strike had been crushed, and Debs and seventy other union members were under indictment for ignoring the injunction which had evolved as the other part of Olney's strategy, and which at last provided capital with the ultimate weapon it had dreamed of to use against labor.

*   *   *

The use of the injunction as a strikebreaking device had been considered and experimentally tried on various occasions in the eighties in both Federal and state courts. In the former, it had proceeded naturally from the equitable interests of the Federal receivers in bankruptcy where, it was readily alleged, these interests were jeopardized by work stoppages on railroads in receivership. In the state instances, the rationale was more nebulous; a Massachusetts court in 1888 contended that strikes and boycotts constituted "a continuous unlawful act, injurious to the plaintiff's business and property, and . . . a nuisance such as a court of equity will grant relief against."[58]

Injunctions were issued early in the 1894 strike by Federal judges in several circuits, but for the employers this was a piecemeal remedy. On their behalf, Olney envisioned a blanket or omnibus restraining order, and in Chicago he enjoyed the enthusiastic cooperation of four men who were to draft and enforce the new instrument. Joining with Federal attorneys Milchrist and Walker were District Judge Peter S. Grosscup and Circuit Judge William A. Woods, who were fully as zealous as the Attorney General in seeking to bring the full force of the law against the labor side of this struggle. Grosscup's unqualified commitment to the idea of untrammeled capitalism was well known;* Woods, as the subsequent official inquiry was to document, had accepted numerous past favors from the carriers.[59]

Both judges met with the Federal attorneys in Milchrist's office to review the draft on which Milchrist and Walker had spent a feverish night; Grosscup would, later that day, grant the injunction prayed for, and Woods subsequently would try the violators. The instrument was all inclusive, a dragnet described by one observer as an order which "punishes an individual for doing a certain thing, and is equally merciless if he does not do it." It named the twenty-four railroads, all engaged in interstate commerce, and averred that they were in need of protection from a conspiracy on the part of the strikers to disrupt the movement of the mails and to impede interstate commerce. They also needed protection in their contract rights, it was declared, since Pullman Palace Cars were "indispensable" to the successful operation of the trains and to accede to the union demand for non-use of the cars would be to violate their contract with Pullman.[60]

The injunction explicitly directed Debs and certain other union officers, as well as an unidentified number of strikers, to desist from any activities, and to

---

*See page 36.

abstain from "ordering, directing, aiding, assisting, or abetting in any manner whatever" anyone else in any activities intended to impede interstate commerce, interfere with the mails, loiter near or injure any railroad property, or —most fundamentally—attempt by coercion, threats or persuasion to induce any employee to leave his job. The injunction was, as the delighted General Managers Association described it, "a Gatling gun on paper."[61]

Debs fully agreed; as he was to tell the Strike Commission, the Pullman dispute was broken up "not by the Army, and not by any other power, but simply and solely by the action of the United States courts." Although most newspapers had denounced the strike as senseless and ruinous, some protested at once against the absolutism inherent in the injunction. The *New York World* called it an "outrageous stretch of Federal power" and predicted that the American people "will never consent that the power of the Federal government shall be placed at the disposal of railroad managers when they quarrel with their employees, while the government recognizes no reciprocal obligation to secure the employees in the enjoyment of their rights and privileges."[62]

*   *   *

There were many who entertained doubts as to the legitimacy of the labor injunction. In the first place, it introduced a process of equity jurisprudence, traditionally reserved for the extraordinary protection of private rights, into the area of public law. Secondly, once introduced into this new environment, it made possible a criminal prosecution without a jury trial, since the violation of the injunction could be punished by summary contempt. Thirdly, it was directed in the main at a large group of unidentified persons, so that it revived and placed in the hands of the courts a power of unlimited scope unknown since the abolition of the general warrant. Finally, notice of the injunction was construed as effective if it were placed in media or areas where the affected parties could be presumed to see it. While Debs and other named persons were personally served, the strikers at large were presumed to be served by publication of the instrument in the newspapers, by reading it to any mobs who would listen, and by fastening it to the walls of railroad buildings and the sides of boxcars.[63]

The effectiveness of the labor injunction as compared with normal criminal process was demonstrated in the fateful fortnight in July following its issuance. A Federal grand jury was in session considering possible indictments against Debs and other union officials, but the evidence came in slowly and the trials which would follow promised to be long-drawn out. Without waiting for the grand jury's action, Milchrist and Walker prepared and filed criminal informations against the union leaders on behalf of the United States government, alleging violation of the injunction. The principal allegation was that in defiance of the writ, Debs and others had sent telegrams to strike leaders urging them to continue their struggle against the carriers. Following the arrest of the defendants, the telegrams were read as evidence; Judge Woods listened to a few, and then ruled that the evidence sustained the charge.[64]

Three of Chicago's leading attorneys came forward to offer Debs' defense

—the eighty-year-old Lyman Trumbull, friend of Lincoln and for half a century one of the leading constitutional lawyers in the nation; S. S. Gregory, a well-known practitioner in the civil courts who argued the impropriety of transferring the injunctive process to criminal law; and Clarence S. Darrow, for whom this case would mark the start of a long career in labor and criminal law. Essentially, the defense was a challenge to the jurisdiction of the court and a question of the constitutionality of prosecuting a criminal charge without a jury trial.

Predictably, Woods rejected both arguments. Jurisdiction, he declared, was conferred by the Sherman Anti-Trust Act since the strike was manifestly a conspiracy in restraint of trade. As for the use of an equity process in criminal proceedings, Woods ruled that any acts of private persons directed against other private persons could be enjoined if there was a reasonable prospect that the acts would result in injuries to private interests which might also be chargeable as crimes. "Strikes by railroad employees," Woods concluded, "have been attended generally, if not in every instance, with some form of intimidation or force." In the instant case, he declared, "it was impossible that a strike which aimed at a general cessation of business upon the railroads of the country should succeed without violence."[65]

The cause was thus lost in Woods' court. In an effort to test the constitutional propriety of the labor injunction. Debs' three attorneys obtained permission to argue for a writ of habeas corpus in the Supreme Court of the United States. In the spring of the memorable term of 1894—in May 1895, a week after the Income Tax Case and five months after the Sugar Trust decision—the high tribunal would hand down the third of its crucial rulings. To uphold this sweeping new power of equity in criminal law, Gregory contended before Fuller and his colleagues, "would be absolutely destructive to liberty and intolerable to a free people. . . . No man could be safe; no limits could be prescribed to the acts which might be forbidden nor the punishment to be inflicted." To prosecute acts of violence which followed upon strikes and lockouts, added Darrow, it was not necessary to extinguish the right to strike itself. Strikes and lockouts, he observed, "are incidents of industrial life. They are not justified because men love social strife and industrial war, but because in the present system of industrial evolution to deprive workingmen of this power would be to strip and bind them and leave them helpless as the prey of the great and strong."[66]

Justice Brewer, the pious Kansan, read the unanimous opinon of the Court. He who so often was to decry the invasion of state and private interests by the Federal authority was now to declare that when any private disputes were "such as affect the public at large, and are in respect of matters which by the Constitution are entrusted to the care of the nation, and concerning which the nation owes the duty to all citizens of securing to them their common rights, then the mere fact that the government has no pecuniary interest in the controversy is not sufficient to exclude it from the courts."

Upon resorting to the courts, Brewer continued, the government had the right to ask for a judicial order compelling obedience to its laws, and upon the defiance of the order to seek penal sanctions against the offenders. With this manifestly impeccable reasoning—clouded only by the fact that the paramount sovereignty of the Federal government was being committed permanently to the disadvantage of one class in American society—the petition was denied.[67]

Capital's long search for the ultimate legal weapon to blunt the labor attack had come to an end. It would be thirty-seven years before the Norris-LaGuardia Anti-Injunction Act would rescind the judicial doctrine pronounced in the spring of 1895. Meantime, the *laissez-faire* entrepreneur would use his advantage well; in the period between 1895 and 1932, the labor injunction would be sought from the Federal courts in more than one hundred and twenty major cases.[68]

4/Fire on the Prairies

IN THE QUARTER of a century which followed the Civil War, the American farmer began his long and steady decline from the dominant position he had occupied in the early decades of the republic. The Jeffersonian ideal of the self-reliant and productive husbandman as the vital force in a free society continued, long after the fact, as the most characteristic national political stereotype. From Illinois' rail-splitting Abraham Lincoln of the 1860's to the Lyndon B. Johnson of the 1960's with his elaborate reminiscences of hard times in the Pedernales Valley of Texas, the rustic symbolism of American life would be carefully preserved. But the harsh reality of the situation was that after the middle of the nineteenth century the farmer had already ceased to be in control of economic events, however desperately he continued to cling to his control of political processes—and the farmer himself was at least vaguely aware of this fact. It had first become apparent with the growth of the interstate railroads; the Union Pacific and the Central Pacific, completing the first transcontinental line in 1869, had begun to close the door on the pioneer era in the very process of opening up the nation's last great land areas to settlement.

The railroad problem of the following generation was essentially the extension of a more complex and ultimately more decisive factor in the decline of rural domination of the economy. The census figures from 1870 to 1900 told the story: in these three decades the population of the United States doubled and the percentage of urban population increased from 20 to 30. (In the next three decades the urban percentage would pass 50.) In 1870 there were 663 communities of more than 2,500 population—most of them, however, under 5,000; by 1900 there were more than 1,700, including three cities exceeding a million persons each. On every ledger, the balance was moving steadily toward the superior position of the industrial urban complex. By 1890 the value of manufactured goods in the United States first passed the total value of agricultural products, but ten years later the nation could report sixteen industries each of whose products annually amounted to more than $200,000,000 in value.[1]

The handwriting was on the wall for at least some to read: Henry George lugubriously observed in 1886 that "it needs no reference to census tables to prove that under present conditions the small American freeholder is doomed." With increasing technological efficiency in agriculture itself and the rising cost of farm production and marketing, George concluded, "ownership of land must tend to concentrate, and an increasing proportion of the people to become tributary to the rest."[2]

Like a magnet, the steadily developing industrial centers began to draw the resources—material and human—from the hinterland toward themselves along the radiating lines of the network of railroads. The farmer, who once had freighted his goods by wagon or river barge to a nearby market, now watched his grain and cattle loaded onto cars which then disappeared into the vast distances leading eastward toward the new cities. The Civil War period had provided enormous expansion opportunities for agriculture; the Homestead Act of 1862 had thrown open the acreage of the Great Plains and thereby made possible the creation of the most remarkable grain-producing economy the world had ever known. But with the expansion had come dependence—first upon the railroads which carried the produce of the farms and ranches to markets beyond the Mississippi and from there, on great steamers, beyond the ocean itself; but more fundamentally, upon the urban centers from which the farmer's own necessities were purchased, where prices for everything were established and where, as he found to his dismay, his mortgages were being gathered into the expanding portfolios of Eastern banks.

Thus, within a matter of a few years—substantially less than a generation —the farmer found himself compelled to deal with a strange and disturbing array of forces which had placed themselves across his lifelines to markets. It was a cruel prospect, the more so since he had been powerless to influence the march of events to this point. Henceforth, predicted the disillusioned Ignatius Donnelly, one of the most ardent advocates of Congressional railroad subsidies in the late sixties, national life would be a contest "between the few who seek to grasp all power and wealth, and the many who seek to preserve their rights as American citizens and freemen."[3]

In the early seventies the farmer made his first effort to regain control of his own destiny, if not of the national destiny, by electing to challenge the growing power of the railroads. As carriers of his grain and livestock, these were the agencies which most immediately affected his well-being; in particular, their continual manipulation of rates for the transportation of wheat, corn and cattle could destroy any hope of a profitable sale before the shipments had even gotten under way. Many a section of land across the great West was owned by the railroads themselves, the result of the lavish bounties which the Congresses of the sixties had granted to promote the construction of lines. And many a bankrupt village, cut off from access to markets by the ruthless competition between the roads, bore mute testimony to the life-and-death nature of the problem. Rebates to favored shippers, offset by the volume they shipped; underbilling and underclassification—shipping expensive articles at the rate of cheaper ones; distribution of boxcars to accommodate certain individuals and localities and to handicap others; disproportionate long and short haul differentials; basing point systems which arbitrarily varied rates for shipments from the West or South—the variety of tactics employable by the railroads to keep the farmer in subjection appeared to be endless.[4]

It was obvious to many, and particularly to a government worker from Itasca, Minnesota named Oliver H. Kelley, that the farmer needed a unifying organization through which he could first learn and then apply techniques of economic counterattack. Kelley, an ardent Mason, favored the idea of a secret society and in 1867 had led in the formation of just such a group, the Patrons of Husbandry, with a foundation, he wrote, "laid on *solid nothing*—the rock of poverty—and there is no harder material."

The original concept of the Patrons, or the National Grange, as it was soon to be called, was avowedly nonpolitical, but it was evident almost from the outset that its practical value lay in its capacity as a unified force to bring the corporation antagonist to terms. By 1873 the Grange could claim three-quarters of a million members, and these men made their purpose clear: "We want the price of every necessary article of consumption or daily use lowered," wrote the Grange historian, James McCabe, "and whatever man or combination of men [seeks] to prevent the realization of this demand is the enemy of the public."[5]

Thus it was, in the ultimate irony of events, that the Jeffersonian yeoman, individualist that he had been, found himself obliged to meet the threat of organized economic power by turning to organized efforts at economic regulation. The farmer, fighting against a steadily constricting encirclement of a corporate society, created the first regulatory agencies and thus speeded the day of government participation in the economic movements of the twentieth century.

*   *   *

The bitterness of agrarian resentment had its roots in the consequences of the shameless overselling of railroad projects in the middle of the century. Promoters of rail lines had approached county and town governments with extravagant descriptions of the roads which would soon be built; to help finance these projects, the local governments issued bonds in enormous quantities— far out of proportion to prospective revenues with which to pay them off, but rationalized by the assurances that once the railroad had been built the increase in population would provide the additional tax money for amortization. Now, twenty-five and thirty years later, the stark facts were that no roads had ever been built, no remarkable growth in population (and hence taxpayers) had come about—and the bonds were being presented for payment. The promoters, having issued stock in the imaginary railroads in such excess as to insure their bankruptcy, had then sold the municipal bonds to Eastern investors and had long since disappeared from the scene. But under the inflexible rule of the common law, the bonds had been issued under authority of the local governments, and the present holders were *"bona fide* purchasers for value" who were entitled to payment.[6]

The judiciary was adamant; if there had been fraud, or at least failure of performance, in the agreements between the local governments and the promoters, that was a matter between the issuers of the bonds and the promoters —but as between the "innocent" present owners of the bonds and the issuers there was an inescapable obligation to pay. Often, it was suspected, there was a shadowy identity between the original promoters and the present "innocent" creditors. But in any case the hard fact was that if the securities were to be paid off, the tax burden on the unlucky local citizens had to be fearfully increased. And the courts were insistent; repudiation by a governmental body was considered un-American and anti-capitalistic as well as illegal. The plea of distress to the locality, the Supreme Court lectured a small Wisconsin town in 1873, was a "vicious" attempt to evade "an honest debt."[7]

Where state courts showed a tendency to sympathize with the desperate plight of their local government units, bondholders' attorneys promptly petitioned for removal of the cases into the Federal courts, on the classic claim of diversity jurisdiction: The creditors were Eastern banks and the defendants were impoverished yeomen of the Western prairies, and thus, in suits between citizens of different states, the litigation could be carried on in courts whose sympathies, if they evinced any, were likely to be for "innocent" creditors. As Judge Dillon, the avid devotee of free enterprise and authority on municipal corporations, was to observe, the uniform enforcement of these claims was also in the best interest of the municipalities, since it insured that their credit in the bond market would remain unimpaired.[8]

There was simply no escape for the hapless victims of the supersalesmen of the railroad mania; state legislative attempts to extinguish the debts or to limit the amount of taxes the communities could levy to pay them were struck down by the Federal judiciary, and in some instances the Federal courts virtually became receivers for local revenues to insure that the bondholders obtained their full due. The sense of a conspiracy to strip the farmer twice—first in the sale of worthless railroad stock and then in the compulsion to redeem the securities his local government had issued to purchase the stock—bred a virulent hatred of the courts and the law of capitalism.[9]

As for the areas which had in fact been accommodated by railroad construction, the denizens often asked themselves if they were much better off. Enormous tracts of rich timberland had been granted from the public domain, either state or federal, to subsidize the railroad construction, and the carriers were selling off logging rights to favorites at lavish profits. But even worse was the chronic problem of the rates charged the farmer himself, who had come to the great grainlands between the Mississippi and the Rockies to plant and reap in the expectation of shipping to the stockyards and elevators to the East.

After backbreaking labor and the constant threats of storm or drought, he all too often found both the railroads to carry his produce and the elevators to store it united in a scheme to bleed him white.

*   *   *

In the spring of 1870 the people of Illinois assembled in constitutional convention at Bloomington in an atmosphere charged with the urgency of drastic action. The *Prairie Farmer,* a leading voice of the agrarian reformers, proposed that a parallel "Producers' Convention" be called for the same time and place to insure that the constitution makers took proper measures for curbing "the present tendency to monopoly and extortionate charges" by railroads. More particularly, the *Farmer* was intent upon securing constitutional action to bring under public surveillance the grain elevators of the Chicago area which, it was widely alleged, enabled the carriers to tighten their grip on the producers' throats by short weights and unconscionable storage rates. A new constitutional clause rather than simple legislation was essential, it was declared, because the railroads had consistently bought out previous Illinois legislatures.[10]

Prodded by these demands, the convention drafted resolutions enumerating and condemning the carriers' rate maneuverings and wrote a constitutional article declaring all places "where grain or other property is stored for compensation" to be "public warehouses" subject to state inspection and regulation. By means of this article, the committee on miscellaneous corporations reported to the convention delegates, it was hoped to meet the complaints of shippers throughout the West, that by short weights and similar devices the roads regularly defrauded them of "five to ten bushels of grain per carload," and that by refusing to deliver the shipments to any elevators but those in which the particular line had a financial interest the shippers were still further put at the mercy of the carrier.

The proposed article was approved by the convention and adopted by a statewide election that summer, and the following year the Illinois legislature—sixty-five of whose members had organized into a club "to look after the interests of the producing class" and to "secure such legislation as will relieve the necessities of the agricultural and mechanical interests of the State"—enacted four statutes regulating the shipping and warehousing of grain under the supervision of a railroad and warehouse commission. Within three years, comparable "Granger laws" had been enacted in Iowa, Kansas, Minnesota and Wisconsin.[11]

The Illinois Warehouse Act of 1871 implemented a broad new concept in American constitutionalism—the right of the public to intervene when the conduct of private business affected the public interest. Under Chief Justice Taney in the late 1830's the United States Supreme Court had affirmed certain state powers to regulate banking and to administer quarantine inspection of incoming vessels in American harbors, but the element of public welfare affected by these commercial activities had been fairly evident.[12] Not so in the case of purely private businesses operated for the accommodation of other private individuals, as the railroad lawyers now hotly contended in rising to the challenge of the Granger laws.

For many a middle-class American, sympathetic in the abstract with the farmer's plight, the introduction into the national life of the regulatory agency in the form of rate-fixing commissions was a profoundly disturbing innovation, in sharp contrast to the Jeffersonian-Emersonian tradition of independence. If the government was to claim a right to regulate railroads by virtue of their having initially been the grantees of public land, it was argued, why could not the farmers equally be subjected to regulation by virtue of their settlements under the Homestead Act? But the most common argument of the capitalists was that the Granger laws were communistic—"an organized, active and influential idiocy," said J. Sterling Morton of Nebraska, later to be Grover Cleveland's Secretary of Agriculture. The railroad interests, for their part, made it clear that they intended to fight the regulations and the acts creating the regulaing agencies to the courts of last resort.[13]

The major case in this contest was precipitated by a criminal action brought by the Illinois warehouse commission against two Chicago grain elevator men, Ira Y. Munn and George L. Scott, and defense counsel for Munn and Scott promptly challenged the constitutional validity of the 1871 law. The grain elevator business was private, not public, despite the constitutional declaration that the elevators were public warehouses, the defendants' briefs contended. The elevators depended upon no franchise from the state to conduct their business, and for the state to inhibit the use of their business in such manner as to prevent their realizing a full profit amounted to depriving them of their property without due process of law.

It was the type of argument which would be raised regularly, and more often than not successfully, over the next three quarters of a century by corporate enterprises resisting the regulatory efforts of state and national governments. In the spring of 1873, when the case was carried to the Illinois supreme court, the railroads had ample reason for optimism. As was later confirmed, the members of the court, in a conference on the case in April, had agreed "with scarcely a dissenting voice, that the act prescribing maximum rates for the storage of grain was unconstitutional."[14]

But law and politics are separate balances in the scales of economic justice, and before a formal judicial opinion on the *Munn* case could be written, the balance suddenly shifted. One of the members of the court resigned in May, and in June the term of another expired. To tip the scales in their favor, the Grangers now turned to the summer elections, pledged to throw the weight of their votes behind candidates for both the trial and appellate courts who would "sustain the Constitution and laws of this State."

The two Granger-endorsed candidates for the high court narrowly edged their competitors in the voting; that September the reorganized court ordered rearguments in the warehouse case and in January 1874 a majority of five to two upheld the constitutionality of the law.[15] The state legislature, the majority declared, had the authority to regulate any business in the public interest, and limitations upon the use and enjoyment of private property in these instances were not equivalent to the deprivation of the property. It was a statement of constitutionalism to strike cold dread into the hearts of conservatives; the ruling "is the advance guard of a sort of enlightened socialism," said the *New York Tribune*.[16]

On writ of error, challenging the constitutional doctrine, the *Munn* case was carried to the United States Supreme Court, in company with four other cases challenging the Granger laws in Iowa, Minnesota and Wisconsin. The manifest significance of the issue brought into the arena some of the leading railroad specialists of the land—William G. Goudy, for thirty years a leader of the Chicago bar, found the *Munn* case the pathway to the general counselship of the Chicago and Northwestern Railway, while William Pitt Clough, defense attorney in the companion Minnesota case, would become general counsel for the Northern Pacific and later, with A. P. Hill and J. P. Morgan, one of the organizers of the Northern Securities Company.[17]

The attack upon the rate regulations probed every possible loophole in the public law. Goudy traced authorities from Magna Carta to the contemporary Thomas M. Cooley, whose article of faith was expressed in the dictum that every law "which directly proposes to destroy or offset individual rights, or does the same thing by affording remedies leading to similar consequences, is unconstitutional and void." The Iowa case and the Federal court case in Wisconsin involved essentially the same sets of facts as in *Munn v. Illinois;* while in state cases in Wisconsin and Minnesota the test took the form of attempts by the railroads to compel shippers to pay more than the fixed rates, relying on the doctrine of the *Dartmouth College Case* against impairment of contracts.[18]

The concerted challenge invited the Supreme Court to frame a categorical reply, which in due course was stated by Chief Justice Waite but documented, from all the evidence, by Associate Justice Joseph P. Bradley, himself an experienced railroad lawyer.[19] Tracing the principle of regulation to seventeenth-century England, where Lord Hale had ruled that any port where shippers must unload must be required to make reasonable charges, Waite declared that any comparable facility "is a business in which the whole public has a direct and positive interest." Where the common law recognized the right of government to regulate such business affected with a public interest, the Court concluded, the legislature was clearly within its constitutional authority to amplify the common law.[20]

Justice Field, with his colleague William Strong, protested in dissent that the holding was "subversive of the rights of private property"; Lord Hale, Field shrewdly pointed out, had spoken of public wharves and public ferries, not privately owned grain elevators. Field's insistence on this distinction planted the germ of dissipation in the Waite-Bradley doctrine which would grow in the generation to follow.[21]

*   *   *

But, in the late seventies, *Munn v. Illinois* seemed to be the perigee of the conservative outlook and the apogee of agrarian hopes. For the capitalist the prospect seemed glum. Unless a Federal constitutional amendment was enacted affirming the sanctity of private property, declared Charles C. Marshall, a New York attorney, it was apparent that "against the whim of a temporary majority inflamed with class-prejudice, envy or revenge, the property of no man is safe."[22]

His cause for alarm seemed to be well founded, for in the year after *Munn* Congress had dealt another blow to the heretofore unrestrained freedom of the railroad empire by passing the Thurman Act, which aimed at halting the systematic looting of the Union Pacific and Central Pacific by requiring their owners to establish sinking funds to retire the lines' grossly swollen indebtedness. Sustaining the Thurman Act in a test case the next year, Waite had declared such legislation a reasonable exercise of the government's power, as grantor of the carriers' charters, to protect the public interest involved.[23] To the *laissez-faire* capitalist, chafing on the verge of his most daring adventures, the public interest doctrine thus pronounced on two occasions by the Waite Court seemed the negation of all his ambitions. Without full freedom of contract, complained Frederick N. Judson, a St. Louis corporation lawyer, "the right of holding property is worthless, . . . and life itself is without hope or happiness."[24]

As it was to turn out, neither Marshall nor Judson had as much cause for pessimism as they professed, nor the agrarians as much ground for optimism. Two members of the bench, including the tenacious and durable Justice Field, had dissented strongly in *Munn,* and Bradley had joined them in the *Sinking Fund Cases.* The number would steadily be reinforced in the coming decade, and even Waite was to retreat from some of the logical consequences of his own doctrine before his death. In 1886 he was to declare that "limitation is not the equivalent of confiscation" (virtually the same phrase, but with precisely the opposite meaning, of the Illinois court in *Munn*), and that regulation could not assume the form of "a taking of private property for public use without just compensation, or without due process of law."[25]

Two years later, Field himself was able to deliver the majority opinion in a case concerning the constitutional authority of a Georgia rate-fixing commission; it was not alone the fact that a business might be affected with a *public interest,* he contended, that was the paramount requisite for authority to regulate, but the fact that there was a *public use* inherent in the nature of the business which justified its regulation. Two years later, in 1890, the power of regulatory commissions was sweepingly curtailed in a six-to-three opinion that an industry had a right, under due process, to have the *reasonableness* of the regulated rates judicially reviewed.[26]

From the broad constitutional test of the presumption of public interest to the narrow constitutional test of the proof of public use, and finally to the subjective constitutional test of reasonableness, the Court over the years directed the regulatory power of government into a progressively more constricted area. Finally, in *Smyth v. Ames,* the Court invalidated a Nebraska rate regulating statute with the vague statement that administrative regulations were unreasonable if they denied a "fair return" on the "fair value" of the private property.[27] Thus it was, by 1898, that the agrarian reformers found themselves maneuvered back almost to the position in which they had been prior to *Munn* in 1877. Waite's rule in the Granger cases remained dormant if not moribund while the Fuller Court developed a rationale which, as Seymour Thompson described it, automatically subjected "the legislation of the states to judicial superintendence."[28]

The Granger movement had been the first passage of arms between the farmers and the capitalists. If its legislative accomplishments had fallen short of their objectives, they had not been without significance. The principle of governmental power to regulate certain private commercial activities which were found to affect the public interest had been asserted in American constitutional law, however relentlessly it might be reduced in scope by later decisions. In addition, the Granger experiments had demonstrated to the agrarians some of the techniques of economic strategy to be applied in the political arena. But it was also clear that the farmers would have to redouble their efforts if they expected to win a more lasting victory. Already, the curtain was rising on the second act in the farmers' political drama.

*   *   *

Even before the Court began the attrition of the doctrine in the Granger cases, the Granger movement itself had spent its momentum. Since it had never been conceived as an organized political force, it lacked the sort of identification which gave both the Democratic and Republican parties so powerful an emotional appeal to the yeomen of the late nineteenth century, while on the economic side the Granger attempts to found agricultural cooperatives, Granger-owned banks, and centralized purchasing of consumer goods were generally foredoomed by the lack of available directorial experience and the looseness of a voluntary program of action. The cooperative movement was ahead of its time, and the business of supplying consumer goods direct to the farm buyer was accommodated by an enterprising new concern, Montgomery Ward and Company, which appeared on the scene.

In politics, having fallen short of their legislative goals of controlling the railroads and banks, the agrarian reformers now shifted their hopes for relief to a new—or, rather, recurring—theme of cheap money. "The relation of the West to the East is that of debtor to creditor," observed a Western editor in the post-Civil War era. The East accordingly favored "concentration of the volume of currency," while the West sought its expansion. "Until the West becomes rich enough to become independent of the East in financial matters," the writer concluded, "this contest will continue."[29] The Civil War, in fact, had exacerbated the currency issue; in the course of that struggle, gold had gradually disappeared from circulation and the government had turned to the issuance of paper money—"greenbacks"—secured simply on the credit of the United States.

By 1870 it was reported that more than $400,000,000 of such paper money was in circulation, and the proposals to recall it and resume specie payments periodically stirred up vigorous farm protests. A man who had borrowed $100 in currency when it was worth $75 did not relish the liability to repay it in dollars to be worth 100 cents each. Yet the pressure of creditor interests mounted steadily during the decade, and Congress' continuing vacillation on the question of resumption was blamed in part for the panic of 1873. By 1879, Congress overrode the objections of the cheap money bloc and authorized the retirement of the greenbacks. The immediate reaction of the debtor classes was to organize for political counter-revolution.

The Greenback Party was the natural heir to the Granger movement, appealing as it did primarily to the agrarian interests, feeding upon the grievances of a class perpetually finding itself at a disadvantage in its efforts to deal with urban economic forces. The cycle of borrowing to meet current needs, and borrowing again to pay off the previous notes when they fell due, seemed to be endless, and always the money for repayment seemed to require more of the borrower's sustenance than he gained in benefits from the new loans. His only hope, the cheap money advocates told him, was to compel the government to make greater quantities of money available; paper money was the Greenbackers' touchstone, but bimetallism gradually became the more sophisticated alternative.

If silver were added to gold as the standard of currency, wrote W. H. ("Coin") Harvey, a proper economic balance could be achieved, for "as two legs are necessary to walk and two eyes to see, so were these two monies necessary to the prosperity of the people."[30] Before the battle cry of "free silver" was raised, however, the paper money question had to be disposed of; the Greenback Party, accordingly, became the transitional medium between the free association of the Grangers and the organized crusade of Populism. Moreover, the formal political machinery of the Greenbackers provided advanced training for many of the men who had been led into public life by the Granger movement.

Many of these were forceful characters, far from the charlatans and buffoons the Eastern press made them out to be. Donnelly of Minnesota might be quixotic and occasionally inconsistent, but he understood perfectly the handicaps under which the farmer labored. So did James B. Weaver of Iowa, and "Sockless Jerry" Simpson and William A. Peffer of Kansas. Conservatives in their midst, like J. Sterling Morton of Nebraska, and conservatives in the East, like Charles A. Dana of the *New York Sun*, might profess dismay and contempt; but in the elections of 1878 the Greenbackers sent fifteen men to Congress and in 1880 polled 308,000 votes for Weaver as their candidate for President, as well as capturing a number of seats in Midwestern legislatures.

The results of the Presidential election left the Republican Party shaken; James A. Garfield won by a plurality of less than 10,000 votes out of a total of more than 10,000,000 cast. Had the Democrats been conciliatory to the Greenbackers, the GOP twenty-year grip on the White House would have been broken. E. L. Godkin, writing in November of that year, warned the Republicans that their party would have to seek some new answers to changing national problems. "Nothing kills a political party sooner than having no legislative end in view—that is, having no policy capable of being embodied in legislation, or promoted by legislation," he wrote.[31]

Economics provided the barometer of political pressures in the Midwest; for a brief period from 1879 to 1884, farm production made a slight recovery from its long postwar decline, and the Greenback movement entered a corresponding state of quiescence. But the long-term statistics indicated no change in the farmer's worsening position. Corn which had sold for 73 cents a bushel in 1869 had dropped to 36 cents a decade later, rallied to 63 in 1881 but by the end of the eighties had fallen to 28. Wheat fared somewhat better until the invasion of the world market by new producing countries in the middle nineties, but to grow the wheat cost as much as 19 cents more than the market price. And always the volume of farm mortgages—for which Westerners paid substantially higher interest rates than did Eastern farmers—continued to accelerate. In Kansas alone, in the decade of the eighties, between 75 and 90 percent of the farms were mortgaged, at an average interest of 9 percent, and more than a third of the mortgages were foreclosed.[32] The farmer's problem did not seem to diminish with the gradual return of prosperity, and a North Carolina editor expressed the growing sense of futility and desperation:

> There is something radically wrong in our industrial system. There is a screw loose. The wheels have dropped out of balance. The railroads have never been so prosperous, and yet agriculture languishes. The banks have never done a better or more profitable business, and yet agriculture languishes. Manufacturing enterprises never made more money or were in a more flourishing condition, and yet agriculture languishes. Towns and cities flourish and "boom" and grow and "boom," and yet agriculture languishes. Salaries and fees were never so temptingly high and desirable, and yet agriculture languishes.[33]

*　　　*　　　*

Eloquent though it was, this description of the situation did not suggest a solution. The Western shipper might continue to point out that it regularly cost him one bushel of grain to send two bushels to market, and when grain sold for a dime a bushel in Colorado and brought a dollar a bushel to a broker in New York, the unconscionable inequity could not long be endured. In vain could a man like Sidney Dillon, president of the Union Pacific, invite the agrarians to compare the cost of carrying a ton of wheat a mile by railroad with the cost of its carriage by a man or a horse; it was not a question of the farmer's carrying wheat, said the *St. Paul Pioneer Press,* but of carrying "three blanket mortgages"—one on his farm to purchase seed for planting, another on his machinery to plant and cultivate and harvest, and another on the crop itself in advance of its reaping and sale.[34]

Yet the Granger legislation of the seventies had come to naught, and the Greenback movement of the eighties had failed to shake the dominant political parties from their apathy toward the agrarian problem. The one major accomplishment in Congress, the result of years of advocacy, had been the Interstate Commerce Act of 1887, but after the substantial limitations placed upon the powers of the Interstate Commerce Commission by judicial opinion, this statute seemed to have disappointed more hopes than it vindicated.

In point of fact, the Interstate Commerce Act represented the all-important next step after the Granger laws. As the latter had introduced the administrative regulatory agency into state constitutional law, so the Federal statute had extended the concept into national law. This was, perhaps, a momentous enough accomplishment, and it had been sharply challenged by conservatives, even agrarian representatives, in the course of the Congressional debate. "I do not believe in commissions," flatly declared Representative William C. Oates of Alabama; moreover, he argued, the commerce clause of the Constitution had been intended only to regulate state actions affecting commerce and not the actions of private individuals engaged in commerce between the states. The argument paraphrased the position of Representative John H. Reagan of Texas, who contended that all that Congress could do was to create a cause of action which an individual might bring against an interstate shipper.[35]

Yet, to the majority of the lawmakers, it was evident that if state regulations could not reach the real rate offenses, Federal regulations were the only alternative. The Supreme Court itself had made this clear the year before, in denying to the states any jurisdiction over interstate commerce.[36] Senator Shelby M. Cullom of Illinois offered the alternative to the Reagan approach: where Reagan proposed a statute enumerating practices to be prohibited in interstate commerce and leaving it to private shippers to sue for damages where such practices could be proved, Cullom favored the recently developed British plan of combining fact-finding powers and fact-trying processes within a single specialized agency.[37] When the Cullom bill was eventually adopted into law, the modern Federal administrative commission was born.

*   *   *

It was to be an oddity of constitutional history that the courts never formally dealt with the ultimate question of the constitutionality of the regulatory concept. They were content, even zealous, to hedge the process about with restraints, often to reduce the new commission to virtual impotence. But even the most confirmed *laissez-faire* jurists seemed tacitly to accept the concept itself as within the ambit of American constitutional theory. In part this was to be explained by the gradual crystallizing of the regulatory procedure in the states during the early period of railroad building and corporation growth. By 1869 the Supreme Court had declared that a state agency could properly regulate the activities of an insurance business even though the conduct of the business carried it across the state line; and in one of the Granger cases of 1877 the Court was heard to observe that "until Congress undertakes to legislate" on interstate matters the individual states could exercise regulatory authority to the extent of their jurisdiction over the business.[38]

Even in the *Wabash* case, when the Court retracted this latter doctrine and denied the states the power to reach interstate commercial activities, the intimation was clear that such regulation was the province of the Federal government. As early as 1875 the Court had expressed in dictum the view that "this is but one country" and commercial intercourse should be kept free from unreasonable burdens. "This is demanded," said the Court, "by the 'general welfare,' and . . . interference with it will demand from the national legislature the exercise of all the just powers with which it is clothed."[39]

The specific question of the constitutionality of the Interstate Commerce Act was answered affirmatively in 1894 by a five-to-four majority of the Court, on a matter of the procedural validity of granting witnesses before the Commission protection from criminal liability for admissions in their testimony. In a complementary opinion two years later, the Court even more positively affirmed the constitutionality of the procedure under the Act.[40] But this was not to say that the Court was abandoning *laissez-faire* economics in the main; as with the state regulatory efforts which had been upheld in principle and nullified in practice, the Interstate Commerce Commission was to find its powers piecemeal diminished by judicial decision.* The agrarians, watching the steady emasculation of the statute in the nineties, now turned to the third and final act of their drama.

*   *   *

"The people are aroused at last," wrote the editor of the *Chicago Western Rural* in the summer of 1890. "Never in our history has there been such a union among farmers as now." The Farmers' Alliance, after a decade of moribund existence, was reviving the promise it had once held out of providing a monolithic opposition to the railroad-banking combinations which bedevilled the husbandman. At the 1887 convention in Minneapolis, the old Granger credo of government regulation of carriers had been extended to a suggestion of government ownership, while the Greenback Party's currency platform had been rebuilt with planks advocating free and unlimited coinage of silver at a ratio favorable in comparison with gold.[41]

Alliance memberships were skyrocketing, touching off optimistic predictions of a million or even two million members in the immediate future. Overtures were being made to regional counterparts—the Southern Alliance and the Agricultural Wheel, in particular—and to the Knights of Labor who met the same year in Minneapolis. In fact, the following year witnessed the formation in Minnesota of a Farmer and Labor Party which formally adopted the more radical ideas of the day—woman suffrage, workmen's compensation, the eight-hour day, and the secret ballot—and turned loose the durable and

---

*Cf cases cited in Appendices D and E.

ubiquitous Ignatius Donnelly on a fresh round of lectures and stump speeches.[42]

Political action was now the avowed policy of the agrarians; to develop any program without this as its basis, Donnelly wrote in the *Forum,* was to arm the farmer with a gun that would not shoot. Washington Gladden, in the same magazine, warned the American public that the farmer "has waited long for the redress of his grievances; he purposes to wait no longer." General Weaver was to write in his book, *A Call to Action,* in 1892, that rural America was prepared to desert both of the major political parties and launch permanently upon its own party organization. "A vast and non-sectional union" of Western and Southern men of the soil was discovered by Hamlin Garland when he returned to the Middle Border after a sojourn in literary Boston in the early nineties.[43]

The agrarian uprising, wrote William A. Peffer, was not intended to assault the traditions of the Republic; it was defensive rather than offensive, but it had come at last to be the farmer's only recourse.[44] These were the words of disturbed but temperate men, but the urban newspapers seldom treated them as such. Instead, the Western leaders who sought to win a serious hearing in the East were more than likely to be linked with demagogues like "Blue Jeans" Williams of Indiana and "Heifer-Calf" Gillette of Iowa; while the storm gathered fury, the East laughed.

The Western reformers, in the nature of things, were a study in contrasts to the congeries of railroad lawyers, wealthy retired executives and party hacks who dominated Eastern politics. Most of them, now and later—Donnelly, Simpson and Weaver among the rebels of the seventies and eighties, Bryan who embodied in himself the transition from Populist to Progressive, and finally men like Norris and Beveridge and LaFollette who assumed leadership in the new century—were a volatile mixture of idealism, provincialism and fundamentalism. Their political creed was simplistic, if somewhat more elaborate than the tenet Donnelly proclaimed in 1870: "Wherever amid the fullness of the earth a human stomach goes empty, or a human brain remains deadened in ignorance, there is wrong and crime and fraud somewhere."[45]

An Irish immigrant, reared in Philadelphia and educated for the bar, Donnelly had moved to Minnesota in the mid-fifties to found a model farming community at Nininger. In the sixties he was in the United States Congress, ardently supporting the land grants to encourage the building of the transcontinental railroads. The seventies found him alternating from Liberal Republicans to Grangers to Greenbackers, and the eighties were marked by literary efforts, including a book on the imagined continent of Atlantis and another on the chronic dispute over Bacon's authorship of Shakespeare. Ingenuous and ebullient, Donnelly was an orator rather than an oracle, a bellwether rather than a political philosopher.[46]

The rationale of agrarian reform politics was supplied by Jerry Simpson of Kansas, deliberately cloaking his subtleties in the hayseed character created

for him by the press corps. Yet one newspaperman, William Allen White, remembered him as a self-educated man who "had read more widely than I, and
often quoted Carlyle in our conversations, and the poets and essayists of the
seventeenth century . . . He accepted the portrait which the Republicans made
of him as an ignorant fool because it helped him to talk to the crowds that
gathered to hear him. They expected little, and got much." In the House of
Representatives, Simpson attracted attention by his continual jibes at the silk
hats and silk socks of the Eastern leaders; but his genuine interest in serious
lawmaking won him the friendship of Speaker Tom Reed, and his competence in floor discussions led Champ Clark to describe him as one of the best
debaters in Congress. "The real Jerry Simpson," said White, "profited from the
fame of his own effigy."[47]

James Baird Weaver of Iowa was the grand old man of the agrarian crusade; a brigadier general in the Civil War, he came closer in personality and
convictions to the typical small freeholder of the prairies and plains. He was a
staunch prohibitionist, a reflex-action opponent of corporations, and an ardent advocate of cheap and plentiful money. Like many a politician of the
time, he was not above acting like a professional G. A. R. veteran when solicit-
ing votes, but his general reputation as a political leader less chimerical than
Donnelly and more fervent than Simpson made him the most logical choice
as a candidate behind whom crusaders of all types could unite.[48]

These were the men who appealed to the conscience of the new industrial
society, who reproachfully reminded the rest of America of its abandoned loyalty to the old economy of husbandry and modest freeholds—and who, now
that their pleas had been scorned, girded for a final battle with iniquitous
change.

        *   *   *

The torch had been put to the parched prairies, drained of resources and
hope after more than thirty years of disappointment, drouth, bankruptcy, and
the sense of failure of the once shining American dream. More than a thousand
covered wagons had passed through Omaha in 1891—headed East. There was
an incipient sullen hatred manifest in the gatherings of men in faded patched
overalls and their women in equally faded sunbonnets, to hear Mary Ellen
Lease urge them to raise less corn and more hell. "We meet in the midst of a
nation brought to the verge of moral and material ruin," Ignatius Donnelly
wrote into the platform of the Alliance meeting in St. Louis in 1892. "From
the same prolific womb of governmental injustice we breed the same two great
classes of tramps and millionaires." The time had come, said Jerry Simpson,
"for the final struggle between the robbers and the robbed." That fall, the
People's Party which had become the political arm of the Alliance polled more
than a million votes, and captured twenty-two electoral votes for Weaver as
candidate for President.[49]

A prairie fire, in the age when the primordial grasslands still towered, often
waist deep, in an unbroken rippling mass to the horizon, was a terrifying spec-

tacle for those who experienced it and for the Easterner who read about it in shuddering fascination. With a roar that seemed to shake the earth, heat that could be felt for miles, and flames that obscured the sky, it came with the speed and devastation of a tornado across the endless expanse of plains. There was no course but to run before it, a deadly race between human and holocaust which only ended when the one or the other was exhausted in death.

So the day of wrath appeared to those who now witnessed the Populist uprising; the steady gathering of force and fury in a mounting roar of out-rage at the money power, the railroad robber barons, the entrenched and com-fortable dwellers in the capitals and the courts. From scores of obscure villages and crossroads they came, from the ruined cotton farms of the South and the grasshopper-infested sodhouse "provings" of the West, as well as from the spent farms of Illinois and Indiana. They were the betrayed, the men who had first survived and then merely outlived the challenges of the frontier. Their strength had been spent bringing forth the fruits of the earth only to see these gathered up and enjoyed by others who had never sown.

The hour had come, the Populists declared with messianic fervor, to recap-ture the Jeffersonian dream; they were resolved to catalog every burning need the people had come to realize in their years of denial and degradation. At Omaha on July 4, 1892, they had come together, more than 1,400 delegates from thirty-two states. "Assembled on the anniversary of the birthday of the nation," their manifesto had declared, they proposed "to restore the govern-ment of the Republic to the hands of 'the plain people,' with whose class it originated." "We believe," the platform continued, "that the powers of gov-ernment—in other words, of the people—shall be expanded . . . to the end that oppression, injustice, and poverty shall eventually cease in the land." To speed the day, the Populists declared for "free and unlimited coinage of silver and gold at the present legal ratio of sixteen to one," a graduated income tax, government ownership of transportation, and the repossession of "land now held by the railroads and other corporations in excess of their actual needs," to be held for "actual settlers only."[50]

"The army of discontent is organizing," wrote the worried editor of the *American Journal of Politics* in 1894, and he saw it fraught with "tendencies dangerous to the state." In a mounting panic, the *New York Post* urged that the country admit no more states from the West "until we can civilize Kansas." But it was from Kansas' northern neighbor that the thunderbolt was finally de-livered. On a sweltering July afternoon at the 1896 Democratic convention in Chicago, the West threw down the gage: "There are those who believe," said the speaker, "that if you will only legislate to make the well-to-do prosperous, their prosperity will leak through on those below. The Democratic idea, how-ever, has been that if you make the masses prosperous, their prosperity will find its way up through every class which rests upon them."

The great cities, he went on, "rest upon our broad and fertile prairies. Burn down your cities and leave our farms, and your cities will spring up again as if by magic: but destroy our farms and the grass will grow in the streets of every city in the country." With Biblical righteousness, the oratory swept to its thundering climax: "You shall not press down upon the brow of labor this crown of thorns, you shall not crucify mankind upon a cross of gold."[51]

*   *   *

William Jennings Bryan had provided rural America with its long-sought Peerless Leader. Years after his recurrent Presidential campaigns were over, men would relive the thrill of his Chicago speech or follow the tanbark Chatauqua trail to the threnody of his oft-delivered oration on "The Prince of Peace." From the turgid waters of the Platte to the fundamentalist confrontation at Dayton, Tennessee three decades later, Bryan would remain a living reminder to a changing America of the homely and homespun fabric of its yesterday. In 1896, seizing the torch from the Populists, the Democratic nominee touched off a succession of wild alarms throughout the industrial areas.

The Democratic platform of 1896 struck three mighty blows at the epochal constitutional decisions of the previous year. The planks had been presaged by the keynote address of Senator John W. Daniel of Virginia, which blamed the current government deficit upon the Supreme Court's having "reversed its settled doctrines of a hundred years" in the Income Tax Case. Governor J. S. Hogg of Texas followed with a declaration that the Debs injunction had been deliberately drafted to accommodate a "protected class of Republicans" in industry which "proposes through Federal courts, in the exercise of their unconstitutional powers by issuance of extraordinary, unconventional writs," to destroy the labor movement.[52]

The language of the platform planks was unequivocal—indeed, it suggested that steps would be taken, if the party was victorious, to undo the wrongs done by the decisions of 1895. It was declared to be "the duty of Congress to use all the constitutional power which remains" after *Pollock,* "or which may come from its reversal by the Court as it may hereafter be constituted," to reassert an income tax power. As for "government by injunction," the platform condemned it as "a new and highly dangerous form of oppression . . . in contempt of the laws of the states and rights of citizens."[53]

Conservatives everywhere professed to be aghast. Former President Harrison was drafted by the Republicans to inveigh in a campaign speech against the party which preferred that "government by the mob" be substituted for "government by the law enforced by the court decrees." Even the incumbent Attorney General Harmon felt compelled to denounce the statements of his own party's nominee in attacking the Debs injunction. As a matter of fact, Cleveland and the Eastern Democrats were having no part of Bryan in any event, and could only applaud Republicans like Chauncey Depew who excoriated the alleged plans of the Democrats for "wild . . . constitutional and economic changes."[54]

The quasi-religious fervor of the Democratic-Populist crusade, and Bryan's own fervent Bible quoting, brought ecclesiastical conservatives, as well as presumably objective academicians, into the fray. Archbishop Ireland of Minnesota, whose words would not fail to impress thousands of immigrant Roman Catholics who were potential voters for a reform party, wrote a letter warning that the Bryan campaign was corrupted by a "spirit of socialism." Professor J. Laurence Laughlin of the University of Chicago was unsparing in his repeated characterizations of Bryan and his followers as "ignorant, unthinking minds, oppressed by a sense of inferiority," while Mr. Dooley found the Democratic-Populist alliance made up of "anny ol' thing that the other parties had rijicted." The Reverend Thomas Dixon, responding to Republican businessmen's hints that bimetallism might mean the end of church donations, charged the Nebraska candidate with being "a slobbering, mouthing demagogue, whose patriotism is in his jawbone." Many bankers publicly announced that every farm mortgage in their portfolios would be called in as soon as it came due if Bryan were to become President, and William Allen White wrote in his *Emporia Gazette* that "the election will sustain Americanism or it will plant Socialism."[55]

*   *   *

In the end, the prairie fire was quenched; it drowned at the Mississippi and Ohio, for Bryan lost every state east and north of those rivers, and even the strongholds of Iowa, Minnesota and Wisconsin. "God's in His heaven," Mark Hanna telegraphed to William McKinley as the returns came in. For the fundamentalist yeoman, however, it seemed that God had forsaken the elect. McKinley won by a margin of more than half a million popular votes and almost 100 electoral votes. In all branches of the Federal government and in all of the populous states, the agrarian challenge had been smashed.

Thoughtful men, like the University of Wisconsin's historian Frederick Jackson Turner, might ask how much of the values of American life had been destroyed in the bitterness of the campaign, but alarmists like Goldwin Smith looked with dread toward the elections of 1900. For Smith, English-born belle-lettrist and student of American history, the future offered only the prospect of cataclysm. Having failed to effectuate legislation which would meet their objectives, and having lost in the political arena, what remained for the discontented elements in the nation but to turn to violence?[56]

Turner's question went unanswered, and Smith's premonitions proved unfounded. The incontrovertible truth was that in three successive assaults—led by the Grangers, the Greenbackers and the Populists—the farmers had failed to turn the glacial advance of the new order. They simply had lacked the strength, both in numbers and in ideas; their proposed remedies for the suspected sickness in the economic body seemed to the majority of Americans to be worse than the disease.

Conservatives never ceased to dread the possibility of a union of the agrarians and the restless urban masses which would create the overriding force which each was seeking; but an effective union, except on a regional basis, never materialized during the half-century of the reform struggle.

There was a fundamental incompatibility between the two groups in the nineteenth century—the agrarians, intellectually, were nativists, committed to an exaggerated but indigenous creed of individualism; the militants of the cities were largely foreign-born and alien-tongued, taking their inspiration from the collectivist dogma of the new European radicals.

By the end of the nineties, a growing number of Americans conceded that the struggle to recapture the past had been lost, was predestined to have been lost. The real need was to come to grips with the new ways, to humanize them and convert their energies. Since the control centers of the new America were urban centers, the reform leadership gradually but inexorably began to pass from the agrarians to the city liberals. The fire on the prairies was banked and smouldering, but the fury it had fed in 1896 was now a matter of history. When political redemption came—like the agrarian revolt, it would be in three waves —its main leaders would be products of the new society itself.

5/Progressives in Power: First Fruits

"WE WANT NO WARS of conquest," declared William McKinley in his inaugural address on March 4, 1897, adding that "we must avoid the temptation of territorial aggression." Thirteen months later his administration would formally declare war on Spain, and less than two years later the United States would add Puerto Rico to its territorial possessions and assume power over the Philippines, Cuba, and an assortment of islands formerly ruled by Madrid. The swift turn of events dazzled the American people at the same time it caught them unprepared for the consequences. From a thinly populated country with vast areas of its own interior still to be settled, and beset by conflicts in both industry and agriculture, the United States had overnight become a world power.

Domestically, the Spanish-American War was a diversion from the unsolved problems on the farms and in the factories, and its benefits for the Republicans were evident in the campaign for McKinley's reelection. Where "free silver" had been the burning issue of 1896, imperialism was the issue of 1900; and while Bryan and the Democrats would vent upon the expansionists the same degree of righteous condemnation that they had poured out upon the gold standard, both McKinley's popular and electoral vote margins of victory were even larger.

With its new and unaccustomed global position, the United States was moved still further away from the economic, social and legal localisms of its earlier history. Where Europe had been its primary point of reference in foreign policy and domestic interest—with the possible exception of the West Coast's antipathy toward the importation of cheap Oriental labor—the horizon now immeasurably widened. The development was not alone the result of the war; for the past decade the nation had found itself being drawn with increasing frequency into the arena of international affairs. Canadian and Bering Sea fisheries disputes in 1888 and 1892 had been a by-product of growing American maritime activity which led in course to a confrontation with rival fishing interests. The Berlin Conference of 1889 had made the United States one of the members of a tripartite protectorate over the Samoan Islands, climaxing a decade in which American efforts to develop a naval station in the far Pacific had come athwart British-German colonial rivalries in Africa and the Near East. In 1895 a dispute with London over the Venezuelan border with British Guiana had led to a bold assertion of the Monroe Doctrine by Richard N. Olney, by then Cleveland's Secretary of State, in a phrase that stirred the national pride to depths it had not known since the war with Mexico: "Today the United States is practically sovereign on this continent, and its fiat is law upon the subjects to which it confines its interposition."[1]

Finally, in the context of the war with Spain, Congress had come to the climax in a twenty-year dialogue on the question of annexation of the Hawaiian Islands, a subject in which American sugar interests had shown a capacity for intrigue equal to any Cecil Rhodes or other imperial agent of the European powers. Since 1875, when a treaty had permitted duty free entry of Hawaiian sugar into the United States, substantial production of this commodity had been built up with the aid of American dollars. The McKinley Tariff Act of 1890, placing all foreign sugar on the free list, abruptly ended the lucrative advantage of the American producers in the islands, and indeed it was estimated that in 1891 the Hawaiian sugar interests had sustained a loss of $12,000,000 in depressed prices. The succession to the Hawaiian throne that same year of a strongwilled nationalist, Queen Liliuokalani, had set the stage for a revolution fomented by Sanford B. Dole, chief justice of the islands' supreme court.

Born in the islands of missionary parents, Dole combined a reformer's zeal with the essential premise that native peoples must ultimately accept the guidance of the superior Anglo-Saxon heritage. He had already led one revolution against the native monarchy and was quite prepared to mount another. In 1893, Dole had the enthusiastic support of the annexationist-minded United States minister, John L. Stevens, who supplied the Marines to drive Liliuokalani from her throne, then took it upon himself to recognize Dole as president of a new republican government and helped draft a proposed treaty of annexation. The scheme had run aground in Cleveland's administration, the President denouncing the whole affair as an unconscionable interference with Hawaiian sovereignty. In any case, Cleveland reported to Congress in withdrawing the treaty from consideration, the "mission of our nation is to build up and make a greater country out of what we have, instead of annexing islands."[2]

Cleveland's position was to be overruled when McKinley took office. For the Republicans, annexation was a logical next step in a steady national advance into the Pacific, consequent to the policy inaugurated by the Congresses of the eighties demanding "a navy second to none" and in furtherance thereof establishing a Pacific naval center at Pearl Harbor. (It was a unit of this mod-

ern ironclad fleet of the new navy era, the U.S.S. *Maine,* which was blown
up in February, 1898 at Havana.) Sentiment against annexation was substantial, nevertheless; Senator Champ Clark of Missouri called it "a bait for our
cupidity" prepared by "agents of the Hawaiian sugar kings." In the end, the
opposition was thwarted; in place of a treaty requiring a two-thirds majority
of the Senate, the annexationists accomplished their end through a joint resolution requiring only a simple majority of both houses of Congress.[3]

*   *   *

The last years of the nineties, as well as witnessing the sudden transformation of the United States into a major power, also witnessed the passing of
the long depression which had exacerbated domestic affairs for parts of three
decades. The floodtide of prosperity was even more exhilarating; "fundamental
changes in the commercial and industrial conditions of the United States,"
said one observer, had made "the years 1898 and 1899 in many respects the
most remarkable in the history of the nation. It was in 1898 that the United
States exceeded Great Britain for the first time in the volume of domestic ex-
ports. . . . In less than three years—that is, between 1897 and 1900—so great
were the trade balances in our favor that over a billion dollars in American indebtedness was wiped from the ledgers of Europe."[4]

Bank clearings doubled between 1894 and 1899, railroad receiverships in
1899 were lower than for any previous year since 1882, and the country attained record production in coal, corn, copper, cotton, iron and lumber. All
sections of the country benefited from improving conditions. Farm prices,
which had declined so drastically during the previous thirty years, picked up
as the decade ended and more than doubled between 1900 and 1910. The
South began moving steadily toward an industrialization which would give
better balance to its economy, so long committed to a one- or two-crop agriculture. In New England and parts of the Midwest, although the rural
population accelerated its decline in favor of the urban, the farmers who remained found better prices for their crops and thus a better living for their
families.[5]

The centralized control of American business continued unabated. After
New Jersey liberalized its corporation laws to make possible the modern holding company, more than fifty major trusts or holding companies came into
being, most of them in the years immediately following the war with Spain.
Railroads continued to be the aristocrats of industry, and in this period they
completed a process of consolidation which was remarkable even for an age
of trust-building. A contemporary chart showed six major financial groups—
dominated by the Morgan interests and interlocked in directorates and in stock
ownership; the five allied groups which completed the aggregate of control included the Pennsylvania railroad syndicate, Vanderbilt, the Moore brothers,
a Gould-Rockefeller combination, and Harriman in association with Kuhn,
Loeb & Company. Their total capitalization was more than $9,000,000,000 and
their miles of lines exceeded 164,000.[6]

But other giants had appeared in the shadows of the railroads and the Standard Oil Trust: the Amalgamated Copper Company, the American Smelting and Refining Company, the Consolidated Tobacco Company, and United States Steel Corporation. The census of 1900 would enumerate more than seventy interstate trusts, each having a capital in excess of $10,000,000.[7]

Much of the antipathy for labor remained in the capitalist world; David M. Parry, president of the National Association of Manufacturers, was to declare in 1903 that all labor was "socialistic" and the unions understood only "the law of physical force." In the fall of that year at Chicago a Citizens' Industrial Association was created to provide a clearing house for employer groups in all parts of the country. Its manifesto stated: "The present industrial conditions have become so deplorable by reason of the indefensible methods and claims of organized labor that the time has come when the employing interests and good citizenship of the country must take immediate and effective measures to reaffirm and enforce those fundamental principles of American government guaranteeing free, competitive conditions. In its demand for the closed shop organized labor is seeking to overthrow individual liberty and property rights, the principal props of our government."[8]

*   *   *

There were some spectacular exceptions to this psychology. With the assistance of a young attorney named Louis D. Brandeis, Boston's department store magnate Edward A. Filene created a cooperative association of employees which approached the partnership of management and labor of which Powderly had once dreamed. "It rests with this century, and perhaps with America," Brandeis told the association in 1905, "to prove that as we have in the political world shown what self-government can do, we are to pursue the same lines in the industrial world."[9]

While Brandeis and Filene were unique, it could not be denied that a new outlook had come to Americans of all ranks of life in 1900. Aware that the fundamental problems of the old century remained, they were now disposed to abandon old proposed solutions for new. Populism, in the final analysis, had been a program born of agrarian despair; the new age called for a positive approach deriving from the optimistic conviction that a changing society could be made to be a better society. In a sense, the Progressive Movement began as an anomaly; it emerged in a period of prosperity and material well-being when social conscience was supposed to be lulled.

But the needs for reform voiced by the progressives in the first years of the new century arose from their awareness of the fact that many flaws lay beneath the smiling surface of the economy. Ray Stannard Baker phrased the *caveat:* "The American has need of his own 'Recessional'—lest we forget our own grave national deficiencies and national faults. We can feed ourselves, we are great and powerful; but we have our own galling Negro problem, our rotten machine politics, our legislative bribery, our municipal corruption, our giant monopolies, our aristocracy of mere riches, any one of which is a rock upon which the ship of state, unless skillfully navigated, may go to its destruction."[10]

If the message stirred any forebodings among the ranks of the middle class, it was at the moment intermingled with concern at the speed with which events were moving. The war with Spain had climaxed a rapid metamorphosis from a politically introverted nation into one on which world responsibilties had suddenly been thrust. Before the first decade of the new century was half over, the automobile would have ceased to be a novelty, and two years into the new century Wilbur and Orville Wright would begin their historic experiments with flying machines on the sand dunes of Kitty Hawk, North Carolina. With these developments, the machine age became mobile, and life in the United States and around the world would move henceforth at an inexorably increasing pace.[11]

*   *   *

The "short and glorious war," begun in the spring and ended in the summer of 1898, spurred expansionist sentiment to brilliant encomiums. "We hold the other side of the Pacific," exulted Henry Cabot Lodge in a letter to Henry White after hearing of the victory at Manila Bay, "and the value to this country is almost beyond recognition." The event seemed the vindication of the "big navy" program to give America a dominant world position, consistent with the contemporary teaching of Admiral Alfred Mahan that control of world ocean communications was the key to national strength.[12]

American business, suddenly discerning a vast foreign market now becoming accessible, declared that the achievement of Dewey's squadron in the Philippines "has placed all American industry and interests on a stronger footing for any conceivable future." The possessions being wrested from Spain were, in the opinion of the *New York Commercial,* true "treasure islands," with the Philippines themselves "the richest islands in the world." The manifest destiny that had placed in American hands, half a century before, a fabulous area from Texas to the Pacific Coast, had now bestowed the strategic and economic control of the ocean itself upon this peculiarly favored people.[13]

Amid the outburst of enthusiasm, certain constitutional issues were quick to intrude themselves. Under what clause of the national charter, asked Senator George G. Vest of Missouri, was the United States authorized to acquire and hold territory for any purpose but prospective statehood—a possibility which, in his view, could not even be remotely entertained with reference to former Spanish colonies? On December 6, 1898—four days before the peace treaty was signed in Paris—Vest introduced a joint resolution denying such authority of acquisition, supporting it with the observation that a colonial system of territorialism "can exist in no free country, because it uproots and eliminates the basis of all republican institutions, that governments derive their just powers from the consent of the governed."

The words formed both a eulogy and an elegy; they echoed from a simpler era of a close-knit, homogeneous society which had long ago vanished. They were to be answered in terms of a new concept of sovereignty inherent in the Federal structure not expressed so much as taken for granted by the Constitution, a concept, as the expansionists maintained, latent until the hour had come when it would in the nature of things quicken into a living element of national government.

The Supreme Court itself had anticipated this attribute of sovereignty essential to the growing responsibilities of the United States of the post-Civil War generation. Justice Bradley had articulated it as a first principle of constitutional law in 1871 with the assertion that the United States "is not only a government, but it is a national government, and the only government in this country that has the character of nationality." In 1893 Justice Gray had reiterated the concept in yet more emphatic terms: "The United States are a sovereign and independent nation, and are vested by the Constitution with the entire control of international relations, and with all the powers of government necessary to maintain that control and make it effective."[14]

In Congress, the expansionists chose Connecticut Senator Orville H. Platt to give the response to Vest. Beginning with the statement that "expansion has been the law of our national growth," Platt urged that the right to acquire territory was not withheld from the national government by the Constitution, that "in the right to acquire territory is found the right to govern it," and that if the power to acquire is unlimited the power to govern is unlimited as well. The Senator traced the details of American expansion from the Louisiana Purchase (upon which President Jefferson had entertained gnawing constitutional doubts) to the contemporary acquisition of some fifty guano islands under the international law of discovery and occupation. Such acquisitions, by a variety of devices, had been simple exercises of a sovereignty inherent in a national state, Platt concluded; the chief constitutional pronouncement of pertinence was the clause directing Congress to make "all needful rules and regulations" for the government of territory of the United States. This, indeed, was the crux of the expansionist theory; territories were to be governed under organic laws enacted by Congress itself.[15]

Governments, said Platt, derive their just powers from "the consent of some of the governed," thus placing a gloss upon a cardinal tenet of the Declaration of Independence. He had valid enough technical arguments to support his case: women, minors, illiterates and residents of the District of Columbia and Alaska were ineligible to vote. This, for Platt, did not lessen the ultimate democratic benefit of American government, for the United States was a "government of a great people . . . that can be trusted to do right" with respect to non-consenters under their jurisdiction; these would be assured "the largest measure of liberty consistent with good order and their general well-being."

The Vest resolution was eventually talked to death. Congress in the main concurred in the view expressed by Senator Lodge, that "the power of the United States in any territory or possession outside the limits of the states themselves is absolute."[16]

*   *   *

Having accepted the argument that the nation had inherent power to acquire and hold territorial possessions which were neither prospective states nor colonies, the government and the governed (particularly those whose consent was required) now faced a larger question: If the Constitution permitted territorial acquisition, did the Constitution itself apply in full force to these territories? Or, in the catchphrase of the day, did the Constitution follow the flag? For the most part, both the expansionists and the anti-expansionists were in agreement with the Senator from Nevada, Francis G. Newlands, that "the ignorance and inferiority" of the population in the new territories "makes free constitutional government impractical or undesirable." The real issue, however, was economic: were imports from these new territories to be exempt from customs charges—and therefore competitive with native manufactures?

To answer this question in terms of the constitutional requirement of uniform duties and the prohibition of duties on shipments between states was to raise the ultimate question: If some requirements of the Constitution (i. e., the clauses on imports and duties) were applicable, was not all of the Constitution applicable? In Congress, the expansionists had their answers ready. Platt quoted from a contemporary article in the *Forum* that "foreign soil acquired by Congress is the property of and not part of the United States," and under such circumstances was not subject to constitutional guarantees. Others added that to impose certain Anglo-Saxon institutions such as jury trial and criminal process by indictment, upon aboriginal peoples not familiar with the principles, could amount to a denial of justice rather than its promotion.[17] In the end, Congress devised a territorial government for Puerto Rico embodying these prevailing convictions; the economic tradition of protectionism was preserved by levying an excise on goods shipped between the United States and its new possession, even though limiting it to fifteen percent of the regular duties on foreign goods and providing for its termination in 1902.[18]

Such a manifest effort at rationalization was promptly tested in the courts; the judicial answers to the questions, however, were as equivocal as the arguments in Congress. A test case against the customs officers of the port of New York alleging illegality in the collection of the duties on imports from Puerto Rico resulted in a five-to-four majority against the government. Justice Brown, speaking for the scant majority, rejected the argument that "a country may be domestic for one purpose and foreign for another," and found the customs duties improperly collected. The dissenters, including Justice White, firmly denied that territory acquired by treaty was automatically incorporated into the United States; the question of when it might be incorporated was, in their view, a legislative and not a judicial one.[19] In another case decided the same day, Brown confused the issue by shifting his position and conceding that Congress had the authority to determine when specific constitutional provisions should be extended to newly acquired territories. His opinion, added to the reiterated theory of "incorporation" by the former minority of four, tended to affirm the expansionist interpretation as narrowly as the earlier case had denied it.[20]

The lengthy reviews of constitutional history in the opinions in the Insular Cases tended to be prolix rather than enlightening; the only articulate doctrine to emerge from the contradictory decisions was, in fact, the "incorporation" theory of White. Until Congress chose to "incorporate" territory into the United States the territory was without the pale of uniform and universal constitutional guarantees. This theory neatly accommodated the rationale of expansionism in Congress, a rationale that the nation had apparently accepted, or at least had not found repugnant, by returning substantial Republican majorities to Congress, and reelecting McKinley, in 1900. The Constitution might not immediately follow the flag, as Mr. Dooley observed, but "the Supreme Court follows th' illiction returns."[21]

*   *   *

Although the national government in the 1900 elections appeared to be remaining safely in conservative hands, a groundswell of change was developing at the state and municipal level. It was overdue; Baker's "Recessional" had accurately identified the rottenness of government among the states and cities of the land as the most massive corruption in history. Lincoln Steffens would soon be publishing his muckraking articles in *McClure's* and *Everybody's* on "The Shame of the Cities," to awaken the American people to the far advanced state of disease in their local governments.

William Marcy Tweed, Tammany boss of New York in the decade after the Civil War who led raids on the city treasury netting between $100,000,000 and $200,000,000, had made his name synonymous with municipal corruption, but his conviction and imprisonment had done little to deter imitators. As the cities contracted with private developers for utilities, street railways, waterworks and other services, franchises went up for bid and lined the pockets of a long list of political vassals. Because the cities, dependent on the state legislatures for their powers until the home rule movement began in Missouri in the late seventies, could not perpetrate their own corruption without aid from the state, the traffic in bribery was thoroughly integrated.[22]

The decay in government was a by-product of the economic opportunism that became the national theme in the generation after the Civil War. As the industrial corporation developed its own ruthless morality, political bosses were quick to observe the methods and also to discern the points where their interests met. Banking and railroad commissions, corporation charters, the law enforcing machinery of the states systematically came under the control of political and financial power groups. Thomas N. McCarter, former attorney general of New Jersey, regarded the partnership of capital and public officials as highly satisfactory; they had "everything in the state worth getting," he was quoted as saying, "except Trenton street cars and Elizabeth gas."[23]

Together with corruption in government was the steady corrosion of life itself in the looted cities. The unanswered needs of housing and public health, social welfare for abandoned families, and the anomalies of a legal system never designed to accommodate the conflicts bred of a modern industrial economy loomed fully as large and threatening as the rot in government. This was the culture bed in which the Progressive Movement germinated.

Jane Addams and her Hull House settlement began in Chicago as early as 1889, but it was another ten years before Illinois established the nation's first juvenile court. Altgeld was one of the first reform-minded governors, but his flouting of conservative opinion in pardoning the Haymarket anarchists in 1893 reduced his effectiveness. But by the end of the nineties, the movement toward redeeming government and answering the voices of social conscience was clearly under way.

It was led, singularly enough, by men of wealth who had come to an awareness of the need to turn their talents to the public service. Hazen S. Pingree, four-time mayor of Detroit and subsequently governor of Michigan in 1896, was one example; his call for a reexamination of all public franchises and his "potato patch" program for unemployed heads of households quickly attracted national attention. Samuel M. ("Golden Rule") Jones, a business leader whose concern for his employees even outdid Filene of Boston, became mayor of Toledo the next year, as did millionaire James D. Phelan in San Francisco. In 1901, as McKinley began his second term, Seth Low became mayor of New York and Thomas L. Johnson mayor of Cleveland, all of them men of large fortunes dedicated to cleaning up municipal politics.[24]

The exposé journalists helped along the cause; Steffens, Ida M. Tarbell and Jacob Riis turned out a torrent of articles attacking corruption in industry, politics and the professions, impurities in foods and drugs, the exploitation of women and children in labor and in morals. The time had come, as a correspondent wrote to Senator Albert J. Beveridge of Indiana in 1902, to bring an end to a society "of fraud and filth and lies."[25]

*   *   *

A Wisconsin governor, a New York prosecuting attorney and a Boston "lawyer for the people" epitomized the progressive revolt as the new century opened. Robert M. LaFollette, who inherited the agrarian spirit of protest and would lead Republican insurgents for the coming quarter of a century, had begun, like many another reformer, in comfortable orthodoxy. From 1885 to 1891 he had been a party regular in the House of Representatives; in the following decade, while he sought unsuccessfully for further public office against the entrenched machine, he completed his education in the need for a more equitable political system. In 1900, at the age of forty-five, he entered the statehouse in Madison. He intended, as he loved to recall in later years, to convert Wisconsin into a laboratory of social experiment.[26]

LaFollette was the first to effect the union of agrarian reform and urban radicalism anticipated but never realized in the eighties and nineties. His progressive bloc for the next thirty years would operate within the conventional framework of the state Republican Party, but it was LaFollette's energy and personality which eventually pushed his reform program through the Republican legislatures. In three successive sessions, a growing volume of social and economic concepts were enacted into law—the direct primary, a greatly strengthened rate-fixing commission to supervise railroads, a state civil service, banking regulations, minimum wages for women, conservation statutes, and a tighter control over franchises granted to private users of public resources. By 1906, when LaFollette moved on to his career in the United States Senate, the "Wisconsin idea" had become the synonym for modern democracy.[27]

Reform as it was needed in the metropolitan areas was led, in the last year of LaFollette's governorship in Wisconsin, by a brilliant but little-known attorney in New York. Charles Evans Hughes would serve as special counsel for two state legislative investigating committees; the first exposed the machinations of the gas and electric power trust and resulted in the creation of a state public utility commission, while the second uncovered a systematic pattern of insurance manipulation which affected policyholders and political relationships in all parts of the nation. Through weeks of meticulous interrogation of unwilling witnesses, Hughes documented the unconscionable inflation of assets, indefensibly high consumer rates, and dangerous adulteration of the gas sold by the trust to the public. Six months later, he employed the same techniques to elicit from insiders in half a dozen major insurance companies a far more sensational story of six- and seven-figure largesses to favored executives, an interstate program of lobbying and graft to prevent enactment of stringent regulatory statutes, and a catalog of fact-juggling techniques by which policyholders were regularly defrauded of benefits which accrued to the manipulators in their stead.[28]

A dozen regulatory statutes recommended by Hughes were adopted by the New York legislature and in the fall of 1906 Hughes himself was elected governor. The progressivism of Hughes, as compared with that of LaFollette, emphasized the difference between the reform mentality of the Midwest and that of the metropolitan East. LaFollette and the insurgents of the farm belt would always be required to deal from a position of minimal political strength, while Hughes, after Taft's debacle, would become the logical successor to Roosevelt as the leader of the Republican moderates of 1916. LaFollette's program was essentially one of humanitarian reform; Hughes' chief legislative victory was in the creating of a body of state administrative law which would serve as a model for dealing with the economic system of the new century.[29]

In Louis D. Brandeis, the humanitarianism of the Western progressives and the sophistication of the Eastern reformers were effectively merged. Like Hughes, Brandeis would be a scourge of the entrenched selfish interests in the insurance industry; like LaFollette, he would be the advocate of effective legal protection for women and other exploited groups. Touring the Pennsylvania coal fields in 1902 to observe at first hand the issues and effects of the great strike there; acting as unpaid attorney for policyholders in Massachusetts to protect them against the repercussions of the Hughes insurance probe in New York; tackling the massive reorganizational problems of traction companies and intercity railroads; serving as special attorney for four different states in defending women's minimum wage laws; acting as chairman of the arbitration board in the New York garment workers' strike of 1910—in the first decade of the new century, Brandeis became one of the most active forces in the whole spectrum of reform.[30]

These were the prototypes of the men and women who generated the Progressive Movement. They were one with Upton Sinclair exposing the working conditions in the Chicago stockyards in 1906, John Spargo awakening the public conscience with *The Bitter Cry of the Children* in the same year, sociologist Edward A. Ross making his pioneer studies of the economic and social seedbeds of crime, and Walter Rauschenbusch pointing modern Christianity toward its social responsibilities.[31] Within the first few years of the new century, the ferment of change was at work throughout American life; an accident of history accelerated its early extension to the national scene.

*   *   *

The Insular Cases, decided in the spring of 1901, validated the nation's tentative ventures into expansionism in the foreign field. That autumn, the assassination of McKinley propelled Theodore Roosevelt into the Presidency and thus set the stage for another kind of expansionism on the domestic scene.

For Roosevelt, three fundamental convictions galvanized his policy on entering the White House: The first, as he wrote in retrospect, was "the theory that the executive power was limited only by specific restrictions and prohibitions appearing in the Constitution or imposed by the Congress under its constitutional powers. My view," he continued, "was that every executive officer . . . was a steward of the people bound actively and affirmatively to do all he could for the people, and not to content himself with the negative merit of keeping his talents undamaged in a napkin. I declined to adopt the view that what was imperatively necessary for the Nation could not be done by the President unless he could find some specific authorization to do it. My belief was that it was not only his right but his duty to do anything that the needs of the Nation demanded unless such action was forbidden by the Constitution or the laws."[32]

Such a view had not been expressed by an American President since Lincoln—and, not surprisingly, the occupants of the White House in the intervening forty-six years had been uniformly uninspired and uninspiring. Even Cleveland, whose career both in New York and in Washington had shown certain striking parallels to Roosevelt's, had held no such concept of the breadth of his responsibility and authority. Republican leaders, reared in the generation of Congressional rather than Presidential dominance, were hardly reassured by Roosevelt's words. His brother-in-law, Douglas Robinson, wrote him in a lengthy letter immediately after McKinley's death that "there is a feeling in financial circles here that . . . you may change matters so as to upset the confidence . . . of the business world, which would be an awful blow to everybody."[33]

Roosevelt promised Robinson and Mark Hanna that he would "go slow";

but already in December 1901 as Henry Adams returned from Europe to his residence on Lafayette Square across from the White House the movement of change was readily discernible. Of the party's elder statesmen in these circumstances, Adams wrote: "To them at sixty-three, Roosevelt at forty-three could not be taken seriously in his old character, and could not be recovered in his new one. Power, when wielded by abnormal energy, is the most serious of facts, and all Roosevelt's friends knew that his restless and combative energy was more than abnormal . . . With him wielding power with immeasurable energy in the White House, the relation of age to youth—of teacher to pupil— was altogether out of place; and no other was possible."[34]

The would-be teachers to the pupil in the White House—men like Senators Hanna and Joseph Foraker from Ohio, Nelson M. Aldrich of Rhode Island and Thomas Platt of New York, and "Uncle Joe" Cannon of Illinois who would become Speaker of the House of Representatives in 1903—chafed at the programs endorsed by "that cowboy" in the President's chair. These programs, indeed, were the epitome of Roosevelt's second basic policy conviction; the Republican party in his view had failed to discern the current of modern history, even though it had been right "during the last decade of the nineteenth century to uphold the interests of popular government against a foolish and illjudged mock-radicalism." The agrarian reformers and the silver bloc he condemned as men "who claimed to be radicals" and who with "their allies among the sentimentalists were utterly and hopelessly wrong." In resisting the wild-eyed demands of the Democrats and Populists, Roosevelt wrote, the Republicans had thrown themselves "into the hands not merely of the conservatives but of the reactionaries. . . . These men still from force of habit applauded what Lincoln had done in the way of radical dealing with the abuses of his day; but they did not apply the spirit in which Lincoln worked to the abuses of their own day."[35]

Never one to be plagued by self-doubt, Roosevelt found his own party remiss in failing to perceive that the continued frustrations of the American people over the past generation essentially violated the national (and Rooseveltian) ideal of fair play. His own formula for qualification for public office was relatively simple: "courage, honesty, and a democracy of desire to serve the plain people." He hoped that Hanna and his cronies in Congress would see the reasonableness of returning to the Lincoln-Roosevelt concept of a radical activism on behalf of the common man. "When," he wrote, "I was forced to abandon the effort to persuade them to come my way . . . I achieved results only by appealing over the heads of the Senate and House leaders to the people, who were the masters of both of us."[36]

Roosevelt's certainty of the strength of the Presidential office and the moral obligation to wield this strength to achieve the yearnings of the average citizen quickly fired the public imagination. Or, more accurately, it could be said that his own colorful pursuit of "the strenuous life" and his capacity for coining the fighting phrase roused the admiration of the everyday American. "The square deal" connoted a return to the balance of interests for which the Populists had argued in vain; speaking softly and carrying a big stick suggested the patriarchal authority of the gradually dimming Victorian age; and the increasing references to "malefactors of great wealth" stirred the hope that at last a champion had been found to ride against the trusts.

What the average man did not perceive, and what the Congressional and party conservatives viewed with dread, was Roosevelt's ultimate conviction— the third of his basic policy ingredients—that "the state, like the county or municipality, [is] merely a convenient unit for local self-government, while in all National matters, of importance to the whole people, the Nation is to be supreme over states, county, and town alike."[37] The Rough Rider was honest enough to perceive that this was the only course to follow into the new century, and courageous enough to carry the concept of Federal government to its logical extreme (albeit he wrote the actual words after he had left the White House). "Men who understand and practice the deep underlying philosophy of the Lincoln school of American political thought are necessarily Hamiltonian in their belief in a strong and efficient National government," he added, "and Jeffersonian in their belief in the people as the ultimate authority, and in the welfare of the people as the end of Government."

The individualism which had been the ideal of Jefferson, Roosevelt observed, had been essential to an age of pioneering and winning of a continent; by the time of his first full year in the White House, in 1902, "the need had been exactly reversed." Yet he found Congress hamstrung by the conviction that government was powerless to interfere with individual freedom even when that individualism was being employed to create an industrial power greater than the power of government itself.[38]

*   *   *

As for the judiciary, Roosevelt stated that for the past quarter of a century the courts had been "on the whole the agents of reaction," and "always, or wellnigh always, their action was negative action against the interests of the people, ingeniously devised to limit their power against wrong, instead of affirmative action giving to the people power to right wrong."[39]

The Supreme Court which the White House contemplated in January 1902 had changed but little since the epochal year 1895. Chief Justice Fuller would, in fact, outlive the Roosevelt administration, and only the consumptive Justice Jackson and the almost senile Justice Field had departed, their places filled by equally conservative Justices Rufus Peckham and Joseph McKenna. In his own seven years in office, Roosevelt would appoint only three members to the bench—Oliver Wendell Holmes, Jr., to fill the "Massachusetts seat" of Justice Gray; William R. Day, a former Secretary of State under McKinley; and his own Secretary of the Navy and Attorney General, William H. Moody. Entering a decade in which the constitutionality of the legislative experiments of the Progressive Movement in the states would be periodically challenged, there was little to indicate that the Court had departed significantly from its jurisprudence of the nineties. Fuller, Brewer, McKenna and Peckham preserved the traditional conservative commitment to a rigidly circumscribed concept of government regulatory authority; Harlan continued steadfast in dissent, and White continued to vacillate with a mild inclination toward liberalism.

Thus the three new men named to the Court by Roosevelt could not insure a permanent reversal of ideological position, or a limit to what the President repeatedly condemned as "negative action." To be sure, the Rough Rider had a blunt and specific definition of a desirable appointee: "a constructive statesman," ever able to keep before him an awareness of "his relations with his fellow statesman . . . in other branches of the government."[40] Day seemed to measure up to these requirements, for while his background in practice had been the familiar breeding ground of conservatives—corporations and railroads —his work as Secretary of State had attracted unusual public approval. As a member of the postwar settlement commission, he had insisted that Spain be compensated by a payment of $20,000,000 for the Philippines rather than asserting their annexation by right of conquest. Roosevelt was satisfied that Day's personal sense of honor would enhance his objectivity on the bench.[41]

Moody seemed equally promising; both Holmes on the Supreme Judicial Court of Massachusetts and Fuller on the Supreme Court of the United States had expressed a high opinion of him as an attorney. "I have always liked his way of stating things," the Chief Justice wrote to S. S. Gregory, an old Chicago colleague. Fate denied Moody a chance to prove his worth on the bench; plagued by rapidly worsening health, he was compelled to resign after four years, at the age of fifty-nine.[42]

Thus it was to be the sixty-one-year-old Oliver Wendell Holmes upon whom the Court of the twentieth century would be built. Fate, as it was to turn out, had not altogether frustrated Roosevelt and the progressives in their effort to infuse fresh vigor into the judiciary; what John Marshall and later Joseph Story had been to the constitutional thought of the early nineteenth century, Holmes and later Brandeis were to be to the constitutional thought of the twentieth. The latter-day collaborators had much the harder task, for they carried the permanent minority argument, providing the transitional rationale from the lonely protests of Harlan between the late seventies and 1910, to the ultimate conversion of the Court in the thirties.[43]

Holmes was a conservative, but for him conservatism was not a synonym for immutable principles; rather, it was a process of continual testing of alternatives and a requirement that the advocates of change prove their case. Life, he repeatedly declared, consisted at the last of successive experiments, and progress was the logical consequence of the "felt necessities of the time." Above all else, Holmes was a pragmatist. In 1873 he had written that "it is no sufficient condemnation of legislation that it favors one class at the expense of another; for much or all legislation does that; and none the less when the *bona fide* object is the greatest good of the greatest number." The most that should be expected of legislative reform, he declared in the first dawning of the reform movement, "is that legislation should easily and quickly, yet not too quickly, modify itself in accordance with the will of the *de facto* supreme power in the community, and that the spread of an educated sympathy should reduce the sacrifice of minorities to a minimum."[44]

Roosevelt had hesitated before appointing Holmes; the tolerant skepticism, the readiness to concede the argument against interest, in particular when the interest was his own, the disdain for panaceas, were all very well in a philosopher (which Holmes was). But was he "sound" on the matter of reform? "The labor decisions which have been criticized by some of the big railroad men and other members of large corporations, constitute to my mind a strong point in Judge Holmes' favor," the President wrote to Henry Cabot Lodge. But could he be relied on in every circumstance to oppose the element on the Court which "stood for such reactionary folly as would have hampered well-nigh hopelessly this people in doing efficient and honorable work for the national welfare?" He did not wish to put on the court, the President told Lodge, "any man who was not absolutely sane and sound on the great national policies for which we stand in public life."[45]

Roosevelt needed to fill the vacancy on the bench so that the initial test case in his reform program would be heard before a full Court. He weighed the pros and cons and nominated the Massachusetts jurist; it would be several test cases later before he would know whether his decision had been right.

*   *   *

In February, 1902, catching both the political and business communities by surprise, the Attorney General on behalf of the White House announced that a suit was being instituted in the Federal court in Minnesota to secure dissolution of the Northern Securities Company. The launching of the attack upon this adversary was as dramatic as it was essential to Roosevelt's plan for implementing the Square Deal. "Just before my accession," he wrote—in fact, it had been in November, 1901, when the new President was preparing his first address to Congress—"a small group of financiers desiring to profit by the governmental impotence to which we had been reduced [by the Sugar Trust decision of 1895] had arranged to take control of practically the entire railway system in the Northwest."[46]

This was the Rough Rider's view. The incorporation papers filed in New Jersey had simply described a concern to be capitalized at $400,000,000 with authority to buy or sell securities of certain railroads. Specifically, the railroads were the Northern Pacific and the Great Northern. The charter and companion papers had been drafted by attorneys for J. P. Morgan and Company, and plans to put the new corporation into operation had been made in the Northern Pacific offices in New York at a meeting attended by E. H. Harriman, James J. Hill, William Rockefeller and others.[47]

For these men and for Morgan himself, launching the first full-scale holding company was a logical and legal step toward eliminating waste—particularly the kind of waste wrought by the titanic Harriman-Hill contest of the previous May over the control of the Northern Pacific. Since 1885, Morgan had quietly and efficiently been reducing the chaos which had followed the railroad-building era of the mid-nineteenth century, and by the opening of the twentieth, most Eastern railroads had been reorganized on an efficient management basis. It seemed logical to turn now to the Western lines and undertake a similar job, with the newly accessible Asian markets of the Pacific as the goal of a combined rail and steamship system. Finally, there was the apparent clarity of the law of the land; since the Sugar Trust Case in 1895, government attempts at bringing prosecutions under the Sherman Act had made only small judicial gains.[48]

"That cowboy" in the White House, however, did not share the industrialists' and financiers' conviction that an uncontrolled and systematically expanding business organization was the answer to the national economic need. "Of all forms of tyranny the least attractive and the most vulgar is the tyranny of mere wealth, the tyranny of a plutocracy," Roosevelt wrote. Stung by the taunt, and outraged that the government had struck the first blow without the courtesy of advance warning, Jim Hill struck back with an equally acid comment: It was hardly the type of fair play the President so often extolled, he said, "that we should be compelled to fight for our lives against the political adventurers who have never done anything but pose and draw a salary."[49]

The business community saw the purpose of the Northern Securities suit to be an effort to reverse the decision in the Sugar Trust Case—as, indeed, Roosevelt himself conceded it to be. "It was necessary to reverse the Knight case," he wrote later, "in the interests of the people against monopoly and privilege." Wall Street was aghast; if this fundamental interpretation of the antitrust statute was to be overturned, what would the President do next? To try to find out, Morgan paid a special call to the White House in the company of Senators Hanna and Depew and later was reported to have told Roosevelt that if "we have done anything wrong, send your man to my man and they can fix it up." The President and "his man"—Attorney General Philander C. Knox—replied that their objective was not to "fix up" but to prosecute illegal combinations.[50]

However Morgan might have regarded Knox's reply as a betrayal of his own class interests, there was no doubt that the Attorney General was firmly in Roosevelt's camp. He was, as a matter of fact, a holdover from the McKinley administration, a boyhood friend of the late President and, just prior to accepting his Cabinet appointment, one of the leaders in the formation of the Carnegie Steel Corporation. He shared Roosevelt's conviction that where the limits to capitalistic freedom had been defined by law, it was the government's responsibility to prosecute the law with full vigor. Although he was not the prototype of the reformer of the Progressive Era, he was the prototype of the able professional in government administration. Knox would be the officer to examine the title of the French company engaged in the construction of the Panama Canal, and upon his recommendation the United States would conclude the purchase of rights to complete that vital waterway. He drafted the bill creating the Department of Commerce and Labor in 1903, and helped strengthen the law on the rate-making powers of the Interstate Commerce Commission.

Knox left the Cabinet in 1904 to fill the unexpired term of Pennsylvania's Senator Matt Quay—put into that position, it was alleged, by the Pennsylvania Railroad Company in order to get him out of the Attorney Generalship. If it was respite from anti-trust suits that was sought by this move, the Pennsylvania and other corporations were disappointed. Roosevelt merely moved Moody from Navy to Justice. The Rough Rider and the Massachusetts attorney were close personal friends, and the same coordination in effort continued between the President and the Attorney General's office. Indeed, the success of Roosevelt's much-touted trust-busting policy turned upon the rapport between him and his chief legal officers—or, conversely, the success of Roosevelt's Attorneys General in the anti-trust field might have been greater had not the Chief Executive been so irrepressible in trumpeting the news of what he intended to do with the errant corporations.*[51]

Knox's Northern Securities case was followed by Moody's Beef Trust Case —and that one, indeed, by a rapid-fire series of initiated actions against alleged conspiracies in lumber, oil, paper, salt and tobacco. Moody, however, meticulously prepared the government's briefs for the cases, and they were still in early stages when, with Justice Brown's retirement, Roosevelt with characteristic impulsiveness selected his Attorney General for the vacancy on the Court. The President did not stop to reflect that when and as these particular prosecutions might come before that tribunal, Moody as Justice would doubtless disqualify himself and thus diminish, rather than add to, the reform vote on the bench.

With his third choice to head the Justice Department, Roosevelt drew from the front ranks of the reform movement itself—Charles J. Bonaparte of Baltimore, grand-nephew of Napoleon but a fervent advocate of social justice. A leader of a clean-government movement in Baltimore, a future founder of the National Municipal League and a driving force in state and national civil service movements, Bonaparte's natural ebullience was an extension of Roosevelt's own, and if anything the trust-busting era promised to move at a still faster pace. A descendant of the Corsican conqueror of Europe and the ardent veteran of San Juan Hill now in command of plans for the assault on the old order—it was enough to make the wealthy and proud wring their hands in dismay.[52]

_____

*Cf. Ch. 6 following.

6/Trust-Busting in
Practice and Politics

T HE FIRST TEN YEARS of the operation of the Sherman Anti-Trust Act
had produced a nondescript record: three different Presidents and five
different Attorneys General directed the execution of the law during this period, and while both Harrison and Cleveland inveighed against the trust evil,
only one of the five men in charge of the Department of Justice—Judson Harmon—had shown any enthusiasm for active prosecution. Only three major
cases reached the Supreme Court on this question in the nineties. In the first
eight years of the new century, to the accompaniment of trumpetings from the
White House under the volatile Roosevelt, there were sixteen major actions
against combinations in restraint of trade. In the four years following under
Taft, there were eighty; despite the whoop and holler of the Rough Rider it was
in the administration of his successor, who would be damned by progressives
in 1912 for defusing the Square Deal, that trust-busting attained its high-water
mark.[1]

There were several explanations for the slow development of momentum.
Either the statute, as Richard Olney firmly believed, was a mere reiteration of
common law and thus did not give the government any new powers for prosecution of business combinations, or it was an unprecedented definition of
government authority which, if constitutional at all, required a whole new body
of evidence to implement it. Alternatively, the American people after two decades of experience with large-scale corporate organization of the economy
would have a different perspective in 1912 for the issues which had seemed so
simple of solution in 1890. To oppose trusts as monopolies was as appealing to
politicians in either year as to oppose sin; to make the more sophisticated distinction between centralized control of management and production as a matter
of efficiency and indiscriminate destruction of competition as a matter of
waste, required more time for thought in both legislature and courtroom. Thus
the trust-busting movement, as an expression of general constitutional reorientation to a new society, was a composite of political extravagance and slowly

maturing jurisprudence, accelerated or retarded by the attitudes of various Presidents and their Attorneys General.

Olney had dealt the Sherman Act a near-fatal blow at the outset, with an equivocal prosecution of the Sugar Trust which all but invited the Court to accept the brief of the trust attorneys; and by choosing a case already dismissed by the lower courts he had left the Supreme Court with little choice, if it accepted jurisdiction at all, but to deal exclusively with the constitutional issue. The *Knight* case had thus made a harsh distinction between the process of transporting goods in interstate commerce, which the government presumably could regulate, and the corporate entities which accounted for the manufacture, distribution or sale of the goods themselves, which it was insisted the government could not reach. Olney had expressly instructed United States attorneys in the field not to initiate anti-trust actions until the constitutional test in *Knight* was accomplished; thereafter, he saw even less reason for them to undertake litigation under the law.[2]

Harmon's first task in succeeding Olney in Justice, therefore, was to resuscitate the statute and its administration—first by urging Congress to clarify the practices to be subject to prosecution under the law, second by encouraging his field attorneys to resume the initiative in gathering evidence for possible prosecutions, and finally by guiding new test cases to the Supreme Court to narrow the doctrine in *Knight*. But the task was complicated by the fact that Olney still was in the Cabinet—having been moved from Justice to State—and still was unalterably convinced that the Sherman Act gave the government no novel powers of business regulation. Repeatedly, Olney advised Cleveland that this had been "the final conclusive interpretation from the Supreme Court." The President, torn between the arguments of his two Cabinet officers, was relegated to a policy of ambivalence, and his message to Congress in December 1896 undertook to incorporate both viewpoints.[3]

Meantime, Harmon was seeking to revive the zeal for enforcement which Olney, and Miller before him, had dampened. His letters of instruction to United States attorneys throughout the country encouraged them to act on their own initiative, and in Tennessee they struck a responsive chord. In November 1896 the Federal district attorney there, James Bible, advised Harmon that he had accumulated evidence to support a prosecution of a combination controlling cast-iron pipe throughout the Southeastern United States. Delighted, the Attorney General sent him the briefs on a test case from Kansas which Harmon was bringing to the Supreme Court for review, and by early January Bible wrote his superior that "I think I have got my trust friends beat. I am informed that they will admit my bill [of complaint] but deny the constitutionality of the Act of July 2, 1890." Three weeks later Bible wrote Harmon: "I am interested in this case as I never was in any other."[4]

Meantime, the Kansas test case was proceeding according to the Attorney General's plan. It had begun in 1892 as a suit to enjoin a contract fixing freight rates between eighteen Western railroads; the Circuit Court had denied the petition for the injunction on the ground that the Sherman Act did not apply to railroads since they were covered by the Interstate Commerce Commission Act. Following this decision the United States attorney Joseph W. Ady had written to Attorney General Miller that the decision "is one of such far-reaching importance, and . . . if correct, goes so far toward emasculating all of the useful features of the anti-trust law, that I deem it of the utmost importance" that a review be taken. Olney, who succeeded Miller, was not disposed to take action until he had tested the Sherman Act in the Sugar Trust Case, and it was not until Harmon came into office that *United States v. Trans-Missouri Freight Association* was prepared for review.[5]

Harmon argued the case for the government before the Supreme Court in December, just as Cleveland was preparing his final message to Congress. The Court's opinion, reversing the lower courts and finding for the government, was not handed down until late the following March, when both Cleveland and Harmon had left office. Justice Peckham, speaking for the five-to-four majority, rejected the carriers' argument that a rate-fixing contract had no relationship to the flow of commerce itself. Railroads, on the contrary, were "instruments of commerce, and their business is commerce itself." Nor were railroads exclusively covered by the Interstate Commerce Commission Act: "If the agreement be legal it does not owe its validity to any provision of the Commerce Act, and if illegal it is not made so by that act." The statute on its face, declared the majority, applied to all contracts and other activities which reasonably could be found to restrain trade.[6]

White, speaking for the dissenters, advanced the argument which he was to develop over the course of the years seeking to distinguish "reasonable contracts" from "unreasonable" restraints of trade. Like Olney, looking to the past, and Roosevelt and Taft, looking to the present, White perceived that a sweeping condemnation of all processes of combination and centralization would indiscriminately affect essential business processes which were demanded by an industrial economy seeking to serve an enormous geographic and political area. Until a "rule of reason" as White conceived of it could be applied to various types of business agreements and combinations, the majority doctrine in his view was "tantamount to an assertion that the act of Congress is itself unreasonable."[7]

Despite misgivings such as these, the narrow victory for the government was a substantial qualification of the extreme *laissez-faire* doctrine of the Sugar Trust Case of two years before. The change of political administrations and the characteristic turnover of attorneys in the Justice Department raised brief doubts as to what the next step should be. William D. Wright, Bible's successor in Tennessee, wrote to the acting Attorney General, J. E. Boyd, inquiring whether the new administration wished to continue an appeal in the case against the Addyston Pipe & Steel Company, where the government had lost in the trial court just before the *Trans-Missouri Freight Association* decision. The McKinley administration replied affirmatively; indeed, the govern-

ment case was to be argued in the Circuit Court of Appeals by Bible and
Edward B. Whitney, who had been on the brief with Harmon in the *Freight
Association* case.[8]

A singular combination of jurists dealt with the appellate judgment in
February 1898; Justice Harlan, the lone dissenter in *Knight,* was the Supreme
Court participant on the Sixth Circuit, together with William Howard Taft
and Horace Lurton, both of whom would later ascend to the high tribunal.
Joseph McKenna, the new Attorney General, would be on the bench when
Addyston came there for final review. Although all except Harlan were constitutional conservatives, their unanimity—and their reliance on the doctrine
set out by the majority in the *Freight Association* case—attested to the general conviction that the extreme rule in *Knight* needed to be circumscribed.

The combination of companies manufacturing and selling pipe under
price-control agreements, said both the appellate and Supreme Courts, was
a conspiracy in restraint of trade under the *Freight Association* holding.
Peckham, quoting extensively from the appellate court opinion of Taft, affirmed
the appellate judgment in favor of the government and thus significantly
complemented the *Freight Association* doctrine: not only railroads as part
of interstate commerce, but actual goods carried in interstate commerce on
conditions which restrained trade in such goods, were proper subjects of the
Sherman Act. Two and a half years after he had left office, Harmon had won
his argument with Olney; there still remained the task of resolving White's
demand for a distinction between reasonable and unreasonable activities in
this area.[9]

*   *   *

Trust-busting was a description of an interplay of politics, policy and
jurisprudence which reached its climax in the first decade of the new century.
For the average American, scarred by the experience of industrial ruthlessness
in the last Victorian generation, the constitutional proposition was simple
enough: If bigness led to monopoly and monopoly was evil, it was government's task to break up monopoly and the correlative bigness of industry. The
more complex alternative—regulation rather than destruction of large industrial
combinations—was neither immediately apparent nor acceptable. Regulation,
by definition, was public surveillance of capitalistic behavior, and while one
example of such a development existed in the Interstate Commerce Commission, the extension of the concept was to be long and labored.

The half-century of public policy toward the interstate system of communications represented in the telephone and telegraph industries illustrated
the difficulty. From the mid-eighties until 1913, the American Bell Telephone
Company fought a running series of battles with both private and government litigants. Private adversaries challenged the validity of Bell patents, while
the government alternated between its own tentative efforts to rescind certain
patents and its even more tentative efforts at prosecuting the growing tele-

phone combine as a monopoly. Independent local telephone systems showed a lively disposition to compete successfully with Bell, but it was obvious that the national interest required a unified long-distance network of communications. The control of the Western Union Telegraph Company by Bell, on the other hand, was a ready-made issue for the anti-trust advocates.

To launch an indiscriminate attack upon the telephone and telegraph industry was both irrational and impractical; it was not until the age of trust-busting had passed its zenith that a compromise could be worked out between the Attorney General's office and the vice-president of the American Telephone and Telegraph Company, N. C. Kingsbury, whereby the telephone corporation divested itself of ownership of Western Union, agreed to discontinue the practice of buying out competing telephone systems, and undertook to connect its long-distance facilities with local independent systems. The Kingsbury Agreement was a compromise between the letter of the anti-trust laws and the process of government regulation. It was not until 1921 that Congress gave tentative authority to the Interstate Commerce Commission to supervise the further merger of communications companies; the full-scale regulatory commission did not appear until 1927 and, seven years after that, in the modern form of the Federal Communications Commission.[10]

Trust-busting was thus an interval between the extreme *laissez-faire* mentality represented in the Sugar Trust Case of 1895, and the administrative regulatory process which took firm root in the early years of the New Freedom. The deliberate modification of the Sugar Trust doctrine in the freight rate and iron pipe prosecutions re-established the concept of government power to control excesses in the free enterprise system. It now remained for the Square Deal to test the ultimate limits of that power through its own enforcement of the Sherman Act.

*   *   *

"I intend to be most conservative," Roosevelt assured his brother-in-law upon moving into the White House, "but in the interests of the big corporations themselves and above all in the interest of the country I intend to pursue, cautiously but steadily, the course to which I have been publicly committed again and again, and which I am certain is the right course. I may add that I happen to know that President McKinley was uneasy about this so-called trust question, and was reflecting in his mind what he should do in the matter."[11]

Within ninety days, the Rough Rider had made known what he was planning to do in the matter. Attorney General Knox, a carryover from the McKinley Cabinet, was firmly convinced that the Northern Securities Company was a conspiracy under the Sherman Act, and his office had prepared a detailed memorandum on the suspicious degree of overcapitalization of the holding company. The capital stock of the company, "although issued merely to take over by exchange the underlying stocks" of the Great Northern and

Northern Pacific, "exceeds the sum of the capital stocks of the two companies by $122,000,000." It was reasonable to assume that other uses for the substantial surplus money were envisioned.[12]

The *Freight Association* decision had also given Knox reason to assume that, under the doctrine that railroads themselves were interstate commerce, the weight of the Sherman Act as now interpreted would favor the government. The Attorney General personally conducted the prosecution in the Circuit Court in Minnesota, where a judgment for the United States was obtained in the early spring of 1903. He reiterated the argument on the appeal to the Supreme Court in December: Every combination in restraint of trade was to be considered illegal under the statute, and the restraint did not have to be either total or unreasonable since the plain purpose of Congress was to prohibit all action "shutting out the operation of the general law of competition." The very existence of the power to restrain trade is itself a restraint, he continued—sounding at this point very much like an echo from the White House. Even an agreement to attempt restraint was not necessary, the government's brief went on, if it could be shown that the parties "act together in pursuance of a common object." Finally, Knox declared, the fact that for nearly a decade the government had acquiesced in the creation of groups analogous to the Northern Securities Company did not estop it from inaugurating the present action nor could its previous inaction be cited as conceding that such combinations were exempt from the statute.[13]

The opposing counsel were impressive men with impressive arguments—among them was John G. Johnson, who had led the phalanx against the Sherman Act in the Sugar Trust Case—and their briefs relied heavily on that case. They decried the government's use of an equity proceeding to dissolve the corporation under clauses of the statute which were criminal in nature and should have compelled the prosecution to produce evidence of a specific violation of the act. Finally, they relied upon the doctrine developed in the *Knight* decision, that the relationship between the corporation and the commerce it implements should be distinguished from the relationship between the corporation and its stockholders.[14]

In the five-to-four majority in favor of the government, the victory for Roosevelt was substantially less than what superficially it appeared to be. Harlan, speaking for himself and three associates, accepted the government's argument that the law prohibited any combination whether reasonable or unreasonable if it had the effect of restraining commerce. His lengthy opinion also took pains to refute the several arguments advanced by Johnson and his associate counsel, in an effort to edge the Court further from the extreme position in the Sugar Trust Case and further along the road it had begun to take in 1897 in the *Freight Association* case, and 1899 in *Addyston*.[15]

But the Harlan opinion represented the view of only four Justices; the government victory came on the fortuitous fact that Justice Brewer, consistently hostile though he was to the idea of government intervention in the free enterprise process and specifically critical of Knox's proposition that combinations were illegal even if reasonable, nevertheless filed a concurring opinion finding the Northern Securities combination to be unreasonable.[16]

White, speaking for Fuller, Holmes and Peckham, dissented on the ground that the current case was controlled by the *Knight* rule of 1895, and that the rule required a distinction between stock ownership and the restraint of interstate commerce. The Sugar Trust of 1895 might concededly effect a monopoly in sugar, he said, but the statute was "decided not to extend to the subject, because the ownership of the stock in the corporation was not itself commerce."[17] Holmes, in a separate dissent, phrased the issue somewhat differently; the purpose of the act, in its own words, he pointed out, was not to insure competition but to forbid restraint of trade by combination or conspiracy. The common law, said the man acknowledged to be the leading historian of that law, defined such restraint as a denial of the field to third parties, while the facts of the Northern Securities case indicated merely that the combination sought a control over two or more railroads. To find that this violated the spirit and letter of the Sherman Act, Holmes said, required reading into the statute words which were not there.

"Great cases, like hard cases, make bad law," said Holmes, in words that seemed to be addressed directly to the White House. "For great cases are called great, not by reason of their real importance in shaping the law of the future, but because of some accident of immediate overwhelming interest which appeals to the feelings and distorts the judgment." The excitement of the anti-trust question thus had developed "a kind of hydraulic pressure which makes what previously was clear seem doubtful, and before which even well settled principles of law will bend." The government's case, the dissent observed, rested at last upon the conviction that "somehow or other the statute meant to strike at combinations great enough to cause just anxiety on the part of those who love their country more than money, while it viewed . . . little ones . . . with just indifference." If Congress had actually sought such an end, a different constitutional question would be involved; but to construe the existing law as Knox would argue, Holmes concluded, would "mean the universal disintegration of society into single men, each at war with all the rest."[18]

*   *   *

Roosevelt, "dee-lighted" with the outcome of the case, had no time to ponder over Holmes' dissent or to express surprise that a man he had put on the Court in the conviction that he would be "sound" on such matters should have found against the government. "I congratulate you, the inspiring and unwavering cause of it all," the President had written Knox the previous spring when the case had been won in the Circuit Court. Now he was even more exuberant: the Sugar Trust decision, he boasted, "I caused to be annulled by the Court that had rendered it."[19]

Already the Rough Rider was charging on; the Beef Trust, so called, had come under scrutiny of Knox's staff only a few weeks after the Northern Securities litigation had been launched. A letter from the Attorney General to all Federal attorneys in the field asked for evidence of the extent and operation of such a trust for use in proceedings "which may be instituted at Chicago rather than as the basis for such proceedings in your own district." As the *Freight Association* case had encouraged him to proceed against the railroad holding company, now the decision in *Addyston Pipe & Steel Company* seemed to Knox to point the way for the prosecution of the packers. For "an important element in the *Addyston* case was the combination among separate dealers, which is a very different thing from one aggregated trust corporation; . . . interstate sales constitute interstate commerce, and . . . this is so even if the production or manufacture is limited to one state." Thus, Knox concluded, the Court was now prepared to distinguish between the Sugar Trust doctrine and the activities of the Beef Trust.[20]

Meantime, the use of the commerce clause of the Constitution as a medium for the implementing of the Federal police power was upheld in 1903 with a five-to-four majority for the government in *Champion v. Ames,* affirming a statute prohibiting the dissemination of lottery tickets across state lines. The commerce clause, said the Court, implied a power to prohibit as well as to regulate goods seeking to enter the stream of commerce, whenever the police power of the United States could best be exercised through prohibition.[21] Early in the same year, Congress had passed a bill strongly urged by both Knox and Roosevelt for the expediting of cases brought under the Sherman Act,* and shortly thereafter had approved the creation of a Bureau of Corporations within the recently established Department of Commerce and Labor. Rounding out Knox's zealous program for administration of the anti-trust law was his establishment of a position of Assistant Attorney General for the full-time supervision of actions to be brought under the Sherman Act.[22]

William H. Moody succeeded Knox in the summer of 1904 with an even greater zeal for vigorous prosecution of the statute. Where Knox had concentrated on civil actions against alleged monopolies, Moody proposed to invoke the criminal provisions of the law as well. It was desirable, declared the ardently progressive *New York World,* that violations of the anti-trust law be treated "as something more than a kindly admonition to go and sin no more." The newspaper heartily approved of Moody's plan to add a criminal prosecution of individual packers to the civil suit against the Beef Trust, which had already been won by the government at the trial court level and was en route to review in the Supreme Court.[23]

A unanimous Court sustained the government in January 1906, in an opinion handed down three weeks after the case was argued. Although Holmes, who read the opinion, had little enthusiasm for the Sherman Act, he took the occasion to broaden the scope of the commerce clause itself by enunciating

---

*Cf. Appendix C.

his "stream of commerce" theory: Commerce was not a mere technical concept as the Sugar Trust decision had assumed, he declared, but was a practical concept "drawn from the course of business." When cattle or other subjects of trade were sent from one state to another for sale, the subjects remained in "a current of commerce among the states" until the sale was consummated —thus substantially extending the length of time in which the subjects remained within the scope of the commerce clause and the Federal regulatory power.[24]

Again Roosevelt was exultant over the judicial decision, and he wrote gratefully to his Attorney General: "I have heard again and again already— notably from Judge Day—of the profound impression made by your argument" in the Beef Trust case, adding that "you do not know how pleased and proud I am."[25] The decision took away part of the disappointment for Moody's criminal suits against the packers, when the Bureau of Corporations in the spring of 1905 unexpectedly filed a report exonerating the individuals. Both the Attorney General and his Chief Executive were chagrined at the finding, which could be offered by the defense counsel in the criminal suits as a rebuttal to the Justice Department's charges. It amounted, said Moody, to permitting a criminal to escape punishment by confessing his sins.[26]

*   *   *

For all the fanfare of trust-busting, the ultimate fact was that only the Northern Securities and Beef Trust cases were significant prosecutions under the Sherman Act which were carried to conclusion by the Roosevelt administration in its seven years in power. The President was vociferous enough in discussing what his Department of Justice had in store for malefactors, and vast amounts of essential paperwork were done by both Moody and Bonaparte as Attorneys General as foundations for actions which were carried through by the Taft administration. There were many explanations for this turn of events: it was certainly not the first time that a crusader (or one who, like the Rough Rider, liked to wear the habit of a crusader) found it easier to assail an evil when out of office than to cope with it effectively once he had attained the office. Moreover, in Roosevelt's case, there was the elemental fact that he had long since recognized that the issue of the trust, and the over-simple solution of anti-trust legislation, was not the real fundamental.

"Much of the legislation directed at the trusts would have been exceedingly mischievous had it not been entirely ineffective," the President said early in his administration. He was but reiterating doubts he had entertained as governor of New York.[27] The ultimate course of action, he sensed, had to be a choice between two concepts: the Anti-Trust Act as ordinarily adopted assumed the inherent evil of business combination and hence assumed the inherent superiority of a decentralized economy. Alternatively, a truly efficient organization of business enterprise on a national scale manifestly held a potential for monopoly—unless subject to interstate surveillance by the Federal power.[28]

For Roosevelt, the desirable solution would have been a modification of the existing legislation to deal with the evils of big business rather than to treat big business as an evil in itself. But throughout his administration he was never to find a means of effectuating this proposition without being caught on one or both horns of a dilemma: in the popular mind, the idea was firmly established that a trust, or any formal incorporation of large-scale enterprise which came under that convenient heading, was to be fought uncompromisingly by any reformer as evidence that he *was* a reformer. In the Senate of the United States, the spokesmen of *laissez-faire* were convinced that the Sherman Act itself had been an unconscionable extension of Federal authority and to talk of further legislation to make it more effective was to suggest a broader definition of Federal power which would be an even greater evil.[29]

To speak softly while carrying a big stick had a peculiar domestic meaning while Roosevelt was filling out McKinley's unfinished term. He was acutely aware that in 1900 had been "kicked upstairs" into the Vice-Presidency on the assumption of the party bosses that he would thereafter be safely in oblivion. If, by the fortuitous and tragic circumstances of McKinley's death, a reform governor had found his way into the White House in 1901, there was no certainty that the conservatives who still controlled the Republican Party would countenance his renomination in 1904. Congress could not thus be pushed too roughly toward a goal of anti-trust reform which the upper house, at least, was unwilling to attain.

Thus Roosevelt sought to unlimber the executive power in the anti-trust law whenever Congress proved too recalcitrant on matters of regulatory legislation; on the other hand, he kept it in check where its use threatened to provoke a conservative revolt within the party. In the summer of 1902, the President told audiences in New England and the Middle West that "those gentlemen of large means who deny that . . . evils exist are acting with great folly," but on the other hand, in the same political junket, he declared that the power of government itself must be used "with wisdom and self-restraint."[30]

As the election year approached, the Rough Rider gave increasing weight to every political consideration. Pleased though he was by the Court majority in the Northern Securities case, the President worried that, coming as it did in the spring of 1904, it might alienate business support for the Republicans; arguments before the Court on the Beef Trust Case were postponed until after the November election. During the fall of 1903 Roosevelt had persuaded himself that Mark Hanna intended to seek the nomination for himself, or at least to withhold it and the accompanying big business support from the President. There was no evidence to corroborate this view, and Hanna himself died that winter, thus leaving Roosevelt virtually unchallenged for renomination.[31]

Anxious as he was to secure a four-year term in office in his own right, Roosevelt could now devote his worries to what the Democrats would do. Obviously, their opportunity lay in appealing to the business community and exploiting its fears of the trust-busting incumbent; and in place of the twice-defeated Bryan they nominated a conservative and colorless New York state judge, Alton B. Parker. The issue, as it turned out, was never seriously in doubt. Roosevelt won by a margin of two and a half million popular votes and an electoral vote margin of 336 to 140. Having been returned to the White House in his own right, the natural exuberance of the Rough Rider led him to make two indiscreet remarks. One was that, having now attained his highest ambition, he would "under no circumstances . . . be a candidate for or accept another nomination"; the other was a reference to the restraint he had exercised in the trust-busting program until the election. Now that it was over, he declared: "Watch out for me!"[32]

The conservative majority in the Senate, shaken but not unseated, indeed intended to watch out for him.

7/The Big Stick in Court and Congress

"THE RIGHTS AND INTERESTS of the laboring man will be protected and cared for," wrote George F. Baer, president of the Philadelphia & Reading Coal & Iron Company, in the spring of 1902. However, he went on, the protection would not come from unions and their leaders but from "the Christian men to whom God in His infinite wisdom has given control of the property interests of this country." The rights and interests which Baer felt so competent to look after were illustrated by the statistics of the previous year, when the average annual wage of coal miners in the chief mining states of the East had amounted to $560 and the number of fatal accidents in the mines had reached 441. Baer, who had succeeded Franklin B. Gowen in command of the Reading empire, spoke the same language as his predecessor.[1]

In the seven years since the great Pullman strike in Chicago, organization of working men had been spectacular. The American Federation of Labor, founded in 1886, by the end of the century was able to count among its affiliates three-fifths of the union members of the country; and Samuel Gompers, the shrewd product of the London slums and the New York cigar workers' informal schools of dialectic, had successfully led the labor movement away from politics into a program of systematic and concerted economic tactics in dealing with management. In 1901 a bridge between capital and labor had been constructed in the form of the National Civic Federation—Mark Hanna was its president and Gompers its vice-president —and optimistic prophets looked to a day of regular arbitration of most if not all employment questions through such a medium.

Education of the general public in the problems of the laboring classes had also begun through such groups as the National Consumers' League, established in 1898 to boycott sweatshop products, and the National Child Labor Committee, formed in 1904 to undertake its thirty-year campaign to do away with the ruthless exploitation of the young in industry. The four great railway brotherhoods had, following the Pullman debacle, been able to devise an amicable process of review of wages and working conditions with the carriers which preserved labor peace on the transcontinental lines until the catastrophic rise in living costs during the first World War.[2]

The story was different in the field of mining, however. It was true that in 1897 the United Mine Workers had effectively organized the bituminous coal fields in Ohio after a spectacularly successful strike. The success was due in part to the ability of men like Hanna to see the handwriting on the wall; with labor advances in other sectors of the American economy and the shocking neglect of living and working conditions in a hazardous occupation, common justice and common sense pointed to the imminence of reform in this industry. But the anthracite regions of Pennsylvania, serving the major population centers of the East, presented an employer resistance as hard as the coal itself. Since the smashing of the Molly Maguires in the seventies, a proprietary empire had been developed under the control of eight railroads which monopolized the transportation system and, through their subsidiaries, controlled the output of the mines as well.

John F. Mitchell, the youthful, vigorous and intelligent head of the U.M.W., pointed to the intolerable conditions in the area—long hours of labor, often uncompensated beyond the fixed weekly wage; unconscionable prices for everything sold through the company stores; filthy living quarters provided by the company towns. In lieu of a strike, Mitchell offered to submit the case of the Pennsylvania miners to an independent board of review, such as the National Civic Federation or a group of Roman Catholic churchmen whom the foreign-born miners would trust. If these fact finders, said Mitchell, "decide that the average annual wages received by anthracite mine workers are sufficient to enable them to live, maintain and educate their families in a manner comfortable to established American standards and consistent with American citizenship, we agree to withdraw our claims." The owners, led by Baer, dismissed the proposal; "mining," said Baer, "is a business and not a religious, sentimental or academic proposition." In May, 1902, 140,000 Pennsylvania miners walked off their jobs.[3]

The responses of Baer and Mitchell to the issues of 1902 were conditioned by their backgrounds and the mentality of industrialism as it had been carried forward from the nineteenth century. Their own careers illustrated the sharp cleavages in opportunity bred by the system: Baer, a successful Reading lawyer, had come to the attention of railroad magnates by winning a succession of suits against them—whereupon they retained him as their own counsel. J. Pierpont Morgan then made Baer his representative in his plan for combining the various coal-carrying lines having terminals in New York City, and with Morgan's backing it was but a short step to the presidency of the Reading Railroad. Having attained this pinnacle just the previous year, Baer had no intention of yielding any of the spoils of his own victory to what he insisted was nothing but an organized plan of extortion.[4]

John Mitchell began his career in the coal mines of Illinois at the age of twelve, and by the time of the Reading strike he had logged nearly two decades of experience from Colorado and Wyoming to Pennsylvania. He had also witnessed the quixotic efforts of the Knights of Labor and had concluded that the best means of advancing the miners' interest was a strong independent union of their own. His membership in the United Mine Workers dated from the desperate labor struggles of the early nineties, and by 1898 he had become the national president of the organization. If Baer spoke the language of Morgan, Mitchell spoke—through the medium of common experience—the unarticulated desires of the polyglot immigrants of the anthracite fields. It was said that these mute multitudes trusted only two men—the priest who assured them of the comfort of their familiar religion in a strange land, and John Mitchell who stood prepared to fight for their future.[5]

*   *   *

"There will be strikes," observed Senator Hanna, "as long as there are hot-headed and unreasonable men on both sides or either side." Unlike the railroad employers in the Pullman strike, the Pennsylvania mine owners made no effort to appeal to public sympathy. Rather, their attitude from the outset was one of insolent contempt. Their leaders, Roosevelt wrote to Hanna, demonstrated "extraordinary stupidity and bad temper," while such a devout friend of capitalism as ex-President Cleveland wrote to the White House offering his support in any way the Chief Executive might be able to use it to bring both sides to a negotiating conference. But Presidents past or present held little awe for Baer; toward Mitchell, whose statement of the workers' case was consistently temperate, Baer manifested a glowering hate. After a fruitless White House confrontation, he advised newspaper interviewers that he and his associates objected "to being called here to meet a criminal, even by the President of the United States."[6]

Confident that the Federal power could not reach a labor dispute within the borders of a single state, and oblivious to the mounting public panic at the threat of a coal famine as autumn came on, Baer reiterated from the comfort of his Philadelphia estate that the problem could be simply solved by a return of the miners to work. Although fellow capitalists elsewhere did not admire the Pennsylvania operators' indifference to a mounting public distress, there was nonetheless a certain grim satisfaction in Wall Street that the Rough Rider who had had the temerity to put teeth back into the anti-trust program should now be getting his comeuppance. Roosevelt, the restless activist, seemed to find himself in a position where, even by his broad concept of the executive power in the public interest, he had no constitutional authority to do anything. "I am at my wits' end how to proceed," he confessed to Henry Cabot Lodge.[7]

Yet, when the national interest desperately required intervention, the President was confident that the public would support almost any tactic he could think of to meet the crisis. If the governor of Pennsylvania, he told Matt Quay, the veteran Senator from that commonwealth, should ask for Federal assistance to deal with the problem, the Army would be on its way to seize and operate the mines forthwith. Quay, whose domination of the Pennsylvania political scene was such that he could reply with confidence concerning the governor's reaction, assured Roosevelt that the request would be made.

But the President was keenly aware of the tenuous legal and political basis for his action; he lacked the color of emergency which had clothed the intervention of Hayes and Cleveland. Thus he was more interested in Quay's relaying the prospect of intervention to the mine operators. Apparently persuaded by the Senator that Roosevelt would take action if pushed that far, Baer and his associates at length gave grudging consent to arbitration—although on their own terms. Far from leaving it to the White House to appoint the members of the commission, the operators insisted that no labor representative be included; specifically, they proposed an Army engineer, an expert mining engineer, a Federal judge from Pennsylvania, someone familiar with the business factors in coal mining, and an eminent sociologist.

Roosevelt was astute enough to find commission members whose qualifications could be construed with sufficient liberality (and imagination) to accommodate the operators' conditions and yet achieve a balance of interests. E. E. Clark, a high official in the Order of Railway Conductors, was named to the commission under the denomination of an "eminent sociologist," while a little extra persuasion enabled the President to enlarge the commission to include Bishop John L. Clark of Illinois, a churchman highly regarded by the workers. The following spring the commission awarded a ten percent wage increase and called for the reform of a list of abuses in the employment context, although it rejected the United Mine Workers' bid for recognition.[8]

*   *   *

The vigorous role played by the White House in the coal strike crisis brought paeans of approval from the country in general, yet Roosevelt, reflecting on "an intervention that never happened," confessed that had he actually been compelled to seize the mine properties, he would have subsequently been the target of an equal amount of abuse. Once "the solution was accomplished and the problem ceased to be a problem," he observed, the inevitable reaction would have been an *ex post facto* carping that there ought to have been a less extreme and less questionable course of government action discovered. He was not the last President to experience the outrage of men who, after having "settled down to comfortable acceptance of the accomplished fact," indulged in the luxury of denouncing the action which accomplished the fact. (Another President—Harry S. Truman, half a century later—would find a bitter refutation in the courts of the Rooseveltian theory of the responsibilities of public stewardship in the crisis of a crippling strike.)[9]

Roosevelt, in 1903, could accept the coal strike settlement with the sense of relief that it had not come to a court test. The intervention he had contemplated as a last resort would have been, he conceded, an exercise of executive power "not required by the Constitution." While he was prepared to take the extreme measure because he was persuaded the executive responsibility to protect the public interest justified it, he was quite aware that a judicial test of this theory of responsibility would have been argued before unsympathetic judges. Federal and state courts, Roosevelt wrote, had come uniformly to "the view that while Congress had complete power as regards the goods transported by the railways, and could protect wealthy or well-to-do owners of these goods, . . . it had no power to protect the lives of the men engaged in transporting the goods," or the well-being of the workers in the railroad-controlled mines which produced the goods.[10]

Despite the victories in the Northern Securities and Beef Trust cases, the President clearly discerned that the issues of economic justice—in terms of curbing capitalistic excesses or enforcing workers' rights—faced an uphill struggle before the courts. The cases which came on to mark the reform efforts of the first years of the new century—the gestation period for the Progressive Movement—were to justify his pessimism more often than not.

*   *   *

The pivotal doctrine in the conservative response to attempts at reform legislation was the inviolability of the individual's right of contract. This doctrine, asserted more than eighty years before as a "No Trespassing" notice to states in their efforts to regulate business activity,[11] seemed to the *laissez-faire* capitalist the irreducible first principle on which American constitutionalism must rest; the alternative, in his view, was socialism and chaos. In 1897 Justice Rufus Peckham had undertaken to reaffirm the doctrine in rejecting a state effort to regulate the content of insurance contracts. Due process of law, said the Court, guaranteed "not only the right of the citizen to be free from the mere physical restraint of his person," but emphatically "to be free in the enjoyment of all his faculties; . . . and for that purpose to enter into all contracts which may be proper, necessary, and essential to his carrying out to a successful conclusion the purposes above mentioned."[12]

Peckham was willing to concede that freedom of contract was not so fundamental a right as to be immune from the operation of other regulations which Congress might constitutionally enact. The commerce clause, he stated in a case two years later, empowered Congress to prohibit the individual from making "those private contracts which directly and substantially, and not merely indirectly, remotely, incidentally, and collaterally, regulate to a greater or less degree commerce among the states."[13] But Peckham was one of two dissenters in the 1898 decision upholding a Utah statute regulating the hours of labor in mines and related industries; it was Justice Brown in this case who declared that the Federal Constitution, the supreme law of the land, "should not be so construed as to deprive the states of the power" to make their local laws "conform to the wishes of the citizens as they may deem best for the public welfare." The police power of the states should, like the power of Congress under the commerce clause of the Constitution, be defined with sufficient reasonableness to safeguard the general health and safety of individuals.[14]

In 1905 Peckham had the opportunity to speak again on the subject; in place of the Utah eight-hour law applying to the mining industry was a New York law limiting the hours of labor in the baking industry to ten per day or sixty per week. There is obviously a limit to the police power, Peckham declared, and the limit was to be found in the answer to the question of whether the exercise of the power was "fair, reasonable and appropriate," or whether it was "an arbitrary interference with the right of the individual to his personal liberty, or to enter into those contracts in relation to labor which may seem to him appropriate or necessary for the support of himself and his family." Moreover, the Justice pointed out, "the liberty of contract relating to labor includes both parties to it. The one has as much right to purchase as the other to sell labor."[15]

The only basis for New York's legislation being upheld, said Peckham, was its public health aspect and the doctrine that laws affecting public health are to be broadly construed. But the Court majority could find nothing inherently injurious to health in the nature of the baking industry, as contrasted with mining. The primary effect of the law, therefore, was to seek to reduce the bargaining inequalities as between the workers and the employer in the labor contract—and to uphold the statute under these circumstances would be an unwarranted interference with the freedom of the individual to make the best contract he could.

Justice Holmes, in a separate dissent, stated bluntly that the majority opinion was based "upon an economic theory which a large part of the country does not entertain." "The liberty of the citizen to do as he likes so long as he does not interfere with the liberty of others to do the same," he continued, "has been a shibboleth for some well-known writers"; but the Fourteenth Amendment, so piously recognized in the majority opinion, "does not enact Mr. Herbert Spencer's *Social Statics.*" Indeed, said Holmes, "I think that the word 'liberty' in the Fourteenth Amendment is perverted when it is held to prevent the natural outcome of a dominant opinion, unless it can be said that a rational and fair man necessarily would admit that the statute proposed would infringe fundamental principles as they have been understood by the traditions of our people and our law."[16]

This, of course, was precisely the point of difference between the legal traditionalists and the accelerating Progressive Movement. It was the fundamental conviction of men like Peckham that laws regulating hours or conditions of labor *would* infringe fundamental principles like that of freedom of contract. Reared in comfortable circumstances in Albany and Philadelphia, with a young gentleman's year in Europe as prelude to his study of law, and ensconced in a genteel legal and political career during the Civil War, Peckham had virtually no personal experience with the human relations or conflicts in postwar industrial development, while his observance of political accommodation of new social ideas at the state capital level in the eighties had not stimulated a sympathy for the ideas themselves. And the Justice was only typical of most of his generation of jurists: men who took for granted the unchangeableness of legal principles in the face of accelerating change in every other circumstance of life.

In 1905, observing the Washington scene after another of his periods abroad, Henry Adams commented of the older members of the bench and other branches of government that "a nineteenth-century education was as useless or misleading as an eighteenth-century education had been to the child of 1838"—the year both he and Justice Peckham had been born. [17] It was, of course, a matter of attitude rather than age. Holmes, for example, had been born in 1841, and his dissent was not only a rebuke to the crystallized legalism of Peckham but a call to his fellows of the minority (Harlan and Day) to recognize that the viability of constitutionalism lay in defining changing frames of reference for changing circumstances. It would be only toward the end of his long tenure on the bench that Holmes would be able to discern a degree of understanding among his colleagues of this basic proposition.

*   *   *

The cases arising midway in the opening decade of the twentieth century revealed the gradually widening gulf between the liberals of the old century and the new, as much as they confirmed the chasm between the conservative majority and the dissenters. Harlan and Holmes had both dissented in the New York wage case; but the fundamental difference in their constitutionalism was more dramatically emphasized three years later when the validity of the Erdman Act came before the Court. Here Harlan wrote the majority opinion, reasserting the commitment of the Court to the tradition of the widest possible freedom of contract in the individual and rejecting the Congressional attempt to outlaw "yellow dog" non-union agreements in railroad labor relations.

The spectre of the Pullman strike had hung over Congress in the middle years of the nineties, and as the hysteria of 1894 receded there was a proportionate rise in the number of proposals to encourage peaceful arbitration of labor issues in the railroad industry. No less an advocate of the carriers' interests than Richard Olney, who had broken the Pullman strike and hounded Debs to the penitentiary, helped draft the original plan for a Federal statute to establish arbitration procedures in railroad labor questions. Congressman Constantine Erdman of Pennsylvania had enlarged upon the Olney proposals, and the bill which eventually took his name was submitted to the 54th Congress, as he told his colleagues in the House of Representatives, with the formal endorsement of both labor and management groups.

The chief opposition to the measure came from men who protested their friendship for the workers. Congressman James G. Maguire of California, for one, feared that arbitration might prove a trap for employees, frozen in a status quo while the arbitrators deliberated indefinitely. In any case, declared Maguire, the law would amount to a "surrender of the individual liberty of all American laborers," and as a form of industrial slavery might well violate the spirit and perhaps the letter of the Thirteenth Amendment.[18]

On June 1, 1898 the Erdman Act became law (although Representative Erdman himself had retired from Congress the previous fall). Its most zealous friends hailed it as the first step in a series of statutes which, it was confidently predicted, would provide for the arbitration of virtually all labor issues in any type of interstate commerce. But, for all their relief at seeing a major body of labor relations made subject to voluntary arbitration, the operators of the railroads viewed Section 10 of the statute with profound misgiving. This section, fixing criminal liability on employers who knowingly and wilfully discharged or penalized employees for membership in unions, had all the appearance of being the forerunner of the union shop. Unless this section outlawing the "yellow dog" contract by which workers were compelled to forswear unions was formally challenged, it was feared the power of government to introduce and perpetuate the union principle in labor negotiations would be established *sub silentio*.[19]

The test case presented itself on the Louisville & Nashville line, in the eastern district of Kentucky, precipitated by the discharge of a union worker, O. B. Coppage. The United States secured a formal indictment of the L & N agent, William Adair, under Section 10 of the Erdman Act, and the case proceeded to trial in the Federal district court. Judge Andrew Cochran chose to assess the validity of the section against "yellow dog" contracts in terms of the statute as a whole, and concluded that Congress was within its powers under the commerce clause to legislate on the subject of labor issues involving interstate railroads. Given this permissible area of legislation, the court found it to be a reasonable exercise of legislative discretion to insure an equality of representation on the part of both labor and management by protecting the workers' representation from anti-union tactics. So finding, Cochran upheld the statute and the outlawing of "yellow dog" contracts as constitutional.[20]

Attorney General Bonaparte pursued the same line of reasoning in answering Adair's appeal to the Supreme Court. The whole of the statute, he argued, should be considered as a unit, and the purpose of Congress in drafting the law should be taken into account in determining the constitutional authority to enact the law and the freedom of Congress to devise the particular details of the law as it was disposed to do. Counsel for Adair, led by Benjamin D. Warfield, undertook to direct the Court's attention away from the commerce clause and to the proposition made famous by Judge Cooley, that the individual has a fundamental right "to refuse business relations with any person whomsoever, whether the refusal rests upon reason, or is the result of whim, caprice, prejudice or malice." With his reasons, argued Warfield, "neither the public nor third persons have any legal concern."[21]

To find Justice Harlan, the veteran dissenter, so readily accepting the carriers' argument for freedom of contract and so sweepingly declaring, in the majority opinion, that the "yellow dog" contract section was unconstitutional, seemed to the legal profession and the general public an incredible reversal of roles. The only equality which Congress could lawfully stipulate in labor arbitration, said Harlan, was the equality of the right of the employer to fix the conditions under which he would offer employment, and the right of the employee to determine whether he would accept the conditions. This was the equality consistent with the due process concept to the Fifth Amendment, the opinion declared, "and any legislation that disturbs that equality is an arbitrary interference with the liberty of contract which no government can legally justify in a free land."[22]

It might be, Harlan speculated, that Congress could make criminal the refusal of an employer to abide by a contract privately agreed upon between the employer and the workers in which discharge for union membership was specifically prohibited; but this was not the matter at issue. The only alternative was to find an overriding public interest vested in the commerce power; but, said Harlan, a labor contract was an agreement between man and man, and had no consequences affecting the interstate transportation of goods such as to make it a legitimate subject of Congressional action.[23]

*   *   *

These words from the man who had so often protested against the excesses of *laissez-faire* capitalism brought a stammering of explanations from his admirers in retrospect. They recalled the forebodings of Congressman Maguire and suggested that Harlan in the *Adair* case was essentially consistent with his lifelong and instinctive opposition to any interference with the liberty of individual action.[24] But Holmes, in dissenting, discerned the basic problem which would have to be faced when a new constitutionalism was devised to deal with the new society emerging in the twentieth century.

Holmes quickly disposed of the "involuntary servitude" charge against the Erdman Act; to argue that the law compelled employers to hire anyone they did not wish to hire, or to prevent them from discharging anyone for good cause, was to ignore the basic Congressional objective, which "simply prohibits the more powerful party to exact certain undertakings" from the disadvantaged party in labor negotiations. The fundamental question, Holmes went on, was whether government could regulate the private employment relation at all.

> Where there is, or generally is believed to be, an important ground of public policy for restraint, the Constitution does not forbid it, whether this court agrees or disagrees with the policy pursued. It cannot be doubted that to prevent strikes, and, so far as possible, to foster its scheme of arbitration, might be deemed by Congress an important point of policy, and I think it impossible to say that Congress might not reasonably think that the provision in question would help a good deal to carry its policy along. But suppose the only effect were to tend to bring about the complete unionizing of such railroad laborers as Congress can deal with, I think that object alone would justify the act. I quite agree that the question what and how much good labor unions do, is one on which intelligent people may differ; I think that laboring men sometimes attribute to them advantages, as many attribute to combinations of capital disadvantages, that really are due to economic conditions of a far wider and deeper kind; but I could not pronounce it unwarranted if Congress should decide that to foster a strong union was for the best interest, not only of the men, but of the railroads and the country at large.[25]

Harlan, looking at the word "liberty," saw the whole spectrum of political freedoms which made up the heritage of the nineteenth century; Holmes, looking at the phrase "liberty of contract," saw the word "contract" as an instrument of economic strategy in the emerging corporate society of the twentieth century. For Harlan, "liberty" was a universal; for Holmes, in an economic context it was relative, and to make a categorical imperative of a political concept when applied to a technical economic concept was to become entrapped by doctrines in which the word "has been stretched to its extreme."[26]

The *Adair* case, linking the liberal reformer Harlan with conservatives like Brewer, Brown and Fuller and the vacillating White, pointed up the fundamental incapacity of the older liberalism to cope with the unfamiliar and unprecedented propositions inherent in the new industrialism. Harlan's reaction to "liberty of contract" in terms of a conventional and ideal concept of "liberty" was, in the final analysis, irrelevant. Justice McKenna's separate dissent, in which he argued acceptance of the lower court's test of the statute as a unity, was technically impeccable but, in its way, as fully committed as Harlan's to the traditions of the past. Only Holmes, in this and other dissents, pointed to the dim shape of a future constitutionalism which would recognize a kind of democracy made up, as he phrased it later, of "conflicting desires to be accomplished by inconsistent means."[27]

*   *   *

Yet Holmes, who could assert that "to have doubted one's own first principles is the mark of a civilized man" and who generally accepted the fact that the emerging society of industrial America sought to stress "the criterion of social welfare as against the individualistic eighteenth-century bill of rights," was enough of a pragmatist to decline "to take the general premise as a sufficient justification for specific measures."[28] So it was that, within a month of the *Adair* dissent, Holmes would be part of a unanimous Court which would find labor organizations liable under the Sherman Act for tactics which amounted to a conspiracy in restraint of trade.

Enactments of Congress, in the final analysis, were to be understood either in terms of the plain meaning of the words of the act or in terms in which Congress made clear its intentions in drafting the act. The Sherman Anti-Trust Act of 1890 had been subjected to enough judicial gloss during the first decade of its existence to lend credence to the charge that the courts did not intend to give it the full dimensions originally conceived by Congress. The Roosevelt administration, with its zealous effort to revive the anti-trust movement, had urged that the courts give the broadest reasonable application to the statute's opening proposition: "Every contract, combination in the form of a trust or otherwise, or conspiracy in restraint of trade . . . is hereby declared to be illegal." The words were plain in their meaning; they must accordingly, it was argued, be applicable to any combination—of labor as well as of capital.

Richard Olney, as Attorney General, had dismissed the proposition as too broad to be literally applicable; and Justice Holmes, in private commentary, condemned the entire statute as a concoction of economic ignorance and incompetence. But the fact was that the law was on the books, and if it applied to any combinations it applied to all, until Congress by fresh legislative action should declare otherwise. This was the basis of unanimity in the Court's opinion on the Danbury Hatters' Case, where the Court found a secondary boycott organized by a union to be evidence of an intention or conspiracy to block off the flow of commerce as it affected its primary employer.[29]

Dietrich Loewe and his partners operated a hat manufacturing business in Danbury, Connecticut. In the spring of 1901, organizers of the United Hatters of America, led by Martin Lawlor and others, undertook to compel the company to recognize the union. Upon rejection of the union demand, Lawlor and his associates turned to wholesale dealers in a variety of states in an effort to persuade them not to do business with the Danbury concern. Loewe and his associates, thereupon, brought suit under Section 7 of the Sherman Act seeking triple damages for injuries resulting from the boycott.

In the original trial of the issue, union counsel demurred to the argument presented by Loewe and his associates; both the Federal district court and the Circuit Court of Appeals sustained the demurrer, and the case came on certiorari to the Supreme Court. Fuller, delivering the opinion, found that the judgments of the lower courts should be overruled: "The combination charged falls within the class of restraints of trade aimed at compelling third parties and strangers involuntarily not to engage in the course of trade except on conditions that the combination imposes."

The common law liability for such obstruction of commerce was well established, said Fuller, and the statute adopted by Congress, if anything, "has a broader application than the prohibition of restraints of trade unlawful at common law." He quoted Holmes' opinion which had upheld an earlier Wisconsin anti-trust law: "No conduct has such an absolute privilege as to justify all possible schemes of which it may be a part. The most innocent and constitutionally protected of acts or omissions may be made a step in a criminal plot, and, if it is a step in a plot, neither its innocence nor the Constitution is sufficient to prevent the punishment of the plot by law."[30]

*   *   *

Three weeks after this decision another unanimous Court, speaking through Justice Brewer, upheld an Oregon maximum-hour law for women and denied that it was an unconstitutional interference with liberty of contract. To accept the argument advanced by counsel, which depended upon a minimum of legal rules and upon an elaborate summary of the most advanced sociological findings of the day, was a sign of the times. Even while accepting the argument, Brewer sought to preserve the older values of the judicial conservatives. It should be remembered of constitutional issues, he said, that they

> are not settled by even a consensus of present public opinion, for it is the peculiar value of a written constitution that it places in unchanging form limitations upon legislative action, and thus gives a permanence and stability to popular government which otherwise would be lacking. At the same time, when a question of fact is debated and debatable, and the extent to which a special constitutional limitation goes is affected by the truth in respect to that fact, a widespread and long-continued belief concerning it is worthy of consideration.[31]

Yet Brewer was acknowledging the newer constitutionalism set out in the brief of the special counsel for Oregon, a fifty-two-year-old Boston attorney whose conviction was that the new American society depended upon social justice unfettered by the crystallized formulae of older law. The position of the traditionalists, said Louis D. Brandeis in another context, placed upon the reformers and the legislatures the burden of proving a law constitutional, instead of requiring those who challenged the act to establish its unconstitutionality.

In this juxtaposition, the advocates of laws accommodating social and economic change had to overcome the social and economic prejudices of the men on the bench as much as they had to deal with the literal issues of the law. Recognizing this fact, however, Brandeis concluded that the brief for reform would have to deal proportionately less with the literal issues of law and substantially more with subjects of economics and sociology . . . which embody the fact and present problems of today."[32]

To persuade a Court which, only three years before in the New York bakery case, had found a maximum-hour law unconstitutional, Brandeis had to distinguish the Oregon law from the New York decision. Accordingly, he opened his argument with an approving quotation from *Lochner* that no law could be sustained if it could not be shown to have a reasonable relation to public health and welfare, or if it was an arbitrary interference with personal liberties of the individual. However, Brandeis then contended, "if the end which the legislature seeks to accomplish be one to which its power extends, and if the means employed to that end, although not the wisest or best, are yet not plainly and palpably unauthorized by law, then the court cannot interfere." To determine the degree of public interest warranting legislative action in the case of a law limiting the daily hours of women employees to ten, Brandeis then concluded, the evidence of modern social research must be relied upon and the court should properly take judicial notice of these non-legal data.[33]

Another Boston attorney, Joseph H. Choate, had dismissed the invitation to argue the Oregon maximum-hour law with the observation that he saw no reason why "a big husky Irishwoman should not work more than ten hours a day in a laundry if she and her employer so desired." The reasons Brandeis marshalled ran to more than a hundred pages in his brief; they were assembled from a long list of statistical and scientific studies by factory inspectors, commissioners of hygiene, social welfare committees and legislative investigations, in state after state and many foreign countries. Exhaustively documented in the printed brief and dramatically summarized in the oral argument, Brandeis drove home to the Court the consistent theme of all the materials: long hours of labor had a direct and undesirable social effect upon the health, safety and morals of working women which only a statute limiting the hours could meet.[34]

"He not only *reached* the Court, but he *dwarfed the Court*," wrote an observer who heard Brandeis in oral argument on the related question of minimum wages five years later. For, the writer continued, "here stood a man who knew infinitely more, and who cared infinitely more, for the vital daily rights of the people than the men who sat there sworn to protect them." Against the massive array of social considerations in the Oregon case, even the *laissez-faire* majority could not muster a response. Brewer, critically but admiringly, said of Brandeis' materials that they were not, "technically speaking, authorities, and in them is little or no discussion of the constitutional question presented to us for determination, yet they are significant of a widespread belief" that women as a group in industrial society were entitled to special legislative protection.[35]

*   *   *

The responsibility of industrial society for the frequent injuries and deaths of employees in hazardous occupations was another concern of the Progressive Movement. The remedy, it was clear, lay in state and Federal legislation, for the common law all but exonerated the employer under any circumstances where the injury could be shown to have resulted from the worker's own negligence or from the negligence of a fellow employee. In modern industry with complex and dangerous machinery, the requirement that the man on the job prove that his injury was not the result of his own or another worker's acts was becoming as unjust as it was unrealistic. In 1906, Congress responded to labor appeals for relief by a statute abolishing the common law doctrines with reference to interstate carriers.[36]

A badly divided Court found the statute unconstitutional by an almost accidental combination of Justices. Only two—White and Day—joined in what was formally denominated the opinion of the Court; the remaining three who made up the narrow majority against the statute—Peckham, with Brewer and Fuller—wrote a concurring opinion in which they disavowed the general premise of the Court's opinion while acquiescing in the result. For the dissenters, Moody prepared a long opinion in essence averring that if Congress had the power to regulate interstate commerce, it could necessarily regulate any personal actions affecting that commerce—a proposition in which White and Day seemed to agree.

Harlan and McKenna concurred with Moody, but in a separate opinion. Holmes, whose intellectual isolation from the rest of the Fuller Court was becoming increasingly apparent, briefly admonished his colleagues that "as it is possible to read the words in such a way as to save the constitutionality of the act, I think they should be taken in that narrower sense." Since the tenor of White's opinion was that if the words were read in a narrow sense (which he and Day were unable to bring themselves to do) the law could be upheld, the fortuitous combination which led to the five-to-four decision against the statute might readily have been six-to-three in favor of it.[37]

The splintering of constitutional interpretation in this case attested to the breakdown in the philosophies of the members of the bench in the face of the continuing challenges of political reform and economic change. For White, the intellectual crisis presented by the great issues raised under the Square Deal and later under Woodrow Wilson's New Freedom aggravated a native disposition to prolixity, and his tedious and all but obscurantist opinion in the Employers' Liability Case was a study of a man watching his old assumptions wash away in the torrent of new causes. The case was decided on January 6, 1908; three weeks later would come *Adair,* on January 27; the Danbury Hatters' Case was decided on February 3, and the Oregon maximum-hour law was decided on February 24. Thus, in a matter of less than eight weeks, some of the most ingrained propositions of *laissez-faire* industrialism had been subjected to successive periods of scrutiny. The mounting agony of doubt, even when the doubt was smothered, was manifest in the disparate discussion in the Employers' Liability Case.

Nowhere on the Court was this agony to be so prolonged as in the mind of Edward D. White, both as a member of the Fuller Court and as Chief Justice in his own right. He dissented in the New York Bakers' Case in 1905, when the majority invalidated the state regulation of working hours; but a decade later he would also dissent in *Bunting v. Oregon,* when the majority upheld a state maximum-hour law. He concurred in a holding for the constitutionality of New York's workmen's compensation law, but dissented in the same term of Court when the majority upheld a similar Washington state law. White perhaps sensed the ultimate issue which would confront the Court in the middle of the twentieth century—the duty, as he expressed it, "to uphold and perpetuate the great guarantees of individual freedom as declared by the Constitution" while at the same time striving to "sustain the authority of the Union as to the subjects coming within the legitimate scope of its power." Yet he floundered throughout most of his judicial career, vainly seeking to preserve increasingly artificial aspects of the dichotomy of state and Federal areas of power within a steadily unifying economic unit which was the United States. It was this inevitable frustration which brought him considerably short of greatness as a jurist; continually he caught glimpses of the new America, but periodically he shrank from the swiftness of the prospect of change. His ambivalence pervaded his writing, which became a prolonged *apologia pro sua vita* but led to the inescapable criticism that his works were "models of what judicial opinions ought not to be."[38]

White readily accepted the argument that Congress could legislate on all matters, including employers' liability for accidents, in the area of interstate commerce. His sole reason for finding the statute invalid was that if its language was broadly construed it could be found to apply to matters within a given state as well. A law which thus "interblended" matters properly the subject of Federal jurisdiction and those outside the jurisdiction was, in his opinion, invalid. Peckham and his associates eagerly agreed that the statute was invalid; they declined, however, to substantiate White's view that employer liability as defined in the law could under any circumstances be a matter of Congressional authority.

The particular point on which the first Liability Case turned was readily enough disposed of; that same spring Congress amended the law to make it specifically apply only to interstate affairs, and in 1912 a second Liability Case was brought before the Court, with a unanimous opinion affirming the statute.[39]

*   *   *

In the fall of 1908, as the Roosevelt administration was entering its final phase, another question of constitutionalism in an increasingly cosmopolitan America presented itself: To what degree does the Constitution, through the Fourteenth Amendment, extend to citizens of states the privileges and immunities guaranteed to them by the Bill of Rights as citizens of the United States? In a sense, the question was premature. In the quarter of a century during which the American people had first come to grips with the problems of urbanization, monopoly, the interstate corporation, unionization of labor, social legislation and related subjects, the role of the Federal government in the enforcement of individual rights had not assumed the clarity of definition that would come in the next half-century.

A Federally guaranteed right, it was assumed, could be asserted by a citizen of the United States only when he was in a Federal or interstate situation; in most conditions of life, the rights or immunities of the individual depended on the constitutional posture of his state of citizenship. In this context, the provision of the Fourteenth Amendment that "no State shall make or enforce any law which shall abridge the privileges or immunities of citizens of the United States" related to only a small area of law.

When the question was presented, it was the moderate Moody who delivered the opinion of the eight-to-one majority rejecting the proposition that the Fourteenth Amendment extended all or most of the Bill of Rights to citizens of the states. And it was Harlan, the old-fashioned liberal in one of the closing dissents in his long career, who urged that a constitutional restraint on government in the interest of individual liberty was equally essential against states as against the Federal power.

Two directors of the Monmouth Trust & Safe Deposit Company of New Jersey, Albert C. Twining and David C. Cornell, had been indicted for allegedly giving false information to a state bank examiner. Twining and Cornell did not testify in their own defense at the ensuing trial, and in his charge to the jury the presiding judge called the jurors' attention to the fact. On conviction and affirming of their conviction by the New Jersey courts, the defendants sued a writ of error in the Supreme Court alleging that this procedure of instruction to the jury, permitted under New Jersey law, violated the Fourteenth Amendment injunction that a state could not abridge the privileges or immunities of Federal citizens.[40]

Moody acknowledged the argument of Twining's counsel that the privilege against self-incrimination had been well established by the time of the Constitutional Convention of 1787. It appeared in the constitutions of most of the original states and by 1908 was to be found in all but two—New Jersey and Iowa. But this fact, to the majority of the Court, only suggested that "it has been supposed by the states that, so far as the state courts are concerned, the privilege had its origin in the constitutions and laws of the states, and that persons appealing to it must look to the states for their protection." To hold otherwise now, Moody observed with unknowing prophecy, would diminish the power of the states and would subject their fundamental law to review in the Federal courts.[41] To demonstrate the contrary, Moody cited decisions of the Supreme Court specifically denying the proposition that the Second, Fifth, Sixth or Seventh Amendments were incorporated into the Fourteenth.[42]

Harlan wrote a lone but vigorous dissent, pointing out that even if the Federal privilege against self-incrimination were not considered to extend to New Jersey through the opening part of the citizenship sentence of the Fourteenth Amendment, there was reason to find New Jersey in violation of the remaining provision of the same sentence, that no state "shall deprive any person of life, liberty or property without due process of law." But, Harlan insisted, the intention of Congress in drafting the Amendment was to insure that all privileges and immunities of citizens of the United States should be protected from state infringement; and the basic privileges and immunities having been set out in specific Amendments to the Constitution, principally in the Bill of Rights, it should follow that these were rights, "which, after the adoption of the Fourteenth Amendment, no state could impair or destroy."[43]

*   *   *

Twining v. New Jersey presented a question for the future, for the constitutional structure of the nation as it would become long after the tenure of

Fuller and his immediate colleagues. The case was decided at the beginning of the twenty-first term of the Court under the Chief Justice; two and a half years later, on July 4, 1910, Fuller would die in office at the age of seventy-seven. Harlan, born the same year as his Chief, would die the year after Fuller. The arch-conservative Brewer would precede them in the spring of 1910, and the equally conservative Peckham in the fall of 1909. *Twining*, therefore, became virtually the final constitutional milestone for a bench which had remained remarkably homogeneous throughout a quarter of a century. The period had begun in the seedtime of the government regulatory process with reference to capitalism, had passed through the excitement of Populism and the Square Deal, and was coming to its close on the eve of the progressive uprising which would herald the New Freedom.

On every hand the signs pointed to the preparation for more sweeping changes—in the passing, in four successive years, of four veterans of the Supreme Court; in the increasing agitation in Congress for a variety of Amendments to the Constitution itself;* in the general assumption, in the election of 1908, that William Howard Taft's administration would carry on the momentum of reform developed under Theodore Roosevelt; and in the steady increase in the reform laws being adopted by state governments as well as being advocated in Congress.

The first decade of the twentieth century, indeed, had recorded some spectacular modifications in the rationale of American government, both Federal and state. Creation of the Department of Commerce and Labor in 1903 had placed the administrative study of metropolitan economic activity on a level with Agriculture in the Cabinet. The Hepburn Act of 1906, although lacking the plenary powers the trust busters had envisioned, greatly strengthened the rate-policing authority of the Interstate Commerce Commission. In the same year a statute regulating the hours of consecutive work permitted of railroad employees was a beginning step toward an ultimate framework of laws on maximum hours.

Roosevelt's great personal interest in the natural resources of the country and their conservation marked the beginning of an effective Federal program of forest preserves, national parks and policies of regulation of the disposition of the mineral wealth of the land. The Pure Food and Drug Act and the Meat Inspection Act, both passed by Congress in 1906, had substantially advanced the principle of Federal surveillance of production and traffic in items materially affecting the public health. Even the panic of 1907, which John D. Rockefeller had blamed on the Rooseveltian attack on big business, resulted in one of the most carefully considered pieces of legislation yet to be drafted on the chronic problem of an inelastic national currency—the Aldrich-Vreeland Act of 1908—which in turn prepared the way, five years later, for the creation of the Federal Reserve System.[44]

---

*See Appendix B.

Political advances in state government in the same decade, led by the "Wisconsin Idea" of Robert M. LaFollette, added impetus to the Progressive Movement. A state income tax, a strong railroad commission, and that near cure-all for the political ills of the age, the direct primary, all were adopted in Wisconsin in 1902 and 1903. In the initiative and referendum, Oregon, in 1902, adopted another political concept dear to the hearts of reformers and in 1904 improved upon Wisconsin's electoral measure with a preferential primary statute.

Popular interest in, and emotional response to, the challenges of the day was whetted by the rising sensational journals, both newspapers like Joseph Pulitzer's *New York World* and magazines like *McClure's, Everybody's,* the *Independent* and the *Outlook.* Through articles in these periodicals, or through more detailed treatment in books, Lincoln Steffens exposed "The Shame of the Cities," Ida M. Tarbell wrote a critical economic history of the Standard Oil Company, and Jacob Riis looked at the slums and told the rest of the world "How the Other Half Lives."

The era of Roosevelt, Hughes and LaFollette—and of Governor Woodrow Wilson of New Jersey—was a period of fervent and militant faith in the masses, who, as Louis Post of Chicago put it in 1906, "are better to be trusted than any one class," and the means of attaining more honest and efficient government, Post concluded, "is more intense democracy." There was, perhaps, one particularly significant characteristic of the reform movement of the first decade of the new century, now that the movement was showing prospects of attaining goals which had proved so elusive to the rebels of the seventies, eighties and nineties: this was the fact that the effective crusades of the Progressive Movement were, in many instances, led by city dwellers rather than by agrarian spokesmen. The voices of the latter tended more and more to form a background chorus to the main argument.

Bryan, aside from the fact that he spoke in terms of a fallaciously simplified economics, was readily recognizable as the voice of the moral righteousness of the rural nineteenth century America. The charges against the contemporary industrial system so often leveled by Bryan were generally conceded by the electorate in 1900 and 1908; they simply preferred more sophisticated leaders to undertake the search for the solution to their problems. Instead of Bryan and the Democrats, it was the congeries of urbane radicals like Roosevelt and Hughes of New York, LaFollette of Wisconsin, Albert J. Beveridge of Indiana and Hazen S. Pingree of Michigan—all Republicans, even though non-conformists—who carried many of the progressive propositions to fruition.

*   *   *

Theodore Roosevelt after his sweeping popular victory in 1904, like Franklin Roosevelt after his landslide in 1936, looked boldly toward his new term with confident plans for great legislative advances. In each case the President was to come to grief at the hands of entrenched conservatives in his own party. For the second Roosevelt, progressivism was to be saved by the substantial reform statutes enacted before his reelection which were validated by a judiciary which was prevailed upon to shift its ideological poles. For the first Roosevelt it was a matter of bulldozing through a recalcitrant Congress a minimum number of statutes and leaving a bitterly resentful Old Guard in control of the party. The seeds of 1912 were sown in the legislative struggle of 1906.

Thus, in his message to Congress in December, 1904, the Rough Rider had called for a broad extension of Federal regulation over railroad rates and over corporation practices in general, employers' liability in industrial injuries, slum clearance, the abolition of child labor, and a long list of other socially advanced proposals. Republican conservatives in Congress, zealously backed by the railroad and corporation lobbies, chose to test their strength on the issue of railroad rate regulation, and managed to smother the bill in the Senate through the spring of 1905. Roosevelt's strategy, in his renewed proposals to Congress the following December, was to narrow his range in the hope of concentrating progressive strength behind a few measures.[45]

It became evident at once that the Rough Rider had charged directly into the most sacrosanct premises of *laissez-faire* capitalism; in his proposal that Congress enact stringent regulatory legislation over price-fixing, the inspection of corporate records and the labor relations of employers, the President was greeted by screams of outrage from the united conservative press of the country. It was, declared one editorialist, "an amazing program of centralization" which was calculated to do away with the state-Federal relationship and bring about a socialist dictatorship. Congress was flooded with protests—many dispatched by spurious agencies like the "Alabama Commercial and Industrial Association," created by railroad propagandists solely to pour abusive compositions into the anti-Square Deal ranks. In a Senate solidly dominated by men like Senators Nelson M. Aldrich, W. B. Allison, Joseph Foraker and J. C. Spooner, for whom free enterprise was the crowning achievement of economics, the reaction to Roosevelt's proposals was apoplectic.[46]

Congressman Peter Hepburn of Iowa had launched the new administration attack in January 1906 with a bill sweepingly extending the powers of the Interstate Commerce Commission over the rate-making of interstate railroads, and seeking to give the Commission a subpoena authority to examine the carriers' books. The degree to which the proposals reflected the temper of the country— fired by a succession of railroad rate scandals the previous fall—was reflected in the alacrity with which the Hepburn Bill passed the House of Representatives; the vote was 346 to 7.[47]

The bill as it came to the Senate proposed to give the Interstate Commerce Commission authority, in the case of a shipper's complaint that a carrier's rates were unreasonable, to determine and enforce a reasonable rate. The "railroad Senators," as their critics called them, planned to amend the bill—recognizing that the groundswell of popular demand for some sort of regulatory law was too great to resist—to insure court review of any rates set by the Commission, and a stay of the new rates until the process of review had been completely exhausted. With the generally known conservatism of the judiciary in such matters, such an amendment could substantially reduce the impact of the Hepburn measure.

The insurgents, led by the recently come LaFollette, proposed a countermeasure which would deny judicial review of Commission rates. Roosevelt concluded that his ultimate chance of success lay between the extremes; at least, it was a case of winning some of the wavering "railroad Senators" to his course. The Hepburn bill as it stood, he accordingly wrote Senator Chester Long of Kansas, was "as far as we could with wisdom go at this time."[48] The President himself had watched over the drafting of the original measure, with the principal work being done by William Z. Ripley, the nationally reputed railroad economist, Attorney General Moody, Paul Morton, a former executive of the Santa Fe, and William Howard Taft. Nor was Roosevelt opposed to a reasonable opportunity for judicial review of specific rates; his concern was that the appeal to the courts should not become a means of stultifying the relief for shippers and consumers which was his primary objective.[49]

There still remained the question, however, whether the bill in any effective form could be pushed through the Senate at all. Aldrich, the Republican boss, was not prepared to concede the White House the votes to do the job; the veteran of many past battles against reform, he knew precisely the men he himself could count on in his own party, and the way to win dissident Democrats to his coalition. A realist at all times, the patrician Rhode Islander took into account that certain of his customary allies—Republicans under pressure from the farmer-dominated legislatures of the West—would have to part company with him for the time being. But if he could keep the opposition scattered, leave the bill open to attack on the Senate floor, and denigrate it in any way as an administration measure, Aldrich remained confident that if the statute passed at all it would be substantially less objectionable to the business community.

The battle was joined early in February. Since the Senate committee on interstate and foreign commerce, to which the bill had been referred, was dominated by administration men, Aldrich arranged for it to be reported onto the floor for amendments, where it would be subject to attack from all sides. In the process, the Republican leader also arranged that the floor manager for the bill should be the Democratic demagogue, "Pitchfork Ben" Tillman of South Carolina, a man whom Roosevelt himself personally loathed.[50]

The feeling was reciprocated. Tillman was the Southern counterpart of the messianic reformers of the Greenback and Populist uprisings in the West, and his terms as governor of South Carolina in the early nineties had been marked by sweeping legislative and constitutional changes, including stringent regulation of intrastate carriers, establishment of a state-owned liquor dispensary—and redistricting which effectively disfranchised the Negro. Like "Sockless Jerry" Simpson of Kansas, Tillman cultivated a backwoods appeal as a ticket to Congress. "Send me to Washington and I'll stick my pitchfork into his old ribs!" was his campaign slogan in 1894. The ribs belonged to the portly and conservative Grover Cleveland, but a decade later they were those of Theodore Roosevelt. Pugnacious and irascible, Tillman's reaction to all issues was essentially visceral; in February 1902 he had provoked a furious fist fight with his colleague from South Carolina, John L. McLaurin, which had evoked a formal censure from the Senate. The White House had immediately recalled an invitation to a state dinner honoring the visiting Prince Henry of Germany; but this rebuff did not incense Tillman so much as Roosevelt's famous breakfast with the Negro educator, Booker T. Washington, the next year.[51]

With such a man in control of the administration bill in the Senate, Aldrich had not only effected a supreme irony but he had made it extremely difficult for communications in strategy to flow between the White House and the Capitol. In addition, by compelling the President to follow the lead of the radical agrarians, Aldrich fed the fears of the Senate moderates that the Hepburn bill would now give the Interstate Commerce Commission virtually confiscatory powers. Eventually, the confident Republican leader reasoned, Roosevelt would have to accept his amendments in return for sufficient support to get the bill enacted.

The Rough Rider, however, was to prove to be an astute enough strategist himself. He permitted Tillman to assume management of the rate bill, marshalling "radical" Southern Democratic and Western Democratic and Republican opposition to the Aldrich amendments. At the same time, the President had no intention of permitting the extremists among the reformers to have their way; in a letter to "Uncle Joe" Cannon of the House on February 19, Roosevelt emphasized that appellate review of Commission rates was essential "to avoid raising the constitutional question." Moody and his predecessor, Knox, now the Pennsylvania "railroad Senator," were at work on the type of amendment which the administration wanted.[52]

Permitting Tillman and his agrarian radicals to raise in conservative minds the fear of an all-powerful administrative agency emerging from the bill, Roosevelt continued to work with Moody, Knox and Allison of Iowa on an amendment which would provide for review by the judiciary and an injunction power which the Commission would be permitted to meet with arguments in open court. When, in early May, the administration amendment was offered, Tillman was apoplectic; Roosevelt, he shouted to the Senate, had been guilty of deliberate double dealing and betrayal. The President, now confident that he had the votes to get the measure through, sent a lengthy letter to Senator Lodge dismissing the Tillman charge as "a deliberate and unqualified falsehood." Thereafter the Senate, by a vote of 71 to 3, passed the measure.[53]

*   *   *

For all the fanfare over the Square Deal, the Hepburn Act was the only major piece of legislation sponsored by the White House which found its way through the Aldrich phalanx. A Pure Food and Drug Act and a Meat Inspection Act were also adopted in June 1906, but only with substantial modifications of the original progressive goals. Roosevelt was never as successful in playing off the various Senate elements against each other, and Aldrich, having suffered one of his rare setbacks, carefully rebuilt his defenses against fresh attacks. Roosevelt steadily found himself more isolated from Capitol Hill, and his relations with Congress steadily deteriorating. For their part, Congressmen did not hesitate to blame the White House for the brief but cataclysmic financial crisis that beset the nation in 1907; Republican reactionaries widely quoted a Georgia Democratic newspaper which described the President as "our chief panic-maker," while the independent Republican *Springfield Republican* accused him of "egotism of a very aggressive nature," and August Belmont flatly declared that he was solely to blame for "the present precarious condition of the financial interest of the United States."[54]

In his final message to Congress on December 8, 1908, Roosevelt seized the opportunity to review in detail the unfinished work which he was confident his successor would carry on, and to strike at the opposition which had thwarted or limited so much of the reforms of his administration. In particular he directed his criticism at the courts: "The rapid changes in our social and industrial life," he reminded Congress, made it essential that "in applying to concrete cases the great rule of right laid down in our Constitution, there should be a full understanding and appreciation of the new conditions to which the rules are to be applied." He continued: "What would have been an infringement upon liberty half a century ago may be the necessary safeguard of liberty today. What would have been an injury to property then may be necessary to the enjoyment of property now. Every judicial decision involves two terms—one, as interpretation of the law; the other, the understanding of the facts to which it is to be applied."

In the nature of the case, Roosevelt went on, every time the courts expressed a judgment on a constitutional matter "they necessarily enact into law parts of a system of social philosophy; and as such interpretation is fundamental, they give direction to all lawmaking. The decisions of the courts on economic and social questions depend upon their economic and social philosophy; and for the peaceful progress of our people during the twentieth century we shall owe most to those judges who hold to a twentieth-century economic and social philosophy, and not to a long outgrown philosophy, which was itself the product of primitive economic conditions."

As he had done in his message the previous year, the Rough Rider enumerated a long list of specific reforms, including a new Federal income tax, national incorporation of interstate business in order to strengthen the administrative supervision of these activities, limitation of the use of the labor injunction, national workmen's compensation, a universal eight-hour work day, and so on. Many of these would come to fruition under Woodrow Wilson, and some would have to await another Roosevelt in the White House. But as this Roosevelt saw it, legislative accommodation of many of the reform goals was imperative if the working classes were not to bear out the Socialist predictions of a mass uprising. Following the Supreme Court's invalidating of a workmen's compensation law in 1908, Roosevelt had written privately to Justice Day that for the Court to continue in its present view would be to breed a revolution, and it might become necessary "to have a revolution, because the condition of the worker would become intolerable."[55]

*   *   *

The furore created by Roosevelt's last message to Congress, and the criticism of the legislators which was implied in his gratuitous comment that the Employers' Liability Act was so sloppily drafted as to have made inevitable the Supreme Court's invalidating of the statute, gave the conservatives such excuse as they needed to launch a counterattack. Senator Aldrich of Rhode Island drafted a resolution of condemnation and inquiry, and on January 4, 1909 the House of Representatives voted overwhelmingly to reject a Presidential communication to it as lacking in respect for Congress. Nicholas Murray Butler, up to then a warm friend of Roosevelt, wrote him sorrowfully that "a President, whether right or wrong, cannot afford to argue with his adversaries, after the fashion of a private citizen, either in a state paper or in a formal public address." The gulf between the retiring President and the Republican party and Congress was not thereafter to be closed.[56]

A final blow to the trust-busting movement had come in the summer of 1908, after the government had successfully prosecuted Standard Oil of Indiana in the Federal District Court, with Judge Kenesaw Mountain Landis levying a fantastic fine of $29,240,000 for violations of the Sherman Act. The Circuit Court of Appeals reversed the judgment; on that bench sat Judge Peter S. Grosscup, the jurist who had aided in drafting the famed Debs injunction in 1895. Roosevelt wrote to his Attorney General, Bonaparte, declaring that the government would again prosecute the oil company for accepting railroad rebates, and that the appellate ruling "amounts precisely and exactly to saying that the biggest criminals in this country should be shielded and the law of Congress nullified, and that it should be done in the most adroit and meanest of ways."[57]

The President told an interviewer in the *Washington Post* that "there is absolutely no question as to the guilt of the defendant nor of the exceptionally grave character of the offense." To permit the judiciary to thwart the lawful actions of the executive in the protection of the public weal, he wrote William Allen White, means that there is "altogether too much power in the bench."[58]

The torrent of recrimination grew in volume as the end of Roosevelt's administration came on. In part, it was the product of a recurrent friction struck off by Congress whenever it is joined with a vigorous and capable President, but in this case the conflict was heightened by an awareness that the Executive was past his period of power, and, so far as the conservatives were concerned, it was already time to prepare the counter-revolution. James W. Van Cleave of the National Association of Manufacturers wrote to Taft upon his election that he rejoiced to know that "Americanism still reigns supreme in the United States," while on March 3, in the closing hours of the old Congress, Senator Isidor Rayner of Maryland tartly observed that on the morrow the country would "have a President, I am sure, who will obey the requirements of the law, who will not evade the obligations of the Constitution, and who, I think, knows by heart the limitations of executive power."[59]

The bitterness of this and similar expressions attested to an antagonism which had prevailed throughout most of Roosevelt's second term; it also reflected the pent-up resentments of the *laissez-faire* advocates at all that had been advanced in the name of the Progressive Movement of the past seven years. Above all, it signalled the intention of the conservatives to seize the initiative and use their numerical superiority to bring the national government back to the comfortable order of things in McKinley's day.

The steps were taken almost as soon as the new President was inaugurated. Of Taft and his associates following the ceremony, Senator Jonathan Dolliver of Iowa observed that the Chief Executive was "surrounded by good men who know exactly what they want." Within two weeks of the inauguration, the bill which would become the Payne-Aldrich Tariff Act, anathema to the progressives and the epitome of the protectionist tradition, was introduced; it dispelled any lingering doubts as to the program of the Old Guard, or any hope that it had either died or surrendered. For the next four years, the Progressive Movement would be held largely in check, until its backed-up force would burst forth in the floodtide of 1912.[60]

PART II

The Crucible
of Change

The Constitution of the United States is not a mere law-yer's document; it is a vehicle of life, and its spirit is always the spirit of the age.

Woodrow Wilson, *Constitutional Government in the United States*, p. 67 (1908)

Chart II   THE WHITE COURT

| 1904 | 1905 | 1906 | 1907 | 1908 | 1909 | 1910 | 1911 | 1912 | 1913 | 1914 | 1915 | 1916 | 1917 | 1918 | 1919 | 1920 | 1921 | 1922 | 1923 | 1924 | 1925 | 1926 |

Row 1 — Presidents of the U.S.

- T. ROOSEVELT (1904–Mar. 4, 1909)
- TAFT (Mar. 4, 1909 – 1913)
- WILSON (Mar. 4, 1913 – 1921)
- HARDING (Mar. 4, 1921 – Aug. 3, 1923)
- COOLIDGE (Aug. 3, 1923 – 1926)

Rows 2–10 — Justices of the Supreme Court

- FULLER (D.-Ill.) — to Jul. 4, 1910
- MOODY (R.-Mass.) — Nov. 29; Jan. 3
- VAN DEVANTER (R.-Wyo.) — Jan. 3, 1911 –
- LAMAR (D.-Ga.) — Jan. 3, 1911 to Jan. 2, 1916
- BRANDEIS (D.-Mass.) — Jun. 5, 1916 –
- McKENNA (R.-Calif.)
- STONE (R.-N.Y.) — Mar. 2, 1925
- DAY (R.-Ohio) — Mar. 18; to Nov. 13
- BUTLER (D.-Minn.) — Jan. 2
- PITNEY (R.-N.J.) — Mar. 18, 1912; to Dec. 31
- SANFORD (R.-Tenn.) — Feb. 19
- HARLAN (R.-Ky.) — to Oct. 14, 1911
- HUGHES (R.-N.Y.) — Oct. 10, 1910 to Jun. 10, 1916
- CLARKE (D.-Ohio) — Oct. 9, 1916 to Sep. 18
- SUTHERLAND (R.-Utah) — Oct. 2
- BREWER (R.-Kan.) — to Mar. 29, 1910
- HOLMES (R.-Mass.)
- WHITE (D.-La.) / WHITE (Chief Justice) (D.-La.) — Dec. 19, 1910 to May 19, 1921
- TAFT (R.-Ohio) — Jul. 11; Sept. 23 (Chief Justice)
- PECKHAM (R.-N.Y.) — to Oct. 24, 1909
- LURTON (D.-Tenn.) — Jan. 3, 1910 to Jul. 12, 1914
- McREYNOLDS (D.-Tenn.) — Sept. 5, 1914 –

Row 11 — Attorneys General

Moody | Bonaparte (Dec. 17) | Wickersham (Mar. 5) | McReynolds* (Mar. 5) | Gregory (Sep. 3) | Palmer (Mar. 5) | Daugherty (Mar. 1) | Stone (Apr. 7) | Sargent (Mar. 17)

Row 12 — Solicitors General

Hoyt (Jul. 1) | Bowers (Apr. 1) | Lehmann (Dec. 12) | Bullitt+ (Aug. 30) | Davis (Sep. 3) | King (Nov. 21) | # (Jun. 1) | Beck (Jul. 1) | Mitchell (Jun. 4)

* McReynolds   # Frierson
+ Bullitt

Row 1 — Presidents of the U. S.
Rows 2–10 — Justices of the Supreme Court
Row 11 — Attorneys General
Row 12 — Solicitors General

The shaded portion of the Chart represents the Court during White's Chief Justiceship (Dec. 19, 1910—May 19, 1921). Because of its shorter duration, it naturally shows less change in composition than Fuller's Court. Still, it is worth noting that three of Taft's five appointments to the Court were of short duration (Hughes, Lamar and Lurton) and gave Wilson his three opportunities to make his appointments to the bench. This left two of Taft's appointees (Pitney and Van Devanter), two of Theodore Roosevelt's (Day and Holmes), one of McKinley's (McKenna) and one of Cleveland's (White). Seven of the nine members of the Court had a pronounced longevity of tenure either before or after White's Chief Justiceship, as indicated in the rows of the chart extending to either left or right of the shaded area.

8/Trustee of the Square Deal

"WE HAVE GOT in our new President," Justice Holmes wrote to Sir Frederick Pollock in March of 1909, adding that Taft's inaugural address "did not seem to me remarkable—although I am told that Mr. Roosevelt called it the best since Lincoln, no doubt because it promised to pursue the reforms of 'my distinguished predecessor.' As I am rather skeptical about the reforms I was less impressed."[1]

The inaugural address was, indeed, unremarkable; the most affirmative passage in it declared that "American business can be assured of that measure of stability and certainty in respect to those things that may be done and those that are prohibited which is essential to the life and growth of all business. Such a plan must include the right of the people to avail themselves of those methods of combining capital and effort deemed necessary to reach the highest degree of economic efficiency." Whether this vague generality alluded to the conviction, shared by Roosevelt and Taft alike, that the existing anti-trust statutes were too categorical, linking "good" and "bad" combinations under the same condemnation of effecting a restraint of trade, was open to speculation, to say the least. So, also, was Taft's apostrophe to the Square Deal general enough to mean whatever the listener might have wanted it to mean. At most, the *Boston Transcript* decided, it suggested that "calm persistence" would take the place of Roosevelt's "strenuous insistence" upon reform.[2]

Taft himself seemed amused by the uncertainties on all sides which attended his address and his first activities in office. The inaugural had been held in the wake of a fierce snowstorm which had swept Washington the day before, and it moved the new President to quip, "I always said it would be a cold day when I became President." But the signs of change were there, for those who chose to look for them, even before he had taken office. In February Taft had observed to William Rockhill Nelson of the *Kansas City Star*: "Mr. Roosevelt's function has been to preach a crusade against certain evils. He has aroused the people to demand reform. It becomes my business to put that reform into legal

135

execution." This could be interpreted as a pause in progressive legislation, a consolidating of positions seized by the previous administration—or it might mean an effort to bring the policies of government more definitely back toward center, for Taft had added: "The people who are best fitted to do this, without injury to the business interests of the country, are those lawyers who understand corporate wealth, the present combination, its evils, and the method by which they can be properly restrained." Such men in key positions in his Cabinet, Taft went on, would be listened to with more respect by Congress than men representing "the more radical members of the party."[3]

The announcement of Cabinet selections was a much clearer indication to the general public of what the incoming administration conceived as its basic character, and it certainly gave Roosevelt his first substantial doubts as to the readiness of his successor to follow without deviation the trail blazed by the Rough Rider. By instinct Taft turned to lawyers, the group with whom he was most at home and the profession where his real interest would always lie; and in his Cabinet there was unmistakably a preponderance of the type of "lawyers who understand corporate wealth." Six of the nine positions were filled with representatives of the bar, and three of these were fundamentally to affect policy. Philander C. Knox of Pennsylvania, Roosevelt's first Attorney General, was named the new Secretary of State, and was reported to have advised Taft on the selection of most of the other Cabinet members. Although he had ably handled the government's prosecution of the Northern Securities Case, and prepared the way for the Beef Trust Case in the first Roosevelt administration, his faith in the essential rightness of American big business processes was fundamental. In his new office Knox would inaugurate the policy of insisting upon substantial foreign concessions to insure the safeguarding of American investments abroad—"dollar diplomacy," it came to be called.[4]

For his own Attorney General, Taft passed over Roosevelt's hint that Charles Bonaparte be retained, and offered the post to George W. Wickersham of New York. It was less a matter of disapproving of the one as having a positive preference for the other. To Bonaparte and several others who had been led to assume that they would be retained in the new administration, Taft wrote that since he would face different problems in his administration he felt it necessary to have "somewhat different personnel in the Cabinet." Yet, to the jealously watching associates of the retired President, it seemed in this appointment that the trust-busting cause had been betrayed; in place of Bonaparte, the Baltimore liberal, the new Chief Executive had appointed a partner from his own brother's Wall Street law firm.

Here, as in so many of his acts as President, William Howard Taft was to display an astute understanding of the temper of the times which the masses never were to appreciate. In Wickersham, Taft was obtaining the services of a man who understood perfectly not only the methods and needs of modern business, but its excesses and their evil consequences. His four years in charge of the Department of Justice would be marked by a vastly larger number of anti-trust actions than the Square Deal had accounted for in seven—and in the end it would be Wall Street which would be clamoring for his removal from the Attorney Generalship. A cultivated gentleman of the old school, who regularly read classics in French, Italian and Spanish and was a connoisseur of the arts, he was in the first quarter of the twentieth century reminiscent of what Henry Adams had been to the last quarter of the nineteenth.[5]

Above all, Wickersham understood the supreme danger, as he put it in a phrase in 1911, of "uncontrolled centralization of power in private hands." The key words in the phrase were "uncontrolled" and "private." As a firm believer in capitalism, the Attorney General did not understand that the anti-trust laws were intended to destroy or cripple the system. He viewed combination—as did both Roosevelt and Taft—as a natural and necessary development of economic efficiency; but he was aware—as they were—of the difference between efficiency and monopoly. The answer to him was a form of government surveillance to promote efficiency and to control monopoly. Because he discerned, in a legal system then lacking the machinery for such surveillance, the steady growth of the threat, he seized upon the only (though imperfect) weapon at his command, the Sherman Act, and set out to slay giants.

Wickersham unhesitatingly took over Bonaparte's dossiers on a number of trusts, and added a substantial number of others of his own initiative: actions were instituted or continued against United States Steel, Standard Oil, International Harvester, and combinations in cash registers, meat packing, powder and sugar. In the course of his administration, he would strive unsuccessfully for a Federal incorporation statute which had been favored by both Roosevelt and Taft; he conceived of the Commerce Court which was born under an unfortunate stigma of being a suspected intragovernmental device for short-circuiting anti-trust prosecutions; and he shared with the Chief Executive the conviction that a harmonious interrelationship between Justice, the Interstate Commerce Commission and the new Department of Commerce and Labor was necessary for a realistic development of public policy relating to modern business.[6]

Far from being Taft's most reactionary appointment, Wickersham as Attorney General proved to be his most forward-looking. His lawyerlike work with his special assistants, Frank B. Kellogg and James C. McReynolds, paved the way for the key anti-trust decisions in the new White Court. His whole administration was an object-lesson in the effectiveness of the government prosecution of policy and of litigation as it was dependent upon the intelligence, vision and ability of this Cabinet officer.

*   *   *

It was in his selection of Richard A. Ballinger as Secretary of the Interior, ironically enough, that Taft set the stage for the irreparable split between himself and the Roosevelt forces. An attorney from the state of Washington, widely experienced in the conservation problems of the West, and with a term as a reform mayor of Seattle, Ballinger seemed to present excellent credentials. In 1907 he had been appointed Commissioner of the General Land Office by J. R. Garfield, Roosevelt's Secretary of the Interior—a turn of events which was to haunt him and Taft when the President selected him for Garfield's position in the new administration.

Garfield was the *beau idéal* of the conservationists whose cause had reached its zenith under Roosevelt. Indeed, the vociferous protest when Garfield was not required was an indication of how fundamental a place conservation had come to occupy in the credo of the Progressive Movement. Nevertheless, the tragedy of the Taft administration was magnified by the sudden avalanche of publicity which gathered about a departmental dispute which normally would have attracted little or no attention.

As a skilled attorney, Ballinger readily discerned the frequent anomalies in the policy positions assumed in conservation matters by Garfield in Interior and Gifford Pinchot in the Department of Agriculture's Division of Forestry under the ardent prodding of Roosevelt. As an expert in mining law, Ballinger saw even greater gaps in the legislative definition of government authority in this area of natural resources. But these were bloodless arguments compared to the emotionalism of the progressives, particularly a field man for the Forest Service, Louis R. Glavis, who found records of Ballinger's tenure as Land Office Commissioner which, to the Roosevelt conservationist, suggested the new Secretary had condoned coal-land claims in Alaska which were possibly fraudulent.[7]

A quirk of fate in the special Congressional investigation of the Ballinger matter brought together three men who would be subsequent colleagues on the Supreme Court a decade later. Senator George Sutherland was one of the majority of conservative Republicans who were hand-picked for the investigating committee; Louis D. Brandeis, the humane and liberal Boston attorney, was selected as special counsel for the complaining witnesses Glavis and Pinchot. And William Howard Taft, destined for disaster as a result of the whole Ballinger affair, would figure embarrassingly in the denouement of the investigation.[8]

From late January until the middle of May, the hearings presented a spectacle of conservative obstructionism and Brandeisian persistence that left the administration thoroughly shaken. Brandeis introduced evidence tending to suggest that Glavis had been dismissed for wrongdoing based upon a finding which was after the fact. When the record of the finding was requested of Attorney General Wickersham, he replied that it had been lost from the files. Witnesses also lost their memories when Brandeis confronted them on the stand, and Ballinger himself presented a spectacle of uncertainty when the attorney examined him.

After weeks of frenetic argument between complainants' counsel and the Republican majority on the committee, a sensation broke on May 14 when F. M. Kerby, a stenographer in the Department of the Interior, gave a story to the newspapers describing how he had helped prepare a letter dictated by Assistant Attorney General Oscar W. Lawler, for Taft's signature, extolling Ballinger's virtues and in the process exonerating him in the Glavis charges. By singular coincidence, Wickersham found the Lawler "memorandum" on the same day and forwarded it to the investigating committee with a statement that it had been prepared by Lawler, left at Taft's summer home in Massachusetts and returned to Wickersham in New York "about a week later." To round out the incredible trilogy of public utterances on this day, the White House released a statement that the President had dictated the statement "personally as the result of his own in vestigation."[9]

The sensational ultimate question—who or how many might be lying among the highest government officials whose names had been brought into the record—was summarily disallowed by the committee. "We are not here to investigate the President of the United States!" Senator Elihu Root shouted with passion, and Sutherland added with equal fury: "To inquire into this is an insult to the President, and I, for one, do not propose to be a party to it." Brandeis had succeeded in forcing the entire conservative establishment to condemn itself.[10]

Glavis' dismissal, Pinchot's vehement attack on Ballinger's general policies, the outraged accusations of the conservationists that the Western mining and timber interests had captured the Interior Department, the sensational editorial treatment of the issue in *Collier's Weekly,* and the Congressional investigation which exonerated the Secretary—these events, from the fall of Taft's first year in office until the middle of 1910, stamped indelibly upon the public mind the picture of an administration bent on nullifying the reform advances under Roosevelt. Inexorably, the shifting weight of politics began to bear down upon the Republicans; in the elections of 1910, the Democrats captured twenty-six governorships, the control of the House of Representatives and, through a coalition with the Insurgent Republicans, the effective control of the Senate as well.[11]

*   *   *

In the fall of 1909, as the Pinchot-Ballinger issue was beginning to assume its lurid proportions, Archie Butt wrote to his sister-in-law: "So much in the President's character can be explained by his complacency. He believes that many things left to themselves will bring about the same result as if he took a hand himself in their settlement." Still, Taft only compounded the troubles for himself growing out of the Ballinger case when he was compelled to review the issues. A lawyer with a lawyer's ingrained insistence upon circumspect procedure, Taft could wholeheartedly respond to Ballinger's marshalled evidence of the general absence of authorization for many of the procedures carried out in the conservation programs under his predecessor. Taft's course of action thereupon was obvious; he set to work, through the lawyers in Interior, to draft legislation to continue, on a legitimate statutory foundation, the program which Roosevelt had pursued under his personal theory of Presidential stewardship.

In this, Taft undertook to act in a fiduciary capacity for the Roosevelt conservation program; he ordered a large number of water-power sites returned to the public domain for private entry because he found no authority under existing law to have removed them in the first place. Both Garfield and the Bureau of Forestry, the President declared, had "gone far beyond legal limitations" in these removals. But, accepting the proposition that it was a responsibility of government to preserve as much as possible of its natural resources, Taft urged Congress to provide the proper legal authority. It had, in fact, been a reactionary Republican group in Congress which had denied to Roosevelt the power to remove lands from entry by executive order; once Taft had prevailed upon Congress to rescind the restriction, he proceeded to remove from private entry more land than Roosevelt had done even in defiance of the restriction.[12]

Again, when Ballinger at length resigned from the Secretaryship of the Interior, Taft demonstrated his support of the conservation program by appointing as his successor an even more ardent conservationist, Walter Fisher. In spite of all of this, however, as so often in his administration, there seemed to be a continuing conspiracy of circumstances to make the President's actions seem hostile to the Progressive Movement generally. The dénouement of the Ballinger-Pinchot affair was the necessity of removing Pinchot himself for a public admission of insubordination; the Forester invited the dismissal, but the result was a cacophony of recrimination directed at Taft.[13]

*   *   *

Toward the end of the Ballinger crisis, Butt again wrote his sister-in-law that Taft "expected all sorts of troubles to come up in his administration, but I think he had hoped to be spared this one." By now, the public furore over the conservation question, culminating in the dismissal of Pinchot, was phrased repeatedly in terms of a break between Taft and Roosevelt. The Presidential statement of the case against Pinchot was judicious in its balance, and Butt expressed the plaintive hope that Roosevelt "will not be led into taking any side until he himself has looked into the matter." As for Taft, he wrote, "I know how sick at soul he is."[14]

It was a cruel turn of fate for a man who had consented with genuine reluctance to be drafted for the job he now had to fill. In principle, although his own sympathies generally lay with the old order of things, Taft conceded that his consent to the draft implied his commitment to the policies of his sponsor. Taft's tragedy as Chief Executive lay in the very meticulousness with which he sought to meet this commitment. Where Roosevelt had led a series of charges against a host of social and economic ills, Taft undertook to lay a legislative basis, after the fact, to support the charges. Taft's contribution was to be a statutory validation of the Square Deal, enacting the measures for which Roosevelt had never been content to wait—or able to get Congress to adopt. Yet, for the more zealous reformers chafing to experience the thrill of new San Juan Hills, Taft's approach from the outset appeared to be retrogressive where it was intended to be retroactive.

*   *   *

Judicial reform was another dogma of the Progressive Movement, and to this Taft could respond with wholehearted sympathy. Again, however, in the carrying out of the reform he was destined to be castigated as a reactionary, for what Taft saw as the greatest need was procedural reform, while the liberals thought in terms of a revision of the substantive law and its interpretation. Nevertheless, Taft's program for modernizing the Federal judiciary was a farsighted one, and in its ultimate dimensions—some attained in his Presidency and others during his Chief Justiceship—it provided a far more efficient medium for the administration of justice irrespective of the philosophies of the judges. In its simplification of procedure, expedition of trials and appeals and consequent reduction of the expense of litigation, it materially contributed to the Progressive Movement's objectives of aiding the little man in society.[15]

Until Fuller's Chief Justiceship, the structure of the Federal judiciary had remained virtually unchanged since the Judiciary Act of 1789, which had defined the jurisdiction of the Supreme Court and created two types of trial agencies—District Courts, whose jurisdiction was limited primarily to admiralty and criminal cases, and Circuit Courts, with general jurisdiction in most other areas of Federal law.* Except for the establishment of a specialized Court of Claims in 1866, this system of two kinds of trial courts and a single appellate tribunal, the Supreme Court, had continued without taking into account the growth of both the country and the volume of justiciable issues. In 1891 an intermediate appellate system was established by the Circuit Courts of Appeals Act; most cases from the Federal trial courts were made reviewable in these new tribunals, with limited rights of appeal from them to the Supreme Court. With the revival of anti-trust litigation under Roosevelt, an Expediting Act was passed in 1903, requiring Federal courts to give precedence to any suits arising out of injunctions issued in anti-trust actions and providing for direct appeal to the Supreme Court.[16]

Congress during Taft's administration, and with the President's unreserved support, moved to legislate other procedural reforms. On the eve of his inauguration—March 3, 1909—the first of a series of statutes had been adopted. This was the Federal Criminal Code, prepared by the Department of Justice but wholeheartedly supported by Taft as a member of the Roosevelt Cabinet. The following year the Expediting Act was amended to provide for the convening of three-judge courts in any cases where the Attorney General certified the public importance of the cause in litigation; appeals from these tribunals also lay direct to the Supreme Court.[17]

But the Judicial Code of 1911 was the climax to this period of statutory

---

*Cf. Appendix C.

modernization of the judiciary. It disposed of the overlapping system of trial courts dating from 1789 by vesting general trial jurisdiction in the District Courts and abolishing the old Circuit Courts (often confused by laymen with the Circuit Courts of Appeals); it broadened the final appellate jurisdiction of the intermediate courts, erased a long list of obsolete procedural requirements, and enlarged the removal power by which cases were transferred from state to Federal courts. It fell substantially short of Taft's full program for judicial modernization, which included such advanced ideas as the merging of law and equity, but it encouraged the Supreme Court to take the initiative in supplementing the legislation with a modernization of the equity rules for all Federal tribunals. The reform of equity practice, an admirer wrote to Taft after the 1912 elections, "will mark your administration as distinctively as did the 'Justinian Code' in the first half of the Sixth Century."[18]

Still, these were progressive steps which were too technical for the layman to appreciate, and again it was Taft's fate to suffer a hostile reaction even in this program of judicial modernization. In 1909 he had supported the creation of a Court of Customs Appeals as a means of channeling complex excise litigation into specialized agencies competent to adjudicate the issues. The following year he signed a measure creating a Commerce Court, designed to adjudicate the technical issues arising in rulings of the Interstate Commerce Commission. But in 1913 the outgoing administration would abolish this court, in response to progressives' complaints that it had been intended to thwart the business-regulating activities of the Commission. The short life of the Commerce Court was taken as an added inference of the essential reaction of the Taft judicial reforms; the proper perspective for these reforms would not be attained until he lobbied through the principal complements to it during his Chief Justiceship.[19]

*   *   *

Still more keenly did the President feel the disappointments of his office when, in the summer of 1910, the Chief Justiceship of the United States became vacant upon Fuller's death. The central ambition of Taft's life had been to occupy that position, and in 1905, when it had briefly appeared that Fuller might retire, Roosevelt had given every indication that the position would be given to him. Indeed, Roosevelt had made Taft his first choice on each of the three occasions when an Associate Justiceship became vacant. Each time the offer had been declined—the first two times, apparently, because it was thought that Fuller was about to step down. The third time—after which Moody was appointed—Taft had hesitated; how often, after all, could a man expect to have any seat on the Supreme Court come within his grasp? But by then, 1906, the Presidential boom had already begun, and Taft's ambition gave way to the conflicting ambition of his wife, who wished only to see her husband in the White House.[20]

Now, when at last the Chief Justiceship was open, Taft could only console himself with the realization that a succession of deaths was giving him, as President, an opportunity to revitalize the Court with insightful selections to fill the vacancies. His first appointment had hardly been felicitous: Horace H. Lurton, a judicial craftsman whom Taft had known and admired since the days when both had served on the Federal circuits, was in his sixty-sixth year when he came onto the Court in December 1909, succeeding Justice Peckham. Characterized by the progressives as a reactionary, Lurton made little contribution to the Court's constitutional jurisprudence, serving only five years before his death.

The second appointment had come five months later, following the death of Justice Brewer. All factions generally applauded—Roosevelt followers because it was a progressive advance, Taft supporters because it was an astute political maneuver. Hughes of New York was a man who, like Taft, nourished ambitions for the Chief Justiceship; but, unlike Taft, he also was assailed by the hope that the Presidential lightning might strike. Fate was reserving a unique compensation for these ambitions; Hughes would see the White House slip from his grasp by the narrowest of margins, but he would become the only man to serve two separate terms on the Court (and the second term would, in fact, be in the Chief Justiceship).[21]

The New York governor was a reformer to appeal to the progressives on the strength of his investigations of the gas trust and insurance scandals and the modernized system of administrative regulation which he had introduced as chief executive of the state. For Taft, Hughes was young enough to fit the President's prescription for a successor to Fuller who might be able to "revise the entire procedure of this country and put it more in line with that of Great Britain," whose judicial system Taft greatly admired. But there were several reasons—among them, apparently, the fact that the Chief Justiceship opened so soon after Hughes' appointment—why the President decided against advancing him. Hughes was confirmed as Associate Justice on May 2, 1910; Fuller died on July 4, and Hughes met with his brethren on the bench for the first time in October. When he had offered the Associate Justiceship to Hughes in April, Taft had hinted at the possibility of succeeding Fuller, but in the same letter, anxious to avoid the appearance of committing himself, he had added a postscript warning that "conditions change, so that it would not be right for me to say by way of promise what I would do in the future."[22]

*   *   *

What conditions changed, in the four and a half months following Fuller's death, was a complex question. Taft received abundant advice, both solicited and unsolicited. William J. Hendrick, former attorney general of Kentucky, wrote two days after the Chief Justiceship became vacant expressing the hope that the President would choose forward-looking men for this and other prospective vacancies; "it is important," Hendrick declared, "that they should come to that great Court without the seal of Rockefeller and Company upon them." Lyman Abbott, editor-in-chief of *The Outlook* (for which Roosevelt was a contributing editor), also perceived that the Court "will be practically new when you are through with your appointments," and endorsed Hughes for the Chief Justiceship. He had "great executive power and . . . a dominating personality" and thus would be a good prospect to unify the new bench. Even Justice Harlan had a recommendation in the wake of Fuller's demise: William R. Day, Roosevelt's second appointee, he suggested, was "a first-class lawyer—sagacious, cautious, as firm as a rock, and eminently wise in consultation. And what has become a necessary qualification in a Chief Justice," Harlan added, shrewdly divining Taft's prescription for the office, Day "has a fine executive power and is a 'man of affairs.' "[23]

It gradually became known that Taft contemplated breaking with tradition and promoting someone among the incumbents on the Court, an insider who would be familiar with the administrative problems of that tribunal and able to act, as his title suggested, as the chief judicial officer of the whole Federal court system. The statutory reforms on the judiciary to date represented an important advance, but in Taft's view Congress still had much to do in this area, and the Chief Justice seemed to him the logical person to make the case to the legislators.[24] The aim to find a seasoned jurist for the Chief Justiceship militated against Hughes' candidacy. There was also the fact that Roosevelt, who had not been enthusiastic about the New Yorker's sharing the spotlight of reform in the heyday of the Square Deal, might be mollified if Hughes were not advanced. For those who, in late 1910, were seeking to patch up the relations between the present and past occupants of the White House, the naming of Hughes would "add perplexity to a situation which is now working out for the best."[25]

The delay in filling the position was becoming a source of embarrassment. Another vacancy had developed in late November when Justice Moody, Roosevelt's third appointee whose deteriorating health frustrated the prospect of a long judicial tenure, took advantage of a special act of Congress and retired.[26] In his place Taft soon nominated Willis Van Devanter, chief justice of Wyoming and a man whom as President then, and as Chief Justice later, he always regarded as a particularly incisive thinker and sound lawyer.[27] Feeling the need to settle the matter of Fuller's successor—indeed, he would submit the nomination with that of Van Devanter—Taft now sent Attorney General Wickersham to sound out the various Justices as to their own preferences.

Hughes, according to the Attorney General's interviews, was welcomed as a colleague but not supported by his brethren for the Chief Justiceship because of his lack of judicial experience. Still, three of the Justices—Day, Holmes and Lurton—told Wickersham that they assumed the President had already decided on Hughes. Harlan, apparently reconsidering his July recommendation, suggested to the interviewer that he would support Hughes if the President would first appoint the aging Kentuckian "as a final ornament to his judicial career," a suggestion that Taft impatiently rejected. Discounting these elements in the canvass, the first choice of the majority of Justices, according to Wickersham, was Edward D. White. Since this was reported to be Roosevelt's preference, and appeared to fill the President's own requirements, the decision at last was reached.[28]

The White appointment had numerous political advantages; he was a Democrat, a Confederate veteran, and a Roman Catholic. Having first come to the Court in 1894, he possessed the wealth of experience that Taft was seeking as a means of furthering the statutory reform of the Federal judicial system. A moderate who had frequently paired with Harlan in dissent and occasionally in a majority supporting progressive legislation, he was generally acceptable to the liberals. While his writing left much to be desired, Holmes observed to Pollock, "his thinking is sound, especially in the legislative direction which we don't recognize as a judicial requirement but which is so, especially in our Court, nevertheless."[29]

By elevating a member of the bench to the Chief Justiceship, Taft in effect gave himself an extra choice in the matter of vacancies on the Court. Now, to fill the vacancy in the ninth seat remaining from Fuller's death, he nominated Joseph R. Lamar of the Georgia supreme court, a man reported to him to have "no entanglements or extreme tendencies of thought."[30] In the twenty-one months since he had taken office, Taft had now had the opportunity to place four men of his choice upon the Court and to seek out a Chief Justice who, he expected, could expedite judicial matters and continue understandingly the campaign for modernization. Before his Presidency was over, Taft would have the chance to make a fifth appointment, when he chose New Jersey Justice Mahlon Pitney to succeed Harlan.[31]

How successful Taft had been in his selections was less evident as time went by. Administratively, White was a disappointment; he definitely did not share the President's view that members of the Court should approach Congress on the matter of judicial reform, and the discursive character of his opinions, which became more pronounced as years went on, made painfully clear his native inability to organize and trim. Yet, among the new members, at least two—Hughes and Van Devanter—were considered to be exceptionally keen thinkers. In the case of the latter, the accuracy of the description depended upon the viewpoint of the observer. An articulate analyst of the issues in a case under discussion, Van Devanter pleased both Hughes and, later, Taft with his manner of guiding his Associates to salient points in the course of the regular weekly conferences of the Court. But his almost total inability to commit his thoughts to writing seriously impeded the work of the Court, and the habit approached a neurosis as the years passed. Van Devanter was instinctively a politician—his dabbling in Wyoming party affairs continued long after he came onto the bench—and his equal instinct in favor of vested rights was to make him, in a brief time, a doctrinaire foe of reform and an outspoken opponent of the New Freedom and later of the New Deal.[32]

How "new" the new Taft Court was, therefore, could not be determined from the background or subsequent performance of its added members. Lamar, who coveted the appointment and was considered to have won it as a recognition of the established conservatism of the South, was to contribute only one significant constitutional opinion in his six years on the bench, and this was an invalidation of a labor union boycott. In general, during White's Chief Justiceship, there would be relatively little to distinguish the jurisprudence of his Court from the majority position of the immediate past.

*   *   *

If the Court changed little in philosophy, the Constitution itself was to undergo a swift series of changes through amendment in this decade. Half a century had elapsed since any alteration in the document had been seriously considered, although scores of ephemeral proposals regularly could be expected in any session of Congress.* For nearly fifteen years, since the Income Tax Case of 1895, a steady stream of proposals to override the *Pollock* decision had been introduced into Congress; but these and other recurrent subjects, seldom reappearing after being referred to Congressional committees, were primarily significant for what they revealed about constituents' sentiments. Amendments to repeal earlier Amendments, particularly the Fourteenth after it became a base for an increasing amount of adjudication, were regularly advanced by reform groups.

In the first years of the Square Deal, a flurry of anti-trust proposals appeared, giving way shortly thereafter to suggested amendments providing for the popular election of Federal judges and, joined with that, the popular election of the President. The greatest number of proposals, in each new Congress from 1901 to 1913, dealt with the popular election of Senators. Woman suffrage and prohibition enjoyed a certain small but consistent support throughout this period, although a larger number of proposals dealt with a related social subject, the threatened dissolution of the patriarchal family system in the face of new economic relations of the individual, taking the form of amendments to frame varying constitutional statements on divorce, marriage, and child welfare.[33]

Outside of the government, political and legal philosophers of the time raised the question of what subjects were permissible for consideration as amendments—what were, in other words, the implied limitations upon the amending power itself. George Ticknor Curtis, brother of a Supreme Court Justice and a son-in-law of Joseph Story, who had culminated a brilliant career at the bar of the Court with a definitive constitutional history of the United States, warned that the answer to the question was of fundamental importance to the new century about to begin. An old-line Federalist, Curtis concluded that the Ninth and Tenth Amendments, asserting the permanent division of powers between the nation and the states, were a gloss upon the Fifth Article of the Constitution and beyond the reach of the amending

---

*Cf. Appendix B.

power. In truth, the Fifth Article itself contained only one extant limitation upon that power: "that no State, without its Consent, shall be deprived of its equal suffrage in the Senate."[34]

In part, the theoretical dialogue was a revival of the Federalist-v.-state sovereignty debates of the early years of the Constitution. The question of whether the Federal government and the Constitution were creations of the states had fallen into abeyance in the interim, or rather had been answered by the movement of history itself. The Civil War, confirming the fact that the Union was indissoluble, and the declaration in the opening section of the postwar Fourteenth Amendment that all persons "born or naturalized in the United States, and subject to the jurisdiction thereof, are citizens of the United States and of the States wherein they reside," had provided a new focus for constitutional theory. It had tended greatly to amplify Chief Justice Marshall's earlier assertion that the Constitution had been the creation of the people rather than of the states, and that the Constitution itself was the best evidence of the existence of a people of the United States as distinguished in their interests, rights and immunities from the people of the states, or the states themselves.[35]

Another dimension in the discussion was provided by the veneration in which the Constitution had come to be held by the population at large. Inchoate though the idea was, the passing generations had evolved an ethical standard of constitutional limitation upon the powers of government independent of the specific provisions in the document; as William E. Seward, Lincoln's Secretary of State, put it, there was "a higher law . . . which regulates our authority." *Laissez-faire* scholars like Cooley, Dillon and Tiedemann proceeded from there to assert limitations upon the powers of the people to alter the economic system as well.

The nature of the fifteen Amendments which had been adopted within the first century of the Constitution might have provided an answer to the philosophical questions now being raised: the first eight had been specific restraints upon the Federal government with reference to certain enumerated privileges and immunities of the people; the next three had asserted restraints upon the Federal government with reference to the rights of the states; the Twelfth was a reform of the electoral machinery originally established in Article Two; while the Civil War and Reconstruction Amendments had been an amalgam of individual privileges and immunities and of restraints upon the states in the Federal system. By 1870, then, when the Fifteenth Amendment had been ratified, the amending process had been employed for almost every kind of change which could be conceived.[36]

*   *   *

As for the immediate question of an income tax amendment, the only hesitation among the reformers concerning its endorsement was prompted by the evidence that the Court itself, in the decade since the *Pollock* decision, had been moving steadily away from the position it had taken in that case. A tax on the sales income represented in business exchanges had been held valid in 1899; inheritance and succession levies had generally been upheld the following year; and in 1902 and 1904 other taxes on business franchises, closely analogous to a tax on income, had all been affirmed.[37] There was, accordingly, a substantial sentiment for simply reenacting an income tax law in Congress—in effect, inviting the Supreme Court to reverse the *Pollock* case.

To a legal purist like Taft, such a maneuver, even if successful, appeared to be a gratuitous weakening of public confidence in the Court itself; this confidence, to men of his turn of mind, rested upon the assumption of absolute values rather than relative ones. Elihu Root described the tactic as a step toward inevitable conflict: if the Court should yield to popular demand reflected in a Congressional reenactment of a tax once declared invalid, what opinion would the people hold of the capacity of the bench for objective justice? Or if the Court refused to yield, would this not set the popular branches of government against the idea of an independent judiciary?[38]

Taft himself, while still a member of Roosevelt's Cabinet, had expressed approval of the principle of a general income tax, but his orderly mind perceived that a constitutional amendment was the desired solution to the problem of the *Pollock* rule. The opposition of the conservatives within his own party had deterred him from any action at the beginning of his term; rather, he waited until the conservatives themselves were maneuvered into a position where they could not oppose it. The opportunity came in the clash over the tariff bill which was to become the Payne-Aldrich Act—a bit of legislation which was used by the Roosevelt wing of the party to document Taft's capitulation to the Old Guard but which, in any case, provided him with the lever he sought to advance the cause of the constitutional amendment.

The insurgent Republican revolt against the conservative domination led to an effort to hamstring the tariff bill by proposing an amendment establishing a general tax on income as a part of the bill. Aldrich and his cohorts turned to the President, as party leader, to seek to drive the insurgents off; and he offered to do so on two conditions: the Aldrich forces would accept a bill drafted by the Attorney General, placing an excise tax on the privilege of doing business as a corporation and measuring the tax by the income of the corporation; and the President would support the alternative proposal of the insurgents and the Democrats for an income tax amendment.[39]

Taft, whose fate it seemed to be to appear as the villain of the reform era, thus got the Sixteenth Amendment on the way to ratification; but his accomplishment was lost in the outraged oratory of the insurgents at his support of the strongly protectionist tariff law, while the Amendment, not being ratified until the last month of his administration, was identified in the popular mind with the flurry of progressive legislation which heralded Wilson's New Freedom.

The substantial nature of Taft's victory on the tax question was demonstrated by the action of the Supreme Court itself when the corporation excise tax came under the concerted attack of fifteen different groups of litigants seeking a reaffirmation of the *Pollock* doctrine. In March 1910 when the appeals were first argued before the Supreme Court, six states had ratified the Income Tax Amendment; in January 1911 on reargument before a full Court, nine had done so. However, by that time two states had specifically rejected the Amendment and three others had passed the opportunity to consider it. To those who clung to the hope that the *laissez-faire* position of the mid-nineties could be preserved in the face of threatened reform, it was reasonable to argue that the struggle to secure the necessary thirty-six ratifications might be defeated, and in such case it was of primary importance to destroy the constitutional claims of the Amendment's forerunner, the corporation excise tax.[40]

(Perhaps spurred on by the trial of the issue in the Court, with the co-incidental meeting of a number of state legislatures and ratifying conventions in the sixty days between reargument and decision, seventeen more ratifications were obtained. It is reasonable to surmise that the Court, if not following the election returns, at least discerned the handwriting on the wall.)

The procedure in challenging the tax closely followed the strategy of the *Pollock* case: In Vermont, a guardian for a minor sought an injunction in the Federal court for that district to restrain the directors of the family corporation from complying with the Federal tax law; upon demurrer and dismissal of the petition, an appeal was taken to the Supreme Court. In fourteen similar suits from Illinois, Massachusetts, Minnesota, New York and Ohio, appeals were joined with that from Vermont, and argued by a phalanx of attorneys fully as distinguished as and numerically larger than those who had come together in the cause of Pollock and others in 1895. Among those arguing before the Court or filing briefs against the tax were the attorney general of Vermont, John G. Sargent; ex-Senator Foraker, who had lost his bid for a third term in 1908 when his fellow Ohioan had been sent to the White House; and William D. Guthrie, one of the original counsels in the 1895 Income Tax Case. Altogether, eleven oral arguments were made in the two days in 1910 and the three in 1911 when the case was heard.[41]

The arguments covered all conceivable challenges to the government's authority. Aside from the reiterated charges that the tax was an income tax in disguise, it was contended that the power to tax a corporation rested with the state that created it, that the tax was arbitrary and unequal in its levying and that classification of corporations for the purpose of the tax was a denial of due process, that the income or value of a corporation's property was not an equitable measure of the value of its franchise, that some corporation income was derived from its investments in tax-exempt securities, and so on. The government's position was more succinctly, but equally effectively, argued through its vigorous and highly successful anti-trust lawyer, Solicitor General Lloyd W. Bowers, and supported by a brief prepared by Wickersham; it pointed to the trend of recent cases by which the Court had circumscribed the *Pollock* rule—as well as boldly reciting the rule from earlier decisions which had been considered overruled by *Pollock*.[42]

In the end, the Court had little difficulty making its decision; the unanimous opinion was delivered by Justice Day, affirming the tax as an excise, and hence an excise upon the privilege of the corporation franchise unaffected by the fact that some of the corporation income by which the tax was measured might be derived from sources exempt from income tax. Nor did the tax interfere substantially with the essential functions of the states by levying upon the instrumentalities of business chartered by them. Justice Harlan, the sole survivor and conspicuous dissenter of the 1895 case, could only have heard with gratification Day's observation that "the right to select the measure and objects of taxation devolves upon Congress, and not upon the courts, and such selections are valid unless constitutional limitations are overstepped."[43] After this opinion, the decline of *Pollock* was steady; it only remained for the Sixteenth Amendment, when it was ratified, to apply the *coup de grace*.

*   *   *

Two months after the corporation tax case, the Court handed down its decision in the long-drawn-out suit to secure the dissolution of the Standard Oil trust. The first attack, by Roosevelt's administration, had been directed against the Standard of Indiana and had failed in the Circuit Court of Appeals with the dismissal of the spectacular $29,000,000 fine assessed by the trial court. The renewed attack, directed against the parent corporation in New Jersey, was to be substantially more successful, and it was carried to success by the less spectacular methods which Taft preferred to the trust-busting fanfare of his predecessor. After the government victory in the lower court in 1909, Taft wired congratulations to the special prosecutor, Frank B. Kellogg, for the "thorough preparation and presentation, on your part, of the government's case."[44]

The intricate structure which had been developed by John D. Rockefeller and his associates over the years since the early eighties now included nine separate (but closely controlled) Standard Oil companies and some sixty-two related corporations in various parts of the industry. This concentration of power in the oil trust, as Taft later wrote, had been a prime factor in the devising of the original Sherman Act, and in the following generation Standard Oil and Rockefeller came to be treated, jointly and separately, as synonyms for the trust problem and the abuses of business combinations in general.

The proliferating system of control in the oil industry in the decade since the Sherman Act had been carefully documented by Kellogg in preparing his case, while a journalistic indictment of the Rockefeller empire had already been returned. Miss Tarbell's muckraking history, the product of five years of investigation, appeared first as a series of articles in *Mc-Clure's* in 1902 and 1903. Before and following this work, Economist Richard T. Ely's *Monopolies and Trusts,* published in 1900, and John Moody's *The Truth About the Trusts,* published in 1904, drew largely from statistics on Standard Oil to underline their case for more vigorous prosecution of government surveillance.[45]

Rockefeller, who always considered the business combination less as a monopoly than as a coordinated program of "men who had the combined brainpower to do the work," professed to be at a loss at the pervasiveness of the hostility directed at him. His habitual refusal to make public replies to the attacks magnified his troubles; as a matter of fact, he had divested himself of all but a nominal association with Standard Oil by 1897—a fact that Miss Tarbell's generally accurate though critical history failed to make sufficiently clear to the large readership of her book.

In this charged atmosphere, the new career in philanthropy to which Rockefeller was turning his attention was, for another decade, to be castigated by the public as "tainted money"—the phrase coined by Washington Gladden in 1905 in protesting a Rockefeller gift of $100,000 to the Congregational Board of Foreign Missions. Although, by the time of the government prosecutions, Rockefeller had come to accept the repeated advice of his associates to seek to create a new public image, several of his philanthropies were undertaken or proposed in extremely awkward juxtaposition to the anti-trust cases against Standard Oil. A $32,000,000 gift was announced just prior to the sensational Landis fine in 1907; even worse in timing from a publicity standpoint was Rockefeller's effort to secure a private bill from Congress incorporating under a national charter the major philanthropy which several years later was successfully established under New York law as the Rockefeller Foundation. Within the week, Standard Oil attorneys filed their briefs on the appeal from the Kellogg prosecution in the Supreme Court.

Attorney General Wickersham urged the President to use his influence in Congress to have the bill withdrawn; "the vast wealth of Mr. Rockefeller was achieved largely by methods which the law has denounced," Wickersham wrote, and with the anti-trust case against Standard Oil now entering its final stages, the government and the American public would, in his view, be placed in a highly compromising position if "the Congress of the United States should assist in the enactment of a law to create and perpetuate in his name an institution" to carry out activities financed by funds originally acquired through the organization of the oil trust. The bill was thereupon withdrawn.[46]

*   *   *

For Chief Justice White, who read the eight-to-one majority opinion in the case in May of 1911, this was not only the first major public law decision to come before his Court, but it presented also the opportunity for which he had been waiting since 1897 to make a judicial critique of the Sherman Act's indiscriminate prohibition of all combinations affecting the flow of trade. That the statute tended to force the Court into a position of judging only the fact of combination, and not the "goodness" or "badness" of the combination, was a fundamental weakness that had been conceded by Roosevelt and Taft alike, while for the political reformers it had presented the problem of bringing labor combinations under the same restraints as business combinations. What was needed, as White developed it in the course of his 20,000-word opinion, was a "rule of reason" by which the beneficial or deleterious effects of economic combinations could be assessed.

The over-inclusive language of the Sherman Act, White observed, if taken literally would be a denial of justice by leaving the courts no authority for considering a specific case on the merits; it put the legislature in the position of "assuming the matter to be decided." But the truth was that "judgment must in every case be called into play" to determine whether the acts in question amounted to a restraint of trade "within the intendment" of the statute. To argue to the contrary, the Chief Justice declared, would be to hold that the law could not be enforced because of its uncertainty. If, however, the intention of the law was to proscribe "undue restraints" of trade and commerce, that left a "rule of reason" as the only practical means of testing the acts of parties charged with violation of the law.[47]

Applying these criteria to the case before it, the Court found Standard Oil generally guilty of violation of the Sherman Act: "The exercise of the power which resulted from that organization fortifies the . . . conclusions," said White; the result of its expansion which was manifestly to extinguish the means by which competition could be maintained, and the splitting up of the national market into districts where the expansion could be intensively developed, "all lead the mind up to a conviction of a purpose and intent which we think is so certain as practically to cause the subject not to be within the domain of reasonable contention."

Having thus devised and then applied his "rule of reason," White turned to the practical problem of dissolving a trust which had become so thoroughly rooted in American economic life. He felt it imperative that the lower court decree be modified, "in view of the magnitude of the interests involved, and their complexity," by extending the deadline for the dissolution from thirty days to six months, and by rescinding the injunction which would have prevented any Standard Oil concerns from engaging in interstate commerce until the dissolution was completed, since this would have resulted in a serious injury to the consuming public denied access to these products.[48]

The practical necessity of exercising restraint in applying the decree was an eloquent testimony to the intricate effect of such a business combination upon the national life. Even more than White's "rule of reason," the economic facts pointed to the necessity of revising and improving the effectiveness of the Sherman Act. As for the rule itself, Harlan's dissent was a vigorous condemnation of it; while he agreed that Standard Oil was guilty of violation of the law, the majority opinion put "words into the anti-trust act which Congress did not put there." In a mannerism which had become familiar to his colleagues and Court spectators over the years, the now aging Kentuckian pounded the bench and warned that the "rule," which purported to distinguish "good" combinations from "bad," would in practice be a loophole by which many a trust could escape liability altogether.[49]

White had occasion to defend his rule against Harlan's criticism two weeks later, when the Court disposed of the second of the major anti-trust cases begun in the Roosevelt administration and painstakingly carried to final adjudication by the Taft administration. The American Tobacco Company and twenty-eight other companies had been ordered by the Federal trial court to dissolve their interlocking relationships, and an appeal was carried to the Supreme Court to test the order. The crux of the government's complaint in this case was essentially a product-control practice which was tacitly effected by some companies and formally implemented in writing by others, with an attendant combination of certain marketing activities.

The government argument also invited an extension of the White doctrine, corroborating a memorandum which Wickersham sent to Taft in the fall of 1911: "We have gone on for twenty odd years," he observed, "in the face of the Sherman law, to be sure, but nevertheless with the current of a real economic tendency towards cooperation and consolidation, until we have brought about a condition of industrial and business organization which must be disentangled, or the life of the Republic is in danger of being throttled." The problem, Wickersham warned, was that the network had to be "disentangled intelligently and with careful regard to the common wealth," lest the whole system of modern capitalism be destroyed.[50]

Where the universal control of the oil industry in the Standard Oil Case was discerned by the Court as a prospect which rendered the restraint of trade "unreasonable," the elements in the Tobacco Trust Case were a mixture of "unreasonable" and "reasonable." Moreover, in White's view, to order a dissolution of the trust would not reach the evil that the anti-trust law sought to remedy, since it would leave unaffected many practices which had essentially become trade customs observed by businesses outside the trust. The "reasonable" approach to the problem, he concluded, was in effect to decree a reorganization of the combination rather than its complete dissolution.[51]

Harlan concurred in part, and contented himself with a reiteration that the "rule of reason" amounted to "judicial legislation." This, in the earlier stages of the two anti-trust suits, had been Taft's view as well, but the President now chose to applaud the doctrine as a proper means of making the Sherman Act itself more effective. To a certain degree, he was being carried

along by the force of events; Wickersham had opened the second half of
Taft's term with a succession of prosecutions of a wide variety of monopolies.

The return to the competitive system of classical capitalism, however,
was not easy, as the decrees in both the Standard Oil and Tobacco Trust
litigation had demonstrated. The complexities of twentieth-century economics made a certain degree of industrial consolidation inevitable as well
as desirable. The White Court undertook by judicial interpretation to make
the Sherman Act less rigid and more conformable with the realities of the
new economics. The Department of Justice, under Wickersham, sought a
new legal regime through the encouragement of consent decrees, under
which the prosecuted firms negotiated with the government for a reorganization of their structures in line with the Tobacco Trust ruling, after which a
formal judgment confirming the negotiation would be entered.[52]

*   *   *

The ultimate objective, however, was legislative reform, which Roosevelt
and Taft had both envisioned as a national incorporation statute. This had
been one of the key recommendations in the final report of the Industrial
Commission in 1902, following its exhaustive study of the evolution of the
industrial system at the turn of the century. While Wickersham drafted a
bill providing for Federal chartering of firms in interstate commerce at the
start of the Taft administration, the measure never received any enthusiastic
response in Congress. Alternative legislation creating a new Commerce Court
—to hear railroad cases appealed from decisions of the Interstate Commerce
Commission—visited another political debacle on the President as his administration entered its last strife-torn stages: critics of the Court at its inception
had predicted that it would be a device for thwarting Commission regulations,
and when a substantial number of the Court's rulings tended to reverse
the Commission, popular outcry led to Congressional abolition of the specialized tribunal in the last days of the Taft administration.

As the President considered his position in 1912, he had good reason
to wonder why he had fallen to such low political estate. In terms of effective
legislation, as well as in terms of the volume and results of his administration's anti-trust efforts, he had substantially more to show as solid accomplishments than Roosevelt had achieved in almost twice the length of time.
The prolonged struggle to offset the effect of the Income Tax Case of 1895
had been relatively successful in the courts while an unequivocal constitutional amendment was well on its way to adoption. The country had grown
in a variety of respects, and the fears aroused by the panic of 1907 had been
generally laid to rest. Even in terms of personal appeal, his friends asked
themselves why Taft was unable to attract a popular response; while he
lacked the dash and color of the Rough Rider, his very size and characteristic rumbling chuckle should have borne out the aphorism that the world
loves a fat man.

But Taft, in the final analysis, was simply out of his element in the Presidency, insofar as this position called for political adroitness, an appeal to popular imagination, and a vociferous recital of the aims and accomplishments of his leadership. The methodical work of his staff and party supporters in Congress, pushing through such legislation as he advanced, was unspectacular and—what was a greater misfortune—was overlooked in the outcry against certain of his actions which seemed to flout the reform movement.

The President's opposition to a limited prohibition law, which he believed was unconstitutional, brought down on him the wrath of the "dry" advocates who were assuming a steadily larger influence in the Progressive Movement. His opposition to the bill proposing the admission of Arizona because its constitution provided for the initiative, referendum and recall of any government official—the epitome of the reforms advocated in this era —confirmed in still more voters' minds the idea that Taft was a reactionary. Most damning of all, of course, was the furore that had been precipitated by the Ballinger-Pinchot episode, which was readily translatable in the popular mind into a calculated plan to sabotage the Roosevelt conservation program. Finally, for all and sundry who suspected the Republican party of being the hired agent of the moneyed classes, the Payne-Aldrich tariff was cited as the ultimate betrayal. Pledged in 1908 to reform the tariff, the Eastern Republicans in Congress had revised it upward—and Taft had borne the blame.

The Taft administration was thus to be characterized—in large measure unjustly—as an interval in the Progressive Movement which had gained such momentum under the Square Deal. It was foredoomed to defeat, largely by the insistent revival of the reform slogans on which the Democrats were now capitalizing, partly by the decision of Roosevelt to contest the nomination in the Republican primary elections, and substantially by the lukewarm regard of the conservatives in Taft's own party. Taft had been intelligent enough to perceive that reform of the industrial system through increasing government surveillance was the cardinal necessity of the time, and he had had the moral courage to act contrary to his own preferences for the world as it had once been. That world, and particularly that America, was about to undergo an ordeal of change which would move it an eternity away from the age known to Taft and his contemporaries.

9/The Road to Armageddon

I N THE FALL of 1909, as William Howard Taft was embarked upon his term as trustee of the Square Deal, an event occurred which profoundly affected the political philosophy of the ex-President, and focussed the attention of the nation upon the logical consequences of the Progressive Movement itself. This was the publication of *The Promise of American Life,* by Herbert Croly, a profound albeit turgidly written treatise which Walter Lippmann was to describe four decades later as "the political classic which announced the end of the Age of Innocence with its romantic faith in American destiny and inaugurated the process of self-examination."[1]

The author was the son of highly educated immigrant parents, the father, David, from Ireland and the mother, Jane Cunningham, from England. Both were devotees of August Comte, and introduced the boy early to the positivist philosopher's concept of the solidarity of the interests of humanity. A leisurely education at Harvard in the nineties subjected him to the broadening views alternately presented by William James, by Royce and by Santayana. The following decade as editor of the *Architectural Record* provided him with an essential synthesis of concepts of social reorganization already manifested in the artistic rebellion and the efforts of the new architecture to articulate some of the features of the emerging high-energy technology around it.

"From the beginning Americans have been anticipating and projecting a better future," Croly wrote. "The better future is understood by [them] as something which fulfills itself." But the lesson of the industrial society which had emerged at the end of the nineteenth century, Croly continued, was that this future "will have to be planned and constructed, rather than fulfilled of its own momentum." The accelerating momentum of American life was in itself a promise of a better future, he went on, for when "the great majority of the poor in any country are inert and are laboring without any hope of substantial rewards in this world, the whole associated life of that community rests on an equivocal foundation."[2]

The Constitution, in Croly's historical summary, was "the expression not only of a political faith, but also of political fears. It was wrought both as the organ of the national interest and as the bulwark of certain individual and local rights." The early Federalists, or Hamiltonians, saw it as an instrument to preserve and defend both personal liberty and personal property; the Jeffersonians regarded it as the statement of a sovereignty which represented a potential encroachment upon local democracy.[3]

In the ensuing one hundred and twenty years since the Constitutional Convention, Croly concluded, the settling of a continent and the rise of an industrial economy made necessary a political organization capable of "an increasing amount of centralized action and responsibility . . . precisely because of the growing centralization of American activity." To preserve the Jeffersonian ideal of the greatest degree of equality and opportunity for the individual, the Hamiltonian ideal of a central authority to insure uniform guarantees of the Jeffersonian objectives was essential.[4]

*   *   *

Roosevelt, emerging from his big game hunt in Africa to tour the capitals of Europe, became aware of the Croly treatise in the mail which had accumulated for him at the American embassy in Paris. In April 1910 he wrote Senator Lodge that he had ordered a copy of the book to be sent to him in care of the embassy in London; and thus, as he started home from more than a year abroad, his mind quickening with anticipation of the political issues on the domestic scene with which he would soon be in contact, the thesis in *The Promise of American Life* became particularly absorbing.[5]

He had not been entirely isolated from developments in Washington during his weeks on safari; in the early spring of 1910, on the White Nile, he had received a visit from his ex-Chief Forester, Gifford Pinchot, and had listened to a detailed report, from Pinchot's viewpoint, of the controversy with Ballinger. While Roosevelt admitted to Lodge that under the circumstances he did not see how Taft could have followed "any course save the one he did," he prefaced the comment with a number of expressions of regret.[6]

To the intimations from Lodge and Elihu Root that the Taft administration was in trouble and might need Roosevelt's help in the Congressional campaigns that summer and fall, Roosevelt hinted at his dissatisfaction: "You do not need to be told that Taft was nominated solely on my assurance to the Western people especially, but almost as much to the people of the East, that he would carry on my work unbroken; not (as he has done) merely working for somewhat the same objects in a totally different spirit, and with a totally different result, but exactly along my lines with all his heart and strength."[7]

This characteristically proprietary and paternalistic view of the requisites for legitimacy of the Taft administration was circulated in due course among private and subsequently public circles. Roosevelt's triumphal tour of the continent, after his months in the jungles, with crowned heads gladly receiving him and treating his stay less as a social affair than as an official state occasion, built up a public enthusiasm in the United States which made his return a major event. The incumbent President, yearning for a personal confrontation which he felt might restore the onetime cordiality between them, was persuaded not to go to New York for the homecoming because the acclaim for the man out of office would leave the Chief Executive of the United States in almost total shadow.[8]

The size of the crowds who turned out to greet the returning hero and accompany him to City Hall for the elaborate round of welcomes prompted Henry Watterson of the *Louisville Courier-Journal* to compare it with Napoleon's return from Elba. Speaking from the Southern and Western traditional suspicion of Europe and monarchies, Watterson observed that Roosevelt was coming back "the European nominee for President of the United States," and warned his countrymen "to consider Theodore Roosevelt as they have never considered him before; to take him more seriously than they have ever taken him," since he returned amid the mounting cadence of demand that he run again in 1912. The Jeffersonian in Watterson spoke out as he reminded the American public of the choice that Roosevelt's candidacy would present:

> If the Government of the United States under our written Constitution of checks and balances be a failure—as many think it—and if there be needed for its executive head a strong man having the courage to take all the bulls of corruption by the horns, and, regardless of obsolete legal restraints, to shake the life out of them, then, indeed, Theodore Roosevelt would seem to be fitted by temperament, education and training for the work. He is a patriotic man with humanitarian proclivities. He is an incorruptible man. He has shown himself fearless of the consequences. If the people are sick and tired of the slow processes of constitutional procedure; if they want in the White House a President, who, disregarding the letter of the law, will substitute his own interpretation of its spirit and intention, . . . Theodore Roosevelt fills the bill to perfection, for he comes directly from the family of the Kings of Men and is a lineal descendant of Caesar and Cromwell.[9]

This modern Caesar, as Watterson saw him, crossed his Rubicon on February 9, 1912, when a petition signed by seven Republican governors—Chester H. Aldrich of Nebraska, Robert P. Bass of New Hampshire, J. M. Carey of Wyoming, W. E. Glasscock of West Virginia, Herbert S. Hadley of Missouri, Charles S. Osborne of Michigan, and William R. Stubbs of Kansas—was formally presented to him. The petition declared that "a large majority of the Republican voters of the country favor your nomination, and a large majority of the people favor your election"; it demanded to know whether Roosevelt would accept such nomination. Two weeks later, he replied: yes, he would accept.[10]

*   *   *

"Upon what food doth this our Caesar feed?" Watterson and many other Americans might have asked themselves when, as a preface to his reply to the governors' petition, Roosevelt addressed the Ohio constitutional convention at Columbus on February 21. "I believe in pure democracy," he told the gathering. "With Lincoln, I hold that 'this country, with its institutions, belongs to the people who inhabit it. Whenever they shall grow weary of the existing government, they can exercise their constitutional right of amending it.' "

"I am emphatically a believer in constitutionalism," Roosevelt went on, "and because of this fact I no less emphatically protest against any theory that would make of the Constitution a means of thwarting instead of securing the absolute right of the people to rule themselves and provide for their social and industrial well-being." Such a false interpretation of constitutional power, he declared, occurs whenever the people's representatives, "whether on the bench, in the legislature or in executive office," deny that the government has "the power to right grave social wrongs."

Among the wrongs the Rough Rider discerned was the prominent one of the abuse of capitalism through unfair competition or unfair destruction of competition; yet he had come to the conclusion, he said, that "it is both futile and mischievous to endeavor to correct the evils of big business by an attempt to restore business conditions as they were in the middle of the last century." The approach of modern government, Roosevelt went on, should be to recognize "that modern business conditions have come to stay, in so far at least as these conditions mean that business must be done in larger units," and that regulation rather than abolition should be the means employed to safeguard the public interest.

With increasing boldness, Roosevelt ticked off the other elements of modern constitutionalism—the power in government to control wages, hours and conditions of work, the direct primary, the popular election of Senators, the electoral franchise for women, the initiative and referendum and the recall of all erring public officials whether elected or appointed. Finally, to cap the climax, Roosevelt urged the state constitution makers to consider a proviso for the recall of judicial decisions which the people considered unjust. For, said the ex-President, justice "between man and man, between the state and its citizens, is a living thing whereas legalistic justice is a dead thing."[11]

The die had been cast, and the New Nationalism—in Roosevelt's view, a plan of Hamiltonian centralism to insure the ultimate attainment of Jeffersonian egalitarianism—had been proclaimed. The resulting struggle for delegates, the impassioned primary efforts from coast to coast, the Republican convention itself with the walkout of Roosevelt supporters, the call for a separate Progressive Party to stand at Armageddon and battle for the Lord—one followed the other in a chain reaction.

In the end it was less an Armageddon than a *Götterdämmerung,* with each side foredoomed to defeat. Taft's role, after the steamroller of party regularity provided him with renomination, was nothing more than to keep Roosevelt from winning; while Roosevelt, who was realistic enough to know that the party split had assured the Democrats of victory, saw his role as the opportunity provided by destiny to awaken the country to the understanding that it, too, had long since crossed a Rubicon.

*   *   *

Americans inevitably asked themselves, as the long Republican reign disin-
tegrated, how it had come to pass that the once cordial relations between the
Rough Rider and his hand-picked successor had turned to ice. Part of the
answer was to be found in the Roosevelt personality. He chafed in the wings
whenever anyone else was on stage; he had resented Hughes as governor winning loud plaudits from the reformers in the midst of his own administration;
he would be consumed with frustration when Woodrow Wilson assumed the
leadership of the Progressive Movement in its second period of power. With
Taft, Roosevelt never overcame his disposition to treat him as his vice-regent,
and it was characteristic that he should declare in print, in the spring of 1912,
that Taft had been "disloyal to our past friendship" as well as to "every canon
of ordinary decency."[12]

Men who were intimates of both Presidents—Elihu Root, for one—were
persuaded until the actual break that each would perceive that their differences
were essentially matters of approach and execution rather than of objectives.
"Taft wanted to hear both sides and then reflect. Roosevelt wanted to hear and
then jump," wrote Root in retrospect. Moreover, Root concluded, Roosevelt
in entering the race in 1912 raised issues which had not been publicly advocated
during his Presidency, so that it was not proper to charge Taft retroactively
with failing to continue them. The most sensational of these—reflecting the
Rough Rider's long-standing dislike of judicial conservatism—was his demand
for a legislative power of recall of "erroneous" decisions, and this utterance in
itself would incline a circumspect and conventional lawyer like Root toward a
circumspect and conventional lawyer like Taft. As early as March, 1912 Root
concluded in a letter to United States Ambassador Robert Bacon in Paris that
the chief effect of such statements by Roosevelt was that of "throwing Taft
into high relief in the public mind as the representative of conservative constitutionalism." The result, he was convinced by then, was that neither man
could be elected.[13]

Taft was never able to articulate the accomplishments of his own administration—least of all to his predecessor. The number of big business prosecutions
during his Presidency had actually so alarmed a conservative spokesman like
the *New York Sun* that it declared Taft to be more of a threat to free enterprise than Socialism or anarchy. Yet in the final analysis it was Taft's un-
questioning reverence for the rule of law—of which the Sherman Act was a
fundamental ingredient by now—that made his support of the anti-trust actions so unequivocal. Taft's touchstone was the legality of government regulation; Roosevelt's was the power of government to destroy obstacles to social
progress.[14]

In his current state of mind, the Rough Rider saw enormity in every act
of the occupant of the White House, and in some a deliberate effort to dis-
credit Roosevelt himself. Taft's decision, in the fall of 1911, to authorize the
Department of Justice to proceed with an anti-trust suit against the United
States Steel Corporation was the supreme affront. The prospective action

alarmed the business community as no other anti-trust prosecutions had done; it was hardly arguable that the Standard Oil Trust had tended unreasonably to restrain trade, and in the American Tobacco Company Case the Court with the government's brief paving the way had made the belated distinction between reasonable and unreasonable combinations in industry.[15] But the Steel Corporation, it was generally argued, had brought stability to American heavy industry without centralization of control. While it might be over-extravagant, as one correspondent put it, to find that "it has been the greatest single force in this country since its organization for the steadying of business and the resulting prosperity to the masses," the charge of monopoly was difficult to credit after the government's position in the Tobacco Company Case.[16]

But the explosive feature of the Steel Corporation suit lay in its political rather than its economic implications. A major part of the government's case for a monopoly rested upon the corporation's acquisition in 1907 of the Tennessee Iron & Coal Company—with the explicit approval of then President Roosevelt. As competent a lawyer as Taft, and a Chief Executive chargeable with the knowledge of the argument being prepared by his own Attorney General, could hardly be conceived as missing the clear implication—that Roosevelt had knowingly acquiesced in the violation of the Sherman Act.[17] Taft could not be unaware of his predecessor's role in the Iron & Coal Company purchase; Roosevelt declared, without any denial on Taft's part, that they had discussed it in 1907. In the fall of 1911, they had again communicated concerning it in connection with Roosevelt's plan to testify before a special investigating committee of the House of Representatives. The investigation itself had received such publicity that the action of the Department of Justice would, for that reason if no other, normally come to the President's attention for review.[18]

Roosevelt could only take the action, tied as it was to the Coal & Iron Company purchase as the key to the monopoly charge, as a crude effort to smear him. He struck back through his contributed column in *The Outlook* with a characteristically vigorous defense of his own actions and a ferocious attack upon the government's arguments. The inconsistency of the Steel Corporation suit in the light of the now-established "rule of reason" and the growing acceptance by reformers of the preferability of controlled growth rather than categorically proscribed growth, gave substantial force to Roosevelt's countercharges.[19]

There was no doubt that the Steel Corporation business was handled with singular ineptitude so far as party harmony and public relations in general were concerned. It vastly widened the gulf between the principals, clouded the administration's own anti-trust policy in the light of the Tobacco Company Case, and came to nothing in the end. Ten years after the action was begun, it dragged finally to a dismissal.[20] By then it was merely a *coup de grace* to the whole trust-busting era. Its chief mischief was done in the spring of the crucial electoral year in which Theodore Roosevelt needed no such added goading to bring himself and his onetime protege down in a crashing defeat.

*   *   *

The credo of the New Nationalism—the legacy of Croly's 1909 volume—was boldly expressed at the Bull Moose convention in August of 1912. It was keynoted in the speech of Senator Beveridge of Indiana, one of the earliest prototypes of Republican insurgency and, like Roosevelt, an avid student (as well as maker and writer) of history. Reared in the harsh conditions of rural poverty in the post-Civil War era in Indiana and Illinois, Beveridge had displayed an oratorical brilliance in college that presaged his career in politics—and particularly reform politics where oratory could be its most inspirational. He came to the Senate in 1899, at the age of thirty-six being one of the youngest men in history to attain such a place. The flamboyant appeal of the Square Deal made him an unswerving Roosevelt man, and the Payne-Aldrich tariff "revision upward" in 1909 convinced him that Taft had betrayed progressivism from the outset.

Beveridge and LaFollette indeed spearheaded the revolt within the Republican ranks which made inevitable the secession from the party convention in 1912, and the creation of the new party of the Bull Moose. As the drive for Roosevelt delegates to the Republican convention got under way, the Indiana orator was drafted for impassioned appeals from Massachusetts to California. He went into the third party movement reluctantly; he understood perfectly that it was only an extension of Theodore Roosevelt's immense popularity, magnified by the conflicts of the current year but foredoomed to die with this campaign. But the issue of economic equality and social justice, he also knew, would not die with this campaign, and the way to remind the American people of that fact was through the example of the Progressive Party.[21]

"We stand for a nobler America," Beveridge told the thousands of delegates crowded into the convention at Chicago. "We stand for a broader liberty, a fuller justice. We stand for social brotherhood as against savage individualism. We stand for an intelligent cooperation instead of a reckless competition. . . . We stand for equal rights as a fact of life instead of a catchword of politics."

"We have more than enough to supply every human being beneath the flag," the speaker went on. "There ought never to be in this Republic a single day of bad business, a single unemployed workingman, a single unfed child. American businessmen should never know an hour of uncertainty, discouragement, or fear; American workingmen never a day of low wages, idleness, or want. Hunger should never walk in these thinly peopled gardens of plenty."

This was idealism, of course, and superb oratory, but it remained to set out the explicit concepts of the New Nationalism. "We mean to try to make little business big, and all business honest, instead of striving to make Big Business little, and yet letting it remain dishonest." The new party meant also, Beveridge continued, to seek to abolish child labor, insure woman suffrage, and develop care for the aged. "How," he asked, "is the workingman with less than five hundred dollars a year, and with earning power waning as his own years advance," to support both parents and children in their dependent periods?

"It is questions like these," Beveridge declared, "we must answer if we are to justify free institutions." To the conservative argument, which would be re-iterated down the next two decades, that government action on such questions would fly in the face of the Constitution, Beveridge replied: "The Progressive Party believes that the Constitution is a living thing, growing with the people's growth, strengthening with the people's strength, aiding the people in their struggles for life, liberty, and the pursuit of happiness, permitting the people to meet all their needs as conditions change."

Fervently the speaker came to his close: "Not reluctantly, then, but eagerly, not with faint hearts, but strong, do we now advance upon the enemies of the people. For the call that comes to us is the call that came to our fathers. As they responded, so do we:

> "He has sounded forth a trumpet that shall
>   never call retreat,
> "He is sifting out the hearts of men
>   before His judgment seat;
> "Oh, be swift our souls to answer Him,
>   be jubilant our feet,
> "Our God is marching on."[22]

The booming organ, taking up the hymn as the speaker concluded, could only dimly be heard in the roar that shook the hall. "A great speech, Albert!" Roosevelt told him. There had not been one like it since Bryan's "Cross of Gold" address of sixteen years before; there would not be another until a new Roosevelt's first inaugural address twenty-one years later. The fervent credo of the New Nationalism stood halfway between them in time, but it looked toward the day of the New Deal rather than to the apostrophe to the agrarian past delivered by Bryan. The men and women who made up the Progressive Party convention were the products of the economic issues of the new century: social workers, prominently led by Jane Addams; university professors of the type of Richard T. Ely, who had first challenged the concept of *laissez-faire;* union organizers and leaders, liberal businessmen and militant churchmen crusading for an end to child labor, social insurance for the unemployed, retirement benefits for the aged.

Roosevelt kept the gathering at its high pitch of emotion the following day with his own "Confession of Faith," with which he also introduced the platform on which the new party would stand. In addition to what had already been advocated, he reiterated the need for an administrative agency to police the activities of interstate commerce, and called for a comprehensive reform of the national currency.

The nationalism of Hamilton, Croly had written, "can be adapted to democracy without an essential injury to itself," but the democracy of Jefferson "cannot be nationalized without being transformed." From a "democracy of indiscriminate individualism," it must become one in which its members are united "by a sense of joint responsibility for the success of their political and social ideal."[23] It was the final awakening to self-consciousness of a people of the United States, as distinguished from the people of the separate states, for which the New Nationalism was sounding its call.

In answer to these clarion statements, the Taft followers—dispirited and resentful of both their present leader and the former leader who had deserted them—took refuge in charges that the new party was "seeking to pull down the pillars of the temple of freedom and representative government," or that it was made up of a dangerous cabal of "political emotionalists or neurotics." These were words that Taft himself had used the previous February, when it first became evident that a fatal breach had developed in the party; after his perfunctory acceptance speech at the Republican convention in June, Taft himself made no more addresses for the duration of the campaign.

*   *   *

The real struggle of 1912 was not between the New Nationalism and old-line Republican *laissez-faire,* but between the New Nationalism and Woodrow Wilson's New Freedom. The latter, as it turned out, was an amalgam of Jeffersonian individualism and a qualified borrowing of Croly's criticisms of contemporary society. In Wilson's view, reform should stop short of any comprehensive governmental intervention into the manipulations of the economic system. Accordingly, in the electoral triumph of the New Freedom, *laissez-faire* was in fact to receive a reprieve, and thereafter to enjoy another decade of vigor, before it was finally done in by the Great Depression. Of the three major candidates in 1912, only Roosevelt was bold enough, or possibly perceptive enough, to describe for the American people the shape of the future.

Nevertheless, the result of the vote in November was an overwhelming triumph for the Progressive Movement: Wilson polled 6,293,019 popular votes, Roosevelt 4,119,507, and Socialist Eugene V. Debs 901,873—a total of more than 11,000,000 votes for political reform as against Taft's 3,484,956. Thanks to the vagaries of the constitutional machinery of an Electoral College (a negative and anti-democratic process which, half a century after the revolution of 1912, remained to be excised from the body politic), Wilson received 435 electoral votes to Roosevelt's 88; the Republican candidate, for the first time since 1856, ran an abysmal third with only 8 electoral votes. There could hardly be any question of the affirmative voice of the American people in favor of change and correction of their system of political economy.

Still, the statistics were susceptible of several equally plausible interpretations: Wilson, it was obvious, was a minority President when his popular vote was compared with the combined vote for Roosevelt and Taft. If the latter's repeatedly uttered, but repeatedly discounted, protestation that he was not a spokesman for or captive of the Old Guard was to be taken at face value, then it might be said that the American voter had chosen between the slow-paced, juridically deliberate approach of Taft and the overnight transformation from past to future that Roosevelt advocated, in favor of the course of the New Freedom which lay somewhere in between.

At fifty-six, Wilson and his philosophy and temperament also lay some-where in between the Jeffersonianism of the past and the welfare economy of the future. His own history had been a succession of signal victories in the wake of apparent defeats. After an unhappy and unsuccessful attempt to prac-tice law, he had turned to an academic career, and in the process of conversion had produced a work on *Congressional Government* which had become a uni-versally accepted authority. Elected president of Princeton University in 1902, he had modernized and restructured the undergraduate and graduate study programs, and when alumni and academic opposition had blocked the full dimensions of his reforms on the campus, he had been nominated and elected governor of New Jersey.[24]

In the two years at Trenton, Wilson's vigorous leadership in a progressive legislative program had won national attention; the direct primary, employers' liability legislation, strengthened administrative control over public utilities and a surveillance of public officials under a corrupt practices act were all pushed through in short order.

At the close of the 1911 session of the New Jersey legislature, Wilson could truthfully write: "I got absolutely everything I strove for—and more besides." The *Jersey Journal* corroborated the view: "No Governor has ever achieved so much in so short a time. In less than four months he has turned New Jersey from one of the most conservative and machine-dominated states into a leader in the forefront of progressive commonwealths." Here, said the editor of a North Carolina paper who was destined to play a role in Wilson's White House career, was a political leader who could answer the extravagant demands of the New Nationalism, while in distant Texas another newspaper commented that Wilson was "the most hopeful figure in American politics."[25]

With this, Wilson moved from New Jersey onto the national stage, touring the country to give a series of speeches that were generally received with en-thusiasm. His luck remained with him, for had the country still been watching the performance of the New Jersey state legislature in 1912, the bright promise might suddenly have dimmed. While the governor stumped the rest of the coun-try seeking the Presidential nomination, the untended barricades against cor-ruption and partisan politics were overrun and many of the advances of the previous year turned back. The session ended in a barren and hostile setting; it had, said Wilson on his return to the scene, done little but "try to amend and mar the wonderful things we accomplished last year."[26]

There was little or no time to waste in regrets, however, if the Democratic nomination was to be won. The convention itself was a formidable test of the Wilson strength, with Bryan, Champ Clark and Oscar W. Underwood of Ala-bama contesting with the New Jersey hopeful for the nomination. Victory came on the forty-sixth ballot. Then had come the weeks of doubt, as the Bull Moose charged well into the lead in terms of popular issues and audience re-sponse.

Roosevelt had chosen to focus his campaign on the argument that the Sherman Act had proved inadequate to deal with the problem of business combination in the twentieth century. He argued the creation of a second major administrative agency in the Federal government, similar to the Interstate Commerce Commission, to regulate and control corporation growth and activity. Wilson found the means to attack this proposal by characterizing it as "accepted and regulated monopoly" which would perpetuate "the existing alliance between government and big business." He added a warning to labor that any government program which insured the continued development of the great industrial combination would be a deathblow to the union movement. Wilson's arguments were backed up by an article in *Collier's Weekly* by Louis D. Brandeis, rejecting the Rooseveltian argument that modern conditions made trusts inevitable: "No conspicuous American trust owes its existence to the desire for increased efficiency," Brandeis wrote. "No conspicuously profitable trust owes its profits largely to . . . efficiency." No trust, in fact, could operate profitably in a market where free enterprise remained; and when it had bought up its competition, there was no evidence that it thereafter became more efficient.[27]

Roosevelt's attacks upon Wilson's Jeffersonian liberalism—he considered the Democratic candidate "a rather impotent, generally inept, academic wrist slapper"—in William Allen White's opinion "forced Wilson . . . to a firmer and perhaps more advanced liberalism than he otherwise might have taken." Between Roosevelt's swashbuckling and Brandeis' cool rebuttals of Roosevelt's proposals as superficial progressivism, Wilson tended to articulate his own program more effectively. Under Brandeis' guidance—the two had only met personally in August, 1912—Wilson countered the New Nationalism with the query, "Shall we regulate competition or monopoly?" And he made effective use of Clark Howell's parody on Roosevelt's famous peroration: The Bull Moose, he declared, stood at Armageddon "to battle for the trusts."[28]

Just as Roosevelt in 1904 had served the American people well by awakening them to the existence of abuses in their economic system, wrote Brandeis in *Collier's,* so Wilson now was needed to deal intelligently with the abuses. The Rough Rider was a born agitator who was able "not only to arouse men but to create a following"; but the time had now come for "that calm, careful, hard thinking which is essential to sound judgment on legislation." Roosevelt had led the assault on the citadels of selfishness; Wilson, wrote Brandeis, brought the blueprints for building a modern democracy.[29] The first fruits of progressivism had been exhilarating. It remained, now in midsummer, to weed out and cultivate.

By early October, the tide had turned in Wilson's favor. In part, it was the logical consequence of the massive split in the Republican organization, and in part it was the inability of the country to go to the ultimate extreme of centralized government which the Progressive Party advocated. One of the most ardent of the Progressives recognized this; in the aftermath of the election, Robert M. LaFollette wrote that "a nation of ninety million people, demanding plain, simple justice, striving for educational, political and industrial democracy, turned to Woodrow Wilson as the only present hope."[30]

*   *   *

In the irony of events, two developments initiated by the retiring Taft administration came to maturity in the first five months of 1913 and further strengthened the reform program which Wilson was to undertake. On February 25 a House committee under Congressman Arsène Pujo of Louisiana filed its year-long study of the alleged "money trust" and the concentration of financial and banking resources in the metropolitan areas of the United States. The Pujo committee report confirmed the steady acceleration of the trend toward centralization of money and credit, through merger of banks and trust companies, interlocking directorates, and acquisition of interests in insurance companies and public utilities. The following year Brandeis would make the report the basis of a widely read book, *Other People's Money and the Banker's Use of It.* Before 1913 was ended, the report would have provided a substantial part of the material needed to support the case for the Federal Reserve Act.[31]

On May 31, with the first Wilson Congress already launched upon its work, the Seventeenth Amendment to the Constitution was declared adopted by Secretary of State Bryan. Not only did this promise, if the Progressive Movement continued its momentum in 1914 and 1916, to introduce a substantially more liberal note into the Senate, but the adoption of the Seventeenth Amendment less than five months after the Sixteenth substantially weakened the argument that it was neither desirable nor practicable to revise the Constitution with any degree of frequency. Indeed, the Eighteenth Amendment had already been foreshadowed by the passage, in the last days of the Taft Congress, of the Webb-Kenyon Act prohibiting interstate shipment of liquor into states with local "dry" laws; Taft's veto, which Congress overrode, suggested that an amendment would be the only constitutional basis for such legislation.[32]

The popular election of Senators was a logical ingredient in the democratizing effect of the various reform movements of the nineties and the early years of the new century. The original concept of the senior branch of Congress consisting of representatives of the states, while the House was made up of representatives of the people, embodied the theory that the Federal government was a strictly circumscribed authority derived from such powers as the states and the people of the states were disposed to delegate to it. In practice and historical experience, both houses of Congress had long since developed a sense of nationality in the conduct of their business which emphasized the irrelevance of the theory; it would be half a century more, however, before the reapportionment decisions of the Supreme Court would affirm the alternative theory that all members of Congress were the Senators and Representatives of the people of the United States.

The resistance to the Seventeenth Amendment in Congress itself had come less from an appeal to the state representation concept than from more material considerations. State courthouse machines which had long controlled the choice of Senators, and Senators who had retained party influence through their connection with the state courthouses, had the most to lose. Almost equal in concern were the interests of many Southern Senators who preferred election by an all-white state legislature to a campaign in which Negro votes might be a factor. In the face of the continuing clamor for direct elections by the people, these interests steadily lost ground.

Many liberals shared the view of William Allen White that the Seventeenth Amendment would pave the way for a more liberal jurisprudence. From the early nineties to the present, White declared, the courts had been consistently hostile to legislation. "The forces of altruism," he wrote, "are manifest in the rising democratic institutions in the cities and the states. The opposing forces of greed are manifest in the judicial worship of property rights as against human rights in many courts." Federal judges were appointed subject to the advice and consent of the Senate; and the Senate, said White, for the past twenty years had been dominated by men "chosen by railroad attorneys through the state bosses who influenced the state legislatures. Hence property is the dominant thought of our courts . . . But when people change their United States Senators the courts will change, and the courts will amend the Constitution to suit the people."[33]

It did not work out quite that neatly; another quarter of a century lay ahead before the composition of the Federal judiciary would be substantially changed. But the optimism seemed justified in the fall of 1912; for the second time in the same generation, the American people were to have the opportunity to deal with the abuses in their economic system.

10/Progressives in Power: Midsummer

W OODROW WILSON ENTERED the White House the heir to the reform desires of the majority of the American people as they had been whetted by Theodore Roosevelt and pent up by William Howard Taft. He had, by all appearances, moved further to the left of center than he had originally intended under pressure of the campaign itself, and now the time had come to put his program into action. "His first four years in the White House," wrote William Allen White, "left no doubt as to his liberal intention. Those years left considerable doubt about the efficacy of his liberalism." He labored, said White, under three handicaps—his lack of personal contact with the men who were the moving forces of practical politics, "his major delusion that he had a first-class mind," and his lack of feel for the mechanics of national government which could only have come from prior experience in Congress or Cabinet.[1]

In addition, Wilson took over a national administration at a time when the country had already undergone a substantial and significant amount of change, and was in the process of assimilating its new political concepts. The Seventeenth Amendment had climaxed a process of direct elections of public officers which had now become general in all the states, compelling a radical reorientation of party political processes. The Sixteenth Amendment, preparing the way for a reorganization of the national tax structure and with this the financing of expanding functions of government, had only recently been adopted. A number of legislative projects of the Progressive Movement in the states had now been enacted into law: more than half of the states now had the initiative and the referendum in some form, and a definite majority of the states had both prohibition and woman suffrage statutes or constitutional amendments on the subjects. What Wilson himself had done in New

169

Jersey as its governor, many other reform leaders had done in other states. The result was that many battles in a peaceful revolution had already been won by the time the New Freedom came to Washington.[2]

*   *   *

In the selection of his Cabinet, Wilson was confronted with one of the first tests of his capabilities as a political leader and of his instincts as the agent of the Progressive Movement. Foremost in urgency was the necessary disposition of the expectations of William Jennings Bryan, the Nebraska Commoner who had fought the fight both for reform and for the party since 1896. There was little choice but to make him Secretary of State in view of his manifest desire for the post as the chief preferment of the new administration—though in the face of the fact that Bryan had virtually no qualification other than native intelligence for the leadership of the foreign policy of the United States. In Wilson's view, it was a case of hoping to offset Bryan's reputation for radical demagogy by the fanatical devotion of thousands of his followers which could be translatable into Congressional support for administration measures. In any event, the Bryan appointment enhanced the portrait of Wilson himself as a liberal.

For Secretary of Labor—a separate Cabinet position created by Congress on the day of Wilson's inauguration—the President chose retiring Congressman William B. Wilson of Pennsylvania, who before his three terms in the House of Representatives had been executive secretary for the United Mine Workers. This appointment, too, won the new President the approval of reform groups and the prospect that Congress would be well disposed to consider any programs advanced through the President by the new department. Three other nominally progressive members were also named— Josephus Daniels, North Carolina newspaper publisher and party wheelhorse, as Secretary of the Navy; Judge Lindley M. Garrison of New Jersey as Secretary of War; and William Gibbs McAdoo of New York as Secretary of the Treasury. McAdoo, a self-made lawyer who by 1902 had become president of the company which built and operated the Hudson River tunnels, would succeed Wilson himself in the leadership of the Democratic Party in the twenties, and would provide a certain continuity from the New Freedom to the New Deal in a term as Senator from California in the thirties.[3]

A neat balance of nominal conservatives represented the rest of the Cabinet: Interstate Commerce Commissioner Franklin K. Lane of California, as Secretary of Interior, would suffer from renewed attacks of the Pinchot-led conservationist forces in a controversy over private leasing of tidelands oil reserves. David F. Houston, president of Washington University in St. Louis, as Secretary of Agriculture, was the target of agrarian bitterness over his successful blocking of rural credit legislation. Congressman William C. Redfield of New York, as Secretary of Commerce, showed himself more than receptive to the expression of the big business viewpoint, but his chief burden to bear was the resentment of the liberals that Wilson had yielded to outcries of the business community and had appointed Redfield rather than Brandeis, his first choice.[4]

Brandeis, in fact, had been Wilson's first choice for the office of Attorney General, but again he had been talked out of the idea. As "the people's lawyer," the brilliant Boston attorney would have given the New Freedom a complexion of total commitment to the most aggressive propositions of the Progressive Movement. Wilson held him in high personal regard, although they had first met only the previous August as the campaign was approaching its climax. Brandeis had provided Wilson with the rationale of the anti-trust program with which to answer Roosevelt and the Progressive Party: restoration and preservation of competition in interstate business, with administrative regulation directed primarily to that end.

Intellectually and economically, Brandeis appealed to the new President as the desirable choice to carry out such a program once the campaign had been won, but the uproar from the respectable and comfortable elements of Boston drowned out his proposal. The best men, wrote the well-to-do and conservative historian James Ford Rhodes, were aghast at the first suggestion of Brandeis as a Cabinet appointee; and Elbert Hubbard, belle-lettrist and exponent of rugged individualism, told Wilson that "Brandeis does not represent America," going on to recite a catalog of damnation including "Business-Baiter, stirrer-up of strife, litigious lurer of hate and unrest, destroyer of confidence, killer of values, commercial coyote, spoiler of pay envelopes."[5]

Wilson quailed before the calumnies, although they were to be as nothing compared to what was to come when he nominated Brandeis as an Associate Justice of the Supreme Court a few years later. He then fell back upon an alternate who came almost with equal recommendations as an anti-trust lawyer and a suspected radical—James C. McReynolds, one of the leading prosecutors under Attorney General Wickersham. The President was impressed with the report that McReynolds had resigned as special counsel for the government when Wickersham had proposed to the Court the reorganization rather than the dissolution of the Tobacco Trust; the action, McReynolds had contended, "nullified the effects of the victory."[6]

The final Cabinet position, the Postmaster Generalship, was given to Congressman Albert S. Burleson of Texas, an old-line spoilsman who was destined to become the first of the Red-baiters in government after the first World War. His support of the entrenched political interests in the Southern states substantially undermined the Progressive Movement in this crucial decade.[7]

In addition to these members of his official family, Wilson required a confidante and aide to serve in the capacity that Taft had provided for Roosevelt in a later day. This spot was filled by Colonel Edward M. House, and turned his attention to the rising governor of New Jersey as the best an urbane and wealthy Texan who had become a kingmaker in state politics hope of the Democrats to return to national power. His deft handling of Wilson's candidacy before the nominating convention, and his direction of the campaign which followed, solidified a warm personal relationship which was to continue until, at Versailles in 1919, their ways would part. House, said the President's son-in-law, "possessed an extraordinary political clairvoyance, a subtle feeling for the inwardness of events and the drifts of public opinion."[8] Since these essential attributes of leadership were sometimes less than adequate in Wilson—and, indeed, his implacable bitterness at disagreement and opposition was a flaw which ultimately proved fatal—an aide like House was of fundamental importance.

*   *   *

House, as a matter of fact, earned a niche in history partly by virtue of his lasting longer in Wilson's favor than most of his onetime associates. Like many another academic intellectual, the President tended to regard sentiment and personal ties as signs of human frailties, and enthusiasm or the candid exchange of viewpoints as a presumption upon his own mental superiority. There had been Colonel George Harvey, editor of *Harper's Weekly* and a leading force in Wilson's campaign for the New Jersey governorship; he left the Wilson circle after a well-publicized quarrel on the eve of the Presidential canvass. Joseph Tumulty, a faithful Irishman who made no pretensions to intellectual parity, also survived rather well until, toward the end of Wilson's life, he was cast out in a public excoriation which made Wilson admirers cringe in mortification.

"Wilson's chief blunders as a liberal came from the vice of exalting his faults as virtues," William Allen White observed. "He was proud of his single-track mind, and apparently did not try to consider many things at once." If he was concentrating on foreign policy, he would be oblivious to "some monstrously reactionary" step by his associates in domestic policy.[9] He was, said Senator John Sharp Williams of Mississippi, "the best judge of measures and the poorest of men I ever knew." Robert Lansing, who would succeed Bryan in the State Department, felt that "intuition rather than reason played the chief part in the way he reached conclusions and judgments." It was generally recognized, early in his administration, that the only advice he considered was that which confirmed his own convictions.[10]

Yet the appraisal of men like Lansing, White and Williams did not do Wilson full justice. Few men in American history—if any—had come to the Presidency with as much previous reflection on the functions of the office. He had been preparing himself, Wilson once told an inquirer, since he had been graduated from Davidson College in 1897. Roosevelt, it was true, had had definite convictions about the potential of the Chief Executive's position, as he had about most things, but it had been an accident of politics that had first put him into office. Still, Roosevelt's administration had prompted Wilson to revise his own concept: In 1885 he had described the United States as a government foredoomed to indecision by virtue of the primacy of Congress and the inevitability of stalemate or compromise in deciding policy. After Roosevelt's example of how a powerful President could carry out policy unsupported by a conservative legislature, Wilson by 1908 was prepared to acknowledge that an Executive elected by an unequivocal mandate from the voters was indeed "the only national voice" the country had. "Let him once win the admiration and confidence of the country," Wilson declared, "and no other single force can withstand him, no combination of forces will easily overpower him."[11]

Wilson, in an age when state governments had proved more responsive to progressive legislative proposals than Congress, concluded in any case that the best preparation for the White House was administrative and executive experience in the states. He could point to Cleveland and Roosevelt (and might have pointed to Hughes) as contemporary examples. Cleveland's troubles with Congress might have given him pause—after all, it was in the period of Congressional domination of the national government that Wilson's first major book on the subject had been written. As for Roosevelt's ability to force a few basic reform measures through Congress, and to govern by executive authority in the alternative, the general progressive triumphs in the states between 1910 and 1912 had made Wilson's task of legislative initiative somewhat easier: men like Joseph T. Robinson of Arkansas and George W. Norris of Nebraska had been elevated from the lower House to the upper, the red-bearded J. Hamilton Lewis had replaced the conservative Shelby M. Cullom from Illinois, and both Thomas J. Walsh of Montana and Harry Lane of Oregon began their long crusading careers at this time.[12]

The Democratic sweep in 1912 was reflected in the 63rd Congress; the Senate had fifty-one Democrats to forty-four Republicans, the House 291 Democrats to 127 Republicans. Where party discipline was effective, there were excellent prospects for enacting the various reform measures to which the party platform had committed the new administration; and Wilson undertook to establish a personal bond between the White House and the Congress by reviving a practice, not observed since Jefferson's day, of appearing personally to deliver his major messages to the lawmakers.

Foremost on the agenda was the downward revision of the tariff—a perennial demand of reformers in the interest of lower consumer prices which was consistently countered by the argument that, after a century of protectionism, the tariff was a part of the fabric of the whole economy. The platform plank, indeed, had recognized this intimate relationship and had promised that revisions would "not injure or destroy legitimate industry." More importantly, the tariff question represented a test of the New Freedom program generally; it was the question on which the Taft administration had first hit shoal water and the Payne-Aldrich Act had remained as a reproach to the Republican pledge of 1908 and a target for the Democratic promise of 1912.

To steer the tricky course through Congress, as administration leaders recognized, the Wilson forces needed to maintain a solid front against the extreme demands of the insurgent Republicans led by LaFollette, the traditional protectionism of the regular Republicans and the sectional interests of various Democratic Representatives and Senators. The delegation from Louisiana opposed relaxing the sugar duties, the spokesman from North Carolina the textile duties, the men from Massachusetts the leather goods duties. Yet the tenor of the New Freedom was elimination of special privileges in the whole body of Federal law. While constitutional issues were not involved in the tariff bill developed by Congressman Oscar W. Underwood of Alabama, the good faith of the Wilson administration and its capacity to implement its legislative program was the underlying issue of the bill.

In the end, the measure which made its way past the numerous obstacles in both houses was a sweeping triumph for Wilson; not only did it greatly expand the list of duty-free goods to become available to the American buying public, but it provided the vehicle for the first general income tax law in implementation of the Sixteenth Amendment. The income tax provision effectively rebutted the argument that the substantial across-the-board reductions in ad valorem rates in the Underwood bill would threaten the government with a deficit before the year was out. More importantly, the first objective of the New Freedom had been won, and for Wilson, as a London observer remarked, the statute "raised him at a single stage from the man of promise to the man of achievement."[13]

*   *   *

The character of the Underwood tariff law bespoke the philosophy of the New Freedom in general; it eschewed the extremism of the Progressive Party platform in favor of a middle course. This was to be evidenced further as the administration advanced upon its next and more challenging goal, the reform of the money and banking system of the United States. Again, an obstacle-strewn course lay ahead: the LaFollette Republicans and the Bryan Democrats now had a common interest in striking an epochal blow at the shadowy but long-suspected "money trust"; the conservatives in both parties looked favorably toward the so-called Aldrich plan for a great central reserve association of private banks, the product of the studies of the National Monetary Commission etsablished by the Aldrich-Vreeland Act of 1908. Between these extremes, the Wilson forces again raised their banner proclaiming "special privileges to none."

The particular privileges at which the reformers aimed had been described in detail by the Pujo Committee report earlier in 1913. In its opening statement the report had observed: "Whether under a different currency system the resources in our banks would be greater or less is comparatively immaterial if they continued to be controlled by a small group." The accelerating concentration of monetary resources was convincingly documented by the committee; in the decade between 1901 and 1911, it reported, the twenty largest banks in New York City increased their percentage of the total bank holdings in the metropolitan area from 34 to 42 percent. And the report concluded: "Far more dangerous than all that has happened to us in the past by way of elimination of competition in industry is the control of credit through the domination of these groups over our banks and industries. It means that there can be no hope of revived competition and no new ventures on a scale commensurate with the needs of modern commerce, or that could live against existing combinations, without the consent of those who dominate these sources of credit."[14]

The fact was that the banking system of the United States, to the extent that it was a system at all, was not adapted to the economic concentration of business and industry which had occurred in the past forty years. The national bank program which had been developed in the sixties was essentially an unconnected group of private institutions which had no means of developing a cooperative and coordinated plan of response to fluctuating economic needs. It was, as one contemporary banking authority put it, "a breeder of panics."[15] And panics, depressions and deflation had been the recurring story of national finance in each decade since the seventies. Both conservatives and progressives agreed on the fundamental need—a centralized administration of the monetary system, responsive, as Croly had put it, to the centralizing activities of the American people. The chief point in dispute was whether the administration should be public or private.

"Our banking laws must mobilize reserves," Wilson said in a second message to Congress on June 23, 1913. In addition, he declared, any legislative program must prevent "the concentration anywhere in a few hands of the monetary resources of the country or their use for speculative purposes in such volume as to hinder or impede or stand in the way of other more legitimate, more fruitful uses. And," he concluded, "the control of the system of banking and of issue . . . must be public, not private, must be vested in the government itself, so that the banks may be the instruments, not the masters, of business and of individual enterprise and initiative."[16]

The words soothed the Bryanites in Congress; the financial community was reassured by the fact that the chairman of the House banking committee, which had charge of the measure, was the conservative Carter Glass of Virginia. Nevertheless, the bankers felt impelled to warn against the prospect of public control. That October, at the convention of the American Bankers' Association in Boston, Arthur M. Reynolds of Des Moines, acting president of the association, described the proposed Glass bill as "an invasion of the liberty of the citizen in the control of his own property by putting under government management enormous individual investments and a branch of the country's business which should be left to individual effort."[17]

The Federal Reserve Act which eventually emerged from the six-month debate was, as the *New York Tribune* described it, "the Aldrich plan modified to suit the tempo of the country." Paul M. Warburg of Kuhn, Loeb &

Company, the father of the Aldrich plan and a vocal critic of the Congressional proposal, conceded his satisfaction with the final measure. Henceforth, he told reporters, he looked for "the gradual elimination of bond-secured currency, of scattered reserves, of immobilized commercial credit, and of pyramiding of call loans on the Stock Exchange."[18] The objective of decentralizing the monetary system was achieved through the establishment of twelve districts with a Federal Reserve Bank in each, while centralized administration was provided by a Federal Reserve Board of seven (later eight) members including the Secretary of the Treasury and the Comptroller of the Currency. The district banks were bankers' banks, holding the cash reserves of members of the system and rediscounting their commercial and agricultural paper at rates which could be adjusted to changing financial conditions. Federal Reserve notes issued by the reserve banks augmented the circulating money supply.

"Mr. Wilson's Currency Bill is a charter of new freedom for the business world," declared a Republican newspaper after the measure had passed Congress and been signed into law.[19] It was, as the predominant theme of commentary had it, one of the most important pieces of economic legislation in the country's history, providing for a currency system responsive to regional needs and backed by a readily transferable fund of reserves.

Experience would demonstrate the need for substantially more authority to be vested in the Board, a need which eventually was met by the Banking Act of 1935; and the Reserve System was committed to the classical concepts of the gold standard as a limit to the money supply, until the emergency measures of the Great Depression provided government bonds as an acceptable collateral. But the ultimate test of the efficacy of the act was its susceptibility to revision and refinement; the calamity cries of the insurgents that it had legalized the money trust were disproved by its own record, while the hostility of the national banks melted in the face of reality. By the spring of 1914, Secretary McAdoo could report that all but eighteen of the country's national banks had come into the system.[20]

*   *   *

The policy of the New Freedom concerning the trust problem was the final major concern of the administration in its first two years in office. As it eventually worked out, the policy was ambivalent; in the Clayton Anti-Trust Act, as one observer put it, Wilson advanced the proposition that "competition should be given a complete test before being virtually abandoned in the laws of the country"; while in the alternative the Federal Trade Commission Act looked to the creation of the second major administrative regulatory agency, charged with "governmental regulation and control of great industrial corporations as complete as are government regulation and control of railroads today" by the Interstate Commerce Commission.[21]

In the end, this ambivalence dissipated the potential of both of the measures, and in the judicial reaction of the early twenties the power of the

Federal Trade Commission was still further curtailed. At the time of Congressional consideration of the two measures, however, the anti-trust program begun under Roosevelt and Taft was being continued by the Justice Department. Attorney General McReynolds, critical though he had been of the tendency of his predecessor to compromise issues with defendants in anti-trust proceedings, utilized the consent decree, and even the informal agreement, with substantial success during his short term in office. It was his zeal for the prosecution of anti-trust matters, in fact, which particularly recommended him to Wilson for the vacancy on the Supreme Court which developed in 1914.[22]

McReynolds used the consent decree technique to break up the plans of the American Telephone & Telegraph Company to secure control of all communications systems in the United States. In the process, he secured agreement on the release of the Western Union Company from the A. T. & T. combine in the Kingsbury Agreement. The Attorney General turned to formal court proceedings, in both civil and criminal law, in another major suit aimed at dissolving the monopoly developed by J. P. Morgan through control of the New York, New Haven & Hartford Railroad. The main objectives of the civil action were obtained in the late summer of 1914 when another consent decree was entered. With the resignation of McReynolds, with the new policy on business combinations suggested by the Clayton and Federal Trade Commission laws—and above all, with the onset of war—the trust-busting fervor of the previous decade steadily waned.[23]

The Federal Trade Commission, established by legislation enacted in September 1914, was Wilson's alternative to Roosevelt's plan to accept the business combination as a fact of modern life: it would restore competition by policing methods of unfair competition. Under Section 5 of the statute, the Commission outlawed "unfair methods of competition," but failed to define these methods; the apparent intent of the administration was to leave the Commission as free as possible to assess specific practices on the merits. The Court of the next decade, intent on reducing the scope of the statute, found the absence of legislative definition a mandate to supply a restrictive judicial definition.[24] In the decade after that, when the New Deal surveyed the shambles of the *laissez-faire* economy, it would require a spate of regulatory agencies to deal with the problems which, throughout the twenties, the courts forbade the FTC to approach.[25]

Still, both the Federal Trade Commission Act and the Clayton Act were largely the product of Brandeis' recommendations to the President. "The first essential of wise and just action is knowledge," said the man whom the business world called a dangerous radical; until the fact-finding and informational functions were performed, he went on, government could not "deal intelligently with the problem of the extent to which trade agreements among competitors should be permitted." Essentially a pragmatist like Holmes, Brandeis urged that the legislative power of the Commission would in many instances lead industry itself to discern the abuses which in its own interest should be resolved. The naivity which this proposition reflected in the light of experience tended unduly to depreciate the substantial practical benefit to the business community which did result from the cumulative effect of Commission studies over the years.[26]

To a certain degree, the Clayton Act undertook to be specific where the Federal Trade Commission Act was general. It prohibited price discriminations substantially contributing to monopoly, interlocking directorates in major industries, and acquisition of stock in competing firms which had the effect of lessening competition. Three methods of relief were provided: court injunctions, cease and desist orders from the FTC, and civil suits for treble damages where the plaintiff could establish specific instances of unfair competition. The act sought to correct a judicial gloss upon the Sherman Act by specifically exempting farm and labor organizations from the provisions of the anti-trust laws, and undertook to abolish the use of the injunction in labor disputes.

The result of the Wilson legislative program in the matter of trust control was not enthusiastically received. An administration newspaper in New York said only of the Clayton Act that "it might have been worse," while the *San Francisco Chronicle* called it "an outrageous interference with the constitutional powers of the states." Its explicit description of illegal practices at once raised the question of whether all unspecified practices were beyond the reach of the law, while the sweeping criminal sanctions for violation of the statute were condemned as a threat to "put every business executive at an indeterminate risk of criminal indictment and punishment."[27] Coupled with the failure of the Federal Trade Commission to produce any spectacular results in the exposure and condemnation of instances of unfair competition, the applause which had greeted the tariff and Federal Reserve laws gave way to a suspicion that Wilson had failed the progressive cause.[28]

*   *   *

Fundamentally, the uncertainties of the first Wilson administration were bred of an unwillingness on the part of the President to break with Jeffersonian traditions, the conflicting advice he received from the liberal and conservative elements so carefully balanced in his Cabinet, and the failure to perceive that business thinking itself was turning away from the crudities of the earlier day. A conspicuous example of the changing psychology of capitalism—however suspect its sincerity might be—had been the voluntary resignation of J. P. Morgan & Company executives from more than thirty boards of directors, and the announced intention to withdraw from still others in the near future.[29]

The fact was that the economic frames of reference in the United States were gradually changing, and were about to be subjected to a cataclysmic change resulting from the European war in which America herself was soon to be involved. But aside from that, there were a number of other factors affecting the domestic scene: the steady and rapid growth of population which had characterized the nineteenth century had noticeably slackened with the beginning of the twentieth, while the accelerating rate of production of consumer goods was beginning to satisfy many of the demands which, unsatisfied in the previous generation, had fed the streams of unrest. From a population increase of nearly 26 percent for the first three decades after the Civil War, the rate dropped to 21 percent in the nineties and in the first ten years of the new century, and then to less than 15 in the war decade. Meantime, in the twenty years from 1899 to 1919, the number of wage earners in manufacturing industries doubled, and the value of products added by manufacture increased sixfold.[30]

Concurrent social trends which were only dimly sensed by contemporaries were, in retrospect, seen to be of even greater significance. At the turn of the century, 40 percent of the population lived in urban centers of 2,500 or more inhabitants; by 1920, the percentage was 51.4. Thus the trend away from the agrarian standards of American life, the values and landmarks of a predominantly agrarian society, which had been prospective in the decades of the Granger, Greenback and Populist movements, had become a reality in the period in which the Progressive Movement came to its high-water mark. To a certain degree, the inability of the New Freedom to come to grips with the problems it surveyed was due to its unawareness that it was seeking to devise legislative procedures familiar to the nineteenth century to apply to economic conditions of the twentieth.

To reformers and conservatives alike in 1913 and 1914, the functions of the economic system were determined by a natural law which was manifested by a competitive process and—after Darwinism provided the analogy —was discernible in the survival of the fittest. The reformer approached the issue with a stress on the perpetuation of the competitive process; the conservative placed stress upon the survival of the fittest. To neither political progressive nor industrial conservative—and least of all to judicial exponents, with the rare exceptions of a Holmes or a Brandeis—had the concepts of a new school of economists become recognizable, much less acceptable. Nevertheless, since the opening of the century, men like Richard T. Ely, Thorstein Veblen and John R. Commons had been documenting the fact of the existence of a new economics and pointing out the consequences of its existence.

The formation of the American Economic Association in 1885 had contained in its statement of principles the opening declaration: "We regard the State as an agency whose positive assistance is one of the indispensable conditions of human progress." To this Ely urged a supplementary assertion that "the doctrine of *laissez-faire* is unsafe in politics and unsound in morals," which the new association felt too strong to endorse. Nevertheless, the formation of the group was itself a challenge to conventional ideas of the nineteenth century, to be taken more seriously than the utopian criticisms of either Edward Bellamy or Henry George. The association, more-over, stimulated a series of searching studies of American constitutionalism and its economic base. J. Allen Smith, an attorney turned economist, antic-ipated Charles A. Beard in his 1907 volume, *The Spirit of American Govern-ment,* which traced the elements of self-interest in the origins of the Con-stitution and condemned judicial review of Congressional enactments as a "monarchical survival."[31]

Yet Smith, one of the most articulate of the critics of the old order in the Progressive Era, was to present a study in contradictions in the latter part of his career which characterized many another reformer in this period of wrench-ing changes in American political polarity. From the great intellectual adven-tures of the Square Deal and the New Freedom, Smith came to conclude, in the aftermath, that "normalcy" should provide a limit to the "positive assistance" of government which he and other youthful rebels had formerly held so essen-tial. In his posthumous work, *The Growth and Decadence of Constitutional Government,* published in 1930, Smith decried the suggestions made amid the collapsing structures of the economy to strengthen the authority of the state to deal with the crisis. At the time of his death in 1924 he was bitterly criticizing the plan to abolish child labor by constitutional amendment, as an example of the limitations on personal freedoms which were the consequence of the demise of *laissez-faire.* He was the prototype of disillusioned New Dealers of the following decade, who shrank from the consequences of the revolution they helped to foment.[32]

*   *   *

In the same year that the American Economic Association was formed, Woodrow Wilson had written in his *Congressional Government* that "there is plain evidence that the expansion of federal power is to continue," because conditions favored "a centralization of governmental functions such as could not have suggested itself as a possibility to the framers of the Constitution." The dilemma which he discerned in this situation was presented by the fact that many problems could be dealt with only by government intervention, but the necessary degree of intervention which would be required to bring these problems under effective control could "be embraced within its juris-diction by no possible stretch of construction, and the majority of them only by wresting the Constitution to strange and as yet unimagined uses."[33]

Now, thirty years later, Wilson found himself responsible for the steering of the ship of state down a steadily more precipitous channel with the land-marks of the past beginning to drop from his view. He had been, as Ely had observed him in the teacher-graduate student relationship at the Johns Hop-kins University of the eighties, essentially a conservative in his preference for the reassuring values of Jeffersonian America. In the White House, as in the governor's office in New Jersey, Wilson faced up to the inevitability and the inexorability of a rapidly broadening function of government accom-panied by an essential broadening of the constitutional standards of governmental responsibility and authority. Having largely predicted the developments to the present, Wilson asked himself where the end was to come, and what the consequences of the new experiments in political economy were to be. Having come so far so fast in his first two years in office, he undertook now to conciliate some of the elements in American life which had been so drastically affected by the legislative innovations of his first Congress.[34]

By the beginning of 1915, the wave of reforms which had inundated Congress tended to subside. The Bryan Democrats and the Republican insurgents urged that the momentum should not be allowed to be lost, but their voices were gradually being drowned in the chorus of opposing advices. Nor did the nation at large seem to demand the continuance of change which had seemed so unanimous in 1912. Toward the end of 1913 a business depression had set in which the conservatives promptly attributed to Democratic animosity toward capitalism. By the end of 1914 and in the early months of 1915 unemployment rose sharply and manufacturing declined in proportion. The accelerating pace of the European war was causing alarm among political and business leaders, and the ideological division within the Cabinet was being exacerbated by Secretary Bryan's vehement protests against preparedness discussions.

The elections of 1914 had further dampened the reform fervor, as Democratic majorities in both houses of Congress were substantially reduced. Looking toward 1916, Wilson's advisers warned that continued decline in party fortunes would breed disaster. Thus, in a confusion of new developments, beneath which lay an elemental doubt as to the consequences to democracy itself of the unprecedented expansion of governmental assertions of power in the first Wilsonian Congress, the administration's program by 1915 seemed to drift toward a halt.

Although the New Freedom implied a continuation of the vigorous antitrust actions of the Justice Department, as they had been brought to a climax by Wickersham, the eight years under Wilson witnessed a steady diminution of this program. In large degree this reflected the Brandeisian influence on the President, confirming Wilson's own conclusion that it was not the size of modern business but its methods which called for regulation. The Federal Trade Commission and Clayton Acts both adhered to the proposition that if government retained the power to define unfair trade practices and regulate or prohibit them, the gains in efficiency and economy from healthy corporate growth would remain to benefit all society. As a logical consequence of this principle, the waning of the trust-busting impulse was inevitable.[35]

The coming of the World War also made inevitable the diversion of the primary efforts of the Justice Department into other channels. Thomas W. Gregory, a onetime classmate of McReynolds at the University of Virginia, and a protege of Colonel House, succeeded to the Attorney Generalship in the fall of 1914. Within two years he would be called upon to administer a vast and unprecedented legislative program related to wartime controls, Selective Service, alien property custodianship, and profiteering. An old-line progressive himself, Gregory was fated to reorient the programs of the Justice Department so that his administration would constitute the transition from the early hopes of the social reformers to the reaction of his successor, A Mitchell Palmer.*[36]

*   *   *

The decline in progressive fervor in the 63rd Congress was accompanied by a resumption of hostile judicial pronouncements which foreshadowed difficulties for future reform legislation. There had been some prospect, after Taft's appointment of Hughes, that the intellectual orientation provided by Holmes' jurisprudence would become more effective on the Court; but Hughes and Holmes, with whom Justice Day was usually associated, were little more than a confirmed minority. In the late summer of 1914 Wilson had nominated Attorney General McReynolds for the seat on the Court made vacant by the death of Justice Lurton. The appointment appeared to have been prompted by a desire to relieve the Cabinet·of the abrasive effect of the irascible Tennesseean's personality, rationalized by the argument that McReynolds' vigorous antitrust prosecutions in the Justice Department would suggest a measure of increased judicial sympathy for future government prosecutions to come before the Court.[37]

Any optimism concerning McReynolds, if the progressives had seriously entertained it, was dashed almost from the moment he came onto the bench; he was the lone dissenter in an opinion striking down an Arizona statute seeking to restrict the number of aliens employable in any given business concern.[38] On the other hand, the leaven of Hughes' carefully reasoned opinions in support of state assertions of police power for general welfare contributed to a definite, albeit transient, revival of the spirit of *Munn v. Illinois*. In the spring of 1912 Hughes had written the opinion upholding the rate-making powers of the Minnesota Warehouse Commission, declaring that the "power of Congress to regulate commerce among the several states is supreme and plenary," and that whenever Congress should determine upon "the necessity of Federal action" the Federal authority would preempt the field. Until such time, as in the Minnesota rate question, state assertion of administrative authority over matters affected with a public interest was not to be held invalid merely because of a prospective but inchoate development of Federal power.[39]

This opinion, closing a vast loophole between state and Federal authority through which the railroads had been operating free from any restraint, was complemented two years later in a decision asserting the primary of ICC rate-making power over that of a state, where the intermixture of local and interstate commerce required the assertion of a uniform Federal administration.[40] Taken together, the two Hughes opinions presented a practical system of dovetailed state and Federal authority which, if it had been analogized and extended to other areas of administrative regulation, might conceivably have reduced the friction between state and national sovereignties in many areas of law. The judicial generation which followed the Minnesota and Shreveport rate

---

*Cf. Ch. 12.

cases, however, like that which followed *Munn,* neglected to extend the precedents established therein, and by the time Hughes returned to the bench, changed conditions had made a preemptive and pervasive Federal administration essential in many of these fields.[41]

The lingering insistence on untrammeled freedom of contract was the issue which served to warn the progressives, in the fall of 1914, the *laissez-faire* jurisprudence was still firmly in control of the constitutional thought of the White Court. As it had been seven years before in a question of Federal authority over labor relations in railroads, the "yellow dog" contract and the legal capacity to outlaw it through state action was presented in a case carried from the Kansas supreme court, which had upheld a Kansas statute on the subject. The six-to-three majority applied the Hughes rationale in the rate cases —in reverse: a subject of legislative action which was forbidden by the freedom of contract rationale of the Constitution was forbidden to the states as effectively as to Congress. To limit an employer's freedom to offer employment on his own terms, the majority declared, was an unconstitutional interference with his contractual rights.[42]

Holmes, in a brief but telling dissent, accepted the argument of the Kansas attorney general, John S. Dawson, that there was constitutional authority inherent in the state to legislate "in order to establish the equality of position between the parties in which liberty of contract begins." In a lengthier dissent in which Hughes joined, Day pointed out that unions represented an interest which had been recognized by state law, and that it was a reasonable exercise of legislative discretion to preserve the right of union membership in the bargaining relationship. Freedom of contract, said Day, does not mean a sacrifice of rights as a condition of accepting employment.[43]

The majority opinion in *Coppage v. Kansas* relegated the Hughes rationale of the rate regulation cases to a limited constitutional applicability. In the matter of freedom of contract, the ideal of *laissez-faire* economics remained unassailable for another generation.

"The labor question will never be advanced toward solution by proclaiming it to be a matter of antagonistic individual rights," Herbert Croly wrote in 1909. "It involves a fundamental public interest—the interest which a democracy must necessarily take in the economic welfare of its own citizens." The logic of national and centralized organization of industry was equally applicable, he believed, to national and centralized organization of labor. Moreover, anticipating both the Wagner and Taft-Hartley acts, Croly warned that both capital and government were estopped from asserting a right to curb labor power when they insisted that labor itself was a matter of free contractual bargaining.[44]

In the winter of 1914-15, Brandeis testified before Wilson's Commission on Industrial Relations that the solution to the labor question depended on eliminating the "juxtaposition of political democracy and industrial absolutism." The agitation over wages, hours and working conditions was, in the final analysis, a concern over symptoms, said Brandeis; the basic question was when labor and management would be recognized in law and economics as essential and co-equal elements in the capitalistic process. Since "no one with absolute power can be trusted to give it up even in part," government in its own interest, as well as in the interest of labor, was required to assert its authority in bringing about the equality.[45]

Croly and Brandeis were voices of the 1930's; to the conservative of 1915, they were the voices of heresy and madness. To Woodrow Wilson, who had accepted Croly's critique only with elaborate qualifications, the time was approaching when he had to come to terms with the critique of Brandeis. Twice before, in matters of Cabinet appointments, he had been dissuaded from an attempt to put "the lawyer of the people" into the service of the government; his firmness in the matter of Brandeis' appointment to the Supreme Court was to bring the New Freedom to its brief climax.

11/The Brief Climax

THE ELECTION YEAR of 1916 opened on a scene of general confusion in both the Democratic and Republican parties, and in both the areas of domestic and foreign affairs. Foreign affairs in particular presented a bitterly divisive series of issues which had broken out almost the moment Wilson had taken office. The sporadic revolution in Mexico, begun in 1910, reached a crisis in February, 1913 with the assassination of the liberal leader Francisco Madero and the seizure of power by the reactionary General Victoriano Huerta. Wilson had adopted a policy of "watchful waiting," which gradually assumed a more affirmative character with the dispatch of American naval units to Vera Cruz to blockade the port to arms shipments. Predictably, incidents led to armed clashes and in April, 1914 to the American bombardment of the port and occupation of the city. A mediation conference in Niagara Falls, Ontario that June led shortly thereafter to Huerta's withdrawal from office and the *de facto* recognition of Venustiano Carranza as president.

Far more menacing was the outbreak of the European war in August, 1914; in rapid succession Imperial Germany declared war on Russia and France, and on the heels of that declaration invaded Belgium. The day after the invasion began, Britain joined France and Russia as a belligerent. The suddenness of the events, and the appalling dimensions of the onslaught which immediately became apparent, filled Americans with dismay. As a people, despite their experiment in imperialism at the turn of the century, they still clung to the tradition of isolation from European affairs, and indeed, the Spanish-American War had been essentially a combination of hemisphere adventurism and Pacific expansion rather than European involvement. As a world power—questionable as its military strength might be in 1914—the United States had no moral or diplomatic commitments to either side. The chief emphasis of American foreign policy since 1908 had been the development of treaties of arbitration among the leading nations of the world, first under Root and later under Bryan as Secretaries of State.

On August 19, Wilson issued a formal proclamation of American neutrality, calling upon his fellow citizens to exemplify the spirit of the proclamation by being "impartial in thought as well as in action." For the moment, a majority of his countrymen were inclined to subscribe to the idea; even Theodore Roosevelt, who would soon be merciless in his criticism of administration policy toward the conflict, expressed his support of the proclamation. The pressure of various groups seeking to commit the nation to one side or the other, warned a Midwestern newspaper, should alert the citizenry to "attempts at abuse of our neutrality" and demanded vigilance "to guard it against the slightest infraction."[1]

There was, if anything, an inchoate disposition to support Germany against the Allies in popular sympathy. Not only did Americans cling to the schoolbook version of the righteousness of the Revolutionary War against British tyranny, but the influx of German immigrants in the mid-nineteenth century had resulted in an impressive contribution of these skilled and educated newcomers to the national wealth, both material and cultural. Added to this was the antipathy for Czarist Russia on the part of Jewish refugees from her pogroms, and the articulate hatred of British authority among Irish immigrant groups. Offsetting these several factors, however, was the general American revulsion at Germany's invasion of a virtually defenseless Belgium, neutralized by international agreement for almost a century, and a mounting clamor of protest at unrestrained submarine warfare which climaxed in the sinking of the British passenger steamer *Lusitania* in May, 1915 with the loss of more than a hundred American lives.

These developments in foreign relations had profoundly unsettling effects upon domestic politics. For the Progressive Movement, modern warfare was a negation of all of the principles of social justice upon which the domestic reforms of the past generation were predicated. The sudden and dramatic resignation of Secretary of State Bryan in protest against the increasing sternness of Wilson's notes to Germany following the *Lusitania* disaster made clear the depth of the schism. "To remain a member of the Cabinet," Bryan told the President, "would be unfair to the cause which is nearest my heart—the prevention of war." He followed this with a public statement that the present issue was a fundamental conflict between systems—the old system of force, with war as its inevitable consequence, and the system of persuasion which "contemplates a universal brotherhood established through the unifying power of example."[2]

For the Republicans, the prospect of a split in the Democratic ranks as a result of the mounting preparedness controversy was tempered only by the awareness that Roosevelt—the chief hope of the insurgents and now all but restored to the party fold—was alienating the pacifist element in the Progressive Movement even more completely than Wilson. Still, it was the Democrats who had the most to lose; not only was the party badly split on the issue of preparedness—Representative Claude Kitchin of North Carolina had already an-

nounced formation of a bloc to smother any legislative proposals on the subject in the House Military Affairs Committee of which he was chairman—but
the war generally was blamed for bringing the push for more reform legislation
to a halt.

Even the announcement of Wilson's engagement and coming second marriage slightly more than fifteen months after the first Mrs. Wilson had died, welcome relief though it provided to the grim headlines of the European conflict,
had serious political implications. Women in many parts of the nation condemned the marriage as unseemly in its haste, while men blamed it for the
President's neglect of party leadership in December, 1915, when the new Congress received the long-expected proposal for the national defense. When, in
February, 1916, Secretary of War Garrison resigned in a dispute over the role
of the National Guard in the prospective preparedness program, the administration seemed indeed to be on the verge of disintegration.

The Garrison resignation came in the midst of a full-scale Democratic revolt against administration policy in the matter of enforcing neutrality—itself
a tactic in derogation of Wilson's national defense bill. Where Wilson and his
new Secretary of State, Robert Lansing, were insisting upon Americans' rights
of travel aboard any commercial vessels of any flag, the Congressional rebels
proposed resolutions denying passports to those who sought to sail on belligerents' ships and forbidding clearance of armed vessels calling at American ports.
The proposals were a manifest invasion of the executive function and a measure of the extent of party hostility to Wilson's general program. It required a
swift and massive mobilization of party strength, as well as substantial
Republican assistance, to beat down the revolt and secure the tabling of the
resolutions in early March.

With the New Freedom bogged down in the preparedness debate, and with
Wilson's popularity apparently plummeting and his leadership of both his
party and the government apparently faltering, the prospects for his reelection
in November did not inspire enthusiasm among his closest associates. For the
Republicans of all hues, the likelihood of unseating Wilson after one term as
they had unseated Cleveland seemed increasingly substantial. Elihu Root, in a
New York speech in February, and Henry Cabot Lodge, in a speech at Lynn,
Massachusetts in March, delivered the opening blasts in what was to become a
steady barrage of criticism of the administration.

* * *

Amid the prevailing confusions of the winter of 1915-16, Wilson dropped
a bombshell of his own which shattered the Senate, Wall Street and the conservative legal establishment of the nation. He nominated Louis D. Brandeis for
the seat on the Supreme Court vacated early in January by the death of
Justice Lamar.

As the shockwave of surprise passed, the screams of calamity began to rise.
"Incredible," "a ghastly joke," "a great national disaster," were characteristic
comments from conservative sources. William Howard Taft, now a Yale Law

School teacher with time to reflect on the three opportunities he had passed over to ascend the bench himself, and time to wonder whether destiny would knock on yet one more occasion, wrote that the news was "one of the deepest wounds that I have had as an American and a lover of the Constitution." The fact that, in the weeks following Lamar's death, a number of newspapers and men of affairs had urged upon Wilson the propriety of naming the ex-President to the bench did nothing to soften the blow which Brandeis' nomination dealt to Taft's own interests. Added to this was the bitter memory of Brandeis' role, as counsel for the complainants during the Ballinger-Pinchot furore, in focussing public attention on the widening discrepancies between the statements on which the Taft administration had staked its own veracity.[3]

Even more of a blow did the Brandeis nomination deal to Senator Lodge of Massachusetts; indeed, the shrewd maneuver by which Wilson put his Senate adversary out on a limb was something which Lodge would remember, a few years later, when the Treaty of Versailles came up for debate. A New England aristocrat with a particular distaste for the polyglot immigrants who were crowding into the electorate and a supreme hostility to those who challenged the *status quo* buttressed by the courts, Lodge instinctively would have reacted to the candidacy of this militant Jewish liberal by invoking Senatorial privilege to ask rejection as a nominee personally obnoxious to him. But it was not that easy. To raise the ethnic question directly was to jeopardize his own electoral base in Massachusetts as well as the prospects for defeating Wilson in the Presidential campaign in the fall. For the moment, Lodge could only rage impotently at the turn of events.[4]

Wilson had certainly weighed all of the political considerations in determining upon his nomination. He was acutely aware of his prospective loss of large blocs of progressive votes in the wake of the disenchantment of the past few months, and he knew that these votes had to be won back, even at the loss of some conservative Democratic votes, if he was to carry the day in November. Added to this was his awareness that his first appointment to the Court— McReynolds—had been a serious mistake so far as liberalizing the jurisprudence of the bench was concerned. That error could be offset only by finding someone who would be beyond doubt a spokesman for enlightened constitutional principles.

But outweighing these several considerations was Wilson's conviction of the ability of Brandeis as a person; from their first meeting in August, 1912, Wilson had appreciated the soundness of the Boston lawyer's analysis of the economic issues on which the New Freedom had to be established. Brandeis' counsel had been regularly sought by the President on recurring occasions after the election, and Wilson had made it clear to all his advisors that he regretted having followed their urging not to have made the "people's attorney" a member of his Cabinet from the outset.[5]

Now the question was to be the ability of the administration to push the nomination past the determined opposition which was manifestly taking shape.

A special subcommittee of the Senate Judiciary Committee had already been named to hold hearings on the qualifications of the candidate, and Lodge among others had suggested the line of attack to be followed: "I have before me the proofs of Brandeis' action in several cases," he wrote to Arthur D. Hill, a leading Boston attorney, which seemed to him to be "in the highest degree unprofessional, if there is any standard of unprofessional honor." He then observed: "If the Bar Associations have nothing to say against his appointment I do not believe that they will find that Senators are anxious to plunge into a very disagreeable contest, as this is sure to be."[6]

The Boston bar did not miss the cue; on February 11, the Senate subcommittee received a formal memorial from fifty-five leaders of that community amounting to a remonstrance against the nomination. The petition itself was rather vague. An appointment to the Supreme Court, it said, "should only be conferred upon a member of the legal profession whose general reputation is as good as his legal attainments are great." Brandeis, it went on, introducing a theme which was to be played recurrently during the coming months, lacked the "judicial temperament" needed for objective consideration of issues, and did not have "the confidence of the people." Among the signers were President A. Lawrence Lowell of Harvard; Charles F. Choate, counsel for the New Haven Railroad; Charles Francis Adams, historian and sometime reformer but in this crisis a defender of his social class; Hollis R. Bailey, an officer of the American Bar Association; and William L. Putnam, a director of the American Telephone & Telegraph Company.[7]

The subcommittee let it be known that it was prepared to explore every phase of Brandeis' public—and probably private—life, over the four decades of his law practice. In addition to the private practice which had made him independently wealthy, Brandeis had figured in a dozen major public issues since 1893 which had made him one of the best-known attorneys in the nation. An eighteen-year struggle for public control of the Boston transit system had been won in 1911, and a six-year battle over the reorganization of the New Haven had come to an end in 1913—two resounding campaigns against the entrenched wealth of the Hub City which accounted for the readiness of its respectable citizens to sign the remonstrance against his nomination. These persons remembered, also, his 1905 crusade against unconscionable insurance rates and the successful effort to break up the monopoly in insurance which had operated so lucratively for the past generations.

Outside New England, Brandeis had been in the public eye since his famed briefs in the Oregon minimum-wage and maximum-hour cases which had been followed by other appearances as counsel in related cases from California, Illinois and Ohio. He had also appeared, at various times since 1910, as special counsel before the Interstate Commerce Commission arguing the case for substantial reforms of railroad rate schedules—a particularly sore point with many vested interests, as the subcommittee hearings were to reveal. In 1916, as his nomination was being debated, Brandeis was completing his sixth year as chairman of the board of arbitration in a New York garment workers' strike.[8]

"By your zeal for the common good, you have created powerful enemies," Judge Charles F. Amidon of the Federal District Court in Fargo, North Dakota wrote Brandeis when the nomination had been announced. He added: "You will be accused of everything, from grand larceny to a non-judicial temperament." The attack was not long in coming. At the opening hearing of the subcommittee on February 9, Clifford Thorne of Des Moines, chairman of the Iowa state railroad commission, appeared to testify against Brandeis' behavior in the ICC rate cases affecting freight charges from Midwestern shipping points. An insurgent Republican himself, Thorne declared that Brandeis had "betrayed" the reform cause by his opinion finding that the railroads had presented a valid case for higher rates than the shippers had been prepared to allow.

Thorne's testimony was promptly refuted by other participants in the ICC hearing; John M. Eshleman, lieutenant governor of California, pointed out that Brandeis' function before the Commission had been to serve as an impartial representative of the public interest rather than as an attorney for the shippers. The result of the rather irrational criticism of Brandeis' role in the Five Percent Rate Case, as it was called, was in fact to build up his image as an objective administrator rather than a doctrinaire enemy of big business.[9]

The threshing out of the rate case results was followed by the testimony from Clarence W. Barron, editor and publisher of the *Wall Street Journal,* who had written that the Brandeis nomination had been "an insult to New England and the business interests of the country." Barron charged that Brandeis had "betrayed" a former client, the United Shoe Machinery Company, and had wrecked the financial structure of the New Haven and other railroads. Sidney Winslow, president of the shoe company, followed with complaints that Brandeis, after serving as attorney and director for the company, had used his inside information to aid in anti-trust suits against the company.

A sign of the extent of organized opposition to the nomination was the announcement, while Winslow was testifying, that a New York appellate attorney, Austen George Fox, had been retained to conduct the campaign of the opposition. The aspect of a formal trial of the nominee was heightened by the request of the administration forces, through Attorney General Gregory, to appoint George Anderson, Federal district attorney from Boston, to develop the "facts" for the subcommittee in the course of its hearings.[10]

The dramatic high point in the hearings was reached in mid-March, when a memorial signed by seven past presidents of the American Bar Association, including Taft and Root, was submitted to the subcommittee in opposition to the nomination. By now the fight was a weekly feature of the mass periodicals, and in columns of Croly's *New Republic* and the social welfare magazine *The Survey* the personal animosity of each of the signers of the memorial was promptly documented. LaFollette of Wisconsin dismissed them as "sleek respectable crooks." In the majority report of the subcommittee filed on April 1, Senator Thomas J. Walsh of Montana summarized the tenor of the opposition: "The real crime of which this man is guilty is that he has exposed the iniquities of men in high places in our financial system. He has not stood in awe of the majesty of wealth."[11]

Wilson elected to follow the strategy of letting the opposition talk itself out, with each specific charge methodically rebutted by other spokesmen from government or the legal profession. Then, in May, it was arranged that the President would be invited to advise the Senate of his reasons for submitting the nomination. In his letter, Wilson pointed out that the objections to Brandeis had come almost unanimously from men who hated him "because he had refused to be serviceable to them in the promotion of their own selfish interests," added that he had carefully investigated the nominee's professional and personal qualifications, and unequivocally announced his interest in "the confirmation of the appointment by the Senate."[12] Moving in for the final attack, administration leaders—McAdoo, Gregory and Burleson in the vanguard —served notice on party regulars that the time had come to be counted, while the insurgents under LaFollette had already been marshalled for action. The Judiciary Committee, by a vote of ten to eight, reported a recommendation that the appointment be confirmed on May 24, and on June 1 the Senate as a whole finally approved Brandeis by a vote of forty-seven to twenty-two—with twenty-seven not voting.

Onto the bench beside Holmes and Day—and, for a short remaining time, Hughes—now came another of the advocates of a flexible and responsive constitutionalism in the twentieth century. Of Brandeis' confirmation, Attorney Anderson in Boston exulted in the triumph of "freedom from the trammels of race prejudice; freedom from subservience to the money power; freedom to think and to act and to speak as men ought to think and act and speak in a real democracy."[13]

*   *   *

The Brandeis nomination had been the most dramatic evidence of a maturing conviction in Wilson's mind that the reform cause needed to be put back in motion. Primarily this was dictated by the looming battle for reelection, but in his new legislative program the President showed evidence that he was prepared to move from the moderate progressivism of the New Freedom to the more militant progressivism which had been the hallmark of the New Nationalism. The experience of his first four years in office had placed Wilson's own philosophy of progressivism in a new perspective: before 1912 he had assumed that the function of Congressional legislation was essentially to police interstate affairs so that state administration would be more effective; now in 1916 he had come to accept the view that national problems required national administration.

Wilson's changing philosophy of government, hammered out on the anvil of experience, was reflected in remarks he made a month after the November election, in a speech before the Washington Gridiron Club: "The day of cold thinking, of fine-spun constitutional argument is gone, thank God. We do not now discuss so much what the Constitution of the United States is as what the constitution of human nature is, what the essential constitution of human society is, and we know in our hearts that if we ever find a place or a time where the Constitution of the United States is contrary to the constitution of human nature and human society, we have got to change the Constitution of the United States."[14]

It was not immediately evident that the Constitution would require changing, either by amendment or by the continued replacement of *laissez-faire* jurists with broader constructionists. The basic consideration was the need and opportunity for implementing a series of nationalistic laws which would demonstrate the administration's commitment to permanent reform. Congress, Wilson was assured by one of the party leaders in the House in early June, was "now working like a well-oiled machine," ready to turn out any legislation which the White House earnestly wished to push through. The National Defense Act, finally hammered out after six months of debate, was signed into law on June 3; before the summer was over a Council of National Defense authorized by the Army Appropriation Act would be established with a view to coordinating the resources and productive processes of the nation including such correlative subjects as engineering, education and medicine.[15]

While these were in the nature of emergency measures under the pressures of the increasingly threatening European conflict, they were to have a fundamental effect on American society in its peaceful and domestic affairs before the end of the decade. But long-term, non-emergency measures of domestic economics which had long been tending toward a national administration were also being advanced through this session of Congress. The Federal Farm Loan Act, a favorite progressive principle which had become more ardently advocated after the Federal Reserve System came into being, was passed in mid-July; with its organization into twelve districts with a Federal Farm Loan Bank in each district and farm cooperatives as members of the district banks, the system offered farmers long-term loans at rates substantially lower than those offered by commercial institutions. In 1913 Wilson had resisted the plan as both paternalistic and an invasion of state responsibilities; now he accepted it as a necessary national answer to a national problem.[16]

In August the Farm Loan Act was supplemented by the Federal Warehouse Act, authorizing licensed and bonded warehouses to issue against certain specified agricultural commodities receipts which could be used as collateral for loans. On September 1 came the Federal Child Labor Law prohibiting the shipment in interstate commerce of manufactured goods where the manufacture had involved the employment of children under fourteen for more than eight hours a day or six days a week. Two days later, on the eve of a threatened national railroad strike, Congress passed the Adamson Act establishing an eight-hour working day on interstate railroads. Complementing these statutes—virtually planks taken from the Progressive Party platform of four years before—were the Kern-McGillicudy measure establishing a system of workmen's compensation for Federal employees, and a provision in the Revenue Act of 1916 which appropriated Theodore Roosevelt's 1912 campaign proposal and created a non-partisan tariff commission.[17]

The veritable flood of reform bills passing through Congress in the summer of 1916 prompted a leading New York Democratic newspaper to call it "the most important program of progressive domestic legislation ever enacted by a single administration since Washington's." There was not too much exaggeration in the statement; having committed himself intellectually to a strong Federal administration, and realizing how fundamentally it departed from the traditional Democratic position favoring decentralized governmental authority, Wilson was working against time on three fronts. There was, in the short run, the political capital to be made of these legislative accomplishments in the imminent Presidential campaign; there was, also in the short run, the prospect of substantial involvement, perhaps all-out involvement, in the war with its inevitable moratorium on domestic advancement. And there was, in the long run, the need to remake the Democratic party in the new Wilsonian image as the party of nationalism. As matters turned out, the short-term objectives were attained; repudiation of the Wilsonian image, by the party and by the public, would come in 1920 as the product of a disparate combination of factors.[18]

*   *   *

On June 10 Charles Evans Hughes sent a telegram to the Republican National Convention in Chicago accepting the party's nomination for President; the same day he forwarded a brief note to the White House resigning as Associate Justice. By return mail, Wilson accepted the resignation. It had not been a surprise to anyone; for months, the tenor of political comment had been that the reform governor of New York and the moderate progressive on the Supreme Court was the only hope for reuniting the Republican party and the best prospect for defeating Wilson in November. Taft's overwhelming defeat in 1912 had removed him completely from consideration, while Roosevelt's bolting of the party then, insuring its loss and the Democratic victory, made it impossible to consider him seriously as a coalition candidate.

Reunion of insurgent and conservative elements of the Republican party aside, the party leaders believed that the Wilson record in foreign affairs was his most vulnerable spot. An all-out attack upon his conduct of international matters in Mexico and other Latin American critical areas, but above all in the European war, was the obvious strategy to be followed. It was the means of reuniting the conservatives Root and Lodge with the insurgent Roosevelt—all of them proceeded to outdo each other in bellicose oratory and in unrestrained castigation of the Wilsonian course. Yet Hughes himself was ambivalent. He was unable to make convincing answers to the Democratic demands to know what he would have done under the circumstances of German aggressiveness on the high seas and documented cases of German conspiracies within the United States itself.

Hughes was handicapped by the fact that, for the past half-dozen years, he had completely kept out of touch with politics. The instinct for campaigning with its exaggerated claims and charges had been dulled in the detached and objective atmosphere of the Supreme Court. In addition, his sympathies for the domestic reforms which had been effected by the Wilson administration kept him from attacking them on principle. It was in the increasingly desperate situation presented by the war overseas that he found the strongest justification for his running for the office at all. While he shared with Wilson the longing to let the cup of involvement pass, he was most effective in his insistence that the preparedness program had been postponed too long and contemplated too modest and too leisurely an implementation.

Too hollow, also, was the Democratic slogan that Wilson "kept us out of war"; both Hughes and Wilson were acutely aware, in the late summer of 1916, that the time remaining to keep out of the war had all but run out. The wishful thinking of the agrarian sections of the nation, and the interior of the country generally, was in contrast to the slowly growing awareness of the public in the East that a final confrontation was rapidly approaching. While the neo-jingoism of Roosevelt was more embarrassing than persuasive, the East inclined to believe that Hughes and the Republicans might offer the hope of a more rapid and more effective program of national security in the face of fearsome danger.

So it was, in November, that the Eastern states began giving their electoral votes to Hughes. The returns during the evening of November 7 pointed to a narrow but consistent Republican lead. All of New England except New Hampshire; all of the Middle Atlantic states with their sizable electoral vote; all of the states north of the Ohio with the exception of Ohio itself; and the progressive strongholds of Wisconsin, Iowa and Minnesota—all were reported in Hughes' column. The Democratic *New York World* conceded defeat; after all, the loss of New York's forty-five electoral votes was assumed to be a blow from which no candidate could recover. Yet neither candidate was rash enough to claim victory; throughout the following day the returns were awaited from the Far West where a slow rise in Democratic strength revived administration hopes. It was not until the evening of the 9th, when the Republican chairman in California conceded that his state had gone for Wilson by some three thousand votes, that the candidates and the country had their final answer.

Again, as in 1912, Wilson found himself a winner by a plurality rather than a majority. Although his popular vote of 9,129,606 was an increase of nearly three million over his earlier record, Hughes polled more than Roosevelt and Taft combined in 1912—8,538,221. The Socialist candidate, Allen L. Benson, received 585,113 votes, a drop of three hundred thousand from Debs' record of four years before; but the Prohibition Party candidate, J. Frank Hanly, won 220,506 votes, slightly more than his counterpart in 1912. The electoral vote between the major candidates was 277 to 254. Not until the election of 1960 would there be another contest so close.

*   *   *

The election result, said most commentators, was a vote for continued reform legislation at home and continued avoidance of war abroad. During the month following the election, there seemed to be a prospect that peace might be subject to fruitful discussion. Early in September, in fact, the German Ambassador to the United States, Count Johann von Bernstorff, had advised the White House that his government desired to know whether the good offices of the United States would be offered if Germany was prepared to guarantee the restoration of Belgium. Wilson had replied that he would take no steps until after the election in the matter of possible mediation; in any event, he was unsatisfied with the prospect of what Germany's other terms might be. Although, by the summer of 1916, Allied counter-attacks on the Western Front and Russian offensives in the east had finally halted the two-year advances of the Imperial German armies, there was no reason to believe that the Kaiser was prepared to do more than settle for the gains he had won to this point.

Thus by December the purported peace feelers had stopped; the Allied Powers, unduly optimistic about the turn of the tide at this time, were no more disposed than the Central Powers to wish for peace on the terms that could presently be obtained. The resumption, early in 1917, of unlimited submarine warfare, the sudden collapse of both Russian and Italian military power and the failure of British and French offensives led to a serious worsening of the situation. The extension of attacks to United States merchant vessels and the interception of a note from German Foreign Secretary Alfred Zimmermann to the Imperial Minister in Mexico offering to make common cause against the United States in event of war, galvanized public feeling against Germany. On April 6, a joint Congressional resolution declared the country to be at war with the Central Powers.

The impact of a machine age war on American society was to be the final catalyst in the transformation of the looseknit individualistic standards of the frontier and small town into a permanently integrated economy. For the first time in its history, as well as in the history of the rest of the world, a nation was committing itself to a war which demanded the conversion of peacetime uses of virtually every phase of human activity, on farms, in mines, in factories and schools. The very speed and efficiency of the change to a centrally administered program of mobilization, training (or retraining, as the case might be), and transportation of men and material alarmed some observers.

Nicholas Murray Butler wrote Congress expressing the hope that the wartime income and excess profits taxes would be understood to be emergency measures and not a precedent for permanent tax policies. Apostles of a strong Federalism, however, saw the lessons learned of wartime emergency as a demonstration of what might be the normal order of things. "Part of the efficient response to an emergency," wrote Charles Merz in the *New Republic,* "consists

in taking the shortest road to readiness." Where the shortcut amounts to a "re-
modeling of our national organization so that it operates more efficiently and
more humanely," he concluded, it was hard to justify going back to something
less efficient and less humane when the emergency had passed.[19]

In 1914 Lord Grey had made his long-remembered remark about the lights
going down in all the capitals of Europe, dimming the last glimpses of a vanishing world. In America in the early summer of 1917, there was perhaps less
of a sense of a way of life about to pass into history. The automobile age was
reflected in such important news reports as the replacement of stagecoaches by
motor buses in Yellowstone Park, and the introduction of a driver's license law
in New York. Patrons of the new silent drama, the motion picture, had a choice
between Douglas Fairbanks in "In Again, Out Again," and Charlie Chaplin in
"Easy Street." A hint of economic things to come was the price of cotton on
the New York Exchange on April 19—21½ cents a pound, the highest since
the Civil War; in Chicago, when May wheat rose to $3.25 a bushel the Board
of Trade ordered a discontinuation of trading. In August the Texas senate removed James "Pa" Ferguson as governor, whereupon his wife, "Ma," was
promptly elected in his place, the first woman to hold such office in American
history; but in the nation's capital suffragettes were less successful, with ten
arrested for picketing the White House in August, and forty-one arrested in
November.[20]

As labor, both skilled and unskilled, attained a premium value, a massive
migration of Southern Negroes to Northern industrial centers began. As manpower dwindled, womanpower was recruited to take its place, and the old
stigma against women's employment in any but a genteel and limited group of
occupations swiftly disappeared. In women's traditional place in the home, too,
the war effort was promoted through observance of meatless, wheatless, sugar-
less and butterless days, while the *New York Herald* reported that fifty society
leaders had agreed upon "Spartan simplicity" when the dinners of the social
season were served.

So, in a short sequence of months, American domestic institutions under-
went a succession of sweeping changes; to the average man in 1918, it almost
seemed that he had looked away for a fleeting moment and all of his familiar
landmarks had vanished. Mass production of every type of commodity, still
tentative and experimental in many cases in 1916, had become a virtually
universal technique of industry by 1918; with farm labor drained off, the farms
themselves became mechanized. The airplane, a novelty when Wilson first
took office, developed a new generation of operators for a new medium of
transportation, while the vital role of motor transportation, demonstrated in
France, accelerated the growth of the highway system of the twenties. Hundreds of thousands of impressionable young Americans embarked in the American Expeditionary Force to the tune of "Over There," and returned to the re-
frain, "How're ya gonna keep 'em down on the farm, after they've seen Paree?"

In a word, emancipation from traditional frames of reference was the net product of the war experience on the American mind.

*   *   *

Ill-prepared, and belatedly facing the prospect of conflict, the United States moved with spectacular speed once the die was cast. On March 31 a General Munitions Board had been established by the Council on National Defense, to coordinate the assembling of raw materials and the manufacture of armaments. On April 14 a Committee of Public Information under George Creel was established to unite American public opinion behind the war effort. Ten days later the Liberty Loan Act was passed by Congress; on May 15 came the Selective Service Act; and on June 15 came the Espionage Act. The American people, so long regarded by Europe as indolent and incapable of self-discipline, overnight were transforming themselves into a fighting state; Marshal von Hindenberg, in defeat, was to pay them the ultimate tribute: "They understood war." Or, at least, their public leaders understood the need for decisive action, and the average American acquiesced in the steps which drafted him into military service—nine and a half million men between 18 and 45 years of age were registered in June 1917.

In the face of the national emergency, the courts found adequate constitutional authority for the wartime measures. The draft law was upheld by a Federal district court in Michigan in July as a necessary incident to the power of the government to raise an army, and in August a Federal court in Georgia rejected the argument that the draft violated the Thirteenth Amendment prohibition against "involuntary servitude."[21] The following year Chief Justice White spoke for a unanimous Supreme Court in upholding the Federal government's power to raise and dispatch armed forces abroad.

In one of his more cogent opinions, White observed that the existence of a nation implies the capacity to enforce its sovereign authority; the transition from the Articles of Confederation to the Constitution had this as one of its primary objectives and effects; and even the seceding states of the Confederacy had retained from the Federal Constitution the assertion of the power to raise and maintain armed forces for the common defense. So much more, said the Court in a pregnant holding, the obligations of Americans to the national need had been confirmed by the Fourteenth Amendment which "broadened the national scope of the government under the Constitution by causing citizenship of the United States to be paramount and dominant instead of being subordinate and derivative."[22]

The economic power of Congress in the emergency was another constitutional issue which the Court considered in a suit challenging the Adamson eight-hour work law of 1916. Speaking for himself and four colleagues (McKenna, unable to accept the broad statement of governmental power in the majority opinion, concurred separately), White affirmed the validity of the statute with the observation that "the public interest begets a public right of regulation to protect it." More than that, the Chief Justice declared, "although an emergency may not call into life a power which has never lived, nevertheless emergency may afford a reason for the exertion of a living power already enjoyed." If Congress may legislate to prevent the interruption of interstate commerce, he concluded, it may also legislate to regulate the conditions which if unregulated would lead to such interruption.[23]

In this brief climax of progressive philosophy on the Court, White was joined by Holmes and Brandeis, the generally pedestrian Pitney, and Hughes' replacement of the previous year, Justice John H. Clarke. Taken together, the propositions in the Selective Draft Cases and in *Wilson v. New* offered a prospect of Federalism which, as events were to show, was ahead of its time by a generation or more. The paramountcy of a Federal citizenship was a fact of peace as well as war, and the efficacy of an innate power of government demonstrated under emergency conditions should not, as Merz had pointed out, irrationally be deactivated when it might be equally efficacious under normal conditions. But the highlights of this jurisprudential proposition were to be thrown into shadow by the hysteria and revulsion which was soon to sweep the country, and Holmes and Brandeis were to settle back to their long and often thankless course of dissent in the age of normalcy.

*   *   *

While domestic reform legislation by tacit understanding was held virtually in abeyance after the declaration of war—the Smith-Hughes Act for Federal grants in aid of vocational training was enacted in February of 1917—the Progressive Movement did attain another long-time objective in the successful campaign in Congress to draft and submit a prohibition amendment to the Constitution. Wartime psychology, as a matter of fact, augmented the prohibitionist argument: the need to conserve the grain which normally would go into manufacture of alcoholic beverages, and the public animosity toward German-American identification with the brewing industry, were both powerful contemporary arguments.

As a matter of fact, prohibition had been a subject of persistent advocacy for most of a century. Temperance had become an article of faith with many American church groups, while civic reformers never tired of citing the parasitic effect of the corner saloon upon working class family life and the wages of the breadwinner. Since 1895 the Anti-Saloon League had been advocating abolition of intoxicants at the state and Federal constitutional levels and by 1914 there were fourteen states "dry" by statewide prohibition, while more than half of the remainder of the country had local option laws to the same effect. The strength of the national Prohibition Party ticket in 1916 was attested not so much by the more than two hundred thousand votes it polled as by the fact that within twelve months thereafter the number of totally "dry" states had virtually doubled.[24]

The practical politics of the campaign of the Anti-Saloon League won the admiration of the most sophisticated observers. "There are no shrewder politicians in America," wrote a fascinated correspondent in the *Independent* in 1914. The League concentrated on identifying "dry" political candidates of either major party—and included in its endorsement even an imbiber who committed himself to prohibition. For the most part, however, it adhered to the ascetic and messianic persuasion of its general counsel, Wayne B. Wheeler. The nemesis of saloonkeepers in more than two thousand prosecutions brought in the course of twenty years, the author of a long list of state and national prohibition statutes, and the campaign manager for the swift ratification of the Eighteenth Amendment, Wheeler came to embody the caricature of the tight-lipped, gaunt and disapproving teetotaler who represented the moral indignation of rural America from which the prohibition movement derived its primary strength.

As it turned out, the final drive through Congress for the Eighteenth Amendment was guided smoothly down a path already well paved. In 1913, just as the Taft administration was expiring, the Webb-Kenyon Act prohibiting interstate shipment of liquor into "dry" states had been passed by Congress, and in 1917 the Supreme Court had upheld its constitutionality.[25] In the same year, the Selective Draft Act prohibited the sale of intoxicating liquor on military bases or to servicemen in uniform. And in August the Lever Food-Control Act had empowered the President to impound distilled spirits intended for alcoholic beverage production if they were found needed for munitions manufacture, and to limit the amount of food products consumed by the distilleries if they were found to be needed for the war effort.[26]

Although the wartime requirements were the prohibitionists' most telling arguments, it was becoming reasonably likely that the war itself would be over before ratification of the Amendment could be effected. Wheeler's forces, quite aware of the urgency of the situation, organized a vigorous thirteen-month campaign to secure the necessary state ratifications. Even so, the major industrial states held out till the last—Pennsylvania, New Jersey and New York were among the last five to approve the proposal, and Vermont, the thirty-sixth required state to ratify, did not act until January 1919—more than two months after the Armistice.

*   *   *

The implications of emergency controls over the nation dictated by the war were readily discerned and decried by constitutional conservatives. Food control legislation was opposed in Congress for its tendency, as Senator Thomas P. Gore of Oklahoma put it, to "turn over the business of our country to one individual"—even though the individual was the Chief Executive or his deputy, a brilliant engineer named Herbert Hoover, who had accomplished a monumental task of getting millions of tons of food through Allied and German blockades to starving Belgium. Senator Lodge said of the penal sanctions in the bill that they went "some distance beyond that once venerated instrument, the Constitution of the United States." Other leaders in public life looked about them at the restrictions placed upon transportation and communications, upon labor relations and housing, and upon almost every activity in American life, and asked themselves whether a war to make the world safe for democracy had not in fact imperiled democracy—which they equated with maximum individual freedom—at home.[27]

The Lever Act, indeed, did give conservatives reason to pause; its preamble declared that, controls over food and fuel being necessary for the common defense, these industries were affected with a public interest which made them subject to Federal regulation. Senator James Reed of Missouri saw this proposition as an infringement upon the Tenth Amendment reserving undelegated powers to the states or the people. The Amendment, he argued, required the advocates of a Federal authority over any subject to carry the burden of proof. Senator John W. Weeks of Massachusetts added that the power vested in the President by the bill as proposed would make him a dictator in law if not in fact. What fundamentally agitated the conservatives, however, was not the necessary concentration of authority in the Chief Executive in time of national emergency—Senator Lodge was heard to aver, in fact, that many of the emergency statutes being introduced into Congress were only declaratory of a plenary authority vested in the President as Commander-in-Chief by the Constitution. The crux of the matter was the principle that in any time or on any subject which manifestly affected the national interest, a Federal authority might be asserted.[28]

*   *   *

Although it was the conservatives who worried most, it was the liberals who suffered most in the aftermath of the rush of centripetal power during the war years. For more than a generation, the vociferous criticism of public affairs and the conduct of governmental business had been the common characteristic of the independent political forces which had made up the Progressive Movement. The agrarian radicals of the late nineteenth century had become the nucleus of insurgency in the established major parties by the early twentieth century, while urban dissidents had gravitated into the Socialist and more militant Socialist Labor parties. For all of them, the stoppage of domestic reform which came with entry into the European war directed their potential for protest to national affairs connected with the war itself. In this they ran headlong into the controls over acts and expressions established by emergency legislation in the form of the Espionage, Trading with the Enemy, and Sedition Acts.

The legislation against disaffection reflected the wave of public resentment at obstructionist activity of German-American groups in the months immediately preceding the declaration of war. The campaign of 1916 had focussed public attention on what Roosevelt contemptuously called the hyphenated groups, and Wilson himself observed, on the eve of the war, that "the spirit of ruthless brutality will enter into the very fiber of our national life, infecting Congress, the courts, the policeman, the man in the street," as the American people closed their minds as well as their ranks for the struggle. It was not democracy's finest hour when a leading clergyman, the Reverend Henry Van Dyke, urged the government to "hang every one who lifts his voice against America's entering the war," and a leading historian, William Roscoe Thayer, warned against "the total pollution of our people by letting loose of the Prussian moral sewers."[29]

The initial denunciations were directed at the enemy abroad; but it was the easiest of steps to swivel the guns and level them at the alleged enemy within, identified most readily as the noncomformist. The regimentation of American society reached its climax in the Sedition Act of 1918, with the absolute proscription of "disloyal, profane, scurrilous, or abusive langauge about the form of government of the United States, or the Constitution of the United States," the armed forces, the American flag, or the war effort of the nation. The penal sanctions included fines up to ten thousand dollars and imprisonment up to twenty years, or both. A major provision of the law was the empowering of the Postmaster General to refuse delivery of anything which in his opinion was calculated to encourage the spread of the proscribed activities. The Justice Department, in implementation of this and related wartime controls, directed its three hundred field operatives to be on the alert for all signs of disaffection in chance remarks and suspicious acts; another hundred members were added in the following twelve months.

Volunteer spy hunters and witch hunters proliferated in response to Attorney General Gregory's announcement that "complaints of even the most informal or confidential nature are always welcome." Gregory had approved the creation, in the summer of 1917, of a private group known as the American Protective League, whose announced function was to guard against neutrality violations. By the following year the League claimed a membership of a quarter of a million persons, with branches in more than six hundred communities, and proudly announced that as an "auxiliary of the Department of Justice" it was conducting thousands of investigations of individuals in aid of the loyalty and preparedness program. Only McAdoo, among the wartime Cabinet members, appeared to view the League with alarm; the abuses of individual rights by persons thus functioning under color of official authority, he wrote the Attorney General, was a threat as grave as any that had ever confronted American freedoms.

While Gregory replied with an ardent defense of the League, he did send out a circular to his official operatives admonishing them that "protection of loyal persons from unjust suspicion and persecution is quite as important as the suppression of actual disloyalty." But in the fall of 1918—although Gregory advised Wilson that it was in violation of his direct orders to the contrary —a collection of badge-flaunting League members and military units in uniform staged a series of "slacker" raids in New York City which prompted the *Evening World* to accuse the "Department of Injustice" of feeding on the gratuitous slanders of "perfervid females and members of Amateur Patriots' Associations" to destroy civil liberties.[30]

A nation which had not, since the days of the Founding Fathers in the Constitutional Convention, taken time for philosophical reflection in the midst of the business of conquering a continent, now found itself, in the throes of a war unparalleled in history, compelled to consider the question whether the "unalienable rights" of their Declaration of Independence and the guarantees of their Bill of Rights were absolute or relative. Did the Constitution unequivocally insure freedom of expression and assembly, freedom from unreasonable searches and seizures, and indeed, life and liberty themselves, against infringement at all times and under all circumstances? This was the ultimate issue posed by the explosion of Federal regulatory legislation in the emergency of 1917-18. Upon the answer would rest not only the peacetime framework of constitutional liberties but the structure of twentieth century Federalism in general.

*   *   *

The question was presented to the Supreme Court on January 9 and 10, 1919, when two anti-war propogandists, Charles T. Schenck and Elizabeth Baer, appealed their convictions in the Federal court for eastern Pennsylvania under the Espionage Act. Schenck, as general secretary of the Socialist Party, had been responsible for the preparation and printing of fifteen thousand copies of a circular to be sent to men who had been screened as eligible for the draft. The leaflets recited the first section of the Thirteenth Amendment, characterized military conscription as a crime against humanity, and urged the reader to "assert your opposition to the draft." Not to do so, the circular added, was itself a denial of the rights which it was the duty of American citizens to maintain.

In answering the question, the Court had to take into account the thesis and antithesis set out in an earlier case which had been adjudicated in the trial and intermediate appellate courts on the constitutionality of the Espionage Act in relation to the First Amendment.[31] The validity of a wartime sedition provision, Judge Learned Hand had asserted, depended on the government's ability to prove the danger to the general welfare directly resulting from the utterance. It was of the essence of constitutional freedom, said Hand, "that the state point with exactness to just that conduct which violates the law. It is difficult and often impossible," he added, "to meet the charge that one's general *ethos* is treasonable." An objective standard to test the danger at which the statute aimed was the only safeguard against an arbitrary application of the statute to any unpopular speech, Hand concluded:

> Political agitation, by the passions it arouses or the convictions it engenders, may in fact stimulate men to the violation of law. Detestation of existing policies is easily transformed into forcible resistance to the authority which puts them into execution, and it would be folly to disregard the causal relation between the two. Yet to assimilate agitation, legitimate as such, with direct incitement to violent resistance, is to disregard the tolerance of all methods of political agitation which in normal times is a safeguard of free government.[32]

Justice Holmes, speaking for a unanimous Court, acquiesced in the doctrine expounded by Hand, who had granted an injunction restraining the government in the prosecution under the statute, but also accepted the argument of the appellate court which had reversed the ruling and dismissed the injunction.[33] With reference to Schenck, Holmes conceded that "in many places and in ordinary times the defendants, in saying all that was said in the circular, would have been within their constitutional rights. But the character of every act depends upon the circumstances in which it is done." The most liberal interpretation of the First Amendment, Holmes declared, would "not protect a man in falsely shouting fire in a theater and causing a panic. It does not even protect a man from an injunction against uttering words that may have all the effect of force," he added, citing a 1911 decision proscribing speech in a labor dispute.[34]

"The question in every case," said Holmes, "is whether the words are used in such circumstances and are of such a nature as to create a clear and present danger that they will bring about the substantive evils that Congress has a right to prevent. It is a question of proximity and degree." If the tendency of the words is to make the danger real, the intention should be punishable even though the danger does not materialize into fact.[35] Holmes reiterated the principle in a companion case upholding the conviction of Jacob Frohwerk, who had published articles in a Missouri German language newspaper urging resistance to military recruiting,[36] and in another case upholding the conviction of the veteran dissident, Eugene V. Debs, for an anti-draft speech at Canton, Ohio, where, Holmes said, liability derived from the intention of some parts of the speech to incite resistance to the law even where the general theme of the speech was constitutionally protected.[37]

*   *   *

The relativism of Holmes' clear and present danger test in the *Schenck, Frohwerk* and *Debs* cases led inevitably to a parting of the ways as subsequent issues, in the wake of the Armistice, came before the Court. Relativistic tests were essentially subjective; they lacked the insistence upon proof beyond reasonable doubt which was inherent in Hand's objective standard. So it was, in the fall of 1919, that Holmes and Brandeis left the majority and sought to differentiate between the earlier cases of actual attempts at interference with the war effort and the subsequent cases of criticism of policy. In the end, it was a case of subjective judgments as to the applicability or non-applicability of the "tendency" test of the utterances; the moderately liberal Justice Clarke spoke for the majority in two of the three cases, and the conservative McKenna in the third, while Holmes and Brandeis wrote a total of four dissenting opinions in all three.[38]

In *Abrams v. United States,* Holmes strove earnestly to define the logical limits to the clear and present danger doctrine. The freedom guaranteed by the First Amendment, he urged, should indeed be considered absolute except in cases of national emergency which "makes it immediately dangerous to leave the correction of evil counsels to time." But the manifest problem was how to determine when an emergency began and when it ended. As Brandeis pointed out in his dissent in *Schaefer v. United States,* in the penumbra of war or other emergency, if not actually in peacetime, an intolerant majority would have little difficulty in finding tendentious and therefore disloyal any unpopular expressions.[39]

Holmes, like the rest of the country, was trying to find his way back to an *ante-bellum* regime, but the way was a gauntlet to be run between disintegrating loyalties. The collapse of the Central Powers in the fall of 1918, the Republican capture of Congress in the elections at the same time, the Bolshevist revolution in Russia, the disillusionments at Versailles and the bristling hostility of the Senate to which Wilson presented the peace treaty—climaxed by the sudden and serious physical decline of Wilson himself in the fall of 1919 —were closing the gates on the Progressive Movement. After two decades of general advances on social and economic fronts, a general weariness of crusading at home and abroad had clearly set in. Already, while the First Amendment cases were being decided, the Court majority had begun the judicial repeal of many fundamental statutory enactments of the New Freedom.

* * *

In the twilight of the Progressive Movement, several remaining objectives were yet to be won. The Nineteenth Amendment—the fourth change in the Constitution in less than a decade—was submitted by Congress in June, 1919 and declared ratified by August of the following year, making woman suffrage a privilege of national citizenship. The Transportation Act of 1920, liquidating the wartime government administration of the railroads, substantially strengthened the rate-making powers of the Interstate Commerce Commission; and the treaty-making power of Congress was significantly activated as a source of expanding national sovereignty. In affirming the capacity of Congress to attain a legitimate national objective through the treaty power, Holmes offered to the American people a last glimpse of a nationalism which was already disappearing behind the clouds of a reviving *laissez-faire:*

The supremacy clause of the Constitution—like all words in the Constitution, said Holmes for the majority—was intended to "have called into life a being the development of which could not have been foreseen completely by the most gifted of its begetters. It was enough for them to realize or to hope that they had created an organism; it has taken a century and has cost their successors much sweat and blood to prove that they created a nation." The question of the power represented in the treaty provision of the supremacy clause "must be considered in the light of our whole experience, and not merely in that of what was said a hundred years ago."[40] Holmes perceived the lights going down upon the midsummer of progressivism; his dissent in *Abrams* was a legacy for a distant future: "But when men have realized that time has upset many fighting faiths, they may come to believe even more than they believe the very foundations of their own conduct that the ultimate good desired is better reached by free trade in ideas—that the best test of truth is the power of the thought to get itself accepted in the competition of the market; and that truth is the only ground upon which their wishes safely can be carried out. That, at any rate, is the theory of our Constitution. It is an experiment, as all life is an experiment. Every year, if not every day, we have to wager our salvation upon some prophecy based upon imperfect knowledge. While that experiment is part of our system I think that we should be eternally vigilant against attempts to check the expression of opinions that we loathe."[41]

12/The Nullification
of Reform

T HE COUNTERATTACK ON the Progressive Movement began in the hills of western North Carolina as the nation's attention was shifting to the prospect of formal war with Germany. Roland H. Dagenhart, an employee in a Charlotte cotton mill, on behalf of himself and two minor sons, brought a suit in the Federal court to enjoin the United States attorney, W. C. Hammer, from enforcing the Keating-Owen Child Labor Act of 1916. The lower court granted the injunction, holding the law unconstitutional, and an appeal was taken to the Supreme Court, where it was argued in April, 1918 and decided that June.

The real questions in issue were indicated by the importance of the attorneys appearing against the government, and the tenor of their argument before the Court. Morgan J. O'Brien, a leader of the New York bar, and four associates were joined in Dagenhart's case and their brief went directly to the point of *laissez-faire* doctrine which was to be reiterated throughout the coming decade: If Congress, by regulating any activity affecting the production of goods entering the stream of interstate commerce, was to be able thus to reach economic subjects heretofore considered solely within the jurisdiction of the states, what would be left of the police power of the states? In the case of the child labor law, ran the argument, the intention of Congress was not the ordinary regulation of commerce itself but the use of the regulatory power to prohibit an economic act which the majority in Congress considered undesirable; in such case, the Court was urged "to see that such prohibition invades none of the rights of the state under its reserved power, and none of the rights of a citizen, secured to him by the Fifth Amendment." The brief closed with quotations from Taft's 1913 *Lectures on Popular Government,* Wilson's treatise on constitutional government, and Elihu Root's Princeton lectures on the Constitution in 1915, all of which were alleged to be "against the constitutionality of this statute."[1]

By a five-to-four division, the usually moderate Justice Day speaking for the majority and the usually conservative Justice McKenna being numbered among the dissenters, the Court upheld Dagenhart's petition for the injunction. Congressional power to prohibit harmful goods from interstate commerce, said Day, was clearly not involved in this statute, since the goods themselves were eligible for shipment after thirty days. The alternative effect of the law, accordingly, was to compel the states to exercise their police power in eliminating child labor in the stipulated industries; but no such power, said Day, was vested in Congress. "Thus," the majority opinion concluded, "the act in a twofold sense is repugnant to the Constitution. It not only transcends the authority delegated to Congress over commerce, but also exerts a power as to a purely local matter to which Federal authority does not extend. The far-reaching result of upholding the act cannot be more plainly indicated than by pointing out that if Congress can thus regulate matters entrusted to local authority by prohibition of the movement of commodities in interstate commerce, all freedom of commerce will be at an end, and the power of the states over local matters may be eliminated, and thus our system of government be practically destroyed."[2]

With this ringing review of judicial horribles, Day added a misreading of the Tenth Amendment, asserting that it expressly delegated powers to the Federal government and reserved all other power to the states or the people. As Congressional critics of the decision promptly pointed out, the term "expressly" was conspicuously absent from the Amendment and had been considered and rejected by the draftsmen of the Bill of Rights.[3]

The reaction to the *Dagenhart* case was one of surprise and anger. It ran counter to the 1911 case upholding the Pure Food and Drug Act, in which the Court had observed that the commerce power of Congress was virtually without limit. In 1913, in upholding the use of the commerce power to control the interstate white slave trade, McKenna in speaking for the Court had declared that "the powers reserved to the states and those conferred on the nation are adapted to be exercised, independently or concurrently, to promote the general welfare, material and moral."[4]

Holmes, speaking for himself, Brandeis, Clarke and McKenna, cited the earlier decisions as having made it clear "that the power to regulate commerce and other constitutional powers could not be cut down or qualified by the fact that it might interfere with the carrying out of the domestic policy of any state." Whether the subject matter was impure foods, prostitution, or the social evil of exploited labor of youth, said Holmes, it "is enough that, in the opinion of Congress, the transportation encourages the evil." As for the argument that the statute interfered with the sovereign interests of the states, Holmes emphasized that when states "seek to send their product across the state line they are no longer within their rights. If there were no Constitution and no Congress their power to cross the line would depend upon their neighbors. Under the Constitution such commerce belongs not to the states, but to Congress to regulate."[5]

The question of child labor was manifestly tied to regional and local interests; since 1880 the number of persons under sixteen employed in industry had steadily declined, largely as a result of the introduction of machine processes which made their work uneconomical. On the other hand, the Southern cotton mills enormously increased their use of child labor in this period. Whole families were commonly employed and the combined wages of the children and parents had come to be essential to subsistence. In 1905 a North Carolina mill operator had decried "the emissaries of Northern fanaticism, prejudice, and envy" who had come to study working conditions and propose laws which would restrict "the people of this great and free state." States' rights, as on so many occasions, became the touchstone of freedom from interference with an established and profitable industrial system.[6]

In Congress, the reaction to the *Dagenhart* case was vocal and positive; Senator Robert L. Owen of Oklahoma spoke at length against the principle of judicial review generally, and in particular decried the circumstances under which a one-vote margin on the Court nullified a policy expressed by both houses of Congress and signed into law by the President. Socialist Representative Meyer London of New York warned that "if this decision remains the law of the land, it will be impossible for . . . Congress to cure by legislation any of the social or industrial evils which legislation in all civilized countries of the world tries to meet."[7]

Determined to meet the challenge of the Court head-on, Congress debated a variety of devices to re-enact the child labor prohibition. The analogy of the Webb-Kenyon Act, denying shipment by interstate commerce into states forbidding goods to be manufactured by child labor as they prohibited intoxicating liquors, was one proposal; the use of the mails or the war powers to control the traffic was also urged. In the end, it was determined that a new child labor law would be made to rely on the taxing power of the United States; the use of the tax authority for purposes of regulation had been upheld on several occasions by the courts. Accordingly, a substantial levy on the employment of child labor in manufacturing became part of the Revenue Act of 1919.[8]

*   *   *

To renew the conservative attack upon a Federal income tax, now unequivocally authorized by the Sixteenth Amendment, was a more difficult task, but the *laissez-faire* capitalist did not shrink from it. To be sure, the Court had not made it easier for him in its 1916 ruling where Chief Justice White had found "no escape from the conclusion that the Amendment was drawn for the purpose of doing away for the future with the principle upon which the *Pollock* case was decided."[9] White considered that the effect of the Amendment was to place income taxes within "the category of indirect taxation to which [they] inherently belonged"; but the business community now urged the proposition that the

Amendment merely removed the rule of apportionment from a direct tax on income. If the Court would accept this definition, it would then be possible to narrow the accompanying definition of income and thus reduce the amount of property interests subject to the tax.

Since, for the capitalist and investor, a major source of income was the periodic stock dividend, the tax liability under the Sixteenth Amendment and its implementing statutes would be substantially reduced if the Court could be prevailed upon to define such dividends as capital until sold or converted. The argument was intriguing enough to attract the services of no less a figure than Charles Evans Hughes as counsel for the stockholder, while a brief *amicus curiae*—also favorable to the argument—was submitted by former Attorney General George W. Wickersham. It was contended by these attorneys that a stock dividend represented no gain or income for the stockholder since it was a "mere readjustment of the evidence of a capital interest already owned," and hence could not be considered income taxable within the meaning of the Amendment. If the implementing act of Congress was intended to reach property as well as money, the argument continued, "it must still be property that constitutes gain or income."[10]

By another five-to-four opinion, the Court adopted the argument and in the process substantially reduced the prospective reach of the income tax laws. Justice Pitney, for the majority, agreed that "the essential matter" was that income was "a gain, or profit, something of exchangeable value *proceeding from* the property, *severed* from the capital . . . *received* or *drawn by* the recipient (the taxpayer) for his separate use, benefit and disposal." The Amendment, said Pitney, "applies to income only, and what is called the stockholder's share in the accumulated profits of the company is capital."[11]

Holmes, in a brief dissent, declared that the "known purpose of this Amendment was to get rid of nice questions" spun out by technicians in finance and law. He added, "I cannot doubt that most people not lawyers would suppose when they voted for it that they put a question like the present to rest." It remained for Brandeis, the lifelong student of finance techniques in industry and insurance, to give his colleagues a basic course in economics as well as in constitutionalism. Stock dividends, he pointed out, were a device long used by financiers to keep accumulated profits for corporate purposes while in effect also distributing these profits to stockholders. In any case, he went on, they were profits and hence income, and since the Sixteenth Amendment empowered Congress to levy taxes on income "from whatever source derived," the scope of the power should be measured by "the substance of the transaction, not its form."

The effect of the majority decision, Brandeis concluded, was to insure that "the owners of the most successful businesses in America will . . . be able to escape taxation on a large part of what is actually their income. So far as their profits are represented by stock received as dividends, they will pay these taxes not upon their income, but only upon the income of their income. That such a result was intended by the people of the United States when adopting the Sixteenth Amendment is inconceivable."[12] Inconceivable though it might be to the men who had worked for sixteen years to effect the Amendment, it was, as Thomas Reed Powell put it, a case of one five-to-four decision being overruled by a constitutional amendment which in turn was narrowed in its application by another five-to-four decision.[13]

*   *   *

A third major goal of the counterattack was the Clayton Anti-Trust Act, "Labor's Magna Carta," as Samuel Gompers had described it in the fall of 1914. A key provision in the statute, and a challenge to the whole rationale of *laissez-faire,* was the proposition that "the labor of a human being is not a commodity or article of commerce. Upon this proposition the law based its exemption from anti-trust liability of labor and agricultural organizations and the prohibition of the injunction in labor disputes except in cases of threatened injury to property. The protection of labor was further provided by recognizing the legality of strikes, peaceful picketing and boycotts, and by stipulating that in cases of contempt outside the court room the union was entitled to a jury trial.[14]

Between October, 1914, when the Clayton Act was passed, and January, 1921, when the constitutional test of the Act came to a climax, a massive shift in political and economic weight had occurred. The Act was signed into law as part of a grand advance on all fronts by the reformers and insurgents in Congress which reached its zenith in the torrent of social legislation in the summer of 1916. This was followed by a vintage judicial year for labor, with a succession of favorable court decisions at both the state and national level.[15] Thereafter had come the cataclysmic reorientation of the economy in response to the demands of the war, and the post-Armistice demobilization of men and industry. On the heels of this came the frustrated negotiations at Versailles and the collapse of Wilson's leadership for the last twenty months of his administration. The mounting disillusionment of the postwar years bred both hysteria and reaction. As labor was identified with the radical movements of such groups as the International Workers of the World and the general strikes which paralyzed communities from Boston to Seattle, the hysteria and the reaction were quickly focused upon the unions and their leaders.

Adding to labor's troubles was the severe depression which set in as the decade ended. The swift return and discharge of hundreds of thousands of men from the military services glutted the employment market, while the overproduction on the farms caused a disastrous fall in the price of agricultural commodities. Business leaders did not hesitate to blame labor for a substantial share in the hardships which were being visited on the American people; B. C. Forbes declared in his magazine of finance and industry that "unionized labor is blindly antagonistic to wage reductions, no matter how thoroughly reductions may be warranted by conditions."[16]

The litigation which had been initiated to test the Clayton Act had reflected the changes of the seven years; the suit had been started before the final passage of the statute, but brought to hearing thereafter. The ruling in the Federal District Court for the Southern District of New York, handed down in April, 1917, had denied an employer's petition for an injunction against union organizers and striking employees. "The right to strike for higher wages and to improve conditions of labor have been firmly established and recognized by the Federal courts," said Judge Martin T. Manton, and "if lawful means are used to effectuate it, such means cannot be made to reach back and taint the purpose itself with unlawfulness."[17]

A year later, in May, 1918, the Circuit Court of Appeals sustained the judgment on the affirmance of two of the three judges; but the content of the opinions was eloquent in its distaste for the statute in general. Judge Henry Wade Rogers, dissenting, levelled two principal charges against the Clayton Act: the secondary boycott, he declared, "is a combination formed to injure the trade, or business, or occupation of another," and for Congress to condone it by legislation was to flout the elemental principles of justice. In addition, he urged, the rights of labor set out in the statute were rights it enjoyed at common law. Accordingly, a statute declaratory of the common law invited application of common-law doctrine, and therefore "if the acts complained of in this case would not have been lawful prior to the passage of the Clayton Act, they are not lawful now."[18]

Judge Charles M. Hough, though not questioning Congress' constitutional right to enact the statute, upheld it with a complete lack of enthusiasm. "We are earnestly told," he observed, that the legal status of the secondary boycott "gives to the workman the choice of being a pariah or a guildslave, and to the employer a doubtful escape from bankruptcy by the path of commercial servitude. If this be true (and the writer is not disposed to question it) the result is imposed by act of Congress; the remedy is political, not judicial."[19] Judge Learned Hand concurred in Hough's finding, but not, he added briefly, "in all the expressions in his opinion."[20]

A year and a half later, in January, 1920, the case was argued before the Supreme Court, and a year later, on January 3, 1921, by a six-to-three division, the lower courts were reversed. Pitney, for the majority, ruled that the Sherman Act's prohibition against any kind of combination in restraint of trade was applicable unless the Clayton Act amendments placed the defendants outside the scope of the prohibition. But the latter statute, he argued, immunized unions and their members from the anti-trust laws only while they were "lawfully" carrying out their "legitimate" purposes. Nothing in the law, Pitney concluded, will "exempt such an organization or its members from accountability where it or they depart from its normal and legitimate objects, and engage in an actual combination or conspiracy in restraint of trade." The Clayton Act was intended, according to the majority, to apply to employers and employees negotiating directly with each other on matters of compensation or conditions of work, and anything beyond that was beyond the privileges of the law. Even so construed, it was contended, the exemptions granted by the statute amounted to "a special privilege or immunity to a particular class, with corresponding detriment to the general public," and for that reason also should be held to the narrowest meaning of the words of the law.[21]

Finding that secondary boycotts were a threat to inflict damage which the courts could enjoin, the majority ruled that the employers were entitled to an injunction. Brandeis, speaking for himself, Holmes and Clarke, protested that the Clayton Act was a fundamental change in the common law and a modification of the Sherman Act as well. "The change in the law by which strikes once illegal and even criminal are now recognized as lawful," said the minority, was not due "to the rejection by the courts of one principle and the adoption in its stead of another, but to a better realization of the facts of industrial life." Yet the evolution of an enlightened common law jurisprudence had required clarification by statute, Brandeis said bluntly, because "the social and economic ideas of judges, which . . . became translated into law, were prejudicial to a position of equality between workingman and employer"; and because of this "dependence upon the individual opinion of judges, great confusion existed as to what purposes were lawful and what unlawful," with the result that Congress was properly brought into the dialogue to "declare what public policy in regard to the industrial struggle demands."[22]

*   *   *

It was, as Holmes described it, "a good dissent," but Brandeis was speaking for a dwindling minority both on the Court and in the nation. Politically, the New Freedom was by now a disappointing memory, with its days swiftly running out. Warren G. Harding and the regime of "normalcy" were about to take over the government, while on the Court Chief Justice White was completing his twenty-seventh year on the bench. Whether it was true, according to stories circulated then and thereafter, that he had promised William Howard Taft, the man who had appointed him Chief Justice, that he would continue to hold the seat until another Republican President could appoint Taft to succeed him, White's death that spring would at least create the opening for which the ex-President had waited so long. Already, before the broken Wilson could be decently removed from the White House, reaction was running at flood tide. Less than ninety days after the judicial emasculation of the Clayton Act, Brandeis, in a private letter, made another observation on the contemporary scene: "Europe," he wrote, "was devastated by war, we by the aftermath."[23]

Meantime, the dismantling of the reforms of the previous decade proceeded at a steady pace, extending into a wide variety of secondary statutes. A 1913 statute providing for Supreme Court appellate review of District of Columbia public utility commission valuations was nullified as a non-judicial process; an amendment to the Federal judicial code which sought to preserve the rights of labor under state laws on workmen's compensation was held to be an attempt to transfer Federal legislative power to the states; a provision for taxing the incomes of judges in office when the revenue act was adopted was held to violate the Constitutional provision against reducing judges' salaries while on the bench; a portion of the Federal estate tax relating to certain types of testamentary trusts was ruled confiscatory; and—after the pressure of wartime emergency had passed—price control features of the Lever Act were found to be unconstitutional.[24]

The ultimate tragedy of reaction born of wartime disillusionment and hysteria was epitomized in the record of Wilson's last Attorney General, A. Mitchell Palmer. An oldtime insurgent—he had attracted considerable attention for his advocacy of a child labor law in the last Taft Congress, and had engineered the support of the Pennsylvania Democratic delegation to the 1912 convention that led to Wilson's nomination—Palmer had served the Progressive Movement well in three terms in the House of Representatives from 1908 to 1914. In 1917 Wilson had appointed him Alien Property Custodian, trustee of some $600,000,000 in property owned by or owed to enemy aliens. Two years later, Attorney General Gregory resigning to return to private practice, Palmer was considered the logical choice to succeed him—ironically, as events were to prove, because both labor and employers were said to endorse his objective approach to problems of the administration of justice.[25]

The swift metamorphosis from progressivism to reaction in Palmer's case only represented on a larger scale what was happening to the American people generally in this period of militant discontent. The frustration of many idealists in the wake of the Armistice and the Peace Conference, the cynicism with which many union leaders seized the advantages which the reform legislation of the pre-war years had offered them, and the frightening spread of radical agitation throughout the capitalistic order all tended to demoralize the reform forces. For thousands of Americans in 1919 and 1920, the changes in society which they had so ardently supported in the heyday of the New Freedom had created a new environment which they disliked, and the ensuing all-out war had utterly destroyed any possibility of returning to the settled order of things they could remember, with increasing nostalgia, as the years passed. "The spirits of the liberals," William Allen White recalled, "were bewildered."[26]

Further demolishing the liberal position was the rise of the Communist autocracy in Russia and the wave of anarchy and radical hoodlumism in America. In February, 1919 the Senate appointed a special committee to investigate Bolshevik activities in the United States, and the Department of Justice herded more than fifty Reds from the West into Ellis Island for deportation. On the eve of the traditional international leftist celebration of May Day, the New York Post Office electrified the country by its discovery of sixteen packages containing dynamite bombs, each package addressed to a selected official in state or Federal government marked by the anarchists for assassination. A month later, a bomb actually did wreck the residence of Attorney General Palmer, the only casualty being the bearer of the bomb, who was blown to bits.[27]

Although there was no specific provision in the Constitution for the expulsion of undesirable aliens, the Supreme Court had ruled as early as 1892 that this was an inherent right of sovereignty, and Congress in 1903 and 1907 had enacted legislation enumerating a variety of disqualifying factors in the case of immigrants or aliens already in the country. The Act of February 5, 1917 had substantially enlarged this list, and it had been revised and further supplemented in 1918. The proper administrative process for implementing the deportation laws had not been clearly defined, but Palmer had no hesitation in acting under the authority of the statutes. In 1911, a Federal court had critically observed that such proceedings were usually in the hands of a government inspector "who acts in it as informer, arresting officer, inquisitor, and judge."[28] For Palmer, convinced by now that the wave of radicalism was totally alien and required the most ruthless application of force to meet it, this was an advantage rather than a deterrent.

Within a matter of weeks the Department of Justice had assembled a detailed index of more than sixty thousand radicals throughout the country. Using this information as its lead, Palmer's force thereupon instituted a series of raids to concentrate the suspected aliens in detention centers throughout the land. As individual cases were examined, those determined to be guilty of illegal acts were then referred to immigration authorities for deportation. In December, 1919, an American transport sailed for Russia—the presumed point of origin—with nearly two hundred and fifty Reds who were being expelled. There would be two or three more such sailings, Palmer informed a New York audience the following February, as the alien radicals were ferreted out and processed for deportation.[29]

With both Wilsons—the President and the Secretary of Labor—ill to the point of being incapacitated, Palmer had virtually a free hand in his drive against the Reds. His chief Cabinet cohort proved to be Postmaster General Burleson, who was more than zealous in his program of denying the mails to leftist publications. But it was Palmer against whom the main criticism was directed; to have rounded up thousands of persons, both alien and citizen, without warrants was a flagrant violation of the Fourth Amendment guarantee against unreasonable searches and seizures. Judge George W. Anderson of the Federal court in Massachusetts severely castigated the government investigators for the arrest and detention of hundreds of men and women in raids in that state, with a rifling of all their possessions and subsequent confinement incommunicado—indeed, anyone who came to inquire about them was also arrested—all without any indication that "a single search warrant was obtained or applied for."[30]

Senator Joseph I. France of Maryland added his indictment of the Attorney General by vigorously condemning the agents of "a department which disgraces the very name of justice" whose methods were "search and seizure without warrant, brutality, torture, perjury, provocation of crime, the holding of prisoners without sentence and the sentencing of prisoners without sense." More than one third of the persons arrested and held for trial in the Massachusetts raids were freed by the court upon finding no evidence against them, while the Assistant Secretary of Labor, Louis Post, refused to institute deportation proceedings against another large bloc of men and women to whom, he ruled, the law simply did not apply. Palmer bitterly condemned Post's action. "By his habitually tender solicitude for social revolution and per-verted sympathy for the criminal anarchists of the country," the Attorney General declared, "he has consistently deprived the people of the enforce-ment of a law of vital importance to their peace and safety."[31]

The hatred of militant radicals—and the readiness of the age of normalcy to attribute both militance and radicalism to any criticism of the existing order —was to become an article of faith for the majority of the nation in the post-war decade of prosperity. As the deportation frenzy waned, a domestic case arose to focus the attention of the country on the question of the chance for justice to be expected by unlettered immigrants caught in the toils of the law. The case, growing out of a payroll robbery and shooting in South Baintree, Massachusetts would keep the issue before the nation until 1927, when the accused and convicted men were finally executed, leaving a legacy of reason-able doubt not yet removed. The names of the defendants were Nicola Sacco and Bartolomeo Vanzetti.

*   *   *

The judicial attack upon reform legislation did not confine itself to Federal statutes. Indeed, the first groundswell of reform had been among the state legislatures, and in attacking these as well as the Congressional enactments the *laissez-faire* interests made their intentions clear: No government authority, either state or national, was to be permitted to interfere with the freedom from liability so long enjoyed by the employer classes in the decades after the Civil War. The obvious point at which to begin this phase of the campaign was in the vaguely defined area between state and Federal jurisdiction; the courts themselves, over the years of constitutional development, had been equivocal on the question of coordinate and concurrent powers of the two sovereignties.

On May 21, 1917 the Supreme Court in three successive opinions cut to pieces the New York and New Jersey workmen's compensation laws in the no man's land between state and Federal areas of jurisdiction with the net result that injured claimants were left without effective remedy and employers without substantial liability. In the first two cases, the state compensation commissions had given awards to railroad workers injured without fault on the part of the railroad; where the carrier had been guilty of no negligence in whole or in part, the Federal Employers' Liability Act* provided no right of recovery, so that the only source of relief was offered by the state acts. Justice Van Devanter, always solicitous of carriers' interests, spoke for a seven-man majority in ruling that Congressional legislation on the subject had completely preempted the field. Preemption, said Van Devanter, meant that the intention of Congress in its legislative action should qualify any rights under state laws

---

*See Appendix D, p. 349.

so that they would not be inconsistent with the Congressional intent; it would follow, accordingly, that where Congress had manifestly intended that carrier liability to injured employees should depend upon carrier negligence, a state law permitting employee recovery without carrier negligence would "interfere with the operation of a law of Congress."[32]

Brandeis, in a dissent joined by Clarke, declared that the "field covered by Congress was a limited field of the carrier's liability for negligence, not the whole field of the carrier's obligation arising from accidents. I find no justification," he said, "for imputing to Congress the will to deny to a large class of persons engaged in a necessarily hazardous occupation and otherwise unprovided for, the protection afforded by beneficent statutes enacted . . . in a field peculiarly appropriate for state action."[33]

In the third case of this date, the state compensation law was all but decimated in an opinion delivered by Justice McReynolds, already rivalling Van Devanter in the excess of his conservatism. In a narrow five-to-four opinion the majority held the New York statute unconstitutional as it applied to workers in maritime trades; these trades came under Federal admiralty jurisdiction as stipulated by the Constitution, except as the Judiciary Act of 1789 had permitted claimants to avail themselves of certain common-law remedies. But compensation for injuries to be determined and awarded by a non-judicial administrative board, said McReynolds, was a remedy unknown to the common law, and to permit such a state provision to stand would interfere with "the proper harmony or uniformity" of the Federal law.[34]

Holmes, in a brief but stinging dissent, pointed out that "maritime law is not a *corpus juris*—it is a very limited body of customs and ordinances of the sea"; any remedies not provided by such a limited body of jurisprudence would come from the common law, and the common law "is not a brooding omnipresence in the sky, but . . . always is the law of some state." It is "too late to say," Holmes went on, "that the mere silence of Congress excludes the statute or common law of a state from supplementing the wholly inadequate maritime law of the time of the Constitution"; if state sovereignty meant anything, it meant the constitutional authority to provide by statute a remedy where neither Federal law nor the common law of the state so provided. To this Pitney added, in a separate dissent, the observation that in interstate commerce, where Congress' paramount authority was express, state law could still operate in areas where Congress had not asserted its jurisdiction. How much more should state authority be valid, he argued, in cases where the extent and exclusiveness of Congress' authority was only implied.[35]

The irony of the matter was that, in their zeal to limit the degree of government regulation of employers' freedom of action, the *laissez-faire* advocates were quite prepared to cite the preeminence of Federal authority at the expense of the states. Thereafter, by circumscribing the Federal power in the same subject-area, the encroachments of public authority could be contained on all fronts.

The insulation of employer and entrepreneurial interests from state regulation was advanced in another five-to-four decision in which the Court struck down a 1914 Washington state law abolishing fees charged to job seekers by employment agencies. Ignoring the evils which the law sought to correct, McReynolds in the majority opinion conceded that "abuses may, and probably do, grow up in connection with this business," but contended that this was insufficient reason for the government to abolish it. In truth, the statute did not abolish the agencies, but only the practice of making the employee pay the fee for listing the job; the agencies were essentially compelled by the rule of the statute to seek their fees from the employers. To McReynolds, however, this was wrong in principle. "Fundamental guarantees of the Constitution," he declared, "cannot be freely submerged if and whenever some ostensible justification is advanced and the police power invoked."[36]

Even the conservative McKenna was found among the dissenters in the case. The current practice of employment agencies, he briefly noted, was a "demonstrated evil," and the police power of the state could validly be directed against it. Brandeis, in a separate dissent joined by Clarke and Holmes —"Note me as agreeing with you vehemently," the latter had written—undertook to analyze the social and economic factors that confirmed the evil and therefore justified the exercise of the police power. That power, said Brandeis, the state should be able to exercise "whether the end sought to be attained is the promotion of health, safety or morals, or is the prevention of . . . general demoralization." Once the state had acted in an area which in its sovereign judgment required action, the only challenge to its authority would turn upon the question whether the action was arbitrary or unreasonable or unrelated to the object sought to be attained; and this, said Brandeis, "is obviously not to be determined by assumptions or by *a priori* reasoning. The judgment should be based on a consideration of relevant facts, actual or possible—*ex facto jus oritur*. That ancient rule must prevail in order that we may have a system of living law."[37]

Two objectives—one short-term, the other long-term—Brandeis pointed out as justifying the state's legislation in the case of the employment agencies. The one concerned the specific abuses of the agency practice—extortionate fees, discrimination against job-seekers, misrepresentation as to the length of the promised employment and the conditions of work. A lifetime spent in the investigation of the seamy facts of the labor market gave the Justice the factual background for his argument. Added to this, however, was the larger, "chronic problem of unemployment—perhaps the gravest and most difficult problem of modern industry." Expert opinion, Brandeis emphasized, was unanimous in supporting a government-regulated system of employment offices as a step toward the solution of the problem. It was logical, economical and morally proper that the states—the laboratories of social experiment, as LaFollette liked to describe them—should devote their inherent lawmaking authority to the incorporation of the prospective solution into law.[38]

McReynolds and his coalition of change-resisting colleagues insisted upon denying to the states the power to reform the existing economic system. In thus stunting the growth of state power, the conservatives permitted the problem to grow instead, until at a future date it attained such proportions that only a national power could cope with it.

*   *   *

Men like Van Devanter and McReynolds—soon to be joined by others of their persuasion—ignored the repeated warning of Holmes that the Constitution, and specifically the Fourteenth Amendment, should not be construed as an obstacle to "the making of experiments that an important part of the community desires." They declined to recognize the need for change in decision-making which Roscoe Pound was describing as the adjudication of "interests, claims, demands, not rights; of what we have to secure or satisfy, not exclusively of the institutions by which we have sought to secure or satisfy them, as if those institutions were ultimate things existing for themselves."[39] The Court majority, for almost two decades, would continue to be concerned above all else with defining the law in immutable terms, terms which had originated in a scale of values which they were determined to perpetuate.

In this process, another tactic in the attack upon reform legislation was to resort to the time-tested proposition of freedom of contract. McReynolds spoke, again for a five-man majority on the Court, in a 1918 case invalidating a Missouri statute which undertook to bar insurance companies doing business in the state from forfeiting policies for default in payment of premiums, if three full years of premiums had in fact been paid into the policy. An insurance contract made with a company chartered in New York was a New York contract, McReynolds declared, and Missouri law could neither reach the contract nor forbid Missouri residents to enter into such a contract. To hold otherwise, he said, would "sanction the impairment of that liberty of contract guaranteed to all by the Fourteenth Amendment."[40]

Brandeis, whose career in public service had reached an early climax in his investigation of the abuses of insurance practice in Massachusetts, led the dissenters in this case. The test of constitutionality in any act of government affecting freedom of contract, as he was so often to point out, was whether the subject of the contract was reasonably within the scope of state regulatory power, whether need for regulation was legitimate, and whether the means used for the purpose of regulation were appropriate to the end in view. Here, answering his questions, Brandeis noted that the subject of the contract was insurance "—a subject long recognized as being within the sphere of regulation of contracts"; the need for regulation arose from the need for protection of the net value of insurance policies by prohibiting forfeiture provisions; and the means of effecting the regulation was the statute stipulating that parties to the insurance contract should dispose of the net value of the policy on which a loan had been secured only in certain limited ways, with a provision for commutation of any balances into extended insurance.[41]

Since, as Brandeis also emphasized, insurance had been held not to be interstate commerce, it was to the states that the policyholder had to turn for any protection, and to hold with the majority was to "deny to a state the full power to protect its citizens in respect to insurance." If neither the state nor the Federal government had authority to assert a protection for the individual against corporate entities in the economic arena, Brandeis was to ask in scores of cases to come, where did protection for the individual lie? To this, the *laissez-faire* majority on the Court had its own answer.

*   *   *

On November 2, 1920 two decades of the Progressive Movement came to an end. In a political campaign in which the chief characteristic of the electorate was apathy and the tenor of election talks was ambivalence, the Republicans captured the White House and both Houses of Congress. A genial but incompetent Ohioan, Warren G. Harding, and a close-mouthed Vermont-born governor of Massachusetts, Calvin Coolidge, rode into the Presidency and Vice-Presidency by a smothering seven million majority over the Democratic candidates, Ohio Governor James M. Cox and an Assistant Secretary of the Navy named Franklin D. Roosevelt. "Not heroics but healing; not nostrums but normalcy," was the GOP candidate's announced program, while other party campaigners emphasized that, Federal government having become a big business, it was time for a businessman's rule to take over.

The only other dominant chord in the threnody of politics was the merciless condemnation of Wilson in the last years of his administration. William Roscoe Thayer, whose intransigence as a conservative rivalled his reputation as a historian, dismissed the retiring President as "an egoist who happened to be President of the country under abnormal circumstances." The sense of political loss after military triumph was directed consistently toward the man whose tactless handling of the Republican Senate had contributed substantially if not decisively to the defeat of the Treaty of Versailles.

This was the conservative thesis, but the progressives had turned from Wilson with an equal sense of disillusionment: In 1917, on the eve of the war, they had been persuaded that Wilson had betrayed the cause of domestic reform; then, when they had been brought around to the view that the war itself presented the opportunity to extend social change to a worldwide scene, the collapse of the peace plans led to the accusation that Wilson had failed the cause abroad as well as at home. "The wistfulness of leaders of a lost cause," wrote Glenn Frank, "tinges their belligerent disappointment."[42]

William Howard Taft, waiting expectantly in the wings as the Republican takeover approached, pronounced a post-mortem on the New Freedom which took on particular significance in view of his own appointment to the Supreme Court which would at last materialize in the following summer. The Wilson regime above all else, he wrote, had been guilty of "a latitudinarian construction of the Constitution of the United States to weaken the protection it should afford against socialistic raids upon property rights, with the direct and inevitable result of paralyzing the initiative and enterprise of capital necessary to the real progress of all. He has made three appointments to the Supreme Court," Taft noted, adding that Wilson had been "greatly disappointed in the attitude of the first of these upon such questions. The other two represent a new school of constitutional construction, *which if allowed to prevail will greatly impair our fundamental law.*"[43]

With God in his Heaven and Harding in the White House, however, Taft noted with optimism that the future might be safe. With four members of the current Court already past the age of seventy, he wrote, "the next President will probably be called upon to appoint their successors. There is no greater domestic issue in this election," he concluded, "than the maintenance of the Supreme Court as the bulwark to enforce the guaranty that no man shall be deprived of his property without due process of law."[44]

The end of the Wilson administration, as it turned out, was also virtually the end of the White Court; the Chief Justice died in May, 1921 and by the start of the October term Taft had been installed in his place. The new Court would insure, for a decade to come, that the "latitudinarian construction" of the Constitution would be kept in check. As for the new government which was coming into office, thoughtful commentators viewed it with misgiving at the same time that they looked back on the last Wilson years as an era of tragedy.

What, indeed, said an editorial writer in the *Nation,* "could be a greater tragedy than to have ruled eight years and to have left so few enduring marks upon our institutions; to have preached . . . to one's countrymen for eight years, only to yield office to the most material, the most sightless administration ever to begin its rule in America." "Probably only an Aeschylus could do Woodrow Wilson justice today," concluded the writer as Harding took office. He wrote at the last: "Certainly no element of the somberest Greek tragedy will be lacking in Washington when Woodrow Wilson leaves office."[45]

PART III

The Decade of Normalcy

We have no concern with the future. It has not come yet.

Oliver Wendell Holmes, J., in *Barker Paint Co. v. Painters Union,* 281 U. S. 462 (1930)

Chart III   THE TAFT COURT

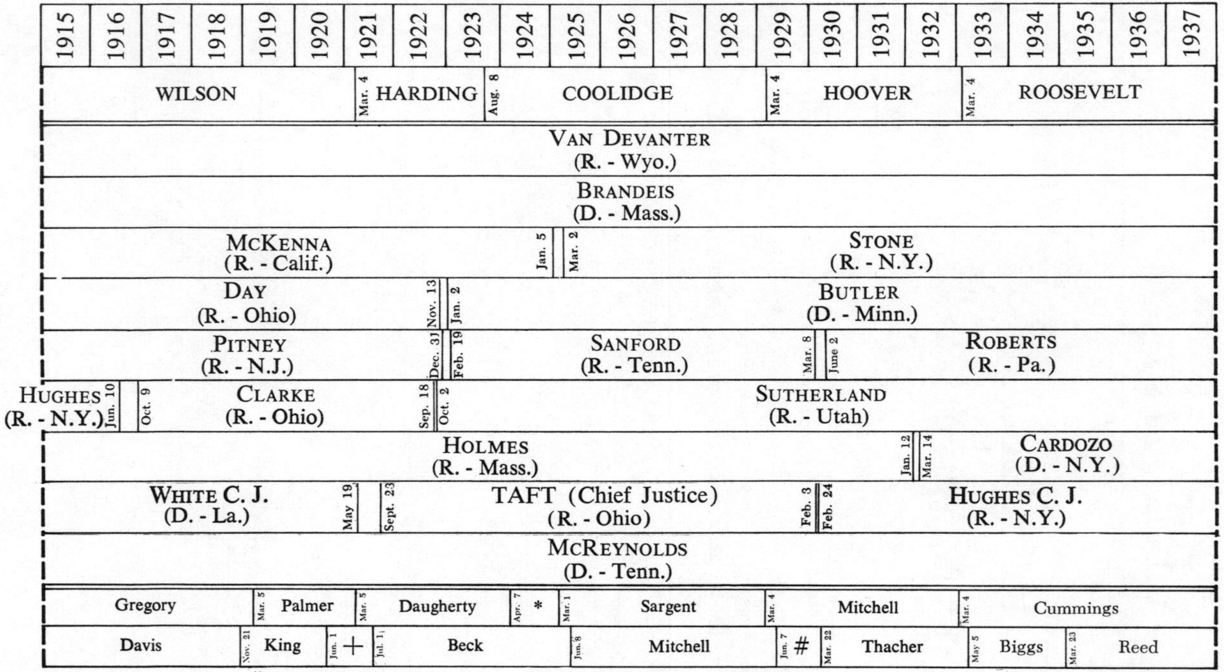

Years: 1915 1916 1917 1918 1919 1920 1921 1922 1923 1924 1925 1926 1927 1928 1929 1930 1931 1932 1933 1934 1935 1936 1937

Row 1 — Presidents of the U.S.
- WILSON
- HARDING (Mar. 4, 1921)
- COOLIDGE
- HOOVER (Mar. 4, 1929)
- ROOSEVELT (Mar. 4, 1933)

Rows 2–10 — Justices of the Supreme Court
- HUGHES (R.-N.Y.) 1910 – Jun. 10 / Oct. 9
- McKENNA (R.-Calif.) – Jan. 5
- DAY (R.-Ohio) – Nov. 13
- PITNEY (R.-N.J.) – Dec. 31 / Jan. 2 Feb. 19
- CLARKE (R.-Ohio) – Sep. 18 Oct. 2
- HOLMES (R.-Mass.)
- WHITE C.J. (D.-La.) – May 19
- TAFT (Chief Justice) (R.-Ohio) Jul. 11 / Sept. 23 ... Feb. 3
- McREYNOLDS (D.-Tenn.)
- BRANDEIS (D.-Mass.) Mar. 2
- STONE (R.-N.Y.) Mar. 2
- SUTHERLAND (R.-Utah) Jan. 12
- SANFORD (R.-Tenn.) Mar. 8
- BUTLER (D.-Minn.) June 2
- ROBERTS (R.-Pa.)
- VAN DEVANTER (R.-Wyo.)
- CARDOZO (D.-N.Y.) Mar. 14
- HUGHES C.J. (R.-N.Y.) Feb. 24

Row 11 — Attorneys General
- Gregory
- Palmer (Mar. 5)
- Daugherty (Apr. 7)
- Sargent (Mar. 1)
- Mitchell (Mar. 5)
- Cummings (Mar. 4)

Row 12 — Solicitors General
- Davis
- King (Nov. 21 / Jun. 1)
- +
- Beck (Jun. 8)
- Mitchell (Mar. 1)
- Thacher (Mar. 22)
- Biggs (May 5)
- Reed (Mar. 23)

* Stone
+ Frierson
# C. E. Hughes, Jr.

Row 1 — Presidents of the U.S.
Rows 2-10 — Justices of the Supreme Court
Row 11 — Attorneys General
Row 12 — Solicitors General

The shaded portion of the Chart represents the Court under Taft's Chief Justiceship. Like Fuller, Taft was junior to all his colleagues when he took office; but three resignations from the bench quickly gave him colleagues closely associated with him in ideology, while his own appointee (Van Devanter) remained. Two Wilson appointees (Brandeis and McReynolds) continued throughout this period, as did Theodore Roosevelt's appointee (Holmes). Midway through Taft's tenure on the Court the last nineteenth-century appointee of McKinley (McKenna) resigned.

13/Bulwark Against Change

ALTHOUGH WARREN G. HARDING was in office only two and a half years, he was able to make the four appointments to the Supreme Court which Taft had hopefully anticipated as the best assurance that the rights of property would be firmly asserted for the foreseeable future.

To Taft himself, it seemed for a tantalizing interval after White's death as if the opportunity to ascend the bench, which he had thrice passed by, would not materialize a fourth time. It was common knowledge in government and legal circles that the ex-President was eager, even impatient, for the appointment. As for Harding, he was already demonstrating his congenital incapacity to make decisions. There were, to be sure, some political debts to be paid, including one owed to his campaign manager, ex-Senator George Sutherland of Utah. Appointment to the Court, and preferably to the Chief Justiceship, was a reward for service which, Sutherland took pains to let Harding know, would not be inappropriate.

Taft himself, as Chief Executive, had given substantial consideration to Sutherland when he had been filling Supreme Court vacancies. It would be hard for him to argue against such an appointment if his advice was solicited; on the other hand, Taft repeatedly told close associates as well as the President that White "many times in the past . . . had said he was holding the office for me and that he would give it back to a Republican administration."[1] Harding was disturbingly vague. While he relayed word through his Attorney General, Harry M. Daugherty, that Taft was his choice for the Chief Justiceship, he was thinking of waiting for a second opening on the Court so that he might simultaneously submit the names of Taft and Sutherland to the Senate.[2] Meantime, there was a brief threat in the form of Charles Evans Hughes, who was reported interested in returning to the bench he had left five years before. In this case also, Taft could hardly withhold an endorsement if he were asked. Not only had he appointed Hughes originally, but after the close defeat in the

1916 election he had written the New Yorker that the most serious consequence was Hughes' loss to the Court.

"What Wilson will do to the Court now, the Lord only knows," Taft had
observed. "I hope that the brethren on the bench will stay in the harness as
long as possible to prevent any more injury than is inevitable." The ex-President had reason for his concern; with Hughes' departure from the Court,
only two of Taft's original appointees remained, and the nightmare appointment of Brandeis had taken place in the meantime. Still, all had turned out
better than he had expected. Van Devanter was strong, and Pitney had at
least "remained in the harness" until a conservative administration was back
in power—while Wilson himself had obliged by adding McReynolds to the
conservative lineup.[3]

In any event, Taft's worries proved groundless; Hughes was named Secretary of State, and Sutherland was placated with a temporary appointment
to the United States Shipping Board. On the last day of June, 1921 Harding
sent Taft's name to the Senate; it was promptly approved. It was, the new
Chief Justice noted, forty years after he had entered public office first as
assistant prosecutor in Hamilton County, Ohio, and eight years since he had
left the White House, as he believed then, to return to a quiet life of private
practice in Cincinnati. Fate had guided him, instead, to a professorship in law
at Yale University, with time to write and lecture on "the evangel of constitutionalism" and to seek to correct some of the "erroneous doctrine taught in
our universities." His appointment to the Court was generally applauded; only
four insurgent Senators voted against it, and only the most adamant reform
journals had words of criticism. "Partly, he is the beneficiary of an unconscious
law of compensation: he was very bad as President, therefore he must be great
as a judge," wrote a contributor—reportedly, Felix Frankfurter—in the *New
Republic*.[4]

More important than this superficial and fallacious assumption, the writer
went on, was the problem of the "recurring failure on the part of the public
to grasp the real significance of the Supreme Court in the political life of the
nation, to appreciate that when members of the Court decide [major cases]
they move in the field of statesmanship." Most important of all was "the fact
that [the appointment] measures the present temporary triumph of reaction.
Labor is cowed, liberalism is confused, and the country's thinking generally is
done in the storm-cellar." Taft's appointment, the writer concluded, diminished
the prospect that the Court would "be able to function as a living organ of
the national will and not as an obstructive force of scholastic legalism."[5]

*   *   *

Taft's philosophy of constitutionalism and his concept of the true business
of the Federal judiciary were well enough known. Shortly after his coming to
Yale, he had undertaken to delineate the basic difference between his and the
progressives' concepts of government, in a type of apology for his own administration. "The change advocated by the social reformers," he had written,

"is really that the object of law should be social interests and not individual interests. They unjustly assume that individual rights are held inviolate only in the interest of the individual to whom such rights are selfishly important and not because their preservation benefits the community." "We recognize," Taft continued, "the inequalities existing between social classes in our communities, and agree to the necessity of new legal conceptions of their duties toward each other. But we have been driven by circumstances into an attitude of opposition. The proposals made for progress have been so radical, so entirely a departure from all the lessons of the past and so dangerous to what we regard as essential in preserving the inestimable social advances we have made . . . that we have been forced to protest."[6]

The conflict of ideologies precipitated by the Progressive Movement in general Taft decried as breeding "the lack of respect for law and the weakened supremacy of the law. The idea seems to be growing," he told a group of law students at the University of Kentucky, "that any small class that has some particular reform which it wishes to effect in its own interest may accomplish that . . . against the whole body politic and social." To the complaint that the courts had been generally hostile to such legislative initiative, he replied that "such a view ignores entirely the recklessness with which members of legis- latures have refused to consider the question of their powers at all, and have avowedly passed any law that seemed popular."[7] Executives of state and nation had abetted legislative excesses, Taft wrote on another occasion, but any "dif- ference between the Executive and the Supreme Court on a question of the power of Congress must always result in a victory of the Court . . . The Court is a continuous body, and the law of its being is consistency in its judicial course. Presidents come and go but the Court goes on forever."[8]

His moral obligation as President to carry through the reforms initiated by his predecessor he felt did not require defense or apology. But "the momen- tum that such a popular movement acquires prevents its stopping at the median line," he told the American Bar Association after two years of the New Free- dom. The indefinite extension of experimental legislation in the interest of gov- ernmental regulation was now becoming a threat to "that freedom of trade and unrestricted initiative which has helped so much the material progress of the country heretofore."[9] On another occasion he admonished the public that neither it nor the world was going to be saved by an "overwhelming mass of ill-digested legislation"; it would remain for the Court to determine whether certain legislation was so very ill-digested that it had to be rejected by the body politic.[10]

This was the new Chief Justice's matured philosophy, and as he took his long-awaited place on the Court Taft made it clear that he intended to take as many positive steps as possible to implement his convictions. In particular, he proposed to be consulted—and indeed intended to advise the White House of his preferences—in the matter of selections to fill other vacancies on the Court as they occurred. It was vital, he repeatedly told associates, to insure that this last fortress of *laissez-faire* should be protected from the inroads already made by men like Holmes, Brandeis and Clarke. Wilson's two liberal appointees, Taft did not hesitate to declare, were committed to the reform plan to "break down the guarantees of the Constitution," while Holmes he repeatedly described as a "noisy dissenter."[11]

*   *   *

If Harding did not take advantage of Taft's offer of advice in the matter of his next Court appointment, it was because the choice—Sutherland—had been predetermined. Moreover, there was no doubt that in the Utah conservative, articulate and capable in the craft of jurisprudence, the Chief Justice was obtaining a valuable ally against the "latitudinarian" minority. Indeed, that minority had been drastically reduced by the vacancy which opened for Sutherland; Justice Clarke, despairing of the future for reform and concerned with the equally diminishing prospect for world organization to preserve peace, had submitted his resignation in the early fall of 1922.

The departure of Clarke from the Court applied a *coup de grace* to the whole era of the New Freedom, as the broken Wilson acknowledged in a poignant letter to his erstwhile appointee. "It has deeply grieved me to learn of your retirement from the Supreme Court," Wilson wrote. "Like thousands of other liberals throughout the country," he added, "I have been counting on the influence of you and Justice Brandeis to restrain the Court in some measure from the extreme reactionary course which it seems inclined to follow." As for Clarke's successor, Wilson went on, "I have seen no reason to suspect him of either principles or brains, and the substitution is most deplorable."[12]

It did indeed seem incredible that so much could have occurred in six short years to destroy almost completely the bright promise of reform in 1916. At that time the *New York World* had hailed Clarke as "singularly like Brandeis in having been a successful corporation lawyer whose practice served only to quicken his sympathies and activities for the causes of political and social justice." Clarke had first attracted national notice as the special assistant to Cleveland Mayor Tom Johnson in a municipal drive to overturn an unconscionable traction franchise. He had been sponsored for the vacancy on the Court created by Hughes' resignation by Ohio's Newton D. Baker, to the editorial applause of the *Cleveland Plaindealer* which predicted that Clarke and Brandeis would "take to the nation's highest court a sympathy with aspirations of the average man, woman and child, and an appreciation of their rights under the laws."[13]

Clarke's compulsive sense of public duty manifested in his early law career, in his two years as United States District Court judge and five on the Supreme Court, as well as his ensuing years of labor (in association with George Wickersham) for the League of Nations Non-Partisan Association, offer a tempting speculation as to the course of constitutional law had he remained on the bench. His opinions in these cases consistently followed those of Brandeis, while his critical view of the decisions of the early Hughes Court culminating in his public support of Franklin D. Roosevelt's Court reorganization plan of 1937, suggests that the long period of liberal minority might have been significantly shortened had he remained. Holmes and Brandeis were left alone to carry the thankless burden of protest. With the addition of Harlan F. Stone in 1925 and Benjamin Cardozo in 1932, Clarke would have given the Hughes Court a liberal majority on the eve of the New Deal—and the cataclysm of the 1937 Court fight might never have occurred.

However it might have worked out, the fact remained that it did not. Clarke's reputation as a liberal was well enough established, at the time of his resignation from the bench, that there was a brief flurry of speculation that he would be the Democratic nominee for President in 1924, leading a crusade to revive the New Freedom and carry on Woodrow Wilson's work. That, too, proved to be merely the stuff of dreams.[14]

The English-born Sutherland, like his colleague and fellow conservative Justice Van Devanter, had grown up in the Far West and had made a career of corporation and railroad practice as well as building a political dynasty of his own. During his brief legal study at the University of Michigan, he had been a student of the conservative Cooley, and the fundamental philosophy of *Constitutional Limitations* became the lodestar of his own career. From 1900 to 1912 he had been a key figure at Republican National Conventions, had served one term as Congressman and two as Senator, and in the campaign of 1920 had developed such an intimate relationship with the President-elect that he had been denominated "the Colonel House of the Harding administration." As Senator he had crossed swords with Brandeis in the Ballinger-Pinchot dispute, and again as Senator had joined in the delaying tactics by which Brandeis' appointment to the Court had been contested. As president of the American Bar Association he had made his own philosophy abundantly clear in his address on "Private Rights and Government Control."

Society, Sutherland had told the organized bar, was a struggle for supremacy between liberty and authority—the one, "the desire of the individual to control and regulate his own activities in such a way as to promote what he conceives to be his *own* good"; the second, "the desire of society to curtail the activities of the individual in such a way as to promote what it conceives to be the *common* good." The liberty of the earlier day, Sutherland went on, was essentially the liberty of person and conscience; of the present day, "the liberty to order the detail of one's daily life for oneself—the liberty to do honest and profitable business—the liberty to seek honest and remunerative investment." For Sutherland as for Taft, the process of control had itself gotten out of control: "We have developed a mania for regulating people." He warned: "The errors of a democracy and the errors of an autocracy will be followed by similar consequences. A foolish law does not become a wise law because it is approved by a great many people. The successful enforcement of the law in a democracy must always rest primarily in the fact that on the whole it commends itself to a universal sense of justice, shared even by those who violate it."[15]

"Liberty consists at last in the right to do whatever the law does not forbid," Sutherland concluded, "and this presupposes law made in advance —so that the individual may know before he acts, the standard of conduct to which his acts must conform—and interpreted and applied after the act by disinterested authority—so that the true relation to one another of the conduct and the law may be clearly ascertained and declared."[16] It was in recollection of sentiments such as these that Taft sent a warm note of welcome to the bench: "Our views are very much alike," the Chief Justice wrote to Sutherland, "and it is important that they prevail."[17]

*   *   *

Harding's third appointment to the Court came sixty days later, when Justice Day, a middle-of-the-road moderate who had occasionally vacillated to the "latitudinarian" side, submitted his resignation. For Taft, this presented the golden opportunity to clinch beyond doubt a *laissez-faire* majority for the Court. With himself and Sutherland, Van Devanter and McReynolds, there was needed only one more appointee of like persuasion to make the constitutionalism of the bench "staunch and strong." While McKenna and Pitney could generally be counted with the conservatives, the one was virtually senile and the other verging on a nervous breakdown which would, before 1922 was out, bring on his resignation as well. But at the moment it was the replacement of Day which concerned the Chief Justice, and he went to work in earnest to see that the right choice was made.

It was politically important, he reminded Harding through various emissaries, including Attorney General Daugherty, that a Democrat be considered, and Taft's own first choice among such prospects was the onetime Solicitor General under Wilson, now a highly successful Wall Street lawyer, John W. Davis. The man who would be the Democratic candidate for President in 1924, however, declined to be considered, so that the next choice appeared to be Pierce Butler of Minnesota, who had the added political factor of being a Roman Catholic as White had been. The Chief Justice wrote to Butler in detail concerning the most effective manner of presenting his candidacy to the White House. At the same time, he kept busy depreciating the candidates recommended by the hard-core progressives in the Senate: Judge Benjamin N. Cardozo of the New York Court of Appeals Taft dismissed as "a Jew and a Democrat . . . [and] what they call a progressive judge," while the equally distinguished Learned Hand, he warned Harding, "would almost certainly herd with Brandeis and be a dissenter."[18]

Compared with these dangerous "subversives" as the Chief Justice described them, Butler's single-minded devotion to the *status quo* seemed more than enough to offset his manifest intellectual limitations. Indeed, it almost

seemed that Taft sought him the more eagerly since it was apparent that
with Butler, Van Devanter and McReynolds as reflex-action conservatives
the main argumentation could be conducted by the Chief Justice and Sutherland.

The extent to which Taft devoted his energies as Chief Justice to promoting Butler's candidacy added a remarkable episode to the history of the
Supreme Court. He enlisted a wide number of attorneys to drum up endorsements—from Minnesota's Congressional delegation through the Western hierarchy of the Church, to spokesmen for local bar associations from
California to New York. Harding accepted the testimonials and in due
course sent the nomination to Capitol Hill. Thereupon Taft sent an urgent
letter to Butler advising him to "have all your friends in St. Paul, Minneapolis and elsewhere center their attention on the Senate." The judiciary
committee in particular was the bull's-eye of the target.[19]

To the general public, the Minnesotan epitomized the Horatio Alger
legend of the poor farm boy who rose to millions; since his legal services
for such lines as the Burlington, the Great Northern and the Northern Pacific
had provided him with his fortune, the railroads in his thinking could
do virtually no wrong. He was, in fact, recognized as expert in the accounting
processes requisite in rate-setting, but his unshakable conviction that the
carriers' rate claims were always just made his appointment to a position
where such claims would often be in adjudication seem particularly irrational.[20]

The Senate insurgents—LaFollette of Wisconsin and Norris of Nebraska
among the leaders—sought to commit Butler's nomination to the Judiciary
Committee and then, if not to bury it, to exact from the nominee an understanding that he would not sit on cases involving rate valuations of railroads. Butler himself answered the committee ambivalently; in any event,
he found no difficulty in determining in numerous rate cases thereafter that
he did not need to disqualify himself.[21]

Butler's dogged hostility toward dissent and nonconformity had been
demonstrated amply in his tenure as a regent of the University of Minnesota. Cases of several faculty members, vaguely charged with having been
"pro-German" during the wartime and postwar hysteria, or with being
particularly critical of capitalistic economics, who had been harassed out
of their positions while Butler was on the governing board, gave the judiciary
committee additional bases to challenge his judicial temper. One faculty
member who had felt the brunt of his attacks described him as "a personality
of intense and unmitigated prejudice, accustomed to permitting the prejudices a free and unchecked expression in word and deed, even to the point
of offensiveness." Another Minnesotan wrote the Senate Committee that
his services for a Minneapolis public utility had resulted in a rise for consumers of electricity from 80 cents to $1.31 per unit. The appointment,
warned another writer, would be "a piece of gross stupidity."[22]

Despite the misgivings of the liberals, the committee eventually reported out the nomination to the Senate floor without dissent. Thereupon the Senate went into executive session—with debate on the nominee behind closed doors—to take its final action. LaFollette was reported to have spoken at length against the candidate specifically and against the caliber of men being put onto the Court in general; but he knew the cause was lost. Moreover, the new appointee was likely to remain on the bench for some years; at fifty-six, Butler would be the youngest member of the Court. Confirmation finally came on December 21, 1922, with sixty-one Senators voting for him, eight voting against, and twenty-seven not voting.[23]

*   *   *

In December, 1922, Pitney's resignation gave Harding his third opportunity within four months to fill a vacancy on the Court. After the conservative victory in the Butler appointment, this came almost as an anticlimax, and the selection of Edward T. Sanford of the Federal District Court in Tennessee was accepted by Taft with the observation that advancement of lower court judges to the high bench was a desirable thing for the morale of the judiciary as a whole. The soft-spoken Sanford was hardly to be characterized as an ideologue in any case; during his seven years on the Court, he was almost automatically to be found concurring in any opinion written or supported by Taft.

Sanford did, indeed, seem so close to his Chief as to give Taft two votes on any constitutional question. They had known each other since the days of the Roosevelt administration; both had been born into moderately affluent circumstances, had been well educated and traveled broadly. As always, Taft showed a particular regard for a jurist of competence and craftsmanship, and Sanford's years on the District Court more than adequately qualified him on that score. His constitutional conservatism was quite in accord with the Chief Justice's frequent aphorism that "the cornerstone of our civilization is in the proper maintenance of the guarantees of the Fourteenth Amendment and the Fifth Amendment." Their affinity was dramatized in the final coincidence of their careers: they died on the same day in 1930.[24]

It had been Taft's unique good fortune to be in a strategic position on both occasions, slightly more than a decade apart, when a series of vacancies opened up on the Supreme Court within a short span of time, thereby making possible a coordinated series of appointments which had the prospect of giving the Court a more uniform jurisprudence. True, the appointments Taft made as President had not come to full flower of expectation; White as Chief Justice had lacked the capacity for administrative organization that Taft had hoped for, and several had served too briefly. But now, as Chief Justice guiding the appointments of another President, he could look forward to a comprehensive plan of judicial improvement at the same time that he could feel confident of the Court's capacity to resist dangerous new doctrines.

With three carry-over conservatives and three appointed under his direction, he had the Holmes-Brandeis minority safely contained.

In point of fact, the juxtaposition of Holmes and Brandeis on the one hand, and Taft and Sutherland on the other, was to provide the constitutional dialogue of the decade with a remarkable intellectual quality. Van Devanter, whom Taft highly admired, furnished the underlying rationale for the dominant conservative view, but Sutherland's power of articulation was substantially greater. With the exception of McReynolds, whom Taft himself deprecated as "too stiff-necked and too rambunctious," the tribunal represented an even-tempered aggregation. The new members of the Court were welcomed by the octogenarian Holmes as definite improvements over "some of our older generation" who tended to treat "a difference of opinion as a cockfight and often left a good deal to be desired in point of manners."[25]

Except for the replacement of McKenna by Harlan F. Stone in 1925, the Court from January 1923 to January 1930 continued unchanged. Indeed, Butler, McReynolds, Sutherland and Van Devanter would "remain in harness" through most of the New Deal era, the Old Guard who died hard and never surrendered, although gradually their once monolithic majority diminished to a querulous minority. Meantime, in the heyday of normalcy, they conducted a remarkable conversation: Holmes, urbane and skeptical, ever insisting that "the first call of a theory of law is that it should fit the facts"; Brandeis, reminding his colleagues that the doctrine of *stare decisis* "does not require that we err again," and that "the logic of words should yield to the logic of realities"; Butler, always reiterating that the Court construe the Constitution "in the light of the principles upon which it was founded"; Van Devanter, admired by all members for his analytical powers, who would be the author and lobbyist for Taft's climactic judicial reforms; Sutherland, firm in the conviction that the economics of the nineteenth century remained "untouched by the impact of life under conditions of modern mass production"; and McReynolds, who never changed, a study in "inflexible and unyielding consistency," the "prototype of the rugged individualist, believing firmly in man living independently and untrammeled" by the requirements of an interdependent society.[26]

*　　　　*　　　　*

The decade of normalcy found the majority and minority views on the Court echoed in Congress; Holmes and Brandeis had their legislative counterparts in Borah of Idaho, Walsh of Montana, Norris of Nebraska and LaFollette of Wisconsin. But in the White House, the philosophy of the executive branch was as firmly committed to *laissez-faire* as it had ever been in McKinley's day. With Chief Executives as unfit as Harding, as phlegmatic as Coolidge and as unquestioningly adulatory of big business as Hoover, the center of political gravity tended to shift back to the conservative majority on Capitol Hill.

The three occupants of the White House in this decade presumably reflected the preferences of a wide majority of the American people in the
wake of the Progressive Era. At least, no candidate of the "out" party was
able to make a serious contest of the elections of 1920, 1924 or 1928.
Demoralized and defensive after the collapse of Wilson's program and person,
the Democrats ran Governor James M. Cox against fellow-Ohioan Harding,
and were defeated by a margin approaching two to one. Seeking to outbid
the Republicans for the conservative vote the next time, they chose Wall
Street lawyer John W. Davis, and lost by a margin of *more* than two to
one. Shifting to the opposite tactic in 1928, the Democrats put forward
Governor Alfred E. Smith of New York (a liberal only by contrast with the
total conservatism of Hoover)—and this time their defeat, aggravated by
the prohibition-repeal dichotomy and the intolerance fanned against Smith's
Roman Catholic faith, was a debacle of the greatest magnitude of all.

Members of the Republican Cabinets varied widely in ability. Hughes,
Frank B. Kellogg and Henry L. Stimson in State conspicuously raised the
level of administration of American foreign affairs, while Andrew W. Mellon
in Treasury and Herbert Hoover in Commerce ran their departments with
impeccable (if bloodless) efficiency. The rest of the Cabinet officers were
substantially lower in caliber. Justice only slowly recovered from the shattering experience under Daugherty, and Harlan F. Stone, who succeeded
him, was in office barely long enough to rehabilitate the morale of the staff.
Neither John G. Sargent, who served for the remainder of Coolidge's administration, nor William D. Mitchell, Hoover's Attorney General, displayed
great initiative in the enforcement of Federal law—although it could be
said in their defense that the impossible task of seeking to make prohibition a
viable constitutional principle was a thoroughly unnerving assignment.

Thus the nation proceeded into the postwar decade, embittered by the
dregs of diplomatic frustration found in the cup of military victory, dazzled
by the technological explosion which was still in process of eruption, unable
to gauge the magnitude of the changes which these developments portended.
The Harding administration's disgraceful record shook the average American's
faith in the political process, just as, at the end of the decade, Hoover's
incapacity for action in the face of disaster was to destroy the party he had
sought so zealously to lead. In the end it would be Coolidge who would,
of the three Republican Presidents, most aptly reflect the temper of the
twenties. "Back of him," wrote William Allen White, "were the urgent
purposes of the American democracy, the Hamiltonian faith that 'the rich'
are indeed the 'wise and good,' the Republican creed which identifies wealth
with brains." The United States Chamber of Commerce, White concluded,
"was Coolidge's alter ego."[27]

*   *   *

The prolonged dialogue between the preponderant conservative majority
and the liberal minority on the Supreme Court began in Taft's first year

with a case calling in question the constitutionality of an Arizona anti-injunction statute. William Truax had operated a non-union restaurant in the city of Bisbee, and when his employees struck for higher wages and union recognition he had sought unsuccessfully to obtain an injunction against one Corrigan and others. An appeal from the state supreme court had been argued before Chief Justice White's bench in April, 1920, and even before his death, had been restored to the docket for reargument. Reargument eventually was had before Taft's Court in October, 1921, and in December a five-to-four majority held the state law in contravention of the Fourteenth Amendment. As Taft put it, speaking for the narrow majority, "the legislative power of a state can only be exerted in subordination to the fundamental principles of right and justice which the guarantee of due process in the Fourteenth Amendment is intended to preserve."

A state law denying to employers the right to petition a court to enjoin striking employees or discharged employees from picketing and boycotting the business was for Taft a taking of the employer's property without due process of law. While no one, employer or worker, had a vested right in any rule of the common law, said the Chief Justice, the Fourteenth Amendment assured everyone that the legal protection of his property was not to be arbitrarily denied by legislative action. "Immunity granted to a class, however limited, having the effect to deprive another class, however limited, of a personal or property right," is a denial of the equal protection of the laws, he went on. "The Constitution was intended—its very purpose was—to prevent experimentation with the fundamental rights of the individual."[28]

The dissents—Clarke and Pitney, who had not yet retired from the Court, joined with Holmes and Brandeis—illustrated for Taft the precarious balance in which the "proper" construction of the Constitution hung. Holmes, the ingrained pragmatist, pointed out that business, rather than being "property" in itself, was in reality "a course of conduct and, like other conduct, was subject to substantial modification according to time and circumstances, both in itself and in regard to what shall justify doing it a harm." Harm itself, he added, was essentially a relative concept in determining the rights and liabilities of members of an economic society: "Legislation may begin where an evil begins. If, as many intelligent people believe, there is more danger that the injunction will be abused in labor cases than elsewhere, I can feel no doubt of the power of the legislature to deny it in such cases." To use the Fourteenth Amendment to cut off the opportunity for social experiment in "the laboratories of the states," as La-Follette so often called them, "even though the experiments may seem futile or even noxious," said Holmes, was to compound contemporary problems rather than to encourage the search for their solution.[29]

The right to carry on a business, said Brandeis in his companion dissent, was a valuable right subject to the protection of law, except where the law itself might determine that it was to be curtailed. The standards by which the determination was to be made must necessarily change with the times, he added: "Practically every change in the law governing the relation of employer and employee must abridge, in some respect, the liberty or property of one of the parties, if liberty and property be measured by the standard of the law theretofore prevailing." "Nearly all legislation," he continued, "involves a weighing of public needs as against private desires; and likewise a weighing of relative social values. . . . What, at any particular time, is the paramount public need, is, necessarily, largely a matter of judgment." If the judgment of the peope in legislative assembly had been exercised, said Brandeis, the resulting legislation could hardly be described as arbitrary and unreasonable, even less an unequal protection of the laws.[30]

This was to be the recurring theme of the constitutional argument for the remaining decade of *laissez-faire:* the concept of the immutable character of constitutional guarantees and prohibitions in the face of continuing changing facts of economic life, countered by the argument that the constitutional provisions themselves have force and significance only as they apply to sets of facts in their contemporary context. For the conservative, legal history taught that the meaning the words of the Constitution had for the framers was to be the only rule of construction, while for the liberals, the degree to which the society of the twentieth century had changed from that of 1787 was to be the measure of change in the meaning of the literal text and the capacity of the Constitution to cope with the issues presented by the living generation.

In the succession of economic issues presented in the constitutional cases of the twentieth century, the conservative majority was firm in its conviction that, unless a specific and literal authority could be found in the state or Federal Constitution, the individual in American society was beyond governmental restraint—or governmental help, as the case might be. For such a proposition, said a militant critic of the Court, the only alternative was direct action—in effect, industrial warfare: "If in future years *Truax v. Corrigan* comes back to plague us in terms of defiance of the courts, we shall know where to assess the blame."[31]

14/The Jurisprudence of Prosperity

Ow far the american people had drawn back from the advanced positions they had assumed in the midsummer of progressivism was dramatically illustrated in the judicial and Congressional dialogue on the child labor issue. The Court had already stated its position in *Hammer v. Dagenhart*: the commerce power, the majority opinion ruled, could not be made a device for reaching an alleged social evil. In the brief climax of the reform fervor under Wilson, Congress had sought to answer the judicial challenge by writing a second child labor law under color of the taxing power. Now, in *Bailey v. Drexel Furniture Company*, an eight-to-one majority struck down this statute also. The effect, wrote Edward S. Corwin, was to make "the Court the supervisor of the purposes for which Congress may exercise its constitutional powers."[1]

"It is the high duty and function of this Court," declared Taft for the majority, ". . . to decline to recognize or enforce seeming laws of Congress, dealing with subjects not entrusted to Congress, but left or committed by the supreme law of the land to the control of the states." Although the Court had "gone far to sustain taxing acts as such, even though there has been ground for suspecting" that the primary purpose of the statute was regulation or prohibition rather than revenue, Taft insisted, the subject of the regulation in those instances was a subject properly under the jurisdiction of the Federal government. Here, it was maintained by the majority, the use of the taxing power was improperly directed to a subject the majority considered to be in the domain of the states. "The good sought in unconstitutional legislation," concluded the Chief Justice, "is an insidious feature because it leads citizens and legislators of good purpose to promote it without thought of the serious breach it will make in the ark of our covenant, or the harm which will come from breaking down recognized standards."[2]

The *Drexel* case gave Taft his first opportunity to phrase his concept of the role of the Court in the justiciable questions of the postwar society. The role had two primary responsibilities, in his view: in the first place, it was to distinguish between areas of legislative power which were state or Federal (or neither, so far as regulatory power might be involved), and in the second place, to preserve for the American people the fundamental doctrines of constitutional law which had been handed down from the past. These principles, he had written a decade before, are fundamentally necessary "checks upon the hasty action of the majority." There had been entirely too much hasty action in the recent past, and Taft intended to check it. The figures would bear him out, for in the course of his Chief Justiceship more state and Federal legislation would be invalidated than in any other period of the twentieth century Court.*[3]

The ultimate reply to a categorical judicial denial of Federal power was, of course, a constitutional amendment; at least three such amendments—the Eleventh, Thirteenth and Sixteenth—had specifically overridden specific Supreme Court rulings.[4] *Drexel* provided the impetus for a fourth such effort; the dialogue which the effort was to provoke was in turn to measure the declining reform fervor of the country.

*   *   *

For many leaders of American thought in the postwar era, the proposal of the child labor amendment was like an axe laid at the root of liberty itself. "Probably if the American people were directly asked whether they desired to change their form of government, their reply would be overwhelmingly in the negative," wrote Nicholas Murray Butler in 1924. "There are, however, other ways of overturning or changing a government than by the method of direct attack. . . . Every attempt to make uniform by the force of federal power the conduct and activities of citizens in the several states, is an undermining of the foundations." Certainly, Butler conceded, national needs had to be met by national efforts; but he rejected the idea that this meant governmental effort. "It should be rather a national effort by the people acting with substantial uniformity and singleness of purpose through their state and local governments and through their activities in the sphere of liberty."

The attempt to insure Negro suffrage through the Fifteenth Amendment, declared the Columbia University president, had been the first intrusion of Federal authority into the liberties of the individual citizens of the states, and the prohibition amendment had been the second. The proposed child labor amendment he viewed as a deliberate plan to introduce "a more far-reaching series of changes in our family, social, economic and political life than have heretofore been dreamed of by the most ardent revolutionary." "The fundamental fallacy which underlies this new American revolution," he concluded, "is that the terms national and governmental are convertible in our American system. Distinctly they are not so convertible. There are

*See tables in Appendix D.

many interests and causes that are national without in any wise being the proper concern of government. Under a free and democratic constitution of society, the burden of proof must always be upon those who would transfer any activity from the sphere of liberty to the sphere of government."[5]

This apostrophe to individualism, in a glossary where national need and governmental action were contradictory terms and where liberty and government tended to be treated as mutually exclusive concepts, was the matured philosophy of the man whom most upper-class, successful Americans considered the embodiment of the material and cultural opportunities of a free society. Butler represented for them the ideal of the academician with a grasp of the realities of everyday American life. Although he had studied abroad in the eighties, he had been one of the relatively small number of Americans who had earned both his undergraduate and graduate degrees in a native institution. His practical grasp of university administration which had made him dean of the Columbia faculty of philosophy at the age of twenty-eight and president of the university at thirty-nine had also led to his participation in the creating of its pioneer Teachers College and later the broadening of the entire curriculum in response to the broadening activities of business and professional life in metropolitan society.

Since 1888 when he had first attended the Republican National Convention as a delegate, and at every such convention since 1904, Butler had become the Nestor and Mentor of the Republican Party. His capacity to speak frankly, as one critic observed, was in inverse proportion to his own political ambitions—he had received New York's backing as a favorite son at the 1920 convention—but his philosophy was consistently in favor of "not . . . more legislation, but infinitely less," and, with this, less "popular interference with representative institutions." He acknowledged that the capitalistic system of the twenties cried for reform, but he never abandoned the hope that it would ultimately reform itself. Morality, a spirit of public service and fair play, as he repeatedly proclaimed, would dispel the public demand for "government suppression."[6]

In rejoinder to men like Butler, the advocacy of the child labor amendment in Congress revitalized the old Progressive fervor; with the opening of the Sixty-eighth Congress, a total of twenty-eight bills on the subject was introduced. Representative Israel M. Foster of Ohio, chairman of the House Judiciary Committee, in reporting out the principal bill favorably, told his colleagues that it was intended to strike at "conditions that interfere with the physical development, education and opportunities for recreation which children require," and to forbid the hiring of boys under eighteen to operate railroad locomotives or mine elevators or engage in other hazardous industrial jobs. Congressman Meyer Jacobstein of New York cited his experience in seeking to persuade business to reform itself, as Butler so ardently urged; the stock excuse he received was that if an employer in one state refrained or was restrained from using this cheap form of labor he simply lost out to a competitor elsewhere who refused to do so. Senator Medill McCormick of Illinois, when the amendment reached the upper chamber, added that if child labor "is tolerated in one section of the country, it injures all the people in every other section of the country. Unless Congress be empowered by a constitutional amendment to act, the evil which had been checked [by the second Child Labor Law] will grow now."[7]

Men like Senators James W. Wadsworth, Jr. of New York and James A. Reed of Missouri had their answers to the liberal argument. Wadsworth, a prosperous gentleman farmer, voiced the opposition of the urban Republican *laissez-faire* capitalist; Reed, a Democratic Kansas City attorney, articulated the fears of the Southern and Western farm belt that the proposal would destroy the age-old division of labor within the agrarian family. At bottom, their arguments echoed the sentiments of Congressman John J. McSwain of South Carolina, who had said in the House debate that "the constant enlargement of the Federal power is dangerous to the liberties of the people and to the safety of America," or, as Representative Harry B. Hawes of Missouri had put it, the amendment sought to nationalize an issue which should be left to "personal inclination and state statute."[8]

In Wadsworth's view, constitutional reference to a subject like child labor presaged "an imperial government whose territory will be divided into . . . provinces instead of . . . sovereign states," while Reed categorically declared that the amendment was intended to introduce into the United States the Bolshevik plan of government control of children. To these arguments, Senator Samuel M. Shortridge of California cogently replied that though "there are certain questions properly within the jurisdiction of the states," there was also the fundamental fact of "national citizenship" and the object of the amendment was "to lodge in Congress or in the government the power to protect the national citizenship." Finally, as Senator Joseph T. Robinson of Arkansas asked his colleagues: "If three-fourths of the states constituting this Union ratify the amendment," could it be said that the amendment "constitutes an infringement of any of the fundamental principles upon which this government rests?"[9]

In the light of the history of the attempted ratification of the amendment, Robinson's words acquired a particular irony.

*   *   *

"The real issue," said the *New Republic* as the ratification issue now came on, "is the old one of state rights. The federal government, which alone holds jurisdiction co-terminous with the American business field, is without adequate powers of regulation. The states have sufficient regulatory power, but because they are arbitrary fragments of the national economic unit, they are unable to use it effectively. In the no-man's land between state ineffectiveness and federal incompetence, business may build up an economic state of its own, unhampered by regulation, insured against attack by the constitutional safeguards of property."[10]

To Owen R. Lovejoy, general secretary of the National Child Labor Committee, the amendment offered the opportunity to abolish night work and dangerous occupations for adolescents, as well as to eliminate the inequities and irregularities in the regulatory statutes of individual states. For former Ambassador William E. Gonzales, a South Carolina publisher, however, the adoption of the amendment meant nothing less than to "forever surrender to the Federal government the absolute power over, and paternalistic control of, their own citizens which [the] states are better qualified wisely to employ."[11]

For the reformers, the reaction of the states was not only disappointing but—as it became evident in retrospect—served notice that the crusading zeal which had once lit the prairie skies had died down. In part the lack of enthusiasm for the Child Labor Amendment was to be explained in terms of hostility of the farmer to the idea (misrepresented as it was by opponents with more crass motives) that the proposal was intended to proscribe normal and beneficial work by young children on the family farm. There was also the serious misgiving of many religious or educational leaders, like Cardinal O'Connell of Boston, and George F. Peabody and Oscar T. Crosby, who resisted in principle the intrusion of the state into the family relationship. Still another factor was the temper of the mid-twenties which President Charles W. Eliot of Harvard described as a "reaction from the heroic temper" of the Progressive era.[12] But of greatest concern of all was the manifest disposition of agrarian leaders to leave the field to the opposition— or to join it. The case of Senator Albert B. Cummins of Iowa, onetime a scourge of extortionate railroad rates, who now co-sponsored a bill conferring upon the carriers a munificent rebate for the profits accrued by the government under its wartime operation of the lines, was symptomatic of the almost complete withdrawal of the former militants of the West. Once again, the reform movement which so long had drawn its strength from the soil would be transplanted to the hotbeds of the urban centers.

In any event, the statistics were sobering. By the end of 1925 only four states had ratified the amendment, three had failed to muster the necessary majority to ratify, and sixteen states had specifically rejected it. "For the present the tide is running irresistibly against any proposed progressive legislation which the business interests now in control of American politics have any sufficient interest in defeating," declared the *New Republic,* adding that the amendment's rejection would "render the task of raising the standards of state legislation more rather than less difficult."[13] Aside from the manifest fact that a three-fourths majority for the amendment could not now be mustered unless some of the negative state actions could be reversed, there was the constitutional question of whether with the passage of time such a proposal had not expired. Congress had not, as it would in subsequent amendments, set a terminal date for leaving the question before the states, and the opponents of the amendment sought for a *coup de grace* by arguing that an indefinite continuation of consideration of the proposal was inconsistent with the amending process itself. By the time the Supreme Court answered the question, it had become moot.[14]

In the two decades that passed before Congress again attempted to assert its authority on the question of exploited child workers, a new generation had appeared in the several branches of government. The dissent of Holmes in 1918, President Franklin D. Roosevelt would tell Congress in the spring of 1937, "spoke for a minority of the Supreme Court" but "for a majority of the American people." Both *Hammer v. Dagenhart* and *Bailey v. Drexel Furniture Co.,* said Attorney General Robert H. Jackson in testifying in favor of the new assertion of legislative authority, represented a "perversion of our Constitution" which needed to be expunged. In June 1938 the Fair Labor Standards Act, including the prohibition of child labor in interstate commerce, was passed by Congress.[15]

To find the 1938 statute constitutional, and to implement the proposition in the now moribund Child Labor Amendment, the Court was to be compelled to overturn the earlier child labor cases, and this it did by a unanimous decision in 1941. To the old arguments that the matter was one solely for the states, Chief Justice Stone answered that the power of Congress over interstate commerce was complete in itself, and was unaffected by "the exercise or non-exercise of state power." Nor were the purposes for which Congress asserted its commerce power to be evaluated by the judiciary: "Congress, following its own conception of public policy concerning the restrictions which may appropriately be imposed on interstate commerce, is free to exclude from the commerce articles whose use in the states for which they are destined it may conceive to be injurious to the public health, morals or welfare, even though the state has not sought to regulate their use."[16]

Dealing directly with the argument of the majority in *Hammer v. Dagenhart,* "that Congressional power to prohibit interstate commerce is limited to articles which in themselves have some harmful or deleterious quality— a distinction which was novel when made and unsupported by any provision of the Constitution"—Stone declared that it had long since been abandoned and had no force. "The conclusion is inescapable," he went on, that the 1918 decision "was a departure from the principles which have prevailed in the interpretation of the Commerce Clause, both before and since the decision. . . . It should be, and now is, overruled."[17]

Twenty-three years had been required to come to that conclusion.

*   *   *

For the reformers of the 1920's it was cold comfort to speculate on the possibility that at some distant future time there might be a change of judicial climate. "If the Fifth Amendment prevents Congress from attempting to deal with industrial disputes by wage legislation, the Fourteenth Amendment prevents states from enacting similar legislation," mourned Francis B. Sayre, Wilson's son-in-law, following the decision striking down the minimum wage law of the District of Columbia in 1923. "This decision," he declared, "makes forever impossible all other legislation along similar lines involving the regulation of wages."[18]

The vehement pronouncement of the majority opinion by Justice Sutherland seemed aimed at serving notice on Congress that this was precisely what the Court was saying. The statute itself, fixing a minimum wage for women workers, sounded very much like the Oregon law for which Attorney Brandeis had argued so eloquently two decades before; Justice Brandeis, who had provided much of the background for the District of Columbia law, felt constrained to remove himself from the present decision. But the attorneys general of California, Kansas, New York, Oregon and Wisconsin, and nine distinguished reform lawyers including Senator Hiram W. Johnson of California, filed briefs *amici curiae* in support of the statute. Felix Frankfurter argued the case for the appellants, the minimum wage board of the District of Columbia; he cited a long catalogue of decisional precedents where the "Brandeis brief" of the Oregon case had cited sociological authorities, seemingly anticipating Sutherland's readiness to dismiss the latter as irrelevant.[19]

Government reports and social welfare commentary Sutherland dismissed, indeed, as "interesting but only mildly persuasive." What was far more persuasive, in his view, was the ominous fact that the minimum wage law "takes account of the necessities of only one party to the contract. It ignores the necessities of the employer by compelling him to pay not less than a certain sum, not only whether the employee is capable of earning it, but irrespective of the ability of his business to sustain the burden." The result, contended the majority opinion, was to compel a payment by an employer "upon a basis having no causal connection with his business, or the contract, or the work the employee engages to do." "The moral requirement, implicit in every contract of employment, viz., that the amount to be paid and the service to be rendered shall bear to each other some relation of just equivalence, is completely ignored."[20]

The 1918 statute in the District of Columbia differed from the 1903 Oregon law by the difference which had developed in the rights of women whom both laws were intended to protect, said Sutherland. "In view of the great—not to say revolutionary—changes which have taken place . . . in the contractual, political, and civil status of women, culminating in the Nineteenth Amendment, it is not unreasonable to say that these differences [between the sexes] have now come almost, if not quite, to the vanishing point." The most significant economic fact to be discerned in these circumstances, said the Justice, is the emancipation of women from the doctrine that they needed special protection in the labor market.[21]

Taft, with Sanford faithfully echoing him, reluctantly dissented from Sutherland's eloquent apology for freedom of contract. However, he felt compelled to observe, "it is not the function of this court to hold Congressional acts invalid simply because they are passed to carry out economic views which the court believes to be unwise or unsound." As for the Nineteenth Amendment, Taft went on, it "did not change the physical strength or limitations of women."[22]

"The criterion of constitutionality," said Holmes in a separate dissent, "is not whether we believe the law to be for the public good." If it embodies a proposition which reasonably could be entertained by reasonable men, and no specific constitutional prohibition intervenes, he went on, no court should have a basis for denying to the legislative branch the power to enact a statute on the subject. Liberty of contract, he observed, was a "dogma" which had been read into the Fourteenth Amendment by analogy from "the vague contours of the Fifth," and since "pretty much all law consists in forbidding men to do some things that they want to do, . . . contract is no more exempt from law than other acts." As for the District of Columbia law in question, Holmes pointed out, it "does not compel anybody to pay anything. . . . It is safe to assume that women will not be employed at even the lowest wages allowed unless they earn them, or unless the employer's business can sustain the burden."[23]

*   *   *

In the *Adkins* minimum-wage case, Taft found himself caught in the crossfire between Sutherland and Holmes. While the instinct for judicial consistency led him to accept the rule established in the Oregon wage and hour cases (*Muller* and *Bunting*) and thus rendered him unable to concur with Sutherland, he recoiled from the heretical commentary of Holmes with reference to the "dogma" of freedom of contract. Freedom of contract was a fundamental ingredient in the Taft Court's jurisprudence of substantive due process (distinguished from procedural due process by its emphasis upon the constitutional subjects which were beyond the reach of government); Holmes' denigration of this concept as an "innocuous generality" was a truer measure of the difference in the conservative and liberal viewpoint even when he and Taft were technically in agreement as to the constitutional validity of the particular statute.

Substantive due process was a generality, beyond question; it was less readily discernible as an innocuous concept, for indeed it was developed as a pragmatic alternative to the more mystical "natural law" to which the earlier nineteenth-century courts had made reference. Under the sympathetic nurture of the Fuller Court, it had expanded into a protective cover for property rights (as it would in later years become for personal rights) against what the courts conceived to be arbitrary infringement by the government. *Adkins* thus represented the zenith of a constitutional principle which had been articulated very early in Fuller's own Chief Justiceship; in 1889 Fuller had declared that all governmental power was limited by "those fundamental principles of liberty and justice which lie at the base of all our civil and political institutions." Thirty-four years later, Sutherland could conclude that "the good of society as a whole cannot be better served than by the preservation against arbitrary restraint of the liberties of its constituent members."[24]

In between these concepts, Chief Justice White's "rule of reason" had appeared as a natural transitional medium; in the final analysis, substantive due process was the application of what the Court itself found to be reasonable. For Sutherland and the majority in *Adkins,* it was the inviolability of freedom of contract. For Taft, it was freedom of contract as qualified by the ruling cases like *Muller* and *Bunting*; the contrary rule in *Lochner v. New York,* he said, appeared to have been rejected *sub silentio*. For Holmes, the test of reasonableness was the reasonableness of the remedy as it appeared to any segment of intelligent members of society and as it was acceptable to the legislative branch. In the succession of cases presented to Taft's Court, where the issue of substantive due process arose, these points of view might as readily diverge into dissent or converge into a unanimous opinion, but the ultimate polarity of the interpretations within the concept itself was the fact of real significance which would emerge from the 1920's.

Meantime, the Minimum Wage Case stood in the way of further efforts at legislative reform in this direction. It would be fourteen years before it would follow the fate of the Child Labor Cases.[25]

*   *   *

The convergence of the disparate concepts of substantive due process into unanimity was illustrated a few weeks after the *Adkins* decision in a case which brought the Court again to the public interest doctrine first enunciated in *Munn v. Illinois*. In the years since 1877, the doctrine that a business clothed with some degree of public interest must be subject to some degree of public control had been carried from perigee (in the public utility rate cases of the nineties) to apogee (in Chief Justice White's opinion in *Wilson v. New*). Taft, speaking for the Court, undertook—in a case involving the authority of a Kansas state court of industrial relations—to summarize and categorize the instances in which free enterprise might be subject to the public interest rule.

There were three such categories, said the Chief Justice: foremost were those enterprises "which are carried on under the authority of a public grant"—railroads and public utilities—where discontinuity at the pleasure of the management or ownership was prohibited by law; a second group consisted of businesses which consistently had been subject to regulation from colonial times to the present—inns and hotels, and public conveyances such as taxicabs; while the third group included businesses which, "though not public at their inception," had subsequently been held subject to regulation by government pronouncement.[26]

It was the third category, obviously, which provided the basis for litigation, and Taft hastened to assert that "the mere declaration by a legislature that a business is affected with a public interest is not conclusive of the question whether its attempted regulation on that ground is justified." In the case before the Court, the Kansas legislature had declared the business of preparing food for human consumption to fall within the public interest doctrine and then had proceeded to assert authority to fix wages and hours and compel arbitration of labor disputes through its administrative industrial relations agency. But, said the Chief Justice, it was novel constitutional theory to contend that "the business of the butcher, or the baker, the tailor, the wood chopper, the mining operator, or the miner was clothed with such a public interest that the price of his product or his wages could be fixed by state regulation."

> To say that a business is clothed with a public interest is not to import that the public may take over its entire management and run it at the expense of the owner. The extent to which regulation may reasonably go varies with different kinds of business. The regulation of rates to avoid monopoly is one thing. The regulation of wages is another. A business may be of such character that only the first is permissible, while another may involve such a possible danger of monopoly on the one hand, and such disaster from stoppage on the other, that both come within the public concern and power of regulation.[27]

To Taft the conclusion was obvious: since food processing was not a monopoly, the public interest doctrine could not be applied in such a manner as to reach the question of wage and hour regulation. The primary public concern, with the proper sanitary safeguards in food processing, was adequately covered by food and drug statutes, and in this area of law the public interest doctrine would also fall short of the power to deal with labor conditions. For Sutherland, the argument was impeccable; it went far toward reviving, in full vigor, the *laissez-faire* ideal of maximum freedom from governmental restraint. As for Holmes and Brandeis, the merits of the specific case did not seem to them to present a practical basis for dissent.

Holmes could accept, on the one hand, the broad proposition in Taft's opinion that a statute intended for one purpose should not be artificially extended to another, unrelated one, while he waited for a case in which the divergence of philosophies on the public interest principle could be more incisively expressed.* Brandeis found the reasoning in the Wolff case acceptable on two counts: he told the Chief Justice, in a memo attached to the draft of the opinion, that he welcomed its effect of discouraging a trend toward compulsory arbitration (the friend of labor fearing that this would sap the slowly gathering bargaining strength of labor); while *Wilson v. New,* affirming the power to regulate labor conditions in interstate carriers, he told Taft, properly belonged in his first category of activities affected with a public interest and was not precedential in the third.[28]

The formalistic effect of devising categories of constitutionalism was to limit the Court liberals' ideological freedom of movement. Taft's three

---

*Cf. his dissent in *Tyson v. Banton*, p. 296.

categories of private enterprise to which the public interest doctrine was variously applicable, set out in *Wolff*, neatly complemented Sutherland's four categories in *Adkins* as permissible areas of restraint on freedom of contract—one of these was the business affected with a public interest, another the governmental power inherent in public works contracts, a third consisted of state and Federal legislation explicitly concerned with wage rates, and the fourth concerned hours or conditions of work.[29] Establishment of these categories tended to compel the government to assume the burden of proof in cases questioning the validity of any regulatory legislation. In Taft's view, this was salutary in its braking of the "trend of those who would improve society by collectivist legislation [and] increasing the functions of government."[30]

*   *   *

The postwar hysteria against unpopular opinions and minority rights presented a paradox within the context of *laissez-faire* emphasis upon maximum freedom of the individual. It was, of course, the economically orthodox for whom this freedom was intended; but the paradox developed from the fact that, in denying the guarantees of the First Amendment to defendants under state sedition laws as in the previous decade the Court had denied them to defendants under Federal sedition laws, the conservatives were led to extend the rule of the First Amendment to the states through the Fourteenth. While the rule of the First Amendment remained the restrictive one originated in *Schenck, Frohwerk* and *Abrams,* the time would come when this rule would be overturned—leaving the guarantees of this portion of the Bill of Rights applicable to the states and inviting the extension of the rest of the first eight Amendments through the Fourteenth in the same manner. Thus the key sedition cases of the twenties, although they sustained the convictions of the defendants, prepared the way for a proper guarantee of rights of national citizenship in subsequent years.

Anomalies abounded. The conservative McReynolds, in an opinion of the Court holding unconstitutional a Nebraska law prohibiting the teaching of foreign languages in elementary schools, averred that the Fourteenth Amendment protected the individual's right to train his children according to the dictates of his own conscience. Two years later McReynolds again spoke for the Court, striking down an Oregon law making attendance at public school mandatory; in addition to invading parental rights, said the opinion, the statute destroyed property rights in private schools.[31]

Even more anomalous was the pivotal case in 1925 in which the conservative majority, while sustaining the constitutionality of a New York statute on criminal anarchy, opened wide the door through which the restrictions placed upon the Federal government by the First Amendment could ultimately be placed upon the states through the Fourteenth. Justice Sanford, speaking for the majority of seven, declared that while the Court

assumed that the First Amendment freedoms "are among the fundamental
personal rights and 'liberties' protected by the due process clause of the
Fourteenth Amendment from impairment by the states," it simply remained
for the Court to apply to the New York issue the "clear and present danger"
test which Holmes had enunciated with reference to the Federal sedition statutes of the wartime decade.

For the majority, the fact of incendiary utterance was enough to establish
the danger. For Holmes, speaking for himself and Brandeis in dissent, this
narrowed free speech to a meaningless group of words: "Every idea is an
incitement. It offers itself for belief, and, if believed, it is acted on unless some
other belief outweighs it. . . . If, in the long run, the beliefs expressed . . .
are destined to be accepted by the dominant forces of the community, the only
meaning of free speech is that they should be given their chance and have their
way."[32]

To permit the legislature to define the limits of permissible speech was, in
Holmes' view, an arbitrary reduction of the universality of the constitutional
guarantee, as much as was for Taft the legislative declaration of the public
interest character of a business. If it was the province of the judiciary to determine on the merits and the facts whether the public interest doctrine was
applicable, it should equally be the province of the judiciary to determine
the applicability of the "clear and present danger" doctrine. Thus the dissenters, through the long period of their minority, undertook to compel the
majority to broaden the base of constitutional construction even while upholding restrictive statutes.

"The majority opinions determined the cases," wrote Harvard's Zechariah
Chafee in retrospect, but the dissents in *Gitlow v. New York* would "determine
the minds of the future." Without dissent, the Court in *Gitlow* implied the
extension of the guarantee of the First Amendment through the Fourteenth
to the states and thus established the principle of a Federally protected individual right against local as well as national government. When the Court
should be persuaded that the guarantee should not be subject to legislative
limitation, the certainty as well as the universality of the constitutional right
would at last be clear. It would be half a dozen years before the first fruits
of this labor would appear, and nearly thirty before it reached full maturity.[33]

The 1927 case of *Whitney v. California* demonstrated further the long
educative process which was required to reach the ultimate goal of complete
enjoyment of First Amendment freedoms. Anita Whitney, convicted under
California's criminal syndicalism statute, like Benjamin Gitlow lost the appeal
to the Supreme Court but won a significant small advance on the larger issue.
Sanford, for the majority, retreated slightly from his position in *Gitlow* by
accepting Holmes' argument that the Court rather than the legislature was the
proper arbiter of the question of the limits to be placed upon the constitutional
guarantee. To be sure, the Justice had no difficulty in finding the California
statute comfortably within these limits, while Brandeis, with Holmes concur-

ring, found no basis for invalidating the statute, since the constitutional issue had not been adequately presented. Nevertheless, Brandeis felt that the ultimate question which remained to be reached was the one Holmes had articulated in *Abrams* a decade earlier:

> Those who won our independence by revolution were not cowards. They did not fear political change. They did not exalt order at the cost of liberty. To courageous, self-reliant men, with confidence in the power of free and fearless reasoning applied through the processes of popular government, no danger flowing from speech can be deemed clear and present, unless the incidence of the evil apprehended is so imminent that it may befall before there is opportunity for full discussion. If there be time to expose through discussion the falsehood and fallacies, to avert the evil by the processes of education, the remedy to be applied is more speech, not enforced silence. Only an emergency can justify repression. Such must be the rule, if authority is to be reconciled with freedom. Such, in my opinion, is the command of the Constitution. It is, therefore, always open to Americans to challenge a law abridging free speech and assembly by showing that there was no emergency justifying it.[34]

*   *   *

But it was in the area of economics rather than in dialectics that the conservative credo was most broadly developed. On some questions, the Court conceded readily enough that the United States had emerged from the war decade as a unified national system which required national legislation if any legislation were permissible. The Transportation Act of 1920 was twice upheld as to provisions which extended the power of the Interstate Commerce Commission into the area of intrastate rates, if this was required to effectuate equitable interstate schedules, and permitted the recapture of profits in excess of a fair return as legitimate administrative regulation in the public interest.[35]

In upholding the 1921 Packers' and Stockyards Act, the Court endorsed Holmes' "stream of commerce" doctrine of two decades earlier and pointed toward the time a decade thereafter when it would extend the rationale of the commerce clause to all phases of economic production.[36] Complementing these affirmations of Federal power, the Court in 1922 pronounced its "doctrine of unconstitutional conditions" which states were forbidden to impose on interstate corporations in denial of Federally guaranteed rights.[37]

But to recognize the preeminence of Federal authority was not to say that Federal authority itself had become coextensive with interstate capitalism. The proper power to determine the fact of unfair competition in the postwar industrial process, said McReynolds in a 1920 decision emasculating the regulatory power of the Federal Trade Commission, must lie with the judiciary; where the Court had the ultimate responsibility for interpreting the law, it should assert the authority to define the practices the law was intended to control. McReynolds justified the Court's intervention into FTC rulings on the ground that only by reviewing the evidence submitted to the Commission could it decide whether the Commission's findings of fact were supported thereby. The beneficial effect of these rulings on the *laissez-faire* system was manifest. In the remainder of the 1920's, Commission orders to cease and desist, directed at interstate corporations, were overturned by the Court majority on dozens of occasions.[38]

*   *   *

Protests against the prevailing judicial tenor inevitably tended to be muted by the general euphoria of the golden decade of prosperity. To the superficial observer, the well-being of the times appeared to be general; the enthusiasm with which all America had converted to the automobile age was only the most prominent evidence that a totally new society had been born. Domestic living had been revolutionized by a torrent of electrified labor-saving devices; telephone communications and radio entertainment had become almost universal; varieties of fresh and tasty foods and of fine quality clothing were readily available in neighborhood stores; the motion picture industry had mushroomed into a network of theaters reaching into every hamlet; urban living developed an antidotal country club culture.

The American of 1925 had become all but a distinct species from the American of 1895. The fundamental difference, wrote Columbia sociologists Robert and Helen Lynd, was that the earlier American found the frame of reference for his life in an "intrinsic satisfaction" in his vocation, while the contemporary American was concerned almost exclusively with what his earning capacity meant in terms of the new luxury goods which had suddenly become available.[39]

The features of American life which were most conspicuous in the twenties were essentially features of an urban society. It was not without significance that the census of 1920 confirmed that for the first time the percentage of the population in urban centers had passed 50. The trend had become discernible four decades earlier, but it would be four more decades before it would precipitate the critical issue of reapportionment of political strength to reflect the social shift. The first World War, like the second, proved to be an agent of acceleration for the centralizing as well as the proliferating of economic productivity; scores of new industries and services were themselves spawned by the new activities in which Americans of the twenties found themselves engaged.

The automobile required the construction of a network of hard-surfaced highways, which in turn invited the country to take to the road and thereupon introduced the vacation resort, the roadside diner and the motor court to the national scene. In the seven years between 1917 and the end of 1923 the Ford Motor Company manufactured its first million cars; it had turned out its two millionth by mid-June of 1924. The manufacture of drugs and cosmetics, the proliferation of drug stores and beauty shops, the saturation of the consumption process with installment buying and chain-store distribution of goods—all assiduously promoted by a multi-million dollar advertising industry—represented the *leitmotif* of the decade of prosperity.[40]

If poverty tended to be accentuated by the concentration of the disadvantaged into the growing urban centers, it was met by a munificent increase in private charities. The community chest became a medium of organized middle-income philanthropy complementary to the large-scale contributions of the growing number of individual foundations; their combined annual support for the relief of the needy was reported to have reached nearly a billion dollars by 1925. These economic good works not only reflected the gospel of the social responsibility of wealth first preached by Andrew Carnegie, but vindicated a fundamental article of faith in the *laissez-faire* system: the care of the indigent was a matter of public conscience through private giving, not through governmental paternalism. Only when the prosperity of the decade collapsed would it become evident that private charity could not cope with more than a fraction of the total need.

Meantime, the publication of the tax returns on 1923 income, as provided by law, revealed that John D. Rockefeller, Jr. had paid a tax of $7,435,169, Henry Ford $2,467,946, and Secretary of the Treasury Andrew Mellon $1,173,987. Two years earlier the Bureau of the Census reported that the total national wealth, at a figure somewhat above $320,000,000,000, represented an increase of 72 percent in a decade. And in 1926 Stuart Chase, writing in the *New York Times,* estimated that the cash value of all resources, raw materials and manufactured products in the United States represented about 40 percent of the wealth of the entire world.[41]

It was the best of all possible worlds to many an American, and the national mood was one of general complacence which remained unshaken amid scandals in high public office and spectacular crime on the cities' streets. The largess for the veterans of the World War stuck to the fingers of various officers of the Veterans' Bureau as it flowed from the public treasury; a small-time Ohio lawyer who became Harding's Attorney General devoted most of his administrative effort to spreading rumors of other executive departments and their wrongdoing while obstructing any inquiry into the activities of his own; and a Senate crony of the new President, Albert B. Fall of New Mexico, found the Secretaryship of the Interior the most tempting opportunity of all. Fall found no difficulty in arranging for a transfer to his department of the vast oil reserves under the custody of the Department of the Navy—whose Secretary Edwin Denby was the most pitiable figure in Harding's incredible Cabinet—after which he secretly leased the two greatest, Teapot Dome and Elk Hills in Wyoming, to private exploiters Harry F. Sinclair and Edward L. Doheny.

Harding, as warm hearted as he was inept, died before the full measure of his cronies' betrayal of the President and the nation became known. Coolidge, as honest as he was small-minded, was not to be held accountable for the spectacular corruption that a Senate investigating committee eventually documented in the Teapot Dome scandals. A political regime which could survive this and a succession of companion exposures without upsetting the even tenor of prosperity had little to fear from a moral accounting at the polls. In the fall of 1924, Coolidge was returned to the White House with a popular vote of more than 15,000,000 over the 8,000,000 for the Democrats' John W. Davis and the Progressives' Robert M. LaFollette, who polled 4,800,000.

*   *   *

For Taft, Harding's death and the shock of the Cabinet scandals, with the successive resignations of Daugherty, Denby and Fall, abruptly ended the Chief Justice's program for controlling the general administration of Federal justice through a succession of advices (often unsolicited) from the Supreme Court to the White House. He was never to be able to establish the same degree of *rapport* with Coolidge or with Hoover, and the remaining judicial appointments of his Chief Justiceship were notably distinguishable from those which had been made by Harding.

The first one was foreshadowed in Coolidge's appointment to the vacant Attorney Generalship—a man unknown to Taft except as a former dean of Columbia University's law school and subsequently a successful Wall Street lawyer. Harlan F. Stone, indeed, was all but unknown to the political community in general, although the *Washington Star,* in applauding the appointment of a manifestly successful and urbane attorney to the shattered Department of Justice, spoke vaguely of him as "a level-headed, brainy, conservative-progressive."[42] In the following year, the Chief Justice came to respect the new appointee highly, and when, in 1925, Justice McKenna was finally persuaded to retire, Taft strongly endorsed (although he did not initiate) the President's decision to elevate Stone to the bench. That the Senate insurgents—now beginning to regain their vocal powers—disapproved of the Wall Street and Amherst College associations with Coolidge which in their view were Stone's chief credentials, was an added persuasion for Taft that the choice was right.[43]

Indeed, as the midpoint in the decade came on with the inauguration of Coolidge, Taft had reason to believe that the main battles to secure the Constitution from insurgent attack had been won. In thirty years the solidarity of the conservative position had not been so complete; Holmes, at eighty-four, and Brandeis, at sixty-nine, presumably would retire sometime within the coming four years in which a safe Republican President could be counted on to rectify the errors of the appointments of Theodore Roosevelt and Woodrow Wilson. Even with the surviving two "latitudinarians," the good feeling within the Court itself was something that had not been approached since Fuller's administration, and in this Holmes himself concurred: "It is very pleasant with the present Chief," he remarked on several occasions.[44]

The American public generally regarded the Chief Justice with approval. "In the areas of his historic blunders . . . President Taft was a fat man; today, treading the primrose majority path of the Supreme Court, he is only the size of every tall man," observed Charles W. Thompson, veteran Washington correspondent. The physical analogy struck him as apt; the cumbersome behavior of Taft's White House career had given way to a deft and confident judicial administration. "He was a good President at the wrong time," Thompson continued, adding that "in the eighties or nineties, where he belonged, he would have been reckoned an intelligent Progressive. As a judge his only fault is one which he shares with the majority of the Federal bench: he believes a little too strongly in the existing order."[45]

For Taft himself, approaching the midway point in his own decade of the Chief Justiceship, the accolade seemed unqualifiedly appropriate.

15/Prohibition:
A Socio-Legal Sketch

T HE FAILURE OF the Eighteenth Amendment—whether the failure was as real as it was apparent—took place in a singular context of silence in constitutional commentary. There was, to be sure, voluble enough argument over detail, but relatively little on principle or theory. It was not legal argument but astute and patient grass-roots politics which had accounted for the original success of the prohibition movement: a generation of state legislative victories and a steady accretion of "dry" strength in both House and Senate. The amendment, when it eventually was proposed, had been debated in Congress essentially in terms of economics—the wartime savings of grains for food rather than distilled beverages—and the final drive through both houses encountered comparatively little opposition. Ratification proceeded with equal expedition; the first state, Mississippi, registered its approval in less than four weeks after the amendment was submitted by Congress, and in a matter of fifteen minutes of deliberation in both houses of the state legislature. Twelve months later the needed thirty-sixth state, Nebraska, completed the process.[1]

It was a remarkable achievement, particularly in view of the fact that neither major party had ever endorsed the idea of national prohibition and no major Presidential candidate had ever devoted significant comment to the subject. In retrospect, the amendment appeared to have been the beneficiary of three major circumstances which converged at this point in time: while the "dry" faction steadfastly denied that the amendment was intruded into the constitutional system under the cover of the war, it was undeniable that it derived substantial stimulus from the general atmosphere of public dedication and self-denial bred by the war effort. In addition, the question of abstinence was presented as a moral issue so universally endorsed by white Protestantism that it maneuvered the most rational opposition onto the defensive. Finally, there was the manifest fact that the mainspring of the prohibition movement was agrarian. Traffic in alcoholic beverages had always been essentially an urban enterprise, and the liquor issue could readily be converted into a symbol of the iniquities of urbanism which rural-dominated legislatures instinctively attacked as a threat to the yeoman virtues of the past.

As New Year's Day of 1920—the date prescribed for prohibition to go into effect—drew near, the country seemed generally to anticipate a change in the national character, bearing out the prophecy of the Anti-Saloon League of New York that "a new nation will be born." In Washington, D. C. a New Year's Eve watch-night service of temperance workers in national convention listened raptly to William Jennings Bryan speak on a text from Matthew 20:2 —"for they are dead which sought the young child's life." In Norfolk, Virginia, the oldtime evangelist Billy Sunday rhapsodized that with the abolition of intoxicants, "slums will soon be only a memory. We will turn our prisons into factories and our jails into storehouses and corncribs. Men will walk upright now, women will smile, and the children will laugh. Hell will be forever for rent."[2]

*   *   *

Yet the opposition was not entirely prostrate. It seized upon one argument: that the ratification of the amendment by state legislatures did not reflect the wishes of the people of the states, and that where the state laws provided for a referendum on actions of the legislature, the ratification could validly be challenged. The test of this proposition occurred in Ohio; it ended in disaster for the "wets." The prohibitionists, victorious in the legislature, petitioned for an injunction to prevent the secretary of state from drawing upon the public funds to conduct a referendum. On an appeal to the Supreme Court, a unanimous bench sustained the injunction on the ground that, while the referendum was permissible with reference to state legislation, it could not be used to vary the method of ratification—whether by legislatures or conventions—of an amendment to the Federal Constitution. The prescription of the method was the exclusive right of Congress, the Court ruled, and a state legislature in ratification of an amendment was discharging a Federal rather than a state function.[3]

One week after this opinion, the Court disposed of a group of seven cases which raised the question of the validity of the Eighteenth Amendment in general, and of the Volstead Act which implemented it. In two original suits, the states of Rhode Island and New Jersey petitioned to enjoin the Executive Department of the government not to enforce the Volstead Act; in four companion cases, Federal court denials of similar injunctions in Kentucky, Massachusetts, Missouri and New Jersey were appealed, while in a fifth case, the granting of an injunction by the Federal court in Wisconsin was also appealed. Dozens of briefs were filed, and oral arguments required ten court days distributed throughout the month of March, 1920; twenty-one states, through their attorneys general, filed briefs *amici curiae*, and a total of fifty-two lawyers eventually figured in the cases in varying degrees.

Rhode Island v. Palmer thus became the medium for the definitive argument on the constitutional issues of prohibition, and on the theory of the constitutional structure of the Federal system, which took place in the "dry decade." Attorney General Herbert A. Rice of Rhode Island set the keynote for the anti-Amendment case in his brief: The Amendment, he contended, was predicated upon the existence of a Federal element in a police power which had been conceived by the framers of the original Constitution to have rested exclusively in the states. The term "amendment" in Article V, Rice declared, referred only to court procedure; the Constitution as a whole "being viewed as a great legal process, warrant, or commission, the principle of amendment which had been applied for centuries to judicial processes and legal documents became directly applicable. And as amendment was always limited to the jurisdiction of the process, or to the purpose of the pleading, or to the scope of the legal document, the term was especially appropriate in relation to a written Constitution designedly limited in all these respects."[4]

The argument was supported in a brief submitted by Elihu Root and William D. Guthrie—the latter unchanged in his conviction of a narrowly circumscribed Federal power which he had insisted upon in the Income Tax Case of 1895: "That the power to amend the Constitution does not include the power of independent legislation by the amending agents is clearly indicated by the rulings both in the national and state courts that the proceedings of Congress and of the state legislatures are not ordinary legislation," so that Congressional resolutions proposing amendments and state legislative resolutions ratifying the proposals are not acts of legislation in themselves. Upon this fine technical distinction, Root and Guthrie contended that the language of the Eighteenth Amendment, prohibiting "the manufacture, sale, or transportation of intoxicating liquors" in the United States, was ordinary legislation improperly cast in the form of a constitutional amendment.[5]

Ironically, the counter-argument of twenty-one states supporting the amendment was to insist upon a necessary Federal power complementing that of the states. Charles Evans Hughes, joining the state attorneys general on these briefs *amici curiae,* flatly asserted that the Constitution "is not a compact between the states. It proceeds directly from the people." If the police power were to be confined to the states as the "wet" argument ran, "then this court has acted without authority in its almost daily application of the due process clause of the Fourteenth Amendment to state legislation."[6] To this same general effect was the brief of Wayne B. Wheeler, general counsel of the Anti-Saloon League, contending that the people of the United States had unlimited power to write into their Constitution whatever they wished, and that once a subject had been so incorporated, the source of legislative authority was the amendment and not necessarily the general police power.[7]

As it turned out, the arguments of counsel were considerably more eloquent than the opinions of the Court. The seven-to-two majority was highly ambivalent in its own decision. Van Devanter spoke for himself and four colleagues, while White and McReynolds filed separate concurring opinions and McKenna and Clarke filed lengthy separate dissents. The formal opinion of the Court, upholding the Amendment and the implementing Volstead Act, was criticized by White as stating "only ultimate conclusions, without an exposition of the reasoning by which they had been reached." He then undertook to give his own reasons for dismissing the petitions for injunctions against the government, but with indifferent success. Characteristically obtuse although uncharacteristically brief, White devoted most of his opinion to refuting the argument that Section 2 of the Amendment, vesting concurrent enforcement power in Federal and state governments, cancelled out the power of each. With tart honesty in his even briefer concurrence, McReynolds observed that it was "impossible now to say with fair certainty what construction should be given" to the Amendment, and that he accordingly preferred to "remain free to consider these questions when they arrive."[8]

*   *   *

The clearest commentary of all had been made by one who did not participate in any of the cases but who would soon become the presiding member of the Court. William Howard Taft, although supporting the principle of national prohibition because it had been made the law of the land, nevertheless observed:

> A national prohibition amendment to the Federal Constitution [has been] adopted against the views and practices of a majority of the people in many of the large cities and in one-fourth or less of the states. The business of manufacturing alcohol, liquor, and beer will go out of the hands of the law-abiding members of the community, and will be transferred to the quasi-criminal class. . . . In the communities where the majority will not sympathize with a Federal law's restrictions, large numbers of Federal officers will be needed for its enforcement. . . . The reaching out of the great central power to brush the doorsteps of local communities, far removed geographically and politically from Washington, will be irritating in such states and communities and will be a strain upon the bond of the national union.[9]

For Congressman Andrew J. Volstead of Minnesota, a small-town lawyer who had first come to the House in 1903 on the wave of agrarian reform, the prohibition amendment represented the day of judgment for the demon rum. He was not a member of the Anti-Saloon League, he told the House in introducing his drastic implementing statute, nor did he consider himself a "crank" on the subject. Nevertheless, he contended, the statute must set the minimum of permissible alcoholic content so low that it would be impossible to manufacture an intoxicant within the law. To those who were urging a milder minimum—3.45 percent alcohol for beer, as against his proposed one-half of one percent—he warned that to fail to make prohibition absolute was to "face a situation that will be infinitely worse to deal with."

The measure was indeed drastic and uncompromising. It had been written, as House members charged without meeting denials, by Wheeler of the Anti-

Saloon League and his associates who were "riding roughshod over the country." Drawing upon more than twenty years of experience in plugging loopholes in state "dry" laws, the drafters of the Volstead Act undertook to wipe out every vestige of traffic in "alcohol, brandy, whiskey, rum, gin, beer, ale, porter and wine, and in addition thereto any [spirituous,] vinous, malt, or fermented liquor, liquids and compounds, whether medicated, proprietary, patent or not, and by whatever name called." The act forbade anyone to "manufacture, sell, barter, transport, import, export, deliver, furnish or possess" anything which fell under the definition of the prohibited goods. Throughout the summer of 1919 the debate continued, but when the vote on the measure at last came, in October, the House majority in its favor was almost three to one, and in the Senate it was approved without even a roll call. Wilson vetoed the act on the ground that it improperly combined in one measure both emergency wartime prohibition and the constitutional prohibition intended to take effect in January. Congress, dominated by "dry" forces, shouted down the technicality and promptly passed the act over the veto.[10]

To finance the enforcement process for the Volstead Act, Congress proceeded to appropriate $2,200,000 for the period ending June 30, 1920. By the end of fiscal 1929, it would have appropriated more than $88,000,000.[11] Other statistics, published by the Treasury Department in 1930 as a summary of the decade of prohibition, were even more eloquent: In the ten-year period, there were more than half a million arrests for liquor law violations; the number of captured stills, distilleries and related items of apparatus for liquor manufacture totalled more than 1,600,000; the total of seized spirits in various stages of preparation for the illicit market exceeded 185,000,000 gallons; more than 45,000 automobiles and 1,300 boats and launches were taken by the revenue officers; and the total value of all confiscated properties was reported at $136,-144,544.50. In this period, more than 500 Federal agents were killed or wounded.[12]

This was the story in retrospect. At the outset, nothing but optimism as to the effectiveness of the prohibition administration was expressed. The first commissioner of prohibition in the Treasury Department, John F. Kramer of Ohio, announced on January 4, 1920: "We shall see that [liquor] is not manufactured. Nor sold, nor given away, nor hauled in anything on the surface of the earth or under the earth or in the air." On January 31, however, George W. Ashworth, director of the Customs Office, advised the House of Representatives appropriations committee that wholesale smuggling of liquor across the borders of the nation was already approaching mammoth dimensions, and that only "an infinitesimal quantity" was being intercepted. Two weeks after that, two agents of the Internal Revenue Service were arrested in Baltimore and charged with corruption in the enforcement of the liquor law.[13]

In the face of these early alarms, the prohibitionists professed complete faith in the future. The manifest fact that the corner saloon had gone completely out of business made it easy to declare that the "dry" law had been an unqualified success. The steady increase in reports of corruption in the ranks of law enforcement officers did little to dampen the general enthusiasm. "Each year," Wheeler told a Senate judiciary subcommittee in 1926, "the Congress that has been elected has been dryer than its predecessor." Before prohibition, it was proudly pointed out, arrests for drunkenness had been at the rate of two out of five offenders, while now they were at a rate of nine out of ten. Where the statistics came from, and whether in themselves they suggested an accelerating rate of alcoholism, was not discussed.[14]

The dawn of sinlessness predicted by the Anti-Saloon League was still rosy on the horizon; for the moment, the clouds seemed to be scattered and the day of righteousness still promised to be fair.

*   *   *

Ambiguities seemed to spring up like dragon's teeth sown in all too fertile soil. What, it was demanded, was the practical effect of the second section of the Amendment, that "Congress and the several states shall have concurrent power to enforce this article by appropriate legislation"? Concurrent power had not heretofore been suggested in any wording of the Constitution, although the courts over the years had played with the concept and developed a somewhat esoteric catalog of propositions concerning it. The White Court had stumbled over itself in attempting to come to grips with the issue in *Rhode Island v. Palmer,* and now Taft, speaking for a unanimous Court, sought to state something less equivocal. He rejected the contention that "in vesting the Federal government with the power of country-wide prohibition, state power would be excluded." While the first section of the Amendment, said Taft, obviously extinguished any state power to protect or regulate liquor traffic, the second section did not cut down or displace prior state laws not inconsistent with it. "Such laws derive their force . . . not from this amendment, but from the power originally belonging to the states, preserved to them by the Tenth Amendment, and now relieved from the restriction heretofore arising out of the Federal Constitution."[15]

The opinion, as it soon turned out, did not help much with the general situation. It reassured the states that they could supplement the Federal prohibition enforcement program if they elected to do so, but it did not charge them with responsibility for doing so. Section 2 might well have been interpreted more affirmatively, and by requiring the states to assist in enforcement would have substantially contributed to the effectiveness of the Amendment itself.* Unable to call upon state law enforcement officers and courts to aid in running down offenders, the Federal authority had to be expanded to such degree as a "dry" but laconic Congress would make possible. While at least three-fourths of the states in fact had various types of prohibition laws at the start of the twenties, no concerted effort was ever made to revise them in any

---

*Taft, quite properly, was distinguishing between concurrent power, with its options, and joint power, which would have made the Amendment much more difficult to implement.

pattern of uniformity. Indeed, New York and several other states soon repealed their own statutes on the subject, immediately increasing the strain on the thinly spread Federal enforcement network.[16]

The Volstead Act had its own share of ambiguities. It was, in the first place, concerned exclusively with shutting off the supply of intoxicants, and hence placed virtually all of its emphasis upon the criminal liability of the manufacturer and distributor. The consumer, whose thirst would ultimately determine the degree of public compliance with the law, was all but ignored by the enforcement system. Private stocks he might have possessed when the statute went into effect he could continue to keep for his personal use, and his home was specifically exempted from the search and seizure provisions of the law unless it could be established that he was engaged in manufacturing for sale any illicit beverage. In addition, if he suddenly discovered an ailment which his family doctor determined to be subject to treatment with spirituous medicines, the law permitted a licensing of certain wines and related liquors for this purpose.[17]

*   *   *

Overshadowing the question of the constitutional theory to be extrapolated from the Eighteenth Amendment, or the matter of the loopholes in the Volstead Act, was the fact that American life in general, at the moment the attempt to enforce prohibition was inaugurated, was undergoing a succession of cataclysmic reversals of attitude. By the beginning of 1920, when the national liquor laws went into effect, the country was rapidly losing its zeal for reform and abstinence which had climaxed in the Wilson years. The Harding appeal for normalcy was the acknowledged keynote of the time, and was most often translated into a sense of individual freedom as distinguished from individual obligation.

A striking illustration of this shift in national psychology was provided by the impact of the Nineteenth Amendment, itself almost contemporary with the Eighteenth. The political equality extended to women by this enactment enhanced the significant degree of economic equality, or at least independence, which women had discovered in the new markets for their services and labor created by the war and manpower shortage. If the returning doughboys would find it hard to settle down again into old ways, the American woman found it even harder—and, indeed, she was never to return to the subordinate status which had been her lot prior to the World War and the Amendment. The whole image of woman had changed, with her skirts and her hair becoming short at virtually the same instant, and her parity with males in the matter of smoking and drinking becoming an accepted element in her emancipation.

Another factor affecting the national psychology, and thus the context of the prohibition effort, was the general awareness that prosperity—ultimately, even wealth—was within the reach of a greater proportion of adult Americans than it had ever been for any comparable group of people in history. As the national economy converted itself, with only a brief decline in the process, from concentrated war production into mass production for a voracious consumer public, the spending of money and the installment plan of paying for the many new luxuries became a compulsive element in public behavior. It also became an article of faith, as the means of insuring the perpetual motion of prosperity. As the president of the Baldwin Locomotive Works, benignly assessing the substantial rise in wage levels in this period, said: "The wage earners constitute the majority of our population. These people are the spenders of the nation, and upon their ability to spend freely the great business of our country depends. Manufactured products of all kinds must be furnished them as well as the necessary staples of life. It is the wage of these people that makes good times or bad."[18]

With money came the means of acquiring the elusive but only slightly diminished quantities of alcoholic beverages presumably driven out of existence by prohibition. Many a middle-class American might brew his own at home, usually producing a foul-tasting intoxicant whose chief virtue was that it was unlikely to be as potentially poisonous as the redistilled commercial alcohols that were offered by many bootleggers. But for the growing numbers of affluent city dwellers, the night club or the speakeasy was becoming the accepted medium for purchase and consumption of spirits of a better vintage, even though many of them were shamelessly adulterated and all of them were extortionate in price.

These establishments provided the meeting-ground for two characteristic elements of postwar American society—the rebellious generation of youth which had been freed from parental restraints in the process of women's emancipation and the consequent redefining of relationships within the family, and the modernized crime syndicates created by the gangster and the racketeer. The first bootleggers and smugglers had prepared the way for the armed and organized mobs which quickly followed; while the early entrepreneurs of an illicit liquor traffic were interested only in transporting the product to the consumer, the tempting and obvious opportunity to "muscle in" and take over the business could hardly be overlooked. A hijacker with a gun took over a rumrunning consignment; unable to appeal to law enforcement agencies (even bribed ones) for protection, the bootlegger's only recourse was to hire his own gun. Thereafter, it was a matter of marshalling larger underworld forces and equipping them with more sophisticated armament.

In a society where to an increasing degree Americans were doing things on an associational basis—in clubs, chambers of commerce, industrial organizations, committees and similar groups—it was totally logical that crime should also organize. The control of the liquor traffic led to the control of the manufacture of liquor as well, and then to its sales outlets. Before the middle of the decade, almost all major night clubs and "blinds" were either owned by big-time criminals or paid "protection" money to them. Arnold Rothstein, the financier of the New York underworld, and Al Capone, the gang leader of Chicago, became public figures representative of a well-known peerage of criminal overlords who scarcely attempted to conceal their identities or business connections. With liquor law enforcement becoming increasingly demoralized, state and local officials systematically corrupted, and a mobile army of gunmen at their command, the gangsters of the mid-twenties had less to fear from government than from jealous rivals in the rackets.

*   *   *

Yet, obviously, it was the insistent and insatiable thirst of law-abiding citizens which constituted the unstable base for the prohibition effort. "There would be little traffic in illegal liquor if only criminals patronized it," Herbert Hoover was to observe at his inaugural in March, 1929. By then the problem had reached a stage which threatened to undermine the process of law in every field of national life, and the new President warned: "Our whole system of self-government will crumble either if officials elect what laws they will enforce or citizens elect what laws they will support. The worst evil of disregard for some law is that it destroys respect for all law."[19]

Earnestly the prohibition forces cast about for fresh means of attacking the problem, and for the most part the courts gave them consistent support on constitutional issues which arose in course. Even before the Eighteenth Amendment had gone into effect, the judiciary had unhesitatingly rejected the argument of a major New York brewery that the wartime prohibition statute had deprived it of property without due process. Nor did the Amendment diminish liability under pre-existing state liquor laws, the Court declared; moreover, the Volstead Act was held to be broad enough to enjoin any type of liquor manufacture as a nuisance. While a private home could not be searched without reasonable belief that it was a site of illicit traffic, liquor en route to the home could be seized, and a state law making the existence of a still on anyone's premises *prima facie* evidence of violation of the prohibition laws was upheld against a charge that the statute violated the Fifth Amendment.[20]

A question arose early in the decade concerning liquor aboard ships coming into American ports; the Supreme Court ruled that the sale of such liquor within the quarantine area was illegal, thereby sealing off quantities of alcoholic beverages while the vessels were in American waters. Statutes in California and New York were held to be constitutional which limited the amount of medicinal liquor that physicians could prescribe or pharmacies could issue, and a Kansas statute forfeiting title to any automobile found to be used in transporting liquor was also held constitutional. The Eighteenth Amendment, said the Court in a sweeping opinion in 1925, gave the Federal government plenary authority to enforce prohibition by any reasonable legislation, and hinted strongly that state statutes would enjoy equally broad interpretation.[21]

Yet the floating bar, in the form of a yacht or other vessel riding just outside the marginal seas over which the United States had jurisdiction, and the rumrunner in the form of a high-speed, seagoing craft of foreign registry presented peculiar problems in both constitutional and international law. In January, 1924, the State Department concluded a unique anti-smuggling treaty with Great Britain, and in May and June made similar pacts with half a dozen other nations, in which the cooperating powers agreed to "raise no objection" to searches and seizures of private boats under their flags whenever there should be "reasonable cause for belief that the vessel has committed or is committing or attempting to commit an offense against the laws of the United States . . . prohibiting the importation of alcoholic beverages." Unprecedented as this stipulation was, the treaties went further and, instead of confining the search or seizure to the traditional three-mile limit of sovereignty or the twelve-mile limit for customs purposes, extended the rights of the United States to such a distance from the coast as "can be traversed in one hour" by the suspected vessel.[22]

While experts mused over a variety of problems created by these "rum treaties," a dramatic practical demonstration of the liabilities involved was provided in March, 1929 by the pursuit of the *I'm Alone,* a vessel of Canadian registry overtaken by Coast Guard cutters forty-eight hours after the original sighting, and two hundred miles off the coast of Lousiana. The *I'm Alone* had been cleared from Belize in British Honduras with a cargo of liquor for Hamilton, Bermuda; she was five hundred miles off course when hailed by the Coast Guard's *Wolcott* and, it was reported by American authorities, she was known to be equipped with 200-horsepower auxiliary engines. Pursuit began near the twelve-mile limit and continued for two days until a companion Coast Guard vessel, the *Dexter,* joined the chase and eventually sank her. All but one of the crew were rescued and taken to New Orleans, where a six-year battle of lawyers began over the logical extreme to which the treaty rights could be carried. In 1935, after the Eighteenth Amendment had been scuttled, the United States paid an indemnity of $50,000 to Canada upon the findings of an international commission.[23]

*   *   *

To range over thousands of miles of ocean watching for small, swift and elusive liquor runners while staying within the technical limits of treaty formulae which were themselves the subject of substantial legal questioning, was a monumental responsibility. Even more demanding, as the years of prohibition multiplied, was the task of balancing law and morals in the constitutional context, as dramatized in the 1926-28 litigation known as *Olmstead v. United States.* The original trial, in the Federal court in Seattle, was hailed by contemporary newspapers as the biggest criminal prosecution in the history of the Volstead Act—ninety persons were indicted in the beginning, and twenty-three ultimately were found guilty. But when, two years later, the Supreme Court upheld the convictions by a five-to-four majority, the opinion was darkly condemned by a national magazine as "the Dred Scott decision of prohibition," and the dissent of Justice Brandeis was hailed as a counterpoint to Hoover's call for popular respect for government: "If the government [itself] becomes a lawbreaker, it breeds contempt for the law."[24]

Roy Olmstead's liability was hardly in question; even the prohibition agents confessed admiration for the efficiency of the system by which he had undertaken the legal acquisition of Canadian liquor, transshipped it to hidden points in the Puget Sound area, and supplied it in undiluted quality and at reasonable prices throughout the Pacific Northwest. Many Seattle citizens of high standing described him as "the good bootlegger," a kind of Robin Hood (or Peter Pan) who had found a means of tempering an unreasonable law. His downfall came about through an assumption that the guarantees of the Fourth Amendment against unreasonable search and seizure, and of the Fifth against self-incrimination, presented a securely interlaced legal barricade between the prosecutors and his thinly-concealed activities in defiiance of the Eighteenth. To the moral question of whether one or more provisions of the Constitution might be narrowed from their established construction to accommodate another provision, Olmstead had taken for granted that the answer would be "no"; the judicial majority opinions in the end held the opposite.

The constitutional morality of the wiretapping issue—on which Olmstead's attorney had attacked the admissibility of the evidence obtained by the government—was first raised in the dissenting opinion of Circuit Judge Frank H. Rudkin in San Francisco. Wiretapping, explicitly forbidden by Washington state law and in Rudkin's view equally forbidden by the Fourth Amendment, represented a betrayal of the values on which the Constitution itself was predicated. "If such ills as these must be borne," he warned, "our forefathers signally failed in their desire to ordain and establish a government to secure the blessings of liberty to themselves and their posterity."[25]

Taft, for whom this case would be the medium for the last major constitutional opinion of his career, saw the moral issue in *Olmstead* not as the impropriety of constricting the guarantees of the Fourth and Fifth Amendments in order to enforce the Eighteenth, but rather as the need to preserve the integrity of the constitutional mandate embodied in the Eighteenth by avoiding a broad but academic interpretation of the Fourth and Fifth. From the outset he had expressed himself as "discouraged about the liquor situation," by which he meant a foreboding of the damage it would do to an orderly society. His answer had been to assert a strict liability with reference to persons found in violation of the prohibition statute. An existing law was to be enforced; this was a sufficient reply both to the opponents of prohibition in general and to the advocates of a modified implementing statute.[26]

The rationale of the prohibition cases, Taft suggested to his brother Justices in 1924, was not "introducing any new law and new principle of constitutional construction, but . . . only adapting old principles and applying them to new conditions created by the change in the national policy which the Eighteenth Amendment requires." Accordingly, Taft supported a majority opinion holding that to deny a private party access to liquor he had put in a warehouse, for private use in his home, was not to deprive him of property without due process. He sided with the majority in declaring that the Amendment nullified a treaty commitment to permit passage of sealed liquor shipments across the

United States from Canada to Mexico. He found no double jeopardy in a case of four men convicted, on the same set of facts, under a Washington state prohibition statute and under the Volstead Act. The problems under the liquor laws were hydra-headed, but Taft could find no recourse but to press an all-out support of the Amendment even at the expense of other constitutional guarantees; search and seizure, as in the case of liquor discovered in an automobile, he declared was not unreasonable where there was probable cause for the action.[27]

For the Chief Justice, the issue in the *Olmstead* case was simpler than in the automobile case; in wiretapping, he declared, there was neither search nor seizure. The Fourth Amendment, he observed, was directed historically against general warrants and writs of assistance whereby government agents could forcibly enter private premises and carry off records. "The language of the Amendment," he concluded, "cannot be extended and expanded to include telephone wires reaching to the whole world from the defendant's house or office." Congress might enact legislation to protect telephone messages and thus "depart from the common law of evidence"; for the Court to do so, Taft said, would be to give "an enlarged and unusual meaning to the Fourth Amendment." "A standard which would forbid the reception of evidence if obtained by other than nice ethical conduct by government officials would make society suffer and give criminals greater immunity than has been known heretofore."[28]

Three of the four dissenters—including the pedestrian and arch-conservative Butler—wrote opinions in criticism of the Taft view. Quite aside from the constitutional guarantee, declared Holmes, "the government ought not to use evidence obtained, and only obtainable, by a criminal act." The instant case, he went on, required a choice between the desirable object of apprehending and prosecuting lawbreakers, and the equally desirable principle that the government should not itself break the law. Nor was the obloquy lessened by the fact that the evidence in the Federal court was obtained by violating a state law. "We have to choose, and for my part I think it a less evil that some criminals should escape than that the government should play an ignoble part."[29]

For Brandeis, the narrow historical interpretation of the Fourth Amendment was irrational. "Clauses guaranteeing to the individual protection against specific abuses of power," he declared, must continually be adapted to a changing technology. Where the original concern of the Amendment had been forcible entry into private premises, the principle of protection against invasion of privacy was the basic issue and must be applied against newer and subtler means of invasion. Most irrational of all, he insisted, was the argument that "the intrusion was in aid of law enforcement. Experience should teach us to be most on our guard to protect liberty when the government's purposes are beneficent. Men born to freedom are naturally alert to repel invasion of their liberty by evil-minded rulers. The greatest dangers to liberty lurk in insidious encroachment by men of zeal, well-meaning, but without understanding."[30]

The confused moral issues presented in the *Olmstead* case epitomized the contradictions and inconsistencies with which the prohibition problem had bedevilled the nation. Americans, whose constitutional principles heretofore had been relatively uncomplicated—a rule of national life written into the Constitution was the accepted standard of conduct thereafter—were increasingly disturbed by confrontation with the ancient philosophical question: What is the obligation of the good man respecting a bad law—assuming the law in fact to be bad? While the decade of prohibition was to record more than a hundred proposals for repeal of the Eighteenth Amendment, the nation was not yet prepared to face the fact that to expunge any part of the Constitution was to confess to the tentative and mutable nature of the whole document. They preferred not to accept the logical consequences of Holmes' proposition that the Constitution was "an experiment, as all life is an experiment." As the twenties wore on, there was growing self-doubt with reference to the matter of prohibition. The battle of the American people in the prohibition era was with themselves, and the integrity of the rule of law was the ultimate issue.

*   *   *

By the end of 1925 it was becoming commonplace for local communities to work out a new version of local option—in this case, the option being as to how vigorously, if at all, the liquor laws should be enforced. Agrarian states, where prohibition sentiment had always been strong, gave full force to the law through their own officers and through cooperation with Federal agents. Urban areas, indifferent or hostile in the matter, tended to withdraw their own law enforcement machinery and to discourage or even corrupt the national prohibition agents in their midst. Periodically, new drives to round up and stamp out the illicit rings of liquor traffic were announced and carried out —with little visible effect on the prevalence of violations or the attitudes of the citizenry.

"The very fact that the law is difficult to enforce is the clearest proof of the need for its existence," Wheeler told a Senate judiciary subcommittee in the spring of 1926. It was an oversimplification, to the same degree as the "wet" argument that prohibition had been responsible for the organized crime of the day. The Eighteenth Amendment, it became clear in retrospect, was only one factor in the massive growth of racketeering in the twenties. Even at its height, the liquor trade represented only one interest of the gangsters, who diversified their activities in many fields—gambling, prostitution and similar pursuits.

Wheeler's testimony before the Senate committee was part of an extended series of hearings in the spring of 1926 looking toward a greatly enlarged governmental effort to cope with the problem of liquor. General Lincoln C. Andrews of the Prohibition Bureau urged a drastic expansion of Federal authority through control of medicinal liquor, bonding of grain growers, broader power to confiscate suspected stores of commercial alcohol, and enlarged search and seizure authority. But 1926 was a Congressional election year, and Andrews' program was expensive as well as controversial. An administration which intended to campaign on its record of economy in public office did not respond with enthusiasm to the recommendations.[31]

Turning from legislative to executive sources of help, Andrews—Senator Beveridge, at least, identified him as the instigator—proposed to President Coolidge that state, county or municipal officers in effect be deputized as agents of the Treasury Department for prohibition enforcement purposes. The executive order of May, 1926 authorizing such appointments caught the public by surprise, and then precipitated a torrent of protest. The Republican *New York Herald-Tribune* scathingly condemned the action as reversing "the whole trend of Mr. Coolidge's governmental philosophy, which has stressed the importance of state government and the necessity of respecting its integrity." Beveridge, the old progressive, attacked the executive order as an unthinking step in the direction of centralization which "will radically and fundamentally change our form of government and change it at once." Blaming the retired General Andrews, Beveridge added that if "this military and bureaucratic exposition of constitutional law is sound . . . if local officers can be made national officers to execute one national law in a particular locality they can be made agents of a general and centralized government to enforce other laws in every locality."[32] Incredulous at the vehemence of the reaction, Coolidge announced that the order would stand. As matters turned out, however, no state or local officers were ever appointed under it, and thus one more effort to deal with the prohibition question was frustrated.

Indeed, it appeared to the "dry" majority and the enforcement agents in government that circumstances were conspiring to insure that they received less help rather than more. The use of undercover agents was piously censured as unworthy of a free nation; in particular, a "front" for Treasury officers known as the Bridge Whist Club, where suspected bootleggers were entertained at public expense while being encouraged unwittingly to incriminate themselves, was loudly condemned as immoral as well as an improper expenditure of public funds.[33]

The "wet" opposition was becoming increasingly vocal, at the same time. A sudden rise in the number of deaths from alcohol poisoning—which the "drys" identified simply as alcoholism—led to charges that the government was becoming an accessory to the murder of its citizens. Because the Volstead Act demanded that industrial alcohol include virulent ingredients which were difficult to remove, the illicit redistilling of such alcohol for bootleg purposes was unlikely to extract all of the poison. It was hardly an answer to the moral question to say that the deaths were the wages of sin, and though the government did not yield to demands that the law be modified in this respect, the prohibitionists were to a degree put on the defensive.[34]

*   *   *

To the "drys" and even the majority of "wets" as the second half of the prohibition decade got under way, the constitutional principle expressed in

the Eighteenth Amendment seemed impregnable. Wilson's son-in-law and former Secretary of the Treasury, William Gibbs McAdoo, told the Ohio bar association in January, 1927 that in the Volstead Act Congress had taken a step
which was now irreversible, for since it "has passed a valid and constitutional
enforcement act, thereby performing the affirmative duty imposed by the
Eighteenth Amendment, any act of Congress in breach of this duty would be
unconstitutional." Had Congress never legislated in implementation of the
Amendment, McAdoo opined, the judiciary would have been powerless to invade the legislative function and order Congress to act; once it had discharged
its "affirmative constitutional duty to pass a statute," however, Congress was
powerless to repeal it, for the Court in upholding the Amendment would have
to find such a repeal invalid.[35]

The argument, strained as it was, reflected the tenor of the period. To
weaken the Volstead Act would be to weaken or even nullify the Amendment.
The better course, it seemed, would be to make the statute still more stringent.
This, in fact, was done in the closing days of the Coolidge administration, with
the enactment of the Jones Law, substantially increasing the amount of the
fines and imprisonment which could be imposed. At the same time, however,
the growing ambivalence of public opinion in the matter was reflected in a
clause admonishing the courts to "discriminate between casual or slight violations and habitual sales of intoxicating liquors or attempts to commercialize
violations of the law."[36]

Still, the problem of practical administration of the prohibition system
continued to grow. In three years, the Department of Justice had reported in
December, 1928, smuggling across the Canadian border had increased by 75
percent, while the production of industrial alcohol had almost doubled in six
years. While President-elect Hoover manfully praised prohibition itself as "a
great social and economic experiment, noble in motive and far-reaching in purpose," he conceded that much remained to be done to make the enforcement of liquor laws effective. "An organized, searching investigation of fact
and cause" was essential, he declared; and early in his administration he
created a commission to carry out the study. Headed by one-time Attorney
General Wickersham, the National Commission on Law Observance and Enforcement undertook an eighteen-month investigation which, as it turned
out, was to sound the death knell for the "noble experiment."[37]

Aside from the statistics on the administrative program and the criminal
law, the Commission advised it was necessary to recognize that "a significant
change has taken place in the social attitude" of the American people. Conduct at social gatherings which would have been unthinkable a generation
earlier, changes in the classes of drinkers and the use of liquor in localities
where it was formerly banned, all added up to a "quite frank disregard of
the declared policy of the National Prohibition Act." Once more, the moral
rather than the legal effect of prohibition was advanced as a primary concern: the "effect on youth of the making of liquor in homes, in disregard

of the policy, if not the express provisions of the law, the effect on the families of workers of selling [liquor] in homes, . . . and the effect on working people of the conspicuous newly acquired wealth of their neighbors who have engaged in bootlegging" had to be weighed against the gains that could be documented with reference to the Amendment.[38]

"We expect legislation to conform to public opinion, not public opinion to yield to legislation," the Commission continued. But why, it asked, had the Eighteenth Amendment been ratified so swiftly and by such substantial majorities, only to flounder thereafter in a morass of public apathy or antipathy? Partly, said the answer, it was a matter of distinguishing between temperance or moderation, which appealed to everyone at least in the abstract, and the letter of the law which "makes no distinction between moderate and excessive use" of intoxicants. When this distinction of temperance from prohibition widened into cleavage, the former majority coalition of opinion was destroyed.[39]

Even greater than the ideological difficulties were the practical problems discussed by the report: Economically, the profits to be realized in illicit liquor traffic *were* only to be contrasted with the costs of an effective system of enforcement; the geographic problem of combatting smuggling *was* staggering; the political conflict bred of a Federally administered prohibition in hostile state and local areas *tended* to destroy effective law enforcement either by the national government or by the states. Ethical difficulties had grown out of disjunctive administrative policies—an example was the taxing of bootleggers' income derived from illegal profits in liquor; and, finally, the judicial system had been strained by the added load of what were essentially police-court prosecutions.[40]

"It is a truism that no laws are absolutely observed or enforced," the Commission conceded. However, it continued, when a statute imposing a restraint upon personal conduct is met with a steadily increasing volume of violations, "the collateral bad effects extend to every side of administration, police, and law and order." Because the Volstead Act aimed at "uniformly high observance" of prohibition, "any large volume of intoxicating liquor continually in circulation shows a serious falling short of the goal, and is highly prejudicial to respect for law."[41]

Although the official conclusion of the Commission was that by strengthening the existing administrative process prohibition might yet be made a success, the individual statements of the Commission members were substantially less sanguine. The ultimate prospect—"a proposed amendment to the Constitution simply repealing the Eighteenth"—was considered specifically by the chairman, Wickersham, in his own final statement. The problem at the root of all possible courses of action, he pointed out, was that with or without prohibition "the unrestricted flow of intoxicating liquor" constituted a blight upon the social system which called for some sort of governmental response.[42]

The case for repeal, revision or nullification of the Eighteenth Amendment began to gather momentum in the last years of the decade. The American Federation of Labor and the American Legion both came out in favor of a major overhaul of the liquor laws, and then went the one remaining step to a position in favor of outright repeal. In 1929 Mrs. Charles H. Sabin of New York, first woman member of the Republican National Committee, resigned to become president of a small group calling itself the Women's Organization for National Prohibition Reform; within three years its membership grew from seventeen to more than a million. In 1930 the American Bar Association endorsed a resolution calling for repeal by a vote of more than two to one. So near to abandonment was the "dry" program that in January, 1931—the same month as the Wickersham report—Congressman James M. Beck of Pennsylvania, former Solicitor General of the United States, proposed that Congress simply nullify the prohibition law by refusing to appropriate funds to enforce it.[43]

The collapse of the great bull market in the fall of 1929, and the swift demoralization of the entire *laissez-faire* system in the following months, furnished the final impetus to the repeal movement. Amid the crash of many illusions about the economic and political verities of the twenties, it became easier to admit that the constitutional experiment of prohibition had also been a failure. Rising unemployment and falling tax receipts also offered a blandishment and a means of rationalizing the public act of repudiation: repeal, it was argued, would create many thousands of needed jobs and would provide new sources of revenue from levies upon legal liquor. The Democrats, behind Franklin D. Roosevelt, made repeal a principal plank in their platform for 1932; immediately upon his inauguration, the new President by executive order slashed the funds available to the Prohibition Bureau and requested Congress to modify the Volstead Act. By early April, 1933 beer with an alcoholic content of 3.2 percent—virtually the level which Congressman Volstead had rejected in 1919—was again on sale in many states. In the same month, the first state, Michigan, had ratified the Twenty-First Amendment, and nine months after that the necessary thirty-sixth, Utah, completed the process. Adoption of the prohibition amendment had been swift, but its repeal was even swifter.[44]

*   *   *

The Twenty-First Amendment, like the Eighteenth, was adopted in an atmosphere all but devoid of searching jurisprudential evaluation of fundamental constitutional issues. As with the earlier enactment, many details were discussed: What of the considerable number of state and Federal liquor laws passed prior to 1920, which presumably had been suspended or repealed by implication upon adoption of the Eighteenth Amendment? Were they now spontaneously revived with repeal? What was the present authority of Congress with reference to the regulation of interstate liquor commerce? Was it the same as it had always been, irrespective of either Amendment, or did the Twenty-First imply a policy of restraint upon the commerce power with reference to this subject? What was the significance of the provision in the repeal amendment for ratification by state conventions rather than by state legislatures? Did this foreshadow a reduction in the function of the legislatures in the Federal constitutional system?[45]

These questions were debated, directly and indirectly, in the course of steering the repeal amendment through Congress. Senate Joint Resolution 211, as originally proposed, consisted of four sections: the first specifically repealed the Eighteenth Amendment; the second reaffirmed the prohibition of interstate transportation of liquor into "dry" states; a third section would have preserved the concurrent power concept to assure the Federal government a kind of right of re-entry into the field, and a fourth section provided for ratification by state legislatures within seven years. In the course of debate, the section on concurrent power was deleted and the process of ratification was vested in state conventions rather than in legislatures.[46]

It was noted by a Washington observer that eighteen Senators in 1933 had also been in Congress in 1917 when the Eighteenth Amendment had been introduced; they had originally voted seventeen to one for prohibition, but now they voted thirteen to five for repeal. The reversal of positions was perhaps more dramatic than the ratio of "dry" and "wet" sentiment in the country at large, but it illustrated the decisiveness of the repudiation of the concept. The retrospective condemnation of the Eighteenth Amendment was the more sweeping as it served to rationalize the support now marshalled for its repeal. Said Senator John J. Blaine of Wisconsin, chairman of the judiciary committee: "The Eighteenth Amendment [was] an inflexible police regulation which might be appropriate in a municipal ordinance. . . . Surely, . . . it was never designed that our Constitution would be a compilation of local ordinances regulating the lives, the customs and the habits of our people. But that is exactly the character of the Eighteenth Amendment. It has no place in the Constitution."[47]

To thrust the concept completely outside the pale, Senator Robert Wagner of New York moved to strike the section on concurrent power. "The real cause of the failure of the Eighteenth Amendment," in his opinion, "was that it attempted to impose a single standard of conduct upon all the people of the United States without regard to local sentiment and local habits." The concurrent power section did not in itself preserve a uniform national standard, "but it invited Congress to impose it; and to that end it is . . . a perpetuation of the conflict between government authority and public opinion."[48]

The insistence upon the convention method of ratification of the repeal amendment reflected the widespread conviction—or at least the loudly repeated charge—that the legislatures would not be responsive to the majority wishes of the people in this matter. Both the Democratic and Republican platforms had stressed the need for submitting the proposal to "truly representative conventions in the states" which would be "called for that sole purpose." Senator J. Hamilton Lewis of Illinois asked, "Shall we not be frank?" The reason "was that our people in all the states had seen themselves tricked by legislatures. They had watched some, out of corruption, cheat the constituency. They had seen others . . . exchange one purpose in order to obtain another."[49]

The convention method of ratification—used only sporadically by various states heretofore and never specifically stipulated by Congress—also appealed to those old-line foes of the Eighteenth Amendment who insisted that ratification in that case had not been representative. Many in Congress recalled the bold, though quixotic, declaration of Federal District Judge William Clark of New Jersey in December, 1930 that the prohibition amendment was invalid because it had not been ratified by representative conventions. Anticipating that his argument, substantially negated a decade earlier in *Hawke v. Smith,* would meet "with a cold reception in the appellate courts," Clark quoted copiously from English and colonial history, the records of the Constitutional Convention, the Congressional debates over the Reconstruction Amendments, and various theoreticians in contemporary law journals. His ruling on the prohibition amendment—not drawn, he candidly confessed, from anything in the briefs of counsel in the case—held that since it dealt uniquely with a question of national control over private conduct, it could only be ratified by the people themselves.[50]

In less than sixty days, a sweeping opinion of the Supreme Court disposed of the novel argument, somewhat patronizingly describing it as "a scientific approach to the problem of government." In any case, the choice of the mode of ratification, said the Court, was the exclusive prerogative of Congress, whether the subject of the proposed amendment was the process of government itself or a matter affecting the personal liberty of the citizen.[51] But the opinion tacitly underlined the fact that Congress might elect to stipulate one method of ratification over the other on the basis of the subject matter—or any other basis. It avoided the problem of how to insure that such conventions would indeed be representative of the balance of interests and desires in any particular segment of the American people.

The convention method was elected by Congress for this amendment only. Like so many constitutional hypotheses which remained unanswered during the prohibition decade, its significance for future constitutional processes was lost in the consuming desire of the American people to expunge the record. The Twenty-First Amendment, as one Washington editor observed, was the only possible answer "to thirteen years of foolish attempt to legislate morality by Federal decree." It would henceforth be consigned to a footnote of history as a "costly and absurd mistake."[52]

16/Blueprint for a Modernized Court

N EXT TO "STAUNCH AND STRONG" constitutionalism, Chief Justice Taft considered the modernization of the Federal judicial process to be the greatest need to cope with the complex issues arising from modern American industrialism. As in the fortuitous series of Court appointments which developed in 1910-11 and 1921-22, Taft found a second opportunity in his Chief Justiceship to continue the judicial reforms which he had begun in his Presidency.

"The business of the Court has reached such dimensions that relief is indispensable," retired Justice William Strong had written as long before as 1881. Another decade had passed before Congress had provided a substantial part of the relief by enacting the Circuit Courts of Appeals Act. In 1891 the docketed cases before the Supreme Court exceeded fifteen hundred, but the number of those disposed of in a single term was less than five hundred. By 1921, when Taft ascended the bench, the intermediate appellate courts were handling almost that same volume of cases, but the demands upon the Supreme Court, while numerically less, were qualitatively much greater.[1]

Many factors accounted for the steady growth in the volume of business before the Court. The litigation bred by the interstate railroads and interstate corporations of the seventies substantially added to the dockets of the entire Federal court system; the Interstate Commerce Act of 1887 set the stage for an eighty-year progression of administrative regulatory acts which developed through progressive and conservative cycles of government administration; and the growth of issues in state courts which involved substantial Federal questions added to the reviewable matters which found their

271

way onto the Supreme Court's calendar. Indeed, the litigious nineteenth-century American had come to regard double appeals—first through the state courts and then through the Federal—as a matter of right.[2]

As one of the new judges appointed to the Circuit Courts in 1892, Taft had formed an early conviction that the proliferation of appeals not only was needless and expensive but diminished the effectiveness of the court system in focussing upon fundamental principles of law. In 1910, in his second annual message to Congress, the President and future Chief Justice declared: "No man ought to have, as a matter of right, a review of his case by the Supreme Court. He should be satisfied by one hearing before a court of first instance and one review by a court of appeals. The proper and chief usefulness of a Supreme Court, and especially the Supreme Court of the United States, is . . . so to expound the law, and especially the fundamental law—the Constitution—as to furnish precedents for the inferior courts in future litigation and for the executive officers in the construction of statutes and the performance of their legal duties." Any other business, "not of general application or importance, [will] merely clog and burden the Court," he added.[3]

The judicial legislation which Taft was able to secure as Chief Executive was substantial, culminating in the Judicial Code of 1911; but the burdens upon the court system which he assumed as Chief Justice called for fresh legislative attention. Dockets were still crowded. Taft's plan for a reduced volume of reviewable cases for the Supreme Court was not dealt with until 1916, when Congress slightly enlarged upon the Court's discretionary powers in the use of certiorari and affirmed the finality of cases in bankruptcy and railroad labor questions heard by the Circuit Courts of Appeal.[4]

The number of questions which could come up from the state courts on writs of error, and from the Federal intermediate appellate courts on appeal, however, continued to burden the Supreme Court with more business than it could limit through the discretionary writ of certiorari. As Chief Justice Taft was to point out to Congress in 1924, in addition to scores of questions based on wills and contracts—individual matters which had little more than incidental or accidental features requiring the attention of the highest tribunal in the land—the Court was plagued with routine Federal matters arising under postal laws, Indian treaties, immigration regulations, injuries to private parties caused by government employees, and land claims where the United States happened to be a joint tenant or tenant in common.[5]

"I doubt if there is a single element in the causes which render the administration of justice . . . inadequate so important as its delays," he told the American Bar Association in the first year of his Chief Justiceship. "It is important, of course, that controversies be settled right, but there are many individual questions which arise between individuals in which it is not so important which of the two views of the law should be adopted as that the law should be settled and the controversy ended. . . . Delay works always for the man with the longest purse."[6]

*   *   *

The Chief Justice, who had already demonstrated in his dealings with the White House that he intended to take the initiative in all matters pertaining to the courts, set to work at once to prepare a reform bill for Congress. A committee consisting of Justices Day, Van Devanter and McReynolds, with Sutherland replacing Day after the latter's retirement, undertook the drafting of a measure which was to become known during the next four years as the "Judges' Bill." It embodied what Taft himself described to the Chicago Bar Association in December, 1921 as the three essential steps toward modernization of the court system: a substantial increase in the number of Federal judges, and a system for transfer of judges from light dockets to heavy ones elsewhere; simplified rules of judicial procedure which should be uniform throughout the system; and a substantially reduced category of subjects within the appellate jurisdiction of the Supreme Court.

"A Supreme Court where there are intermediate courts of appeal is not a tribunal constituted to secure, as its ultimate end, justice to the immediate parties," Taft declared. "They have had all that they have a right to claim when they have had two courts in which to have adjudicated their controversy. The use of the Supreme Court is merely to maintain uniformity of decision for the various courts of appeal, to pass on constitutional and other important questions for the purpose of making the law clearer to the general public."[7]

Taft as Chief Justice was to find Congress as cantankerous as he had found it as Chief Executive. Many of the insurgents of the earlier day were still in the Senate, and Taft occasionally found himself asking whether their opposition to his program was as personal as much as it might be a matter of policy. Norris of Nebraska sounded like a hardfisted farmer when he complained at the expense of bringing Federal judges together in a conference where "they will be dined every evening" and "will be run to death with social activities." The amalgam of xenophobia and provincialism of the decade prompted protests against the requested authority of the Chief Justice to assign lower court judges to other, more congested, districts at his discretion. The proposal was compared to the political authority of the English Lord High Chancellor or, more irrationally, to the Prussian military system. Senator John K. Shields of Tennessee objected to the Court members testifying at all before Congress, since this presumed to intrude upon the legislative function.[8]

It early became evident that Taft would have to settle for half a loaf or none at all; the "Judges' Bill" with its three major reform proposals was broken down, and the first of the proposals became the Act of September 14, 1922. It created twenty-four new district judgeships, authorized an annual conference of senior court judges subject to the call of the Chief

Justice, permitted a limited assignment of judges within the circuits, and added an extra appellate judge in the Second, Seventh and Eighth Circuits.*[9]

Never one to hesitate to comment where the welfare of the judiciary was concerned, Taft spoke favorably on the pending bill at the San Francisco meeting of the American Bar Association in August of that year, particularly urging that the certiorari authority therein be retained. It would, he declared, reduce the greatest volume of appeals involving the least important cases— those which did not present "serious constitutional questions or questions of public importance," but merely assured private individuals of "another chance to have questions of importance to them, but not of importance to the public, passed upon by another court." That not all members of Congress subscribed to this proposition was indicated two years later in the continuing debate on other features of the "Judges' Bill," when Senator Tom Heflin of Alabama asserted that "if one man's rights were preserved and safeguarded the court in that action served a just purpose and it could well afford to consider one hundred to two hundred cases if necessary, in order to do justice by even one American citizen."[10]

*   *   *

Gratified though he was by the initial victory in the 1922 statute, Taft did not regard it as even half a loaf. At best, it represented but one-third of the changes he considered indispensable for a modernized court system. There remained the need, in the face of objections like Heflin's, to reduce still more the number of cases to be permitted to come before the Supreme Court, and finally, to make uniform and simplified rules of civil and criminal procedure, with a merging of actions at law and in equity, throughout the Federal system. The sweeping reforms in judicial process which he had observed in a trip to England that summer, and the fact that many state courts had scrapped the multiplicity of old common-law writs in favor of more direct "code pleading," made procedural reform in the Federal courts seem all the more urgent. This reform, however, was not to come about until late in the 1930's.

A Chief Justice as Congress-conscious as Taft would be equally sensitive to unacceptable measures initiated in Congress itself, and would devote an equal amount of his time to fighting them as to urging support for his own legislative program. In 1928 Taft was particularly concerned over a measure which Norris quietly maneuvered onto the floor of the Senate without any prior public hearings. It proposed to deprive the Federal judiciary of much of its diversity jurisdiction—a proposal which jurists and legal scholars themselves frequently advocated as a means of disposing of the easy access to Federal courts deriving merely from the fact that the litigants were citizens or residents of different states.

In this case, Taft opposed the bill because he saw it as a revival of the

---

*On the major legislative remedies for the problems of the Federal courts for the period of this study, cf. Appendix C.

old agrarian radicalism, intended to compel Eastern creditors to sue in state courts friendlier to farm belt debtors. It struck at a principle he had commended to the organized bar early in his tenure on the bench. Diverse-citizenship jurisdiction, he declared, had been the chief insurance to investment capital to underwrite the development of the West, and to extinguish this course of judicial remedy would injure the West by scaring investors away.[11]

Another bill, sponsored by Senator Thaddeus H. Caraway of Arkansas, actually passed the Senate before Taft could rally the opposition—this time, not only the American Bar Association, his standard ally, but the White House itself. The bill would have barred Federal judges from commenting on the testimony of witnesses in trial courts, a prohibition already widely adopted in state courts but in Taft's view a doubtful procedural safeguard which tended to encourage jury leniency toward accused criminals.[12]

But the affirmative modernization of the Federal judiciary was the Chief Justice's paramount legislative interest. The remaining propositions in the "Judges' Bill" were reintroduced by Senator Cummins in January, 1924; for the next twelve months, the measure not only had to meet repeated objections from the Senate insurgents but frequently was sidetracked by Congress' absorbing concern with other matters. The first revelation of the Harding scandals broke in the same month, only shortly after the President's death. Then Congress was engaged in a lengthy debate over a proposed bonus for veterans of the late war, in the form of a subsidy to make up the differential between soldiers' pay overseas and war workers' pay in stateside industry. Although Coolidge vetoed the measure, an election-conscious Congress was able to pass it over the White House rejection. Concurrent with the bonus fight was the prolonged struggle—it was to continue until the crash of 1929—over various proposals for farm relief; in the spring of 1924 the plans for price subsidies and commodity stabilization went down to a staggering defeat, a factor which led thereupon to the creation of a new Progressive Party and a three-party election contest that summer and fall.

When the judiciary bill did come up, it was manifest that the chief objections now as in 1922 lay in the proposal to curtail the "writs of right"—appeals and writs of error—in favor of a wider discretionary power in the Court represented by certiorari. A companion objection was the fact that in the process of limiting Supreme Court jurisdiction, the intermediate appellate courts tended to become courts of last resort on many constitutional questions. Cummins, charged with steering the bill through the Senate, patiently pointed out that in many areas of constitutional law the Circuit Courts of Appeal already were the tribunals of last resort, and that in any case of conflicting rulings by different appellate courts the Supreme Court would grant certiorari routinely. He also stressed that the bill reflected the matured convictions of the Court's most experienced lawyers—McReynolds, Van Devanter and Sutherland. The latter, as a former Senate colleague, carried definite weight with Congress, while Van Devanter represented the

Court in the committee hearings in place of Taft, who had been warned that his zealous lobbying in 1922 still rankled with many Senators.[13]

With Van Devanter and Cummins in the forefront, however, Taft did not intend to remain idle. He arranged for pressure from the Montana bar association to curb the vociferous objections of Senator Thomas J. Walsh, an old-line progressive who decried the limitations upon the individual's right to have his day in the highest court in the land. He drafted a memorandum for Coolidge, hoping to stir the President to action in support of the bill. He sought to persuade state leaders to communicate their endorsements of the judiciary proposals to their Congressional delegation.[14]

In the end, it appeared that the objections to the specific details in the bill were less a matter of fundamental hostility than a concern that such a sweeping reorientation of constitutional procedure be searchingly examined before approval. After the elections in November—in which the neo-Progressive Party made a significant showing but still sustained a defeat with the Democrats—Congress settled down to a final view of the matter and on February 13, 1925 the new judiciary act was finally passed. It gave Taft a substantial victory; the intermediate appellate courts were given final jurisdiction in appeals from Federal district courts in most instances, as well as in appeals from rulings of the Federal Trade Commission and the Interstate Commerce Commission. The statute preserved the writ of error from state courts in matters of constitutional or Federal statutory construction, and provided for direct appeal from the Federal district courts in certain specified circumstances. Most importantly, it gave the Supreme Court a substantially broader discretionary power in the use of certiorari.[15]

Although, as it was to turn out, this was the last of the Chief Justice's administrative reforms to be won in Congress, it was sufficient to earn him a major rank among the men who had served on the bench of the Supreme Court. The Act of 1925 proved to be a masterful accomplishment. Under the broadened discretion of the Court represented in its certiorari powers, Taft himself estimated that 80 percent of the cases formerly carried up for review as of right could now be evaluated and confined to major issues such as the "constitutional validity of statutes, Federal and state, genuine issues of constitutional rights of individuals, the interpretation of Federal statutes when it will affect large classes of people, questions of Federal jurisdiction, and sometimes doubtful questions of general law of such wide application that the Supreme Court may help to remove the doubt." Another benefit of the new statute, the Chief Justice added, was the opportunity it presented to the Court to undertake the first comprehensive revision of its own rules of practice in its history.[16]

*   *   *

For one who idolized Chief Justice John Marshall and hoped that his own constitutionalism would carve a niche beside that of the great Federalist, it was somewhat ironic that Taft's own monumental accomplishments on the

Court should take the form of important but highly technical administrative statutes—the Acts of 1922 and 1925—and a plan for a new building for the Court itself, which he was not to live to see. As a matter of fact, an adequate facility for the Court was an integral part of the process of modernization of the tribunal itself; throughout the national history the Court had been the most conspicuously neglected agency of government as far as physical accommodations were concerned.

In 1800, when the government moved into the new "Federal City," there had been no provision at all for housing the judicial branch, and two weeks before Marshall opened his first term as Chief Justice, Congress made available a small room on the first floor of the unfinished Capitol. The Court moved about the building periodically thereafter until 1860, when it was settled in the former Senate chamber, new wings having been added to accommodate the overgrown Houses of Congress. The Court was still in this location, more than sixty years later, when Taft ascended the bench.[17]

Taft began his campaign for more suitable space in 1923, when the new Senate Office Building was completed; two years later he discerned an opportunity in a bill authorizing fifty million dollars' worth of new public buildings which had come up in the Senate. His first effort to secure an earmarking of part of the funds for a Court building was defeated in part by his old nemesis, Senator Norris, but when the bill went to conference committee to dispose of differences between House and Senate versions, Taft redoubled his lobbying. The proviso for the Court was put back in, and the final conference report on the bill with this recommendation was then accepted by both Houses of Congress. The Chief Justice then maneuvered to get the "right" men in the architectural commission, and to see that the proper location—directly east from the Capitol—was acquired. In December, 1929 Congress approved an appropriation of $9,740,000 for the construction; it was slightly more than two months before Taft died.[18]

*   *   *

In his earnest program for modernizing the judiciary Taft was also sympathetic—or, as some of his critics alleged, hypersensitive—to arguments that the Executive Department should also be vested with broader discretionary powers to cope with modern needs. In *Myers v. United States* in 1926 the Chief Justice undertook to develop this proposition. It only served to widen the split in the Court which, always latent with Holmes and Brandeis, was to become chronic thereafter. Although Taft wrote the opinion for a six-to-three majority, the *Myers* case proved to be a Pyrrhic victory.

However he disliked the aggressive role of the first Roosevelt and Wilson in the White House, Taft perceived that the times called for something less passive than what the complacent Harding and the taciturn Coolidge chose as their Presidential function. He might, subconsciously, have recalled the bitterness of the Ballinger issue during his own administration. In any event, the question of an independent Presidential power of removal, extending to all executive department appointees, afforded Taft the occasion for a judicial pronouncement on the subject. Frank Myers had been appointed postmaster of Portland, Oregon under a statute fixing the tenure of such officers at four years unless removed by the President with the consent of the Senate. Two and a half years later, Myers was removed by the Postmaster General acting on orders from the White House but without any action on the removal by the Senate. Myers then sued for the salary for his unexpired term in the Federal Court of Claims, which denied him relief on the ground that he had not filed within the statutory time limit. The Supreme Court affirmed the ruling, "although for a different reason," as Taft admitted.[19]

Neither the merits of the case nor the constitutional issue involved were as momentous as the exhaustive opinions seemed to imply; if *Myers* was to exemplify Taft's concept of the authoritative expository nature of constitutional review under the modernized procedure of the Court, it was a sandy foundation for the monument to his own jurisprudence. The fact that the argument was sharply divided—not only did three of his Associate Justices dissent, but the detailed *amicus curiae* brief of the distinguished Pennsylvania attorney, George Wharton Pepper, anticipated virtually all of the points in the majority opinion—led each side to pile supporting data on top of each other. Taft's opinion ran to seventy pages, the dissent of McReynolds to sixty-two and that of Brandeis to fifty-five. Only Holmes, also in dissent, was brief; he contented himself with the *riposte* that the majority arguments seemed to him to be "spiders' webs inadequate to control the dominant facts."[20]

The Constitution itself was silent on the subject of the removal power of the President, Taft pointed out, so that it was necessary to review the history of past practice in the matter. Taft explored in exhaustive detail the debates in the First Congress which resulted in a narrow decision in favor of the President's authority to remove a Cabinet officer without consent of the Senate. This was the proper decision, Taft concluded, because "the power of removal, although equally essential to the executive power, is different in its nature from that of appointment." To approve or not to approve a Presidential nominee, he argued, was a legitimate check-and-balance function of the Senate, since the executive was still free to find a person of his choice whom the Senate would not reject. On the other hand, to give the Senate a power to compel the executive to retain an appointee with whom he was no longer satisfied was to invade the executive function and impede it.[21]

Taft also had to dispose of a principle in the landmark case of *Marbury v. Madison*, by his idol John Marshall, where the great Chief Justice had conceded that an appointment created by Congress for a term of years did not give the executive a right of removal. (Marshall, as Taft and every student of history knew, had evaded the consequences of that proposition by holding unconstitutional the act of Congress under which Marbury had brought his suit in the Supreme Court.) The proposition, said Taft, was disposable as dictum which he considered refuted by the practice of the executive throughout most of the nineteenth century; the only strong Congressional pronouncement to the contrary he identified as the Tenure of Office Act adopted by the Reconstruction Congresses in their vendetta with Andrew Johnson. This tainted bit of legislation was repealed in 1887—the year after enactment of the postal law under which Myers subsequently received his appointment.[22]

Anticipating the criticism that the majority holding might undermine the civil service system, Taft pointed out that Myers' office fell within the group of political appointments outside the civil service. "It is the intervention of the Senate in their appointment and not in their removal which prevents their classification into the merit system," he observed. He also cited statements by Presidents Cleveland and Wilson asserting the unlimited nature of the removal power with reference to non-classified appointees.[23]

The lengthy rebuttals of McReynolds and Brandeis showed the other side of the coin of division of powers. "A certain repugnance must attend the suggestion that the President may ignore any provision of an act of Congress under which he has proceeded," McReynolds stated. "He should promote and not subvert orderly government." To hold with the majority, he declared, would be to compromise the principle of balancing of powers which was not justifiable unless specific language could be found in the Constitution to that effect. "Constitutional provisions should be interpreted with the expectation that Congress will discharge its duties no less faithfully than the Executive will attend to his. . . . Generally, the actual ouster of an officer is executive action; but to prescribe the conditions under which this may be done is legislative."[24]

Brandeis pointed out that the President could enforce effective discipline without flouting the statutory requirement by suspending the officeholder in question rather than removing him. As for Andrew Johnson's veto message with reference to the Tenure of Office Act, Brandeis noted that the same President "approved other acts containing the removal clause which related only to inferior officers." He compiled, in one of many detailed footnotes, a chart of Presidents from Johnson to McKinley who had consistently exercised a removal power subject to Senatorial consent—usually manifested in Senate approval of the nomination of a successor. In the final analysis, said Brandeis, separation of powers did not mean that each branch of government was autonomous, and the ultimate purpose of the separation was to insure that no one should be subject to the arbitrary and capricious use of the executive or legislative function.[25]

"I never wrote an opinion that I felt to be so important in its effect," Taft wrote to a friend a month later. His resentment at the lengthy refutations of his own thesis provoked a testier commentary to his brother a couple of days after the opinion. "McReynolds and Brandeis," he wrote, "belong to a class of people that have no loyalty to the Court and sacrifice almost everything to the gratification of their own publicity and wish to stir up dissatisfaction with the decision of the Court, if they don't happen to agree with it."[26]

Loyalty to the Court—conformity in constitutional doctrine or at least parenthetical dissent—had been the touchstone of the jurisprudential rehabilitation which Taft had set as his goal when he became Chief Justice. The 1926 complaints betrayed his dread that the goal would not be attained in his lifetime; the increasing frequency and extent of dissent indicated to him a revival of the "latitudinarianism" which he had sought so long to submerge. In the *Myers* case, the recalcitrance of Holmes and Brandeis was to have been expected, but the defection of McReynolds had been a cruel blow, and the aftermath of the decision could only cast doubt upon what Taft had hoped would be his monumental opinion. The majority holding was castigated as "a positive instigation to strife between the President and Congress" by a leading scholar. In 1935, little more than five years after Taft's death, the Supreme Court would substantially qualify the rule in denying Franklin D. Roosevelt the power to remove a Federal Trade Commissioner without Senate approval.[27]

The fact was that the sands of *laissez-faire* were beginning to run out in the fall of 1926; the Congressional majorities won by conservative Republicans two years earlier were drastically reduced in both House and Senate, while on the Court the hard core of dissenters was about to be enlarged. Stone, the presumably safe Wall Street lawyer, was becoming "subservient to Holmes and Brandeis," Taft wrote to brother Horace in 1928.[28] A law school professor himself for a decade, Taft never ceased to cast the protesting minority in the Court with the "law school claque" which so regularly attacked his most cherished doctrines. In truth, the groves of academe by the latter part of the 1920's were astir with ideas of a modernized jurisprudence and a modernized judicial process which was far removed from the technical advances which Taft had wrought.

*   *   *

The theory of natural rights, which had dominated eighteenth century thought when the Constitution was devised, and the theory of legal rights, behind which the property interests of the nineteenth century entrenched themselves, "served to cover up what the legal order really was and what court and lawmaker and judge were really doing," observed Roscoe Pound in 1923. The statement pointed to the root of the ideological conflict that racked the Court, the legal profession and the political parties from the nineties to the twenties. In the twenties, a confluence of legal and social thought took place which was to provide the kinetic force for the revolution in law and politics in the generation to follow.

It was a striking coincidence that Nebraska—the archetype of the Middle Border, the staging area for the old Populist uprising, and at the same time the native ground of the American farmer with his ingrained conservatism—should have produced three of the most articulate condemnors of the established order in this period. First had come Bryan, the silver-tongued and uncomplicated, whose progress from the "Cross of Gold" speech in Chicago in 1896 to the Scopes anti-evolution trial in Dayton, Tennessee in 1925 epitomized the rise and fall of the politics of moral rejection of the crudities of modern life. Next, overlapping him in time, had come Norris, who strove to combine Bryan's humanitarianism and rule of individual conscience with a pragmatic plan of attack to liberalize the established fact of the new corporate society. Finally had come Pound, the most massive intellect of all, who identified the sociological need of modern jurisprudence, "the adjustment of principles and doctrines to the human conditions they are to govern rather than to assume first principles."[29]

In 1906, when Bryan was preparing for his third and final bid for the White House two years hence and Norris was completing his second term as a Congressman, Pound shocked the American Bar Association at its St. Paul convention with his monumental paper on "The Causes of Popular Dissatisfaction with the Administration of Justice." It was the beginning of more than half a century of critical analysis of the process of revising the legal system "not as a shield to safeguard personal rights and liberties but as a cooperative instrument to satisfy social needs," as one historian later observed. Pound's jurisprudence, he went on, "was a legal philosophy fitted to the realities of social life in an urban order, of economic life in an industrial order, and of political life in an egalitarian order."[30] It pervaded the curriculum of the Harvard Law School when Pound was its dean in the 1920's; it became the credo of the Hughes Court after the great ideological confrontation of the late 1930's; and it provided the foundation for the revitalized doctrine of Federally guaranteed individual rights under the Warren Court of the fifties and sixties.

For Taft, William Graham Sumner provided the soundest economics, Herbert Spencer the most plausible social theory, and Thomas M. Cooley the ultimate authority on constitutionalism. The young rebels in the law schools looked further back than these men to get their ideas of the true basis for the future of American law. More than Blackstone, Mansfield or Bentham, Felix Frankfurter was fond of saying, the most important law reformer of the eighteenth and nineteenth centuries was James Watt, the inventor of the steam engine."[31] In any case, it was during Taft's tenure on the Court that the new ideas anticipated by Pound's St. Paul address, by Holmes' skeptical relativism, by Ernst Freund's 1904 study of the police power, and by Brandeis' famous brief in the Oregon maximum working hours case, converged into a challenging jurisprudence. Rules which had evolved as expressions of "the *mores* of the day," wrote Benjamin Cardozo in 1924, "may be abrogated by courts when the *mores* have so changed that perpetuation of the rule would do violence to the social conscience."

"This is not usurpation," he added. "It is not even innovation. It is the reservation for ourselves of the same power of creation that built up the common law through its exercise by the judges of the past."[32] To this observation Frankfurter added that "American constitutional law is not a fixed body of truth, but a mode of social adjustment." The words were a variant on a theme he had expressed for twenty years, as when in 1912 he had declared that whatever "is reasonably defensible on economic or social grounds, whether or not it accord with our individual notion of economics, cannot be offensive on constitutional grounds."[33] These were the coalescing axioms of a new jurisprudence, sounding strange and ominous to the conservatives on the Taft Court. It was cruel indeed, the Chief Justice often reflected, to hear Pound excoriate some of his most cherished opinions as a "carnival of unconstitutionality," or to find Frankfurter damning them as concepts "antiquated twenty-five years ago."

To the aging jurist, even Herbert Hoover, elected in 1928 to continue the postwar Republican dynasty, seemed like an unreliable modernist. What would become of the Constitution, Taft repeatedly asked close friends and relatives, when he and his trusted colleagues had departed from the bench? While Holmes was eighty-eight when Hoover took office, and Brandeis seventy-three, Taft was less confident than he once had been that they would now be replaced with "safe" men. Worse than that, who would come after Van Devanter, now seventy, or McReynolds and Sutherland, each sixty-seven —or himself, now seventy-two? Only Butler, at sixty-three, and Sanford, at sixty-four, seemed likely to be on the bench for a reasonable number of added years. And, as Taft himself had to concede, neither of them was spectacularly endowed with the type of wisdom needed to deal with the facile and proliferating apologetics of the liberals both in Congress and in the law schools. Youngest of all was Stone, who at fifty-seven already was rumored to be under Presidential consideration as Taft's successor in the Chief Justiceship.[34]

The Court in 1929 was undeniably an old Court, and Taft could only hope that his stalwarts would be able to hang on and hold off the threat of radicalism for as long as possible. Most of them were indeed to do so— thus compounding the ultimate jurisprudential crises with which his successor would have to deal.

17/The Twilight of Laissez-Faire

THE PROGRESSIVE MOVEMENT was in a state of general disorganization at the beginning of the twenties; the New Freedom, which had captured the reform banners of the past decade, was the property of the Democrats, while the Bull Moose had decoyed most of the insurgents from their hard-won positions of influence within the Republican Party. Both Democrats and Republican insurgents had been all but smothered in the Harding election, and it required the normal shifts in political balances to make possible their slight recovery in the Congressional elections of 1922. Thereafter, small though their numbers were, they began to talk in terms of a "bloc"; a month after the November elections that year, LaFollette invited some three dozen Senators and Representatives to meet with him to discuss a common policy on legislation "for the greatest good for the greatest number of the whole people." The administration forces promptly denounced the participants as "smashers of prosperity."[1]

"Fighting Bob" LaFollette was the natural leader of the group. To the country at large he symbolized the old-line reform movement from the Populist crusade to the current critics of the postwar order. It was symbolic that he attended his first Republican political convention in 1896, the year of Bryan's emergence in the Democratic ranks, and would be the third-party candidate for President in 1924, the year before his death. From 1880, when he had been elected to his first public office, through six years in the House of Representatives, another six as governor of Wisconsin, and nineteen in the Senate, his name had been synonymous with social reform and the struggle to control excesses of the economic system. He was the *beau idéal* of the Progressive Movement; the "Wisconsin Idea" of systematic tax reform, codified regulation of railroads and corporations, a state civil service and the innovation of the direct primary represented most of the goals which for reformers elsewhere had proved all but unattainable. A thoroughly practical (and, his critics said,

283

ruthless) politician, he had wrested power from the state Republican machine by creating a machine of his own. Throughout the first four decades of the twentieth century, it would either dominate the so-called major party or would steer its own course under its own name.

Although LaFollette found many things wrong with the postwar state of affairs, he had concluded in the summer of 1922 that the consistent doctrinaire opposition of the Supreme Court majority to the legislative efforts of the previous decade represented the greatest threat to the public welfare. The nullification of most of the New Freedom, he declared, had been marked by "a process of gradual encroachments, uncertain and timid at first, but now confident and aggressive." The day had come, he continued, "when the Federal judiciary must be made—to some extent, at least—subject to the will of the people, or we must abandon the pretense that the people rule in this country . . . . We cannot live under a system of government where we are forced to amend the Constitution every time we want to pass a progressive law. The remedy must adequately cope with the disease, or there is no use applying it."

A single amendment, reforming the process of judicial review, was LaFollette's proposed remedy. The amendment he had in mind would deny to the inferior Federal courts any power to declare an act of Congress unconstitutional, while in cases where the Supreme Court held the act invalid or "asserted a public policy at variance with the statutory declaration of Congress . . . the Congress may by reenacting the law nullify the action of the court."

> Had such been the provision of the Constitution, the action of Congress in enacting the child labor law the second time would have been effective, and we would have had an efficient child labor law today. Had such been the Constitution, it would not have been necessary to wait twenty years to get an income tax law, after the Supreme Court had reversed its former decision upholding the law. Were such now the Constitution, the Congress could by statute speedily correct the indefensible policy asserted by the Supreme Court . . . with respect to labor unions, farmers' associations, and other voluntary organizations. . . .
>
> The Constitution gave to the President of the United States a veto upon legislation, in order that the Executive might be able to protect itself against encroachments. But it also gave to the Congress the power to assert its will by repassing the law, even after it had been vetoed. This was necessary in order to prevent the President from using his veto to block all progress and make himself a despot.
>
> The Constitution did not give the courts a veto . . . Nevertheless, the courts have asserted not a veto power while laws were in the making but have usurped the far greater veto power of nullifying laws after they have been enacted, and by the process of so-called interpretation to declare the public policy. They thus themselves enact what shall be the law of the land.[2]

LaFollette's attack was made originally before a meeting of the American Federation of Labor in Cincinnati, but he read it into the *Congressional Record* after alarmed conservatives cited it out of context in order to launch counter-attacks. Nicholas Murray Butler was drafted to deliver a diatribe against the Wisconsin insurgent at the meeting of the New Jersey Bar Association, the more temperate passages referring to LaFollette as "a destructionist and a re-volutionary." Senator Walter E. Edge hastened to insert Butler's speech in the *Record,* and Senator Frank B. Kellogg of Minnesota took the floor to de-nounce the Cincinnati speech as "subversive of our representative government, the liberties of the people, and the Bill of Rights."[3]

The old embers on the prairies flared up afresh that fall; LaFollette won a landslide reelection to the Senate, while in Minnesota Kellogg went down in defeat before Henrik Shipstead and in North Dakota the conservative Senator Porter J. McCumber lost to the insurgent Lynn J. Frazier. After the debacle of 1920, the Republican majorities in both Houses of Congress were reduced by 1922 to a point where, it was widely asserted, the progressives again held the balance of power.

*   *   *

Alarmed at the prospects for their legislative program, administration leaders called a special session of Congress after the 1922 fall elections. La-Follette saw this as an attempt to push through many of the bills which had been recklessly proposed in the floodtide of reaction in Harding's first year in the White House: strike-control legislation, nullification of many of the con-servation laws, and increased subsidies to American shipping interests.

The "lame-duck" Congress, dominated by men who had just been de-feated at the polls but who would hold office for almost four remaining months, illustrated for the liberals a flaw in the constitutional machinery which was too susceptible of cynical political maneuver. "It was contrary to all reason and precedent," said Norris, "that men who had been repudiated by their own people should continue to mold legislation as representatives of those people. This gave any President who desired to use it enormous power over legisla-tion. On several occasions . . . many of these lame-duck members of Congress were willing to follow the command of the executive and adopt legislation which he desired. For their subservience they were given fat executive ap-pointments."[4]

Caraway of Arkansas sought, rather naively, to meet the problem in the 1922 special session by introducing a resolution calling attention to the specific administration bills, particularly the ship subsidy, which had previously been supported by lame-duck members of both Houses. It was the sense of his resolution that these members ought to abstain from voting on the measure since they did not have "the moral right to support or vote for any measure which the people by their votes have repudiated." The resolution also called upon "chairmen of committees not in sympathy with the people's wishes ex-pressed at the polls" to resign. A roar of laughter in the Senate greeted the reading of the resolution.[5]

Norris, to whom the resolution was referred as chairman of the Senate Judiciary Committee, concluded that it was impractical; what was needed was a modernizing amendment to eliminate lame-duck sessions. In a period when Congress still indulged in the leisurely schedule provided by the Constitution with reference to eighteenth-century delays in transportation and communication, Norris pointed out, it would be thirteen months before the Congress elected in November would meet in regular session. The Norris amendment proposed to advance the meeting of the new Congress to January 4 following the November elections, and the terms of the President and Vice-President from March 4 to January 20. As the amendment was reported out from the Norris committee, it also proposed the abolition of the Electoral College and direct popular election of the President and Vice-President. The Electoral College, observed Norris, had never worked to the benefit of the people and was essentially undemocratic; "the voice of the people should dominate in the most simple, direct fashion in the election of the chief magistrate."[6]

Norris had assumed that the abolition of the Electoral College, included with the other modernizing features of the Lame-Duck Amendment—which also provided for contingencies in the event of death of a President-elect— "would not excite any opposition, and that, under the favorable atmosphere that existed, a long-neglected change would be accomplished easily in this way." The Electoral College provision, however, roused substantial emotional opposition among both liberals and conservatives. Bryan, coming from Nebraska to assure Norris of his support of the Lame-Duck Amendment, urged that the Electoral College provision be withdrawn so as not to dissipate the strength of the basic reform. Whether or not Bryan was correct in his evaluation, the more limited form of the amendment did in fact pass the Senate after two days of debates, in February, 1923.[7]

Bryan had confidently predicted that he could muster substantial Democratic support in the House to aid in passing the amendment; as matters turned out, five consecutive sessions of Congress recorded the reenactment of the proposal by the Senate and the smothering of the bill in the lower chamber. It would be ten years before the amendment finally was passed by both Houses and submitted to the people in the spring of 1932. By the end of that year, it had been ratified; perhaps in their eagerness to end the old regime of the decade of normalcy with which they had become so disillusioned in the depression, the American people were only too ready to put their legislature on a more businesslike basis.[8]

*   *   *

The long decade of normalcy was a lonely time for members of the insurgent bloc in the Senate; if they held a balance of power on some issues, they were more commonly in a futile minority. Nor were they clairvoyant. On occasions, as in their opposition to Stone's appointment to the Court, they fell into the oversimple assumption that a man of moderate conservatism and an associate of wealthy corporate clients could not retain a balanced judgment on the bench. Norris' suspicion of the money power was occasionally distorted by an ingrained dislike for urban life in general which was characteristic of the yeomen who made up his constituents.

But lavish expenditures of money—as in several senatorial elections in which the candidate spent several times the aggregate salary he would receive if elected—could mean, if not corruption, at least a moral decay to be fought against. "With the cynical philosophy of the day, people were not greatly concerned over moral issues," Norris observed when the seat of Senator Truman H. Newberry of Michigan was challenged. Accordingly, in order to catch public attention and focus it upon the issue, the Nebraska Senator facetiously urged that since there had been "a public sale" for the Senate seat and "the price was right," there was no reason why the Senate itself should not confirm the sale. The Harding forces were not amused—nor especially reassured when Newberry was seated by the close vote of 46 to 41. The Michigan incumbent resigned the seat shortly thereafter.[9]

Frank Smith of Illinois, challenged on the basis of the vast sums of money allegedly spent by private utilities to insure his election, eventually surrendered his seat. William S. Vare, Republican boss of Pennsylvania, acknowledged the expenditure of $800,000 in his campaign for a seat, and it was declared vacant after an investigation led by Norris. It was a continuing, wearing campaign to preserve the integrity of the legislative branch in the face of a torrent of abuse from party regulars. For Norris and his handful of associates, the rewards were seldom to be lavish and more often to be only the knowledge that they had been true to their own consciences.

*   *   *

The major accomplishment of the Congressional liberals in the twenties was the perfecting of a legislative formula for stabilizing labor conditions in the railroad industry. For almost four decades there had been a search for a practical statutory program on the subject, with each major enactment somehow falling short of its goals. In 1888 the first experiment in voluntary arbitration supervised by the government was put onto the rolls; its only application was in the 1894 Pullman strike, with results so disastrous for labor that it left the unions with a chronic suspicion of all governmental processes for suspending militant action while negotiations were attempted—a circumstance which seemed uniformly to end in management's advantage.

The Erdmann Act a decade later, creating an official mediation and conciliation service, sought to enlist labor's support by banning the "yellow-dog" contract in interstate commerce. Ten years after that, the Court struck down this section of the statute and with it deflated a substantial body of labor hopes. A 1916 railroad labor act hardly had a fair trial period before the government assumed control of the carriers for the duration of the war, applying its own no-strike policy; the Transportation Act of 1920, returning the carriers to prviate control, undertook to set up a government adjustment board to arbitrate non-wage questions, but without notable response from either side in the industry.[10]

After the "conspicuous failure" of the 1920 statutory effort, as it was characterized by W. N. Doak of the Brotherhood of Railroad Trainmen, management and union leaders came together to undertake to draft their own bill Having then conferred with President Coolidge in January, 1926, the new railway labor plan was introduced in Congress. "Whatever may be the strong or weak points of the new legislation," observed one economist, "neither side is now in a position to claim that the measure was put over on it."[11] But if, officially, labor and management were at one on the basic elements in the legislative plan, this did not dispose of all opposition. Both the National Association of Manufacturers and the National Grange were to express concern that any machinery which helped labor and management to settle their differences routinely was likely to affect the public adversely in increased rates to offset the bargain made within the industry.

The 1920 railroad labor provisions, said Congressman Alben W. Barkley of Kentucky, pleased no one because they implied a compulsory process of settlement of disputes without any machinery for enforcement. Labor resented the implication of compulsion, management resented the inability of the labor board under the statute to make it a reality. The 1926 bill, as Congressman Schuyler Merritt of Connecticut put it, was a recognition of the economic realities of modern industrial society and a concession to human psychology.[12] In its departure from the mechanistic formulae of past legislation, it placed a moral obligation upon both parties in labor relations to undertake to bargain peacefully as a condition for withholding governmental intervention.

The economic bipartisan nature of the bill, commanding the joint support of most labor and management leaders, accounted for its ultimate acceptance by the conservative majorities in Congress. The statute, as enacted in the spring of 1926, recognized a duty in both labor and employer to bargain collectively—thereby, it was hoped, accomplishing the outlawing of the "yellow-dog" contract without making it a legislative stipulation. A presidentially appointed mediation board would act as referee for disputes and seek a basis acceptable to both sides for arbitration which would ultimately become binding on all parties. If the proposals of the mediation board were rejected by either side, the board would refer the dispute to the President, who had power to invoke a sixty-day no-strike period for fact-finding and recommendations.[13]

The essential conservatism of the major railroad unions mollified the conservatives in both industry and Congress, and contributed further to the ultimate acceptance of the 1926 statute. For a decade, since the Adamson law, the eight-hour day had been standard in this industry, and had dispelled employer fears of accelerating costs as a result of reduced working time. National union policies were directed at promoting job security and self-benefiting activities of membership, as in the form of labor-financed banks and labor-sponsored educational programs. Even in an era when *laissez-faire* had become a

gospel amounting to revelation, the concessions to the union movement represented in the statute were not regarded as a major victory for progressivism.
Certainly, most political and industrial leaders did not regard it as a stepping
stone toward a comprehensive reform of labor conditions within the economy.

*   *   *

The railroad brotherhoods had become the aristocrats of labor; for the
great majority of working class men in the twenties, the philosophy of the 1926
statute was totally esoteric. The contrast between the benefits which were
accruing to railroad labor at this time and the hardships which were almost
universal in the next largest labor area—mining—could hardly have been
greater. Norris, gathering data on working conditions in the Pennsylvania coal
fields, was aghast. The individual miner, he concluded, "signed away his liberties" to seek better wages, safer working conditions, more sanitary housing than
the company towns offered—or even the right to quit.

"The condition had become intolerable," the Senator concluded in 1927,
for "there had developed under the system a type of human bondage that en-
slaved the miner to a life of toil without any opportunity to make a decent
effort to improve or to better his condition. . . . Courts had issued injunctions
of the most restrictive character, and through resort to law the mine operators had invoked the aid of government to make it impossible for miners to
organize and strike."[14]

Union membership had dropped precipitously since the end of the war,
and in the bituminous fields in Illinois, Indiana, Ohio and western Pennsylvania
attempts to organize the workers had led to virtual civil war. The United Mine
Workers had suffered a series of crippling defeats in strike attempts between
1922 and 1925. In the latter year, reported the United States Coal Commission,
an almost chronic condition of privately financed martial law obtained, with
deputy sheriffs on company payrolls maintaining order, and union organizers
met with injunctions the moment they appeared.[15]

Since the famous Debs injunction of 1894, this tool of equity had become
a standard bit of equipment in the industrial machinery of the twentieth century. Even before the last years of the nineteenth, the courts for the most part,
said an observer at the end of the decade of normalcy, had found a rationale
"to relate the injunction of labor disputes to time-honored principles." Thus
the ancient practice of enjoining action which threatened "imminent and irreparable injury" to property was readily applied to attempted strikes and
other work stoppages.[16] In these circumstances, courts unsympathetic to the
class struggle of the time took little pains to distinguish between purposes permissible under the common law (such as concerted action by employees on
matters of wages, hours and working conditions) and those which threatened
the property interests or profit position of capital. To make such nice distinc-
tions, observed Holmes, "needs not only the highest powers of a judge and a
training which the practice of law does not insure, but also a freedom from
prepossessions which is very hard to attain."[17]

Holmes, two years after the Debs case, had dissented vigorously from the majority view of the Massachusetts court that "a combination of persons to do what one of them lawfully might do for himself will make the otherwise lawful conduct unlawful." If capital may combine, so may labor, Holmes had argued, and each in fact should be free to combine to "support their interests by argument, persuasion, and the bestowal or refusal of those advantages which they otherwise lawfully control." The right of combination, he added four years later, should also extend to boycotts of non-union shops since "unity of organization is necessary to make the contest of labor effectual."[18]

The majority view was otherwise, and in 1922 the Taft Court declared that the doctrine to be applied in the Federal courts was that unions themselves were suable as entities distinct from their individual members.[19] From this point it was a short step to an almost universal application of both anti-trust actions and injunctions against organized groups of employees.[20]

Justice Sutherland, resuming the constitutional dialogue with Holmes, gave his own reply to the argument that workers might do collectively what they could lawfully do singly; "An act which lawfully might be done by one, may when done by many acting in concert take on the form of a conspiracy and become a public wrong, and may be prohibited if the result be hurtful to the public or to the individuals against whom such concerted action is directed." Where the action of the union falls into the category of a public wrong and threatens to curtail the flow of goods in interstate commerce, Sutherland declared, the arguments that the unions are lawful and that "the ultimate result aimed at may not have been illegal in itself, are beside the point. Where the means adopted are unlawful, the innocent general character of the organizations adopting them or the lawfulness of the ultimate end sought to be attained, cannot serve as a justification."[21]

Brandeis, replying for himself and Holmes, pointed out that "only unreasonable restraints are prohibited by the Sherman law," and that since the act "does not establish the standard of reasonableness," this must be determined by common law. "Tested by these principles," he declared, "the propriety of the union's conduct" in striking plants which recognized only company unions "can hardly be doubted by one who believes in the organization of labor." If refusal to work in such plants can be enjoined under the anti-trust laws, Brandeis concluded, the laws themselves impose "restraints on labor which remind of involuntary servitude." Where the Sherman Act had been construed to permit a combination of capital into a single corporation to control 50 percent of the steel industry, and in another case to permit a combination embracing "practically the whole shoe machinery industry of the country," it would seem strange if Congress "had by the same act willed to deny to members of a small craft of workingmen the right to cooperate in simply refraining from work, when that course was the only means of self-protection against a combination of militant and powerful employers."[22]

That, however, was precisely the interpretation the Court majority intended the law to have.

*   *   *

To reach the majority rule in the Bedford Stone Cutters' Case the Court had followed to the ultimate extreme the nullification of the proposition hopefully set out in the Clayton Act of 1914, that "the labor of a human being is not a commodity or article of commerce," and that labor organizations were not "to be held or construed to be illegal combinations in restraint of trade under the anti-trust laws." In three sweeping decisions in 1921, the Court had slashed at the heart of the intended guarantee by holding, first, that secondary boycotts were not within the protection of the statute; second, that the act did not introduce any new principles into the equity jurisdiction of the Court, thus leaving the injunction power virtually as free as ever; and, third, that the requirements of due process which qualified the interpretations of Federal labor laws applied through the Fourteenth Amendment to state labor laws as well. Three years later, the provision in the Clayton Act for a jury trial in cases of contempt arising out of injunction contests was limited to criminal contempt, leaving labor leaders and unions liable in civil contempt.[23]

In 1926 the Court found a combination of unionized construction firms, which aimed at keeping non-unionized firms out of the Chicago market, to be a conspiracy in restraint of trade.[24] The Bedford Stone Cutters' Case the following spring, therefore, was part of a continuing process of moving labor law further away from the provisions of the Clayton Act which had once been hailed as labor's Magna Carta.[25] "It is for labor to make reply" to this systematic judicial frustration of legislation enacted for its benefit, declared a liberal journal after the *Bedford* decision. "And sooner or later," it predicted, the reply would come, "in this country as in England, through political action."[26]

The first political effort to curb the trend of labor decisions was made by Shipstead of Minnesota in December following the *Bedford* case. His bill proposed to halt the abuse of the injunctive process by stipulating that "nothing shall be held to be property" subject to protection by equitable action "unless it is tangible and transferable." The remedy was to be direct and simple; its chief flaw lay in the fact that a judiciary which had already demonstrated its capacity for tortuous interpretation of apparently plain meanings would not be likely to have trouble finding a means of neutralizing this statutory effort. As Norris and others added, the categorical negative in the Shipstead proposal condemned "many well-settled and beneficent exercises of equitable jurisdiction" which had nothing to do with labor matters.[27]

The time had come, Norris told his judiciary subcommittee associates— Thomas J. Walsh of Montana and John J. Blaine of Wisconsin—to draft a measure which would canvass all the doctrines of labor law which could conceivably furnish a foothold for the labor injunction, and would find the constitutional answer for each. He enlisted five economists and law school specialists to undertake the task: Felix Frankfurter and Francis B. Sayre of Harvard, Donald Richberg of Chicago, Herman Oliphant of Johns Hopkins, and Edwin E. Witte of Wisconsin. "They locked themselves in" the committee room, Norris recalled, "and for forty-eight hours gave their undivided attention and study to every court decision bearing upon the rights of organized labor." When the scholars' draft was reviewed by the subcommittee, the Senators struck everything from the Shipstead bill after the enactment clause, and substituted the new text.[28]

As the Senate liberals girded themselves for an all-out assault by the defenders of the freedom of contract, their cause was aided by the introduction of a companion bill in the lower House by Congressman Fiorello H. La-Guardia. The squat, ebullient Representative from New York was fully to earn the right to co-sponsorship of the anti-injunction law by his eloquent advocacy in the House and on the stump during the next four years. Through La-Guardia's efforts, the bill passed the lower House consistently ahead of schedule, only to die when administration forces in the Senate stalled off action until the end of the session. But LaGuardia's greatest service was in educating a growing number of his colleagues in the facts of life in the labor market of *laissez-faire* capitalism. He read to them a typical "yellow-dog" contract:

> I will perform all work assigned to me. I will not take part in any strike or hinder the conduct of the factory as an open shop or nonunion shop. My employment may be terminated at any time by you or by me upon written notice. . . .
>
> In case my employment is terminated I will for one year thereafter in no way annoy, molest or interfere directly or indirectly with your customers, property, business or employees.
>
> As evidence of my good faith and in consideration of such employment by you, I hereby agree to deposit with you the sum of .... dollars, payable .... dollars herewith and the balance in weekly payments of ....[29]

The primary purpose of the contract, as LaGuardia pointed out on various occasions, was to provide a blacklist of dissidents to circulate among other employers, as well as to provide a basis for seeking a court restraining order when an employer deemed it desirable. "Have you ever seen one of these orders?" the bellicose little Congressman demanded. He then proceeded to describe it: "It is issued against fictitious persons. 'The .... Shoe Factory against Joe Doe, John Roe and Mary Smith, names fictitious, real names unknown to the complainant, and all other persons unknown to the complainant, and unknown to the court, hereby are ordered and enjoined.' Then it describes all sorts of acts. Any person who never saw the order or ever heard of it could be held liable." In the final analysis, declared La-Guardia, the whole system was intended to invoke the judicial equity power to "break a strike; to take one side of an issue; to determine wages and standards of living by the brute force of judicial power—instead of leaving it to a matter of adjustment by free American workers."[30]

Predictably, the conservatives also charged the law with being one-sided, liable to cause the opposite effect of LaGuardia's accusations. It was condemned as "an attempt to take away an inherent judicial power with which the legislature has no right to interfere, while the president of the American Bar Association, Gurney E. Newlin, warned: "Such class legislation is bound to produce undesirable social results, and will be highly detrimental to the welfare of the general public." James A. Emery, general counsel for the National Association of Manufacturers, led an almost marathon attack by lobbyists upon the bill.³¹

In the dying hours of the Hoover administration, the Norris-LaGuardia Anti-Injunction Act finally passed Congress and was signed into law. It was the bankruptcy of *laissez-faire,* attested by three years of rapidly worsening depression, which provided the final impetus. Eighteen years had passed since the Clayton Act had presumably established the principle of untrammeled collective bargaining; but this proposition had not been found in the glossary of normalcy.

*   *   *

Of all the rights believed to be unimpeachable in the *laissez-faire* system, the protection of all of the interests associated with private property was paramount. "The legal conception of property is *of right,*" Justice McKenna declared in 1914, and seven years later he added: "The security of property, next to personal security against the exactions of government, is of the essence of liberty." The same Justice, in 1924, observed with concern the persistent legislative efforts, among the states as well as in Congress, to regulate or curtail one vested right or another, and concluded that the institution he had so consistently praised "has adversaries in this world and different forms [of ownership] excite different degrees of antagonism."³²

One of the sources of antagonism perceived by McKenna was the effort of the Negro, as his numbers in the larger cities grew, to acquire housing outside the overcrowded tenement areas into which he was herded. To meet the threat to property values as these were envisioned by white owners, restrictive covenants were devised and incorporated into contracts of sale to run with the land. A unanimous Court in 1926 quoted a rule from the Civil Rights Cases of the seventies: "Individual invasion of individual rights is not the subject matter of the [Fourteenth] Amendment." The provisions of the Constitution as well as of the statutes governing the District of Columbia, where the issue arose, declared the Court, "do not in any matter prohibit or invalidate contracts entered into by private individuals in respect to the control and disposition of their own property." For almost another quarter of a century, the restrictive covenant was to stand as a barricade against mounting social pressure.³³

The same concern at protecting property from mounting economic pressure came before the Court the next year in the form of a constitutional challenge to a zoning ordinance preserving the residential nature of a suburb

in the path of expanding industrial facilities. Urban growth and conges-
tion, observed Justice Sutherland for the majority of six, required the urban
community to choose between the vested interests of certain property owners
and the prospective interests of others. Where the local community, acting
within its constitutional powers, chose to protect one group at the expense
of the other, this did not infringe upon the due process provisions of the Fourteenth Amendment. "And in this there is no inconsistency," Sutherland declared, "for while the meaning of the constitutional guarantees never varies,
the scope of their application must expand or contract to meet the new and
different conditions which are constantly coming within the field of their
operation. In a changing world, it is impossible that it should be otherwise."[34]

                    *   *   *

Where it was a case of the government arbitrating between competing
private interests, the conservatives might be divided—Butler, Van Devanter
and McReynolds, in fact, dissented in the zoning decision. But where the
question was the regulation of private enterprise in what the government
deemed to be the public interest, the partisans of *laissez-faire* closed ranks.
A state "may not, under the guise of protecting the public, arbitrarily interfere with private business, or prohibit lawful occupations, or impose unreasonable and unnecessary restrictions upon them," Justice Butler declared
for a majority of seven in striking down a Nebraska statute guarding against
short weights in bakery goods. It was sufficient, said the opinion, to uphold
the police power of the state in setting minimum weights; to extend it to
the fixing of maximum weights for different sizes of bread loaves was "essentially unreasonable and arbitrary."[35]

Brandeis' dissent for himself and Holmes—with the characteristic mass
of footnotes marshalling contemporary economic data—replied to Butler
that the only test of arbitrariness was to examine the circumstances on which
the state had based its action. "Knowledge is essential to understanding,"
mused the Justice in an aphorism which was to be oft-quoted thereafter, "and
understanding should precede judging. Sometimes, if we would guide by
the light of reason, we must let our minds be bold." But under the mundane
facts of the instant case, Brandeis went on, no great intellectual adventure
was required: it could readily be determined that the problem was commonly
recognized in the baking industry, and that the statute in question was reasonably likely to solve the problem. To invalidate a state statute on the speculation that it might not solve the problem, he concluded, was to indulge in
"an exercise of the powers of a super-legislature—not the performance of
the constitutional function of judicial review."[36]

"The state has wide discretion in selecting things for regulation," Butler
conceded in a 1926 case, concerned with a Pennsylvania statute prohibiting
the use of certain material in manufacture of bed comforters. "But," he
added, "the number and character of the things permitted to be used in
such manufacture properly may be taken into account in deciding whether

the prohibition . . . is a reasonable and valid regulation or is arbitrary and violative of the due process clause. . . . And it is a matter of public concern that the production and sale of things necessary or convenient for use should not be forbidden. They are to be distinguished from things that the state is deemed to have power to suppress as inherently dangerous."[37]

Holmes, with whom both Brandeis and Stone joined in dissent, made the pragmatic observation that a regulatory or prohibitory statute "is not required to be mathematically precise and to embrace every case that theoretically is capable of doing the same harm." A reasonable likelihood that the regulation "hits the evil where it is most felt" should be sufficient to sustain the police power; to insist upon anything more, he said, was to press the Fourteenth Amendment too far.[38]

The invocation of the Fourteenth Amendment to curb the use of state police power was consistent throughout Taft's Chief Justiceship. If the Court could satisfy itself that the issue concerned an exclusively public right —as, in a South Dakota case, a school district which was found invalid by a judicial decree and was resurrected by a legislative act—the police power was apt to be liberally interpreted; but any private right growing out of a court judgment, it was insisted, should not be "annulled by subsequent legislation." The majority of the Court found no monopoly in an exclusive franchise granted to a taxicab company by a railroad terminal, and denied a New Jersey municipality the power to set up a public taxi stand on the premises. In an Oklahoma case, Sutherland held that a franchise for a cotton gin, obtained on securing a certificate of convenience and necessity, became a property right which could be protected by injunction against competitors who were not required to obtain a like certificate.[39]

In ten cases raising a constitutional question about state legislation regulating various activities of private corporations, Professor Thomas Reed Powell of Harvard Law School found only three to have been decided in favor of the state and only four to have been unanimous. Taft, Powell noted, was with the majority in all divided decisions, and Holmes with the minority in all. The uniform hostility to regulatory laws in cases involving industrial relations, Powell observed, demonstrated that the Court was not "ineffective in protecting the interests of employers against legislative hopes of employees."[40] An unvarying disposition in the majority to set aside a statute which fixed a presumption of liability in railroads in personal injury cases, or a law laying particular procedural requirements on out-of-state corporations, Powell concluded, arose out of "judicial preference and not the Constitution."[41]

*   *   *

The foreshadows of coming jurisprudential events were cast in a series of cases, extending from 1927 to 1932, in which the half-century of the public interest doctrine initiated in *Munn v. Illinois,* subjected to a consistent process of limitation by succeeding conservative generations of jurists, was to be retired in favor of a more pragmatic modern concept. By that time—in the case of *Nebbia v. New York* in 1934—the decade of normalcy had long since passed.

In a five-to-four decision (*Tyson v. Banton*) denying New York the authority to regulate the price of resale theater tickets, Justice Sutherland for the majority undertook to restrict to still narrower confines the doctrine that a state could regulate a business affected with a public interest. "A business is not affected with a public interest merely because it is large or the public are warranted in having a feeling of concern in respect of its maintenance," he observed. "Nor is the interest meant such as arises from the mere fact that the public derives benefit, accommodation, ease or enjoyment from the existence or operation of the business; and while the word has not always been limited narrowly as strictly denoting 'a right,' that synonym more nearly than any other expresses the sense in which it is to be understood."[42]

The public interest doctrine, which in principle could justify a wide range of restrictive legislation, was to be distinguished from the police power, which essentially was concerned that a business not jeopardize the public health or safety, said Sutherland. The public interest doctrine "is not only a more definite and serious invasion of the rights of property, and the freedom of contract, but its exercise cannot always be justified by circumstances which have been held to justify legislative regulation of the manner in which a business shall be carried on." A general power of regulating a business which is lawful on its face and subject to abuse only in particulars was, in Sutherland's view, out of proportion to the mischief to be dealt with. Even if the only manner of reaching the specific abuses would be a general power of regulation, he insisted, this tended to condone "methods precluded by the Constitution. Such subversions are not only illegitimate but are fraught with the danger that, having begun on the ground of necessity, they will continue on the score of expediency, and, finally, as a mere matter of course."[43]

From this argument Brandeis, Holmes, Stone and even Sanford dissented. "We fear to grant power and are unwilling to recognize it when it exists," declared Holmes. "The truth seems to me," he went on, "to be that, subject to compensation when compensation is due, the legislature may forbid or restrict any business when it has a sufficient force of public opinion behind it." Stone, anticipating the day when the demands of the modern economic system would render the niceties of the public interest doctrine irrelevant, observed: "To say that only those businesses affected with a public interest may be regulated is but another way of stating that all those businesses which may be regulated are affected with a public interest. It is difficult to use the phrase free of its connotation of legal consequences, and hence when used as a basis of judicial decision, to avoid begging the question to be decided." To hold a business exempt from regulation is to assume, he said, that there is a competitive economy which will provide its own regulation; to determine whether this is in fact true is a function of the legislature rather than the judiciary, and the judicial function "ends when it is determined that there is a basis for legislative action."[44]

Sutherland's fundamental thesis—that a business was regulable only when it was *"devoted* to public use and its use thereby, in effect, *granted* by the public"—was reiterated the following year in a six-to-three decision invalidating a New Jersey statute controlling employment agency fees. Stone's dissent made still more positive his contention in *Tyson*: "Price regulation is within the state's power whenever any combination of circumstances seriously curtails the regulative force of competition so that buyers or sellers are placed at such a disadvantage in the bargaining struggle that a legislature might reasonably anticipate serious consequences to the community as a whole."[45] In 1932 Brandeis took up the theme even more bluntly: "The notion of a distinct category of business 'affected with a public interest' employing property 'devoted to a public use' rests upon historical error. In my opinion, the true principle is that the state's power extends to every regulation of any business reasonably required and appropriate for the public protection."[46]

The end of the road, which began on the Illinois prairies with the Granger laws of the seventies, was now coming into view.

*   *   *

It was a final ironic turn of fate that Taft, as Chief Justice, should reach the end of his long career during the presidency of Herbert Hoover, whose own position after 1929 seemed to Walter Lippmann to parallel the dénouement of 1912. For the course of American politics, and for the Court itself, the thunderous crash of business prosperity in the stock market catastrophe of October, 1929 sounded the end of a world. The aged Chief Justice did not live long enough into the next year—he resigned in February and died in March—to witness the cruel, steady expiration of so many of the grand illusions on which the decade of normalcy had rested. It was Hoover's fortune to bear the brunt of discontent pent up during the years of Taft's Chief Justiceship.

The nomination of Charles Evans Hughes to succeed Taft seemed unlikely to provoke any objection; it was to be assumed that a conservative Republican President would select a congenial counterpart to fill the position, and there could be little quarrel over Hughes' professional eminence. He was currently the American representative on the World Court, a judicial position in the international sphere which complemented his four years as Secretary of State under Harding and Coolidge. His progressive record as governor of New York had doubtless dimmed in public memory by now, but his six years as Associate Justice were recalled as a period of moderate advances in the direction of constitutional liberalism. On the whole, said the *New York Times,* there had never been "a clearer case of the office seeking the fit man."[47]

Hughes himself had told Hoover that he didn't "want a fight over the nomination," and the President had assured him that this possibility would be carefully investigated before his nomination was submitted to the Senate. But all seemed auspicious; Brandeis apparently reflected the sentiment of the Court when he released a statement expressing the hope that the confirmation would be unanimous, while Norris, chairman of the Senate Judiciary Committee, told the press that he anticipated that the committee would recommend confirmation.[48]

Yet it was Norris who opened the debate on the propriety of confirming the nominee. While the Nebraska Senator, like others who quickly joined in, paid tribute to Hughes' personal abilities, the fight, as it was described by a leading Washington correspondent, "resolved itself with dramatic swiftness into a protest against the social philosophy embodied in the present majority of the Supreme Court itself. It became a popular uprising against the practice aptly described by Senator [Clarence C.] Dill as 'writing into the law of the land economic doctrines that enable organized wealth to pick the pockets of the people under the guise of protecting its constitutional rights.' "[49] Senator William E. Borah of Idaho declared that "under the Fourteenth Amendment the Supreme Court of the United States . . . becomes really the economic dictator in the United States," and with reference to the doctrine of *laissez-faire* he added, "however sincerely that view may be entertained, which places the greatest stress upon the rights of property, I do not feel that I ought to vote for a man as Chief Justice of the United States who will be in a position to advance that doctrine to its full fruition."[50]

Borah also listed the major clients whom Hughes had represented before the Court in recent years—oil companies, the meat packing industry, large manufacturers. There was a reasonable presumption, he suggested, that the nominee shared the view of the capitalists who retained him and the conservative holdovers from the Taft Court: that "practically no restraint ought to be placed upon the vast corporate interests of the United States."[51] Some of the criticism of the nominee was small-minded or irrelevant—Hughes was attacked for having abandoned the bench in 1916 to re-enter politics, or for having been taken in by the corrupt members of Harding's cabinet when he was Secretary of State. But the principal arguments remained on the economic issues of modern constitutionalism. The insistence of the Court upon reviewing utility rates after they had been set by authorized state or Federal commissions, said Dill of Washington, has established "a body of law not written by the Congress, a body of law whose effect reaches into the daily lives of the masses of the people of America." In insulating consumer rates against legislative or administrative adjustment, said Dill, "the last resort of organized capital that plunders the common people of America" has become "the Supreme Court of the United States."[52]

Thus obliquely, the constitutionalism of the Taft Court was excoriated by the protests against the choice for Taft's successor. The insurgents were realists enough to know that, in the final analysis, they did not have the votes to prevent Hughes's seating. A motion to recommit the nomination to the judiciary committee was lost, and the motion to confirm followed immediately—52 ayes, 26 nays, and 18 not voting.[53]

*   *   *

In the case of Hughes, the manifest capabilities of the candidate himself made it difficult for the insurgents to identify him positively with the stand-pat element of the Court. But two months later the rebellion flared up again, with a more vulnerable nominee. Three weeks after Hughes was confirmed, Justice Sanford suddenly died, on the same day as Taft. Since Sanford had been a Tennesseean, Hoover began casting about among Southern prospects to find his replacement, and in early April sent to the Senate the name of a North Carolinian, Federal Judge John J. Parker. Once more, the President had reason to expect that the nomination would not excite opposition. He had been reassured when ten Southern Senators and seven Southern governors had notified him of their support of the particular candidate, while Parker's own twenty-year record on the lower court benches, the Attorney General reported, appeared impeccable.[54]

The difficulty lay in Hoover's inability to read the signs of pent-up resentment at the one-sidedness of *laissez-faire* jurisprudence in the past decade. The President, said one critic, "had chosen an undistinguished candidate for political reasons"—the South, which had split asunder with Alfred E. Smith's candidacy, was indeed worth wooing in the worsening times which attended the mid-term elections—and had "completely ignored the warning provided by the opposition to Mr. Hughes."[55] In the present case, the candidate was considerably more vulnerable, on two counts: he was, as Borah of Idaho told the Senate, "peculiarly identified" with an anti-labor application of the injunction power substantially beyond the limits which even the conservative majority of the Supreme Court had set down; and, as a torrent of telegrams from Negro leaders advised, Parker was remembered for a remark, in the course of a 1920 gubernatorial campaign, that the participation of Negroes in politics was "a source of evil."[56]

With the perennial Norris-LaGuardia Bill outlawing the labor injunction slowly but steadily mustering a prospective majority in Congress, said Borah, and with the hope that a moderate like Hughes (if not a liberal like Brandeis) could be added to the Court, the intransigent conservatives on the bench might at last be curbed.[57] On April 22 the Senate judiciary committee reported unfavorably on the nomination. Both before and after this action, the White House served notice that it would not withdraw Parker's name; and on May 8, by a vote of 39 to 41, the Senate rejected the candidate. It was the first time in the twentieth century that a President had suffered such a rebuff.[58]

"As with Hughes, the attack on Parker in its larger aspects was an at-

tack on the conservative cast of the Supreme Court," said an observer after
the six-week debate had ended. Although Hoover gave no indication that
the debate on both nominations had changed his own concept of the role of
the Court in national life, his alternate nomination—Owen J. Roberts of
Pennsylvania—was approved with relatively little discussion. Roberts' chief
public service had been as special assistant to the Attorney General in prosecuting the Teapot Dome scandals, an assignment in which as in his thirty
years of private practice he had demonstrated high professional competence.
From what meager data could be found, he appeared to be a moderate or
at least a modern-minded man; it would remain for the constitutional challenges of the mid-thirties to reveal his true character.[59]

With the addition of Hughes and Roberts, the more optimistic among
observers predicted that the hard-core conservatives had at last been reduced to a minority, and in a succession of cases in the next few months the
record tended to bear them out. With Hughes writing the majority opinions,
the Court affirmed an Ohio statute providing that a state law could not be
invalidated by the Ohio supreme court if more than one justice dissented; it
upheld two Louisiana statutes, one providing for free textbooks to public
and private schools and the other levying a substantial emergency tax on
oil production; it sustained a New York vocational rehabilitation fund, an
Oklahoma law licensing farmers' cotton gins, and a Texas statute protecting
railroad labor from company unions.[60] It had the appearance, said one
dazzled liberal publication, of a "Hughes rebellion."[61]

First Amendment freedoms, to which the Court had paid lip service
without enforcing them in the twenties, also were hearteningly strengthened.
Invalidating a California statute forbidding the flying of a "red flag," Hughes
spoke for the Court in declaring that "the opportunity for free political discussion to the end that government may be responsive to the will of the
people and that changes may be obtained by lawful means, . . . is a fundamental principle of our constitutional system."[62] A Minnesota statute authorizing a prosecuting attorney to enjoin publication of scurrilous or defam-
atory matter was set aside as a flagrant violation of the freedom of the
press.[63]

*   *   *

The degree to which these decisions retracted the extreme "judicial imperialism" of the decade of normalcy was a matter of speculation, as were
the long-run convictions of the Court majority which pronounced them.
Closer scrutiny of the decisions in the first two terms of the Court under
Hughes—the closing years of the Hoover administration—suggested that
the more liberal construction of the Constitution applied to cases relating to
the police powers of the states. Conscious of the growing disaster of the depression, Hughes was prepared to define the extraordinary powers of the
states in terms sufficiently broad to cope with the problem. "Emergency does

not create power," the Chief Justice was to declare in 1933, but it "may furnish the occasion for the exercise of power."[64]

When the question became one of Federal authority—a fundamental question when, in the national crisis which ushered in the New Deal, the states had exhausted their capacity to deal with the depression—the thinking of the Court majority revealed little change from the vanished era of normalcy. There was no change, indeed, in its opposition to Federal Trade Commission interference with free enterprise, however ruthless. In *Federal Trade Commission v. Raladam Company,* the Court reached a logical extreme in the line of reasoning begun early in Taft's Chief Justiceship, when in effect it held that monopoly could not be regulated unless public deception was established—and that public deception could not be established unless regulable monopoly could be proved.[65] The Court continued its insistence upon reviewing and reducing decrees of the Interstate Commerce Commission regulating railroad charges—in this case, a depression-spawned practice of exorbitant reorganization fees in bankruptcy.[66] The remnants of the Sherman Act still found inconvenient to great corporations were further demolished with an opinion that cross-licensing of patents and pooling of royalties did not violate anti-trust law.[67]

Nor was the state power of regulation to be permitted to spread more than slightly beyond the narrow limits to which the Fuller and Taft courts had long since confined it. The public interest doctrine long ago enunciated in *Munn v. Illinois* and systematically circumscribed over the years, was once more drastically reduced in the spring of 1932; once more ascendant, Justice Sutherland spoke for the six-to-two majority of the Court (including the moderates, Hughes and Roberts) in applying the restraints of the Fourteenth Amendment to a state attempt to regulate private business in the case of *New State Ice Company v. Liebmann.* To use a licensing power to limit the number of firms entering a particular business field, when the field did not represent a natural monopoly or a use of natural resources in which a public interest was manifest, said Sutherland, was both unreasonable and arbitrary.[68]

Within eight months after this case the Hoover administration and the age of *laissez-faire* would receive their *coup de grace.* In his dissent for himself and Justice Stone, Brandeis spoke eloquently in valedictory. "To stay experimentation in things social and economic," he warned, "is a grave responsibility," particularly in a period when, as now, there was "unprecedented unemployment, a catastrophic fall in commodity prices and a volume of economic losses which threatens . . . the stability of the capitalistic system." Whether, by limiting competition to prevent ruin, a state might hit upon a means of dealing with economic collapse generally, said Brandeis, was a question for which social science had no answer. The test of a free enterprise system under these circumstances, he declared, was its readiness to permit experimentation with remedial laws. "This Court has the power to prevent [the] experiment," Brandeis conceded. "But in the exercise of this high power, we must ever be on our guard, lest we erect our prejudices into legal principles."[69]

The words of the dissent were a discerning commentary on the intellectual unpreparedness of the Hughes Court for the magnitude of the challenge already being presented by the deepening depression. The new Chief Justice, seeking to apply the confident assumptions of the decade of normalcy to a decade which was anything but normal, was to find many basic propositions of the constitutionalism of Taft—or of White or Fuller—increasingly irrelevant. For three generations the consistently conservative majority of the Court had insisted upon restricting the regulatory powers of Congress in the interest of the widest possible freedom of private economic functions. Now, as private economic institutions found themselves in the path of disaster, a judiciary and a Chief Executive conditioned to a reflex action against the idea of government intervention found themselves incapable of devising effective rescue. As uncertainty deepened, the initial liberalism of the two new Justices—Hughes and Roberts—quickly evaporated; they dashed for shelter in the comforting and familiar shibboleths of *laissez-faire* jurisprudence. By reestablishing the majority clinging to the old order, even as the old order crumbled, they refused to countenance even a concept of self-preservation.

The constitutionalism which had predominated from 1889 to 1932 was now to be confronted with a depression unparalleled in virulence in the history of Western capitalism, followed by a second World War of substantially greater magnitude than the first. From these successive cataclysms would emerge a society more distantly removed from the decade of normalcy than that society had been removed from the America of the seventies and eighties. Only in the age of Theodore Roosevelt and the first administration of Woodrow Wilson had there been any concerted national effort to bring some degree of order and responsibility to the undiminishing process of developing an interdependent, corporate economy.

William Howard Taft, whose Presidency represented the interval between these efforts and whose Chief Justiceship had coincided with the final years of the old orthodoxy, perhaps reflected as well as any figure in the years between 1889 and 1932 the vacillations of American commitment. In March, 1930 a not always friendly critic of the Chief Justice, noting that in 1912 Taft had been the victim of a political avalanche—receiving the smallest number of electoral votes ever given up to that time to the candidate of a major party—went on to observe: "No one would have ventured to predict that eighteen years later he would stand high in the affection of the American people. It was not so much that Taft changed during these eighteen years, for he did not. It was . . . that the United States reverted . . .

to a frame of mind of which his own temperament was a better expression than before."[70]

Taft's death had been sincerely and universally mourned; it might have seemed in retrospect that his countrymen knew they were also mourning the death of an economic and constitutional age.

APPENDICES

Appendix A

Court Personnel From Fuller to Taft

Each Chief Justiceship represents an administrative chapter in the history of the Supreme Court, although the influence of individual Justices provides the real continuity from one such chapter to another, and the tenure of specific individuals, long preceding a particular judicial administration or continuing long after it, may be more significant than the arbitrary divisions by the tenures of the Chief Justices. The continuity of the Court is illustrated in one dimension, by the Charts which introduce each Part of the volume. The present Appendix complements the Charts with brief summaries of pertinent career data on individual members of the Court.

The Justices are given in the order of their seniority or time of appointment; it is worth noting, for example, that a Chief Justice like Fuller or Taft, appointed from outside the current membership of the bench, begins as a junior to all his Associates. This fact may be more superficial than significant; a Chief Justice who, in Taft's phrase, has the ability to "marshal the Court" may be able to take advantage of his "honeymoon period" to assert his leadership from the outset. In any event, it is the background of the individual jurists, and their tenure in the particular historical context, which is of the greater importance.

"This emphasis upon personal qualifications and characteristics is a manifestation of the twentieth century shift in American jurisprudence from the unrealistic acceptance of the mechanistic theory of judicial interpretation to frank acknowledgement of the subjective element in the decision-making process," wrote Professor John R. Schmidhauser of the State University of Iowa in 1959.[1] Schmidhauser's own studies have assembled a variety of social and economic indices of individual Justices' behavior on the bench. For the purposes of the present work, however, the data have been more narrowly selected, being confined primarily to professional details from which a composite portrait of the Court in each era may be discerned. Detailed biographies of individual Justices, where these exist, are discussed in the Bibliographic Essay.

Between the appointment of John Jay in 1789 and the appointment of Fuller in 1889, fifty men had occupied the variable number of seats on the

Court (including, of course, the eight Associates whom Fuller himself joined). The first group of *curricula vitae* which follows includes the nine Justices who were on the bench in October, 1888, as well as one who was confirmed but who declined the appointment—which tells something of the political conflicts which affected the Court which Fuller took over. The second group covers twelve Justices and two rejected nominees who figured in Fuller's Chief Justiceship, the third group includes the six men named to the Court during White's tenure, and the fourth group the five new men who came onto the bench during Taft's administration.

Each of these groups is introduced by a table summarizing the process of appointment of the individual to the Court, followed by a concise summary of career data for each individual. The name of each Justice in the groups is preceded by a number indicating his order in the succession of members of the Court since the beginning, and this is followed in parentheses by a number indicating the Justice he has succeeded. (For those prior to the period covered by the present work, the name of the predecessor appears in a footnote.) At the end of each of these periods in the Court's development there is a short statistical recapitulation.

1.   The Court as Fuller Found It

The Justices are given in the order of their seniority; short professional sketches follow the table.

Name of Justice	President Nominating	Date of Nomination	Date of Confirmation	Vote on Confirmation*	Date of Commission	Date of Swearing-in
Miller	Lincoln	7-16-62	7-16-62		7-16-62	12- 1-63
Field	Lincoln	3-10-63	3-10-63		3-10-63	12- 7-63
Bradley	Grant	2- 8-70	3-21-70	49- 6	3-21-70	3-23-70
Harlan	Hayes	10-17-77	11-29-77	φ	11-29-77	12-10-77
Matthews	Hayes	1-26-81	†			
	Garfield	3-14-81	5-12-81	24-23	5-12-81	5-17-81
Gray	Arthur	12-19-81	12-20-81	51- 5	12-20-81	1- 9-82
[Conkling	Arthur	2-24-82	3- 2-82	39-21]	‡	
Blatchford	Arthur	3-13-82	3-27-82	φ	3-27-82	4- 3-82
Lamar	Cleveland	12- 6-87	1-16-88	32-28	1-16-88	1-18-88
Fuller	Cleveland	5-20-88	7-20-88	41-20	7-20-88	10- 8-88

*Unless otherwise indicated, confirmation was either unanimous or without recorded dissent.

†Senate refused to act (see sketch following).

‡Conkling declined commission (see sketch following).

φConfirmation in executive session, without record of vote.

36 (28*). SAMUEL FREEMAN MILLER (April 15, 1816-October 13, 1890). Born Richmond, Kentucky; studied medicine, Transylvania University, 1836-38; practiced medicine in Kentucky, 1838-47; read law and admitted to bar in Kentucky, 1847; in Iowa, 1850; practiced law in Kentucky, 1847-50; in Iowa, 1850-52. Miller wrote the majority opinion in the *Slaughterhouse Cases,* 16 Wall. 36 (1873), first major interpretation of Fourteenth Amendment holding Amendment did not inhibit reasonable exercise of states' powers to regulate private enterprise. Served as member of Electoral (Hayes-Tilden) Commission of 1876.

38†. STEPHEN JOHNSON FIELD (November 4, 1816-April 9, 1899). Born Haddam, Connecticut; brother of David Dudley Field, uncle of Justice Josiah D. Brewer (No. 51); A. B., Williams College, 1837; read law in brother's New York office, 1837-41, and admitted to bar in New York, 1841; in California, 1850; practiced law in New York, 1841-48; in California, 1850-57; mayor of Marysville, California, 1849-50; member, California legislature, 1850-51; justice, California supreme court, 1857-63, and chief justice, 1861-63. Retired from Supreme Court of United States, December 1, 1897.

41‡. JOSEPH P. BRADLEY (March 14, 1813-January 22, 1892). Born Albany County, New York; A. B., Rutgers College, 1836; read law in Newark, 1836-39, and admitted to bar in New Jersey, 1839; specialized in corporation and patent law and served as general counsel for various railroads. Senate opposition to his appointment based on charge that Grant was seeking to "pack" the Court with two new Justices (Bradley and Judge William Strong of Pennsylvania), in vacancies existing after Congress restored the Court membership to nine, to override the adverse 4-3 ruling in the first Legal Tender Case, *Hepburn v. Griswold,* 8 Wall. 603 (1870); Bradley and Strong made up part of the 5-4 majority which subsequently reversed *Hepburn* in the second Legal Tender Case, *Knox v. Lee,* 12 Wall. 457 (1871).

44 (37φ). JOHN MARSHALL HARLAN (June 1, 1833-October 14, 1911). Born Boyle County, Kentucky; A.B., Centre College, 1850; studied law at Transylvania University and in father's law office, 1851-53 and admitted to bar in Kentucky, 1853; general practice in Kentucky, 1853-60, 1867-76; served in Union Army, 1861-63, resigning to become state attorney general, 1863-67; previously served as county judge, 1858; member of Louisiana Reconstruction Commission, 1877; member, Bering Sea Commission, 1892.

46 (35§). STANLEY MATTHEWS (July 21, 1824-March 22, 1889).

---

* Peter V. Daniel (1841-62).

† Field was appointed to a tenth seat on the bench, established in 1863 to accommodate a new "Western circuit."

‡ The deaths of Justices John Catron in 1865 and James M. Wayne in 1867 left two positions vacant, and in order to prevent President Andrew Johnson from filling them Congress reduced Court membership to eight. The position for Bradley came when Congress restored the Court to nine in 1870.

φ David Davis, 1862-1877.

§ Noah H. Swain, 1862-1882.

Born Cincinnati, Ohio; A. B., Kenyon College, 1840; read law in Cincinnati and in Columbia, Tennessee, 1840-43; admitted to bar in Ohio, 1844; practiced law intermittently, 1844-61, 1865-77, while editing anti-slavery newspaper, serving as judge, court of common pleas of Hamilton County, Ohio, 1851, and as United States attorney, 1858-61; clerk of lower house of state legislature, 1848-49; served in Union Army, 1861-63, judge of Cincinnati superior court, 1863-65; United States Senator (unexpired term), 1877-81. Senate neglected to act on nomination submitted by retiring President Hayes, claiming it was a political accommodation; President Garfield made renomination a test of party loyalty and secured confirmation by single vote.

47 (34*).   HORACE GRAY (March 24, 1828-September 15, 1902). Born Boston, Massachusetts; A. B., Harvard College, 1845; studied law at Harvard and completed preparation for bar in attorneys' offices, 1848-51; admitted to practice in Massachusetts, 1851; practiced intermittently, 1851-64, while serving as reporter to state supreme judicial court, 1854-64; justice, supreme judicial court, 1864-81, and chief justice, 1873-81. Resigned from United States Supreme Court, July 9, 1902. Gray's wide professional reputation made his appointment the climax to the "rehabilitation" of the Supreme Court after its disastrous decline in public regard during the Reconstruction era, and the few votes cast against his confirmation were essentially a sign of the continuing power struggle between the White House and Congress which climaxed in the Conkling nomination a few weeks later (see next paragraph).

[ROSCOE CONKLING (October 30, 1829-April 18, 1888). Born Albany, New York; studied at Mount Washington Collegiate Institute in New York before going to Utica to read law in attorneys' offices, 1848-50; admitted to bar in New York, 1850; practiced intermittently in New York, 1850-58; became mayor of Albany, 1858-59; served in United States House of Representatives, 1859-67; his control of the Republican machine in the state legislature enabled him to win election to the United States Senate, where he served, 1867-81. President Grant offered him the Chief Justiceship of the United States when it should become vacant, but Conkling declined in favor of continuing his political career. An old-line spoilsman, he considered all Federal appointments in New York as his prerogative, and became bitterly embroiled with President Hayes over White House plans to develop a broader civil service based on a merit system. In 1879 Hayes succeeded in ousting Conkling's henchman, Chester A. Arthur, from the position of Collector of Customs in New York; in the power struggle at the Republican Convention in 1880, James A. Garfield, an anti-Conkling man, was paired with Arthur in an effort to reunite the party. After Garfield's assassination, President Arthur nominated Conkling as an Associate Justice as a gesture of political domination of Congress, on February 24, 1882. A bitter partisan struggle ensued in the Senate, with confirmation being carried by a vote of 39 to 21 on March 2; thereupon, Conkling,

---

* Nathan Clifford, 1858-81.

who had never had any intention of accepting the position, formally declined it.

[Conkling participated in the Congressional debates on the so-called Reconstruction Amendments, and in 1882 as counsel in a case before the Supreme Court he made his famous argument that a primary purpose of the Fourteenth Amendment had been to protect the rights of corporations, in *San Mateo County v. Southern Pacific Railroad Co.*, 116 U. S. 138. The argument foreshadowed an interpretation of the Amendment which the majority of the Court, even without Conkling, tended to apply zealously throughout the next half a century.]

48 (42*). SAMUEL BLATCHFORD (March 9, 1820-July 7, 1893). Born New York City; A. B., Columbia College, 1837; read law as secretary to William H. Seward, 1837-42; admitted to practice in New York, 1842; practiced law, 1842-67, specializing in international and commercial law; United States District Judge, 1867-72; United States Circuit Judge, 1872-82.

Blatchford was a specialist in bankruptcy, maritime law and patents; he contributed little to constitutional jurisprudence.

49 (45†). LUCIUS QUINTUS CINCINNATUS LAMAR (September 17, 1825-January 23, 1893). Born Putnam County, Georgia, of French Huguenot ancestry; a brother, Mirabeau, was second president of Texas Republic; A. B., Emory College, 1845; read law in Macon and admitted to practice in Georgia, 1847; in Mississippi, 1849; practiced in Georgia, 1847-49, 1852-55; in Mississippi, 1849-52, 1855-57, 1864-72; served as professor of law, University of Mississippi, 1849-52, 1866-72; served in United States House of Representatives, 1857-60; in Confederate diplomatic service, 1862, in military service, 1861, 1863-64; again served in House of Representatives, 1872-76; in United States Senate, 1876-85; Secretary of Interior, 1885-87. Despite his record of postwar reconciliation, Senate debated his previous Confederate military service as a possible disqualification, finally confirming, 32 to 28.

50 (43‡). *Eighth Chief Justice.* MELVILLE WESTON FULLER (February 11, 1833-July 4, 1910). Born Augusta, Maine; A. B., Bowdoin College, 1853; studied at Harvard Law School and read law, 1853-55; admitted to practice in Maine, 1855; in Illinois, 1856; practiced law in Illinois, 1856-88, specializing in corporation and real estate law; member of Illinois state legislature, 1863-64. His active participation in Democratic politics had roused substantial inter-party conflicts, which resulted in a barrage of acrimonious charges exchanged by the factions in the Senate and delayed confirmation for some weeks. During Fuller's long tenure he served on the Venezuela-British Guiana Border Commission, 1899, and as the American member of the Permanent Court of Arbitration at The Hague, 1900-1910.

---

* Ward Hunt, 1872-82.
† William B. Woods, 1880-88.
‡ Morrison R. Waite, C. J., 1874-88.

Fuller's Court was the first to be virtually cleansed of the noxious effects of the Reconstruction era, although the number of non-unanimous votes of confirmation indicated the vigorous Senatorial challenge to the Presidential leadership which pervaded the Republican domination of the government and continued in a slightly varied form when Cleveland inaugurated the postwar Democratic revival (see following section).

Although Conkling would have died before Fuller took office, the great Senatorial struggle over his nomination was a virulent symptom of this Republican power push which was part of the background to the judiciary which Fuller took over.[2] Between Justice Miller, the oldest in point of service, and Fuller himself, twenty different men of widely varying capabilities had figured in the checkered history of the Court for this period. Four nominations, including two for Chief Justice, had been rejected by the Senate or withdrawn by the White House in the face of certain rejection, while Lincoln's Secretary of War, Edward M. Stanton, had died after confirmation but before he could take office. The remaining eight among these had served brief and generally undistinguished terms.

Recapitulation

When Fuller became Chief Justice he found a Court whose members' aggregate experience totalled more than 185 years of private practice, twenty-two years of legislative service, nine years in administrative office, and thirty-seven years on the benches of state or lower Federal courts. One Justice had spent more than a dozen years in part-time university teaching, while another had lectured for an even longer period after he came onto the bench.

Law was still a subject learned under the tutelage of practitioners; six of the nine Justices in 1888 had done all of their preparation for the bar in law offices, while the three who took some university work in the subject still found it desirable to complete their reading under a practicing attorney. The educational level of the Court was high; all members had completed an undergraduate course of study, although the length of time required for a degree was variable. Undergraduate colleges represented were Bowdoin, Centre, Columbia, Emory, Harvard, Kenyon, Rutgers, Transylvania and Williams. Of the three Justices who took part of their legal training at universities, two attended Harvard and one Transylvania. One Justice had a degree in medicine and had been a practicing physician.

The time spent in private practice ranged from fifteen to thirty-three years, with twenty-one being the average. Four Justices had had prior legislative experience in the states or in Congress; four had had prior judicial experience; one had been a Cabinet officer, another a state attorney general and a third a Federal District Attorney.

2. The Court Under Fuller, 1888-1910

The Justices listed below appear in the order in which they succeeded members of the Court as Fuller had found it.

Name of Justice	President Nominating	Date of Nomination	Date of Confirmation	Vote on Confirmation	Date of Commission	Date of Swearing-in
Brewer	Harrs'n	12- 4-89	12-18-89	53-11	12-18-89	1- 6-90
Brown	Harrs'n	12-23-90	12-29-90		12-29-90	1- 6-91
Shiras	Harrison	7-19-92	7-26-92		7-26-92	10-10-92
Jackson	Harrison	2- 2-93	2-18-93		2-18-93	3- 4-93
[Hornblower	Clevel'd	9-19-93	1-15-94	24-30]		
[Peckham, W. H.	Clevel'd	1-22-94	2-16-94	32-41]		
White	Clevel'd	2-19-94	2-19-94		2-19-94	3-12-94
Peckham, R. W.	Clevel'd	12- 3-95	12- 9-95		12- 9-95	1- 6-96
McKenna	McKnly	12-16-97	1-21-98		1-21-98	1-26-98
Holmes	Roosevelt	8-11-02*				
		12- 2-02	12- 4-02		12- 4-02	12- 8-02
Day	Roosevelt	2-19-03	2-23-03		2-23-03	3- 2-03
Moody	Roosvlt	12- 3-06	12-12-06		12-12-06	12-17-06
Lurton	Taft	12- 3-09	12-20-09		12-20-09	1- 3-10
Hughes	Taft	4-25-10	5- 2-10		5- 2-10	10-10-10

*Interim appointment, resubmitted after convening of Congress.

51 (46). DAVID JOSIAH BREWER (January 20, 1837-March 28, 1910). Born Smyrna, Asia Minor; nephew of Justice Field and of David Dudley Field; studied at Wesleyan and Yale Universities, receiving A. B. with honors, Yale, 1856; read law in uncle's New York office and graduated, Albany Law School, 1858; admitted to bar in New York, 1858; in Kansas, 1859; practiced intermittently in Kansas, 1859-61, 1863-65; commissioner, United States Circuit Court in Leavenworth, 1861; judge of probate and criminal courts, Leavenworth county, 1862; state district attorney, 1865-69; Leavenworth city attorney, 1869-70; justice, Kansas supreme court, 1870-84; United States Circuit Court judge, 1884-89. Served on Venezuela-British Guiana Border Commission, 1895.

52 (36). HENRY BILLINGS BROWN (March 21, 1836-September 4, 1913). Born South Lee, Massachusetts; A. B., Yale University, 1856; studied law at Harvard Law School and in attorney's office in Detroit, 1856-60; admitted to bar in Michigan, 1860; served as United States deputy marshal, 1861; assistant United States attorney, 1863-68; state circuit judge, 1868; private practice, with emphasis on admiralty law, 1868-75; United States District Court judge, 1875-90. Resigned from United States Supreme Court, May 28, 1906.

53 (41).   GEORGE SHIRAS, Jr. (January 16, 1832-August 21, 1924). Born Pittsburgh, Pennsylvania; studied at Ohio University and received A. B., Yale University, 1853; read law at Yale and in Pittsburgh office of Judge Hopewell Hepburn, 1853-55; admitted to bar in Pennsylvania, 1855; in Iowa, 1855; practiced with brother in Iowa for year, then in Pittsburgh, 1856-92. Since President Harrison neglected to consult the two Senators from Pennsylvania before making the nomination, they opposed Shiras and the judiciary committee reported out his name without recommendation; thereupon the Senate confirmed without recorded dissent. Shiras is chiefly remembered as the Justice who allegedly shifted his vote in the Income Tax Case of 1895. He resigned his seat February 23, 1903.

54 (49).   HOWELL EDMUNDS JACKSON (April 8, 1832-August 8, 1895). Born Paris, Tennessee; A. B., West Tennessee College, 1849; studied law at University of Virginia and completed preparation in law offices in Lebanon, Tennessee, 1849-56; admitted to practice in Tennessee, 1856; general practice in Tennessee, 1856-61, 1865-86; custodian of sequestered property for the Confederate States, 1861-65; served in state legislature, 1880; elected United States Senator, 1881-86; United States District Court judge, 1886-91; United States Circuit Court judge, 1891-93.

[WILLIAM HORNBLOWER (May 13, 1851-June 16, 1914). Born Paterson, N. J.; nephew of Justice Bradley; A. B., College of New Jersey (Princeton), 1871; LL. B., Columbia University, 1875; admitted to bar in New York, 1875; in general practice, 1875-91. President Cleveland's nomination was violently opposed by Senator David B. Hill because Hornblower as an election commissioner had ruled against one of Hill's henchmen; the rejection of the nomination was part of Hill's all-out fight with Cleveland for control of the New York Democratic party. In 1895 Hornblower declined Cleveland's offer to submit his name for another vacancy.]

[WHEELER H. PECKHAM (January 1, 1833-September 27, 1905). Born Albany, New York; studied at Union College; read law at Albany Law School and in father's law office and was admitted to bar, 1854; practiced in New York, 1854-59, 1865-84; failing health led him West to Iowa and Minnesota, 1859-64; served in 1873 as special counsel prosecuting "Boss" Tweed; United States district attorney, 1884, resuming private practice, 1885-1905; one of the founders of the Association of the Bar of the City of New York. Both Senators Hill and Edward Murphy opposed his nomination to Supreme Court because of his militant independence of regular party organization in New York.]

55 (48).   EDWARD DOUGLAS WHITE (November 3, 1845-May 19, 1921). Born Lafourche Parish, Louisiana, son of distinguished leader of state bar; studied at Mount St. Mary's College in Maryland, Jesuit College in New Orleans and Georgetown College in Washington; in Confederate Army, 1861-63; prisoner of war, 1863-65; read law and was admitted to bar in Louisiana, 1868; engaged in private practice, 1868-79, 1881-91; member of state legisla-

ture, 1874; justice of Louisiana supreme court, 1879-80; United States Senator, 1891-93. Cleveland nominated him immediately after New York Senators had invoked "senatorial courtesy" in rejecting Peckham (see above) and under same "courtesy" secured his confirmation. *Ninth Chief Justice* (see Section 3).

56 (54). RUFUS WHEELER PECKHAM (November 8, 1838-October 24, 1909). Born Albany, New York; brother of Wheeler H. Peckham (see above); studied privately in Philadelphia and abroad, read law in father's office and was admitted to bar in New York, 1859; general practice, 1859-69, 1872-81; county attorney, 1869-72; Albany corporation counsel, 1881-83; judge of New York supreme court, 1883-86; judge of New York court of appeals, 1886-95. Senator Hill's power in New York had waned by this time, and he made no attempt to block this nomination.

57 (38). JOSEPH McKENNA (August 10, 1843-November 21, 1926). Born Philadelphia, but in infancy family moved to Benicia, California; graduated from Benicia Collegiate Institute, 1865, and having read law as part of these studies was admitted to bar in California, 1865; practiced intermittently, 1865-85; county attorney, 1866-70; member of state legislature, 1875-76; elected to United States House of Representatives, 1885-92; United States Circuit Court judge, 1892-97; served briefly as Attorney General to President McKinley, 1897. His nomination to Supreme Court was attacked as accommodation of Senator Leland Stanford and the Western railroad lobby, but after some debate he was confirmed without recorded dissent.

58 (47). OLIVER WENDELL HOLMES, Jr. (March 8, 1841-March 6, 1935). Born Boston, Massachusetts, son of distinguished physician and belle-lettrist; studied at Harvard College, leaving before graduation to enter Union Army; thrice wounded in Civil War; LL. B., Harvard, 1866; admitted to bar in Massachusetts, 1867; general practice, 1867-82; editor of *American Law Review*, 1870-73; lecturer, Lowell Institute, 1880, subsequently publishing lectures as classic study, *The Common Law*, 1881; invited to occupy newly created chair of law at Harvard, 1882; judge, Massachusetts supreme judicial court, 1883-1902. Retired from Supreme Court of United States, January 12, 1932.

59 (53). WILLIAM RUFUS DAY (April 17, 1849-July 9, 1923). Born Ravenna, Ohio; A. B., University of Michigan, 1870; studied law at Michigan and in offices in Ravenna, 1870-72; admitted to bar in Ohio, 1872; general practice in Canton, Ohio, 1872-86; judge of state court of common pleas, 1886-89; onset of ill health caused him to resign and decline offers of Federal judgeship and Attorney Generalship under McKinley; Assistant Secretary of State, 1897; Secretary of State, 1898; succeeded William Howard Taft as judge of United States Circuit Court for sixth circuit, 1899-1903. Resigned from Supreme Court of United States, November 19, 1923.

60 (52). WILLIAM HENRY MOODY (December 23, 1853-July 2, 1917). Born Newbury, Massachusetts; A. B., Harvard College, 1876; studied law at Harvard and in law office of Richard H. Dana, Jr., 1876-78; admitted

to practice in Massachusetts, 1878; general practice, 1878-88; Haverhill city solicitor, 1888-90; state district attorney, 1890-95; elected to United States House of Representatives, 1895-1902; Secretary of Navy, 1902-04; Attorney General, 1904-06. Rapidly declining health compelled him to resign from Supreme Court of United States, November 20, 1910.

61 (54). HORACE HARMON LURTON (February 26, 1844-July 12, 1914). Born Newport, Kentucky; studied privately and at University of Chicago; served in Confederate Army, discharged for physical disability, reenlisted and was taken prisoner; graduated from Cumberland Law School, 1867; admitted to bar in Tennessee, 1867; general practice in Clarksville, Tennessee, 1867-75, 1878-86; chancellor in equity, 1875-78; judge, Tennessee supreme court, 1886-93; judge, United States Circuit Court of Appeals, 1893-1909; law professor and dean, Vanderbilt University law school, 1898-1909.

62 (51). CHARLES EVANS HUGHES (see next section).

Recapitulation

During Fuller's long Chief Justiceship, twelve Associates were appointed; since Hughes' period of active service fell almost entirely in the next administration, however, his record is not included in this statistical summary. The eleven others, accordingly, reflect the professional composition of the Court over more than two decades. They represented a total of 185 years of private practice, 25 years of legislative service, and a remarkable total of 112 years of judicial experience on local, state and Federal benches. All but one had studied or been graduated from undergraduate institutions, and the one exception had had broad private schooling. The undergraduate schools included Benicia Collegiate Institute in California, the University of Chicago, Georgetown, Harvard, the Jesuit College of New Orleans, Michigan, Mount St. Mary's, West Tennessee and Yale. Law schools included Albany, Cumberland, Harvard, Michigan, Virginia and Yale, with some collegiate legal work at Benicia.

Experience in private practice ranged from a minimum of five years to a maximum of thirty-seven, with an average of seventeen. The state high appellate courts and the Federal trial and appellate courts were a fertile proving ground, with nine of the eleven having served on one or more. Three Justices had held a total of four Cabinet posts, and four had been local or state prosecutors or both.

3.   The Court Under White, 1910-1921

Justice White was elevated to the Chief's chair by President Taft in a move without historical precedent. The table and sketches which follow cover the professional careers of the Justices who were appointed during his administration, including Justice Hughes whose main service on the bench was under White.

Name of Justice	President Nominating	Date of Nomination	Date of Confirmation	Vote on Confirmation	Date of Commission	Date of Swearing-in
White	Taft	12-12-10	12-12-10		12-12-10	12-19-10
Van Devanter	Taft	12-12-10	12-15-10		12-16-10	1- 3-11
Lamar	Taft	12-12-10	12-15-10		12-17-10	1- 3-11
Pitney	Taft	2-19-12	3-13-12		3-13-12	3-18-12
McReynolds	Wilson	8-19-14	8-29-14		8-29-14	10-12-14
Brandeis	Wilson	1-28-16	6- 1-16	47-22*	6- 1-16	6- 5-16
Clarke	Wilson	7-14-16	7-24-16		7-24-16	10- 9-16

*27 not voting.

62 (51). CHARLES EVANS HUGHES (April 11, 1862-August 27, 1948). Born Glens Falls, New York; studied at Colgate University and received A. B. from Brown University, 1881; A. M., Brown, 1884, and LL. B., Columbia University, 1884; admitted to practice in New York, 1884; general practice, New York City, 1884-1907; professor of law, Cornell University, 1891-93; special counsel for state investigating commissions, 1905-06; governor of New York, 1907-10. Resigned from Supreme Court of United States, June 10, 1916, to become Republican candidate for President.

63 (50). WILLIS VAN DEVANTER (April 17, 1859-February 8, 1941). Born Marion, Indiana; A. B., Asbury (now DePauw) University, 1878; LL. B., Cincinnati Law School, 1881; admitted to bar in Indiana, 1881; in Wyoming, 1884; general practice in Indiana, 1881-84, in Wyoming, 1884-87; state's attorney, 1887-88; member, Wyoming state legislature, 1888; chief justice, Wyoming supreme court, 1889-90; resumed private practice, 1890-97; assistant United States Attorney General, 1897-1903; judge, United States Circuit Court, 1903-10. Retired from Supreme Court of United States, June 1, 1937.

64 (52). JOSEPH RUCKER LAMAR (October 14, 1857-January 2, 1916). Born Elbert County, Georgia; the previous Justice Lamar (No. 49) was a kinsman; studied at University of Georgia and received A. B. from Bethany College in West Virginia, 1877; read law at Washington and Lee University and in law office in Augusta, and admitted to practice in Georgia, 1878; general practice in Georgia, 1878-1903, 1906-10; member, Georgia legislature, 1886-89; justice, Georgia supreme court, 1903-05, resigning for reasons of health.

65 (44). MAHLON PITNEY (February 5, 1858-December 9, 1924). Born Morris County, New Jersey; A. B., College of New Jersey (Princeton), 1879; read law in father's office in Morristown and admitted to bar, 1882; general practice in New Jersey, 1882-94; elected to United States House of

Representatives, 1894-98; served in New Jersey legislature, 1898-1901, and was president of senate, 1901; justice, New Jersey supreme court, 1901-08; chancellor, New Jersey, 1908-12. Resigned from Supreme Court of United States December 31, 1922.

66 (56). JAMES CLARK McREYNOLDS (February 2, 1862-August 24, 1946). Born Elkton, Kentucky; A. B., Vanderbilt University, 1882; LL. B., University of Virginia, 1884; admitted to bar in Tennessee, 1884; general practice, 1884-1903, 1907-13; Assistant Attorney General, 1903-07; Attorney General, 1913-14. Retired from Supreme Court of United States, February 1, 1941.

67 (60). LOUIS DEMBITZ BRANDEIS (November 13, 1856-October 5, 1941). Born Louisville, Kentucky; studied privately and received LL. B., Harvard Law School, 1877; admitted to practice in Missouri, 1878; in Massachusetts, 1879; general practice, 1878-1916; "People's Attorney" for Public Franchise League and Massachusetts State Board of Trade, 1897-1911; counsel, New England Policyholders' Protective Committee, 1905; special counsel in wage and hour cases from California, Illinois, Ohio and Oregon, 1907-14; counsel for *Collier's Weekly* in Ballinger-Pinchot case, 1910; chairman of arbitration board, New York garment workers' labor disputes, 1910-16. Retired from Supreme Court of United States, February 13, 1939.

68 (62). JOHN HESSIN CLARKE (September 18, 1857-March 22, 1945). Born Lisbon, Ohio; completed legal studies at Western Reserve University, 1877; admitted to practice in Ohio, 1878; general practice, Ohio, 1878-1914; judge, United States District Court, 1914-16. Resigned from Supreme Court of United States to work for world peace, September 18, 1922.

Recapitulation

The members of Chief Justice White's Court presented a total of 176 years of private practice, ranging from a minimum of twelve to a maximum of thirty-eight with an average of twenty-five. Four of them had had extended judicial experience, with Justice Pitney having accounted for almost half of this total as both justice and chancellor of the New Jersey high courts. Pitney had also had extended legislative experience in both Trenton and Washington, and Justice Hughes had been governor of New York. Brandeis, Hughes and Mc-Reynolds had attracted national attention in their work as special counsel for a number of investigatory commissions during the Progressive Era.

Hughes, who held a master's degree as well as the usual baccalaureate and professional law degrees, had also taught law at Cornell for two years. Only Pitney had followed the older practice of reading for the bar without formal law school preparation. Undergraduate colleges represented included Bethany College, Brown, Colgate, DePauw, Georgia, Princeton and Vanderbilt; law schools attended in whole or in part were Cincinnati, Columbia, Harvard, Virginia, Washington and Lee, and Western Reserve.

4. The Court Under Taft, 1921-1930

The Taft Court was remarkably stable throughout the decade of the twenties, as the text points out. Holmes, Brandeis, McReynolds and Van Devanter continued through this decade. The five new members of the Court should be considered, in the summaries which follow, in the light of the combined total of forty-three years of prior experience on the Supreme Court itself, represented by their seniors. Such significance as this relationship may have is discussed in the text.

Name of Justice	President Nominating	Date of Nomination	Date of Confirmation	Vote on Confirmation	Date of Commission	Date of Swearing-in
Taft	Harding	6-30-21	6-30-21	*	6-30-21	10- 3-21
Sutherland	Harding	9- 5-22	9- 5-22		9- 5-22	10- 2-22
Butler	Harding	11-23-22	12-21-22	61- 8	12-21-22	1- 2-23
Sanford	Harding	1-24-23	1-29-23		1-29-23	2-19-23
Stone	Coolidge	1- 5-25	2- 5-25	71- 6	2- 5-25	3- 2-25

*Confirmed in executive session; no recorded vote, but four Senators were reported in opposition. Cf. *New York Times,* July 1, 1921.

69 (55). *Tenth Chief Justice.* WILLIAM HOWARD TAFT (September 15, 1857-March 8, 1930). Born Cincinnati, Ohio; A. B., Yale University, 1878; LL. B., Cincinnati Law School, 1880; admitted to bar in Ohio, 1880; practiced law intermittently, 1880-87; assistant prosecuting attorney, Hamilton County, Ohio, 1881; collector of internal revenue, Cincinnati, 1882; judge, Ohio superior court, 1887-90; United States Solicitor General, 1890-92; judge, Circuit Court of Appeals, 1892-1900; President, Philippine Commission, 1900-04; Secretary of War, 1904-08; President of United States, 1909-13; professor of law, Yale University, 1913-21; joint chairman, War Labor Board, 1918. Resigned from Supreme Court of United States, February 3, 1930.

70 (68). GEORGE SUTHERLAND (March 25, 1862-July 18, 1942). Born Buckinghamshire, England; studied law at University of Michigan and was admitted to bar in Utah, 1883; general practice in Utah, with specialties in railroad law, 1883-1901, 1903-04, 1917-22; served in Utah legislature, 1896; United States House of Representatives, 1901-03; United States Senate, 1905-17. Retired from Supreme Court of United States, January 18, 1938.

71 (59). PIERCE BUTLER (March 17, 1866-November 16, 1939). Born Northfield, Minnesota; studied at Carleton College and read law, being admitted to bar in Minnesota, 1888; general practice, with specialty in railroad law, 1888-91, 1897-1922; assistant county attorney, 1891-93; county attorney, 1893-97.

72 (65).   EDWARD TERRY SANFORD (July 23, 1865-March 8, 1930). Born Knoxville, Tennessee; studied at University of Tennessee and received A. B., Harvard College, 1885; LL. B., Harvard Law School, 1889; admitted to bar in Tennessee, 1888; general practice in Tennessee, 1889-1907; Assistant Attorney General, 1907-09; judge, United States District Court, 1909-23.

73 (57).   HARLAN FISKE STONE (October 11, 1872-April 22, 1946). Born Chesterfield, New Hampshire; A. B., Amherst College, 1894; LL. B., Columbia University, 1898; admitted to bar in New York, 1899; general practice in New York, 1899-1903, 1905-10, 1923-25; professor of law, Columbia University, 1903-05, 1910-23, and dean, 1915-23; Attorney General, 1924-25. *Twelfth Chief Justice.*

Recapitulation

The five new men on the Court under Taft had seventy-nine years of practice, an average of sixteen years apiece. Two had had prior judicial experience—fourteen years on the Federal District Court for Justice Sanford, three on state courts and eight on the Federal Court of Appeals for Taft. Taft's four years in the Philippines, four on the Roosevelt Cabinet and four as President of the United States, of course, represented a unique administrative record. Stone's fifteen years as a professor of law was also unique among the records of the Justices.

Undergraduate schools represented among the new appointees of this period included Amherst, Carleton, Harvard, Tennessee and Yale. Among the four who prepared for the bar through law school in whole or in part, the schools represented included Cincinnati, Columbia, Harvard, and Michigan.

The Court Under Hughes, 1930-32

The Hughes Court and its successors will be treated in the corresponding Appendices in the companion volume to this study. However, it is worth noting, for the period from Taft's resignation to the end of the term of Court in June 1932, that President Hoover made three nominations which were approved and one which was rejected, within this period of twenty-eight months. The Hughes, Parker and Roberts nominations, and the debates in the Senate over the first two, constitute a kind of valedictory to the Old Legality; Cardozo's appointment to succeed Holmes, although chronologically within this same period, belongs ideologically with the events preparing the way for the New Legality. More detailed reference to the Hughes Court as a whole, in any case, is left for the companion volume.

Attorneys General from 1889 to 1932

This study of the Court and the Constitution has included some suggestions of the role of the chief legal officers of the government in encouraging or restraining the prosecution of litigation. The personalities and professional sympathies of men like Olney and Harmon in the first decade of the Sherman

Act, and of men like Theodore Roosevelt's three Attorneys General in the era of trust-busting, or of Wickersham in Taft's administration, are definite factors in the definition of the major constitutional issues of their eras. How definite their influence on events may have been, the limitations of space and the paucity of available documents did not permit to be fully explored.

There is enough, it is hoped, which has been set out in the preceding pages to suggest a degree of significance in the role of the Department of Justice. As a Cabinet officer, of course, the Attorney General may be assumed to be the chief agent of administrative policy in such fields as anti-trust activity, labor law and the assertion of Federal power in general. A brief summary of the backgrounds of the occupants of this Cabinet seat from Cleveland's first administration to the end of Hoover's, accordingly, is a desirable complement to the biographical abstracts on the members of the Court themselves.

AUGUSTUS H. GARLAND (June 11, 1832-January 26, 1899). Practiced law in Arkansas, 1850-61, 1865-74; member of Congress of the Confederate States, 1861-65; pardoned by President Andrew Johnson for his service in rebellion against the United States, and successfully challenged the constitutionality of a Congressional loyalty oath statute which would have disbarred him from practice (*Ex parte Garland,* 4 Wall. 333). Governor of Arkansas, 1874-76; United States Senator, 1877-85; Attorney General, 1885-89; practiced law in Washington until his death.

WILLIAM HENRY HARRISON MILLER (September 6, 1840-May 25, 1917). Studied law under the later Chief Justice Morrison R. Waite; practiced in Indiana, 1866-89, most of the time as Benjamin Harrison's law partner; Attorney General, 1889-93; resumed law practice until retirement in 1910.

RICHARD OLNEY (September 15, 1835-April 8, 1917). LL. B., Harvard Law School, 1858; practiced in Boston, 1859-93; Attorney General, 1893-95; Secretary of State, 1895-97; resumed law practice until his death.

JUDSON HARMON (February 3, 1846-February 22, 1927), LL. B., Cincinnati Law School, 1868; practiced in Ohio, 1869-76, 1887-95, 1897-1908; judge, superior court, 1878-87; Attorney General, 1895-97; Governor of Ohio, 1908-12.

JOSEPH McKENNA (see data under first part of this Appendix).

JOHN W. GRIGGS (July 10, 1849-November 28, 1927). Practiced law in New Jersey, 1871-95, while also serving in state legislature at various periods, and as city counsel for Paterson, 1879-82; Governor of New Jersey, 1895-98; Attorney General, 1898-1901; member, Permanent Court of Arbitration, 1901-12; practiced law in New York, 1912-27.

PHILANDER CHASE KNOX (May 6, 1853-October 12, 1921). Practiced law in western Pennsylvania, 1875-1901; Attorney General, 1901-04; appointed to United States Senate and served, 1904-09; Secretary of State, 1909-13; resumed law practice until elected to Senate, serving from 1917 to his death.

WILLIAM H. MOODY (see data under first part of this Appendix).

CHARLES J. BONAPARTE (June 9, 1851-June 28, 1921). LL. B., Harvard Law School. Practiced law in Baltimore, 1874-1906; Attorney General, 1906-09; returned to law practice, 1909-21. Founder of National Civil Service Reform League and National Municipal League.

GEORGE W. WICKERSHAM (September 19, 1858-January 25, 1936). LL. B., University of Pennsylvania. Practiced law in Philadelphia, 1880-83, then in New York, 1883-1909; Attorney General, 1909-13; resumed practice in partnership with brother of William Howard Taft; chairman of National Commission on Law Observance and Enforcement (Wickersham Commission), 1929-31.

JAMES C. McREYNOLDS (see data under first part of this Appendix).

THOMAS W. GREGORY (November 6, 1861-February 26, 1933). Law study, Univ. of Virginia, 1883-84; LL. B., Univ. of Texas, 1885. Practiced law in Texas, 1885-1914, serving also as Austin city attorney, 1891-94. Attorney General, 1914-19, resigning to enter law practice in Washington, 1920-25, after which he retired to Texas.

A. MITCHELL PALMER (May 4, 1872-May 11, 1936). Practiced law in Pennsylvania, 1893-1908; member of United States House of Representatives, 1908-15; Alien Property Custodian, 1917-19; Attorney General, 1919-21; practiced law in District of Columbia, 1921-36.

HARRY M. DAUGHERTY (January 26, 1860-October 12, 1941). LL. B., Univ. of Michigan, 1881. Practiced law in Ohio, 1881-1921, also serving in Ohio legislature, 1890-94. Attorney General, 1921-24, resigning as a result of the oil scandals; acquitted of charges of conspiracy to defraud, 1927.

HARLAN F. STONE (see data under first part of this Appendix).

JOHN G. SARGENT (October 13, 1860-March 5, 1939). Practiced in Vermont, 1890-1908, 1913-24, 1929-39. County attorney, 1898-1900; secretary of civil and military affairs for Vermont, 1900-02; attorney general of Vermont, 1908-12; Attorney General, 1925-29.

WILLIAM D. MITCHELL (September 7, 1874-August 24, 1955). LL. B., Univ. of Minnesota, 1896; practiced law in Minnesota, 1896-1925; Solicitor General, 1925-29; Attorney General, 1929-33; practiced law in New York City, 1933 to retirement.

Solicitors General from 1889 to 1932

Attorneys General sought their chief trial officers from among experienced attorneys, who in many cases left private practice only long enough to discharge the duties of this office, although some were career men in politics and public service. While the effectiveness of the Solicitors General depended fundamentally upon the general policy which their superiors in charge of the Department of Justice were prepared to advance, the ultimate success of government prosecutions depended upon the skill with which attorneys under the Solicitor General prepared the government's cases. Taft, Hoyt, Bowers, Davis and Beck were considered by contemporary professionals to have been among the best legal craftsmen in the group for this period.

GEORGE A. JENKS (March 26, 1836-February 10, 1908). Practiced law in Pennsylvania, 1860-85; member of Congress, 1875-77; Assistant Secretary of Interior, 1885-86; Solicitor General, 1886-89; resumed private practice thereafter.

ORLOW W. CHAPMAN (January 7, 1832-January 19, 1890). Practiced law in New York, 1858-71, 1876-89; state superintendent of insurance, 1871-76; Solicitor General, 1889 to death.

WILLIAM HOWARD TAFT (see data under first part of this Appendix).

CHARLES H. ALDRICH (August 28, 1850-April 15, 1929). Practiced law in Indiana, 1876-86, in Illinois, 1886-92, 1894 to retirement. Solicitor General, 1892-93.

LAWRENCE MAXWELL, JR. (May 4, 1853-February 18, 1927). LL. B., Cincinnati Law School, 1875; practiced in Ohio, 1875-93; Solicitor General, 1893-95; professor of law, Cincinnati Law School, 1896-1912, and visiting lecturer in law, Univ. of Michigan, 1909-16; leader of civic affairs in Cincinnati, 1916-27.

HOLMES CONRAD (January 14, 1840-September 4, 1915). Studied law, Univ. of Virginia, 1860; served in Confederate Army; practiced in Virginia and District of Columbia, 1864-95; Assistant Attorney General, 1895; Solicitor General, 1895-97; resumed practice in Washington, 1898-1914; professor of law, Georgetown University, 1914-15.

JOHN K. RICHARDS (March 15, 1856-March 1, 1909). Practiced in Ohio, 1880-92; city solicitor, Ironton, 1885-89; in state legislature, 1890-92; Ohio attorney general, 1892-96; Solicitor General, 1897-1903; United States Circuit Court judge, 1903-09.

HENRY M. HOYT (December 5, 1856-November, 1910). LL. B. Univ. of Pennsylvania, 1881; practiced in Philadelphia and New York, 1886-97, and also served as officer of banking and investment houses, 1883-93; Assistant Attorney General, 1897-1903; Solicitor General, 1903-09; counsel for Department of State, 1909-10.

LLOYD W. BOWERS (March 9, 1859-September 9, 1910). LL. B., Columbia Law School, 1882; practiced in New York, 1882-93; general counsel, Chicago & Northwestern R. Co., 1893-1909; Solicitor General, 1909 until death.

FREDERICK W. LEHMANN (February 28, 1853-September 12, 1933). Practiced in Nebraska, 1873-76, in Iowa, 1876-90, in Missouri, 1890-1910, 1913 to retirement. Solicitor General, 1910-12. Leader in civic affairs in St. Louis.

WILLIAM M. BULLITT (March 4, 1873-October 3, 1957). LL. B., Univ. of Louisville, 1895; practiced in Kentucky, 1894-1957, except for service as Solicitor General, 1912-13; member of boards of directors of numerous banking and philanthropic organizations; special counsel to government, 1921-22 and 1924-25.

JOHN W. DAVIS (April 13, 1873-March 24, 1955). LL. B., Washington & Lee Univ., 1895; professor of law, same, 1896-97; practiced law in West Virginia, 1897-1913; Solicitor General, 1913-18; Ambassador to Great Britain, 1918-21; founded law firm in New York in 1921 and continued practice there until retirement. Democratic candidate for President, 1924.

ALEXANDER C. KING (December 7, 1856-July 25, 1926). Practiced in Georgia, 1875-1918, including serving as general counsel for several railroads. Solicitor General, 1918-20; judge, United States Circuit Court of Appeals, 1920-26.

WILLIAM L. FRIERSON (September 3, 1868-May 25, 1953). Practiced in Tennessee, 1889-1905, 1909-16; mayor of Chattanooga, 1905-09; city attorney, 1912-15; special judge, Tennessee supreme court, 1916; Assistant Attorney General, 1917-20; Solicitor General, 1920-21; resumed practice, 1921 to retirement.

JAMES M. BECK (July 9, 1861-April 12, 1936). Admitted to bar in Pennsylvania and practiced there, 1884-86; United States District Attorney, 1886-1900; Assistant Attorney General of United States, 1901-03; practiced in New York and Washington, 1903-21, 1925-27; Solicitor General, 1921-25; member, House of Representatives, 1927-34; author of several books, including *The Passing of the New Freedom* (1920), *The Constitution of the United States* (1922), *Vanishing Rights of the States* (1926), *Our Wonderland of Bureaucracy* (1933).

WILLIAM D. MITCHELL (see data under Attorneys General).

CHARLES EVANS HUGHES, Jr. (November 30, 1889-January 21, 1950). LL. B., Harvard Law School, 1912; practiced in New York City, 1912-13; law clerk to Judge Benjamin N. Cardozo, 1914; practiced in Horace Taft's law firm, 1914-16, then founded own law firm, 1916-29; Solicitor General, 1929-30; resumed practice until retirement.

THOMAS D. THACHER (September 10, 1881-November 12, 1950). Studied law, Yale Law School, 1904-06; practiced in New York City; 1906-25; Assistant United States Attorney, Southern District of New York, 1907-08; United States District Court judge, 1925-30; Solicitor General, 1930-33; resumed law practice, 1933-43; New York City corporation counsel, 1943; judge, New York court of appeals, 1943-48.

Appendix B

Proposed Constitutional Amendments, 1889-1932

In 1896 the American Historical Association published a detailed study by H. V. Ames of the University of Pennsylvania on *The Proposed Amendments to the Constitution of the United States During the First Century of Its History*. This work, covering the period 1789-1889, has been complemented by several equally useful compilations covering most of the three-quarters of a century since.[3] While the constitutional propositions represented by the proposed amendments are attributable to Congress or, in the preponderance of cases, to the constituents of individual Congressmen, the subject matter nevertheless tells us something of the constitutional or political ideas of each era. Congress' role as a buffer between the emotional responses of the general public—often in reaction to an unpopular judicial decision—and the independent process of constitutional interpretation by the courts is attested by the literally thousands of proposals which have been advanced in the course of time, introduced *pro forma* and then forgotten.

As of the end of 1968 twenty-five Amendments to the Constitution have been adopted (and five rejected). The first twelve were adopted within fifteen years of the Constitution itself. Three were added in the nineteenth century—and the remaining ten in the twentieth century to date, perhaps reflecting the accelerating social and economic processes of the period covered by the present study.

The present Appendix consisting of Tables I to IV lists the principal subjects in proposed amendments for the decades from the nineties to the beginning of the thirties (that is, Table I covers twelve years as does Table IV).

The statistics were derived primarily from the Congressional compilations which followed the Ames study, but the numerical count of specific proposals differs between the totals in these Tables and those in the Congressional compilations. This is explained by the fact that in the Tables, in order to illustrate more explicitly the variety of subjects proposed as amendments to the Constitution, the several subjects occasionally covered by a single proposed amendment in the compilations have been distributed under separate headings in the Tables.

TABLE I. Proposed Amendments, 1889-1900

Subjects of Proposed Amendments	Congresses and Sessions														
	51st/1st	51st/2nd	52nd/1st	52nd/2nd	53rd/Sp.	53rd/1st	53rd/2nd	53rd/3rd	54th/1st	54th/2nd	55th/1st	55th/2nd	55th/3rd	56th/1st	56th/2nd
Alien suffrage prohibited								2	2						
Amendments: repeal of XV				1					1			2		1	1
referenda on interpretation									1		1	1	1		1
Annexation, admission of states									1		1		1	2	
Anti-lottery provision	2		1												
Anti-trust and related subjects	2		1				1							5	1
Cabinet, eligibility of Congressmen			1							1				1	
Congress: biennial sessions			1												
jurisdiction over crimes	2														
jurisdiction over finance			4												
District of Columbia representation	2														
Domestic relations*	3		4				1		2		2		1	14	1
House of Representatives: elections	1								2		2				1
length of terms							1			2	1			3	
size of membership		1								1					2
Judiciary: eligibility to other offices						1									
limitation of terms							1					1			
popular elections												1		2	
reorganization of courts															
Labor: regulation of hours							1		1		1	1		2	
Legislation: sectarian, prohibited								1	3		2			1	
special, prohibited							1								
Pensions, generally			1									1			
Postmasters: popular elections	3		1												
President: item veto	3		1				3		4		2				

*Includes proposals to disqualify polygamists from public office.

TABLE I. Proposed Amendments, 1889-1900 (Cont'd.)

Subjects of Proposed Amendments	Congresses and Sessions														
	51st/1st	51st/2nd	52nd/1st	52nd/2nd	53rd/Sp.	53rd/1st	53rd/2nd	53rd/3rd	54th/1st	54th/2nd	55th/1st	55th/2nd	55th/3rd	56th/1st	56th/2nd
President (cont'd.)															
limit to veto power									1						
length of term	3		4			1				2			1	3	
number of terms	1		3				1	4							
popular elections	2		7	4		2	1		1						
second Vice-President			1												
succession to President									1					1	
Prohibition of alc. bev.	2							1							
Religion: in public schools	1														
acknowledgement of God							2		3					1	
Senate: popular elections	9	3	25		1	12	2		10		5	1	1	11	
ratification of treaties													1	1	
vacancies, how filled											1				
Taxation: direct, indirect, defined							2		4		1	1			
income tax									1		6	2		10	
miscel. tax plans									1		1			1	
uniform, defined									1					1	
Terms of President, Congress (time of beginning)	7		6		1	1					1				
Woman suffrage	3	1	1	1	2		2		4		1	1		2	
Total amendments proposed	47	4	59	5	2	17	19	8	41	5	27	16	4	63	7
Total reported out of committee	3		7					1			2	2	2	6	
reported out adversely	2		3											6	
debated	3		1								1	2	2	1	1
Total passed by one House											1	2	2	1	1

TABLE II. Proposed Amendments, 1901-1910

Subjects of Proposed Amendments	57th/1st	57th/2nd	58th/1st	58th/2nd	58th/3rd	59th/1st	59th/2nd	60th/1st	60th/2nd	61st/1st	61st/2nd	61st/3rd
Amendments: repeal of XIV	2		1			2	2	2	2	1	2	
repeal of XV			3			3	3	5	5	3		1
Amendments: procedure	2											
Anarchists: deportation, imprisonment	2											
Annexation, etc.	1											
Anti-trust, etc.	5	2		1		1		1				1
Claims against U. S.											1	
Congress: jurisdiction over crime	2											
recall of members								1				
Convict labor, regulation of								1				
District of Columbia representation		1										
Domestic relations	7	4		1		2	1	5	1		1	
Employers' liability							1	1				
Government officers generally:												
popular elections								1				
recall or removal						1						
selection						1						
House of Representatives: elections	1					2						
length of terms					1	2		2			2	
size of membership	1			1	1							
Initiative and referendum								1				
Insurance: Federally issued						1		1				
regulation of private companies						1						
Judiciary: jurisdiction	1			1		1	1	1			2	

TABLE II. Proposed Amendments, 1901-1910 (Cont'd.)

Subjects of Proposed Amendments	Congresses and Sessions											
	57th/1st	57th/2nd	58th/1st	58th/2nd	58th/3rd	59th/1st	59th/2nd	60th/1st	60th/2nd	61st/1st	61st/2nd	61st/3rd
Judiciary (cont'd.)												
limitation of terms								2				
popular elections	1		1	1			3	4			1	
Labor: maximum hours	2		1	1		1		2				
Legislation: limitations on private bills				1			1	1			1	
sectarian, prohibited	1		1			1		1				
Limitations on fortunes and property		2	1	1		1				1		
Postmasters: popular elections							1	1				
President: election by House of Rep.											1	
item veto	2											
limit to veto												1
length of term			1		2	2	2	4	1	1		1
number of terms					2	2	1	2	1	2		
succession to President	2					1	1	3	3	1	1	
Prohibition of alc. bev.								1				
Railroads, regulation of								2				
Religion: acknowledgement of God									1	1		
Senate: length of term					1	1						
popular elections	9	1	4	1	7	7	1	13		4	7	2
vacancies, how filled	1											
Taxation: direct, defined	2		1	1		1		1			1	
income tax	6		2	1	2	2	1	7		4	1	
inheritance tax, etc.	1									1		
Terms of President, Congress (time of beginning)	4	1		3	3	6	3	3		5	9	
Treason, defined	2											

TABLE II. Proposed Amendments, 1901-1910 (Cont'd.)

Subjects of Proposed Amendments	Congresses and Sessions											
	57th/1st	57th/2nd	58th/1st	58th/2nd	58th/3rd	59th/1st	59th/2nd	60th/1st	60th/2nd	61st/1st	61st/2nd	61st/3rd
Woman suffrage	3		1	1		1		2			3	
Total amendments proposed	58	10	17	10	7	40	12	71	7	26	31	8
Total reported out of committee						2			1	2	1	1
reported out adversely							1					
debated						1			1	2	1	1
Number passed by one house									1			
Number passed by both houses, submitted*									1			

*Became Sixteenth Amendment.

TABLE III. Proposed Amendments, 1911-1920

Congresses and Sessions

Subjects of Proposed Amendments	62nd/1st	62nd/2nd	62nd/3rd	63rd/1st	63rd/2nd	63rd/3rd	64th/1st	64th/2nd	65th/1st	65th/2nd	65th/3rd	66th/1st	66th/2nd	66th/3rd
Alien suffrage, restriction				1				2	1	8		1	3	
Amendments: repeal of XI				1										
repeal of XIV	2	1		2										
repeal of XV	1	1		2			1						1	
repeal of XVIII												2	1	
Amendments—procedure	2	2	1	6	3	1	3	2	4	1	1	11	2	
Anti-lynching authority											1			
Anti-trust, etc.	1				1									
Bearing arms; militia					2		3							
Claims against U. S.	1													
Congress: recall							1		1					1
initiative/referendum			1											
Constitutional convention	1							1						
Constitutionality, judicial review		1	1	1			1	1	1			1		
Controls over foods and fuels									1					
Domestic relations			1	2			2	1	3	1		3		
Farm ownership, promoting of								1		1				
Government officers: length of term					1		2		1					
popular elections		1			1		1	1						
recall or removal		2	2											
House of Representatives: elections												1		
lengths of terms	3	1	1	1	3	1	6		3	1				
size of membership														5
Vice-President, former, as member									1					
Impeachment proceedings			1											
Insurance: Federal control of		1			2									

TABLE III. Proposed Amendments, 1911-1920 (Cont'd.)

Subjects of Proposed Amendments	Congresses and Sessions													
	62nd/1st	62nd/2nd	62nd/3rd	63rd/1st	63rd/2nd	63rd/3rd	64th/1st	64th/2nd	65th/1st	65th/2nd	65th/3rd	66th/1st	66th/2nd	66th/3rd
Judiciary: abolition or reorganization of				1										
appointment of Sup. Ct. Justices					1									
disqualification for other offices							1		2					
jurisdiction	2			1			3		2					
limitation of terms	1	5		2	2	1	2		1	2		2		
popular elections		6		1	2		2		1	2	1		1	
Labor: maximum hours			1	1			1			1	1			
prohibiting child labor										2		1		
women, hours of					1					1		1		
Legislation: single subject to bill							1							
sectarian, prohibited									1					
Limitations on fortunes and property					1			1						
Migratory bird administration	1													
Postmasters: popular elections					2									
President: electoral process, change				1			1							
item veto	3			3	2	3	4	4	2	2		3		
limit to veto		1	1	1						2				
length of term	1	6	3	9	1	1	5	1	1				1	
number of terms	1	7	3	9	1	1	4	1	2				1	
nomination procedure														1
popular election	3	3	3	9	2		5	7	2					2
Presidential primary			1	1										
succession (disability)													2	
Prohibition of alc. bev.		1		5	6	3	10	1	13					
Senate: abolition of	1													
bills, procedure on							2							

TABLE III. Proposed Amendments, 1911-1920 (Cont'd.)

Subjects of Proposed Amendments	Congresses and Sessions													
	62nd/1st	62nd/2nd	62nd/3rd	63rd/1st	63rd/2nd	63rd/3rd	64th/1st	64th/2nd	65th/1st	65th/2nd	65th/3rd	66th/1st	66th/2nd	66th/3rd
Senate (cont'd.)														
popular elections	16	1												
President, former, as member						1	1					1	1	
treaty ratification									1			1	1	2
waiver of immunity								1						
Suffrage, denial of					1		1	1	1			1		
Tariff commission							1	1						
Taxation: inheritance and excise					2									
miscellaneous proposals	1	1		1	1								1	1
Terms of President, Congress														
(times of beginning)	4	1		3	1	1	3	1	2		1			3
Trade marks	1			1										
War powers: limit on	1				1	1	2		1	1	1	1		
peace agency established							1							
Woman suffrage	3	4	6	6	3		9	2	11	7	5	13		
Total amendments proposed	46	46	20	70	44	11	78	28	57	27	9	42	15	15
Total reported out of committee	1	4		2	4		1		5	1	1	1		
reported out adversely										1				
debated	1	2*		2	4		1		4	1	1	1	1	
Number passed by one house	1	1							1	1		1		
Number passed by both houses, submitted	1‡								1§			1†		

*One withdrawn. ‡Became Seventeenth Amendment. §Became Eighteenth Amendment.
†Became Nineteenth Amendment.

TABLE IV. Proposed Amendments, 1921-1932

Subjects of Proposed Amendments	67th/1st	67th/2nd	67th/3rd	67th/4th	68th/1st	68th/2nd	69th/1st	69th/2nd	70th/1st	70th/2nd	71st/1st	71st/2nd	71st/3rd	72nd/1st	72nd/2nd
Aliens, disabilities, etc.	2				3		1		3		4	2		1	
Amendments: repeal of XVI		1													2
repeal of XVIII	1	3			3		6	6	9		7	5	7	30	12
Amendments: procedure	10			2	8		6		4		4	4		15	3
Congress: campaign activ. and expend.	1				2		1		1						
campaign procedure	2	2			3		1		1		1				
convening without call of Pres.		1			1										
primary elections	3														
qualifications generally								1	1		1				
waiver of immunity									1		2			1	
Constitutional convention				1		1									
Constitutionality, judicial review				1	1										
Criminal jurisdiction												1		1	
District of Columbia suffrage	2			2	2		2	1	2		2	2		2	
Domestic relations	5		2	2	7		4		4		1				
Equal rights for sexes				2	2		2		2		2			1	
Fuel production, control of		1													
Food prices. control of					1		1								
Government officers: elections	2			1					2						1
recall or removal															
House of Representatives: apportionment (general)														3	
apportionment by professions	1														
concurrent treaty power												1		1	
length of term	2		1	1	1		1				1				
limit on members' wealth						1									

TABLE IV. Proposed Amendments, 1921-1932 (Cont'd.)

Subjects of Proposed Amendments	Congresses and Sessions														
	67th/1st	67th/2nd	67th/3rd	67th/4th	68th/1st	68th/2nd	69th/1st	69th/2nd	70th/1st	70th/2nd	71st/1st	71st/2nd	71st/3rd	72nd/1st	72nd/2nd
House of Representatives (cont'd.)															
limit on number of members	5	1			4	1	2		1	3	1	1	1	2	
vacancies, how filled	1	1			1										
Interstate and foreign commerce								1	1						
Judiciary: appointment of Sup. Ct. Justices					1		1								
limitation of terms	1														
popular election					1		1		1		1	1		2	
Jury trials															
Labor: maximum hours	2									2		1	1	2	1
prohibiting child labor		15		8	29		2			1			1		
women's hours and wages	1	1			4		1		1	1					
Legislation: "concurrent powers"	1								1			1			
sectarian, prohibited											1				
Philippine independence															
President: abolish Electoral College									1		4	1	1	2	
item veto	2				2		1		1	1	1			2	
length of term	1	1		1	2				2						2
number of terms	1			1	2		1								
popular elections	1	2		3	4	1			1		1	2		2	
Presidential disability	1														
Presidential primary				1	1										
treaty powers, limitation									1						
Religion: public money prohibited							1		1						
freedom of, reiterated									1						
Senate: electoral procedure												1			

TABLE IV. Proposed Amendments, 1921–1932 (Cont'd.)

Subjects of Proposed Amendments	Congresses and Sessions														
	67th/1st	67th/2nd	67th/3rd	67th/4th	68th/1st	68th/2nd	69th/1st	69th/2nd	70th/1st	70th/2nd	71st/1st	71st/2nd	71st/3rd	72nd/1st	72nd/2nd
Senate (cont'd.)															
limit on wealth of members							1								
President, former, as ex-officio member										1					
treaty ratification	2				2		1								
Tariff court or commission		1													
Taxation: states' securities taxable	2	3		1	10	1	3				1			7	3
profits, securities taxable	1				1				3						
Treason, defined	1	1			2										
Territory: annexation policy	1														
extension of Amendment XVIII to											1				
Terms of President, Congress (time of beginning)	3			3	10		8		6	2	3	2	1	12	
War (including conscription)	1	2			7		6		5	2	3	2	1	8	
Total amendments proposed	57	37	1	25	117	5	30	10	56	12	38	24	11	144	24
Total reported out of committee					4		1		1	1			3	12	3
debated					7		1		1				1	5	2
Number passed by one house					1		1		1					3	2
Number passed by both houses, submitted					1*									1§	1‡

*Child Labor Amendment (not ratified)   § Became Twentieth Amendment   ‡ Became Twenty-first Amendment

Appendix C

Statutes on the Federal Judiciary, 1889-1932

The Judiciary Act of 1789 established a three-level system of Federal courts which continued with little substantive change for the next century. Under this organic statute, the Supreme Court of the United States was defined exclusively as an appellate review court, except for the limited original jurisdiction stipulated in Article III of the Constitution. The other two types of courts in the Federal system were essentially trial courts which divided the subject-matter of their jurisdiction between themselves: the District Courts were limited to admiralty suits, criminal cases and a few other narrowly defined areas; the Circuit Courts (not to be confused with the later Circuit Courts of Appeals) were the chief trial courts in the Federal structure.

The original states were divided into individual districts for the District Courts, and into three circuits for the Circuit Courts, which were to be presided over by two (later one) of the Justices of the Supreme Court together with the District Court judge of the state where the Circuit Court was sitting. In certain cases the Circuit Court might review cases appealed from the District Court, but the early process of judicial review was normally from any Federal trial court to the Supreme Court, through a system of appeal or, in cases appealed from state courts, on writ of error.[4]

The system, for a small new nation, was reasonably efficacious, although various practical difficulties demanded (and often failed to receive) attention as the country began to grow. With the admission of each new state, the circuit system had to be revised by Congress, while the inconvenience of having Supreme Court Justices ride circuit—particularly after the volume of appellate business began to grow—more than offset the hypothetical advantage of having them keep in touch with the country at the trial level. The practice of circuit riding simply fell into disuse within the first half-century of national growth, but Congress did not get around to dealing formally with the problem until it created the intermediate appellate court system in 1891.

The original act of 1789 was a "compromise between the extreme Federalist view that the full extent of the judicial power granted by the Constitution should be vested by Congress in the Federal courts, and the view of those who feared the new government as a destroyer of the rights of the states, who wished all suits to be decided first in the state courts, and only on appeal by the Federal Supreme Court."[5] The first attempt at reform of the original system was made in the Judiciary Act of 1801; but the Jeffersonians excoriated the law as an attempt by the retiring Federalists to pack the judiciary with persons hostile to the incoming administration. Many of President John Adams' "midnight judges" never in fact filled their appointments, while an appointee under another last-minute statute, David Marbury, engaged in a famous suit with Secretary of State James Madison in a vain attempt to obtain his commission as a justice of the peace. The 1801 act was repealed the following spring by the Anti-Federalists, returning the judiciary to the status established by the 1789 statute and having as one of its unfortunate results "the creation of a precedent against . . . reform."[6]

For most of the nineteenth century, ushered in by this ideological dispute, Congressional enactments tended steadily to enlarge upon the work of the Federal judiciary without undertaking to revise or modernize the machinery of the courts themselves. Beginning in 1833, certain cases were permitted to be removed from state to Federal trial courts, thereby vastly increasing the business of the latter. A Court of Claims, first established in 1855 as a fact-finding agency, was converted into a specialized judicial body to hear claims against the United States in 1866; and since the latter date, appeals have been taken as of right directly to the Supreme Court. In 1869 Congress recognized the fact that most Justices did not consistently ride circuit by creating separate Circuit Court judgeships; but to the extent that this offered any relief to the Supreme Court itself, it was more than offset by the sweeping jurisdictional revision in the Act of 1875 which enlarged the business of the Federal trial courts to include every type of Federal question. The result was that the lower courts "ceased to be restricted tribunals [for suits] between citizens of different states and became the primary and powerful reliances for vindicating every right given by the Constitution, the laws and treaties of the United States."[7]

The fact was that the movement toward uniform, nationally adjudicated rights and liabilities had already set in; the geographic expansion of the country, the Congressional enactments on banking and bankruptcy in the 1860's, and the new Federal questions presented by the Civil War, Reconstruction and the Thirteenth, Fourteenth and Fifteenth Amendments—all added up to justiciable matters to be entertained only by Federal courts. They also added up to an unmanageable volume of work for these courts, so that with the beginning of the second century of national history—the period covered by the present study—the need for successive reforms of the judicial system became insistent. The select list which follows describes the principal legislative efforts of this period to make the judicial machinery more efficient and more responsive to the needs of a unified economic and social order.*

---

*The statutes briefly summarized here, of course, are only selective; a substantial number of other more routine judicial acts also were passed by Congress during this period.

March 3, 1891. Circuit Court of Appeals Act, Ch. 517, 26 Stat. 826.

The Circuit Court of Appeals Act was the first significant reform in the Federal judiciary system since it was established. The intermediate appellate courts created by the statute were given jurisdiction over all reviewable cases from the trial courts except for those entitled to a direct review by the Supreme Court (constitutional questions, construction of treaties, issues of jurisdiction, capital crimes and conflict of laws). The Circuit Courts of Appeals were given final jurisdiction in diversity of citizenship cases, issues litigated under admiralty, patent and revenue laws, and non-capital criminal convictions. The intermediate courts could certify specific questions to the Supreme Court for an opinion, and the Supreme Court could exercise its discretionary power of certiorari to bring up any cases from the appellate court for review.

February 9, 1893. District of Columbia Court of Appeals Act, Ch. 74, 27 Stat. 434.

Because all questions arising in the courts of the District of Columbia are technically Federal questions, much of the docket of the Supreme Court was taken up with relatively minor issues brought on appeal from the trial courts of the District. Since the 1891 statute had not provided for review of District of Columbia appeals in any of the intermediate courts, Congress undertook to correct this oversight by establishing a separate intermediate court within the District itself. The poor draftsmanship of the statute, however, left a number of anomalies in the appellate jurisprudence of the District which were resolved on only a piecemeal basis over a period of years.

July 1, 1898. Uniform Bankruptcy Act, Ch. 541, 30 Stat. 544.

Another oversight in the 1891 statute concerned the relief for the Supreme Court of the great volume of bankruptcy appeals, and the preemption of the subject matter by the Federal courts. The Bankruptcy Act of 1867, until its repeal a decade later, had placed a substantial burden on the Federal courts, but the alternative after repeal was an unsatisfactory confusion of jurisdictions between state and Federal courts. The 1898 statute reasserted exclusive original jurisdiction in the Federal trial courts, with appeal to the new intermediate courts and final review in the Supreme Court limited to cases in which the Court chose to grant certiorari.

February 11, 1903. Expediting Act, Ch. 544, 32 Stat. 823.

In a period of gradual revival of anti-trust activity after the earlier hamstringing of the Sherman Act, both the government and corporations complained of the long delay in determining the constitutionality of certain injunctions issued in anti-trust proceedings. This statute provided that Federal trial courts should give precedence to any suits arising out of an injunction petition, and that an appeal from the trial of such suits could be taken directly to the Supreme Court.

June 30, 1906. Immunity of Witnesses Act, Ch. 3920, 34 Stat. 798.

Following the findings of the Bureau of Corporations in its investigation of the Beef Trust, and the holding of the United States District Court in the initial prosecution of the Trust, that individuals who testified before the Interstate Commerce Commission or the Department of Commerce and Labor were to be immune from criminal liability for practices confessed in their testimony, President Roosevelt sought to have a statutory clarification of the original acts of 1893 and 1903 relating to immunity of witnesses before these agencies. Congress' only response was to stipulate in this statute that the immunity was limited to natural persons and did not extend to the corporations themselves.

March 3, 1909. Criminal Code. Ch. 321, 35 Stat. 1088.

This was the first part of a Congressional program for a comprehensive recapitulation of all statutory provisions concerned with judicial procedure in Federal courts. Because Federal criminal jurisdiction is limited to statutory, rather than to common-law, offenses, the codifying of such statutory crimes was urgently needed. Ch. 3, for example, collected all the then existing civil rights laws; Ch. 7 listed offenses by government officers; Ch. 8 the criminal violations of the postal laws.

June 25, 1910. Amended Expediting Act, Ch. 428, 36 Stat. 854.

This statute further facilitated the judicial process in anti-trust litigation by providing for the convening of three-judge trial courts upon a certification by the Attorney General of the public importance of the cause being litigated. The procedure involved the seeking of an interlocutory injunction by the government. The jurisdiction of three-judge courts was broadened in the judiciary acts of 1925 and 1948. Direct appeal for review lay to the Supreme Court.

March 3, 1911. Judicial Code. Ch. 231, 36 Stat. 1087.

This was the culminating statute in President Taft's program for modernizing the legislative provisions concerning the Federal courts. Under it the old Circuit Courts were abolished and the District Courts made the trial courts of general jurisdiction. The statute also took into account the specialized jurisdiction of two courts created in other ancillary enactments—the Court of Customs Appeals (today the Court of Customs and Patent Appeals), created in 1909 to review findings of the government boards of general appraisers under the tariff acts; and the Commerce Court, created in 1910 to review findings of the Interstate Commerce Commission but abolished in 1913 by popular demand in Congress. The Judicial Code undertook to remove a number of obsolete procedural laws from the statute rolls, extended the removal power to transfer causes from state to Federal courts, and enlarged the final appellate jurisdiction of the Circuit Courts of Appeals.

September 14, 1922. Judicial Conference and Transfer Act, Ch. 306, 42 Stat. 837.

Taft as Chief Justice undertook to continue the modernization program he had begun in his executive capacities a decade before. This statute—part of the "Judges' Bill" described in Chapter 16—authorized the creation of a conference of senior judges of the judicial circuits (enlarged to include other Federal judges as the conference idea proved its worth in later years) whose primary task was to "make a comprehensive survey of the conditions of business in the courts of the United States and prepare plans for assignment and transfer of judges" from districts with light dockets to others with overcrowded dockets.

February 13, 1925. Judicial Code Revision. Ch. 229, 43 Stat. 936.

This was the second major portion of Chief Justice Taft's plan for modernization of the judicial process, which Associate Justice Van Devanter helped steer through Congress. It substantially reduced the number of cases which would automatically come to the Supreme Court on appeals by broadening its discretionary power of certiorari. Judgments in the Court of Claims were made final, as were a broadened group of cases reviewed in the Circuit Courts of Appeals, which now were given final jurisdiction over bankruptcy cases, Federal Trade Commission orders and Interstate Commerce Commission orders under the Clayton Act, and most other subjects except those arising under anti-trust and interstate commerce statutes, appeals from three-judge courts, and certain criminal cases. Cases in state courts involving questions of state law repugnant to the Constitution or in conflict with treaties or statutes of the United States continued to come before the Supreme Court on writs of error.

January 31, 1928. Act Respecting Writs of Error. Ch. 14, 45 Stat. 54.

Writs of error were abolished in favor of simple appeals. This was a minor enactment but symptomatic of the final steps toward modernization and simplification of procedure which were carried out in the next decade by the Hughes Court.

March 23, 1932. Norris-LaGuardia Anti-Injunction Act, Ch. 90, 47 Stat. 828.

After the failure of an attempt to exempt labor organizations from the anti-trust provisions of the Clayton Act of 1913, a prolonged struggle in Congress eventually resulted in this act denying to Federal courts a jurisdiction to issue injunctions in labor disputes except in strictly defined cases. Section 2 of the statute declared the public policy of the United States to be the encouragement of free collective bargaining; Section 3 outlawed the "yellow-dog" contract. Attorney General William D. Mitchell considered the statute unconstitutional because of the latter provision, but Hoover signed it into law. The act signalled the end of the extreme anti-labor policies of the courts and anticipated the major labor statutes of the early New Deal.

Appendix D

Selected Acts of Congress, 1889-1932[*]

"I do not think the United States would come to an end if we lost our power to declare an act of Congress void," observed Justice Oliver Wendell Holmes in 1913; but he added: "I do think the Union would be imperiled if we could not make that declaration as to the laws of the several states."[8] Any review of the statutory provisions which have been invalidated over the years by the Supreme Court will strike the layman, at least, with the relatively high proportion of state laws and municipal ordinances, in contrast to Congressional enactments, which have been the subject of constitutional challenge. Throughout its history the Court has voided no more than a hundred Federal statutes, but more than 750 state and local laws. By far the majority of all such cases have been adjudicated since 1889.

Between 1803, when Chief Justice Marshall pronounced his broad doctrine of judicial review in *Marbury v. Madison* (1 Cr. 137), and 1888 when Fuller became Chief Justice, the Supreme Court invalidated seventeen Federal statutes, 127 state statutes and seven municipal ordinances. Moreover, the process of judicial review carried to the point of invalidating an act of Congress developed slowly; after the cornerstone decision in *Marbury,* more than half a century elapsed before the second such instance of invalidating in *Dred Scott v. Sandford,* 19 How. 393 (1857). But the steady acceleration of justiciable causes to come before the Court after the Civil War, as described in Appendix C, naturally increased the frequency with which legislative acts came to be subjected to judicial review. In the second century of our constitutional history to date, more than sixty Federal laws, 530 state statutes and seventy-five municipal ordinances have been voided.

Another dimension of constitutional change is discernible in the number of earlier decisions of the Court which have been overruled in the course of time. Up to 1889, twenty-three earlier judicial holdings had been reversed; since then, there have been more than ninety. Thus the statistics corroborate the acceleration of change, and the steady consolidating of a constitutional position affirming a predominant Federalism. Indeed, the constitutional decisions

---

[*]With tables of Federal, state and municipal laws invalidated and prior decisions overruled.

of the period from 1889 to 1932 (and through the first term of Franklin D. Roosevelt), hostile though they often were to either state or Federal regulation of the economic system, prepared the way for the movement which is to be described in the companion volume in this present study. For by creating a constitutional vacuum by the series of decisions which dominated the period from *Pollock* in 1895 to the invalidating of the NRA in the early New Deal, the Court found it imperative thereafter to confirm a new capacity in government and to define it as essentially (and often as exclusively) Federal.

A comprehensive list of Federal, state and local laws which have been voided, and judicial decisions which have been overruled, appears in *The Constitution of the United States of America* (Washington, rev. ed. 1965), compiled by the Legislative Reference Service of the Library of Congress, at pp. 1405-1551. This has provided the basis for the statistical tables which follow. The principal Federal statutes for the period 1889-1932, which illustrate Con-

The Fuller Court, 1889-1910

October Terms	Statutes and Ordinances Invalidated				Overruling Opinions
	U.S. Laws	State Laws	Mun. Ord.	Totals	
1889		2		2	
1890		7	1	8	1
1891		4		4	
1892					1
1893	1	1	1	3	
1894	1	2	1	4	1
1895		1		1	1
1896	1	4		5	
1897		3		3	
1898		8	1	9	
1899	2	2		4	
1900		3	1	4	
1901	1	1		2	
1902		3	1	4	
1903	1	3	1	5	
1904		1	3	4	
1905	1	3		4	
1906	1	3	2	6	
1907		4	1	5	
1908	2	3	1	6	
1909*	2	5		7	
Totals	13	63	14	90	4

*Term ended in June 1910; Fuller died July 4.

The White Court, 1910-1921

October	Statutes and Ordinances Invalidated				Overruling
Terms	U.S. Laws	State Laws	Mun. Ord.	Totals	Opinions
1910		9	1	10	
1911	2	1		3	
1912	1	9	2	12	
1913		13	5	18	
1914		19	2	21	1
1915	1	22	1	24	
1916	1	5	1	7	1
1917		12	1	13	2
1918	1	7	3	11	2
1919		8	2	10	
1920*	4	12		16	
Totals	10	117	18	145	6

*White died May 19, 1921.

The Taft Court, 1921-1930 (through 1932)*

October	Statutes and Ordinances Invalidated				Overruling
Terms	U.S. Laws	State Laws	Mun. Ord.	Totals	Opinions
1921	2	9		11	
1922	3	15	1	19	1
1923	2	15	1	18	1
1924	1	6	2	9	
1925	1	14	1	16	1
1926	2	20	2	24	
1927	1	17	4	22	
1928	2	16		18	1
1929†		13		13	1
1930		13		13	2
1931	1	16		17	1
Totals	15	154	11	180	8

*Because the history of the Court in this volume is carried to the close of the 1931 Term of Court in June 1932, the first two and a half years of the Hughes Court have been included in this table.
†Taft resigned February 3, 1930.

gress' efforts to come to grips with changing economic and social issues and the Court's response to these efforts, then follow the tables. The principal state statutes and municipal ordinances are cited in the cases which held them invalid, and appear in the citations in Appendix E.

February 4, 1887. Interstate Commerce Act; Ch. 104, 24 Stat. 379.

This statute inaugurated the administrative regulatory process at the national level, following the initial regulatory processes introduced by the state Granger laws. The first Federal administrative agency, the Interstate Commerce Commission, was established to carry out Congressional proposals to compel railroads to maintain "reasonable and just" rates, abolish pooling, drawbacks and rebates where the effect was to place consumers or shippers at a disadvantage, forbid differentials in rates between long and short hauls over the same line, and empower the Commission to summon witnesses and compel the producing of books and papers in aid of its investigations.

Inherent weaknesses in the administrative machinery created by this pioneering statute, as well as excessively narrow interpretations of the law by the courts, led Congress over the years to enact a steady series of amendments. The most important for the period of the present volume were the Elkins Act of 1903, the Hepburn Act of 1906 and the Transportation Act of 1920, described below. Other amendments included an act of March 2, 1889 (Ch. 382, 25 Stat. 855) making more explicit the rate practices subject to ICC surveillance; an act of February 10, 1891 (Ch. 128, 26 Stat. 743) broadening the Commission's subpoena powers; an act of April 13, 1908 (Ch. 143, 35 Stat, 60) seeking to restrict railroads' issuance of free passes as a means of subverting regulatory bodies; an act of August 24, 1912 (Ch. 390, 37 Stat. 566) limiting railroad acquisition of competing water carriers; and an act of May 29, 1917 (Ch. 23, 40 Stat. 101) regulating the practice of distributing freight cars to favored shippers.

Among judicial decisions which affected the powers of the Commission in its early years—before the several major statutory amendments of the Progressive Era strengthened it—may be cited *Counselman v. Hitchcock* (1892), *Interstate Commerce Commission v. Brimson* (1894), *Brown v. Walker* and *Cincinnati, New Orleans & Texas Pacific Ry. v. ICC* (both in 1896) and *ICC v. Alabama Midland Ry.* (1897), all described in Appendix E.

June 27, 1890. Dependent Pension Act, Ch. 634, 26 Stat. 182.

This statute introduced into American law and politics the service pension broadened to cover dependents of military veterans. Enacted to discharge President Harrison's bid for the G. A. R. veterans' vote two years before, it became a model for enactments relating to dependents of military veterans of the Spanish-American war and of all major American conflicts of the twentieth century.

July 2, 1890. Sherman Anti-Trust Act, Ch. 647, 26 Stat. 209.

Although the statute bore the name of Senator John Sherman of Ohio, its framing was largely the work of Senators George F. Hoar of Massachusetts and George F. Edmunds of Vermont. The law categorically declared: "Every contract, combination in the form of trust or otherwise, or conspiracy in restraint of trade or commerce among the several states, or with foreign nations, is hereby declared to be illegal." Such sweeping generalities invited restrictive interpretations by unsympathetic courts, and while Attorney General Harmon and President Roosevelt periodically urged Congress to make the statute less ambiguous, as well as more capable of distinguishing between "good" and "bad" trusts, no substantive statutory change was effected until the Clayton Act of 1914.

The statute was all but emasculated in the Sugar Trust Case (*United States v. E. C. Knight & Co.*, 1895), was gradually rehabilitated in the cases of *United States v. Trans-Missouri Freight Assn.* (1897) and *Addyston Pipe & Steel Co. v. United States* (1899), and came to a climax in *Northern Securities Co. v. United States* (1904) and *Swift & Co. v. United States* (1906). The emerging of the "rule of reason" doctrine in *Standard Oil Co. v. United States* (1911) and *United States v. American Tobacco Co.* (1911) marked the gradual decline of the "trust-busting" fervor of the generation which followed the passing of the Sherman Act.

July 14, 1890. Sherman Silver Purchase Act, Ch. 708, 27 Stat. 289.

This was one of a long series of legislative efforts to deal with the problem of a viable currency system which would be responsive to the shifting economic balances in the last quarter of the nineteenth century. It began as an all-out effort of Western silverites in Congress to establish bimetallism, but when Eastern conservatives blocked this project the bill in its final form became only a plan for monthly Treasury purchases of silver and the issuance of both gold and silver certificates as currency. Three years later the act was repealed, on November 1, 1893 (Ch. 6, 28 Stat. 4), and the Gold Standard Act of 1900 (see below) completed the rout of the "free silver" bloc.

March 3, 1891. Forest Reserve Act, Ch. 561, 26 Stat. 1095.

Antedating the conservation measures of Theodore Roosevelt, this statute authorized the President to set aside any part of the public domain as forest preserves. It was followed by the Carey Act of August 18, 1894 (Ch. 301, 28 Stat. 422) authorizing the President to grant up to a million acres of the public lands to states in which they were situated, to be used for reclamation purposes.

May 5, 1892. Chinese Exclusion Act, Ch. 60, 27 Stat. 25.

Statutes aimed at curbing the importation of cheap Oriental labor dated back to the Coolie Trade Prohibition Act of February 19, 1862 (Ch. 27, 12

Stat. 340). Between 1882 and 1904, nine different statutes, of which this was the most stringent, sought to deal with the problem. Section 4 of this act, subjecting violators to a year's hard labor before deportation, was found unconstitutional in *Wong Wing v. United States* (1896).

August 27, 1894. Wilson Tariff Act, Ch. 349, 28 Stat. 553.

The income tax provisions in sections 27-37 of this law were found unconstitutional in *Pollock v. Farmers' Loan & Trust Co.* (1895).

January 30, 1897. Indian Liquor Sales Prohibition Act, Ch. 109, 29 Stat. 506.

One of the early Federal prohibition statutes, this law forbade the sale of liquor to Indians on lands held in trust by the United States. The courts' attitude both toward Federal prohibition (in the absence of a constitutional amendment) and toward the question of the use of the commerce clause as a means of implementing the Federal police power, was illustrated in two cases challenging the constitutionality of this statute: *Matter of Heff* (1905) and *United States v. Nice* (1916).

June 1, 1898. Erdmann Act, Ch. 370, 30 Stat. 424.

A major attempt by Congress to devise machinery for arbitration of labor disputes in the railroad industry, this statute established a rudimentary mediation service through the chairman of the Interstate Commerce Commission and the commissioner of the Bureau of Labor. Section 10 of the act, outlawing "yellow dog" (non-union) contracts, was invalidated in *Adair v. United States* (1908).

March 14, 1900. Currency (Gold Standard) Act, Ch. 41, 31 Stat. 45.

Another of the legislative efforts to create an efficient national currency, this statute defined the gold content of the dollar, placed all other forms of American money on a parity with gold, provided for the redemption of legal tender notes and—to meet agrarian currency needs—authorized the establishment of national banks with a minimum of $25,000 capitalization in towns of less than 3,000 population.

June 17, 1902. National Reclamation (Newlands) Act, Ch. 1093, 32 Stat. 388.

The cornerstone of Theodore Roosevelt's conservation program, this statute sponsored by Senator Francis Newlands of Nevada set aside most of the proceeds of public land sales in sixteen Western states to finance the construction and maintenance of irrigation projects.

February 14, 1903. Ch. 552, 32 Stat. 825.

This statute created a new Cabinet position, the Department of Commerce and Labor. The latter became a separate department on March 4, 1913 (Ch. 141, 37 Stat. 736).

February 19, 1903. Elkins Act, Ch. 708, 32 Stat. 847.

This was the first major revision of the Interstate Commerce Act of 1887, defining unfair discrimination against shippers in interstate commerce and fixing criminal penalties for railroads deviating from fixed rates. The statute was less important for its direct effect than for its function as a precedent for the substantial legislative enlargement of the powers of the Interstate Commerce Commission in Congressional enactments of 1906, 1910 and 1920.

June 11, 1906. Federal Employers' Liability Act, Ch. 3073, 34 Stat. 232.

An early labor statute, this law sought to fix liability on all interstate carriers for injuries to employees caused by supervisors' negligence or defective equipment. In the first *Employers' Liability Case* (1908) the statute was held unconstitutional because it extended to intrastate as well as interstate activities. Corrective amendments to the original law in acts of April 22, 1908 (Ch. 149, 35 Stat. 65) and April 5, 1910 (Ch. 143, 36 Stat. 291) resulted in a judicial upholding of the general law in the second *Employers' Liability Case* (1912).

June 29, 1906. Hepburn Act, Ch. 3591, 34 Stat. 584.

The second major overhauling of the Interstate Commerce Act of 1887, this statute vested rate-making authority in the Commission and broadened its jurisdiction to include pipelines and other media of interstate transportation. Its orders were binding until successfully challenged in the courts, thus placing the burden of proof on the carriers. The statute also was widely applauded for its so-called commodities clause, which empowered the Commission to order a separation of ownership of railroads and certain producing industries such as mines, which involved commodities shipped in interstate commerce. The principles set down in the Hepburn Act prepared the way for the development of other regulatory agencies and thus insured the ultimate power of government over a capitalistic system which had to this time largely evaded control.

June 30, 1906. Meat Inspection Act, Ch. 3913, 34 Stat. 669.

Meat inspection had first been the subject of Congressional action in 1890, but the current act, reflecting—in company with the Federal Employers' Liability Act, the Hepburn Act and the Pure Food and Drug Act—the legislative climax to Roosevelt's Square Deal, was much stronger. It provided for stringent Federal inspection of the packing industry, and aimed at elimination of unsanitary and dangerous conditions.

June 30, 1906. Pure Food and Drug Act, Ch. 3915, 34 Stat. 768.

Despite judicial reluctance to recognize a broad medium for the Federal police power in the commerce clause, this statute aimed at enforcing a national prohibition of adulterated foods and drugs in interstate commerce. While courts did in fact circumscribe the statute with many narrow constructions of terms, Congress sought through a long series of amendments to make its intentions more precise, and the general finding of constitutionality in the statute encouraged the courts gradually to broaden the police power potential of the commerce clause.

May 30, 1908. Aldrich-Vreeland Currency Act, Ch. 229, 35 Stat. 546.

Still grappling, with indifferent success, with the problem of an elastic yet stable national currency, this statute represented the boldest Congressional effort to that time to limit circulating notes to those issued by national banks or to state bank notes based only on Federal securities. More importantly, the statute created a National Monetary Commission to investigate the currency systems of leading commercial nations; the Commission's report in 1912 provided one of the bases for the Federal Reserve Act of the following year.

June 18, 1910. Mann-Elkins Act, Ch. 309, 36 Stat. 539.

Senator Stephen B. Elkins of West Virginia and Congressman James R. Mann of Illinois jointly sponsored the bills which emerged into this statute, a substantial broadening of the revisions of 1903 and 1906 of the Interstate Commerce Act of 1887. With President Taft's strong backing, the statute gave the Commission greater powers over rate-fixing and long/short-haul contract clauses, and extended its jurisdiction to include communications as well as transportation facilities. The law also created a Commerce Court as a specialized judicial agency for reviewing Commission rulings; but the apparent inclination of this court to overturn rather than to sustain such rulings led to a popular demand for its abolition, which Congress heeded in 1913.

June 25, 1910. Postal Savings Depositories Act, Ch. 386, 36 Stat. 814.

Both Presidents Roosevelt and Taft had endorsed a measure ardently advocated by Populists of the previous decade, introducing into the American economy a system of postal savings banks which had proved highly successful in Europe. Intended to encourage thrift among low-income groups, the primary effect of the statute was to encourage these groups to overcome their suspicion of commercial banks and to deposit their money with the government agencies rather than hoarding it. The banking community, which had at first condemned the idea as socialistic, subsequently lauded it as a means of educating a certain segment of the public in the practical operation of the capitalistic system.

June 25, 1910. Corrupt Practices Publicity Act, Ch. 392, 36 Stat. 822.

Following the example of New York and other states in passing laws defining corrupt acts in public office, Congress in 1907 had adopted an experimental statute which was substantially strengthened by the 1910 enactment. The latter statute stipulated that public statements of election campaign contributions in the case of the House of Representatives should henceforth be filed with designated authorities. After the Seventeenth Amendment made Senators also subject to popular election, the statute was extended to cover all of Congress.

June 25, 1910. Mann (White Slave) Act, Ch. 395, 36 Stat. 825.

The four statutes enacted between June 18 and 25 represented the high tide of reform legislation under President Taft, the last three being specifically in response to key proposals of the Progressive Movement. This statute created a Federal criminal liability for the transporting of women across state lines for immoral purposes.

March 1, 1913. Webb-Kenyon Interstate Liquor Act, Ch. 90, 37 Stat. 699.

Passed over Taft's veto on the eve of the first Wilson administration, this statute represented the high-water mark (to that date) of the national prohibition movement. Although Taft considered the bill to be an unconstitutional use of the commerce power for police power purposes, the provisions prohibiting the shipment of interstate liquor into states where its sale was forbidden was never directly tested by the courts. The Wartime Prohibition Cases (1919) tended to support the constitutionality of national prohibition under the war powers, and the adoption of the Eighteenth Amendment rendered the question moot.

December 23, 1913. Federal Reserve Act, Ch. 6, 38 Stat. 251.

After half a century of legislative efforts to create a national currency which would be sufficiently elastic to adjust to the needs of a modern economic system, the bill jointly sponsored by Senator Carter Glass of Virginia and Senator Robert L. Owen of Oklahoma became the cornerstone of the New Freedom. By creating twelve Federal Reserve districts, with a Federal Reserve Bank in each, a uniform system of government-controlled "bankers' banks" was established. By empowering member banks (which included all national banks and a steadily increasing number of state banks) to pay out and accept Federal Reserve notes throughout the country, a greatly increased and uniform currency supply was created. By empowering the central Federal Reserve Board to raise or lower rediscount rates, a control over the credit system of the country was also made possible.

Revisions and adjustments in the system were effected through ten other statutes passed by Congress in the decade following the fundamental act: a more precise definition of reserves to be held in regional banks was made August 15, 1914 (Ch. 252, 38 Stat. 691) and a more precise definition of rediscount procedures March 3, 1915 (Ch. 93, 38 Stat. 958). Discounting of commercial paper was covered September 7, 1916 (Ch. 461, 39 Stat. 752) and the creation of branches for reserve banks June 21, 1917 (Ch. 32, 40 Stat. 232). Membership requirements for the Federal Reserve Board were revised

March 3, 1919 (Ch. 101, 40 Stat. 1314). A system of graduated rediscount rates was authorized April 13, 1920 (Ch. 128, 41 Stat. 550) and the capital requirements for member banks were redefined March 23, 1923 (Ch. 252, ss. 401-407, 42 Stat. 1478). Three other statutes dealt with special problems of chartering member banks doing business abroad. By the end of its first decade of operations, as a result of these legislative refinements, the Federal Reserve System was generally considered to have achieved the economic stabilization of the monetary and credit system which had been sought for the sixty years since the Civil War.

September 26, 1914. Federal Trade Commission Act, Ch. 311, 38 Stat. 717.

The second major administrative agency to be established by Congress, the Federal Trade Commission was intended to operate in a manner analogous to the Interstate Commerce Commission, investigating the practices of all interstate corporations except carriers and banks and issuing cease and desist orders in cases where it found unfair business practices. While the FTC was handicapped from the beginning by Congressional failure either to define its authority unequivocally or to vest it with sufficient enforcing powers, its net effect over the years was to educate both the business community and the consuming public to the deleterious effects of trade boycotts, mislabeling and adulterating of goods, artificial maintenance of resale prices, and the like.

With the passage of the Pure Food and Drug Act of 1906, the Federal Reserve, Trade Commission and Clayton Acts of 1914, and the first efforts at farm and labor legislation between 1916 and 1920, Congress committed the nation to a Federally administered program of economic regulation. Although the conservative majority on the Supreme Court throughout the 1920's and early 1930's construed most of these statutes narrowly and in cases like the child labor and minimum wage laws flatly ruled them unconstitutional, the legislative base had been laid for the early New Deal and the ultimate expansion of Federal administration which followed.

October 25, 1914. Clayton Anti-Trust Act, Ch. 323, 38 Stat. 730.

Where the Federal Trade Commission Act dealt indirectly with the trust question by establishing the principle of investigation and regulation, the Clayton Act sought to strengthen the prohibitory features of the original Sherman Act by making more explicit the type of practices considered to be in restraint of trade. These practices included pricing practices which were found substantially tending to contribute to monopoly, certain interlocking directorates, and tying contracts under which the parties agreed not to handle the products of outside competitors. The FTC was directed to apply its cease and desist orders in such cases, with a right to petition for injunctions as a means of enforcement, while injured parties were given a right to seek civil damages triple in amount to the losses sustained.

By stipulating that labor and agricultural organizations were to be exempt from the anti-trust laws, the Clayton Act was first hailed as "labor's Magna Carta." A series of narrow judicial decisions in the twenties, however, all but eviscerated this provision of the law, and the use of the labor injunction in industrial disputes was not effectively curbed until the Norris-LaGuardia Act of 1932 (see Appendix C).

June 3, 1916. National Defense Act, Ch. 134, 39 Stat. 166.

The increasing menace of the European War led to a prolonged debate over preparedness throughout 1915, and after a lengthy Congressional battle resulted in this statute. Like the reform statutes of the New Freedom, this law carried the Federal authority to an unprecedented degree into broad aspects of national life. Besides enlarging both the regular Army and the National Guard, the law created a Reserve Officers Training Corps at colleges and universities, a Citizens' Military Training Corps at military camps, and an inventory procedure for industrial preparedness.

July 17, 1916. Federal Farm Loan Act, Ch. 245, 39 Stat. 360.

Prolonged and insistent demands of farm groups at length wore down Congressional and Cabinet opposition to Federal statutory aid to agriculture, opposition which had held consistently to the idea that these particular subjects were non-Federal. With this reversal of position, Congressional farm policy became a feature of national legislation thereafter. The Farm Loan Act was intended to provide for agriculture the type of economic support which the Federal Reserve Act had provided for banking and currency and thus indirectly for industry and commerce. With a regional organization and a national board comparable to the structure of the Federal Reserve System, the statute provided for memberships to be held by cooperative farm loan associations through which individual farmers could obtain long-term loans at rates substantially lower than those of commercial banks.

A series of amendments were adopted between April 1920 and August 1921, further strengthening the program and laying the base for the Federal Intermediate Credit Bank established in 1923 (see below).

August 11, 1916. United States Warehouse Act, Ch. 313, 39 Stat. 486.

Another goal of the Progressive Movement and the Populists before it—low-cost crop loans—was attained in this companion statute to the Farm Loan Act. This statute authorized bonded warehouses to issue warehouse receipts which were negotiable in themselves and acceptable as collateral for loans. The statute was broadened February 23, 1923 (Ch. 106, 42 Stat. 282).

September 1, 1916. Child Labor Act, Ch. 432, 39 Stat. 757.

This statute undertook to prohibit the flow of goods produced by child labor in interstate commerce, thus using the commerce clause as an implementation of the police power as in the Webb-Kenyon Act (above). This use of the commerce power, however, was specifically ruled unconstitutional in *Hammer v. Dagenhart* (1918).

September 3, 1916. Adamson (Railway Labor) Act, Ch. 436 39 Stat. 757.

The first Federal maximum-hour law, applicable to interstate railroads, was passed on this date, the eve of a threatened nationwide rail strike. The Court upheld the constitutionality of the law by a narrow five-to-four majority in *Wilson v. New* (1917).

May 18, 1917. Selective Service Act, Ch. 15, 40 Stat. 76.

More comprehensive than the four draft statutes of the Civil War period, this law asserted the Federal authority to register and classify for military service all American men from 21 to 30 years of age. It was variously amended, the most comprehensive extension of its effect being in the Man Power Act of August 31, 1918 (Ch. 166, 40 Stat. 955) which registered all American males from 18 to 45 years of age. The governmental powers were generally upheld in the Selective Draft Law Cases (1918).

June 15, 1917. Espionage Act, Ch. 30, 40 Stat. 217.

A drastic assertion of Federal authority under the war powers was represented in this statute, imposing penalties of fines up to $10,000 and imprisonment up to twenty years for obstructing recruiting and training of troops or otherwise aiding the enemy. The Postmaster General was authorized to exclude from the mails periodicals he found to be seditious. Although many of the activities for which such severe criminal liabilities were imposed were defined only in general terms, the constitutionality of the act as a whole was upheld in *Schenck v. United States* (1919).

August 10, 1917. Lever Food and Drug Control Act, Ch. 53, 40 Stat. 276.

The first Federal law to attempt control of production, distribution and pricing of foods and fuels declared essential to the war effort, this statute was also notable for introducing wartime prohibition. It also marked the establishment of important new (albeit temporary) administrative agencies in the Grain Corporation, the Sugar Equalization Board and others, with broad authority over the pricing and distribution of foodstuffs. The War Prohibition Cases (1919) upheld this aspect of the law's administration.

The statute was substantially strengthened October 12, 1919 (Ch. 80, 41 Stat. 297) in an effort to cushion the economic effects of liquidating the wartime controls. The Lever Act was a model for a wide variety of wartime and postwar price and production controls legislated by Congress during and after the second World War.

October 6, 1917. Trading With the Enemy Act, Ch. 106, 40 Stat. 411.

After the outbreak of war, this statute undertook to prevent commercial intercourse between American producers and the enemy nations, established an Office of Censorship to control communications beyond the borders of the United States, and created an Office of Alien Property Custodian to take possession of properties of belligerents and their nationals where found in the United States. The effective operation of many sections of the statute continued long after the war; fourteen amendments were enacted by Congress between 1918 and 1932.

April 10, 1918. Webb-Pomerene (Export Trade) Act, Ch. 50, 40 Stat. 516.

Economic pressures bred by the war—the cutting off of trade with the Central Powers and the opening of markets formerly dominated by England and France—led American exporters to demand a right to form export trade associations which could compete with the long-established European cartels. This statute exempted such American groups from the operation of the anti-trust laws while prohibiting unfair trade practices between themselves. The companion statutes authorizing the Federal Reserve System to establish foreign branches so that American foreign trade could be financed with dollars and American commercial paper made possible the development of the dollar to a parity with the pound sterling as a medium of international trade. Thus the Webb-Pomerene Act contributed substantially to the changing of the character of the national economy as an indirect result of the war.

February 24, 1918. Child Labor Tax Act, Ch. 18, 40 Stat. 1138.

Immediately following the Court's invalidating of the Keating-Owen Child Labor Act of 1916 in *Hammer v. Dagenhart* (1918) as an unconstitutional use of the commerce clause for police power purposes, Congress undertook to reach the same legislative objective through the tax power. The statute, levying a heavy tax on goods produced by child labor and introduced into interstate commerce, was extended November 23, 1921 (Ch. 136, 42 Stat. 306). It was invalidated in *Bailey v. Drexel Furniture Co.* (1922).

May 16, 1918. Sedition Act, Ch. 75, 40 Stat. 553.

Reflecting the rising tide of popular enmity for unpopular or alien ideas in the context of patriotic conformity, this statute, an amendment to the 1917 Espionage Act, prescribed severe penalties for persons convicted of wilfully making statements interfering with the war effort, using "disloyal, profane, scurrilous or abusive language" with reference to the American flag, Constitution or form of government, and the like. While this statute also was unsatisfactorily general in the terms in which it fixed liability, it was upheld in *Abrams v. United States* (1919).

September 19, 1918. District of Columbia Minimum Wage Law, Ch. 174, 40 Stat. 960.

Basing its legislative action on the earlier court decisions upholding state wage and hour laws for women, Congress enacted a statute fixing such wages and hours for women employees in the District of Columbia. The manifest legislative intention was to insure such employees in the Federal District an economic parity with those protected by state laws presumably valid. In holding the statute unconstitutional in *Adkins v. Children's Hospital* (1923), the Court cast substantial doubt on the validity of state laws of this type as well.

October 28, 1919. National Prohibition Enforcement (Volstead) Act, Ch. 85, 41 Stat. 305.

Although vetoed by President Wilson, the statute was passed over his veto by Congress to expedite the taking effect of the Eighteenth Amendment and insuring the continuity of national prohibition which had been effected by temporary wartime statute.

February 28, 1920. Esch-Cummins (Transportation) Act, Ch. 91, 41 Stat. 456.

Implementing the return of railroads to private control after wartime governmental operation, the statute took the opportunity to extend substantially the powers of the Interstate Commerce Commission to authorize consolidation of lines, make definite evaluations of railroad properties, fix rates and determine fair return to stockholders, supervise new issues of securities and establish a revolving fund through a recapture of certain profits above 6 percent for the aid of ailing railroads. A labor arbitration board for the lines was also created.

The Transportation Act of 1920 was a sweeping extension of the Interstate Commerce Act of 1887, and was generally upheld by the Court in *Railroad Commission of Wisconsin v. C., B. & Q. Ry.* (1922) and *Dayton-Goose Creek Ry. Co. v. United States* (1924). The famous *Shreveport Rate Case* (1914), in fact, had encouraged Congress to assert the broad authority set out in the 1920 statute.

June 5, 1920. Merchant Marine (Jones) Act, Ch. 250, 41 Stat. 988.

The Wartime Shipping Board created by Statutes of 1916 and 1918 was reorganized under this act which sought to aid private industry in the development of an American mercantile fleet to exploit the nation's new competitive advantages in world trade. It provided for the sale of government-built ships to private parties, with proceeds up to $25,000,000 available as loans for the construction of other vessels by private groups.

June 10, 1920. Federal Water Power Act, Ch. 285, 41 Stat. 1063.

To encourage the development of water power reserves on public lands, the statute created the Federal Power Commission—another in the steadily developing group of administrative agencies—with authority to license private industry to construct and operate dams, power houses and transmission lines for a maximum of fifty-year leases. The government reserved the right to take over the facilities thereafter.

August 15, 1921. Packers and Stockyards Act, Ch. 64, 42 Stat. 159.

Congress by this statute applied Holmes' "current of commerce" doctrine to regulate the marketing activities of livestock processors and prevent unfair and discriminatory practices. The constitutionality of the statute was upheld in *Stafford v. Wallace* (1922).

August 24, 1921. Grain Futures Trading Act, Ch. 86, 42 Stat. 187.

Complementing the preceding statute, this enactment sought to regulate practices on the national grain exchanges to prevent manipulation and speculation in commodities. In the case of *Hill v. Wallace* (1922) Section 3 of the statute was held unconstitutional as an intrusion into non-Federal areas through the use of the tax power. Taking a cue from the opinion that the commerce clause might be a proper instrument for the same project, Congress enacted a second Grain Futures Trading Act September 21, 1922 (Ch. 69, 42 Stat. 998), which was upheld in *Board of Trade v. Olsen* (1923). The statute was the point of departure for some of the New Deal farm legislation of the 1930's.

February 18, 1922. Cooperative Marketing Association (Capper-Volstead) Act, Ch. 57, 42 Stat. 388.

In another legislative effort to assist agriculture, this statute exempted farm cooperatives and similar associations from the operation of the anti-trust laws. Under the encouragement of the Department of Agriculture, cooperative buying and selling of agricultural products was promoted.

March 23, 1923. Federal Intermediate Credit Bank Act, Ch. 252, 42 Stat. 1454.

The continuing demands of agriculture for economic assistance—reflecting the farmers' chronically worsening position compared with industrialized urban areas—resulted in a modification of the Federal Farm Loan Act of 1916. Under the new act, intermediate credit banks were established through government subscription to make short-term, low-interest crop loans through cooperative producing and marketing associations.

May 20, 1926. Railway Labor Act, Ch. 347, 44 Stat. 577.

A continuing effort by both labor and management, dating from the late nineties, to find a workable system of negotiating an employment contract, resulted in the historic act of this date. By providing for collective bargaining, union recognition, machinery for grievance settlements and arbitration of disputes, the statute was a milestone in legislative promotion of industrial harmony. The statute was found unconstitutional in *Texas & New Orleans Ry. v. Brotherhood of Railway & Steamship Clerks* (1930).

March 2, 1929. Jones (Intoxicating Liquor) Act, Ch. 473, 45 Stat. 144.

After a decade of futile legislative and administrative efforts to make the Volstead Act effective, this statute was the final Congressional attempt to deal with the problem by making the criminal liabilities more severe. With the continuing ineffectiveness of prohibition laws, the movement for repeal of the Eighteenth Amendment got under way.

June 15, 1929. Agricultural Marketing Act, Ch. 24, 46 Stat. 11.

Another chronic farm problem, of uncontrolled production and resulting surpluses, produced a bill endorsed by the Hoover administration for promoting the marketing of farm commodities through a Federal Farm Board. Surpluses were to be systematically purchased and marketed by the Board in cooperation with agricultural associations, with a stabilization of production and acreage limitation through subsidiary agencies in the form of the Cotton Stabilization Corporation, the Wool Marketing Corporation, and others. After an expenditure of more than $180,000,000 without notable success, the program was discontinued on the eve of the New Deal, thus preparing the way for the first of the emergency farm statutes of 1933 and 1934.

January 22, 1932. Reconstruction Finance Corporation Act, Ch. 8, 47 Stat. 5.

As the great depression worsened, the Hoover administration sought to aid private industry by creating a government lending agency, empowered to issue tax-exempt bonds and extend credit to banks, life insurance companies, railroads, building and loan associations and farm mortgage associations. This represented the limit to which the *laissez-faire* economists of the old order were prepared to go in marshalling the powers of government to deal with national emergencies.

February 27, 1932. Glass-Steagall Act, Ch. 58, 47 Stat. 56.

As gold began to drain out of the domestic markets with foreign withdrawals and local hoarding, the administration tried to reverse the trend by diverting three-quarters of a billion dollars in gold from backing the currency to the support of private industry. The failure of this measure to curb the gold drain made inevitable the departure from the gold standard when the New Deal came to power.

July 21, 1932. Emergency Relief and Reconstruction Act, Ch. 520, 47 Stat. 709.

As economic conditions worsened still more, Congress by this act broadened the authority of the Reconstruction Finance Corporation by empowering it to make loans up to $1,500,000,000 for self-liquidating public construction projects and to make temporary loans to states unable to finance local relief projects.

July 22, 1932. Federal Home Loan Bank Act, Ch. 522, 47 Stat. 725.

The final desperate effort of the Hoover administration to deal with economic disaster was this enactment, creating a special banking system designed to afford for home owners the type of discount relief that industry obtained through the Federal Reserve System. Long-term loans repayable in installments were made through building and loan associations and insurance companies to refinance home mortgages and stimulate home building. The immediate goals of the legislation were only partially attained; the collapse of private savings had become so general that there was no significant residential construction to be stimulated. The statute served as an epitaph for the old order which expired with the elections of November, 1932.

Appendix E

Principal Constitutional Cases, 1889-1932

This Appendix has a chronological arrangement, rather than the conventional table of cases (the alphabetical arrangement of the cases cited in this volume appears in the Index). Chronology, and the association of certain men on the Court and in the Executive Department (i.e., the Presidency and the Department of Justice), is particularly significant in the historical analysis which is the primary emphasis of this study. Accordingly, the precise date for the handing down of opinions in these cases, as well as the dates of argument or reargument, the dates when a change in personnel in the Court occurred, a new Presidential term began or the Attorneys General or Solicitors General changed, are all taken into account. The reader will find it useful to correlate the dates in this Appendix with those set out in Appendices C and D as well.

Where the Court is in any manner divided in the opinions in a given case, this also is noted. The Justice who delivers the opinion of the Court itself is in the nature of things an institutional spokesman; the words of the opinion may or may not articulate his own fundamental constitutional view. The latter is more apt to be expressed in a concurring or dissenting opinion, and accordingly these divergent statements in the same case are also noted. There is, finally, a succinct statement of the constitutional issue or rule in the case.

All of the important cases cited in the text appear here, and in addition there is a representative selection of other cases which invalidated state statutes or municipal ordinances, drawn from the compilation in the annotated edition of the Constitution prepared by the Legislative Reference Service of the Library of Congress, to which reference is made in Appendix D. It is neither practical nor necessary to include every decision involving a constitutional point, however minor, under Fuller, White or Taft. Rather, this Appendix undertakes to put into chronological perspective the tenor of constitutional thought on the Court at successive periods within the forty-plus years covered in this volume. It seeks to show the continuity or consistency, as well as the changes and alternatives, which makes up the judicial dialogue between the first administrative regulatory enactments like the Interstate Commerce Act and the Sherman Act, and the end of the Decade of Normalcy.

The principal list which follows covers the period from 1889, Fuller's first full year as Chief Justice, to February, 1930, when Chief Justice Taft resigned. It is preceded by a brief group of cases prior to 1889 which figured significantly in the subsequent work of the Court, and is concluded with a selection of cases under Chief Justice Hughes, from March, 1930 to June, 1932, when the study in the present volume comes to its end.

1873

April 14. Slaughterhouse Cases. 16 Wall. 36.

Argued February, 3-5, 1873. Miller, J., for the Court; Bradley, Field, Swayne, JJ., Chase, C. J., dissenting.

First judicial pronouncement on the Fourteenth Amendment. Upholding a Louisiana statute granting a slaughterhouse monopoly, the majority narrowly defined rights of United States citizens under the Amendments, thus leaving the bulk of civil rights law under state jurisdiction. The dissenters contended that the due process clause of the Amendment should apply against states depriving persons of their property rights.

1877

March 1. Munn v. Illinois. 94 U. S. 113.

Argued January 14, 18, 1876. Waite, C. J., for the Court; Field, Strong, JJ., dissenting.

Prototype of the Granger Cases, sustaining an Illinois statute defining grain elevators as businesses "affected with a public interest" and not unduly interfering with interstate commerce. The decision tacitly recognized the constitutionality of the regulatory administrative agency in state government.

1881

January 24. Springer v. United States. 102 U. S. 586.

Argued April 8, 9, 1880. Swayne, J., for the Court.

Affirmed the constitutionality of a Civil War Federal income tax.

1883

October 15. Civil Rights Cases. 109 U. S. 3.

Argued November 7, 1882; reargued March 29, 1883. Bradley, J., for the Court; Harlan, J., dissenting.

Five cases—from California, Kansas, Missouri, New York and Tennessee —were consolidated in a test of the "public accommodations" section of the Civil Rights Act of 1872. By holding that the Fourteenth Amendment empowered Congress to protect national citizenship rights only from denial by "state action," and did not afford protection against denial of these rights by private individuals, the Court effectively removed the Federal authority from the civil rights area for the next three-quarters of a century.

1885

> *December 21.* San Mateo County v. So. Pac. R. Co. 116 U. S. 138.

Argued March 19-21, 1882; restored to docket October, 15, 1883. Waite, C. J., for the Court.

Unimportant in itself—the opinion merely dismissed the case because the issue was no longer pending before the Court—the oral argument in this case three years earlier had featured Senator Roscoe Conkling's famous declaration, as counsel for the Southern Pacific, that the word "persons" in the Fourteenth Amendment had been intended to extend the protection of due process to "legal persons"—i.e., corporations.

1886

> *May 10.* Santa Clara County v. So. Pac. R. Co. 118 U. S. 394.

Argued January 26-29, 1886. Waite, C. J., for the Court.

Within six months, the Court had accepted the Conkling contention, stating in the present case that further argument on the point was unnecessary, and thus introducing the concept of substantive due process as a protection of corporations against constitutional attack in many of their activities.

> *October 25.* Wabash, St. L. & Pac. R. Co. v. Illinois. 118 U. S. 557.

Argued April 14, 15, 1886. Miller J., for the Court; Bradley, Gray, JJ., and Waite, C. J., dissenting.

Invalidating an Illinois statute forbidding railroads to insert long/short-haul differential clauses in transportation contracts, this case purportedly left such regulation to Congress but in effect created a "twilight zone" where railroads could operate free of either state or Federal authority. This case helped accelerate the movement in Congress to pass the Interstate Commerce Commission Act of 1887.

1888

October 8. THE FULLER COURT (October 1888-June 1910).

Fuller, C. J.; Blatchford, Bradley, Field, Gray, Harlan, Lamar, Matthews, Miller, JJ.

President: Grover Cleveland. Attorney General: Augustus N. Garland. Solicitor General: George A. Jenks.

> *October 29.* Georgia R. & Banking Co. v. Smith, 128 U. S. 174.

Argued October 16, 17, 1888. Field, J., for the Court.

One of the earliest opinions of the Fuller Court held that a state charter to a railroad delegating to it a power of condemnation clothed the railroad with a public use subject to legislative regulation.

1889

> *January 14.* Stoutenburgh v. Hennick. 129 U. S. 141.

Argued December 18, 1888. Fuller, C. J., for the Court; Miller J., dissenting.

Invalidating an act licensing commission salesmen in the District of Columbia, as a burden on interstate commerce.

March 4. President Benjamin Harrison inaugurated.

March 7. William H. H. Miller becomes Attorney General.

May 13. Chae Chan Ping v. United States (Chinese Exclusion Case). 130 U. S. 581.

Argued March 28, 29, 1889. Field, J., for the Court.

Holding that Congressional enactments on the limiting or excluding of immigrants subsequent to a treaty on the subject had the effect of abrogating the treaty provisions as municipal law.

May 29. Orlow W. Chapman becomes Solicitor General.

1890

January 6. Justice Brewer succeeds Matthews.

February 4. William Howard Taft becomes Solicitor General.

March 24. Chicago, Milw. & St. Paul R. Co. v. Minnesota, 134 U. S. 418.

Argued January 13, 14, 1890. Blatchford, J., for the Court; Miller, J., concurring; Bradley, Gray, Lamar, JJ., dissenting.

These early Minnesota rates cases, reversing the state court, held invalid a state law empowering the railroad commission to fix carrier rates without reserving a right of judicial review.

April 14. In re Neagle. 135 U. S. 1.

Argued March 4, 5, 1890. Miller, J., for the Court; Fuller, C. J., and Lamar, J., dissenting; Field, J., not participating.

Affirming a Federal trial court finding that the bodyguard of a Federal officer who kills another reasonably believed to be threatening the officer is not liable to a criminal proceeding under state law. For further references to this case in Field's career, see Appendix A.

April 28. Leisy v. Hardin. 135 U. S. 100.

Argued January 6, 1890. Fuller, C. J., for the Court; Gray, Brewer, Harlan, JJ., dissenting.

This case introduced Fuller's concept of the "unbroken package"—in this case, liquor in its original containers shipped into a state—which as an item in interstate commerce was exempt from a state prohibition law. Reversing *Pierce v. New Hampshire* 5 How. 504 (1847).

May 19. McGahey v. Virginia. 135 U. S. 662.

Argued January 21, 1890. Bradley, J., for the Court.

This was one of six cases from the Virginia supreme court of appeals and two from the United States Circuit Court for the Eastern District of Virginia, all challenging state laws which sought to refinance, reduce or extinguish the original obligations on state bonds. The Court held that such laws impaired the contracts represented in the bonds in contravention of the contracts clause of the Federal Constitution.

May 19. Norfolk & Western R. Co. v. Pennsylvania. 136 U. S. 114.

Argued April 24, 25, 1890. Lamar, J., for the Court; Fuller, C. J., and Brewer and Gray, JJ., dissenting.

A Pennsylvania tax on interstate rail transportation was held to be a burden upon interstate commerce.

May 19. Minnesota v. Barber. 136 U. S. 314.

Argued January 14, 15, 1890. Harlan, J., for the Court.

Minnesota statute requiring state inspection of cattle brought into the state for slaughter held to be a burden upon interstate commerce.

1891

January 6. Justice Brown succeeds Miller.

January 19. Brimmer v. Rebman. 138 U. S. 78.

Argued January 5, 1891. Harlan, J., for the Court.

Rule in *Barber* case applied to similar Virginia law.

May 25. In re Rahrer. 140 U. S. 545.

Argued March 1, 1891. Fuller C. J., for the Court; Brewer, Gray, Harlan, JJ., dissenting.

A Congressional act of 1890 modified Fuller's "unbroken package" doctrine by stipulating that it was Congress' intention that such shipments in interstate commerce were to be subject to the prohibition laws of the states into which they were brought. The act was upheld.

May 25. Pullman's Palace Car Co. v. Pennsylvania. 141 U. S. 18.

Argued October 18, 1888; reargued March 6, 1890. Gray, J., for the Court; Bradley and Field, JJ., concurring; Harlan, J., dissenting.

Modifying the rule in the *Norfolk & Western* case of the previous year, this case undertook to devise a formula for the application of a state tax to interstate rail transportation.

May 25. Crutcher v. Kentucky. 141 U. S. 47.

Argued March 19, 1890. Bradley, J., for the Court; Fuller, C. J., and Gray, J., dissenting; Brown, J., not participating.

Invalidating a state license law as applied to an interstate express line, where rigid regulations were held to be an arbitrary burden on interstate commerce.

1892

January 11. Counselman v. Hitchcock. 142 U. S. 547.

Argued December 9, 10, 1891. Blatchford, J., for the Court.

Under the Interstate Commerce Act of 1887, witnesses were held not compelled to testify in criminal prosecutions without assurance of absolute immunity from subsequent prosecution for the offense under investigation. Relieving individuals of this liability, ultimately recognized by Congress in a statute, was periodically criticized as weakening the act as a whole.

February 28. Field v. Clark. 143 U. S. 649.

Argued November 30, December 1, 2, 1891. Harlan, J., for the Court; Fuller, C. J., and Lamar, J., dissenting in part and concurring in part.

Congress' procedure as to enacting its own legislation was held to be a "political question" beyond the jurisdiction of the Court.

February 29. Budd v. New York. 143 U. S. 517.

Argued March 17, 18, 1891. Blatchford, J., for the Court; Brewer, Brown and Field, JJ., dissenting.

Affirming the "public interest" doctrine of *Munn v. Illinois,* with Brewer expressing the minority position that such state regulatory statutes improperly interfered with private enterprise.

March 21. Charles H. Aldrich becomes Solicitor General.

April 4. Logan v. United States. 144 U. S. 263.

Argued January 26, 27, 1892. Gray, J., for the Court.

Attempts to seize suspects in custody of United States officers were held to be indictable as a conspiracy against government authority.

October 10. Justice Shiras succeeds Bradley.

October 17. McPherson v. Blacker. 146 U. S. 1.

Argued October 11, 1892. Fuller, C. J., for the Court.

Sustaining a Michigan statute providing for electors in Presidential election by districts instead of on a statewide basis, as a subject exclusively within state jurisdiction.

1893

March 4. Justice Jackson succeeds Lamar. Grover Cleveland is inaugurated for second term.

March 6. Richard Olney becomes Attorney General.

March 27. Monongahela Nav. Co. v. United States. 148 U. S. 312.

Argued October 25, 26, 1892. Brewer, J., for the Court; Jackson and Shiras, JJ., not participating.

When Congress asserts its authority over navigable streams by taking of dam and lock constructed under a grant from the state, owners held entitled to reasonable compensation. The question of reasonableness in this case was held to be a judicial rather than a legislative question.

April 3. Virginia v. Tennessee. 148 U. S. 503.

Argued March 8, 9, 1893. Field, J., for the Court.

Holding that interstate compacts require the consent of Congress, although where Congress has accepted a local agreement between states, consent is inferred.

May 29. Lawrence Maxwell, Jr., becomes Solicitor General.

1894

March 12. Justice White succeeds Blatchford.

May 14. Brass v. North Dakota ex rel. Stoeser. 153 U. S. 391.

Argued April 26, 1894. Shiras, J., for the Court; Brewer, Field, Jackson and White, JJ., dissenting.

This decision affirmed the doctrine of the majority in *Munn* and *Budd,* but the dissenters were joined by Justice White, who had joined the Court only two months before, suggesting to conservatives a possible early ascendancy for the minority view.

May 26. Covington & Cincinnati Bridge Co. v. Kentucky. 154 U. S. 204.

Argued April 25, 1894. Brown, J., for the Court; Fuller, C. J., and Field, Gray and White, JJ., concurring.

After a bridge has been constructed under an interstate compact, neither state may attempt unilaterally to regulate its fees, since it has then become an instrument of interstate commerce.

May 26. Reagan v. Farmers' Loan & Trust Co. 154 U. S. 362.

Argued April 4, 5, 1894. Brewer, J., for the Court.

Where a state rate-fixing commission is legally created, the courts have power to review the fixed rates and hold them unreasonable, but the commission rather than the courts has the sole power to fix a new rate.

May 26. Interstate Commerce Commission v. Brimson. 154 U. S. 447.

Argued April 16, 1894. Harlan, J., for the Court; Fuller, C. J., and Brewer and Jackson, JJ., dissenting; Field, J., not participating.

Compelling witnesses to testify before the Commission, the Court held, did not include the power to punish recalcitrants; it was suggested that Congress could empower the courts to enforce a Commission summons in aid of its hearings.

December 10. Plumley v. Massachusetts. 155 U. S. 461.

Argued April 5, 6, 1894. Harlan, J., for the Court; Jackson, J., concurring; Fuller, C. J., and Brewer and Field, JJ., dissenting.

Massachusetts law prohibiting the sale of colored oleomargarine upheld as a valid exercise of the public health power of the state.

1895

January 21. United States v. E. C. Knight & Co. 156 U. S. 1.

Argued October 24, 1894. Fuller, C. J., for the Court; Harlan, J., dissenting.

The Sugar Trust Case, holding that a combination to control most of the sugar supply of the nation was not a combination in restraint of interstate commerce. This narrow interpretation of the Sherman Anti-Trust Act limited its application to transportation as against manufacturing of commodities.

February 7. Holmes Conrad becomes Solicitor General.

April 8. Pollock v. Farmers' Loan & Trust Co. 157 U. S. 429.

Argued March 7, 8, 11-13, 1895. Fuller, C. J., for the Court; Field, J., concurring; White, Harlan, JJ., dissenting; Jackson, J., not participating; "even division" noted by Chief Justice on basic constitutional issue.

The first Income Tax decision, invalidating certain Federal tax levies on income from government bonds and lands but dividing on question of constitutionality of an income tax itself.

April 29. Gulf, Colo., etc. R. Co. v. Hefley. 158 U. S. 98.

Argued April 4, 1895. Brewer, J., for the Court.

Where a state law relates to the same subject as the Interstate Commerce Commission Act, the Federal statute prevails and limits the state law to intrastate commerce.

May 20. Pollock v. Farmers' Loan & Trust Co. 158 U. S. 601.

Argued May 6-8, 1895. Fuller, C. J., for the Court; Harlan, Jackson, Brown, White, JJ., dissenting.

On rescheduling the case and hearing reargument on the constitutional issue, majority held the Income Tax Law invalid. Overruling, among others, *Ware v. Hylton*, 3 Dallas 199 (1796) and *Springer v. United States* (1881— see above).

May 27. In re Debs. 158 U. S. 564.

Argued March 25, 26, 1895. Brewer, J., for the Court.

Sustaining the conviction of labor leader in Pullman strike, for ignoring the labor injunction devised to break the strike.

June 8. Judson Harmon becomes Attorney General.

1896

January 6. Justice Peckham succeeds Jackson.

March 2. Greer v. Connecticut. 161 U. S. 519.

Argued November 22, 1895. White, J., for the Court; Field and Harlan, JJ., dissenting; Brewer and Peckham, JJ., not participating.

Upholding a state law on conservation of game birds, even though affecting interstate commerce, where Congress has not asserted a pre-emptive authority.

March 23. Brown v. Walker. 161 U. S. 591.

Argued January 23, 1896. Brown, J., for the Court; Shiras, Gray, White and Field, JJ., dissenting.

Affirming the immunity provisions of Interstate Commerce Commission Act, as amended, as a limitation on state criminal law.

March 30. Cincinnati, New Orleans & Texas R. Co. v. Interstate Commerce Commission. 162 U. S. 184.

Argued January 30, 31, 1896. Shiras, J., for the Court.

Where intrastate carrier engages to carry interstate traffic, it is regarded as being engaged in interstate commerce and subject to Commission regulation.

April 13. Gibson v. Mississippi. 162 U. S. 565.

Argued December 13, 1895. Harlan, J., for the Court.

While declaring that a state may not exclude Negroes from juries solely because of their race, an exclusion which may be based on other grounds will not qualify the case for removal into a Federal court.

May 18. Wong Wing v. United States. 163 U. S. 228.

Argued April 1, 2, 1896. Shiras, J., for the Court; Field, J., concurring in part and dissenting in part; Brewer, J., not participating.

Invalidating section of Chinese Exclusion Act which subjected offenders to infamous punishment without a judicial trial.

May 18. Plessy v. Ferguson. 163 U. S. 537.

Argued April 13, 1896. Brown, J., for the Court; Harlan, J., dissenting; Brewer, J., not participating.

Upholding Louisiana law segregating facilities on railroad passenger trains; Harlan in dissent made famous remark that "our Constitution is color-blind." The revival of the Harlan position had to await the desegregation cases beginning in 1953.

November 30. Missouri Pacific R. Co. v. Nebraska. 164 U. S. 403.

Argued March 4, 1896. Gray, J., for the Court.

Invalidating a state law authorizing a state agency to compel railroad company to erect additional storage elevators along its right of way on same terms as it has done for certain producers.

1897

January 18. Gulf, Colorado & Santa Fe R. Co. v. Ellis 165 U. S. 150.

Argued November 3, 1896. Brewer, J., for the Court; Gray and White, JJ., and Fuller, C. J., dissenting.

Invalidating a Texas law which would have required railroads to pay attorney fees and court costs for plaintiffs who successfully maintained suit against the roads.

March 1. Allgeyer v. Louisiana. 165 U. S. 578.

Argued January 6, 1897. Peckham, J., for the Court.

Invalidating a Louisiana statute which sought to deny out-of-state insurance companies a license to do business within the state where they had not complied with all requirements of local law. The effect of the decision was to extend "freedom of contract" under the Fourteenth Amendment to its greatest extreme in limiting the reach of state authority over interstate business.

March 1. Chi., Burl. & Quincy R. Co. v. Chicago. 166 U. S. 226.

Argued November 6, 9, 1896. Harlan, J., for the Court; Brewer J., dissenting.

Upholding an Illinois statute which required railroads to assume costs of constructing crossing facilities and maintaining flagmen, as reasonable exercise of state police power.

March 4. William McKinley inaugurated as President.

March 5. Joseph McKenna becomes Attorney General.

March 22. United States v. Trans-Missouri Frt. Assn. 166 U. S. 290.

Argued December 8, 9, 1896. Peckham, J., for the Court; White, Field, Gray and Shiras, JJ., dissenting.

Upholding an anti-trust prosecution of eighteen railroads which combined to fix rates. Counsel for the railroads argued a "rule of reason" to distinguish between "reasonable" and "unreasonable" restraints of trade, a view which Justice White was ultimately to establish in the Standard Oil and Tobacco Trust Cases.

November 18. Interstate Commerce Commission v. Alabama Midland R. Co. 168 U. S. 144.

Argued March 12, 15, 16, 1897. Shiras, J., for the Court; Harlan, J., dissenting.

This case qualified the long- and short-haul rate differential doctrine first discussed in the *Wabash* case, and insisted upon a right of judicial review of findings of fact by the Interstate Commerce Commission, thus substantially circumscribing the Commission's rate-making powers.

July 1. John K. Richards becomes Solicitor General.

1898

January 25. John W. Griggs becomes Attorney General.

January 26. Justice McKenna succeeds Field.

February 28. Holden v. Hardy. 169 U. S. 366.

Argued October 21, 1897. Brown, J., for the Court; Brewer and Peckham, JJ., dissenting.

Upholding a Utah law fixing maximum hours for working in mines as a valid use of the police power to limit freedom of contract where the health and safety of workers in a manifestly dangerous calling was the basis for the exercise of the power.

March 7. Smyth v. Ames. 169 U. S. 466.

Argued April 5-7, 1897. Harlan, J., for the Court; Fuller, C. J., and McKenna, J., not participating.

Invalidating a Nebraska statute fixing railroad rates as contravening the due process clause of the Fourteenth Amendment and not assuring the companies of a "fair return" on a "fair value" of their properties. The rule placed virtually all rate-making by state commissions under court surveillance.

March 28. United States v. Wong Kim Ark. 169 U. S. 649.

Argued March 5, 8, 1897. Gray, J., for the Court; Fuller, C. J., and Harlan, J., dissenting; McKenna, J., not participating.

A child of Chinese subjects permanently resident in the United States was held to be a citizen of the United States under the citizenship clause of the Fourteenth Amendment.

April 18. Hawkes v. New York. 170 U. S. 189.

Argued March 9, 1898. Brewer, J., for the Court; Harlan, McKenna and Peckham, JJ., dissenting.

A New York law denying convicted felons a license to resume practice of a licensed profession held not to conflict with the prohibition against bills of attainder.

April 25. Galveston, Harrisburg, etc. R. Co. v. Texas, 170 U. S. 226.

Argued January 21, 24, 1898. Fuller, C. J., for the Court.

Land grants in state railroad charters held subject to subsequent legislative alteration of charter and not impairing original contract where railroad had not exercised any of its rights in the land.

May 23. Schollenberger v. Pennsylvania. 171 U. S. 1.

Argued March 23, 24, 1898. Peckham, J., for the Court; Gray and Harlan, JJ., dissenting.

Reviving the "original package" doctrine and modifying rule in *Plumley v. Massachusetts* by holding that a state may not prohibit the sale of imported oleomargarine.

December 12. Blake v. McClung. 172 U. S. 239.

Argued November 8, 1897. Harlan, J., for the Court; Brewer, J., and Fuller, C. J., dissenting.

This case distinguished the word "persons" in the Fourteenth Amendment as interpreted by Conkling from the word "citizens," denying rights of citizenship to corporations. The distinction made possible suits by states against foreign corporations with agents or representatives within the state.

1899

February 27. Ohio v. Thomas. 173 U. S. 276.

Argued January 10, 1899. Peckham, J., for the Court; Harlan, J., concurring; Fuller, C. J., not participating.

Another of the cases involving an agrarian legislative campaign against oleomargarine, this case denied to Ohio a power to prohibit the purchase and use of oleomargarine in Federal institutions within the state.

December 4. Addyston Pipe & Steel Co. v. United States. 175 U.S. 211.

Argued April 26, 27, 1899. Peckham, J., for the Court.

Sustained a conviction of perpetrators of a market-allocation plan as in violation of the Sherman Anti-Trust Act, thus complementing the *Trans-Missouri Freight* case in partially rehabilitating the Act after the extreme decision in the Sugar Trust Case.

December 4. Bradfield v. Roberts. 175 U. S. 291.

Argued October 27, 1899. Peckham, J., for the Court.

The first decision under the "establishment" clause on religious freedom in the First Amendment, this case upheld a contract between the District of Columbia and a religious order for the construction of a charitable clinic, maintained by the order, attached to a public hospital.

December 18. Cumming v. Board of Education. 175 U. S. 528.

Argued October 30, 1899. Harlan, J., for the Court.

Upholding a state court ruling that a school board could not be compelled under the Fourteenth Amendment to withhold funds for a high school for white children until matching funds for a Negro high school were provided.

1900

May 14. Knowlton v. Moore. 178 U. S. 41.

Argued December 5-7, 1899. White, J., for the Court; Brewer, Harlan, McKenna, JJ., dissenting; Peckham, J., not participating.

Retreating from the Income Tax Case doctrine, the Court here held that the requirement of uniformity of indirect taxes is "geographic, not intrinsic," and validated excise taxes laid upon "the incidents of ownership."

November 19. Austin v. Tennessee. 179 U. S. 344.

Argued November 9, 10, 1899. Brown, J., for the Court; White, J., concurring; Brewer, Peckham and Shiras, JJ., and Fuller, C. J., dissenting.

Sustaining a Tennessee statute prohibiting the import and sale of cigarettes and modifying the "original package" doctrine by limiting its applicability to specifically addressed consignments.

1901

March 4. President McKinley begins second term.

April 9. Philander C. Knox becomes Attorney General.

May 27. DeLima v. Bidwell. 182 U. S. 1.

Argued January 8-11, 1901. Brown, J., for the Court; McKenna, Shiras and White, JJ., dissenting.

In this, the first of the Insular Cases, the majority held that with the end of the Spanish-American War, Puerto Rico ceased to be a foreign country and imports therefrom could not be subjected to duties without express Congressional authority.

May 27. Dooley v. United States. 182 U. S. 222.

Argued with preceding case. Brown, J., for the Court; White, Gray, Mc-Kenna and Shiras, JJ., dissenting.

Conversely, holding that goods exported from the United States to Puerto Rico were duty free.

May 27. Downes v. Bidwell. 182 U. S. 244.

Argued with preceding two cases. Brown, J., for the Court; White, Mc-Kenna and Shiras, JJ., concurring; Gray, J., separately concurring; Fuller, C. J., and Harlan, Brewer, and Peckham, JJ., dissenting.

Confusing the issue set out in the preceding cases, the majority in its several opinions concluded that the rights of the Constitution did not automatically, immediately and completely extend to newly acquired territory. The effect of the three Insular Cases was to leave the government of such territory solely subject to Congress.

September 3. Theodore Roosevelt sworn in as President.

October 21. Knoxville Iron Co. v. Harbison. 183 U. S. 13.

Argued March 7, 1901. Shiras, J., for the Court; Brewer and Peckham, JJ., dissenting.

In this case, in which future Justice Sanford appeared as counsel for the company, the Court ruled that a state law requiring cash redemption of coal requisitions given employees in lieu of salary was not a denial of due process.

November 25. Cotting v. Kansas City Stockyards. 183 U. S. 79.

Argued November 14, 15, 1899; reargued January 23, 24, 1901. Brewer, J., for the Court; Harlan, Gray, Brown, Shiras, White and McKenna, JJ., "assented to the ruling" without expressing an opinion on the statute involved.

Invalidating a Kansas statute, as a denial of equal protection of the laws under the Fourteenth Amendment, applying to a single, specific stockyard and not to any others.

1902

December 1. Reid v. Colorado. 187 U. S. 137.

Argued October 24, 1902. Harlan, J., for the Court; Brewer, J., dissenting.

Qualifying earlier rulings on state public health authority over imported cattle, the Court held that a state may protect its people from prospective contagion by denying entry where contagion is reasonably in prospect.

December 8. Justice Holmes succeeds Gray.

1903

February 23. Champion v. Ames. 188 U. S. 321.

Argued December 15, 16, 1902. Harlan, J., for the Court; Fuller, C. J., and Brewer, Peckham and Shiras, JJ., dissenting.

The majority asserted a Federal police power—not heretofore unequivocally recognized by the courts—sufficient to prohibit the dissemination of lottery tickets through the mails.

March 2. Justice Day succeeds Shiras.

March 16. Henry M. Hoyt becomes Solicitor General.

November 30. Atkin v. Kansas. 191 U.S. 207.

Argued May 1, 1903. Harlan, J., for the Court; Fuller, C. J., and Brewer and Peckham, JJ., dissenting.

Sustaining a Kansas statute setting eight-hour day for public works projects within the state.

1904

March 14. Northern Securities Co. v. United States. 193 U. S. 197.

Argued December 14, 15, 1903. Harlan, J., for the Court; Brewer, J., concurring; White, Holmes and Peckham, JJ., and Fuller, C. J., dissenting.

By a narrow majority, the government won its anti-trust suit against a holding company (one of whose attorneys in argument before the Court was former Attorney General Griggs). Justice Brewer's concurrence in the official opinion, on the ground that the combination was unreasonable, actually advanced the argument of the four dissenters that the law ought to distinguish between types of business combinations as "reasonable" or "unreasonable."

April 4. National Mutual Bldg. & Loan Assn. v. Brahan. 193 U. S. 635.

Argued February 25, 26, 1904. McKenna, J., for the Court; White, J., not participating.

A New York insurance company doing business in Missouri was held to be subject to the regulations of Missouri authorities. The Court steadily retreated from this view in subsequent years.

May 31. Public Clearing House v. Coyne. 194 U. S. 497.

Argued April 18, 1904. Brown, J., for the Court; Brewer, Holmes and White, JJ., concurring; Peckham, J., dissenting.

Upholding Congressional enactments denying use of the mails for schemes suspected of being fraudulent.

May 31. McCray v. United States. 195 U. S. 27.

Argued December 2, 1903. White, J., for the Court; Fuller, C. J., and Brown and Peckham, JJ., dissenting.

Sustaining a Congressional act of 1886 imposing a discriminatory tax on colored oleomargarine, the Court held that when Congress' tax power was plenary the judiciary could not inquire into the purposes for which the tax power was used.

July 1. William Moody becomes Attorney General.

1905

February 20. Jacobson v. Massachusetts. 197 U. S. 11.

Argued December 4, 1904. Harlan, J., for the Court; Brewer, Peckham, JJ., dissenting.

Sustaining a Massachusetts compulsory vaccination law, the Court opinion rejected a contention that the Preamble of the Constitution standing alone could be regarded as a source of law.

March 4. Theodore Roosevelt inaugurated President in his own right.

April 10. Matter of Heff. 197 U. S. 488.

Argued January 9, 10, 1905. Brewer, J., for the Court, Harlan, J., dissenting.

Although limiting the Indian Liquor Sales Act of 1897 (see Appendix D), the opinion sustained the general principle of a Federal prohibition law.

April 17. Lochner v. New York. 198 U. S. 45.

Argued February 23, 24, 1905. Peckham, J., for the Court; Holmes, Harlan, Day and White, JJ., dissenting.

Invalidating a New York eight-hour day law for bakers, the majority held that this application of state police power interfered with the Federal constitutional guarantee of freedom of contract. Holmes' dissent criticized the majority reasoning on the ground that the Constitution was not intended to embody any specific economic theory.

December 4. South Carolina v. United States. 199 U. S. 437.

Argued April 11, 1905. Brewer, J., for the Court; White, Peckham, and Mc-Kenna, JJ., dissenting.

Proprietary activities of a state (in this case, operation of a state liquor store) as distinguished from its governmental activities held subject to Federal license taxes.

1906

January 30. Swift & Co. v. United States. 196 U. S. 375.

Argued January 6, 7, 1906. Holmes, J., for the Court.

A unanimous Court upheld the government's anti-trust action against the packing industry, with Holmes introducing his concept of the "current of commerce" in which certain local business practices could be found to be part of interstate commerce.

December 17. Justice Moody succeeds Brown. Charles J. Bonaparte becomes Attorney General.

1907

April 15. Patterson v. Colorado. 205 U. S. 454.

Argued March 5, 6, 1907. Holmes, J., for the Court; Harlan and Brewer, JJ., dissenting.

After three-quarters of a century of statutory limitation on the contempt power, this opinion substantially rehabilitated the claim that the judiciary had inherent power to find offenders in contempt.

1908

January 6. First Employers' Liability Case. 207 U. S. 463.

Argued April 10-12, 1907. White, J., for the Court; Fuller, C. J., and Peckham, Day and Brewer, JJ., concurring; Moody, J., dissenting.

A Congressional act doing away with common law concepts of contributory negligence in cases of employees injured on interstate railroads was held invalid because applying in some cases to intrastate lines as well. The statute was amended by Congress and upheld in 1912.

January 27. Adair v. United States. 208 U. S. 161.

Argued October 29, 30, 1907. Harlan, J., for the Court; McKenna, Holmes, JJ., dissenting.

Invalidating the provision of the 1898 Erdman Act which had sought to outlaw "yellow-dog" anti-union contracts in interstate railroads. The case marked the broadening definition of Holmes' own economic liberalism in constitutional interpretation, in his dissent.

February 3. Loewe v. Lawlor. 208 U. S. 274.

Argued December 4, 5, 1907. Fuller, C. J., for the Court.

The Danbury Hatters' Case held the Sherman Anti-Trust Act applicable to labor unions engaged in secondary boycotts.

February 24. Muller v. Oregon. 208 U. S. 412.

Argued January 15, 1908. Brewer, J., for the Court.

Accepting the argument in support of the Oregon law fixing maximum working hours for women, documented by elaborate statistical, social and economic data in the "Brandeis brief," the Court modified its previous position that the Fourteenth Amendment insured freedom of contract against any governmental action.

March 16. Armour Packing Co. v. United States. 209 U. S. 56.

Argued January 20-22, 1908. Day, J., for the Court; Brewer, J., dissenting; Moody, J., not participating.

Affirming the power of the Interstate Commerce Commission under the Elkins Act of 1903 to investigate rate differentials for unfair burdens on shippers.

April 6. Hudson Water Co. v. McCarter. 209 U. S. 349.

Argued March 18, 19, 1908. Holmes, J., for the Court; McKenna, J., dissenting.

Affirming a state's right to prohibit the diversion of water within its borders to other states, and denying that such use of state police power impairs the contract of a company undertaking to make the diversion.

May 9. Berea College v. Kentucky. 211 U. S. 45.

Argued April 10, 13, 1908. Brewer, J., for the Court; Holmes and Moody, JJ., concurring; Harlan and Day, JJ., dissenting.

Upholding a Kentucky law, after granting charter for college education to be offered to both white and Negro students, requiring segregation of classes.

November 9. Twining v. New Jersey. 211 U. S. 78.

Argued March 19, 20, 1908. Moody, J., for the Court; Harlan, J., dissenting.

Rejecting an argument that a state law permitting judges to comment on failure of defendants to testify in their own defense denied rights of national citizenship, the Court declared that the Fourteenth Amendment did not automatically apply the first eight Amendments of the Bill of Rights to the states.

1909

March 4. William Howard Taft inaugurated as President.

March 5. George W. Wickersham becomes Attorney General.

April 1. Lloyd W. Bowers becomes Solicitor General.

1910

January 3. Justice Lurton succeeds Peckham.

April 4. Mo. Pac. R. Co. v. Nebraska. 217 U. S. 196.

Argued March 7, 1910. Holmes, J., for the Court; Harlan and McKenna, JJ., dissenting.

Invalidating a state law which required railroads to construct spurs of track to any private elevator within a minimum distance of its right-of-way, upon the demand of the elevator owner.

April 21. Int. Textbook Co. v. Pigg. 217 U. S. 91.

Argued April 21, 1909. Harlan, J., for the Court; Fuller, C. J., and McKenna, J., dissenting.

Local licensing of out-of-state mail-order distributors of services held to be unconstitutional burden on interstate commerce.

October 10. Justice Hughes succeeds Brewer.

December 12. Frederick W. Lehmann becomes Solicitor General.

December 19. THE WHITE COURT (December 1910-May 1921).

White, C. J., Day, Harlan, Holmes, Hughes, Lurton, McKenna, Moody, Van Devanter, JJ.

1911

January 3. Justice Van Devanter succeeds to White's position as Associate Justice. Justice Lamar succeeds Moody.

January 3. Bailey v. Alabama. 219 U. S. 219.

Argued October 20, 21, 1910. Hughes, J., for the Court; Holmes and Lurton, JJ., dissenting.

Invalidating an Alabama statute requiring individuals to "work out" their debts by service on the land of the creditor—a variation of peonage—as in conflict with the Thirteenth Amendment.

January 3. Muskrat v. United States. 219 U. S. 346.

Argued November 30, December 1, 2, 1910. Day, J., for the Court.

One of a long line of cases in which the Court has consistently declined to give advisory opinions in cases not involving a "case or controversy" within the meaning of the Constitution.

March 13. Hipolite Egg Co. v. United States. 220 U. S. 45.
Argued January 5, 1911. McKenna, J., for the Court.

Sustaining the provisions of the Pure Food and Drug Act of 1906 authorizing seizure of adulterated goods in interstate commerce.

March 13. Flint v. Stone Tracy Co. 220 U. S. 107.
Argued March 17-19, 1910; reargued January 17-19, 1911. Day, J., for the Court.

All but nullifying the original doctrine in the Income Tax Case, sustaining a Federal tax on the income of corporations, this case accelerated the process of judicial reversal of the *Pollock* case at the same time that the Sixteenth Amendment was approaching adoption.

May 3. United States v. Grimaud. 220 U. S. 506.
Argued February 28, 1910 and affirmed by a divided Court; reargued March 3, 1911. Lamar, J., for the Court.

Affirming the constitutionality of conservation statutes of 1891 and 1905, with a distinction between the vesting of broad administrative discretion in the Executive and the unconstitutional delegation of legislative power to the administrator.

May 15. Standard Oil Co. v. United States. 221 U. S. 1.
Argued March 14-16, 1910; reargued January 12, 13, 16, 17, 1911. White, J., for the Court; Harlan J., concurring in part and dissenting in part.

The "rule of reason" with reference to application of the Sherman Anti-Trust Act was applied by the majority in this case ordering the dissolution of the oil combine.

May 29. United States v. Am. Tobacco Co. 221 U. S. 106.
Argued June 3-6, 1910; reargued, January 9-12, 1911. White, C. J., for the Court; Harlan, J., concurring in part and dissenting in part.

The culmination of the "rule of reason" standard was this decision ordering the reorganization rather than the dissolution of the Tobacco Trust. Harlan, in one of his closing dissents, denounced the doctrine as "judicial usurpation."

May 15. Oklahoma v. Kansas Nat. Gas Co. 221 U. S. 229.
Argued April 4, 5, 1911. McKenna, J., for the Court; Holmes, Hughes and Lurton, JJ., dissenting.

Modifying the *Hudson Water Co.* doctrine, the Court in this case distinguished between a state's power to prohibit the taking of its natural resources and its power to deny a right to transport them in interstate commerce once they had been reduced to possession.

May 15. Gompers v. Bucks Stove & Range Co. 221 U. S. 418.
Argued January 27, 30, 1911. Lamar, J., for the Court.

Extending the doctrine in the *Danbury Hatters' Case,* the Court held that an anti-trust order enjoining a secondary boycott in the form of published charges of unfair trade was not infringement upon the freedoms of the First Amendment.

October 20. Southern R. Co. v. United States. 222 U. S. 20.

Argued March 9, 10, 1911. Van Devanter, J., for the Court.

Upholding a Federal statute on railroad safety devices, the Court applied the statute to all cars on interstate trains whether or not engaged in interstate commerce as a "practical necessity" to effectuate the Congressional objectives.

1912

January 15. Second Employers' Liability Case. 223 U. S. 1.

Argued February 20, 21, 1911. Van Devanter, J., for the Court.

Sustaining the constitutionality of the revised law fixing liability for employee injury without reference to contributory negligence.

February 19. Pacific States Tel. Co. v. Oregon. 223 U. S. 118.

Argued November 3, 1911. White, C. J., for the Court.

Dismissing an argument that the Constitution guaranteed to the states "a republican form of government" as non-judicial question.

March 18. Justice Pitney succeeds Harlan.

June 7. Savage v. Jones. 225 U. S. 501.

Argued January 18, 1912. Hughes, J., for the Court.

Sustaining a statute prohibiting the importation of dog food below certain standards, as a valid public health measure not unreasonably burdening interstate commerce.

October 15. William M. Bullitt becomes Solicitor General.

1913

February 24. Home Tel. & Tel. Co. v. Los Angeles. 227 U. S. 278.

Argued October 28, 1912. White, C. J., for the Court.

Holding that the injunctions of the Fourteenth Amendment apply to all persons, natural or "legal," who are agents of state action.

February 24. Hoke v. United States. 227 U. S. 308.

Argued January 7, 8, 1913. McKenna, J., for the Court.

A series of cases, of which this was the first, sustained all phases of the White Slave Act as a valid exercise of Federal police power.

February 25. Income Tax Amendment declared adopted.

March 4. Woodrow Wilson inaugurated as President.

March 5. James C. McReynolds becomes Attorney General.

April 7. McDermott v. Wisconsin. 228 U. S. 115.

Argued January 17, 20, 1913. Day, J., for the Court.

Sustaining the constitutionality of the Pure Food and Drug Law and extending the "original package" doctrine to apply to packages within original shipping package—i. e., those which actually reach individual purchasers and consumers.

May 13. Seventeenth Amendment declared ratified.

June 9. Minnesota Rate Cases. 230 U. S. 352.

Argued April 9-12, 1912. Hughes, J., for the Court; McKenna, J., concurring.

Sustaining a railroad rate fixed by a state commission, the Court held that the exclusive authority of Congress over interstate commerce did not inhibit state action in non-conflicting areas.

June 10. Lewis Pub. Co. v. Morgan. 229 U. S. 288.

Argued December 2, 3, 1912. White, C. J., for the Court.

Amendments to postal laws requiring statements of ownership of periodicals as condition for admission to second-class mail held not an abridgement of First Amendment on freedom of press.

August 30. John W. Davis becomes Solicitor General.

1914

February 24. Weeks v. United States. 232 U. S. 383.

Argued December 2, 3, 1913. Day, J., for the Court.

The Court for the first time held that in prosecutions in Federal courts the Fourth Amendment barred the use of evidence secured through illegal search and seizure.

June 8. Houston & Texas R. Co. v. United States. 234 U. S. 342.

Argued October 28, 29, 1913. Hughes, J., for the Court; Lurton and Pitney, JJ., dissenting.

In this landmark Shreveport Rate Case, the Court held that the Interstate Commerce Act and the commerce clause of the Constitution gave the United States plenary power in rate making. Where the Commission had to fix intrastate rates in order to establish an equitable long- and short-haul ratio, the Federal rate-fixing authority would override and amend a rate set by a state authority.

June 22. The Pipeline Cases. 234 U. S. 548.

Argued October 15, 16, 1913. Holmes, J., for the Court; White, C. J., concurring; McKenna, J., dissenting.

Affirming the Hepburn Act which extended the authority of the Interstate Commerce Commission to regulate pipelines.

September 3. Thomas W. Gregory becomes Attorney General.

October 12. Justice McReynolds succeeds Lurton.

1915

January 25. Coppage v. Kansas. 236 U. S. 1.

Argued October 30, 1914. Pitney, J., for the Court; Day and Hughes, JJ., dissenting.

Complementing the *Adair* case of 1908, this case held unconstitutional a state law outlawing "yellow-dog" anti-union contracts as an interference with freedom of contract.

April 12. C. B. & Q. R. Co. v. Wisconsin R. Comm. 237 U. S. 220.

Argued March 12, 1915. McKenna, J., for the Court.

Holding that when a state requires an interstate corporation to comply with local regulations, the Interstate Commerce Commission is empowered to examine the regulations to determine their potential effect on interstate commerce.

November 1. Truax v. Raich. 239 U. S. 33.

Argued October 15, 1915. Hughes, J., for the Court; McReynolds, J., dissenting.

Invalidating a state law which sought to limit the number of foreign nationals who could be employed by local employers.

December 12. Hadacheck v. Los Angeles. 239 U. S. 394.

Argued October 22, 1915. McKenna, J., for the Court.

Sustaining a city ordinance which required certain businesses to be operated outside the city limits.

1916

January 24. Brushaber v. Union Pac. R. Co. 240 U. S. 1.

Argued October 14, 15, 1915. White, C. J., for the Court; McKenna and Pitney, JJ., dissenting.

The majority opinion declared that the Sixteenth Amendment had been intended to rescind the rationale of the *Pollock* case.

February 21. Tyee Realty Co. v. Andrews. 240 U. S. 115.

Argued October 14, 15, 1915. White, C. J., for the Court; McReynolds, J., not participating.

Following the rule in *Brushaber* and upholding the implementation of the Sixteenth Amendment in the Tariff Act of 1913.

June 5. Justice Brandeis succeeds Lamar.

October 9. Justice Clarke succeeds Hughes.

1917

January 8. Clark Distilling Co. v. Western Md. R. Co. 242 U. S. 311.

Argued May 10, 11, 1915; reargued November 8, 9, 1916. White, C. J., for the Court; McReynolds, J., concurring; Holmes and Van Devanter, JJ., dissenting.

Upholding the constitutionality of the Webb-Kenyon Act and thus sustaining also the West Virginia prohibition law.

January 15. Caminetti v. United States. 242 U. S. 470.

Argued November 13, 14, 1916. Day, J., for the Court; McKenna and Clarke, JJ., and White, C. J., dissenting; McReynolds, J., not participating.

Broadening the interpretation of the White Slave Act by holding that it applied to non-commercial as well as commercial traffic in women for any immoral purpose.

March 4. Wilson begins second term as President.

March 19. Wilson v. New. 243 U. S. 332.

Argued January 8-10, 1917. White, C. J., for the Court; McKenna, J., concurring; Day, Pitney, Van Devanter and McReynolds, JJ., dissenting.

Affirming the eight-hour work day on interstate railroads provided in the Adamson Act. While stressing that this was a temporary measure of limited applicability, the majority opinion nevertheless declared that authority for Congressional control of such subjects was latent in the Constitution.

April 9. Bunting v. Oregon. 243 U. S. 426.

Argued April 18, 1916; reargued January 19, 1917. McKenna, J., for the Court; White, C. J., Van Devanter and McReynolds, JJ., dissenting; Brandeis, J., not participating.

Extending the Oregon statutes relating to maximum hours, first upheld in 1908 with reference to women, to all employees in all industry. The statute also affected minimum wages of women and minors, and this aspect of the law was impliedly upheld as well.

May 21. New York Cent. R. Co. v. Winfield. 244 U. S. 147.

Argued February 29, March 1, 1916; reargued February 1, 1917. Van Devanter, J., for the Court; Brandeis and Clarke, JJ., dissenting.

Holding that the Federal Employers' Liability Act excluded claims for workmen's compensation under state law even where the Federal law did not provide a remedy.

May 21. Erie R. Co. v. Winfield. 244 U. S. 170.

Argued March 1, 1916; reargued February 1, 2, 1917. Van Devanter, J., for the Court; Brandeis and Clarke, JJ., dissenting.

Extending the rule of the companion case to deny relief under state laws where employee was injured after leaving work, on ground that he was still engaged in interstate commerce pre-empted by the Federal law although the Federal law afforded no relief.

May 21. South. Pac. R. Co. v. Jensen. 244 U. S. 205.

Argued February 28, 1916; reargued January 31, February 1, 1917. McReynolds, J., for the Court; Holmes, Pitney, Brandeis and Clarke, JJ., dissenting.

The third of the compensation cases, denying relief under the Federal law where injury occurred in maritime work on vessels owned by railroads subject to the statute.

June 11. Paine Lumber Co. v. Neal. 244 U. S. 459.

Argued May 3, 4, 1915; reargued October 24, 25, 1916. Holmes, J., for the Court; Pitney, McKenna and Van Devanter, JJ., dissenting.

The majority held that a private party could not petition for an injunction against a labor union under the Sherman Act where the petitioner failed to show special injury to himself. This shortlived view of the limits to the labor injunction was to be overturned early in the Taft Court.

June 11. Adams v. Tanner. 244 U. S. 590.

Argued May 7, 1917. McReynolds, J., for the Court; McKenna, Brandeis, Holmes and Clarke, JJ., dissenting.

Invalidating a Washington state law forbidding employment agencies to collect fees from job seekers, as a deprivation of a property right without due process of law.

December 10. Hitchman Coal & Coke Co. v. Mitchell. 245 U. S. 229.

Argued March 2, 3, 1916; reargued December 15, 18, 1916. Pitney, J., for the Court; Brandeis, Holmes and Clarke, JJ., dissenting.

Affirming the right of employees to seek an injunction against union organizers advocating a strike for union recognition.

December 10. Eagle Glass & Mfg. Co. v. Rowe. 245 U. S. 275.

Argued December 18, 1916. Pitney, J., for the Court; Brandeis, Holmes and Clarke, JJ., dissenting.

Reaffirming the rule in the *Hitchman* case.

1918

January 7. Selective Draft Cases. 245 U. S. 366.

Argued December 13, 14, 1917. White, C. J., for the Court.

Half a dozen cases were consolidated in this opinion sustaining the power of the Federal government, both as an inherent element of sovereignty and as a direct consequence of the Constitution's provision in Article I, Section 8, "to raise and support armies."

January 14. Goldman v. United States. 245 U. S. 474.

Argued December 13, 14, 1917. White, C. J., for the Court.

Another draft law decision, sustaining the power of the Federal government to compel military service as not an unreasonable infringement upon individual liberty.

May 20. Peck v. Lowe. 247 U. S. 165.

Argued December 10, 11, 1917. Van Devanter, J., for the Court.

Sustaining the first Income Tax Law passed under the Sixteenth Amendment, in its provision for levying on the net income of a corporation derived from sales of exported goods.

June 3. Hammer v. Dagenhart. 247 U. S. 251.

Argued April 15, 16, 1918. Day, J., for the Court; Holmes, McKenna, Brandeis and Clarke, JJ., dissenting.

The first Child Labor Act decision, narrowly holding invalid the use of the commerce power as a police power to prohibit shipment of goods produced by child labor in interstate commerce where the goods themselves were not inherently harmful. Justice Day's opinion stressed that regulation of child labor was a local issue.

June 3. United States Glue Co. v. Oak Creek. 247 U. S. 321.

Argued March 21, 1918. Pitney, J., for the Court; White, C. J., concurring.

Sustaining a state income tax on domestic corporations even when the tax fell in part upon income derived from interstate commerce.

June 10. Toledo Newsp. Co. v. United States. 247 U. S. 402.

Argued March 7, 8, 1918. White, C. J., for the Court; Holmes, J., dissenting.

Sustaining the broadening contempt power of the judiciary which had been revived in *Patterson v. Colorado,* the Court held that applying such power to newspapers was not infringement of the First Amendment.

November 21. Alexander King becomes Solicitor General.

December 23. Intern. News Serv. v. Associated Press. 248 U. S. 215.

Argued May 2, 3, 1918. Pitney, J., for the Court; Holmes and McKenna, JJ., concurring; Brandeis, J., dissenting.

Sustaining the application of the laws of unfair competition under the anti-trust statutes, the Court held that a news service was entitled to protection from the pirating of its news by another, even though the news itself was part of the public domain.

1919

January 29. Eighteenth Amendment declared ratified.

March 3. Schenck v. United States. 249 U. S. 47.

Argued January 9, 10, 1919. Holmes, J., for the Court.

Applying a test of "clear and present danger," Justice Holmes sustained the wartime Espionage Act against the charge that it violated the First Amendment.

March 3. United States v. Doremus. 249 U. S. 86.

Argued January 16, 1919. Day, J., for the Court; White, C. J., McKenna, Van Devanter and McReynolds, JJ., dissenting.

Sustaining a Federal anti-narcotic drug law as a reasonable use of the tax power as a police measure to outlaw a practice believed contrary to the general welfare.

March 5. A. Mitchell Palmer becomes Attorney General.

March 10. Frohwerk v. United States. 249 U. S. 204.

Argued January 27, 1919. Holmes, J., for the Court.

Again applying the "clear and present danger" test, the Court held a conviction for conspiracy under the Espionage Act was not an infringement upon the First Amendment.

March 10. Debs v. United States. 249 U. S. 211.

Argued January 27, 28, 1919. Holmes, J., for the Court.

Nor would the First Amendment, said the Court in this case, protect one engaged in intentional obstructing of the military operations of the government.

June 9. American Mfg. Co. v. St. Louis. 250 U. S. 459.

Argued April 30, 1919. Pitney, J., for the Court.

Sustaining a state tax which could be distinguished as a tax on business (local) rather than on the goods of the business (interstate).

November 10. Abrams v. United States. 250 U. S. 616.

Argued October 21, 22, 1919. Clarke, J., for the Court; Holmes and Brandeis, JJ., dissenting.

Holding that the advocacy of strikes at war plants amounted to a "clear and present danger" under the *Schenck* rule. Holmes made his famous protest against the proscription of ideas.

1920

January 5. Ruppert, Inc., v. Caffey. 251 U. S. 264.

Argued November 20, 21, 1919. Brandeis, J., for the Court; McReynolds, Day and Van Devanter, JJ., dissenting.

Upholding the Volstead Act against the charge that it arbitrarily deprived brewery owners of property without due process of law.

January 26. Silverthorne Lumb. Co. v. United States. 251 U. S. 385.

Argued December 12, 1919. Holmes, J., for the Court; White, C. J., and Pitney, J., dissenting.

Holding that the Fourth Amendment protects corporations from unreasonable search and seizure in criminal proceedings.

March 1. United States v. U. S. Steel Co. 251 U. S. 417.

Argued March 9, 12-14, 1917; reargued October 7-10, 1919. McKenna, J., for the Court; Day, Pitney and Clarke, JJ., dissenting; McReynolds and Brandeis, JJ., not participating.

Dismissing the long-pending anti-trust suit against the Steel Trust, this case marked the final end of the trust-busting era and the final triumph of the "rule of reason."

March 1. Schaefer v. United States. 251 U. S. 466.

Argued October 21, 1919. McKenna, J., for the Court; Brandeis, Holmes and Brandeis, JJ., dissenting.

The Court began with this case to divide on the circumstances which would constitute "clear and present danger" under the *Schenck* rule, but the majority sustained an absolutist prohibition in the Espionage Act.

March 8. Eisner v. Macomber. 252 U. S. 189.

Argued April 16, 1919; reargued October 17, 20, 1919. Pitney, J., for the Court; Holmes, Day, Brandeis and Clarke, JJ., dissenting.

Limiting the effect of the Sixteenth Amendment by excluding stock dividends from income subject to tax.

April 19. Missouri v. Holland. 252 U. S. 416.

Argued March 2, 1920. Holmes, J., for the Court; Van Devanter and Pitney, JJ., dissenting.

The majority in this case sustained a treaty on migratory bird conservation, executed between Canada and the United States, as vesting in Congress a power not specified in the Constitution. Alarmists claimed that such a construction tended to give Congress a means of evading constitutional restraints.

June 1. William L. Frierson becomes Solicitor General.

June 1. Evans v. Gore. 253 U. S. 245.

Argued March 5, 1920. Van Devanter, J., for the Court; Holmes and Brandeis, JJ., dissenting.

Interpreting the Sixteenth Amendment as not authorizing the United States to "diminish" the salary of a Federal official while in office by imposing the income tax.

June 1. Hawke v. Smith. 253 U. S. 221, 231.

Argued April 23, 1920. Day, J., for the Court.

In two companion cases, the Court dismissed an attempt by anti-prohibitionists in Ohio to compel the question of ratification of the Eighteenth Amendment to be submitted to the people; Congress was held to have sole discretion in determining the method of ratification.

June 7. National Prohibition Cases. 253 U. S. 350.

Argued March 8-10, 29, 30, 1920. Van Devanter, J., for the Court; White, C. J., and McReynolds, J., concurring; McKenna and Clarke, JJ., dissenting.

Grouping a number of cases testing the validity of the Eighteenth Amendment and the Volstead Act, the majority rejected a novel argument that the Amendment was not a subject for constitutional provision.

June 7. Federal Trade Comm. v. Gratz. 253 U. S. 421.

Argued April 20, 21, 1920. McReynolds, J., for the Court; Pitney, J., concurring; Brandeis and Clarke, JJ., dissenting.

The majority held that desist orders of the Commission based on complaints which failed to establish the fact of unfair competition were void. The effect was to substitute the judgment of the Court for that of the Commission in determining the conclusiveness of the evidence supporting a complaint.

August 26. Nineteenth Amendment proclaimed ratified.

November 8. Johnson v. Maryland. 254 U. S. 51.

Argued October 18, 1920. Holmes, J., for the Court; Pitney and McReynolds, JJ., dissenting.

Denying state authority to require license of Federal mail trucks.

December 13. Gilbert v. Minnesota. 254 U. S. 325.

Argued November 10, 1920. McKenna, J., for the Court; Holmes, J., concurring; Brandeis, J., dissenting.

Sustaining a state sedition law as reaching an area in which state and Federal "cooperation" was desirable. This rule was not overturned until *Pennsylvania v. Nelson* in 1956.

1921

January 3. Duplex Prtg. Press Co. v. Deering. 254 U. S. 443.

Argued January 22, 1920. Pitney, J., for the Court; Brandeis, Holmes and Clarke, JJ., dissenting.

Although the Clayton Act had specifically exempted labor unions from anti-trust action, the majority opinion construed this exemption so narrowly—holding that it did not apply to secondary boycotts and certain other strike tactics—as virtually to emasculate the law.

February 28. United States v. Cohen Gro. Co. 255 U. S. 81.

Argued October 18, 19, 1920. White, C. J., for the Court; Pitney and Brandeis, JJ., concurring.

Although the Court did not decide the case until the wartime emergency had passed, it invalidated in this opinion the criminal penalties of the Lever Food Control Act. A related case (*Weeds, Inc. v. United States*) invalidated other major provisions of the statute, establishing a precedent against government controls of commodities which would be cited against New Deal laws a dozen years later.

March 4. Warren G. Harding inaugurated President.

March 5. Harry M. Daugherty becomes Attorney General.

March 7. Milwaukee Pub. Co. v. Burleson. 255 U. S. 407.

Argued January 18, 19, 1921. Clarke, J., for the Court; Brandeis and Holmes, JJ., dissenting.

Affirming the Postmaster General's authority under the Espionage Act to bar subversive matter from the mails.

April 18. Block v. Hirsch. 256 U. S. 135.

Argued March 3, 1921. Holmes, J., for the Court; White, C. J., and McKenna, Van Devanter and McReynolds, JJ., dissenting.

Affirming the power of the government in the District of Columbia to impose rent controls under emergency conditions and for the duration of the "exigency."

May 16. Dillon v. Gloss. 256 U. S. 368.

Argued March 22, 1921. Van Devanter, J., for the Court.

Rejecting another attack on the Prohibition Amendment, the Court held that Congress has complete discretion in determining the length of time an Amendment could lie before the people.

June 1. Burdeau v. McDowell. 256 U. S. 465.

Argued April 11, 12, 1921. Day, J., for the Court; Brandeis and Holmes, JJ., dissenting.

Sustaining the right of the government to retain and use in criminal prosecutions evidence illegally obtained by private parties without the government's knowledge.

July 1. James M. Beck becomes Solicitor General.

October 3. THE TAFT COURT (October 1921-February 1930.)

Taft, C. J., Brandeis, Clarke, Day, Holmes, Lamar, McReynolds, Pitney, Van Devanter, JJ.

December 5. Am. Steel Foundries v. Trades Council. 257 U. S. 184.

Argued January 7, 1919; reargued October 5, 1920; reargued October 4, 5, 1921. Taft, C. J., for the Court; Brandeis, J., concurring; Clarke, J., dissenting.

Invalidating an injunction which sweepingly denied strikers all picketing rights as too broad under the Clayton Act, the opinion nevertheless reaffirmed the *Duplex* rule that the anti-trust laws strictly circumscribed the rights of organized labor.

December 19. Truax v. Corrigan. 257 U. S. 312.

Argued April 29, 30, 1920; reargued October 5, 6, 1921. Taft, C. J., for the Court; Holmes, Pitney, Clarke and Brandeis, JJ., dissenting.

Invalidating an Arizona anti-picketing statute.

December 12. Dahnke-Walker Co. v. Bondurant. 257 U. S. 282.

Argued March 18, 1921; reargued October 10, 1921. Van Devanter, J., for the Court; Brandeis and Clarke, JJ., dissenting.

Rejecting a suit based on a state law rather than on an explicitly stated Federal constitutional right, the majority held that where the plaintiff fails to allege his constitutional right and the issue is based on state law reviewed by a state high court, it will not be heard by the Supreme Court as of right (i. e., only on certiorari).

1922

January 30. Cornelius v. Moore. 257 U. S. 491.

Argued December 15, 1921. McKenna, J., for the Court; McReynolds, J., dissenting.

One of the many prohibition-era cases, denying a claim of deprivation of property without due process where the claimant had acquired an interest in liquor in a warehouse from which he was not permitted to remove it.

February 27. Terral v. Burke Constr. Co. 257 U. S. 529.

Argued January 17, 1922. Taft, C. J., for the Court.

Invalidating an Arkansas statute which penalized foreign corporations for availing themselves of the Federal courts in suits within the state.

February 27. Leser v. Garnett. 258 U. S. 130.

Argued January 23, 24, 1922. Brandeis, J., for the Court.

Rejecting an attack upon the Nineteenth Amendment, the Court dismissed

Maryland's argument that the suffrage amendment arbitrarily added to the state's electorate and thus destroyed its political balance.

February 27. Wisconsin R. Comm. v. Chi., Burlington & Quincy R. Co. 257 U. S. 563.

Argued March 11, 14, 15, 1921; reargued December 5-7, 1921. Taft, C. J., for the Court.

Court declined to extend the rule of the Shreveport Rate Case to permit Interstate Commerce Commission to regulate intrastate rates where intrastate points were remote from interstate portion of the carriers' business.

May 1. Stafford v. Wallace. 258 U. S. 495.

Argued March 20, 22, 1922. Taft, C. J., for the Court; McReynolds, J., dissenting; Day, J., not participating.

Upholding the Packers and Stockyards Act of 1921, the Court extended the "current of commerce" theory to include livestock after it had been unloaded from interstate carriers, as still part of the interstate business transaction.

May 15. Hill v. Wallace. 259 U. S. 44.

Argued January 11, 12, 1922. Taft, C. J., for the Court; Brandeis, J., concurring.

The opinion held the Futures Trading Act of 1921 invalid as an attempted application of the tax power to police power objectives.

May 15. Bailey v. Drexel Furn. Co. 259 U. S. 20.

Argued March 7, 8, 1922. Taft, C. J., for the Court; Clarke, J., dissenting.

Invalidating the Child Labor Tax Law of 1918, thus denying to Congress the use of either the commerce power (in *Hammer v. Dagenhart*) or the tax power as an instrument for dealing with child labor.

June 5. United Mine Workers v. Coronado Coal Co. 259 U. S. 344.

Argued October 15, 1920; reargued March 22, 23, 1922. Taft, C. J., for the Court.

Sustaining a suit for damages to property incurred during a strike, under the civil liability section of the Sherman Act.

October 2. Justice Sutherland succeeds Clarke.

December 11. United States v. Lanza. 260 U. S. 377.

Argued November 22, 1922. Taft, C. J., for the Court.

One of a long line of prohibition cases turning on constitutional claims, this case held that the protection against double jeopardy applied to a second Federal prosecution rather than to separate Federal and state prosecutions.

1923

January 2. Justice Butler succeeds Day.

January 8. Federal Trade Comm. v. Curtis Pub. Co. 260 U. S. 568.

Argued November 17, 1922. McReynolds, J., for the Court; Taft, C. J., and Brandeis, J., dissenting.

Asserting more sweepingly the rule of the *Gratz* case, that the "ultimate determination of what constitutes unfair competition" under the Federal Trade Commission Act is a judicial matter.

February 19. Justice Sanford succeeds Pitney.

April 9. Adkins v. Children's Hospital. 261 U. S. 525.

Argued March 4, 1923. Sutherland, J., for the Court; Taft, C. J., Sanford and Holmes, JJ., dissenting; Brandeis, J., not participating.

Invalidating the District of Columbia minimum wage law for women, holding it to be an infringement upon freedom of contract under the Fifth Amendment.

April 9. Hodges v. Snyder. 261 U. S. 600.

On motion to dismiss or affirm, February 26, 1923. Sanford, J., for the Court.

Affirming a South Dakota court ruling that legislation extinguishing a taxpayer's right of suit is within the power of the state where the right is a public rather than a private one.

April 16. Chicago Board of Trade v. Olsen. 262 U. S. 1.

Argued February 26, 1923. Taft, C. J., for the Court; McReynolds and Sutherland, JJ., dissenting.

Sustaining the Grain Future Trading Act of 1922, drawn by Congress under the commerce power after the Court had invalidated (in *Hill v. Wallace*) a similar statute drawn under the taxing power. The disposition of the Court to find the commerce clause to be a more appropriate vehicle for exercise of the police power was to be a guideline for Congress consistently thereafter.

April 30. Cunard SS. Co. v. Mellon. 262 U. S. 100.

Argued January 4, 5, 1923. Van Devanter, J., for the Court; Sutherland and McReynolds, JJ., dissenting.

Twelve suits were consolidated in this opinion, which affirmed the government's power under the Eighteenth Amendment to prohibit the possession of liquors on ships within the territorial waters of the United States.

May 21. S. W. Bell Tel. Co. v. Pub. Serv. Comm. 262 U. S. 276.

Argued December 8, 1922. McReynolds, J., for the Court; Brandeis and Holmes, JJ., dissenting.

Applying the "fair value" standard to determine a "fair return" in fixing rates for utilities, the case limited the power of state commissions to substitute their judgment for the "honest discretion of the company's board of directors."

June 3. Frothingham v. Mellon. Massachusetts v. Mellon. 262 U. S. 447.

Argued May 3, 4, 1923. Sutherland, J., for the Court.

An original suit by Massachusetts, and an individual suit by a taxpayer, both challenged the validity of Federal grant-in-aid under the Shepard-Towner Maternity Act of 1921. By denying jurisdiction over the question, the Court left to Congressional discretion the whole subject of Federal grants-in-aid in many fields.

June 4. Meyer v. Nebraska. 262 U. S. 390.

Argued February 23, 1923. McReynolds, J., for the Court; Holmes and Sutherland, JJ., dissenting.

Invalidating a state law which prohibited the teaching of modern foreign languages below the high school level.

June 11. Sonnenborn Bros. v. Cureton. 262 U. S. 506.

Argued March 24, 1922; reargued October 5, 1922. Taft, C. J., for the Court; McReynolds, J., concurring.

The "original package" doctrine was further circumscribed by this case, validating a state occupation tax levied on warehousers of goods still in original packages but ready for distribution locally.

June 11. Wolff Pkg. Co. v. Court of Ind. Relations. 262 U. S. 522.

Argued April 27, 1923. Taft, C. J., for the Court.

Invalidating a state law subjecting to a special tribunal the labor problems of businesses declared to be affected with a public interest, the Court held that this public interest could not be arbitrarily attributed by the state but must depend on surrounding circumstances.

August 2. Calvin Coolidge sworn in as President upon death of President Harding.

1924

January 7. Dayton-Goose Cr. R. Co. v. United States. 263 U. S. 456.

Argued November 16, 19, 1923. Taft, C. J., for the Court.

Sustaining, as a general principle, the "recapture" provisions of the Transportation Act of 1920. This enabled the Interstate Commerce Commission to evaluate both intrastate and interstate earnings in determining railroad rates above a "fair return."

February 5. Washington v. Dawson. 264 U. S. 219.

Argued January 8, 9, 1924. McReynolds, J., for the Court; Holmes, J., concurring; Brandeis, J., dissenting.

Invalidating an attempt by Congress to stipulate the applicability of state workmen's compensation laws to cases under Federal admiralty jurisdiction.

April 7. Harlan F. Stone becomes Attorney General after oil scandals force Daugherty to resign.

April 14. Burns Baking Co. v. Bryan. 264 U. S. 504.

Argued October 19, 1923. Butler, J., for the Court; Brandeis and Holmes, JJ., dissenting.

Invalidating a state law regulating the weight of bread as a denial of due process.

June 9. United States v. New River Co. 265 U. S. 533.

Argued April 24, 1924. Butler, J., for the Court; McKenna, J., dissenting.

Holding that courts ought not to substitute their judgment for the findings and conclusions of the Interstate Commerce Commission when the Commission was acting within the scope of its statutory power.

October 20. Michaelson v. United States. 266 U. S. 42.

Argued April 9, 10, 1924. Sutherland, J., for the Court.

Holding unions liable for contempt when striking in defiance of a ruling of the Railroad Labor Board.

1925

March 2. Justice Stone succeeds McKenna.

March 2. Carroll v. United States. 267 U. S. 132.

Argued December 4, 1923; reargued March 14, 1924. Taft, C. J., for the Court; McKenna, J., concurring; McReynolds and Sutherland, JJ., dissenting.

Upholding the right of Federal agents to search private vehicles without warrant where violation of the prohibition law was reasonably suspected, as distinguished from denial of such power with reference to private dwellings.

March 2. Buck v. Kuykendall. 267 U. S. 307.

Argued November 25, 1924. Brandeis, J., for the Court; McReynolds, J., dissenting.

Invalidating a state action denying a license to operate a bus line as an attempt to limit competition rather than as a highway safety measure.

March 4. President Coolidge inaugurated for a full term.

March 17. John G. Sargent becomes Attorney General.

May 25. Coronado Coal Co. v. United Mine Workers. 268 U. S. 295.

Argued June 7, 1925. Taft, C. J., for the Court.

Although ruling that coal mining was not itself interstate commerce—and hence mining unions were not entitled to the protection of the Clayton Act against injunctions—the Court held that a strike interfering with the interstate shipment of coal was a conspiracy in restraint of trade subject to prosecution under the Sherman Act.

June 1. Miles v. Graham. 268 U. S. 501.

Argued March 16, 1925. McReynolds, J., for the Court; Brandeis, J., dissenting.

The Court here declared that a statute subjecting salaries of judges to an income tax did not come under the constitutional rule against diminishing salaries of officeholders while in office, where the judges were appointed after the enactment of the statute.

June 1. Pierce v. Society of Sisters. 268 U. S. 510.

Argued March 16, 17, 1925. McReynolds, J., for the Court.

Invalidating a state law which would have prohibited private school education by requiring all chilldren to attend public schools.

June 1. William D. Mitchell becomes Solicitor General.

June 8. Gitlow v. New York. 268 U. S. 652.

Argued April 19, 1923; reargued November 23, 1923. Sanford, J., for the Court; Holmes and Brandeis, JJ., dissenting.

Although both the majority and minority opinions accepted the proposition that the First Amendment guarantees of free speech extended through the Fourteenth Amendment to the states, the majority nevertheless held that this did not prevent a state from prohibiting anarchistic utterances or publications.

1926

March 8. Weaver v. Palmer Bros. 270 U. S. 402.

Argued December 11, 1925. Butler, J., for the Court; Holmes, Brandeis and Stone, JJ., dissenting.

Invalidating a Pennsylvania law forbidding the use of certain stuffing materials for bed comforters, even when sterilized, as an arbitrary use of the public health power.

May 3. Colorado v. United States. 271 U. S. 153.

Argued March 5, 8, 1926. Brandeis, J., for the Court.

Sustaining the authority of the Interstate Commerce Commission, under the Transportation Act of 1920, to determine the requests of railroads to abandon intrastate branches.

May 24. Corrigan v. Buckley. 271 U. S. 323.

Argued January 8, 1926. Sanford, J., for the Court.

Affirming restrictive covenants against the sale of real estate to Negroes as private action not within the reach of the Fourteenth Amendment.

October 25. Myers v. United States. 272 U. S. 52.

Argued December 5, 1923; reargued April 13, 14, 1925. Taft, C. J., for the Court; Holmes, McReynolds and Brandeis, JJ., dissenting.

Invalidating a Congressional statute denying the President power to remove certain postmasters without Congressional consent, as an improper restraint upon the Executive powers.

November 22. Euclid v. Ambler Realty Co. 272 U. S. 365.

Argued January 22, 1926; reargued October 12, 1926. Sutherland, J., for the Court; Van Devanter, McReynolds and Butler, JJ., dissenting.

Sustaining a zoning ordinance which sought to protect residential districts from encroaching industrialism, as a valid exercise of the police power of the state.

1927

January 3. DiSanto v. Pennsylvania. 273 U. S. 34.

Argued October 27, 1926. Butler, J., for the Court; Stone, Holmes and Brandeis, JJ., dissenting.

The majority opinion invalidated a state license tax on travel agents selling steamship tickets for travel abroad. Stone's dissent introduced the test of whether such taxes affected purely local concerns without infringing upon the national interest—a view that ultimately prevailed in *California v. Thompson* in 1941.

February 28. Tyson & Bro. v. Banton. 273 U. S. 418.

Argued October 6, 7, 1926. Sutherland, J., for the Court; Holmes, Brandeis and Stone, JJ., dissenting.

The majority opinion invalidated a New York law regulating the resale of theater tickets. The dissent contended that the regulating of any local business was reasonably within the jurisdiction of the state.

April 11. Bedford Stone Co. v. Journeymen Stonecutters. 274 U. S. 37.

Argued January 18, 1927. Sutherland, J., for the Court; Sanford and Stone, JJ., concurring; Brandeis and Holmes, JJ., dissenting.

Despite the Clayton Act's specific exemption of labor union activities from injunction, this case substantially broadened the doctrine of *Duplex Printing Press* by defining as unfair competition union efforts to prevent members from finishing products of nonunion labor.

May 16. Whitney v. California. 274 U. S. 357.

Argued October 6, 1925; reargued March 18, 1926. Sanford, J., for the Court; Brandeis and Holmes, JJ., concurring.

Although, as in *Gitlow,* the Court assumed the extension of First Amendment guarantees to the states through the Fourteenth, the opinion nevertheless found valid the state criminal syndicalism law as applying to the factual situation in this case.

1928

February 20. Delaware, Lackawanna, etc. R. Co. v. Morristown. 276 U. S. 182.

Argued January 6, 9, 1928. Butler, J., for the Court; Brandeis and Holmes, JJ., concurring in part and dissenting in part.

Invalidating a local ordinance creating a public taxi stand on premises of privately owned railroad terminal where terminal had given exclusive contract to one taxi company.

May 21. Willing v. Chicago Aud. Assn. 277 U. S. 274.

Argued April 19, 20, 1928. Brandeis, J., for the Court, Stone, J., concurring.

Another in a long catalog of cases where the Court refused to take jurisdiction because it considered that the issue sought a declaratory judgment rather than settlement of a "case or controversy" as stipulated by the Constitution.

May 28. Ribnik v. McBride. 277 U. S. 350.

Argued April 26, 27, 1928. Sutherland, J., for the Court; Sanford, J., concurring; Stone, Holmes and Brandeis, JJ., dissenting.

Invalidating a state law regulating employment agencies and holding that such agencies were not activities affected with a public interest.

June 4. Olmstead v. United States. 277 U. S. 438.

Argued February 20, 21, 1928. Taft, C. J., for the Court; Brandeis, Holmes, Butler and Stone, JJ., dissenting.

By a narrow majority the Court upheld a conviction based on evidence secured by wiretapping, even though in contravention of the Washington state law prohibiting such surveillance.

June 4. Nat. Life Ins. Co. v. United States. 277 U. S. 508.

Argued April 12, 1928. McReynolds, J., for the Court; Brandeis, Holmes and Stone, JJ., dissenting.

Invalidating a section of the Revenue Act of 1921 which laid a tax on state and municipal bonds.

1929

February 18. Frost v. Corporation Comm. 278 U. S. 515.

Argued March 26, 1928. Sutherland, J., for the Court; Brandeis, Holmes and Stone, JJ., dissenting.

Denying the right of Oklahoma to grant a franchise to a cooperative cotton gin in competition with an individual licensee, on the ground that the state was impairing a property right it had already granted to the private licensee.

March 4. Herbert Hoover inaugurated as President.

March 4. William D. Mitchell becomes Attorney General.

May 20. St. L., O'Fallon R. Co. v. United States. 279 U. S. 461.

Argued January 3, 4, 1929. McReynolds, J., for the Court; Brandeis, Holmes and Stone, JJ., dissenting; Butler, J., not participating.

Sustaining an argument that the Interstate Commerce Commission had to take into account all considerations stipulated by the statutes, including in this case the reproduction cost of property upon which rates were being based, the Court substantially limited the discretion of the Commission in determining the bases for its rate fixing.

May 27. Charles Evans Hughes, Jr., becomes Solicitor General.

1930

February 24. THE HUGHES COURT (February 1930-June 1941).

Hughes, C. J., Brandeis, Butler, Holmes, McReynolds, Sanford, Stone, Sutherland, Van Devanter.

March 12. Ohio v. Zangerle. 281 U. S. 74.

Argued February 27, 28, 1930. Hughes, C. J., for the Court.

Affirming argument that an Ohio state constitutional provision that no state law should be declared unconstitutional by the state court if more than one justice dissented, against charge that this was repugnant to the Federal Constitution.

March 22. Thomas D. Thacher becomes Solicitor General.

May 26. Texas & N. O. R. Co. v. Brotherhood of Railway & Steamship Clerks. 281 U. S. 548.

Argued May 1, 2, 1930. Hughes, C. J., for the Court.

Sustaining the right of employees under the Railway Labor Act to a free choice of their representatives for collective bargaining.

June 2. Justice Roberts succeeds Sanford.

1931

February 24. United States v. Sprague. 282 U. S. 716.

Argued January 21, 1931. Roberts, J., for the Court, Hughes, C. J., not participating.

Dismissing a novel holding of the intermediate courts, that the Prohibition Amendment had never been in effect because relating to personal liberties of individuals and thus in conflict with the reserved powers of the people.

April 13. Standard Oil Co. v. United States. 283 U. S. 163.

Argued January 13-15, 1931. Brandeis, J., for the Court; Stone, J., not participating.

Permitting patentees to cross-license oil refining processes when the practice does not tend to create a monopoly.

May 18. Stromberg v. California. 283 U. S. 359.

Argued April 15, 1931. Hughes, C. J., for the Court, McReynolds and Butler, JJ., dissenting.

Invalidating a California "red flag" statute as unconstitutionally denying to American citizens the right to freedom of expression, including unpopular radical opinions and symbols.

May 25. Federal Trade Commission v. Raladam Co. 283 U. S. 643.

Argued April 24, 1931. Sutherland, J., for the Court.

One of a series of cases throughout the years since this Commission was formed, narrowly construing the Commission's powers to prosecute suspected deceptive business practices in favor of private freedom of enterprise. Here the Court declined to uphold a Commission order against claims of an "obesity remedy" manufacturer.

June 1. Near v. Minnesota. 283 U. S. 697.

Argued January 30, 1931. Hughes, C. J., for the Court; Butler, Van Devanter, McReynolds and Sutherland, JJ., dissenting.

Invalidating a Minnesota law authorizing the closing of publications alleged to be guilty of false charges against public officials.

1932

March 14. Justice Cardozo succeeds Sanford.

March 21. New State Ice & Coal Co. v. Liebmann. 285 U. S. 262.

Argued February 19, 1932. Sutherland, J., for the Court; Brandeis and Stone, JJ., dissenting; Cardozo, J., not participating.

Invalidating an Oklahoma law requiring licenses to engage in sale and distribution of ice, as infringing upon individual liberty in violation of the Fourteenth Amendment.

April 11. Burnet v. Coronado Oil Co. 285 U. S. 393.

Argued January 15, 1932; reargued March 16, 1932. McReynolds, J., for the Court; Stone, Roberts and Brandeis, JJ., dissenting.

Holding exempt from Federal taxation public school lands leased to private companies, where a portion of the revenue from the extracted oil from the lands went to public schools.

Bibliography

The large and continuously enlarging volume of literature on the Constitution and the Supreme Court of the United States presents a formidable challenge to anyone undertaking to construct a meaningful bibliography on the subject. Both quantitatively and qualitatively, peculiar problems are involved. On the one hand, legal scholars discussing minutiae of particular constitutional decisions frequently ignore the opportunity to discuss the larger implications of the decisions; on the other, broader studies of Court and Constitution are more often than not tendentious rather than objective.

In such cases, the scholar as a matter of course would seek such original source materials as might be available—but in this subject-area he finds a frustrating paucity of papers and documents. Justices of the Court in particular, for reasons which they deemed good and sufficient, have much too often (from the scholar's viewpoint) destroyed the vital records of their own judicial work. For the period of the present study, Justices who have followed this practice have included Lurton, McKenna, Peckham, Pitney and White. While the loss of Chief Justice White's documents, relating to the crucial thirty years from the early nineties to the end of the Wilson administration, is particularly hard, it would have been conceivable that some insight into the mentality of the Court during these years might have been gleaned from the papers of any of these men.

In the case of Justices for the period of this study whose papers have in fact been preserved and, for the most part, made accessible for research, the most productive lodes have already been well mined: Professor Alpheus T. Mason of Princeton in his definitive studies of Brandeis, Stone and Taft, has demonstrated the importance of such manuscript resources in reconstructing both the attitudes and reactions of the individual jurist and the true perspective of his times. While some members of the bench and academic community have professed dismay at the fullness and frankness of the revelation of the Court's inner workings in such publications as these, the present writer holds to the view that a truer respect and appreciation for the Court as an institution and for the members of the bench as individuals will come from a recognition that both the bench and its members are subject to the human prejudices and second thoughts which come with time and experience.

A comprehensive inventory of papers of the Court and its members has been made by the editors and staff of the Oliver Wendell Holmes Devise of the Library of Congress, which has for a number of years been engaged in a multi-volume project on the history of the Court since its founding. While the magnitude of this undertaking is awesome, and the lack of access to many of the documents for other researchers in this field is regrettable, it is reasonable to expect that many now restricted papers will ultimately be open to all scholars—and the volumes of the history itself, when they appear, should make a substantial contribution to the understanding of the role of the Court in American life.

Some of the principal manuscript collections of value to a study of the Court and the Constitution are in collateral lines. The files of the Department of Justice, deposited in the National Archives for the period of the present volume, provide particularly revealing details of the government's general strategy in some of the major cases of the trust-busting era. These are supplemented by the papers of certain of the Attorneys General, such as Richard Olney, Philander C. Knox and William H. Moody, in the Manuscripts Division of the Library of Congress. Even more important for the political elements in the story, although they have already been extensively worked, are the papers in the same depository for Theodore Roosevelt, William Howard Taft and Charles Evans Hughes. The Hughes papers are nominally restricted, but available to researchers through the cooperation of the Chief Justice's descendants. Another type of primary source material, too often overlooked, is represented in the briefs and related case papers on major constitutional cases, available together with the journals and minutes of the Supreme Court in the National Archives and in the Supreme Court Library.

Attempts to have the Supreme Court tell its own story, *malgré lui*, have been made in two excellent collections edited by Alan F. Westin—*The Supreme Court: Views From Within* (New York, 1961), consisting of fourteen out-of-court commentaries by individual Justices revealing in varying detail some of the activities behind the judicial curtain; and *An Autobiography of the Supreme Court* (New York, 1963), an enlargement of this same approach. The latter volume includes speeches, letters and memoirs of Justices for various periods of Court history, introduced by a perceptive essay by the editor, "Of Free Speech and Judicial Lockjaw," reflecting in another dimension the scholar's regret at the paucity of commentary on their own work by the men who have been the prime movers in our constitutional development.

Westin's essay is followed by a useful bibliography of selected writings by the Justices which need not be duplicated here. It is worth noting at this point, however, that books and shorter papers by and about individual members of the Court provide an insight into their backgrounds and interests which has definite value in forming an estimate of their judicial behavior. Certainly one would do well, in beginning a general assessment of the Court for a given period, to familiarize himself with the basic facts of each Justice's career in some standard reference such as the *Dictionary of American Biography* (New York, 22 vol., 1927-64). As the present study was going to press, a new four-volume biographical dictionary of the Supreme Court was scheduled to appear, edited by Fred L. Israel and Leon Davidson under the title, *The Justices of the United States Supreme Court, 1789-1966: Their Lives and Major Decisions.* With articles on individual Justices written by specialists on the individual or his times, this reference work promises to fill a need of long standing.

The counterpart of such a reference for the judiciary, the *Biographical Directory of the American Congress, 1774-1961* (Washington, 1961), is useful for the highly condensed *curricula vitae* required to put more than 10,000 personal histories within the covers of a single volume. An article by John R. Schmidhauser, "The Justices of the Supreme Court: A Collective Portrait," 3 *Midwest J. of Pol. Sci.* 1 (February 1959), has provoked considerable comment, as has a shorter work, treating selected members of the Court as prototypes of various periods and philosophies, edited by Allison Dunham and Philip B. Kurland under the title, *Mr. Justice* (Chicago, 2d ed. 1964). Most of the major figures of the Court for this period, like Fuller, Hughes and Taft among the Chief Justices and Brandeis, Field, Holmes, Miller and Stone among the Associate Justices, have been the subject of one or more comprehensive works and a number of scholarly articles. The most conspicuously neglected major figure to date is John Marshall Harlan, although Professor Westin is working on a biography.

A selected list of writings by or about members of the Court from Fuller to the beginning of the Hughes Chief Justiceship, including certain listings of their papers, is a fundamental guide to the composite character of the judiciary for this period, viz.:

BRADLEY, JOSEPH P. A group of Bradley's papers is in the New Jersey Historical Society in Newark. His son Charles published a volume of *Miscellaneous Writings* (Newark, 1902) which included a review of his judicial career by Dean William Draper Lewis of the University of Pennsylvania and a critique of his dissenting opinions by A. Q. Beasley. There is an earlier, general study by Courtlandt Parker entitled, *Mr. Justice Bradley of the United States Supreme Court* (Newark, 1893), although it is of little value. Professor Charles O. Fairman of Harvard Law School has written two excellent articles—"The Education of a Justice: Justice Bradley and Some of His Colleagues," 1 *Stanf. L. Rev.* 217 (January 1949), which discusses Bradley's relations with Justices Brewer, Brown, Field and Miller; and "What Makes a Great Justice? Mr. Justice Bradley and the Supreme Court, 1870-1892," 30 *Boston U. L. Rev.* 49 (January 1950). There is also an interesting study by M. C. Klinkhamer, entitled "Joseph P. Bradley: Private and Public Opinions of a 'Political' Justice," 38 *U. Detroit L. J.* 150 (December 1960).

BRANDEIS, LOUIS D. A major group of the Justice's papers is in the University of Louisville Law Library. Equally important is a group of his Supreme Court files which are now in the Harvard Law Library and were the basis of Professor Alexander M. Bickel's excellent *The Unpublished Opinions of Mr. Justice Brandeis* (Cambridge, 1957; Chicago, 1967). The literature on this Justice is already voluminous, and the writings of Brandeis himself in the Progressive Era were substantial. References should be made to his articles in *Collier's Weekly* from 1909 to 1916, as well as to two widely read books by him, *Business—A Profession* (Boston, 1914) and *Other People's Money and How the Bankers Use It* (New York, 1914), a popularization of the report of the Pujo Committee.

Jacob DeHaas published the first of a number of biographical studies in *Louis D. Brandeis: A Biographical Sketch* (New York, 1929), and Irving Dilliard edited a paperback collection under the title, *Mr. Justice Brandeis: Great American* (St. Louis, 1941), each of which contains selections of the Justice's papers and addresses. Other papers were collected by Osmund K. Frankel under the title, *The Curse of Bigness: Miscellaneous Papers of Louis D. Brandeis* (New York, 1934), while some of the best-known of the jurist's views were compiled by Solomon Goldman in *The Words of Justice Brandeis* (New York, 1953). Also of value are Alfred Lief's *Brandeis: The Personal History of an American Ideal* (New York, 1936), his *Brandeis Guide to the Modern World* (Boston, 1941), and his earlier *Social and Economic Views of Mr. Justice Brandeis* (New York, 1930). The most exhaustive studies of this major figure in the Court's history are three books by Alpheus T. Mason—*Brandeis: Lawyer and Judge in the Modern State* (New York, 1933); *The Brandeis Way* (New York, 1938); and *Brandeis: A Free Man's Life* (New York, 1956).

A special study of Brandeis in his early progressive career is Henry L. Staples' *The Fall of a Railroad Empire: Brandeis and the New Haven Merger Battle* (Syracuse, 1947). A. L. Todd reviewed the struggle over the nomination to the Supreme Court in *Justice on Trial: The Case of Louis D. Brandeis* (New York, 1964). The complete text of the hearings before the Senate Judiciary Subcommittee on the *Nomination of Louis D. Brandeis* (Washington, 1916), is still revealing.

In periodical treatment, Freund's "Mr. Justice Brandeis," 70 *Harv. L. Rev.* 769 (March 1957), is important. Of many symposia on the Justice, the one in 11 *St. Louis L. J.* 4 *et seq.* (Fall 1966) is among the most recent, while the famous "Brandeis brief" is analyzed in detail in M. E. Doro, "The Brandeis Brief," 11 *Vanderbilt L. Rev.* 783 (June 1958) and in Clement E. Vose, "The National Consumer's League and the Brandeis Brief," 1 *Midwest J. of Pol. Sci.* 267 (November 1957).

BREWER, DAVID J. The prolific outpouring of works by this member of the Court is the best medium for the study of his fundamental beliefs, particularly since no full-length study of him has been made. A fervent little tract, *The Protection of Private Property from Public Attack* (New Haven, 1891), effectively summarizes his *laissez-faire* philosophy; the strong religious influences of his boyhood and youth in a missionary household was also reflected in several of his works: *The United States: A Christian Nation* (Philadelphia, 1900) and *The Twentieth Century from Another Viewpoint* (New York, 1899).

Brewer was also the author of a series of lectures on *American Citizenship* (New Haven, 1911), and the editor of three multi-volume collections entitled *The World's Best Orations* (St. Louis, 11 vol., 1899), *The World's Best Essays* (St. Louis, 10 vol., 1900) and *Masterpieces of Eloquence That Have Advanced Civilization* (New York, 10 vol., 1908).

A small collection of Brewer papers is at Yale University. A graduate dissertation by Lynford A. Lardner, *The Constitutional Doctrines of Justice David Josiah Brewer* (Princeton, 1938), is useful. Two articles of value are F. Bergan, "Mr. Justice Brewer: Perspective of a Century," 25 *Albany L. Rev.* 191 (June 1961) and R. E. Gamer, "Justice Brewer and Substantive Due Process: A Conservative Court Revisited," 18 *Vanderbilt L. Rev.* 615 (March 1965).

BROWN, HENRY B. Most of the papers of this Justice are in the Burton Historical Collection in the Detroit Public Library. Charles A. Kent published a brief *Memoir of Henry Billings Brown* (New York, 1915) which is the only booklength treatment to date.

BUTLER, PIERCE. Francis J. Brown wrote a graduate dissertation, *The Social and Economic Philosophy of Pierce Butler* (Washington, 1945), and David J. Danelski of Yale University has described in complete detail how *A Supreme Court Justice Is Appointed* (New York, 1964). Although this completes the list of studies on Butler, these two works give the reader a full view of the Court and the times of this Justice.

CLARKE, JOHN H. The Justice's crusade against war is exemplified in his Brown University lectures which were published as *America and World Peace* (New York, 1925). Hoyt L. Warner's *Life of Mr. Justice Clarke: A Testament to the Power of Liberal Dissent in America* (Cleveland, 1959) draws upon the Clarke manuscripts on deposit at Western Reserve University.

DAY, WILLIAM R. The only study of significance is Joseph E. McLean, *William Rufus Day, Supreme Court Justice from Ohio* (Baltimore, 1946).

FIELD, STEPHEN, J. The main group of papers for this important Justice is in the University of California, although a collection of 174 pieces is in the Oregon Historical Society and the manuscript of his *Personal Reminiscences of Early Days in California* is in the California State Library, Sutro Branch. The Field papers were extensively used for the definitive work by Carl B. Swisher, *Stephen J. Field, Craftsman of the Law* (Washington, 1930; Hamden, Conn., 1963). Field's *Reminiscences,* privately published in San Francisco in 1880, also appears in a limited edition entitled, *California Alcalde* (Oakland, 1950). An undated collection of *Opinions and Papers of Stephen J. Field* was published in New York. Chauncey F. Black wrote *Some Accounts of the Work of Stephen J. Field* (New York, 1895), and two doctoral dissertations are Walter R. Gaedecke's *Rights, Interests and the Court: The Jurisprudence of Mr. Justice Stephen J. Field* (Chicago, 1958) and George A. Shipman's *Constitutional Doctrines of Stephen J. Field* (Ithaca, N. Y., 1931).

Three articles of special note are Howard J. Graham, "Justice Field and the Fourteenth Amendment," 52 *Yale L. J.* 851 (September 1943); Wallace Mendelson, "Mr. Justice Field and *laissez-faire,*" 36 *Va. L. Rev.* 45 (February 1950); and Alan F. Westin, "Stephen J. Field and the Headnote to O'Neill v. Vermont: A Snapshot of the Fuller Court at Work," 67 *Yale L. J.* 363 (January, 1958).

FULLER, MELVILLE W. Another of the neglected members of the modern Court, Fuller does have one major study to his credit. Indeed, the work of Willard L. King, a Chicago attorney, in *Melville Weston Fuller, Chief Justice of the United States, 1888-1910* (New York, 1950; Chicago, 1967) is doubly valuable not only for its fullscale study of Fuller's career in law and on the bench but for his locating of the widely scattered papers of and about the Chief Justice. A small group of manuscripts is also in the Library of Congress.

GRAY, HORACE. More than 300 letters to Justice Gray are in the Supreme Court archives; like many papers of the Justices, these are predominantly comments on current issues without great significance. An article by E. B. Davis and H. A. Davis, "Mr. Justice Horace Gray: Some Aspects of His Judicial Career," appears in 41 *A. B. A. Journal* 421 (May 1955), and another by J. M. Smith, "Mr. Justice Horace Gray of the United States Supreme Court," 6 *S. D. L. Rev.* 221 (Fall 1962), completes the significant literature on this subject.

HARLAN, JOHN MARSHALL. Of all the major and colorful figures in the history of the modern Court, the neglect of this Justice by scholars is all but inexplicable. Floyd B. Clarke's monograph, *The Constitutional Doctrines of Justice Harlan* (Baltimore, 1915), is still the only generally available study. Among law review articles of importance are a symposium in 46 *Ky. L. J.* 321 *et seq.* (Spring 1958); Henry J. Abraham, "John Marshall Harlan: A Justice Neglected," 41 *Va. L. Rev.* 871 (November 1955); Edward F. Waite, "How 'Eccentric' Was Mr. Justice Harlan?" 37 *Minn. L. Rev.* 173 (February 1953); Richard F. Watt and Richard M. Orlikoff, "The Coming Vindication of Mr. Justice Harlan," 44 *Ill. L. Rev.* 13 (March-April 1949); and Westin, "John Marshall Harlan and the Constitutional Rights of Negroes: The Transformation of a Southerner," 66 *Yale L. J.* 637 (April 1957). A body of Harlan papers has recently been deposited in the Library of Congress.

HOLMES, OLIVER WENDELL. The studies on this Justice are deservedly the most abundant of any on the modern Court. A definitive biography by Professor Mark DeWolfe Howe of Harvard Law School had produced two volumes prior to Howe's death; hopefully the project will be continued by others. The two volumes—*Oliver Wendell Holmes: The Shaping Years, 1841-1870* (Cambridge, 1957) and *Oliver Wendell Holmes: The Proving Years, 1870-1882* (Cambridge, 1963)—cover in much greater detail the life of the Justice so entertainingly recounted in Catherine Drinker Bowen's *Yankee from Olympus: Justice Holmes and His Family* (Boston, 1944). A masterpiece of succinct analytical biography is Felix Frankfurter's *Mr. Justice Holmes and the Supreme Court* (Cambridge, 1938, 1961), reprinting Frankfurter's 1938 lectures on the subject as well as his essay in the *Dictionary of American Biography*.

Holmes' own professional writing, beginning with his years as editor of the *American Law Review*, was extensive and influential; *The Common Law* (Boston, 1882) is the definitive work on its subject, and his *Collected Legal Papers* (New York, 1920) brought together a number of addresses and articles delivered over the years. His transatlantic correspondence with English men of affairs has been definitively edited by Professor Howe in *The Holmes-Pollock Letters* (Cambridge, 2 vol., 1941) and *The Holmes-Laski Letters* (Cambridge, 2 vol., 1953). Alfred Leif's *Representative Opinions of Justice Holmes* (New York, 1931) and his *Dissenting Opinions* (New York, 1929) may be read with Max Lerner's *The Mind and Faith of Justice Holmes* (Boston, 1943).

Professor Howe, Holmes' literary executor, has effectively catalogued and edited the Justice's papers under his care; other manuscripts are in the Harvard Law Library and in the Library of Congress. A unique feature in the bibliography of this Justice which deserves mention is the bequest he made to the United States, which is now identified as the Oliver Wendell Holmes Devise of the Library of Congress. Under a permanent committee of administration, this bequest has underwritten the multi-volume history of the Court already mentioned, and more recently has financed an annual series of Holmes Devise Lectures given at different American law schools. Among these lectures published to date are Francis Biddle's *Justice Holmes, Natural Law and the Supreme Court* (New York, 1961) and J. Willard Hurst's *Justice Holmes and Legal History* (New York, 1964). In this vein, although not part of this series, is Samuel J. Konefsky's *The Legacy of Holmes and Brandeis: A Study in the Influence of Ideas* (New York, 1956).

The literature on Holmes has always been abundant, but in the past two decades a revisionist trend has set in. It is summarized in Francis E. Lucey, "Holmes—Liberal—Humanitarian—Believer in Democracy?" 39 *Georgetown L. J.* 523 (May 1951), and more recently in a symposium, "Mr. Justice Holmes: Some Modern Views," 31 *U. Chicago L. Rev.* 213 *et seq.* (Winter 1964). See also Samuel Krislow, "Oliver Wendell Holmes: The Ebb and Flow of Judicial Legendry," 52 *Northwestern U. L. Rev.* 514 (September-October 1957). These are sufficient to illustrate the current of contemporary discussion, and specific references are to be found in each of the articles.

HUGHES, CHARLES EVANS. The definitive biography is by Merlo

Pusey, *Charles Evans Hughes* (New York, 2 vol., 1951), which has won the Pulitzer Prize and has become the standard authority on the subject. A useful study by Samuel Hendel is entitled *Charles Evans Hughes and the Supreme Court* (New York, 1951), and is particularly insightful into his period as Associate Justice. Hughes himself published a series of public papers from the time of his New York governorship to his campaign for the Presidency under the title, *Addresses of Charles Evans Hughes, 1906-1916* (New York, 1916), but his most important work was his series of lectures at Columbia University in 1927, published later under the title, *The Supreme Court of the United States: Its Foundation, Methods and Achievements* (New York, 1929,1936).

The Hughes Papers are in the Library of Congress, and are made available to scholars on application to members of the Hughes family. They are of particular value for the period of his Chief Justiceship, which is treated in the companion volume to the present study. Most of the professional periodical literature, for both Hughes and Stone, relates to the periods of their Chief Justiceships and accordingly will be treated in the notes to the companion volume. One brief article relating to the period of Hughes' non-judicial services is J. G. Rogers' "Hughes as Secretary of State," 27 *Am. Bar Assn. Journal* 411 (January 1941); in this same general vein, see also Dexter Perkins' *Charles Evans Hughes and American Democratic Statesmanship* (Boston, 1956).

LAMAR, JOSEPH R. Several hundred of Lamar's letters are in the University of Georgia. His wife, Clarinda H. Lamar, wrote *The Life of Joseph R. Lamar, 1857-1916* (New York, 1926). A more scholarly study, tracing the common ancestry of the two Justices Lamar, is Samuel H. Sibley, *Georgia's Contribution to Law: The Lamars* (New York, 1948).

LAMAR, LUCIUS Q. C. Papers of this Justice are in the Mississippi Department of Archives and History, in the Georgia Historical Society and in the Southern Historical Collection of the University of North Carolina. Wirt Armistead Cate has written *Lucius Q. C. Lamar: Secession and Reunion* (Chapel Hill, 1935), a discerning study which replaces Edward Mayes' *Lucius Q. C. Lamar: Life, Times and Speeches* (Nashville, 1896). There is an interesting article by Daniel J. Meador, "Lamar and the Law at the University of Mississippi," 34 *Miss. L. J.* 227 (May 1963).

McKENNA, JOSEPH. There is a doctoral dissertation by Matthew McDevitt, *Joseph McKenna: Associate Justice of the United States* (Washington 1945).

McREYNOLDS, JAMES C. The bulk of this Justice's legal papers may be found in the University of Virginia. They provide the basis for a dissertation by Stephen T. Early, *James Clark McReynolds and the Judicial Process* (Charlottesville, 1954), supplanting an earlier work by Sterling P. Gilbert, *James Clark McReynolds* (n. p., 1946).

MILLER, SAMUEL F. Miller's own posthumously published *Lectures on the Constitution* (New York, 1891) and an earlier, shorter work, *The Consti-*

tution and the Supreme Court of the United States (New York, 1889), merit examination. A definitive biography is Charles O. Fairman, *Mr. Justice Miller and the Supreme Court* (Cambridge, 1939).

MOODY, WILLIAM H. The Moody papers in the Library of Congress are mostly interesting for his period as Attorney General. There is a highly informative article by P. T. Hoffman, "Theodore Roosevelt and the Appointment of Mr. Justice Moody," 18 *Vanderbilt L. Rev.* 545 (March 1965).

PITNEY, MAHLON. See the article by D. M. Levitan, "Mahlon Pitney —Labor Judge," 40 *Va. L. Rev.* 733 (October 1954).

SHIRAS, GEORGE. There are reported to be papers of this Justice in the possession of the family. Winfield Shiras has edited *Justice George Shiras, Jr. of Pittsburgh* (Pittsburgh, 1953).

STONE, HARLAN FISKE. The definitive biography is Alpheus Thomas Mason's *Harlan Fiske Stone: Pillar of the Law* (New York, 1956), which relies on the Stone Papers in the Library of Congress. Other references will be found in the notes to the companion volume.

SUTHERLAND, GEORGE. A collection of this Justice's lectures at Columbia University appears under the title, *Constitutional Power and World Affairs* (New York, 1919). A biographical study has been published by Joel F. Paschal, *Mr. Justice Sutherland, A Man Against the State* (Princeton, 1951). See also Alpheus T. Mason, "The Conservative World of Mr. Justice Sutherland," 32 *Am. Pol. Sci. Rev.* 443 (June 1938).

TAFT, WILLIAM HOWARD. The bulk of the Taft Papers will be found in the Library of Congress. A work by Herbert S. Duffy, *William Howard Taft* (New York, 1930), is especially informative for his years on the Circuit Court of Appeals. Frederick C. Hicks' *William Howard Taft: Yale Professor of Law and New Haven Citizen* (New Haven, 1945) describes his years between 1913 and 1921. The fullscale biography is Henry F. Pringle, *Life and Times of William Howard Taft* (New York, 2 vol., 1939), but the best study of his judicial career is Alpheus T. Mason, *William Howard Taft, Chief Justice* (New York, 1964). See also Professor Walter F. Murphy's article, "In His Own Image: Mr. Chief Justice Taft and Supreme Court Appointments," 1961 *Supreme Court Review* 159 (Chicago, 1961).

WHITE, EDWARD D. A posthumous collection entitled, *Legal Traditions and Other Papers* (St. Louis, 1927) is interesting. A dissertation by Harold F. Hartman, *Constitutional Doctrines of Edward D. White* (Ithaca, N. Y., 1936), and Sister Marie Carolyn Klinkhamer's dissertation, *Edward Douglas White, Chief Justice of the United States* (Washington, 1943), are the most informative works about this figure. Sister Marie Carolyn has also written an article, "The Legal Philosophy of Edward Douglas White," 35 *U. Detroit L. J.*, 174 (December 1957). A recent work is Gerard Hagemann, *The Man on the Bench* (Notre Dame, 1962), and a promising beginning toward a new biography is the article by W. E. Joyce, "Edward D. White: The Louisiana Years," 41 *Tulane L. Rev.* 751 (July 1967).

As to the subjects of the Court and the Constitution in the twentieth century, perhaps the best one-volume history is to be found in Carl Brent Swisher's *American Constitutional Development* (Boston, 2d ed., 1954), although major events of the later years make a third edition desirable. Some of these events are covered in essays on *American Constitutional History* (New York, 1964), edited by Alpheus T. Mason in honor of Edward S. Corwin. Mason's own *The Supreme Court from Taft to Warren* (Baton Rouge, 1958) is also a valuable, though condensed, survey.

Standard constitutional histories fall progressively shorter of contemporary periods. Thus Andrew C. McLaughlin's *Constitutional History of the United States* (New York, 1935) stops where the New Deal begins; Charles Warren's *The Supreme Court in United States History* (Boston, 2d. ed., 1954) extends only to 1918 in its revised edition. Although tendentious to the point of being emotional at times, Gustavus Myers' *History of the Supreme Court of the United States* (Chicago, 1925) has a certain amount of factual data not readily found elsewhere—particularly for the Fuller Court of the nineties. H. C. Hockett's *Constitutional History of the United States* (New York, 2 vol., 1939) was intended to cover only the first century of independence. Since developments within this period are essential to an understanding of the major events which followed, all of these works are useful to one seeking a background to the present. Complementing the foregoing titles is an older work which contains certain materials consistently omitted from the later books: Hampton Carson's massive volume compiled for the Judiciary Centennial Committee of the New York State Bar Association, published under the title, *The Supreme Court of the United States: Its History* (Philadelphia, 1892).

All of these will presumably be replaced by the multi-volume history of the Supreme Court which for the past decade has been in various stages of preparation under the sponsorship of the Oliver Wendell Holmes Devise of the Library of Congress. Each volume, according to the original plan, is being written by a specialist in the period represented by the volume, thus taking advantage of research in depth while preserving the continuity of the whole. Professor Freund of Harvard is the general editor of the project. Complementing this work on the Court is a contemporary treatise by Professor Bernard Schwartz of New York University, *A Commentary on the Constitution of the United States,* the fourth and fifth volumes of which, completing the work, appeared in the early spring of 1968. The first two volumes appeared under the title of *The Powers of Government* (New York, 1963); the third was *The Rights of Property* (New York, 1965); the final two are *The Rights of the Individual* (New York, 1968). The most substantial work of this type yet to appear in the twentieth century, it summarizes many of the consequences of constitutional development for the century anticipated by the same author in his earlier *The Supreme Court: Constitutional Revolution in Retrospect* (New York, 1957). Schwartz has also restated the basic propositions of American constitutionalism, for British readers, in his admirably concise *American Constitutional Law* (Cambridge, Eng., 1955).

A useful general statement on each Article and Amendment to the Constitution, by Professor Corwin, under the title, *The Constitution and What It Means Today* (Princeton, 12th ed., 1958), has become the classic handbook for students. A comparable summary is Judge Edward Dumbauld's *The Constitution of the United States* (Norman, Okla., 1964). Of various annotated editions of the document itself the most useful is the one periodically issued by the Legislative Reference Service of the Library of Congress, *The Constitution of the United States of America* (Washington, rev. ed. 1965). The current edition reprints Corwin's admirable commentary prepared for the 1952 revision. The most venerated commentary on the Constitution—*The Federalist*—has gone through a great many editions under a great many editors, but one of the most recent, by Jacob Cooke (Middleton, Conn., 1961), is also the most nearly definitive. Reference should also be made to C. Herman Pritchett's *The American Constitution* (New York, 2d ed., 1968).

A landmark study by Felix Frankfurter and James M. Landis, begun as a series of articles in the *Harvard Law Review,* was later published in book form as *The Business of the Supreme Court* (New York, 1928). Two decades later the *Harvard Law Review* incorporated some of the methods of this project into an annual critique of the Court's work, complete with statistical summaries, which continues to date. Among other yearly reviews of continuing value are the annual summaries of the *American Political Science Review,* extending back through most of the present century; the *Annual Survey of American Law,* begun by New York University Law School in 1942, which places constitutional developments in the context of other fields of law; and the *Supreme Court Review,* which has been published by the University of Chicago Law School since 1960.

Many of these references cover the period following the present study, just as the standard constitutional histories cover the period preceding it, but they are all fundamental to a perspective of the period itself. Once past these titles, an enormous mass of commentary confronts the student of the subject. He will find some guidance in a small reference book published by the Bureau of Public Administration of the University of California, edited by Dorothy C. Tompkins under the title, *The Supreme Court of the United States: A Bibliography* (Berkeley, 1959). Another handy reference is Percival E. Jackson, *The Wisdom of the Supreme Court* (Norman, Okla., 1962), a thesaurus of quotations from the opinions and other writings of the Justices.

The present volume has stressed the importance of a professionally competent handling of the government's cases in constitutional litigation, for which the Attorney General and the Solicitor General are primarily responsible. The authoritative study of this function is *Federal Justice* (New York, 1937), by Homer Cummings and Carl McFarland. For the various Presidents and leading Congressional figures, the standard references appear in the Chapter Notes.

Among the scores of specialized studies, a few may be specifically cited here: Corwin's old classic, *The Doctrine of Judicial Review* (Princeton, 1914; Gloucester, Mass., 1963); Irving Brant's *The Bill of Rights: Its Origin and*

Meaning (New York, 1965); Benjamin R. Twiss, *Lawyers and the Constitution* (New York, 1942, 1962); Arnold M. Paul, *Conservative Crisis and the Rule of Law* (Ithaca, N. Y., 1960); Clyde E. Jacobs, *Law Writers and the Courts* (Berkeley, 1954); Paul G. Kauper, *Frontiers of Constitutional Liberty* (Ann Arbor, Mich., 1956); and Donald G. Morgan, *Congress and the Constitution* (Cambridge, 1966).

The periodical literature on these subjects is torrential. A selected group of representative and seminal writings has been compiled by the Association of American Law Schools and published under the title, *Selected Readings on Constitutional Law* (St. Paul, Minn., 1960).

Notes

The notes to the chapters in this volume have been limited to the most productive sources among many which were consulted. Few references are cited for general background facts—e. g., national election results, contemporary public events, and the like—where these are readily to be found in standard histories or current periodicals. On the other hand, citations to documents, court records and case reports have been meticulously listed.

CHAPTER 1   *Apology for the Past*

[1] The quotations are from an editorial by Seymour D. Thompson, in 29 *Am. L. Rev.* 742 (Sept.-Oct. 1895); cf. also Justice Walter Clark, "Constitutional Changes Which Are Foreshadowed," 30 *id*. 702 (Sept.-Oct. 1896); and Sylvester Pennoyer, 29 *id*. 550 (July-Aug. 1895).

[2] *New York World,* May 21, 1895; *Salt Lake Tribune* and *Indianapolis Nonconformist,* quoted in 18 *Pub. Op.* 595 (May 30, 1895).

[3] 25 *Am. L. Rev.* 550 (July-Aug. 1895).

[4] *New York Sun,* quoted in 11 *Lit. Dig.* 125 (June 1, 1895); *Philadelphia Public Ledger,* May 21, 1895.

[5] *St. Louis Post-Dispatch,* quoted in 11 *Lit. Dig.* 126 (June 1, 1896).

[6] Munn v. Illinois, 94 U. S. 113 (1877).

[7] Collector v. Day, 11 Wall. 113 (1871).

[8] Springer v. United States, 102 U. S. 586 (1881).

[9] 9 *Harv. L. Rev.* 198 (1895), citing, in addition to the *Day* and *Springer* cases, Hylton v. United States, 3 Dall. 171 (1796) and Veazie Bank v. Fenno, 8 Wall. 533 (1869).

[10] Case papers in Pollock v. Farmers' Loan & Trust Co., Docket No. 893, file for 1894 Term of Supreme Court (National Archives).

Under the Circuit Court of Appeals Act of 1890, direct appeal to the Supreme Court lay from the Circuit Courts (i. e., trial courts) in "any case that involves the construction or application of the Constitution of the United States," 26 Stat. 826, ch. 517, sec. 5. Beyond that, however, procedure as to docketing and settling dates for argument and reargument were largely discretionary. "The rule of the Court as to petitions for a rehearing is somewhat nebulous and unsatisfactory," confessed Cleveland's first Attorney General, A. H. Garland, in his *Experiences in the Supreme Court with Some Reflections and Suggestions as to That Tribunal* (Washington, 1898), pp. 39-40.

[11] Minutes of the Supreme Court, 1894 Term, p. 304; Journal, same, p. 106.

[12] Minutes, pp. 486-87; Journal, p. 157.

[13] Minutes, pp. 592-93; Journal, p. 193.

[14] *Washington Star,* May 6, 1895.

[15] *Chicago Tribune,* May 18, 1895.

[16] A great deal of speculation has revolved about this matter; the latest and most persuasive theory appears in Paul, *Conservative Crisis and the Rule of Law,* pp. 214-18.

[17] Henry H. Ingersoll, "The Revolution of 20th May, 1895," *Proceedings of the Bar Association of Tennessee* (1895), pp. 161, 162. Ingersoll was an attorney present in the Court on this date, and the details of the activities and behavior in the courtroom then are from his eyewitness account.

[18] Pollock v. Farmers' Loan & Trust Co., 157 U. S. 429, 607 (1895).

[19] Ingersoll, *loc. cit.,* p. 163.

[20] Cf. notes 7 and 8, supra.

[21] Pollock v. Farmers' Loan & Trust Co., 158 U. S. 601, 618 (1895).

[22] Fred Rodell, *Nine Men* (New York, 1955), p. 146.

[23] Cf. Robert F. Reeder, "Chief Justice Fuller," 59 *U. Pa. L. Rev.* 1 (October 1890); cf. note 3 therein.

[24] 26 Cong. Rec. 6637, 6707.

[25] The counsel and the abstracts of their briefs appear in 39 *L. Ed.* (Lawyers' Edition of the Supreme Court reports), 759-809.

[26] 39 *L. Ed.* 785.

[27] id., 768-73.

[28] id., 799.

[29] id., 793.

[30] 157 U. S. 429.

[31] id., 581.

[32] Swisher, Field, ch. xiii; cf. In re Neagle, 135 U. S 1 (1890).

[33] Swisher, *Field,* p. 430; 134 U. S. App. VI (1890).

[34] Cf. 168 U. S., App.

[35] 158 U. S. 671, 674, 677; Ingersoll, *loc. cit.,* pp. 169-71.

[36] 158 U. S. 685.

[37] id., 706.

[38] id., 695.

[39] id., 713-14.

[40] Ingersoll, *loc. cit.,* 177-78.

CHAPTER 2   *The Jurisprudence of Industrialism*

[1] Charles F. Clark, David A. Wells, *Recent Economic Changes* (New York, 1890), chs. 7-11.

[2] Benjamin O. Flower, "The Last Century as a Utilitarian Age," 25 *Arena* 271 (Mar. 1901); Henry Adams, *The Education of Henry Adams* (Boston, 1918), pp. 343-44.

[3] *Historical Statistics of the United States* (Washington, 1960), pp. 283-84, 286, 288; and see also pp. 106ff., 112-21, 128-29. Edward L. Kirkland, *History of American Economic Life* (New York, 1946), ch. 12; and Russell B. Nye, *Midwestern Progressive Politics* (East Lansing, Mich., 1951), ch. 2.

[4] Henry George, *Progress and Poverty* (New York, 1911), Introduction. Ida M. Tarbell, *The Nationalizing of Business, 1878-1908* (New York, 1936), ch. 20.

[5] William G. Sumner, *What Social Classes Owe Each Other* (New York, 1883), chs. 1, 6.

[6] Cf. Tarbell, *op. cit.,* ch. 5.

[7] Cf. biographical sketch on Dodd in 5 *Dictionary of American Biography* (hereinafter cited as *D. A. B.*), 341; Flint, 21 *D. A. B.* 305; and Moore, 13 *D. A. B.* 142.

[8] Tarbell, *op. cit.,* chs. 3-5; Kirkland, *op. cit.,* ch. 11.

[9] 13 *D. A. B.* 143.

[10] Dodd, "Ten Years of the Standard Oil Trust," 13 *Forum* 300, 305 (May, 1892).

[11] Dodd, "The Present Legal Status of Trusts," 7 *Harv. L. Rev.* 157 (October 1893).

[12] Allan Nevins, *Study in Power: John D. Rockefeller* (New York, 1953), I, p. 390.

[13] Tarbell, *op. cit.,* ch. 3.

[14] id., ch. 4.

[15] Henry D. Lloyd, *Wealth Against Commonwealth* (New York, 1894), ch. 1.

[16] John Sherman, *Recollections of Forty Years in the House, Senate and Cabinet* (Chicago, 1895), II, p. 1073.

[17] 21 Cong. Rec., 1768 *et seq.*

[18] id., 2456.

[19] id., 2460.

[20] id., 2467, 2571, 2607, 2609.

[21] id., 2465, 2950, 2981, 6116, 6208, 6312.

[22] 134 U. S. App. VI (1890).

[23] Cf. Swisher, *American Constitutional Development,* chs. 18, 19.

[24] W. H. H. Miller to Frank D. Allen, February 11, 1892. Department of Justice Instruction Book No. 19 (Washington, 1892), pp. 324-25.

[25] Cf. W. H. Taft, *The Anti-Trust Act and the Supreme Court* (New York, 1914).

[26] United States v. Jellico Mt. Coal & Coke Co., 46 Fed. 432, 434 (1891).

[27] Henry James, *Richard Olney and His Public Service* (Boston, 1923), p. 20; Homer Cummings and Carl McFarland, *Federal Justice,* pp. 321-22.

[28] In re Green, 52 Fed. 104 (1892). Cf. Memorandum in Olney Papers, Li-

brary of Congress, cited also in Cummings and McFarland, *op. cit.,* p. 322.

29 United States v. E. C. Knight & Co., 60 Fed. 934 (1894).

30 Budd v. New York, 143 U. S. 517 (1892); Brass v. North Dakota, 153 U. S. 391 (1894); Reagan v. Farmers' Loan & Trust Co., 154 U. S. 362 (1894).

31 Campbell, 3 *D. A. B.* 456; Conkling, 4 *D. A. B.* 346; Slaughterhouse Cases, 16 Wall. 36 (1873); San Mateo County v. South Pac. R. Co., 116 U. S. 138 (1885), arguments of counsel March 19-21, 1882, Docket No. 106 in records of the case in the Supreme Court Library.

32 Johnson, 10 *D. A. B.* 106. See also Benjamin R. Twiss, *Lawyers and the Court: How Laissez-Faire Came to the Supreme Court* (New York, 1942, 1962), pp. 206-08.

33 Twiss, *op. cit.,* pp. 202-06, 210-13.

34 United States v. E. C. Knight & Co., 156 U. S. 1, 12, 13 (1895).

35 id., 37-43.

36 id., 45.

37 Olney to Miss Straw, January 22,1895. Olney Papers.

38 King, *Melville Weston Fuller,* chs. 8, 9.

39 Cf. references on these Justices in the Bibliographic Essay, and also Charles Warren, *The Supreme Court in United States History* (Boston, 1922, 1926), II, esp. pp. 761-62.

40 Cf. Harmon, 8 *D. A. B.* 276, Griggs; 7 *D. A. B.* 627.

41 Cf. Stanford, 17 *D. A. B.* 501.

42 Cf. Hearst, 8 *D. A. B.* 487.

43 Cf. Aldrich, 1 *D. A. B.* 151. See also N. W. Stephenson, *Nelson Aldrich: A Leader in American Politics* (New York, 1930), chs. 6-12.

44 34 *Am. L. Reg.* 89-90 (February, 1895).

45 Cf. Minnesota v. Barber, 136 U. S. 313 (1890); McGahey v. Virginia, 135 U. S. 662 (1890); N. & W. R. Co. v. Pennsylvania, 136 U. S. 114 (1890).

46 Leisy v. Hardin, 135 U. S. 100 (1890).

47 Cf. King, *Fuller,* chs. 11, 13.

48 Allgeyer v. Louisiana, 165 U. S. 578 (1897).

49 Cf. Santa Clara County v. Southern Pacific R. Co., 118 U. S. 394 (1885), and note 31 supra.

50 Smyth v. Ames, 169 U. S. 466, 522, 526 (1898).

51 Hurtado v. California, 110 U. S. 516 (1884).

52 Thomas N. Cooley, *Constitutional Limitations* (Boston, 1868), II, ch. 2. Cf. also Paul, *op. cit.,* p. 233.

53 Christopher Tiedemann, *Constitutional Limitations on Police Power* (St. Louis, 1886), p. 119.

54 John F. Dillon, *Law and Jurisprudence of England and America* (Boston, 1894), pp. 198, 206. Cf. also Taft, "Recent Criticism of the Federal Judiciary," 14 *Am. Bar Assn. Report,* 237 (1895).

55 Lloyd, *op. cit.,* p. 12.

56 29 *Am. L. Rev.* 306 (March-April, 1895).

CHAPTER 3   *The Conservative Crisis*

[1] Phil S. Foner, *History of the Labor Movement in the United States* (New York, 1955), II, pp. 103-04.

[2] Charles E. Russell, *These Shifting Scenes* (New York, 1914), p. 81.

[3] Cf. W. T. Hutchinson, *Cyrus Hall McCormick: Harvest 1856-1884* (New York, 1935), pp. 615-17.

[4] Morris Hillquit, *History of Socialism in the United States* (New York, 1903), p. 245.

[5] Russell, *op. cit.*, p. 106.

[6] Harry Barnard, *Eagle Forgotten: The Life of John Peter Altgeld* (New York, 1938), p. 104. Commons, *op. cit.*, II, p. 393.

[7] Barnard, *op. cit.*, pp. 107-08.

[8] Melville E. Stone, *Fifty Years a Journalist* (New York, 1921), p. 173.

[9] id., p. 173.

[10] Ray Ginger, *Altgeld's America: The Lincoln Ideal vs. Changing Realities* (New York, 1958), p. 51.

[11] id., pp. 53-54; Foner, *op. cit.*, pp. 108-10.

[12] Ginger, *op. cit.*, pp. 56-60; Barnard, *op. cit.*, ch. 12.

[13] Quoted in Foner, *op. cit.*, p. 111.

[14] id., ch. 8.

[15] Cf. Altgeld in I *D. A. B.* 231; Barnard, *op. cit.*, pp. 85ff.; Henry M. Christman, ed., *The Mind and Spirit of John Peter Altgeld* (Urbana, Ill., 1960), pp. 38ff.; Ginger, *op. cit.*, ch. 9.

[16] Christman, *op. cit.*, pp. 63ff.

[17] Barnard, *op. cit.*, pp. 210-15.

[18] Cf. id., ch. 24.

[19] id., p. 14.

[20] Commons, *op. cit.*, II, ch. 1.

[21] Marvin W. Schlegel, *Ruler of the Reading: The Life of Franklin B. Gowen* (Harrisburg, Pa., 1947), p. 96.

[22] Cf. id., chs. 9-11.

[23] Wayne G. Broehl, *The Molly Maguires* (Cambridge, Mass., 1965), ch. 2.

[24] id., chs. 6, 7.

[25] Schlegel, *op. cit.*, pp. 132-34.

[26] Cf. Foner, *op. cit.*, pp. 209-11.

[27] Allan Nevins, *Emergence of Modern America* (New York, 1927), ch. 14.

[28] Cf. Robert V. Bruce, *1877—Year of Violence* (New York, 1959), chs. 1-2.

[29] id., ch. 5.

[30] H. J. Eckenrode, *Rutherford B. Hayes, Statesman of Reunion* (New York, 1930), p. 300.

[31] Bruce, *op. cit.*, chs. 6, 7; Nevins, *Emergence of Modern America*, ch. 14.

[32] id., pp. 388-90.

[33] Bruce, *op. cit.*, ch. 9.

[34] id., ch. 11.

[35] id.

[36] Cf. Felix Frankfurter and Nathan Greene, *The Labor Injunction* (New York, 1930), pp. 2-5.

[37] Cf. Commons, *op. cit.,* chs. 8-13.

[38] Cf. Gompers, 7 *D. A. B.* 369.

[39] Allan Nevins, *Grover Cleveland, A Study in Courage* (New York, 1933), ch. 35.

[40] James, *op. cit.,* Cummings and McFarland, *op. cit.,* pp. 439ff.

[41] Tarbell, *op. cit.,* pp. 240-43.

[42] Pullman, in 15 *D. A. B.* 263; Almont Lindsey, *The Pullman Strike* (Chicago, 1942), ch. 2.

[43] id., p. 26.

[44] id., p. 27.

[45] id., ch. 3.

[46] United States Strike Commission, *Report on the Chicago Strike* (Washington, 1895), pp. 554-57.

[47] Lindsey, *op. cit.,* ch. 5.

[48] id., ch. 6.

[49] Black, "The Lesson of Homestead," 14 *Forum* 14, 21 (September 1892).

[50] Lindsey, *op. cit.,* chs. 6, 7.

[51] id., ch. 13; Nevins, *Cleveland,* p. 614.

[52] Chicago, Burlington & Quincy R. Co. v. Warner, 108 Ill. 544 (1884).

[53] Gustavus Myers, *History of the Supreme Court,* pp. 591-98.

[54] Nevins, *Cleveland,* pp. 616-17; Cummings and McFarland, *op. cit.,* pp. 438ff.

[55] Nevins, *Cleveland,* pp. 421ff.

[56] id., p. 626.

[57] Strike Commission *Report,* p. xlviii.

[58] Sherry v. Perkins, 147 Mass. 212 (1888).

[59] Nevins, *Cleveland,* p. 618; Lindsey *op. cit.,* ch. 12.

[60] Cf. Felix Frankfurter and Nathan Green, *The Labor Injunction* (New York, 1930), pp. 2-5.

[61] Nevins, *Cleveland,* p. 618.

[62] Strike Commission *Report,* pp. 143-44, 146.

[63] Lindsey, *op. cit.,* ch. 12.

[64] id., ch. 12.

[65] United States v. Debs, 64 Fed. 724, 728 (1894).

[66] In re Debs, 39 *L. Ed.* 1092, 1095ff. (1895).

[67] 158 U. S. 564, 577ff.

[68] Cf. Frankfurter and Green, *op. cit.,* App. I, II.

CHAPTER 4 *Fire on the Prairies*

[1] *Historical Statistics of the United States,* pp. 131ff.

[2] George, *op. cit.,* ch. 8.

[3] Ignatius Donnelly's prodigious pronouncements have been edited by Everett Fish in a volume entitled, *Donnelliana* (Chicago, 1892).

[4] William Z. Ripley, *Railroads: Rates and Regulation* (New York, 1922), chs. 4-16.

[5] Nye, *op. cit.,* pp. 41-44.

[6] Cf. Alan Westin, "The Supreme Court and the Populist Movement," 15 *J. Politics,* 3 (February, 1953).

[7] Rees v. City of Watertown, 19 Wall. 107 (1873), denying direct Federal authority to compel a municipality to discharge its obligations.

[8] Weston, *loc. cit.,* p. 4.

[9] id., 3-9.

[10] Cf. C. J. Buck, *The Agrarian Crusade* (New Haven, 1920), p. 128; Charles Fairman, "The So-Called Granger Cases, Lord Hale, and Justice Bradley," 5 *Stanf. L. Rev.* 592-600 (July 1953).

[11] Cf. Swisher, *Field,* ch. 14. The railroad and grain elevator cases, as Justice Field took pains to point out, did not for the most part involve statutes sponsored exclusively by the National Grange, but the term became a popular name used even by the Court thereafter.

[12] Briscoe v. Bank of Kentucky, 11 Peters 257 (1837); Bank of Augusta v. Earle, 13 Peters 519 (1839); New York v. Miln, 11 Peters 102 (1837).

[13] Cf. James C. Olson, *J. Sterling Morton* (Lincoln, Neb., 1942), ch. 15; Fairman, *loc. cit.,* pp. 620-30.

[14] Cf. James K. Edsall, "The Granger Cases and the Police Power," 10 *Am. Bar Assn. Rep.* 288, 298 (1887).

[15] Edsall, *op. cit.,* 315; Munn v. People, 69 Ill. 80 (1874).

[16] Cf. Nevins, *Emergence of Modern America,* ch. 6.

[17] Cf. 24 *L. Ed.* 77-80.

[18] Munn v. Illinois, 94 U. S. 113 (1877); and also Chi., B. & Q. R. Co. v. Cutts, id. at 155; Peik v. Chi. & N. W. R. Co., id. at 164; Chi., M. & St. P. R. Co. v. Akley, id. at 179; St. Peter R. Co. v. Blake, id. at 180; and Stone v. Wisconsin, id. at 181.

[19] Cf. Fairman, *loc. cit.,* 287.

[20] 94 U. S. 113, 131ff.

[21] id., at 136.

[22] Marshall, "A New Constitutional Amendment," 24 *Am. L. Rev.* 908, 912 (Nov.-Dec. 1890).

[23] Sinking Fund Cases, 99 U. S. 700 (1879).

[24] Judson, "Liberty of Contract Under the Police Power," 14 *Am. Bar Assn. Rep.* 231 (1891).

[25] Stone v. Farmers' Loan & Trust Co. (Railroad Commission Cases), 116 U. S. 307, 331 (1886).

[26] Georgia R. & Banking Co. v. Smith, 128 U. S. 174, 179 (1888); Chicago, Milwaukee & St. Paul R. Co. v. Minnesota, 134 U. S. 418 (1890).

[27] Smyth v. Ames, 169 U. S. 466 (1898).

[28] 24 *Am. L. Rev.* 522 (May-June 1890).

[29] Nye, *op. cit.,* p. 53.

[30] Cf. Harvey, *Coin's Financial School* (Richard Hofstadter, ed.; Cambridge, Mass., 1963), ch. 3.

[31] Cf. 27 *Nation* 312 (Nov. 24, 1878).

[32] Nye, *op. cit.,* chs. 1, 2.

[33] Quoted in John D. Hicks, *The Populist Revolt* (Minneapolis, 1931), p. 54.

[34] id., pp. 62ff.

[35] 18 Cong. Rec. 847.

[36] Wabash, St. L. & Pac. R. Co. v. Illinois, 118 U. S. 557 (1886).

[37] 17 Cong. Rec. 3393.

[38] Peik v. Chicago & Northwestern R. Co., 94 U. S. 164, 177 (1877); and cf. Paul v. Virginia, 8 Wall. 168 (1869).

[39] Baltimore & Ohio R. Co. v. Maryland, 21 Wallace 456, 474 (1875).

[40] Interstate Commerce Commission v. Brimson, 154 U. S. 447 (1894); Brown v. Walker, 161 U. S. 591 (1896).

[41] Hicks, *op. cit.,* ch. 4.

[42] id., ch. 5.

[43] Garland, *A Son of the Middle Border* (London, 1914), ch. 28; Nye, *op. cit.,* pp. 104-120.

[44] Peffer, "The Farmer's Defensive Movement," 8 *Forum,* p. 464 (January, 1890).

[45] Cf. Donnelly, 5 *D. A. B.* 369.

[46] Cf. Nye, *op. cit.,* 66-68.

[47] White, *Autobiography* (New York, 1946), 217-18; Nye *op. cit.,* 68-69.

[48] Cf. Weaver, 19 *D. A. B.* 568.

[49] Nye, *op. cit.,* ch. 3.

[50] Hicks, *op. cit.,* ch. 8.

[51] Tarbell, *op. cit.,* ch. 14.

[52] Cited in Weston, "Supreme Court and the Populist Movement," 31.

[53] id., p. 31.

[54] id.. 34-36.

[55] Nye, *op. cit.,* ch. 5; Hicks, *op. cit.,* ch. 13.

[56] Tarbell, *op. cit.,* ch. 15.

CHAPTER 5 *Progressives in Power: First Fruits*

[1] Olney to James A. Bayard, June 20, 1895. *Papers Relating to the Foreign Relations of the United States, 1893* (Washington, 1896), p. 558.

[2] Dole, 5 *D. A. B.* 358; Nevins, *Letters of Grover Cleveland* (New York, 1933), p. 491.

[3] 31 Cong. Rec. 5794, 6712.

[4] Ray Stannart Baker, "The New Prosperity," 15 *McClure's* 86, 88 (May, 1900).

[5] id., 87.

[6] M. G. Cuniff, "Increasing Railroad Consolidation," 3 *World's Work* 1775 (February 1902).

[7] George E. Mowry, *The Era of Theodore Roosevelt and the Birth of Modern America* (New York, 1958), p. 7.

[8] Philip Taft, *The American Federation of Labor in the Time of Gompers* (New York, 1957), pp. 262-64.

[9] Alpheus T. Mason, *Brandeis: A Free Man's Life*, ch. 10.

[10] Baker, *loc. cit.*, p. 88.

[11] Cf. Mark Sullivan, *Our Times* (New York, 1926), I, chs. 11, 15, 18.

[12] Julius W. Pratt, *Expansionists of 1898* (Baltimore, 1936), p. 267.

[13] id., p. 267, n. 94.

[14] Cf. generally 32 Cong. Rec. 93ff, 296ff; and cf. Fong Yue Ting v. United States, 149 U. S. 698, 711 (1893).

[15] 32 Cong. Rec. 296.

[16] id., 297, 958.

[17] id., 287-88.

[18] 31 Stat. 77.

[19] DeLima v. Bidwell, 182 U. S. 1 (1901); and cf. Dooley v. United States, 182 U. S. 222 (1901).

[20] Downes v. Bidwell, 182 U. S. 244 (1901).

[21] Edward J. Bander, ed., *Mr. Dooley on the Choice of Law* (Charlottesville, Va. 1963), pp. 47-52.

[22] A. M. Schlesinger, *The Rise of the City* (New York, 1933), chs. 3, 4.

[23] Cited in Mowry, *op. cit.*, p. 69.

[24] id., 63-64.

[25] id., 89.

[26] Cf. LaFollette, 10 *D. A. B.* 541.

[27] Cf. Belle C. LaFollette, *Robert M. LaFollette* (New York, 1953), I, chs. 9-16.

[28] Merlo Pusey, *Charles Evans Hughes,* I, chs. 14, 15.

[29] id., chs. 17-22.

[30] Mason, *Brandeis*, chs. 7-14.

[31] Hofstadter, *The Progressive Movement* (New York, 1963), *passim; The Age of Reform* (New York, 1955), chs. 4, 5.

[32] Theodore Roosevelt, *Autobiography* (New York, 1925), p. 357.

[33] Henry F. Pringle, *Theodore Roosevelt* (New York, 1931), p. 238.

[34] Adams, *Education*, pp. 417-18.

[35] Roosevelt, *Autobiography*, p. 351.

[36] id., p. 352.

[37] id., chs. 12, 13.

[38] id., p. 423.

[39] id., p. 424.

[40] Pringle, *Roosevelt*, pp. 561-62.

[41] Cf. Day, 5 *D. A. B.* 163.
[42] King, *Fuller,* pp. 308ff, 316ff.
[43] Felix Frankfurter, *Mr. Justice Holmes and the Supreme Court, passim.*
[44] id.
[45] H. C. Lodge, *Selections from the Correspondence of Theodore Roosevelt and Henry Cabot Lodge, 1884-1918* (New York, 1925), I, 517-19.
[46] Roosevelt, *Autobiography,* p. 428.
[47] Pringle, *Roosevelt,* pp. 252ff.
[48] Roosevelt, *Autobiography,* pp. 426-27.
[49] Pringle, *Roosevelt,* p. 262.
[50] id., p. 256.
[51] Cf. Hoffman, "Theodore Roosevelt and the Appointment of Mr. Justice Moody," 18 *Vand. L. Rev.* 733 (October 1954).
[52] Bonaparte, 2 *D. A. B.* 427.

CHAPTER 6   *Trust-Busting in Practice and Politics*

[1] Cummings and McFarland, *op. cit.,* ch. 16.
[2] Cf. Nevins, *Cleveland,* pp. 722-23.
[3] id., pp. 723-24.
[4] Bible to Harmon, Nov. 16, 1896; Bible to Harmon, Dec. 16, 1896; Bible to Harmon, January 16, 28, 1897. Dept. Justice File No. 17922-96 (National Archives).
[5] Ady to Miller, Dec. 1, 1892. Dept. Justice File No. 11136-92. Cf. also Cummings and McFarland, *op. cit.,* pp. 325ff.
[6] United States v. Trans-Missouri Freight Assn., 166 U. S. 290, 307 (1897).
[7] id., at 343.
[8] Wright to J. E. Boyd, Acting Attorney General, Sept. 16, 1897. Dept. Justice File No. 13927-97.
[9] Addyston Pipe & Steel Co. v. United States, 175 U. S. 211 (1899).
[10] Cummings & McFarland, *op. cit.,* pp. 314ff.
[11] Roosevelt to Douglas Robinson, Oct. 4, 1901, in S. E. Morison, ed., *The Letters of Theodore Roosevelt* (Cambridge, 1951), III, 159-60.
[12] Memo, undated, "Overcapitalization," in P. C. Knox Papers (Library of Congress).
[13] United States v. Northern Securities Co., 120 Fed. 721 (1903). Northern Securities Co. v. United States, 193 U. S. 197 (1903).
[14] 43 *L. Ed.* 680-88; and cf. 193 U. S. 268-73.
[15] 193 U. S. at 317ff.
[16] id., at 360.
[17] id., at 364.
[18] id., at 400.
[19] Cummings and MacFarland, *op. cit.,* p. 329.
[20] Undated draft of circular letter to United States attorneys, Knox Papers.
[21] Champion v. Ames, 188 U. S. 321 (1903).

[22] Cummings and MacFarland, *op. cit.,* p. 498.

[23] *New York World* clippings in William H. Moody Papers (Library of Congress).

[24] Swift & Co. v. United States, 196 U. S. 375 (1906).

[25] Roosevelt to Moody, Jan. 9, 1905. *Letters,* IV, 1096-97.

[26] Cummings and McFarland, *op. cit.,* p. 335.

[27] Mowry, *op. cit.,* p. 132.

[28] id., pp. 132ff. Cf. also Pringle, *Roosevelt,* pp. 425-29.

[29] id., pp. 441-42, 478-79.

[30] id., p. 258.

[31] id., ch. 7.

[32] id., pp. 356, 359.

CHAPTER 7 *The Big Stick in Court and Congress*

[1] Pringle, *Roosevelt,* p. 265.

[2] H. U. Faulkner, *The Quest for Social Justice* (New York, 1931), ch. 3.

[3] Pringle, *Roosevelt,* pp. 266-67.

[4] Baer, 1 *D. A. B.* 489.

[5] Mitchell, 13 *D. A. B.* 51.

[6] Pringle, *Roosevelt,* p. 272.

[7] id., p. 269.

[8] id., pp. 276-77.

[9] Roosevelt, *Autobiography,* p. 476.

[10] id., p. 464.

[11] Cf. Dartmouth College v. Woodward, 4 Wheaton 518 (1819).

[12] Allgeyer v. Louisiana, 165 U. S. 578 (1897).

[13] Addyston Pipe & Steel Co. v. United States, 175 U. S. 229 (1899).

[14] Holden v. Hardy, 169 U. S. 366 (1898).

[15] Lochner v. New York, 198 U. S. 45, 52 (1905).

[16] id., at 74.

[17] Adams, *Education,* p. 501.

[18] 29 Cong. Record, 2389.

[19] Ch. 370, 30 Stat. 424.

[20] United States v. Adair, 152 Fed. 737 (1907).

[21] 52 *L. Ed.* 436, 437.

[22] 208 U. S., at 166.

[23] id., 177ff.

[24] Cf. Harlan, 9 *D. A. B.* 269.

[25] 208 U. S., at 190f.

[26] id., 190.

[27] Holmes, *Collected Legal Papers* (New York, 1920), p. 279.

[28] id., p. 307.

[29] Loewe v. Lawlor, 208 U. S. 274 (1908).

[30] id., 283, 299.

[31] Muller v. Oregon, 208 U. S. 412 (1908).

[32] Mason, *Brandeis,* p. 251.

[33] id., pp. 248ff.

[34] id., p. 249.

[35] id., p. 253; 208 U. S. at 421.

[36] Ch. 3073, 34 Stat. 272.

[37] First Employers' Liability Case, 207 U. S. 463 (1908).

[38] Cf. White, 20 *D. A. B.* 95.

[39] Second Employers' Liability Case, 223 U. S. 1 (1912).

[40] Twining v. New Jersey, 211 U. S. 78 (1908).

[41] id., 89, 92, 99.

[42] id., 94.

[43] id., 114, 125.

[44] Pringle, *Roosevelt,* chs. 11-15.

[45] id., p. 420.

[46] id., pp. 421ff.

[47] id., p. 421.

[48] Roosevelt to Long, Jan. 31, 1906; *Letters,* V, 3804.

[49] Cf. John M. Blum, "Theodore Roosevelt and the Hepburn Act: Toward an Orderly System of Control," in *Letters,* VI, 1558ff.

[50] Stephenson, *Aldrich,* pp. 291-96; Pringle, *Roosevelt,* p. 422.

[51] Roosevelt, *Autobiography,* pp. 422-24, 484-85.

[52] Roosevelt to Cannon, Feb. 19, 1906; *Letters,* V., 3821.

[53] Pringle, *Roosevelt,* p. 424.

[54] 38 *Lit. Dig.* 405 (March 19, 1909).

[55] Pringle, *Roosevelt,* ch. 15.

[56] id., pp. 483-84.

[57] id., p. 482.

[58] id., p. 482.

[59] 43 Cong. Rec. 3726ff.

[60] Pringle, *Roosevelt,* Bk. II, ch. 15.

CHAPTER 8   *Trustee of the Square Deal*

[1] Holmes to Pollock, Mar. 7, 1909. Howe, ed., *Holmes-Pollock Letters,* I, 152.

[2] 38 *Lit. Dig.* 405 (March 13, 1909).

[3] Pringle, *Taft,* I, 382.

[4] Knox, 10 *D.A.B.* 478.

[5] Wickersham, 22 *D.A.B.* 713.

[6] Cummings and McFarland, *op. cit.,* pp. 328ff, 498.

[7] Cf. Pringle, *Taft,* I, Chs. 26, 27.

[8] Mason, *Brandeis,* ch. 17.

[9] id., pp. 270-78.

[10] id., 276.

[11] Pringle, *Taft,* I, ch. 30.

[12] Pringle, *Taft,* I, ch. 28; and cf. Archie Butt, *Taft and Roosevelt: The Intimate Letters of Archie Butt* (New York, 1930), I, pp. 348-49.
[13] Pringle, *Taft,* I, ch. 29.
[14] Butt, *op. cit.,* I, p. 202; II, pp. 53-55.
[15] Cf. Mason, *Taft,* ch. 2.
[16] Cf. Frankfurter and Landis, *The Business of the Supreme Court,* ch. 1, 2.
[17] id., ch. 3.
[18] Thomas W. Shelton to Taft, Nov. 9, 1912. Taft Papers (Library of Congress).
[19] Pringle, *Taft,* I, p. 102; Mason, *Taft,* ch. 1.
[20] Pringle, *Roosevelt,* p. 498.
[21] Pusey, *Hughes,* I, chs. 26, 27.
[22] Pringle, *Taft,* I, p. 532.
[23] Hendrick to Taft, July 6, 1910; Abbott to Taft, July 3, 1910; Harlan to Taft, July 11, 1910. Taft Papers.
[24] Pringle, *Taft,* I, pp. 533-35.
[25] Amasa Thornton to Charles D. Norton, Dec. 1, 1910; Thornton to Taft, July 11, 1910. Taft Papers.
[26] Act of June 23, 1910, Ch. 377, 36 Stat. (Part II-Private Bills) 1861.
[27] Pringle, *Taft,* I, p. 534; Mason, *Taft,* pp. 34-36.
[28] Cf. Mason, *Taft,* p. 38.
[29] Holmes to Pollock, Sept. 24, 1910; *Holmes-Pollock Letters,* I, p. 170.
[30] J. E. Dodge telegram to Judson Harmon, Dec. 8, 1910. Taft Papers.
[31] Cf. Otto T. Baumann to Taft, Nov. 4, 1910. Taft Papers.
[32] Cf. Mason, *Taft,* pp. 221-23.
[33] See Appendix B, and also Charles C. Tansill, ed., *Proposed Amendments to the Constitution of the United States,* 69th Cong., 1st Sess., Sen. Doc. 93 (Washington, 1926).
[34] Curtis, *Lecture on the Implied Powers of the Constitution* (Washington, 1885); and cf. his *Constitutional History of the United States* (New York, 1889-96) Vol. II.
[35] Cf. McCulloch v. Maryland, 4 Wheaton 316, 403 (1819).
[36] Cf. Ames, *The Proposed Amendments to the Constitution of the United States During the First Century of Its History,* ch. 1.
[37] Nicol v. Ames, 173 U. S. 509 (1899); Knowlton v. Moore, 178 U. S. 1 (1900); Patton v. Brady, 184 U. S. 608 (1902); Spreckles Sugar Ref. Co. v. McClain, 192 U. S. 397 (1904).
[38] Pringle, *Taft,* I, p. 433; 44 Cong. Rec. 4003.
[39] Pringle, *Taft,* I, pp. 432-35.
[40] Swisher, *op. cit.,* ch. 20.
[41] Flint v. Stone Tracy Co., 220 U. S. 107 (1911).
[42] 55 *L. Ed.* 389, 392-410.
[43] id., 392-400.
[44] Taft to Kellogg, Nov. 21, 1909, cited in Pringle, *Taft,* I, p. 661.

[45] Mowry, *op. cit.,* ch. 5.

[46] Pringle, *Taft,* II, pp. 661-63.

[47] Standard Oil Co. of New Jersey v. United States, 221 U. S. 1 (1911).

[48] id., at 74-82.

[49] id., at 82-106.

[50] Wickersham to Taft, Nov. 4, 1911. Taft Papers.

[51] United States v. American Tobacco Co., 221 U. S. 106 (1911).

[52] id., at 189-93.

CHAPTER 9 *The Road to Armageddon*

[1] Croly, *The Promise of American Life* (Ed. by Arthur M. Schlesinger, Jr.; Cambridge, Mass., 1965), intro.

[2] id., chs. 1, 5, 6.

[3] id., pp. 34-35.

[4] id., pp. 274-75.

[5] Lodge, ed., *Correspondence,* II, p. 378.

[6] id., II, pp. 356, 358.

[7] id., II, p. 367.

[8] Pringle, *Taft,* II, ch. 30.

[9] 40 *Lit. Dig.* 794-99 (April 23, 1910).

[10] Pringle, *Roosevelt,* Bk. III, ch. 5.

[11] Roosevelt, *Works* (New York, 1926), XVII, ch. 13.

[12] Pringle, *Roosevelt,* Bk. III, ch. 4.

[13] Philip Jessup, *Elihu Root* (New York, 1938, 1964), II, pp. 164-66.

[14] id., pp. 179, 180; Pringle, *Taft,* II, ch. 40.

[15] id., II, pp. 669ff.

[16] id., p. 671.

[17] Jessup, *op. cit.,* II, p. 184.

[18] Pringle, *Taft,* II, pp. 670ff.

[19] id., II, ch. 39.

[20] United States v. U. S. Steel Corp., 251 U. S. 417 (1920).

[21] Claude Bowers, *Albert J. Beveridge and the Progressive Era* (New York, 1932), Bk. IV, ch. 7.

[22] id., pp. 426-28.

[23] Croly, *op. cit.,* p. 214.

[24] Cf. Arthur S. Link, *Woodrow Wilson and the Progressive Era* (New York, 1954), chs. 1-3.

[25] Link, *Wilson: The Road to the White House* (Princeton, 1947), ch. 10,

[26] id., ch. 9.

[27] Mason, *Brandeis,* ch. 27; Link, *Road to the White House,* pp. 489-93.

[28] id., ch. 14.

[29] Mason, *Brandeis,* ch. 26.

[30] Cf. 45 *Lit. Dig.* 826 (November 9, 1912).

[31] Pujo Committee, *Report on Concentration of Money and Credit,* 62nd Con-

gress, 2nd Session. H. Doc. No. 504 (Washington, 1913).

[32] Pringle, *Taft,* II, p. 861.
[33] White, *The Old Order Changeth* (New York, 1910), pp. 202-03, 206-07.

CHAPTER 10   *Progressives in Power: Midsummer*

[1] White, *Woodrow Wilson: The Man, His Times and His Task* (New York, 1924), p. 292.
[2] id., p. 293.
[3] Cf. McAdoo, *Crowded Years* (Boston, 1931), chs. 12-16.
[4] Cf. Mason, *Brandeis,* ch. 25.
[5] id., p. 386.
[6] Link, *Wilson: The New Freedom* (Princeton, 1956), p. 110; Cummings and McFarland, *op. cit.,* p. 339.
[7] Link, *New Freedom,* ch. 4.
[8] McAdoo, *op. cit.,* p. 127.
[9] White, *Wilson,* p. 274.
[10] Link, *New Freedom,* p. 70.
[11] Wilson, *Congressional Government* (New York, 1913), ch. 5.
[12] Link, *Progressive Era,* ch. 3.
[13] Cf. 44 *Lit. Dig.* 613-15 (October 11, 1913); 27 *World's Work,* 9-11 (November, 1913).
[14] Pujo Committee *Report,* Sec. 1.
[15] Cf. Brandeis, "Breaking the Money Trust," 58 *Harper's Weekly,* 10 (November 22, 1913); R. L. Owen, "Currency Bill and Financial Panic," 76 *Independent,* 58 (December 5, 1913).
[16] *New York Times,* June 14, 1913.
[17] Cf. 97 *Nation,* 180 (August 28, 1913).
[18] 48 *Lit. Dig.,* 1 (January 3, 1914).
[19] id., p. 2.
[20] Link, *Progressive Era,* pp. 43-53.
[21] id., pp. 67ff.
[22] Cummings and McFarland, *op. cit.,* ch. 16.
[23] id., ch. 16.
[24] Swisher, *op. cit.,* pp. 824ff.
[25] Carl McFarland, *Judicial Control of the Federal Trade Commission and the Interstate Commerce Commission, 1920-1930* (New York, 1931), *passim.*
[26] Mason, *Brandeis,* ch. 27.
[27] 49 *Lit. Dig.* 778ff (October 24, 1914).
[28] Link, *Progressive Era,* ch. 9; *New Freedom,* ch. 14.
[29] Link, *Progressive Era,* pp. 67-68.
[30] *Historical Statistics of the United States,* pp. 593ff.
[31] Joseph Dorfman, *The Economic Mind in American Civilization* (New York, 1939), III, pp. 207ff.
[32] id., pp. 296-98.

[33] *Congressional Government*, ch. 5.

[34] Link, *New Freedom*, chs. 3, 8, 12.

[35] Swisher, *op. cit.*, pp. 573-74.

[36] Cummings and McFarland, *op. cit.*, pp. 348ff.

[37] Cf. Burton J. Hendrick, "Attorney General and Believer in the Sherman Act," 27 *World's Work* 26 (November, 1913).

[38] Truax v. Raich, 239 U. S. 33 (1915).

[39] Minnesota Rate Cases, 230 U. S. 252 (1913).

[40] Shreveport Rate Case, 234 U. S. 342 (1914).

[41] Cf. Pusey, *Hughes*, II, ch. 63.

[42] Coppage v. Kansas, 236 U. S. 1 (1915).

[43] id., at 4-6, 27.

[44] Croly, *op. cit.*, p. 389.

[45] Mason, *Brandeis*, chs. 26, 28.

CHAPTER 11   *The Brief Climax*

[1] Cf. E. T. Devin, "Neutrality of the Law or of the Spirit?" 33 *Survey*, 33 (October 3, 1914); Wilson, "American People and the Great War," 79 *Independent*, 301 (August 31, 1914).

[2] 50 *Lit. Dig.* 1449-52 (June 19, 1915).

[3] Pringle, *Taft*, II, pp. 952-53.

[4] Mason, *Brandeis*, p. 492.

[5] Link, *New Freedom*, pp. 10-15.

[6] Todd, *Justice on Trial*, ch. 4.

[7] Mason, *Brandeis*, ch. 30.

[8] id., p. 687.

[9] id., pp. 468-70.

[10] id., p. 469.

[11] id., ch. 31.

[12] Link, *Wilson: Confusions and Crises* (Princeton, 1964), pp. 357-60.

[13] Mason, *Brandeis*, pp. 504ff.

[14] Cited in Mason, *Taft*, p. 75.

[15] Link, *Progressive Era*, chs. 6, 7.

[16] id., pp. 56-59, 225-26.

[17] id., pp. 226ff.

[18] Cf. editorial "Mr. Wilson's Congress," 103 *Nation*, 251 (September 14, 1916).

[19] 55 *Lit. Dig.* 1-3 (Oct. 2, 1917); Merz, "Growth of Federalism," 10 *New Republic* 256 (March 31, 1917).

[20] William P. Slosson, *The Great Crusade and After* (New York, 1930), ch. 2.

[21] United States v. Sugar, 243 Fed. 423 (1917); Story v. Perkins, 243 U. S. 997 (1917).

[22] Selective Draft Cases, 245 U. S. 366 (1918).

[23] Wilson v. New, 243 U. S. 332, 349-59 (1917).

[24] Charles Merz, *The Dry Decade* (New York, 1931), ch. 1.

[25] Clark Distilling Co. v. Western Maryland R. Co., 242 U. S. 311 (1917).

[26] Ch. 53, 40 Stat. 276.

[27] Swisher, *op. cit.,* pp. 631ff.

[28] id., p. 634.

[29] Cf. Chafee, *op. cit.,* ch. 2.

[30] id., ch. 2.

[31] United States v. Schenk, 253 Fed. 212 (1918); and cf. Masses Pub. Co. v. Patten, 244 Fed. 535 (1917).

[32] id., p. 540.

[33] Schenk v. United States, 249 U. S. 47 (1919).

[34] id., at 52.

[35] id., at 52, citing Gompers v. Bucks Stove & Range Co., 221 U. S. 418 (1911).

[36] Frohwerk v. United States, 249 U. S. 204 (1919).

[37] Debs v. United States, 249 U. S. 211 (1919).

[38] Cf. Chafee, *op. cit.,* chs. 2, 3.

[39] Schaeffer v. United States, 251 U. S. 466 (1920).

[40] Missouri v. Holland, 252 U. S. 416 (1920).

[41] Abrams v. United States, 250 U. S. 616, 630 (1919).

CHAPTER 12 *The Nullification of Reform*

[1] Hammer v. Dagenhart, 242 U. S. 251, 62 *L. Ed.* 1101, 1103 (1918).

[2] 247 U. S. at 276.

[3] id., at 274.

[4] Hipolite Egg Co. v. United States, 220 U. S. 45 (1911); Hoke v. United States, 227 U. S. 308 (1913).

[5] 247 U. S. at 277-81.

[6] Cf. Swisher, *op. cit.,* pp. 584ff.

[7] 56 Cong. Rec. 7692.

[8] Ch. 18, 40 Stat. 1057, 1138.

[9] Brushaber v. Union Pacific R. Co., 240 U. S. 1 (1916); cf. also Tyee Realty Co. v. Anderson, 240 U. S. 115 (1916).

[10] Eisner v. Macomber, 252 U. S. 189-99 (1920); and cf. Brushaber v. Union Pacific R. Co., 240 U. S. 1 (1916).

[11] 252 U. S., at 207.

[12] id., at 219-20.

[13] Cf. Powell, "Supreme Court and the Constitution," 36 *Pol. Sci. Q.* 411 (September, 1920).

[14] Ch. 323, 38 Stat. 730.

[15] Cf. Paine Lumber Co. v. Neal, 244 U. S. 459 (1917); Eagle Glass & Mfg. Co. v. Rowe, 245 U. S. 275 (1917).

[16] P. W. Slosson, *The Great Crusade and After* (New York, 1930), ch. 5.

[17] Duplex Printing Press Co. v. Deering, 247 Fed. 192 (1917).

[18] Duplex Printing Press Co. v. Deering, 252 Fed. 722, 727-42, 744 (1918).

[19] id., at 748.

[20] id., at 748.

[21] Duplex Printing Co. v. Deering, 254 U. S. 443 (1921).

[22] id., at 479-88.

[23] Mason, *Brandeis*, p. 542.

[24] United States v. Cohen Grocery Co., 255 U. S. 81 (1921); and cf. Evans v. Gore, 253 U. S. 245 (1920).

[25] Palmer, 22 *D. A. B.* 510.

[26] Cf. White, *Autobiography*, ch. 83.

[27] Sullivan, *Our Times: The Twenties* (New York, 1935), pp. 167-70.

[28] Chafee, *op. cit.*, ch. 4.

[29] Sullivan, *Our Times: The Twenties*, p. 172.

[30] Chafee, *op. cit.*, ch. 4.

[31] id., ch. 5.

[32] Cf. New York Central R. Co. v. Winfield, 244 U. S. 147, 153 (1917); Erie R. Co. v. Winfield, 244 U. S. 170 (1917).

[33] 244 U. S. at 154-70.

[34] Southern Pacific Co. v. Jensen, 244 U. S. 205, 207-18 (1917).

[35] id., at 218-55.

[36] Adams v. Tanner, 244 U. S. 590 (1917).

[37] 244 U. S., at 597-616.

[38] id., at 607-08.

[39] Pound, *Interpretations of Legal History* (New York, 1923), p. 152.

[40] New York Life Ins. Co. v. Dodge, 246 U. S. 357, 365-77 (1918).

[41] id., at 377-88.

[42] Frank, "Has Wilson Failed?" 98 *Century* 506 (August, 1919).

[43] Taft, "Mr. Wilson and the Campaign," 10 *Yale Review* (n. s.), pp. 1, 19-20 (October, 1920).

[44] id.

[45] "The Passing of Mr. Wilson," 112 *Nation* 328 (March 2, 1921).

CHAPTER 13 *Bulwark Against Change*

[1] Mason, *Taft,* pp. 76ff.; Pringle, *Taft,* II, pp. 955ff.

[2] Mason, *Taft,* p. 78.

[3] Pusey, *Hughes,* I, p. 364.

[4] "Chief Justice Taft," 27 *New Republic* 231 (July 27, 1921).

[5] id., 231.

[6] Taft, *Popular Government* (New Haven, 1913), pp. 231, 234-35.

[7] Taft, "The Attacks on the Courts and Legal Procedure," 5 *Ky. L. J.* 3, 8, 22 (October, 1916).

[8] Taft, "The Boundaries Between the Executive, the Legislative, and the Judicial Branches of Government," 25 *Yale L. J.* 599, 616 (May, 1916).

⁹ Taft, "Presidential Address," 1916 *Am. Bar Assn. Rep.* p. 368.

¹⁰ Taft, *Our Chief Magistrate and His Powers* (New York, 1916), pp. 12-13.

¹¹ Pringle, *Taft,* II, p. 899; Mason, *Taft,* p. 161.

¹² Quoted in Mason, *Taft,* p. 163.

¹³ 53 *Lit. Dig.* 240 (July 29, 1916).

¹⁴ 74 *Lit. Dig.* 15 (Sept. 16, 1922).

¹⁵ Sutherland, "Presidential Address," 1917 *Am. Bar Assn. Rep.* pp. 197, 198, 201, 203.

¹⁶ id., p. 204.

¹⁷ Taft to Sutherland, Sept. 10, 1922. Taft Papers.

¹⁸ Mason, *Taft,* pp. 170-171.

¹⁹ Danilov, *A Supreme Court Justice Is Appointed,* p. 108.

²⁰ id., p. 114.

²¹ Mason, *Taft,* pp. 168-69.

²² M. B. Hodges, "Pierce Butler, Friend of Intolerance," 115 *Nation* 661 (December 13, 1922); Editorial, "Pierce Butler and the Rule of Reason," 33 *New Republic* 81 (December 20, 1922).

²³ Danilov, *op. cit.,* p. 137.

²⁴ Cf. 285 U. S. xxxvii-lvii (1931).

²⁵ Holmes to Pollock, February 24, 1913; *Holmes-Pollock Letters,* II, p. 114.

²⁶ Cf. Frankfurter, *Holmes, passim;* Brandeis, 317 U. S. ix-xlix (1942); Butler, 310 U. S. v-xx (1939); McReynolds, 334 U. S. v-xxiv (1947); Sutherland, 323 U. S. v-xxii (1944); Van Devanter, 316 U. S. v-xliii (1941).

²⁷ White, *A Puritan in Babylon* (New York, 1938), pp. 396, 444.

²⁸ Truax v. Corrigan, 257 U. S. 312 (1921).

²⁹ id., p. 343.

³⁰ id., pp. 355, 357.

³¹ Edit., "Does Mr. Taft Want Direct Action?" 114 *Nation* 32 (January 11, 1922).

CHAPTER 14   *The Jurisprudence of Prosperity*

¹ Bailey v. Drexel Furniture Co., 259 U. S. 20 (1922); Corwin, "Child Labor Decision," 31 *New Republic,* 179 (July 11, 1922).

² 259 U. S., at 37.

³ Mason, *Taft,* pp. 244-48, 262-63.

⁴ Chisolm v. Georgia, 2 Dallas 419 (1793); Dred Scott v. Sanford, 19 Howard 393 (1857); Pollock v. Farmers' Loan & Trust Co., 158 U. S. 601 (1895).

⁵ Butler, "The New American Revolution," 10 *Am. Bar Assn. Journal* 845, 846, 847 (December, 1924).

⁶ Butler, *Why Should We Change Our Form of Government?* (New York, 1912), p. 47; *The Faith of a Liberal* (New York, 1924), p. 248.

⁷ 65 Cong. Rec. 7177, 7180, 7187; and cf. 64 id., 5345.

⁸ 65 Cong. Rec. 7195.

9 id., 9895, 10097, 10139.

10 41 *New Republic* 109 (December 24, 1924).

11 "The Twentieth Amendment: A Symposium," 73 *Forum* 13 (January, 1925).

12 81 *Lit. Dig.* 6 (May 10, 1924).

13 42 *New Republic* 330 (May 20, 1923).

14 Coleman v. Miller, 307 U. S. 433 (1939).

15 Ch. 676, 52 Stat. 1060, 1067.

16 United States v. Darby, 312 U. S. 100 (1941).

17 312 U. S., at 117.

18 Sayre, "The Minimum Wage Decision," 50 *Survey,* p. 150 (May 1, 1923).

19 Adkins v. Children's Hospital, 261 U. S. 525, 527-35 (1923).

20 id., at 557.

21 id., at 560.

22 id., at 562-67.

23 id., at 570-71.

24 In re Kemmler, 136 U. S. 436, 448 (1889); Adkins v. Children's Hospital, 261 U. S. 525 (1923).

25 West Coast Hotel Co. v. Parrish, 300 U. S. 379 (1937).

26 Wolff Packing Co. v. Court of Industrial Relations, 262 U. S. 522 (1923).

27 id., at 539.

28 Mason, *Brandeis,* p. 547.

29 Mason, *Brandeis,* p. 547.

30 Taft, *Popular Government,* p. 229.

31 Meyer v. Nebraska, 262 U. S. 390 (1923); Pierce v. Society of Sisters, 268 U. S. 510 (1925).

32 Gitlow v. New York, 268 U. S. 652 (1925).

33 Chafee, *op. cit.,* p. 325.

34 Whitney v. California, 274 U. S. 357 (1927).

35 Wisconsin R. Comm. v. Chicago, Burlington & Quincy R. Co., 257 U. S. 563 (1922); Dayton-Goose Creek R. Co. v. United States, 263 U. S. 456 (1924).

36 Stafford v. Wallace, 258 U. S. 495 (1922).

37 Terral v. Burke Constr. Co., 257 U. S. 529 (1922), overruling Doyle v. Continental Ins. Co., 94 U. S. 535 (1877).

38 Federal Trade Commission v. Gratz, 253 U. S. 421 (1920); Federal Trade Commission v. Curtis Pub. Co., 260 U. S. 568 (1923).

39 Lynd, Middletown (New York, 1929), ch. 8.

40 id., chs. 17-19.

41 Cf. Federal Trade Commission, *National Wealth and Income* (69th Congress, 1st Sess.; Sen. Doc. No. 126, 1926); National Industrial Conference Board Bulletin No. 5 (1927), p. 34; *New York Times,* August 22, 1926.

42 Mason, *Stone,* pp. 142-47.

43 Mason, *Taft,* pp. 182-83.

[44] Holmes to Pollock, Sept. 18, 1927; *Holmes-Pollock Letters,* II, p. 205.

[45] C. W. Thompson, "The Two Tafts," 1 *American Mercury* 315, 319 (March 1924).

CHAPTER 15   *Prohibition: A Socio-Legal Sketch*

[1] Merz, *The Dry Decade,* pp. 39, 42.

[2] Herbert Asbury, *The Great Illusion* (New York, 1950), pp. 142-45.

[3] Hawke v. Smith, 253 U. S. 221 (1920).

[4] Rhode Island v. Palmer, 64 *L. Ed.* at 949 (1920).

[5] id., pp. 951, 952.

[6] id., p. 959.

[7] id., p. 975.

[8] id., pp. 979, 980.

[9] Cited in Asbury, *op. cit.,* p. 155.

[10] 58 Cong. Rec. 2298-99, 2301.

[11] Merz, *op. cit.,* App. F, p. 329.

[12] id., App. G, pp. 330-31.

[13] id., p. 57.

[14] id., pp. 164, 170.

[15] United States v. Lanza, 260 U. S. 377, 381-82 (1922).

[16] Merz, *Dry Decade,* chs. 4-6.

[17] Asbury, *Great Illusion,* ch. 11.

[18] Cited in Kirkland, *op. cit.,* p. 671.

[19] Cited in Merz, *op. cit.,* p. 244.

[20] The cases in which these rules were enumerated include Rupert, Inc. v. Coffey, 251 U. S. 264 (1920); Vigliotto v. Pennsylvania, 258 U. S. 403 (1922); Lewinsohn v. United States, 278 Fed. 421 (1922); cert. den. 258 U. S. 630 (1923); Cornelius v. Moore, 257 U. S. 491 (1922); Hamas v. Georgia, 258 U. S. 1 (1922).

[21] Cf. Cunard SS. Co. v. Mellon, 262 U. S. 100 (1923); Hixson v. Oakes, 265 U. S. 254 (1924); Lambert v. Yellowby, 272 U. S. 581 (1926); Von Osten v. Kansas, 272 U. S. 465 (1926); Selzman v. United States, 268 U. S. 466 (1925).

[22] Cf. Treaty with Great Britain, signed January 23, 1924, in 43 Stat. Part II, p. 1761; and similar treaties with Norway, p. 1772; Denmark, p. 1809; Germany, p. 1815; Sweden, p. 1830; Italy, p. 1844; and Panama, p. 1875.

[23] Asbury, *Great Illusion,* ch. 12.

[24] Olmstead v. United States, 277 U. S. 438 (1928).

[25] Olmstead v. United States, 19 Fed. 2d, 842, 850 (1927).

[26] Pringle, *Taft,* II, pp. 981-83.

[27] id., p. 984. cf. Cornelius v. Moore, 257 U. S. 491 (1922); United States v. Lanza, 260 U. S. 377 (1922); Carroll v. United States, 267 U. S. 132 (1925).

[28] Olmstead v. United States, 277 U. S. 438 (1928).

[29] id., at 469-71.

[30] id., at 479.

[31] Cf. Merz, *op. cit.,* ch. 8.

[32] Quoted in Merz, *op. cit.,* pp. 191-92.

[33] id., pp. 194-96.

[34] id., pp. 197-99.

[35] Quoted in 13 *Am. Bar Assn. Journal* 117 (March, 1927).

[36] Cited in Merz., *op. cit.,* p. 233.

[37] id., p. 237.

[38] Cf. House Doc. No. 722, 71st Cong. 3d. Sess., *Enforcement of the Prohibition Laws of the United States* (1931), pp. 21-22.

[39] id., pp. 48-51.

[40] id., pp. 52-58.

[41] id., p. 60.

[42] id., p. 162.

[43] *New York Times,* January 18, 1931; and cf. Asbury, *op. cit.,* p. 15.

[44] Asbury, *Great Illusion,* ch. 15.

[45] Cf. discussions in 27 *Ill. L. Rev.* 528 (January, 1932); and 28 id. 950 (March, 1934); and Max P. Rapacz, "Effect of the Eighteenth Amendment upon the Amending Process," 9 *Notre Dame Law.* 313 (March, 1934).

[46] Cf. 76 Cong. Rec. 4138-39.

[47] M. B. Hamilton, "Lest We Forget," 29 *American Mercury* 40 (May, 1933); 76 Cong. Rec. 4143.

[48] id., p. 4146.

[49] id., pp. 4158-59.

[50] United States v. Sprague, 44 Fed. (2d), 967-86 (1930).

[51] United States v. Sprague, 282 U. S. 716 (1931).

[52] 76 Cong. Rec. 4228.

CHAPTER 16   *Blueprint for a Modernized Court*

[1] Cf. William Strong, "The Needs of the Supreme Court," 132 *North American Review* 439 (April, 1881); and cf. Warren, *Supreme Court in United States History,* II, p. 727n; Frankfurter and Landis, *op. cit.,* pp. 295-98.

[2] Pound, "Causes of Popular Dissatisfaction With the Administration of Justice," 25*Am. Bar Assn. Reports,* 395 (1906).

[3] Mason, *Taft,* ch. 2.

[4] Cf. Act of March 3, 1911, ch. 231, 36 Stat. 1087; and ch. 448, 39 Stat. 726.

[5] Cf. Hearing Before Subcommittee of Committee on the Judiciary, 68th Congress, 1st Sess., p. 23, cited in Frankfurter and Landis, *op. cit.,* pp. 261-62.

[6] 46 *Am. Bar Assn. Reports,* 562 (1921).

[7] Taft, "Three Needed Steps of Progress," 8 *Am. Bar Assn. Journal,* pp. 34, 35 (January, 1922).

[8] Cf. Mason, *Taft,* p. 111.

[9] Ch. 306, 42 Stat. 837.

[10] 66 Cong. Rec. 2928.

[11] Cf. Mason, *Taft*, pp. 127ff.

[12] id., p. 143.

[13] id., chs. 4, 5; Frankfurter and Landis, *op. cit.,* ch. 7.

[14] Mason, *Taft*, ch. 5.

[15] Ch. 229, 43 Stat. 936.

[16] Taft, "The Jurisprudence of the Supreme Court Under the Act of February 13, 1925," 25 *Yale L. J.* 1-3, 9, 12 (November, 1925).

[17] Warren, *Supreme Court in United States History,* I., pp. 169-71, 191.

[18] Mason, *Taft*, pp. 133-137.

[19] Myers v. United States, 272 U. S. 108 (1926).

[20] id., p. 177.

[21] id., pp. 121, 122.

[22] id., pp. 141, 145-57, 165-69.

[23] id., pp. 173-74.

[24] id., pp. 178, 182-83, 186.

[25] id., pp. 242, 254, 258 n27, 291-95.

[26] Pringle, *Taft*, II, p. 1025.

[27] Humphreys' Exec. v. United States, 295 U. S. 602 (1935).

[28] Quoted in Mason, *Taft*, p. 228.

[29] Cf. Pound, quoted in Henry Steele Commager, *The American Mind* (New Haven, 1910), ch. 18.

[30] Cf. Commager, *op. cit.,* pp. 380.

[31] Harlan B. Philips, ed., *Felix Frankfurter Reminisces* (New York, (1960), p. 197.

[32] Nathan Cardozo, *The Growth of the Law* (New York, 1924), p. 137.

[33] Frankfurter, "Social Issues Before the Court," 22 *Yale Review* 476 (March, 1933); "The Zeitgeist and the Judiciary," 29 *Survey* 542 (January 25, 1913).

[34] Cf. Mason, *Taft*, ch. 12.

CHAPTER 17   *The Twilight of* Laissez-Faire

[1] Cf. 75 *Lit. Dig.* 5 (December 16, 1922).

[2] 62 Cong. Rec. 9081; cf. also LaFollette, *op. cit.,* II, p. 1057.

[3] id., p. 1057.

[4] George W. Norris, *Fighting Liberal* (New York, 1945), p. 332.

[5] id., pp. 329-30.

[6] id., p. 232.

[7] id., p. 233.

[8] id., pp. 234-42.

[9] id., pp. 216-18; Richard L. Neuberger, *Integrity: The Life of George W. Norris* (New York, 1937), pp. 150-51.

[10] Cf. C. O. Fisher, "The New Railway Labor Act: A Comparison and an Appraisal," 17 *Amer. Econ. Rev.* 177 (March, 1927).

[11] *New York Times,* January 7, 1926; Fisher, *op. cit.,* pp. 178, 180.

[12] 67 Cong. Rec. 4516, 4567.

[13] Ch. 347, 44 Stat. 577.

[14] Norris, *op. cit.,* p. 309.

[15] Kinkaid, *op. cit.,* p. 674.

[16] Frankfurter and Greene, *op. cit.,* p. 22.

[17] Holmes, "Privilege, Malice, and Intent," 8 *Harvard L. Rev.* 1, 9 (1898).

[18] Vegelahn v. Gunter, 167 Mass. 92, 107, 108 (1896); Plant v. Woods, 176 Mass. 492, 505 (1900).

[19] United Mine Workers v. Coronado Coal Co., 259 U. S. 344 (1922).

[20] Frankfurter and Greene, *op. cit.,* pp. 85-133.

[21] Bedford Stone Co. v. Journeymen Stonecutters Assn., 274 U. S. 37, 54-55 (1927).

[22] id., 58, 65.

[23] Duplex Printing Press Co. v. Deering, 254 U. S. 443 (1921); American Steel Foundries v. Tri-City Central Trades Council, 257 U. S. 184; Truax v. Corrigan, 257 U. S. 312 (1921).

[24] Michaelson v. United States, 266 U. S. 42 (1924).

[25] United States v. Brims, 272 U. S. 549 (1926).

[26] Editorial, 50 *New Republic* 262, 264 (April 27, 1927).

[27] Norris, *op. cit.,* 311; Frankfurter and Greene, *op. cit.,* p. 207.

[28] Norris, *op. cit.,* pp. 312-13.

[29] 75 Cong. Rec. 5479.

[30] id., p. 5480.

[31] Editorial, 14 *Am. Bar Assn. Journal,* 201 (April, 1928); Newlin, "Proposed Limitations upon the Federal Courts," 15 *Am. Bar Assn. Journal,* 401 (July, 1929); Norris, *op. cit.,* p. 312.

[32] Leroy Fiber Co. v. Chicago, Milwaukee & St. Paul R. Co., 232 U. S. 340, 350 (1914); Block v. Hirsh, 256 U. S. 135, 165 (1921); United States v. New River Collieries Co., 265 U. S. 533, 544 (1924).

[33] Cf. Civil Rights Cases, 109 U. S. 3 (1883); Corrigan v. Buckley, 271 U. S. 323, 331 (1926); and see Shelley v. Kraemer, 334 U. S. 1 (1948).

[34] Euclid v. Ambler Realty Co., 272 U. S. 365, 387 (1926).

[35] Burns Baking Co. v. Bryan, 264 U. S. 504, 513, 517 (1924).

[36] id., pp. 520, 528, 534.

[37] Weaver v. Palmer Bros. Co., 270 U. S. 402, 412-13 (1926).

[38] id., p. 416.

[39] Hodges v. Snyder, 261 U. S. 600 (1923); Delaware, Lackawanna & Western R. Co. v. Morristown, 276 U. S. 182 (1928); Frost v. Corporation Commission, 278 U. S. 515 (1929).

[40] Powell, "Supreme Court and State Police Power, 1922-1930," 18 *Va. L. Rev.* 270, 304 (January, 1932); id., p. 414 (February, 1932).

[41] id., p. 509 (March, 1932).

[42] Tyson Bros. v. Banton, 273 U. S. 418, 430 (1927).

[43] id., 431, 445.

44 id., 445, 446, 451, 454.

45 Ribnik v. McBride, 277 U. S. 350, 359-75 (1928).

46 New State Ice & Coal Co. v. Liebmann, 285 U. S. 262, 280-311 (1932).

47 Pusey, *Hughes,* II, pp. 650-55.

48 id., ch. 63; and cf. editorial, "The New Chief Justice," 130 *Nation* 238 (February 26, 1934).

49 Paul Y. Anderson, "The Hughes Rebellion," 130 *Nation* 208 (February, 19, 1931).

50 72 Cong. Rec., 3449.

51 id., 3450.

52 id., 3500.

53 id., 3591.

54 Cf. 72 Cong. Rec. 7301, 7690, 7793, etc.

55 62 *New Republic,* 230 (April 16, 1930).

56 105 *Lit. Dig.* 9 (March 17, 1930); *New York Times,* March 26, 30, 1930; 72 Cong. Rec. 7930.

57 id., 7932-33.

58 *New York Times,* April 13, 22, 24, May 8, 1930.

59 Cf. 72 Cong. Rec. 9115, 9217.

60 Ohio v. Zangerle, 281 U. S. 74; Cochran v. State Board of Education, 281 U. S. 370; Ohio Oil Co. v. Conway, 281 U. S. 146; Staten's Rapid Transit R. Co. v. Phoenix Indemnity Co., 281 U. S. 98; Corporation Commission v. Lowe, 281 U. S. 431; Texas & New Orleans R. Co. v. Brotherhood of R. & S. Clerks, 281 U. S. 548. all in 1930.

61 130 *Nation* 208 (February 19, 1931).

62 Stromberg v. California, 283 U. S. 359 (1931).

63 Near ex rel. Olson v. Minnesota, 283 U. S. 697 (1931).

64 Home Building & Loan Assn. v. Blaisdell, 290 U. S. 398 (1933).

65 283 U. S. 643 (1931).

66 United States v. Chicago, Milwaukee & St. Paul R. Co., 238 U. S. 840 (1931).

67 Standard Oil Co. v. United States, 283 U. S. 163 (1931).

68 New State Ice & Coal Co. v. Liebmann. 285 U. S. 262, 278-80 (1932).

69 id.. pp. 306-11.

70 Editorial, 62 *New Republic,* 111 (March 19, 1930).

APPENDICES

1 John R. Schmidhauser, "The Justices of the Supreme Court: A Collective Portrait," 3 *Midwest J. of Pol. Sci.,* 1 (February, 1959).

2 Warren, *Supreme Court,* II.

3 Cf. *Proposed Amendments to the Constitution of the United States* [December 4, 1889—July 2, 1926] (69th Cong., 1st Sess., Sen. Doc. No. 93); *Proposed Amendments to the Constitution of the United States* [December 6, 1926-January 3, 1963] (87th Cong., 2d Sess., Sen. Doc. No. 163).

[4] Cf. Frankfurter and Landis, *op. cit.,* chs. 1, 2.

[5] Charles Warren, "New Light on the History of the Federal Judiciary Act of 1789," 37 *Harv. L. Rev.* 49, 131 (November, 1923).

[6] Erwin C. Surrency, "History of the Federal Courts," 28 *Mo. L. Rev.* 214, 220 (Spring, 1963).

[7] Frankfurter and Landis, *op. cit.,* p. 65.

[8] Holmes, *Collected Legal Papers,* p. 295.

INDEX

Abbott, Lyman, 143, 144
Abraham, Henry J., 404
Abrams v. U.S. (1919), 203-205, 245, 247, 357, *385*
Adair, William, 115, 116
Adair v. U.S. (1908), 114-117, 348, *376, 380*
Adams, Charles F., 189
Adams, Henry, 18, 19, 37, 91, 114, 137
Adams, John, 338
Adams v. Tanner (1917), 217, *383*
Adamson (Railway Labor) Act (1916), 192, 193, 197, 287, 288, *354*, 384
Addams, Jane, 88, 163
Addyston Pipe & Steel Co. v. U.S. (1899), 99, 100, 104, 112, 113, 347, *372*
Adkins v. Children's Hospital (1923), 241-243, 245, 356, *390*
Ady, Joseph W., 99
Agricultural Marketing Act (1929), *358*
Agricultural Wheel, 73
Agriculture: cooperatives, 69, 357; credit banks, 357; farm loans, 192, 353; farm ownership: proposed Constitutional amendments, 331; farm relief, 275; Granger Movement, 33, 63-74, 78, 79; marketing, 358; prices, 82; and railroads, 61-66; surpluses, 358

Alabama Commercial and Industrial Association, 126
Aldrich, Chester H., 158; biography, *323*
Aldrich, Nelson M., 34, 91, 126-130, 148, 174-176; *See also* Payne-Aldrich Tariff Act
Aldrich-Vreeland Currency Act (1908), 124, 174, *350*
Aliens: deportation, 214, 215; proposed Constitutional amendments, 326, 331, 334
Allgeyer v. Louisiana (1897), 36, 112, *369-370*
Allison, William B., 34, 55, 126, 128
Altgeld, John P., 43, 44, 56, 88
American Bell Telephone Co., 100, 101
American Can Co., 21
American Economic Association, 179
American Federation of Labor, 50, 51, 108, 268
American Mfg. Co. v. St. Louis (1919), *385*
American Protective League, 201
American Railway Union, 51, 54
American Sheet Steel Co., 21
American Steel Foundries v. Trades Council (1921), 291, *388*
American Telephone and Telegraph Co., 101, 177
American Tin Plate Co., 21

NOTE: Pages italicized indicate that act, statute or case is summarized in the appendices, or that biography and/or bibliography for Justice, Attorney General or Solicitor General is included in the appendices.

Vose, Clement E., 402
Wabash, St. Louis & Pacific R. Co.
v. Illinois (1886), 72, 73, *363*
Wadsworth, James W., Jr., 238
Wagner, Robert, 269
Waite, Edward F., 404
Waite, Morrison R., 31, 33, 36, 67-69
Walker, Edwin, 56-58
Walsh, Thomas J., 173, 191, 231, 276, 291
Wanamaker, John, 23
War powers: proposed Constitutional amendments, 333, 336; *See also* World War I
Warburg, Paul M., 175, 176
Ware v. Hylton (1796), 368
Warehouse Act (1916), *353*
Warfield, Benjamin D., 116
Warner, Hoyt L., 403
Warren, Charles, 408
Warren (Earl) Court, viii, 281
Wartime Prohibition Cases (1919), 351, 354; *See also* Prohibition
Washington, Booker T., 128
Washington v. Dawson (1924), *391*
Water power, 140, 356, 357; *See also* Federal Water Power Act (1920)
Watt, James, 281
Watt, Richard F., 404
Watterson, Henry, 158
Wayne, James M., 309 n.
Weaver, James Baird, 70, 74, 75
Weaver v. Palmer Bros. (1926), 294, 295, *393*
Webb-Kenyon Interstate Liquor Act (1913), 167, 199, 208, *351*, 354, 381
Webb-Pomerene (Export Trade) Act (1918), *355*
Weeds, Inc. v. U.S. (1921), 387
Weeks, John W., 200
Weeks v. U.S. (1914), *380*
Wells, David A., 18
Western Federation of Miners, 51
Western Union Telegraph Co., 23, 101, 177
Westin, Alan F., 400, 401, 404
Wheeler, Wayne B., 199, 254-257, 264
White, Edward D.: as Supreme Ct. Justice, 14, 16, 32, 86, 87, 93, 99, 100, 103, 117, 120-122, 367, 370; as Supreme Ct. Chief Justice, 146, 151-154, 197, 198, 208, 212, 220, 223, 230, 233, 243, 255, 257, 316, 318; appointment, 145; bibliography, 399, *407;* biography, 313 (chart), *314, 315,* 317 (chart)

White, Henry, 84
White, William Allen, 75, 78, 130, 166, 168, 169, 172, 213, 232
White Court: biographies, 316-318; statutes and ordinances invalidated, 345
White slave traffic, 207, 351, 379, 381; *See also* Mann (White Slave) Act (1910)
Whitney, Anita, 246
Whitney, Edward B., 100
Whitney v. California (1927), 246, 247, *394*
Wickersham, George W., 226; as Attorney General, 136-139, 144, 145, 150, 151, 153, 154, 171, 181, 209, 321; as chairman of National Commission on Law Observance and Enforcement, 266-268; biography, *322*
Williams, James D., 74
Williams, John Sharp, 172
Willing v. Chicago Auditorium Association (1928), *394*
Wilson, James H., 49
Wilson, William B., 170, 214
Wilson, Woodrow, 160, 206, 227, 277, 279; as Governor of New Jersey, 125; Presidential candidate (1911), 165, 166; elected President, 164; as President, viii, 129, 142, 148, 167, 169-178, 180-188, 191-196, 200, 201, 204, 210, 212-214, 219, 220, 224, 226, 232, 235, 250, 256, 258, 302, 356
Wilson v. New (1917), 197, 198, 243, 244, 354, *382*
Wilson Tariff Act (1894), 11, *348*
Winslow, Sidney, 190
Winston, Fred S., 41
Wiretapping, 262, 263, 395
Wisconsin R. Commission v. Chicago, Burlington & Quincy R. Co. (1922), 247, 356, *389*
Witte, Edwin E., 292
Wolff Packing Co. v. Court of Industrial Relations (1923), 243-245, *391*
Women; *See* Labor: women workers; Suffrage; White slave traffic
Women's Organization for National Prohibition Reform, 268
Wong Wing v. U.S. (1896), 348, *369*
Woods, William A., 57-59
Workmen's Benevolent Association, 45
Workmen's Compensation; *See* Labor: workmen's compensation
World Court, 297

World War I, 181, 185-187, 192-202,
213, 353; effects, 248; Federal legislation, 192, 197, 199, 200, 202, 353-355;
Peace Treaty (Versailles), 213, 219
Wright, William D., 99

Writs of Error Act (1928). *341*
"Yellow-dog" contracts; *See* Labor: "yellow-dog" contracts

Zimmermann, Alfred, 195